CW01023913

The Darkest Year

The British Army on the Western Front 1917

Wolverhampton Military Studies No. 35

Edited by Spencer Jones

Helion & Company

To my parents
Sheila & Victor
With love

Helion & Company Limited
Unit 8 Amherst Business Centre
Budbrooke Road
Warwick
CV34 5WE
England
Tel. 01926 499 619
Email: info@helion.co.uk
Website: www.helion.co.uk
Twitter: @helionbooks
Visit our blog at blog.helion.co.uk

Published by Helion & Company 2022
Designed and typeset by Mach 3 Solutions (www.mach3solutions.co.uk)
Cover designed by Paul Hewitt, Battlefield Design (www.battlefield-design.co.uk)

Text © Spencer Jones and contributors 2022
Images open source unless otherwise credited
Maps drawn by and © Barbara Taylor 2022

Front cover: Observation post near Fleurbaix, Christmas 1916 by William Barnes Wollen.
(New Zealand Archives)
Back cover: Column of Canadian infantry on the march, May 1917. (*The Sphere*,
4 August 1917)

ISBN 978-1-914059-98-8

British Library Cataloguing-in-Publication Data.
A catalogue record for this book is available from the British Library.

For details of other military history titles published by Helion & Company Limited contact
the above address or visit our website: http://www.helion.co.uk.

We always welcome receipt of book proposals from prospective authors.

Contents

List of Illustrations

List of Maps

Text

Colour Plates

General Key for All Maps

Formation/Unit National Designators

Red	German
Blue	Allied
ANZAC	Australian and New Zealand Army Corps
AUS	Australian
BR	British
CAN	Canadian
FR	French
Bav	Bavarian
Gd(s)	Guards (British or German)
Ldw	Landwehr
Res	Reserve

British and Dominion Regiments

A&SH	Argyle and Sutherland Highlanders
Buffs	Royal East Kent Regiment
Devon	Devonshire Regiment
EL	East Lancashire Regiment
EY	East Yorkshire Regiment
HLI	Highland Light Infantry
Kings	King's Liverpool Regiment
KRRC	King's Royal Rifle Corps
Lincs	Lincolnshire Regiment
Lond	London Regiment
Middx	Middlesex Regiment
Northants	Northamptonshire Regiment
Queens	Royal West Surrey Regiment
RB	Rifle Brigade
RBks	Royal Berkshire Regiment
RF	Royal Fusiliers
RIR	Royal Irish Rifles
RWY	Royal Wiltshire Yeomanry
SF	Sherwood Foresters (Notts & Derbys)
Suff	Suffolk Regiment

XXXX Army	German trenches/formations
XXX Corps	— **XXXX** — Army to Brigade boundaries (number of crosses denotes which. All armies)
XX Division	Railway
X Brigade	Canal
III Regiment (FR/GE)	Light railway/tramway
II Battalion or Regiment (BR only)	Marsh/inundation
I Company	Sunken road
••• Platoon	
Infantry	
Cavalry	
Multiple units	
(-)/(+) Elements of/on loan ?? Higher Formation	

Abbreviations

AA	Assistant Adjutant
ADC	Aide de Camp
AG	Adjutant General
AQMG	Assistant Quarter-Master General
BEF	British Expeditionary Force
BM	Brigade Major
CAS	Chief of the Air Staff
CB	Companion of the Order of the Bath
CFS	Central Flying School
CID	Committee of Imperial Defence
CIGS	Chief of the Imperial General Staff
CinC	Commander in Chief
CO	Commanding Officer
CoS	Chief of Staff
CRA	Commander, Royal Artillery
CRE	Commander, Royal Engineers
DAAG	Deputy-Assistant Adjutant General
DGMA	Director General of Military Aeronautics
DMA	Director of Military Aeronautics
DMO	Director of Military Operations
DMT	Director of Military Training
DQMG	Deputy Quartermaster General
DSO	Distinguished Service Order
EEF	Egyptian Expeditionary Force
GHQ	General Headquarters
GOC	General Officer Commanding
GQG	Grand Quartier Général [General Headquarters French Army]
GS	General Staff
GSO	General Staff Officer [numerical designation indicates grade, e.g. GSO1]
IGC	Inspector General of Communications
IGS	Imperial General Staff
KCMG	Knight Commander of the Order of St. Michael & St.George
LoC	Line of Communication

MGGS	Major-General, General Staff
MW	Military Wing [of the Royal Flying Corps]
NCO	Non Commissioned Officer
QF	Quick Firing [Artillery gun]
QMG	Quarter-Master General
RA	Royal Artillery
RAMC	Royal Army Medical Corps
RE	Royal Engineers
RFA	Royal Field Artillery
RFC	Royal Flying Corps
RGA	Royal Garrison Artillery
RHA	Royal Horse Artillery
TF	Territorial Force
VC	Victoria Cross
WO	War Office

Notes on Contributors

Dr Jim Beach is Senior Lecturer in 20th Century History at the University of Northampton. His research focuses upon British military intelligence during the First World War. He is the author of *Haig's Intelligence: GHQ and the German Army, 1916-1918* (2013).

Nigel Dorrington graduated with a BA in History from the University of Birmingham in 1986 and completed an MA in First World War Studies at the same university in 2013. Born in London, he now teaches History at Wood Green Academy, Wednesbury. His interest in the First World War grew from a visit to the Ypres and Somme battlefields whilst a student teacher at Nottingham University and from 12 years as a Territorial with 5th Battalion, Royal Regiment of Fusiliers – the descendants of the Royal Warwickshire Territorials of 48th (South Midland) Division. Nigel regularly leads school parties to the 1914-18 battlefields in France and Belgium.

Charles Fair is a former Territorial Army officer who has had a lifelong interest in the British Army of the 1908-45 era. His first book, *Marjorie's War: Four Families in the Great War 1914-1918*, was published in 2012 and is based on a family archive of 800 letters and 400 photographs. He was the Douglas Haig Fellowship's Scholar in 2009 for his essay on the social history of a working class battalion of the London Regiment. Charles is currently undertaking a PhD at King's College London on the selection and training of junior officers in the British Army of the First World War.

Alexander A. Falbo-Wild is a historian, researcher, and professional military educator based in Baltimore, Maryland. He specializes in the history of organizational culture, military operations, media, and combat motivation. Alexander's publications include *Supporting Allied Offensives: 8 August-11 November 1918* (2018) published by The US Center of Military History and 'Rising to the Occasion: the US Army in the World Wars, 1900-45' in Matthias Strohn (ed.), *How Armies Grow* (2019). From 2014-18 he was a Case Method Teaching Fellow at Marine Corps University and an Honorary Historian in Residence with USMC History Division. Alexander then served as Chief Archivist to the Maryland National Guard's Office of the Command Historian from 2018-21. He is currently a history graduate student at Temple University.

Dr Tim Gale is an independent scholar based in London. His publications include two books on the French tank force during the First World War, the subject of his PhD for the Department of War Studies at King's College London. Tim has also contributed a number of chapters for academic works on various aspects of the French army in the 19th and 20th centuries. He is currently researching the wartime career of General Charles Mangin, as well as the Battle of Cambrai. Tim is Assistant Secretary-General of the British Commission for Military History.

Dr Meleah Hampton is a historian in the Military History Section of the Australian War Memorial. She is the author of *Attack on the Somme: 1st Anzac Corps and the Battle of Pozières Ridge 1916* (2016) and numerous articles and essays on the operational conduct of the First World War, particularly on the Western Front. Meleah lives in Canberra with her husband and three children. She is a member of the editorial committee for the Memorial's *Wartime* and the *British Journal of Military History* editorial advisory board and is an ambassador for the Western Front Association in Australia.

Richard Hendry holds undergraduate and Master's degrees in Law and, prior to retirement, spent his working life as a legal academic and then as director of employment law and employee relations for a management consultancy. An independent scholar, Richard earned an MA in the History of Britain in the First World War at the University of Wolverhampton in 2018. He has a particular interest in the work and experiences of the London Regiment's battalions and divisions on the Western Front during 1914-18, but also enjoys examining other aspects of that conflict and wider military history in general.

Dr Simon Innes-Robbins is a retiree with over three decades service as Senior Curator with the Imperial War Museum. His research focuses on the culture, leadership and operational performance of the British Army. Simon's publications include *British Generalship on the Western Front, 1914-18: Defeat Into Victory* (Templer Medal 2004 runner-up), *The First World War Letters of General Lord Horne* (2009) and *British Generalship During the Great War: The Military Career of Henry Horne, 1861-1929* (2011). He is also co-editor of *Staff Officer: The War Diaries of Walter Guinness (First Lord Moyne) 1914-18* (1987) and has contributed chapters to Ian Beckett & Steven J. Corvi (eds.) *Haig's Generals* (2006); Spencer Jones (ed.), *Stemming The Tide: Officers and Leadership in the British Expeditionary Force 1914* (Templer Medal 2013 runner-up); Spencer Jones (ed.), *Courage Without Glory: The British Army on the Western Front 1915* (2015) and Spencer Jones (ed.) *At All Costs: The British Army on the Western Front 1916* (2018).

Dr Spencer Jones is Senior Lecturer in Armed Forces & War Studies at the University of Wolverhampton and serves as Regimental Historian for Royal Regiment of Artillery. His key works include *From Boer War to World War: Tactical Reform of the British Army*

(2012); *Stemming the Tide: Officers and Leadership in the British Expeditionary Force 1914* (Templer Medal 2013 runner-up); *Courage without Glory: The British Army on the Western Front 1915* (2015) and *At All Costs: The British Army on the Western Front 1916* (2018).

Dr Michael LoCicero is an independent scholar and Helion & Company Publishing and Series Editor. Having earned a PhD from the University of Birmingham in 2011, he was previously employed as a contracted researcher at the National Archives, Kew and the Soldiers of Oxfordshire Trust. His publications include a contributory chapter on Brigadier-General Edward Bulfin in the acclaimed Spencer Jones (ed.) *Stemming the Tide: Officers and Leadership of the British Expeditionary Force 1914* (2013); *A Moonlight Massacre: The Night Operation on the Passchendaele Ridge, 2 December 1917* (2014/2021); a contributory chapter chronicling the forgotten battle of International Trench in Spencer Jones (ed.), *Courage Without Glory: The British Army on the Western Front 1915* (2015), a contributory chapter analysis of a large-scale German trench raid at La Boisselle in Spencer Jones (ed.), *At All Costs: The British Army on the Western Front 1916* (2018); the co-edited *Gallipoli: New Perspectives on the Mediterranean Expeditionary Force, 1915-16* (2018) in which he also contributed a chapter on the relatively unknown fighting at Krithia Nullah, November-December 1915 and the co-edited *Catholic General: The Private Wartime Correspondence of Major-General Sir Cecil Edward Pereira, 1914-19* (2020).

Andrew Lock is a Postgraduate Researcher at the University of Suffolk examining the pursuit to the Hindenburg Line and BEF tactical progress in early 1917. He earned a History of Britain and the First World War MA at the University of Wolverhampton in 2017 and is currently employed as a tutor and historical guide in London and on the Western Front battlefields. Andrew has given talks at Western Front Association branches in East Anglia and has lately become a trustee of the Great War Group, a charitable organisation aimed at remembrance and promoting education of the conflict. He has also taken on the role of Archivist and Historian at Blackheath Rugby club and is currently working on a project centred around the club's roll of honour.

Harry Sanderson is a PhD student at the University of Leeds researching training in the British Army and how it affected soldier experience of war, their morale, identity and performance on the battlefield inclusive. Prior to this, he earned an MA in War and Strategy at Leeds and a BA in War Studies at the University of Kent.

Lieutenant-Colonel Simon Shephard completed his 37-year Regular Army career in 2018 and remains an active member of the Army Reserve, serving on the staff of the Army Officer Selection Board, Westbury. He spent nine years in the ranks before commissioning through the Royal Military Academy Sandhurst. Following his attendance on the Chief of the General Staff's 'SOMME 16' staff ride, Simon entered the First World War MA course at the University of Wolverhampton under the direction of Dr Spencer Jones and Professor Gary Sheffield. He has presented his research findings to the Western Front Association, Royal Artillery Historical Society, Royal Engineer Historical Society and various British and Canadian artillery regiments. Simon is particularly interested in how doctrinal lessons from the past can be applied to current and future problems which the British Army seeks to address.

Dr John Spencer is a historian and writer with a particular interest in grand strategy and superior direction of the First World War. He has a BA in International Relations from the University of Lancaster, an MA in First World War Studies from the University of Birmingham and a PhD from the University of Wolverhampton. A journalist with nearly 40 years' experience, John was employed by various regional newspapers and later as Group Managing Editor of the Press Association, the national news agency for Great Britain and Ireland. His most recent publication, *Wilson's War: Sir Henry Wilson's Influence on British Military Policy in the Great War and its Aftermath*, was published by Helion & Company in 2020.

James Taub is the Public Program Specialist at the National World War I Museum and Memorial in Kansas City, Missouri. Hailing from Michigan, he received his MA in War Studies from the University of Glasgow and a BA from Dickinson College. James was previously employed as Education Coordinator for the United States World War One Centennial Commission and currently researches and writes on the First World War whilst conducting public history programmes. His interests lie with the British, French and American experience of 1914-18 with particular focus on the average fighting man.

Dr Tom Thorpe is an independent early career scholar focusing on combat motivation, morale and military group cohesion with a particular interest in the First World War. He is a Trustee of the Western Front Association (WFA) and presenter and producer of the WFA's weekly podcast, *Mentioned in Dispatches*. Tom was, prior to earning his PhD, a public relations professional specialising in health and social care policy, speech writing and stakeholder engagement. He is also an occasional pundit on history subjects for *LBC Radio* and *Sky News*.

The Wolverhampton Military Studies Series
Series Editor's Preface

As series editor, it is my great pleasure to introduce the *Wolverhampton Military Studies Series* to you. Our intention is that in this series of books you will find military history that is new and innovative, and academically rigorous with a strong basis in fact and in analytical research, but also is the kind of military history that is for all readers, whatever their particular interests, or their level of interest in the subject. To paraphrase an old aphorism: a military history book is not less important just because it is popular, and it is not more scholarly just because it is dull. With every one of our publications we want to bring you the kind of military history that you will want to read simply because it is a good and well-written book, as well as bringing new light, new perspectives, and new factual evidence to its subject.

In devising the *Wolverhampton Military Studies Series*, we gave much thought to the series title: this is a *military* series. We take the view that history is everything except the things that have not happened yet, and even then a good book about the military aspects of the future would find its way into this series. We are not bound to any particular time period or cut-off date. Writing military history often divides quite sharply into eras, from the modern through the early modern to the mediaeval and ancient; and into regions or continents, with a division between western military history and the military history of other countries and cultures being particularly marked. Inevitably, we have had to start somewhere, and the first books of the series deal with British military topics and events of the twentieth century and later nineteenth century. But this series is open to any book that challenges received and accepted ideas about any aspect of military history, and does so in a way that encourages its readers to enjoy the discovery.

In the same way, this series is not limited to being about wars, or about grand strategy, or wider defence matters, or the sociology of armed forces as institutions, or civilian society and culture at war. None of these are specifically excluded, and in some cases they play an important part in the books that comprise our series. But there are already many books in existence, some of them of the highest scholarly standards, which cater to these particular approaches. The main theme of the *Wolverhampton Military Studies Series* is the military aspects of wars, the preparation for wars or their prevention, and their aftermath. This includes some books whose main theme is the technical details of how armed forces have worked, some books on wars and battles, and some books that re-examine the evidence about the existing stories, to show in a different light what everyone thought they already knew and understood.

As series editor, together with my fellow editorial board members, and our publisher Duncan Rogers of Helion, I have found that we have known immediately and almost by instinct the kind of books that fit within this series. They are very much the kind of well-written and challenging books that my students at the University of Wolverhampton would want to read. They are books which enhance knowledge and offer new perspectives. Also, they are books for anyone with an interest in military history and events, from expert scholars to occasional readers. One of the great benefits of the study of military history is that it includes a large and often committed section of the wider population, who want to read the best military history that they can find; our aim for this series is to provide it.

Stephen Badsey
University of Wolverhampton

Foreword

The year 1917 is one of a select handful of dates that mark a genuine turning point in world history. It saw the downfall of the Czarist regime in Russia and its eventual replacement by the Bolsheviks, and also the emergence of the United States of America as a truly global power. This set up an ideological clash that was to define much of the 20th century. On the one side was V.I. Lenin's vision of global proletarian revolution and workers' states; on the other, President Woodrow Wilson's similarly universalist agenda of liberal internationalism and capitalism. The conflict between these two ideologies was not resolved until 1989-91, with the end of the Cold War and Wilson's victory and Lenin's defeat, both belated and posthumous. Twenty-one years into the 21st century, the outcome of this struggle appears less clear cut. Perhaps it has simply mutated into different forms.

Aside from these two headline developments, with the luxury of more than a century of hindsight, we can discern other major developments in 1917 that had long-lasting effects. These included the Allies' wrenching of Palestine from the Ottoman Empire, and the Balfour Declaration, which announced that the London government would work towards 'the establishment in Palestine of a national home for the Jewish people.' The Declaration went on to say that 'nothing shall be done which may prejudice the civil and religious rights of existing non-Jewish communities in Palestine', evidence that even at that stage there was some recognition of the sheer complexity of the situation.[1] Following another world war and the unspeakable evil of the Holocaust, 1917 would stand out as a watershed in the development of the Arab-Israeli question, something which even the most clear-sighted could have only dimly discerned in the penultimate year of the Great War.

Superficially, in 1917 the British Empire seemed to be growing in power, with significant forces from the Dominions, India, and colonies deployed alongside troops from the British Isles in theatres across the globe, and new territories being conquered and added to Britannia's realms. In reality, this was a house built on sand. Various forms of nationalism were stimulated by the war, and nationalism is usually bad news for empires. At one extreme was the insurrection in Dublin at Easter 1916, the

---

1   *Modern History Sourcebook: The Balfour Declaration* <https://sourcebooks.fordham.edu/mod/balfour.asp> (accessed 6 January 2022).

consequences of which were still working through in 1917. At the other extreme was the growth of Dominion nationalism in Australia, Canada and New Zealand. At this stage, these nationalisms still firmly located in the context of loyalty to King and Empire, but in the longer term also undermined the solidarity of 'Greater Britain'.

Yet another form of nationalism was spurred on by the demands of total war, in this case the mobilisation of Indian manpower, economy and society during the First World War. In 1917 the Indian National Congress called for self-government. The response of the Secretary of State for India, Edwin Montague was given on 20 August 1917: that the British government wanted 'the gradual development of self-governing institutions with a view to the progressive realization of responsible government in India as an integral part of the British Empire.'[2] This aspiration, eventually embodied in the 1919 Government of India Act, was less than radicals wanted but in retrospect was nonetheless a significant step towards the eventual collapse of the British Empire.

Thus 1917 was a year of major events which had far-reaching consequences – and I could have mentioned many more. This is the background for the discussion of the British Army in France and Flanders during this year, as several of the contributors to this volume acknowledge. This is all to the good, as there has frequently been a disconnect between historical studies of the 'big' events caused by the war and what happened on the battlefield. Indeed, I have come across more than one historian of the Great War who were casually dismissive of the very idea of studying tactics and command, let alone the terrain over which battles were fought. But what happened on the battlefield did matter. The Nivelle Offensive (April 1917) had profound consequences for France which went far beyond the immediate tactical and operational impact.

Similarly, the operational success of Dominion troops undoubtedly played a role in the growth of Dominion nationalism. In 1917, most obviously, the capture of Vimy Ridge by the Canadian Corps in April provided a symbolic coming of age for Canada. The significant role played by British troops, guns, staff officers and commanders in this victory is generally ignored in the popular memory of Vimy, as is the fact that in 1917 the capture of the ridge was a strategic dead-end. These truths simply do not fit the nationalist narrative. Recently, scholarly historians, not least Canadians, have produced a more nuanced picture of the true significance of Vimy, at every level from the minor tactical to the role of myth in nation-building.[3] Other 1917 Western Front battles, notably Bullecourt, Messines and Third Ypres, also played roles in the process of nationalist sentiment developing in the Dominions.

2   *Lord Sinha of Raipur and the Government of India Act 1919* <https://lordslibrary.parliament. uk/research-briefings/lln-2019-0153/> (accessed 6 January 2022).
3   Tim Cook, *Vimy: The Battle and the Legend* (Toronto: Penguin, 2017); Geoffrey Hayes, Andrew Iarocci & Mike Bechtold (eds.), *Vimy Ridge: A Canadian Reassessment* (Waterloo, Ontario: Wilfrid Laurier University Press, 2006)

Today, in 2022, we both know and, crucially, *understand* a great deal more about the First World War in general and the Western Front in particular than we did even twenty years ago. Spencer Jones deserves a share of the credit for his role in this welcome development, as he has edited four volumes of essays, one dedicated to each year of the war. So far, the years 1914 to 1917 have been covered, and a 1918 volume is planned. Each book brings together a diverse and talented group of scholars writing on an eclectic group of topics, and the current volume is no exception. This book is very welcome, for although 1917 is not an 'unknown' year like 1915, there is still much to be explored. Without question, 1917 was a terrible ordeal for the British army, but scholars are divided between those who see the BEF's glass as essentially half empty at the end of 1917 (e.g., huge casualties, minimal territorial gains) and those who see it as half full (e.g., improved weapons and tactical methods and a more experienced army). This is a pretty basic disagreement. Notwithstanding its title, this book offers evidence for both sides in the debate.

Cool, detached, scholarly analysis, such as we find in this book, is badly needed. As the centenary year of 2017 demonstrated, 'Passchendaele' remains an emotive term in the UK, Australia, Canada and New Zealand, with many unable to get past the name, with its resonances of suffering and futility, to engage in analysis. Cambrai is known for its first day and the first mass use of tanks; everything else about the battle is unknown to a lay audience. At least these battles have some name recognition. By contrast, beyond the cognoscenti, 'Messines' and 'Arras' mean very little, while Vimy has a sort of free-floating afterlife existence, detached from the Battle of Arras, of which it was actually an integral part.

My immediate predecessor as President of the Western Front Association, Professor Peter Simkins, has often used the analogy of scholarship as a wall, with individual historians adding bricks to build up the structure. *The Darkest Year: The British Army on the Western Front 1917* adds not one, but a number of important blocks to the edifice. The year 1917 is hugely significant in the creation of the modern world, and thanks to this book we now know a little more about it.

Gary Sheffield
Professor Emeritus, University of Wolverhampton
January 2022

Acknowledgements

This is the fourth volume in a series which explores the British Army on the Western Front year-by-year. It follows on the success of preceding volumes *Stemming the Tide: Officers and Leadership in the British Expeditionary Force 1914* (2013); *Courage without Glory: The British Army on the Western Front 1915* (2015) and *At All Costs: The British Army on the Western Front 1916* (2018).

This volume faced the unique challenge of being compiled during the COVID-19 pandemic. Work had begun in earnest on the volume in February 2020. The following month saw the first of several lockdowns placed upon the United Kingdom, which prevented access to libraries or archives. This posed unique difficulties for research. Furthermore, the gloom caused by incessant lockdowns in the autumn and winter 2020-21 made writing peculiarly difficult. On more than one occasion it was possible to reflect that the title *The Darkest Year* had some resonance with our current circumstances! Yet I owe an immense debt to the contributors to this volume who overcame these obstacles to produce a series of excellent chapters. This book is as much theirs as it is mine.

As always, the work could not have been completed without the assistance of the staff of Helion & Company As with all previous volumes in the series, Duncan Rogers offered constant support and encouragement. Michael LoCicero provided priceless editorial support and served as the image editor for the volume. Special thanks are due to series cartographer Barbara Taylor for yet another fine set of maps.

Many individuals contributed to the volume through shared knowledge and research. Despite us being separated by the restrictions caused by the pandemic, Stephen Badsey and Gary Sheffield were able to provide several important volumes from their own collections when libraries were inaccessible. My colleagues at the University of Wolverhampton, notably John Bourne, Peter Simkins, John Buckley and Howard Fuller provided ideas and constructive comment throughout the project. I am also grateful to members of the Western Front Association who took the time to correspond with me on several points of detail. Finally, I would like to extend a particular thanks to my students past and present. Their enthusiasm for military history is a constant source of inspiration.

In a time when socialising proved challenging, I owe thanks to my friends, particularly Andy, Jake, and Jon for remaining in touch and providing humour and support throughout the pandemic.

Last, but certainly not least, I owe my deepest thanks to my parents for their unstinting love and support. I have dedicated this volume to them as a small token of my love and appreciation.

Introduction

This may well prove to be the darkest year of the war.
Chief of the Imperial General Staff Sir William Robertson, 29 December 1917.

World history pivoted on 1917. Although the 'long nineteenth century' of 1789-1914 is held to have ended with the outbreak of the First World War, a case can be made that this period truly ended in 1917.[1] As A.J.P. Taylor argued, had Napoleon Bonaparte been alive at the beginning of 1917, 'he would have found nothing which surprised him, or which, at any rate, he could not understand': European powers led by kings, emperors and politicians fought for territorial gain. However, by the end of 1917 Napoleon 'would have been bewildered. At one end of Europe was Bolshevism, an entirely new system of thought and government. At the other end of Europe the United States … was beginning to intervene on a scale which would eclipse all the traditional Great Powers.'[2]

Yet all this lay in the future. For much of the year the struggle between the Allies and the Central Powers continued a strategic pattern which had been established in 1915. Britain and France sought to breach Germany's defences on the Western Front; Italy waged war against Austro-Hungary amidst the mountain fortresses of the Alps; and Russia sought to drive back the German and Austro-Hungarian invaders. Britain and, to an extent, Russia, continued their war with the Ottoman Empire, and a multinational Allied force remained lodged, largely impotent, at Salonika in Greece.

The stalemate frustrated the warring powers. The solution seemed to lie in ever greater military effort. Armies grew and battles became ever more intense. As a result, the casualties of the conflict were staggering. From the opening weeks of the war the scale and brutality of combat had shocked observers. The fighting had intensified further in 1915 and 1916. The latter year, marked by the co-ordinated assaults of the Allied general offensive, had been the bloodiest of the war so far. In the west, the

---

1   On the long nineteenth century concept, see Eric Hobsbawm's trilogy *The Age of Revolution: Europe 1789-1848* (1962), *The Age of Capital 1848-1875* (1975) and *The Age of Empire 1875-1914* (1997).
2   A.J.P. Taylor, *The First World War* (London: Penguin, 1963), p.165.

Battle of the Somme and the Battle of Verdun resulted in over one million Allied and German casualties.

Such losses placed unprecedented strain on the home fronts of the warring powers. The scale of sacrifice meant there was no prospect of a compromise peace and European governments remained committed to winning a decisive victory. As 1917 dawned, it was necessary for Allies and Central Powers to undertake 'remobilisation'[3] as nations sought to reorganise their economies, and indeed societies, to sustain the ever-expanding armies at the front. This resulted in centrally directed production on a previously unthinkable scale, defined by the work of the Ministry of Munitions in Britain and the Hindenburg Programme in Germany. Remobilisation ensured the war could be continued, but it placed an immense strain on civilians. Political leaders were cognisant of the cracks that were appearing in society, given vivid example by industrial strikes and civil unrest. Remobilisation could not be sustained indefinitely. It was imperative that the war was won on the battlefield before the home front gave way.

This was the background against which the British Expeditionary Force (BEF) fought its campaigns in 1917. The BEF started the year in a comparatively promising position. It had served a blood-soaked apprenticeship on the Somme in 1916. For all its hardships, this brutal school had taught the Army essential tactical and operational lessons. The BEF emerged from the Somme bloodied but considerably wiser, and began 1917 as a well-equipped, battle-hardened army. Its growing tactical skill was codified by the Training Directorate, formed in January 1917, which translated lessons from the field into practical written advice. Three crucial documents were produced in the winter of 1916-17 which would guide the BEF's tactics and training for the coming year: *SS 135: Instructions for the Training of Divisions for Offensive Action* in December 1916, and *SS 143: Instructions for the Training of Platoons for Offensive Action* and *SS 144: The Normal Formation for the Attack*, both printed in February 1917.[4]

These documents created an outline for future assaults. There were two key elements. The first element was artillery support. Great emphasis was placed on counter-battery fire to crush German guns as a necessary precondition of any assault. Then, on the day of battle, a creeping barrage would proceed slowly but relentlessly across no man's land, providing a curtain of fire that would supress the defenders. The second element was the reorganisation of infantry. The infantry who followed the barrage were now organised into well-armed, tactically flexible platoons. Each platoon was divided into four fighting sections of eight soldiers commanded by a non-commissioned officer. The first was made up of bombers with hand grenades; the second consisted of a Lewis gun team; the third comprised riflemen and scouts; the fourth provided rifle-grenadiers.

---

3   On this point, see William Philpott, *Bloody Victory: The Sacrifice on the Somme and the Making of the Twentieth Century* (London: Abacus, 2010), pp.466-97.

4   For the creation of the SS pamphlet series, see Jim Beach, 'Issued by the General Staff: Doctrine Writing at British GHQ, 1917-1918', *War in History*, 19 (4), 2002, pp.464-91.

A fifth headquarters section of one officer and four men gave tactical direction.[5] The mixture of weapons allowed the platoon to deal with a variety of threats. They could storm an enemy trench, consolidate captured positions, or advance on an enemy strongpoint using their own intrinsic firepower.

Tactical improvements were matched by growing material strength. The Ministry of Munitions produced guns and ammunition at a prodigious rate and the improved logistics system in France, created in 1916, ensured that the gunners of the Royal Artillery were always well equipped.[6] Ammunition was also improving in quality. In 1915 approximately 25 percent of all shells were duds. This figure was little improved for much of 1916.[7] By 1917 the widespread introduction of the advanced No. 106 Fuse, commonly known as the Graze Fuse due to its ability to detonate when it met even the slightest resistance, made high explosive shells far more reliable and effective. Improvements in ammunition were matched by progress in the technical art of gunnery. Shooting 'from the map' using grid references was well understood and fire could be delivered with a degree of accuracy that was almost unthinkable a year earlier. Sophisticated counter-battery techniques such as sound ranging and flash spotting were beginning to give the gunners a significant advantage over their German opponents.[8] In the skies, the Royal Flying Corps lost its technological edge and suffered accordingly in 'Bloody April', but the arrival of advanced fighter aircraft, including the SE.5a and the Sopwith Camel, turned the tide by the summer of 1917.[9]

The BEF was a much-improved fighting force compared to its nadir in 1915. It had learned a great deal and had put its lessons into practice. Yet it did not learn in isolation. It is important to remember that the learning process of armies in the First World War was complicated and multi-dimensional.[10] Some lessons were misinterpreted, others were forgotten, and innovations could become outdated as the war progressed. Perhaps most importantly, the learning process did not take place in a vacuum but is instead best thought of as a learning race. The catalyst for many Allied improvements

5   For a useful summary of how a platoon was intended to function in battle, see John Lee, 'Some Lessons of the Somme: The British Infantry in 1917' in Brian Bond (ed.) '*Look to Your Front': Studies in the First World War* (Staplehurst: Spellmount, 1999), pp.79-89.
6   On this point, see Christopher Philips. *Civilian Specialists at War: Britain's Transport Experts and the First World War* (London: University of London Press, 2020), pp.321-367.
7   Ian Beckett, Timothy Bowman & Mark Connelly, *The British Army and the First World War* (Cambridge: Cambridge University Press, 2017), p.310.
8   Andrew Hinks, 'Punching Above Their Weight? A Study of the Effectiveness and Field Expertise in Sound Ranging and Flash Spotting in the First World War', Unpublished MA Dissertation, University of Wolverhampton, 2017.
9   Peter Hart, *Bloody April: Slaughter in the Skies over Arras, 1917* (London: W & N, 2006)
10 Robert T. Foley, 'Dumb Donkeys or Cunning Foxes? Learning in the British and German Armies during the Great War' in International Affairs, Vol. 90, No. 2, pp.279-298; Jim Beach, 'Issued by the General Staff: Doctrine Writing at British GHQ, 1917-18' in *War in History*, Vol. 19, No. 4, 2012; Aimée Fox, *Learning to Fight: Military Innovation and Change in the British Army 1914-1918* (Cambridge: Cambridge University Press 2017).

was the bitter experience of facing sophisticated German defences. Just as the French and British armies developed ways to master these problems, the Germans sought new methods of their own to counter their opponents.

This process is illustrated by the experiences of 1917. Having absorbed the lessons of the Somme and Verdun, the British Army was well-prepared for a renewal of the type of fighting it had faced in 1916. Yet the German army had learned its own lessons and produced its own tactical and training documents.[11] By 1917 it had evolved a system of defence in depth which moved away from prepared, fixed defences, which were increasingly vulnerable to British artillery fire, and was instead anchored on a checkerboard of lightly held positions which would occupy the crater field of no-man's land. These positions would delay and disrupt the attackers as they advanced.[12] Meanwhile, specialist counter-attack formations waited behind the lines, at a distance sufficient to save them from the worst of the British artillery bombardment, ready to spring forward and drive the attackers back after their cohesion had been broken.[13] The clash between improving British assault methods and advanced German defensive doctrine would define the battles of 1917.

This is a theme which is explored throughout the volume. This volume begins with a series of chapters examining broad issues in the British Army of 1917. To start the collection my own chapter considers the problems of strategy and the growing tension in British civil-military relations. John Spencer continues the exploration of strategy with a study of the decline and eventual fall of the Chief of the Imperial General Staff General Sir William Robertson. The matter of training is examined by Charles Fair, who investigates the growing professionalisation of British officers at the time. This is followed by Tom Thorpe, who looks at morale and cohesion within the British infantry. Jim Beach considers British intelligence analysis, particularly in the context of the Third Battle of Ypres, through a study of the role of Major James Cuffe.

The remainder of this volume consists of chapters that delve into the operational and tactical problems faced by the British Army. Michael LoCicero presents a detailed examination of a German trench raid near Loos in January 1917 and considers its far-reaching military and socio-literary consequences. Nigel Dorrington considers III Corps and its advance to the Hindenburg Line in spring 1917, whilst Andy Lock looks at the bitter fighting experienced by 8th Division and 2nd Australian Division during the same series of operations. Simon Innes-Robbins traces the overall development of British operational art with reference to the ideas of First Army commander General Henry Horne and the victories at Vimy Ridge and Hill 70. Alexander Falbo-Wild explores the important role of the Royal Engineers at the Battle of Arras and

---

11   Tony Cowan, 'The Introduction of New German Defensive Tactics in 1916-1917', *British Journal for Military History*, 5.2 (2019), pp.81-99.

12   A good description of how this worked in practice (and some of the problems the system faced) can be found in Jack Sheldon, *The German Army in the Spring Offensives 1917: Arras, Aisne and Champagne* (Barnsley: Pen & Sword, 2015), p.11.

13   Jack Sheldon, *The German Army at Passchendaele* (Barnsley: Pen & Sword, 2014), pp. xi-xii.

demonstrates that their work was essential to initial British successes. Success is distinctly absent from Meleah Hampton's chapter, which examines the causes of the Australian disaster at First and Second Bullecourt. Harry Sanderson also focuses on defeat in his exploration of the Third Battle of the Scarpe which British official historian Cyril Falls reckoned was the 'blackest' day of the war. Simon Shephard considers the overwhelming importance of artillery at the Third Battle of Ypres and chronicles how the Royal Artillery fought the campaign. James Taub looks at a single, famed action during Third Ypres in his thorough study of 33rd Division at Polygon Wood. Success and failure are mixed in Richard Hendry's detailed examination of 47th (London) Division in two distinctly different engagements at Messines Ridge and Bourlon Wood. Finally, Tim Gale considers the 'dark days' of the nascent tank arm and compares the development and deployment of French and British armour in 1917.

Several themes emerge from these chapters. The first is the difficulty of the year for the Allies. Weary French forces were pushed to the point of mutiny. Russia tumbled out of the war and into the Bolshevik Revolution. The Italians were crushed at the Battle of Caporetto. The United States could offer no material assistance as its army was still mustering in North America. These problems forced the BEF to bear the brunt of the fighting on the Western Front and exposed serious rifts in British civil-military relations.

The second theme is the complexity of operations which the British Army undertook in 1917. In contrast to 1916, where the Somme defined the BEF's war, 1917 was shaped by several major offensives that were markedly different: the advance to the Hindenburg Line, Battle of Arras, Battle of Messines, Third Battle of Ypres, and Battle of Cambrai. The complexity grows still further when one considers that battles often consisted of multiple phases and subsidiary engagements. The ability of the BEF to learn and adapt was sorely tested as it faced new and difficult challenges. Yet, as the only Allied army capable of mounting major attacks, it was essential that the British kept fighting throughout the year.

The final theme is the nature of the learning process. The chapters convey a sense of overall tactical improvement in the British Army which could result in some striking successes. Yet they also make clear that lessons were not consistently applied. Although the revised training and tactics embodied by *SS 143* and its companion documents was ostensibly universal, key principles could be forgotten or ignored. When combined with the increased sophistication of German defensive methods, this could lead to defeat. A further complication was that too often senior commanders of the BEF asked their men to do too much with too little, leading to hasty, narrow attacks that had little chance of success. This had been a problem since 1915 and would remain so until 1918.

These factors made 1917 a difficult and even dispiriting year for the British Army. It could deal significant blows to its German opponent. The opening of the Battle of Arras and the capture of Vimy Ridge, the seizure of Messines Ridge, and the ferocious 'bite and hold' attacks at Third Ypres showed what the BEF could achieve. Yet it also experienced bitter failure. There were errors in the advance to the Hindenburg

Line which led to lost opportunities and significant casualties, whilst the latter stages of the Battle of Arras were poorly directed and resulted in needless bloodshed. Crucially, the BEF could not convert its battlefield successes into the long-desired breakthrough and attempts to press any initial advantage often floundered. The story was repeated throughout the year. After a dramatic opening day, the Battle of Arras degenerated into bloody stalemate in which the Army suffered its highest daily casualty rate of the war. The relentless efforts to breakthrough at Third Ypres failed and left the BEF demoralised and clinging to an untenable salient. The initial success at Cambrai could not be exploited and German counter-attacks regained almost all their lost ground. Facing strategic setbacks and seemingly unable to break the cycle of battlefield attrition, William Robertson's assessment of 1917 as the 'darkest year' of the war for Britain is understandable.

This collection sheds new light on the successes and failures of the darkest year. It reveals the difficulties that are often hidden behind the simple shorthand of the phrase 'learning process' and explores how lessons were learned, forgotten, and then sometimes learned once more. The BEF emerged from 1917 bloodied, weary, but wiser still. It would have need of all its knowledge and skill in the campaigns of 1918.

1

David Lloyd George and British Strategy on the Western Front 1917

Spencer Jones

For the middle winters of war are always the same: grey, timeless, nobody winning.[1]

The winter of 1916-17 was the coldest of the First World War. The foul weather rendered major operations impossible. Soldiers battled the elements rather than each other. In these dark months statesmen and generals found ample time for reflection on the progress of the war. The assessment was an uncomfortable one for Germany and the Central Powers as it was clear that the war was inclining in favour of the Allies. In 1916 the Allied strategy of a 'General Offensive', a series of co-ordinated attacks launched simultaneously on the Western, Eastern and Italian Fronts, had wrestled the initiative from the Central Powers.[2] The Allies had hoped that by overstretching the Central Powers and exhausting their reserves a crack would appear *somewhere* along the seemingly impregnable German and Austro-Hungarian fronts. In this respect the Allies were to be disappointed. At times, notably on the Eastern Front during the opening days of the Brusilov Offensive, or during the bitter September fighting on the Somme, the Central Powers had staggered beneath the blows of the Allied armies. Yet each time the defenders had recovered, the line had been stabilised, and breakthrough remained elusive. Nevertheless, the strategic value of the General Offensive did not only lie in territory gained. By forcing the Central Powers into a summer of prolonged, intense combat, the Allies took advantage of their superior manpower and industrial resources to lock Germany into an attritional *Materialschlacht* – 'material battle' – which it could not win. The German line had held, but under the relentless

---

1   Fred Majdalany, *Patrol* (London: Imperial War Museum, 2020 reprint of 1953 edition), p.1.
2   For discussion of the General Offensive strategy, see Stephen Badsey, 'The Battle of the Somme and British War Plans 1916' in Spencer Jones (ed.) *At All Costs: The British Army on the Western Front 1916* (Solihull: Helion & Co., 2018), pp.33-53.

fire of the Allied guns its tenacity had come at a severe physical and psychological cost.[3]

Military pressure on the fighting fronts was matched by economic pressure upon the home front. In the aftermath of the Battle of Jutland the British naval blockade had tightened.[4] Germany's inability to import foodstuffs was exacerbated by a poor harvest in the autumn of 1916 resulting in the notorious 'Turnip Winter'. By mid-1917 German rations had sunk to a mere 1100 calories per day.[5] This economic erosion placed Germany in a difficult position. Its military leaders believed the German army could hold the line on the Western Front, but there was no hope of decisive victory here. The Eastern Front offered better prospects, but although an offensive here might capture territory it was deemed unlikely to knock Russia out of the war. Yet simply enduring the war without plans for victory asked too much of its beleaguered civilian population. Germany had to do *something* in 1917 or else concede that she had lost the war. Such was Germany's desperation to turn the tide that a nation famed for its army looked to her navy for victory. This led to the ill-advised decision to resume unrestricted submarine warfare in February 1917 in the hope that this would starve Britain into submission before economic blockade and military pressure dragged Germany to defeat.[6]

In contrast, the Allies could approach the year with a certain degree of confidence. Although the General Offensive had not broken the Central Powers, military leaders in Britain and France took satisfaction in the damage which had been inflicted upon them. An atmosphere of 'sober optimism' was observed at the Chantilly Conference in November 1916 as the Allies discussed their plans for the coming year.[7] Allied strategy for 1917 was to launch a second General Offensive. It was agreed that 'general offensives, in the maximum strength that each Army can put in the field, will be launched on all fronts at the earliest moment at which they can be synchronized' with synchronization defined as being within three weeks of one another.[8] The exuberant Henry Wilson thought that the war could be won that year if the British Expeditionary Force was provided with sufficient resources to allow it fight 'two Sommes at once'.[9]

---

3   Tony Cowan, 'Muddy Grave? The German Army at the end of 1916' in Jones (ed.) *At All Costs,* pp.451-74.

4   Keith Neilson, 'The Blockade in 1917' in Douglas E. Delaney & Nikolas Gardner (eds.) *Turning Point 1917: The British Empire at War* (Toronto: UBC Press, 2017), pp.29-51.

5   Alexander Watson, *Ring of Steel: Germany and Austria-Hungary at War 1914-1918* (London: Allen Lane, 2014), p.352.

6   Watson, *Ring of Steel,* p.416-427.

7   Cyril Falls, *Military Operations: France & Belgium 1917,* Vol. I (Nashville, Tennessee: Battery Press 1992 reprint of 1940 edition), p.1 (Hereafter *Military Operations 1917,* Vol. I).

8   Falls, *Military Operations 1917,* Vol. I Appendices, 'Resolutions of the Chantilly Conference', p.1.

9   Keith Jeffrey, *Field Marshal Sir Henry Wilson: A Political Soldier* (Oxford: Oxford University Press, 2006), p.171.

Although it was unlikely that the British alone could fight a campaign on this scale, it was possible that a combined Allied effort could achieve a similar effect.

In purely military terms the idea of a renewed General Offensive held promise. The 1916 offensive had inflicted significant damage on the Central Powers. In 1917 there was reason to suppose that the experienced French army and the now battle hardened British Expeditionary Force would be able to launch a much more effective joint attack than had been possible in the previous year. Its weakness lay in its separation from the views of politicians in Britain and France. Political leaders in the Allied nations worried about the physical, financial, and psychological cost of another year of attritional war. The balance of the fighting in 1916 may have inclined towards the Allies, but it had come at a terrible price and had failed to produce a victory that would convince the weary public that its sacrifices were not in vain. The General Offensive had certainly rocked Germany, but it had also shaken the British and French governments.

Dissatisfaction with the approach to the war was acute in British political circles. In early December 1916 David Lloyd George had ousted incumbent Prime Minister Herbert Asquith and formed a new coalition government. Although by his own admission a layman in military affairs, Lloyd George had always doubted the value of major offensives on the Western Front.[10] His doubts had grown throughout 1916 and by November he complained 'What is our policy? … I have heard of one. People talk of hammering, and of a war of attrition.'[11] His concerns extended beyond the human cost of attrition: as a former Chancellor of the Exchequer Lloyd George understood that attrition was taking a toll not only on British lives but also on British finance. This latter point weighed heavily upon the minds of his new government.[12] In early 1916 Chancellor of the Exchequer Reginald McKenna had warned that the financial cost of the General Offensive meant there was a real risk that Britain would go bankrupt before the Central Powers were defeated.[13] After a year of bitter fighting this prophecy was dangerously close to fruition.

Lloyd George was also worried about the effect which the war was having on British morale. The introduction of conscription in 1916 had not produced the unrest which many politicians had feared. But Lloyd George doubted whether the public would tolerate another year of heavy casualties without clear victories. His fears were not unwarranted.[14] Although the anti-war movement in Britain was small,

---

10   David French, *British Strategy and War Aims 1914-16* (London: Allen & Unwin, 1986), pp.30-32.
11   Quoted in William Philpott 'Attrition: How the War was Fought and Won' in Jonathan Krause (ed.) *The Greater War: Other Combatants and Other Fronts, 1914-1918* (London: Palgrave Macmillan, 2014), p.238.
12   French, *British Strategy*, pp.244-49.
13   Ibid., pp.120-22.
14   J.M. Bourne, *Britain and the Great War, 1914-1918* (London: Edward Arnold, 1989), p.209.

Lloyd George War Cabinet, December 1916. (*The Times History of the War*)

EARL CURZON.

VISCOUNT MILNER.

MR. LLOYD GEORGE.

MR. ARTHUR HENDERSON.

MR. BONAR LAW.

THE WAR CABINET.

fragmented and lacked any real political influence, there were worrying signs that the British public were becoming weary. In May 1917 Britain was rocked by a wave of strikes 'which called into question the willingness of organized labour to continue to accept the leadership of Britain's traditional governing classes.'[15] Although these protests were against workplace conditions rather than the war itself, they nevertheless sent a shudder of fear through the cabinet. There was also unrest across the Dominions, notably in the form of anti-conscription riots in Canada and in the acrimonious campaign that proceeded the second Australian conscription referendum in December 1917.[16]

Beyond these dramatic demonstrations of dissatisfaction there were other, worrying signs that the public were tired of war. In June, the War Office Cinema Committee's feature length documentary *The German Retreat and the Battle of Arras* was a commercial flop, prompting Lord Beaverbrook to acknowledge that 'the public is jaded.'[17] War weariness could find expression in protests. In July, a Women's Peace Crusade rally in Glasgow attracted an estimated 10,000 attendees.[18] Perhaps most famously of all, in July *The Times* published decorated veteran Siegfried Sassoon's statement 'Finished

15   David French, *The Strategy of the Lloyd George Coalition 1916-1918* (Oxford: Clarendon Press, 1995), p.67.

16   Marc Durflinger, 'Vimy's Consequence: The Montreal Anti-Conscription Disturbances, May to September 1917' in Delaney & Gardner (eds.), *Turning Point*, pp.160-88.

17   Stephen Badsey, *The German Corpse Factory: A Study in First War World Propaganda* (Solihull: Helion & Co., 2019), p.180.

18   George Robb, *British Culture and the First World War* (London: Palgrave Macmillan, 2002), p.38.

with the War: A Soldier's Declaration' which condemned the 'political errors and insincerities for which the fighting men are being sacrificed.'[19] The publication of this sensational piece would have been unthinkable a year earlier.

With the public mood darkening it was unsurprising that Lloyd George rejected Wilson's 'two Sommes at once' and sought a different strategy. The problem lay in finding a new approach. Since 1914 British strategy had been shaped by the vision of Lord Kitchener. Formed within days of the outbreak of war, Kitchener's strategy envisaged France and Russia bearing the brunt of the fighting until Britain's New Army was ready to take the field and strike the decisive blow in 1917.[20] The policy promised to defeat Germany and to secure Britain's position in a post-war world by virtue of having a powerful army at the end of the conflict. But the decision to commit the New Army to the Western Front in 1916, a year ahead of Kitchener's original timetable, had signalled the end of his strategy in favour of the Allied General Offensive.

Kitchener's strategy had unravelled due to the urgent need to support France and Russia with more than just British money and munitions. Both Allied nations had suffered dreadful casualties in 1914-15, not to mention the loss of much economically valuable territory to the German invader. In particular, the French urgently needed assistance on the Western Front where the Germans remained within striking distance of Paris.[21] Peripheral campaigns against the Ottoman Empire or elsewhere, as tempting as they might be to the British War Cabinet, did little to help the French in their hour of need. As a result, British forces became ever more committed to the Western Front and Kitchener's conception of holding a powerful, fresh army back until the decisive hour became impossible.

It was this strategic reality which underpinned Britain's involvement in the General Offensive of 1916. To Lloyd George's mind this had been an error, which he blamed on Asquith's acquiescence to military opinion and his refusal to reassert his authority once it became clear that the General Offensive had not produced a breakthrough. There was some truth in these criticisms. Asquith's government had gambled on the success of the 1916 offensive and when this failed to win the war it saw no option except simply trying it again in 1917. Lloyd George condemned them as 'the cabinet of indecision' and, despite his lack of military credentials, he was determined to find an alternative that met Britain's strategic interests better than another year of bloody attritional fighting.[22]

---

19 *The Times*, 31 July 1917. For the wider implications of Sassoon's protest, see Badsey, *Corpse Factory*, p.183.
20 George H. Cassar, *Kitchener's War: British Strategy From 1914 to 1916* (Washington D.C.: Potomac Books, 2004), p.35.
21 Spencer Jones "'To Make War as we must and not as we should like": The British Army and the Problem of the Western Front 1915' in Spencer Jones (ed.), *Courage Without Glory: The British Army on the Western Front 1915* (Solihull: Helion & Co., 2015), pp.32-33.
22 David Lloyd George, *War Memoirs of David Lloyd George,* Vol. I (London, Odhams Press, 1938), p.817-22.

Above all else, Lloyd George was committed to winning a decisive victory over Germany. Rather than prolonged attrition he envisaged a new strategy anchored on the idea of dealing 'knock out' blows to the Central Powers.[23] His concept was general rather than specific, and it owed something to Kitchener's earlier vision. Lloyd George did not necessarily want the British Army to be the force that delivered the blow and preferred the idea of one of Britain's allies bearing the brunt of the effort. The 'knock out' strategy evolved as the war dragged on and led to the related concept of 'knocking out the props' from under Germany by defeating her weaker allies, particularly Austro-Hungary and the Ottoman Empire, but at the outset of 1917 Lloyd George still hoped that the Allies might be in a position to topple Germany that year. Unfortunately for Lloyd George his new vision faced the same problems which had derailed Kitchener's strategy. Both policies relied on Britain's allies having the strength to sustain major operations. Yet by 1917 Britain's allies were weary, and, in the case of Russia, on the brink of complete collapse.

Nevertheless, Lloyd George was not initially discouraged. His desire to chart a new strategic course took two forms in early 1917. First, inspired by news of secret Austro-Hungarian peace proposals, he hoped that a renewed Italian offensive might force Germany's most significant ally out of the war. He proposed reinforcing the Italians with Allied heavy artillery to allow them to deliver a knock-out blow against Austro-Hungary.[24] Despite a cool reception from the Italian military and outright opposition from Chief of the Imperial General Staff William Robertson, he clung to this idea throughout the year.[25] Secondly, he was soon enamoured with new French commander General Robert Nivelle. Nivelle, a French national hero after his victories at Verdun, was a charismatic figure who stood in stark contrast to his taciturn predecessor Joseph Joffre. Nivelle boasted of a bold plan to combine overwhelming artillery fire with skilful infantry attacks, an approach which had served him well at Verdun, to crack open the Western Front within 48 hours and provide 'a splendid harvest of glory for the British and French armies.'[26] The appointment of Nivelle, just two months after Lloyd George had issued his call out for knock out blows, seemed propitious. Once the Italian option had faded away, it was unsurprising that the prime minister backed this bold new commander. Lloyd George was not the only politician to be seduced by Nivelle's promises, but his commitment to the Frenchman's plan would create lasting problems with Robertson and Douglas Haig. Lloyd George's duplicitous attempt to make Haig subordinate to the new French commander during the Calais Conference

23   This celebrated phrase was given in an interview with an American journalist. See Andrew Suttie, *Rewriting the First World War: Lloyd George, Politics and Strategy 1914-1918* (Basingstoke: Palgrave Macmillan, 2005), pp.84-85.
24   Lloyd George, *War Memoirs*, Vol. I, pp.843-45.
25   David Woodward, *Lloyd George and the Generals* (London: Routledge, 2014), pp.135-36.
26   Quoted in David Murphy, *The Breaking Point of the French Army: The Nivelle Offensive of 1917* (Barnsley: Pen & Sword, 2015), p. xv.

of February 1917 poisoned British civil-military relations for the remainder of the year and arguably the rest of the war.[27]

Lloyd George's knock out strategy lasted for as long as Nivelle's star was in the ascendant. The defeat of the offensive in April 1917 and the spasm of unrest it produced in the French army brought it crashing back to earth. The impossibility of a knock-out blow being delivered by one of Britain's allies was now clear. The French army, rocked by mutinous disobedience, was incapable of major offensive operations for the remainder of the year. The Italian option had already been discounted, although it did not prevent Lloyd George revisiting it from time to time, until the disaster at Caporetto in late 1917 removed the possibility permanently. On the Eastern Front, hopes that post-Tsarist Russia would be reinvigorated with patriotic fighting spirit were soon dashed. Beset by internal unrest and with its armies in disarray, Russia could barely sustain its war effort and was in no position to launch a meaningful attack. The disastrous Kerensky Offensive of July 1917, which ended in mutiny and wholesale retreat, was stark evidence of Russia's terminal decline. Finally, there was little hope of assistance from Britain's newest major partner, the United States. The American Expeditionary Force would be in no position to undertake operations until mid-1918 at the earliest.

The inability of France and Russia to launch major attacks did more than dash Lloyd George's dream of a knock-out blow. It also unhinged the General Offensive concept of simultaneous assaults. By summer 1917 Britain had become the only member of the Allies capable of launching a major attack against Germany. This meant that the British Expeditionary Force would have to bear the brunt of war for the remainder of the year. This was a difficult proposition at the best of times, worsened by the fact that Britain was under severe pressure from the German U-boat campaign, which was inflicting dangerous losses on merchant shipping and threatening to force her to the negotiating table unless it could be countered. Thus, within six months of becoming Prime Minister, Lloyd George faced an unprecedented set of difficulties that made his knock-out vision impossible.

A new strategy was required that addressed three key problems. The first problem was the urgent need to counter the U-boat campaign. A full discussion of this aspect of the war is beyond the scope of this work, but it is important to note that it dominated the thoughts of the War Cabinet throughout the spring and summer of 1917.[28] The Royal Navy's initial emphasis on aggressive patrols to counter U-boats proved ineffective and by April the strategic outlook was bleak.[29] The solution was eventually found in the use of convoys, which made it harder for U-boats to find targets and forced them

---

27   For a vivid account of this disastrous meeting and its consequences, see Suttie, *Rewriting the War,* pp.105-14.

28   A detailed account can be found in David Stevenson, *1917: War, Peace and Revolution* (Oxford: Oxford University Press, 2017), pp.13-35, 67-91.

29   John Terraine, *Business in Great Waters: The U-Boat Wars, 1916-1945* (Ware: Wordsworth Editions, 1999), p.766.

to attack in the presence of escort vessels which could strike back. The pressure to introduce convoys had come from the politicians of the War Cabinet and showed the willingness of the Lloyd George government to intervene in military affairs.[30] Yet it was also a significant gamble and, although it relieved some of the pressure on British shipping, it did not remove it entirely. The war at sea would continue to occupy the minds of the War Cabinet throughout the year, for defeating the U-boats also required a thorough reorganisation of British shipping, transport, farming, and food supply.[31]

The second problem was the need to prevent Germany having a free hand which might allow her armies to turn their full force against Russia, or perhaps even France or Italy. The military necessity of this was clear. Fear of Russian defeat had coloured Allied strategy from 1915 onwards, and the precarious state of Russian politics raised the possibility that she could be knocked out of the war in 1917. This would represent a strategic disaster for the Allies. It would remove Russia's vast manpower from the war and allow Germany to transfer reinforcements from the Eastern Front to the Western or Italian Fronts. With the French army incapable of offensive action for the foreseeable future and the Italians only capable of exerting pressure against Austro-Hungary, it was necessary for Britain to maintain the pressure on Germany. This problem was not merely military, but also political. With Russian and French forces paralysed, any British decision to stand on the defensive would give the indication that the Allies had been fought to a standstill. This would embolden the Central Powers and have severe consequences for the mood on the British home front. Furthermore, it would send a damaging signal to the French and Russian governments who had sometimes doubted Britain's commitment to the war.[32]

The third problem was how to maintain the war on the Western Front without bringing Britain – or the Empire – to the brink of collapse. As discussed above there were signs of strain on the home front and the mood in Ireland remained tense after the Easter Rising of 1916.[33] Yet the real danger to Britain was political rather than social. In 1916 Lord Lansdowne had produced a secret memorandum arguing that the Allies could only win a Pyrrhic victory and that a negotiated peace was necessary.[34] This view had some adherents, especially amongst the Liberal politicians who remained loyal to Asquith, and their voices would grow stronger as 1917 wore on.[35] The ideas soon reached the public sphere. In March 1917, Henry Massingham

30   Stevenson, *1917*, pp.86-87.
31   Ibid., pp.83-87.
32   David French, *Lloyd George Coalition*, p.46.
33   John Grigg, *Lloyd George: War Leader 1916-1918* (London: Penguin, 2003) pp.116-18.
34   The National Archives (hereafter TNA) CAB 37/159/32: 'Terms on which a peace might be considered: Need to assess present and prospective resources for the Allies', 13 November 1916. For an examination of Lansdowne's reasoning, see Frank Winters, '"Exaggerating the Efficacy of Diplomacy": The Marquis of Lansdowne's "Peace Letter" of November 1917', *The International History Review*, Vol. 32, No.1, 2010, pp.25-46.
35   David French, *Lloyd George Coalition*, p.199.

published a piece in the *National Review* which made a similar argument, attracting the notice of the War Cabinet and causing Maurice Hankey, the influential Cabinet Secretary, to concede that it presented a 'very logical and interesting case.'[36]

A key reason for the growing pessimism within government circles was Britain's manpower situation. Conscription had sustained the British Army in 1916, but by mid-1917 Britain had passed its manpower peak. Finding soldiers without taking men from essential industry was becoming increasingly difficult. This process had clear military implications, but it also created political anxiety. Removing men from industry threatened a clash with unions which could have severe consequences for the government. Yet doing nothing risked leaving the Army short of men at a critical time. Furthermore, the War Cabinet worried that if the war dragged on into 1918 then the American Expeditionary Force might become the dominant force of the Allied armies and, in a twist on Kitchener's earlier vision, be able to strike the final blow and dominate the post-war world. For Britain this would represent a Pyrrhic victory of the type which Lansdowne feared. This pessimistic line of thought was a serious threat to the government.

The scale of these problems should not be underestimated. In combination they meant that 1917 was a year of 'extreme peril' for Britain that has been compared to the crisis which faced the nation in 1940.[37]

What made these dangers more acute was Lloyd George's unusual position. The price for overthrowing Asquith had been the alienation of a vast swathe of his own Liberal Party. His new government was a coalition dominated by Conservatives who had no intrinsic loyalty to their new prime minister. This placed Lloyd George in a sensitive position which required all his 'adroitness and personal prestige'.[38] The strains of war made this work much harder. The government was not immune from press criticism, especially from the Northcliffe press, and there were moments when there was a risk that Lloyd George might be unseated. A notable example was the publication of the Mesopotamia Commission's report in July 1917. Hankey recalled that in its aftermath 'the irresponsible clamour of our gutter press and a few of the lower class and more disreputable members of the present contemptible House of Commons' reached a fever pitch and meant that 'no one is safe nowadays', including Lloyd George himself.[39] The government survived this stormy period, but it was an indication of the dangers which it faced.

It was against this tempestuous political background that Lloyd George tried to chart a new strategic course. The situation was grave but there were some reasons for optimism. Much of this was due to the fighting power of the British Expeditionary Force. Its trial by fire at the Somme in 1916 had transformed the BEF from a

---

36 Maurice Hankey's Diary, 23 March 1917, quoted in Stephen Roskill, *Hankey: Man of Secrets, Volume I 1877-1918* (London, Collins, 1970), p.372.
37 Grigg, *Lloyd George*, pp.1–10.
38 Ibid., p.8.
39 Hankey Diary 4 July 1917 quoted in Roskill, *Man of Secrets*, p.407.

courageous but inexperienced army into an effective, battle-hardened force backed by the output of a fully mobilised arms industry. Proof of its new strength was given at the first day of the Battle of Arras, 9 April 1917. British forces advanced over three miles and captured at least 5,600 prisoners and 36 artillery pieces.[40] It was the most successful British assault of the First World War to this point. Unfortunately, initial progress could not be maintained. The offensive degenerated into prolonged attritional fighting which revealed that there were still serious weaknesses in the BEF's operational approach. Nevertheless, its opening day served as a clear indicator of how far the BEF had come from the disaster of 1 July 1916. The British Army could now be expected to deal a significant blow to the Germans whenever they launched a set piece attack. Further proof of this point was given by the success of Second Army's assault on Messines Ridge in June.

These battles proved that an operational approach which emphasised careful preparation, overwhelming firepower, and limited objectives had a high chance of success.[41] This concept was a not new one in the British Army: variations of the idea had existed, under the shorthand description of 'bite and hold', since early 1915.[42] By 1917 its value seemed irrefutable. William Robertson emphasised its importance in a letter to Haig dated 20 April 1917:

> At one time audacity and determination to push on regardless of loss were the predominating factors, but that was before the days of machine guns and other modern armament… it seems to me your success [at Arras] was mainly due to the most detailed and careful preparation, to thorough knowledge of the ground by battalions and batteries and the higher units, and to well observed artillery fire… I cannot help thinking that Nivelle has attached too much importance to what is called 'breaking the enemy's front'. The best plan seems to me to be… that of defeating the enemy's army, and that means inflicting heavier losses upon him than one suffers oneself.[43]

In addition to their operational advantages, methodical attacks of this nature had the potential to ease, if not completely solve, Britain's strategic problems on the Western Front. In theory, they could allow the British Army to continue the war and inflict

40   Falls, *Military Operations 1917*, Vol. 1, p.236.
41   For early French adoption of this approach, see Michael Goya *Flesh and Steel During the Great War: The Transformation of the French Army and the Invention of Modern Warfare* (Barnsley: Pen & Sword, 2018), pp.164-185.
42   Jones, 'To Make War as we must', in Jones (ed.) *Courage without Glory*, pp.51-54; Paul Harris & Sanders Marble, 'The 'Step-by-Step' Approach: British Military Thought and Operational Methods on the Western Front 1915-1917', *War in History*, Vol. 15, No.1, 2008, pp.17-42.
43   Grigg, *Lloyd George*, pp.159-60.

stinging damage to the Germans without running the risk of being sucked into a prolonged, attritional battle which would bleed the attacker as much as the defender.

There was an opportunity here for a close alignment of Britain's strategic needs and operational approaches. Lloyd George did not want the BEF to launch major attacks on the Western Front at all, but if it had to be done then he was determined to prevent it turning into an attritional bloodbath that would sap Britain's dwindling manpower. Robertson was convinced that the Western Front remained the decisive theatre and that it was necessary to attack here but recognised the desirability of limited objectives which allowed the BEF to inflict more damage than it received.

Unfortunately, the Prime Minister and the Chief of the Imperial General Staff could not marry their respective visions. This failure owed much to their personal animosity. On paper, the two men had something in common. Both were unorthodox, exceptionally talented individuals who had advanced from humble backgrounds to positions of power. Yet here the similarity ended for their personalities were completely different and their relationship was consequently poor. Lloyd George, who had always been ill-at-ease with soldiers, was frustrated by Robertson's priggish attitude and stubbornness. In turn, Robertson disapproved of Lloyd George's intrigues and found his energetic personality irritating.[44]

This hostility had negative consequences for war policy. Robertson had a personal dislike of Lloyd George which was matched, after the disaster at the Calais Conference in February 1917, by professional distrust. He increasingly saw his role as that of protecting the Army against dangerous political interference. Lloyd George struggled to break down this resistance. He could not charm Robertson in person, and for much of the year he was in no position to engineer a political showdown that might oust him. Lloyd George's confidence in his own military judgement had been shaken after Nivelle's failure and he knew that key members of his own War Cabinet were staunch supporters of Robertson. Any attempt to remove the Chief of the Imperial General Staff had the potential to trigger a wave of resignations which would cause the government to collapse.

Lloyd George attempted to circumvent these problems by seeking alternative sources of military advice throughout the year. The most important of these was Maurice Hankey, who the BEF's Chief Intelligence Officer John Charteris described as '[a man] who is said to know more about everything than anyone else in the Empire'.[45] Lloyd George had a close friendship with Hankey and sought to employ him as a counterweight to Robertson.[46] Hankey resisted this role and refused to be used as a pawn in a clash between politicians and generals.[47] Furthermore, his military views were similar to those of Robertson. He believed in the necessity of fighting Germany

---

44 Ibid., pp.33-34.
45 Roskill, *Man of Secrets*, p.387.
46 Ibid., p.387.
47 Ibid., p.414.

on the Western Front to deny her a free hand elsewhere and often argued with Lloyd George on this point.[48]

It was against this background of strained civil-military relations that the BEF's Commander-in-Chief, Douglas Haig, drew up his plans for a new offensive at Ypres. Haig's vision was the culmination of a long-held British desire for an offensive in Flanders. Given the enduring controversy over the offensive it is easy to forget how much it seemed to promise in 1917. A successful attack at Ypres offered several tantalising prizes. Its military advantages were clear. It would allow the BEF to escape the notorious salient, a perpetually 'active' sector of front which inflicted a constant stream of casualties on its defenders. An advance would also remove the lingering German threat to the Channel Ports. Yet the most important prize lay on the German occupied coast. The Belgian ports of Ostend and Zeebrugge served as bases for German naval forces. Contrary to popular belief, the main threat from these ports were German destroyers that frequently sortied into the English Channel and 'provided a constant menace to the cross-Channel communications'.[49] Small UB Class coastal U-boats also operated from these ports and their mine laying activities were a cause for concern.[50] The capture of these ports promised to end these problems at a stroke and was thus strongly encouraged by the Royal Navy.[51] Success also promised political advantage. Britain had gone to war to protect Belgium and a victory here would be a powerful morale boost. Furthermore, the loss of occupied Belgium would rock the German government, which saw the captured territory as a crucial bargaining chip should a compromise peace become necessary.[52]

It is important to note that in mid-1917 success on this front seemed possible. The terrain of the Ypres salient, dominated by a half-moon of high ground which overlooked the plains to the east and west, was significant. These ridges were crucial to the entire Flanders position. If British forces could seize this high ground, then German positions to the east would be overlooked and vulnerable. This might force the defenders to fall back even further, for the next defensible positions were several miles distant. It would require an advance of around seven miles to clear the ridges.[53] This was distant within the context of the First World War but did not seem impossible considering the three and a half miles which had been covered on the first day of the Battle of Arras.

---

48 Ibid., p.443.
49 Lord Hankey, *The Supreme Command 1914-1918*, Vol. II (London: George Allen & Unwin, 1961), p.679. All references in this chapter are to volume II.
50 Ibid., p.679.
51 Ibid., p.679. See also Geoffrey Till, 'Passchendaele: The Maritime Dimension' in Peter Liddle (ed.) *Passchendaele in Perspective: The Third Battle of Ypres* (London: Leo Cooper, 1997), pp.73-88 and Mark D. Karau, *The Naval Flank of the Western Front: The German MarineKorps Flandern 1914-1918* (Barnsley: Seaforth, 2014).
52 Watson, *Ring of Steel*, pp.260, 462, 466.
53 Gary Sheffield, *The Chief: Douglas Haig and the British Army* (London, Arum Press Limited, 2011), pp.160, 223.

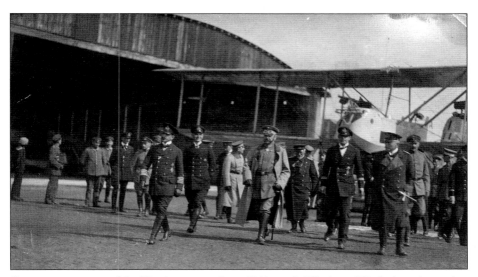

German occupation of the Flanders coast: *Generalfeldmarschall* Paul von Hindenburg inspecting the seaplane aerodrome situated on Zeebrugge Mole, May 1917. (Private collection)

The potential benefits of an offensive here were clear. Yet the concept also had significant weaknesses. It paid little attention to Britain's wider strategic situation. The decline of France and Russia meant that Britain would have to carry out this offensive alone. In 1916 the German army had been able to sustain ferocious battles with the French, British and Russians simultaneously. The idea that in 1917 the BEF *alone* could smash the German army was questionable. Haig does not seem to have seriously considered this problem.[54] This was despite the urging of Robertson. Haig discussed the matter with him and recorded in his diary: 'He wished me to realize the difficult situation in which the country would be if I carried out large and costly attacks without full co-operation by the French. When autumn came round, Britain would then be without an Army!'[55] Haig was undeterred. He had faith that the Russian Kerensky Offensive of July would draw off German troops but made no attempt to revise his vision even after the campaign ended in disaster.[56] Haig's confidence was based on his conviction that German morale was low and that the defenders were on the brink of collapse.[57] This stubborn optimism was arguably Haig's greatest weakness as a commander. It is often attributed to the buoyant intelligence reports produced

---

54 Woodward, *Lloyd George and the Generals*, p.175.
55 Haig Diary 9 June 1917 quoted in John Terraine, *The Road to Passchendaele. The Flanders Offensive of 1917: A Study in Inevitability* (London, Leo Cooper, 1977), p.128.
56 See Douglas Haig's memorandum to his Army commanders, 5 July 1917, reproduced in Terraine, *Road to Passchendaele*, p.185.
57 Haig Diary, 3 August 1917 quoted in Terraine, *Road to Passchendaele*, p.220.

by Charteris, but prior to Third Ypres Charteris was 'rather restrained' and had little confidence that the coming battle would be decisive.[58]

Nevertheless, Haig was in a strong position to pursue his vision. In early May, an inter-Allied conference in Paris had agreed that the timing, objectives, and nature of future offensives in 1917 should be determined by soldiers rather statesmen.[59] There was an initial expectation that a future offensive would be an Anglo-French operation, but by early June it became clear that the French would be unable to make a major attack for the remainder of the year. This alarmed the British government and contributed to the forming of the War Policy Committee, a specialist branch of the War Cabinet, which consisted of Lloyd George, Lord Curzon, Alfred Milner and General Jan Smuts with Maurice Hankey as secretary.[60] The War Policy Committee would meet sixteen times between 8 June and 20 June as it grappled with the problems of the war.[61]

The decisive meeting occurred on 19 June – Haig's 56th birthday – when the chief was summoned to London to lay his plans before the War Policy Committee. He gave a bravura performance. Lloyd George recalled:

> When Sir Douglas Haig explained his projects to the civilians, he spread on a table or desk a large map and made a dramatic use of both his hands to demonstrate how he proposed to sweep up the enemy – first the right hand brushing along the surface irresistibly, and then came the left, his outer finger ultimately touching the German frontier with the nail across…[62]

In John Terraine's choice phrase, 'Lloyd George never forgave that finger-nail.'[63] However, recriminations lay in the future. At the time Lloyd George was impressed with Haig's 'very powerful' statement and 'splendid conception' but challenged him on its practicality.[64] Haig and the politicians would discuss the offensive over the next three days. The debate split the War Policy Committee. Lloyd George and Lord Curzon expressed their scepticism whilst Milner and Smuts were in favour of the operation. Lloyd George and Haig would debate the matter at length: Hankey described it as a 'regular battle royale'.[65]

58   Jim Beach, *Haig's Intelligence: GHQ and the German 1916-1918* (Cambridge: Cambridge University Press, 2015), p.249.
59   Ian Beckett, Timothy Bowman & Mark Connelly, *The British Army and the First World War* (Cambridge, Cambridge University Press, 2017), p.199.
60   Hankey, *Supreme Command*, p.672.
61   Ibid., p.673
62   Lloyd George, *War Memoirs*, Vol. II, p.1277.
63   Terraine, *Road to Passchendaele*, p.145.
64   Grigg, *Lloyd George*, p.164.
65   Hankey Diary 17 June 1917 quoted in Roskill, *Man of Secrets*, p.403.

Three factors turned the debate in Haig's favour. The first was Haig's ability to point to British victories at Vimy Ridge and Messines.[66] The BEF had proved that it could capture formidable German positions at an acceptable cost. Lloyd George was forced to acknowledge these 'brilliant successes' but also pointed out the previous tendency for battles to take the form of 'Brilliant preliminary successes followed by weeks of desperate and sanguinary struggles, leading to nothing except perhaps driving back the enemy a few barren miles – beyond that nothing to show except a ghastly casualty list.'[67] Haig parried this criticism by assuring Lloyd George that he had 'no intention of entering into a tremendous offensive involving heavy losses. His plan was aggressive without committing us too far.'[68]

The second factor was Lloyd George's lack of alternatives. His first proposal was the employment of 'Petain tactics': carefully planned, limited attacks designed to inflict damage on the Germans.[69] This idea certainly had its merits, but Lloyd George's own enthusiasm for it was limited.[70] Instead he returned once more to supporting an Italian offensive against Austro-Hungary with the bold statement 'If success was achieved on the Italian Front… victory in the War was assured. A separate peace with Austria would then be practicable, and having eliminated Austria from the War, Germany would be at our mercy.'[71] Lloyd George's confidence was not shared by either the generals or the War Policy Committee. Lord Curzon noted that the Italians had shown no evidence that they could break the Austro-Hungarian lines.[72] Lloyd George's insistence that British artillery support would be decisive was unconvincing.[73]

The third factor was the unity of military opinion. In private Robertson retained doubts over the Ypres offensive, but in public he backed Haig to the hilt. His summary to the War Policy Committee made his position clear:

> It is a source of deep regret to me that I cannot advise the adoption of the policy so greatly desired by the Prime Minister, for I fully recognize the responsibility which he has to carry. My own responsibility, I may add, is not small in urging the continuance of a plan regarding which he has 'grave misgivings', but I can do no other than say that to abandon it and to attempt to seek a decision in Italy seems to me to be unsound.[74]

---

66 Grigg, *Lloyd George*, p.165; Quoted in Terraine, *Road to Passchendaele*, pp.149-50.
67 Grigg, p.165; Quoted in Terraine, p.163.
68 Lloyd George, *War Memoirs*, Vol. II, p.1289.
69 Terraine, *Road to Passchendaele*, p.163.
70 He devoted a single, brief paragraph to the idea in a much longer memorandum. TNA CAB 27/6: Tenth Meeting of the Cabinet Committee on War Policy, 21 June 1917; see also Terraine, *Road to Passchendaele*, p.161.
71 TNA CAB 27/6; Terraine, *Road to Passchendaele*, p.165.
72 TNA CAB 27/6; Terraine, p.166.
73 On this point, see Grigg, *Lloyd George*, p.172.
74 Quoted in Terraine, *Road to Passchendaele*, p.172.

It was not only the army which favoured the Ypres offensive. On 20 June, Admiral John Jellicoe gave a bleak account of British shipping losses to U-boats stating, 'There is no good discussing plans for next spring – we cannot go on.'[75] The revelation suggested that the elimination of German occupied ports in Belgian might be necessary for national survival. The extent to which Jellicoe's intervention was decisive is debatable – his despair was not shared by the War Policy Committee – but it added powerful support to the military position.[76]

The arguments swung the War Policy Committee behind Haig. Despite his deep misgivings about Haig's plan, Lloyd George did not dare to overrule the unanimous opinion of his political and military advisors. The plan was approved at a 'rough and tumble' War Cabinet meeting on 20 July.[77] The best that Lloyd George could do was to insert a circuit breaker by insisting that the offensive would be halted if it degenerated 'into a drawn out battle of the Somme type' without hope of decisive victory.[78] This proviso was well intentioned but contained a serious flaw: the politicians had no way of determining at what point the offensive, which was certain to be costly even if it gained ground, had become a purely attritional battle. Robertson understood this and highlighted it in a letter to Haig:

> He [Lloyd George] replied that so long as this step-by-step system of advances was adhered to he would back your plan for all it was worth... the Prime Minister asked one of the Cabinet when your operations ought to be stopped, if they did not seem likely to achieve complete success – that is how many losses we ought to incur before stopping. The Cabinet Minister gave a good answer. He said that he could not answer the question merely with reference to losses, and that the time to stop would be when it appeared that our resources were not sufficient to justify a continuance of our effort.[79]

Haig was furious and told Robertson 'to be firmer and play the man, and, if need be resign' if Lloyd George pushed the point.[80] Robertson responded by extracting acquiescence from the prime minister that Haig's views would be considered 'before coming to any decision as to the cessation of the operations.'[81] This agreement disabled Lloyd George's circuit breaker: Haig's unshakeable optimism meant he would *always* believe that the BEF was on the brink of victory.[82]

75   Quoted in Till, 'Maritime Dimension' in Liddle (ed.) *Passchendaele*, p.77.
76   A useful summary of Jellicoe's influence is given in Roskill, *Man of Secrets*, p.405.
77   Woodward, *Lloyd George and the Generals*, p.183.
78   Ibid., p.183; Terraine, *Road to Passchendaele*, p.199; Roskill, *Man of Secrets*, p.413.
79   Robertson to Haig, 18 July 1917, quoted in Terraine, *Road to Passchendaele*, p.199.
80   Quoted in Woodward, *Lloyd George and the Generals*, p.184.
81   Ibid., p.184.
82   For this optimism, see Beach, *Haig's Intelligence*, pp.251, 254, 257-58, 260.

The full story of the Third Battle of Ypres is beyond the scope of this chapter.[83] It was a complex, multi-phase battle that was shaped by appallingly muddy conditions. The BEF gained footholds on the high ground to the east of Ypres but the ambitious objectives which Haig had illustrated to the War Policy Committee were never achieved. The high-water mark was reached in November when the ruined village of Passchendaele was taken by the Canadian Corps after a herculean effort. Yet this reaped no strategic rewards: the final advance placed the BEF in a swamp-like salient that was under constant German artillery fire. An attempt to expand the position through an ambitious night attack in December met with disaster.[84] The noisome conditions in the Passchendaele salient would become emblematic of the entire campaign. In its aftermath, the morale of the BEF plummeted. The campaign would scar the psyche of the army.[85]

The campaign also scarred Lloyd George. He was in an agonising position. He had little faith that the offensive would succeed and had surrendered political control of the battle. His oversight of the campaign was characterised by despair, passivity, and vague attempts to promote an Italian offensive which would allow him to escape the nightmare. But he was trapped in a political quagmire. Ordering a halt to the battle would precipitate a showdown with Haig which he had he neither the personal confidence nor the political strength to win. Haig retained powerful Royal connections and Parliamentary allies which made him politically unassailable.[86] The only hope Lloyd George had of challenging him was via Robertson.[87] But Robertson, despite his own doubts about the conduct of Third Ypres, lived up to his nickname of 'refrigerator'[88] and proved immovable.

The pressure took a physical toll on Lloyd George. On 5 September Hankey found the prime minister 'restless, and neurotic, unstable and rather infirm in purpose, neuralgic and irritable, exacting and difficult to please.'[89] By 8 September Lloyd George was sufficiently ill for the news to reach the national press and he would remain in a

83   Modern scholarly accounts may be found in Robin Prior & Trevor Wilson, *Passchendaele: The Untold Story* (New Haven, Connecticut: Yale University Press, 2002) and Nick Lloyd, *Passchendaele: A New History* (London: Penguin, 2017).

84   For particulars of this tragic final act, see Michael LoCicero, *A Moonlight Massacre. The Night Operation on the Passchendaele Ridge, 2 December 1917: The Forgotten Last Act of the Third Battle of Ypres, Second Edition* (Warwick: Helion & Co., 2014/2021).

85   For a useful summary of the debate, see Alexander Mayhew, 'Making sense of the Western Front: English infantrymen's morale and perception of crisis during the Great War', unpublished PhD, London School of Economics and Political Science, 2018 pp.42, 95-96. See also Richard Grayson, *Belfast Boys: How Unionists and Nationalists fought and died together in the First World War* (London: Bloomsbury, 2014, pp.119-39).

86   Grigg, *Lloyd George*, pp.234-35.

87   Hankey, *Supreme Command*, p.697; Roskill, *Man of Secrets*, p.435.

88   E.L. Spears, *Prelude to Victory* (London: Cape, 1939), p.33.

89   Quoted in Grigg, *Lloyd George*, p.228.

Portraits of exhaustion and despair: Forlorn British captives seized during the early stages of the Third Ypres campaign. (*Illustrierte Geschichte des Weltkrieges, 1914/17*)

'convalescent' state for much of the month.[90] The illness may have been psychosomatic – Lloyd George had a history of such ailments at times of severe anxiety – but its effects lingered for most of the month and left him weak.[91]

This weakness may have contributed to Lloyd George's sudden interest in German peace overtures at the end of September. The proposal arrived at a time when Lloyd George was at a low physical and mental ebb. He had despaired of victory on the Western Front and had accepted that Russia's contribution to the Allied cause was effectively over. After almost a month of convalescence the peace proposal seems to have renewed his energy. He crossed the English Channel to discuss it with the French government immediately. He also discussed it with Robertson and Haig. Robertson thought that the defeat of Russia meant 'the chances of our achieving a military victory were gone' but Haig disagreed.[92] Haig argued that the Germans 'were very worn out and had some very poor material in the fighting line' and showed Lloyd George a cage of exhausted German prisoners to underline the point.[93] Lloyd George admitted these men were 'a weedy lot' and far below the standards seen earlier in the war, although he claimed in his memoirs that the physically fit men had been deliberately removed to promote this impression.[94]

Lloyd George's interest in the peace proposal may have gone even further had it not been for the unanimous opposition of the War Cabinet.[95] This was fortunate for Britain and the Allies. The extent to which the German overtures were serious remains debatable, and their main intention seems to have been to detach Britain from the Allies, or at the very least sow discord between the powers.[96] Lloyd George downplayed his interest in the peace proposal in his memoirs, but his defence has been dismissed as 'supremely misleading' by biographer John Grigg.[97]

Lloyd George's energy in exploring the German peace overture contrasts sharply with his lethargy over Third Ypres. After the war Hankey argued that the prime minister had two opportunities to halt the offensive. The first was 15 August, when positive news from Italy raised the possibility of revisiting his proposals for an attack against Austro-Hungary. The second was during his visit to the front on 25-26 September.[98] Yet the visit of September was largely to discuss the peace overtures and it is not clear if Lloyd George seriously considered ordering Haig to halt Third Ypres on this trip. Hankey defended Lloyd George's inaction on the grounds that 'it is difficult to stop a Commander-in-Chief who believes himself to be on the floodtide

90   Ibid., p.231.
91   Ibid., pp.228–31.
92   Lloyd George, *War Memoirs*, Vol. II, pp.1419-23.
93   Grigg, *Lloyd George*, p.240.
94   Lloyd George, *War Memoirs*, Vol. II, p.1316.
95   Grigg, *Lloyd George*, p.240.
96   Fritz Fischer, *Germany's Aims in the First World War* (New York: Norton, 1967), p.420.
97   Grigg, *Lloyd George*, p.243.
98   Hankey, *Supreme Command*, Vol. II, pp.702-03.

of success.'[99] Hankey might also have added that he too played a role in allowing the offensive to grind on. A diary entry for 15 October noted: 'Breakfast with LG. Afterwards we had a great argument about war policy. I supported Haig's view and LG opposed it.'[100] Curiously, the day after this argument Lloyd George sent a telegram of congratulations to Haig which stated, 'I am personally glad … of renewing my assurance of confidence in your leadership.'[101] Haig was nonplussed and wrote in his diary, 'I wonder why the Prime Minister should suddenly have sent this message?'[102]

Without political intervention, the Third Battle of Ypres continued. The results of the offensive remain deeply controversial. For Prior and Wilson, it was a disastrous campaign with 'dire consequences' for the British Army, which was left bloodied, exhausted and demoralised.[103] Lloyd disagrees, describing the battle as a 'lost victory' for the BEF and noting 'there were few battles as mentally and physically challenging to the German Army as Flanders was in 1917'.[104] There is truth in both these assessments. British and German forces suffered gravely in the battle. Yet the German line held and the British failed to achieve Haig's stated objectives. Third Battle of Ypres inflicted brutal attrition on the German defenders but the psychological damage it caused to the British Army was uniquely severe.

The offensive would have far reaching effects beyond the battlefield. During Third Ypres the British War Cabinet became strangely paralysed.[105] The final sputtering out of the offensive, the false dawn at Cambrai, and the Italian disaster at Caporetto finally shook Lloyd George from his lethargy. He would move to reassert civilian authority over Haig and Robertson at the end of the year, precipitating a bitter showdown that would have consequences for the British Army in 1918. His campaign to oust Robertson is discussed in detail elsewhere in this volume.

Yet Lloyd George could never completely escape from the mud of Flanders. He 'felt the anguish of Third Ypres until the end of his life.'[106] He also surely felt guilty about his failure to exert control over the operation. This, in part, explains his furious efforts to rewrite the history of the campaign in his notoriously unreliable *Memoirs*. What Lloyd George could not accept was the sheer difficulty which Allied strategists faced in 1917. There is a sense of terrible inevitability when examining British strategy in 1917. Dreams of 'knocking out the props' were illusory: Germany had to be fought directly, and the only place to do this was on the Western Front. The declining

99   Ibid., p.703.
100   Hankey Diary, 15 October 1917 quoted in Roskill, *Man of Secrets*, p.443.
101   Quoted in Grigg, *Lloyd George*, p.275.
102   Haig Diary, 16 October 1917, quoted in Grigg, *Lloyd George*, p.275.
103   Prior & Wilson, *Passchendaele*, p.200.
104   Lloyd, *Passchendaele*, pp.292, 296. For Lloyd George, Hubert Gough was the villain of the campaign. See Anthony Farrar-Hockley, *Goughie: The Life of General Sir Hubert Gough* (London: Hart-David, 1975) for a counterpoint.
105   On this point, see Prior & Wilson, *Passchendaele*, pp.185-94.
106   Woodward, *Lloyd George and the Generals*, p.279.

'New Year's congratulations are strictly forbidden': German cartoon depicting John Bull sadly contemplating a litany of Allied setbacks (revolution in Russia; Caporetto; U-boat woes; rainfall in Flanders; Cambrai counter-attack) during 1917. (*Kladderadatsch*, 30 December 1917)

strength of Britain's allies made the task much harder and forced the BEF to bear the brunt of the fighting. This suggested a reconsideration of methods. Yet the fractious nature of British civil-military relations made this impossible. The comparative weakness of Lloyd George's position meant he could not force a political showdown with his generals and ultimately acquiesced to an operation which he did not believe would succeed and which he had no power to constrain. Everything had to be staked on Haig's ambitious plans.

The strategic and battlefield difficulties of 1917 made it was a bleak year for the British war effort. By the end of the year the Allies seemed close to defeat. American forces had not yet arrived in any strength; Russia had been forced out of the war; Italy had been dealt a crushing blow at Caporetto; France had been fought to a standstill and the BEF was close to exhaustion. The political mood was pessimistic. On 29 November, Lord Lansdowne published his previously private memorandum as a 'peace letter' in the *Daily Telegraph*. Echoing President Woodrow Wilson's call for a 'peace without victory', Lansdowne described 'wanton prolongation' of the war as a crime and warned of popular rebellion.[107] A month later, on 29 December, William Robertson grimly reflected, 'This may well prove to be the darkest year of the war.'[108] Yet pessimism is not the same as defeatism. For all the setbacks of 1917, Britain and France remained determined to continue the war, but the failure of Haig's Third Ypres conception meant that direction of the conflict would be realigned by Lloyd George – with controversial consequences – in 1918.

107 D. Newton, 'The Lansdowne "Peace Letter" of 1917 and the Prospect of Peace by Negotiation with Germany', *Australian Journal of Politics and History*, 48 (1) (2002), pp.17-20
108 Quoted in Hugh Cunningham, *The Challenge of Democracy: Britain 1832-1918* (London: Routledge, 2001), p.236.

2

Decline and Fall
Sir William Robertson as Chief of the Imperial General Staff in 1917

John Spencer

At the end of 1916 General Sir William Robertson was at the height of his powers. A year into his role as Chief of the Imperial General Staff (CIGS), his bluff, no-nonsense approach had transformed the military staff at the War Office into an efficient, focussed and loyal machine. The days when the professional head of the army was a mere rubbing-rag for the Secretary of State for War, Field Marshal Lord Kitchener, were long gone. Robertson drove a hard 'bargain' with 'K of K' when, in late 1915, he agreed to fill the boots of a succession of hapless predecessors. As CIGS Robertson would not only be the government's principal military advisor. All orders to the British Army, in all theatres, would be approved by him, even if they still carried the fig leaf imprimatur of the Secretary of State. A dispirited and exhausted Kitchener had accepted the inevitable and, over time, grudgingly acknowledged 'Wully's' focus and drive. Kitchener's death in June 1916 was a blow to public morale, but by then politically at least, he was a busted flush. His successor was not.

David Lloyd George took political control of the War Office on 6 July 1916. From the outset he tackled it with the same vigour and sense of purpose that he had applied to the Ministry of Munitions. The latter half of 1916 saw the fledgling British Expeditionary Force (BEF) graduate from an inexperienced volunteer army to a serious fighting force. The costly first day of the Battle of the Somme was followed by weeks and months of gradual, if expensive, gains and ended with an army bloodied yet educated. Another fighting season beckoned, and the Western Front would be the army's priority. The Secretary of State for War had been shocked by the losses on the Somme, and before the campaign ended in November he had begun to agitate for alternative theatres where, he believed, success would be easier, and cheaper. The notion of victories against other nations of the Central Powers, effectively 'knocking away the props' which supported the German war machine, had already become a familiar Lloyd George argument. It was entirely at odds with Robertson's mantra which was that the principal enemy, Germany, could only be defeated on the principal front, the Western. This fundamental difference of opinion dominated British strategy for the whole of 1917 and came to its climax in October of that year. Exactly 12 months earlier Lloyd George had agitated for allied resources to be diverted to the Balkan theatre to support Romania in its fight against Germany's Bulgarian ally. An acrimonious showdown at the War Committee on 9 October 1916, in which Robertson spoke against this strategy, was the opening round of a new battle at the heart of British civil-military relations.[1] Afterwards, Robertson took it upon himself to remind Lloyd George that 'the CIGS should be able to count upon the Secretary of State for War in regard to the military plans which he puts forward'.[2] This honest, if ill-judged sermonising, which included a thinly-

General Sir William Robertson.

veiled threat of resignation, cut no ice with the Welshman. He had his own views, and: 'You must not ask me to play the part of a mere dummy. I am not in the least suited to it.'[3]

If Lloyd George refused to be a 'dummy' whilst leading the War Office he certainly would not be one as Prime Minister. The collapse of Asquith's coalition government in December 1916 finally gave Lloyd George the power he had craved for so long. Now, at last, he could impose his views on British war policy. But it was not going to be easy. The coming year was, by any measure, a momentous one for the allied cause in the Great War. First, the BEF was placed under the command, albeit temporarily, of a French general untried in the exercise of strategic command. Success at Vimy Ridge quickly turned into bloody stalemate around Arras, while the major French offensive it had been launched to support failed. In the early summer the BEF's Commander-in-Chief (C-in-C) Field Marshal Sir Douglas Haig's success at Messines was followed by the bloody, muddy, and ultimately indecisive slog up the Passchendaele Ridge. The year ended with initial success at Cambrai; a bold initiative which turned, all too quickly, to disappointment. Elsewhere the allied cause suffered

1   The National Archives (TNA) CAB, 42/21/3, War Committee, 9 October 1916.
2   David R. Woodward, *The Military Correspondence of Field-Marshal Sir William Robertson, Chief of the Imperial General Staff, December 1915-February 1918* (London: Army Records Society, 1989), hereafter *MCWR*, Robertson to Lloyd George, 11 October 1916, pp.90-1.
3   Ibid., Lloyd George to Robertson, 11 October 1916, pp.93-96.

from the disintegration of the Russian Empire, a disastrous setback on the Italian front and the continuing open sore that was the stalemate at Salonika. By contrast, in the Middle East a morale-boosting success was one of the few things to celebrate by the year's end.

Each of these campaigns, and other yet more peripheral concerns, fell into Robertson's remit. Each demanded his attention, strategic consideration and ultimately policy advice. Each was dependent upon the support or otherwise of a coalition government and a capricious Prime Minister. For Robertson personally, 1917 was a time of triumph and disaster. A year which began with opportunity and promise ended in frustration, his authority under siege from a politician whose motives he could never understand. This chapter focusses on the events which led up to Sir William Robertson's forced resignation in early 1918; events which paved the way for the Prime Minister to finally rid himself of a soldier with whom he had never seen eye to eye.

For those interested in the history of the British Army in the Great War, David Lloyd George often assumes the role of bogeyman: ambitious, unscrupulous, ultimately venal, a politician who by devious scheming ran rings around honourable, straight-backed soldiers intent only on doing their duty. As with all such easy characterisations this one contains both fact and fiction. Certainly, Lloyd George was the ultimate political operator. Comfortable with deal-making, to the extent of forging shaky alliances with political rivals, he had an almost messianic belief in his own destiny. In this, at least, he had parallels with some in the senior ranks of the army. When Lloyd George moved into 10 Downing Street on 6 December 1916 he did so as head of Britain's second wartime coalition government. A Liberal, he succeeded H.H. Asquith — 'Squiff' to his detractors — with the promise of action where there had been delay, grip where there had been weakness. That, at least, was the official line. In fact, the new Prime Minister had a tiger by the tail. Lloyd George achieved power not with the support of his own party colleagues, but with the acquiescence of his opponents in the Conservative and Unionist Party, whose leading lights made up a substantial proportion of his cabinet. It meant that if he were to govern, he had to compromise, often on issues he felt most strongly about. At every stage of his wartime premiership Lloyd George had to consider the views of his conservative-minded, military-supporting enablers in both Houses of Parliament. While his ministry began on a wave of confidence, this fractious alliance was not acquiescent for long.

All this meant that in early 1917 Robertson and Haig had to deal with a new premier and a new cabinet overtly committed to winning the war. For both soldiers the war could only be won in the west. All other theatres were sideshows to this main event. If Lloyd George and his government were serious about winning the war, rather than agreeing a peace based upon negotiated compromise — and they said that they were — only the defeat of the German army in the field would deliver that victory. Lloyd George thought otherwise. This fundamental difference dominated British military policy in 1917, the darkest year of the war for the allied cause.

As far as the military leadership was concerned, the year began reasonably well. Whilst allowing himself to be persuaded of the virtues of another major offensive on the Western Front, the new Prime Minister was desperate to reduce British casualties. One way to achieve this, he believed, was for the British Army to play a secondary role to their French ally. In order to do so, and in a bid to limit what he saw as the wasteful inclinations of Haig and Robertson, he placed his country's forces under French command.[4] Its significance for this discussion is the impact it had on the Prime Minister's ability to dominate strategic policy. In placing Haig's army under the orders of the French Commander-in-Chief General Robert Nivelle, albeit only for the duration of his eponymous offensive, Lloyd George succeeded in uniting against him not only his Unionist cabinet colleagues, but also much of the British press. Had the French C-in-C's scheme been a success, Lloyd George would have been vindicated. As it was it failed to achieve its grandiose objectives. For so accomplished a politician, antagonising both those who kept him in power, and the barons of Fleet Street, was a bruising experience. Haig and Robertson, so recently cowed by their subservience to their ally, were once again in the ascendant. It meant that throughout the summer of 1917 a chastened Prime Minister could do little other than watch from the side-lines as his generals planned for the long-awaited offensive to conquer the high ground around Ypres and push on to the Belgian coast. As is discussed in detail elsewhere in this volume, that was not to be. By the time the Third Ypres offensive had been grinding on for almost two months, Lloyd George had had enough.

Towards the end of September, he and his French opposite number met at a conference in a train carriage at Boulogne. The business discussed was unremarkable, the decisions apparently uncontroversial, and all was over and done with in less than two hours. Yet for Sir William Robertson's career it was of profound importance.

As was par for the course at such gatherings, the subjects for discussion were the Western, Middle Eastern, Italian and Salonika fronts. The French premier, Paul Painlevé, had been in office for less than a fortnight. Nonetheless, for the previous six months he had served as War Minister, having sacked Nivelle for his failed offensive. The widespread acts of indiscipline which infected the French army in the aftermath of the battle prompted Painlevé to replace him with Philippe Pétain. The experience meant that he knew only too well the fragile state of his country's army. In his view Britain could, and should, do more by taking over more trench line on the Western Front. This French demand was a familiar feature of such conferences and continued to be well into 1918. The British representatives invariably met the request with warm words of sympathy, while doing what they could to avoid formal commitment, resulting in little change, if any, on the ground. This time Robertson once again played a straight bat, avoided detailed commitment and suggested that the best way forward was for the two C-in-Cs to discuss details. Nothing could be done, he insisted, until Haig's offensive was complete and it became clear what could realistically be achieved.

---

4   For an assessment of the Nivelle Offensive (16 April-9 May 1917), see Elizabeth Greenhalgh, *The French Army and the First World War* (Cambridge: Cambridge University Press, 2014), pp.170-219.

Where he was clear, was that 'any great extension of the British line was not consistent with the adoption of a great offensive next spring.' Nonetheless, he acknowledged, as far as the British and French governments were concerned 'the principle of taking over more of the line was already admitted.'[5] In a brief, and apparently innocuous, intervention Robertson had managed to anger both Lloyd George and Sir Douglas Haig. For the Prime Minister, Robertson's words were evidence that, while one enormously costly offensive was still going on, all his principal military adviser could muster as a strategy for the next year was more of the same. Haig did not attend the conference but hosted Lloyd George and the CIGS to dinner that evening. Busy with the planning for the Battle of Polygon Wood, which began the next day, he was told by Lloyd George that Painlevé was anxious that the British should take over more of the line. The Prime Minister also asked him to produce a paper on future British strategy in the likely event that Russia dropped out of the war. A few days later, Haig wrote that a 'bombshell had arrived', in the shape of a letter from Robertson noting that at the Boulogne conference his government had agreed 'in principle' that his army would take over more line from the French. 'Robertson comes badly out of this', Haig wrote in his diary, 'especially as it was definitely stated (with the War Cabinet's approval) that no discussion re. [sic] the operations on the Western Front would be held with the French without my being present.'[6] From Robertson's perspective he had acknowledged a long-standing and almost inevitable strategic reality, but effectively kicked it into the long grass by leaving details to the allied commanders. Haig, however, saw it as sabotaging any prospect of another major British offensive in early 1918. Manpower was short as it was without spreading it even more thinly. It was an ominous development for the increasingly shaky Haig-Robertson alliance, one which, in the eyes of the politicians at least, had been solid and formidable for so long. For Robertson's career as CIGS, 25 September 1917 was the start of a downward trajectory..

Having asked Haig for his views on future British strategy, Lloyd George instructed Robertson to do much the same, with an eye to the Prime Minister's familiar request to consider alternative theatres to the Western Front; in this case against the Ottoman Empire in Palestine. The Prime Minister might have been disappointed, but could hardly have been surprised, when Robertson's appraisal landed on his desk. It took a familiar, strongly pro-Western Front position, with gloomy predictions for the prospects of expanded operations in Palestine. An offensive northwards towards Jerusalem, even if successful, entailed widening the British front from 30 to 50 miles. He predicted at least three costly battles against strong Turkish resistance leading to 'little result beyond the moral advantages which we may gain'.[7] Worse, he calcu-

5   TNA CAB 28/2 IC: Procès-Verbal of an Anglo-French Conference held at Boulogne, 25 September 1917.

6   Haig Diary, 3 October 1917 quoted in Gary Sheffield & John Bourne (eds.), *Douglas Haig: War Diaries and Letters 1914-1918* (London: Phoenix, 2006 [2005]), pp.331-32.

7   TNA CAB 24/28/42, GT 2242: 'Occupation of Jaffa-Jerusalem Line', CIGS to War Cabinet, 9 October 1917, pp.1, 3, 7.

lated that the British force of seven infantry and three cavalry divisions would need reinforcing by three infantry divisions with two more in relief.[8] Those troops had to come from somewhere and this, Robertson claimed, meant that:

> Turkish territory will become, for an indefinite period, the decisive theatre and the West front must meanwhile be delegated to secondary importance. This is because we have not sufficient resources to seek a decision in two theatres at the same time. No country ever has had, or probably will have. The first rule in all wars is to concentrate in the main theatre all forces that can be employed. Any departure from this rule has invariably proved disastrous.[9]

He warned of the consequences if the government insisted on major offensives on two fronts; expecting success from concentrated action in the Middle East would be a 'more dangerous' gamble than usual.[10] The estimate of forces required for a push to Jerusalem increased when General Sir Edmund Allenby, C-in-C Egyptian Expeditionary Force (EEF), reported that he would, in fact, need 14 infantry divisions and another six in relief. This demand, and there is evidence that Robertson and Allenby colluded on the matter, has been described by one authority as 'one of the most absurd appreciations ever presented to a British government.'[11]

More convincingly, Robertson's appraisal reminded the Prime Minister of the advantage the enemy had thanks to its internal lines of communication. The Germans could move 10 divisions a month between east and west fronts. By contrast, the Allies had to move forces long distances, it taking one division four weeks to move from Salonika to Egypt. The Royal Navy, in a supporting document, estimated it would need 100 ships to transport six divisions from France to the Middle East, the force arriving no sooner than the third week of February 1918. This would mean that 'the whole of the traffic in the Mediterranean' would be seriously interfered with, with severe impacts on supplies of coal and wheat to Italy, which was already struggling to resist the Central Powers.[12] On the home front, diverting transports from trans-Atlantic convoys would reduce British imports of food, raw materials and armaments, by up to 1.2 million tons from November 1917 to December 1918.[13] In the months

8   TNA CAB 24/28/42, GT 2242: 'Occupation of Jaffa-Jerusalem Line', CIGS to War Cabinet, 9 October 1917, pp. 4-5.
9   TNA CAB 24/28/42, GT 2242: 'Future Military Policy', CIGS to War Cabinet, 9 October 1917, p.1.
10 Ibid., pp. 1-2.
11 TNA CAB 27/8, WP 52: Allenby to CIGS, 10 October 1917; Woodward, *Lloyd George*, p.206; *MCRW*, Robertson to Allenby, 5 October 1917, p.232.
12 TNA CAB 27/8: WP 54, 'Question of reinforcing the army in Palestine', First Sea Lord to War Cabinet, 9 October 1917, pp.1, 3.
13 TNA CAB 27/8: WP 54, 'Effect on Imports into the United Kingdom of proposed transfer of troops from France to Egypt', First Sea Lord to War Cabinet, 9 October 1917, p.2.

after the United States entered the war in April 1917, Robertson and the War Office had been striving to ensure as many American troops as possible were transported to Europe. British shipping capacity, already stretched to breaking point, was simply not capable of absorbing another major logistical priority without dire consequences.

This was not what Lloyd George wanted to hear. Haig's assessment took a similar line, influenced as it was by the apparent ineffectiveness of Britain's main allies, and the progress of his Flanders offensive. It was produced during the Battle of Broodseinde, at a time when the Third Ypres offensive was still considered, by the C-in-C at least, to be going the BEF's way.[14] Haig's confidence is clear from his diary, which in the week before he submitted his report referred at least five times to the positive progress the BEF was making.[15] Diverting a proportion of his forces away from the Western Front would mean he had to stand on the defensive. If Britain did not conduct an offensive in the west in 1918 there was no prospect of her allies doing so.[16] It seems to have escaped Haig's notice that this was exactly what Lloyd George wanted. He was opposed to another costly offensive on the Western Front, at least until the Americans arrived in force.

Unsurprisingly, Haig's report concluded by advocating further operations in the west in 1918, building on what he believed were the successes of 1917. In the coming year the main weight of the fighting would fall to the British. While he knew the Prime Minister believed there might be alternatives to concentrating on the Western Front, he wanted to stick to the policy of devoting effort and resources to defeating Germany in the west. Haig, somewhat unconvincingly, said he had examined and 'carefully considered' the other options but there was not one of them 'which offers any prospect of defeating the German armies, and until we defeat those armies I see no prospect of gaining the peace we seek'.[17] As for the current campaign, it was:

> … beyond question that our offensive must be pursued as long as possible. I have every hope of being able to continue it for several weeks still and of gaining results which will add very greatly to the enemy's losses in men and moral[e] and place us in a far better position to resume an offensive in the spring.[18]

This was not to Lloyd George's satisfaction. According to Lieutenant-General Sir Henry Wilson, who Lloyd George had begun to consult informally on military policy, when their papers arrived the Prime Minister condemned both Haig and Robertson as:

14 Nick Lloyd, *Passchendaele: A New History* (London: Viking, 2017), pp.212-13; the Battle of Broodseinde (4-8 October 1917) began well with initial objectives achieved.
15 National Library of Scotland (NLS), (Acc.3155/96-97) Field Marshal Sir Douglas Haig (manuscript) diary, 5 and 7 October 1917.
16 TNA CAB 27/8: GT 2243, p.3.
17 Ibid., p.2.
18 Ibid., p.5.

Contemporary cartoon commentary on the BEF's successive offensives (Menin Road Ridge,
Polygon Wood, Broodseinde) to secure Passchendaele Ridge:
'A BIRTHDAY GREETING FOR HINDENBURG. F.M. SIR DOUGLAS HAIG (*sings*)
"O I'LL TAK' THE HIGH ROAD AN' YE'LL TAK' THE LOW ROAD …"'
(*Punch*, 10 October 1917)

… pig-headed stupid and narrow-visioned. Haig has submitted, what LG called, a 'preposterous' paper which sets out to prove that the west front is the *only* front. LG says that, in fact, on Haig's own showing the Western front is a *hopeless* front. Allenby has apparently said that he needs 2 to 1 to beat the Turks and therefore it would follow that it was no use sending troops out there. Haig claims that even if the Boches [sic] are reinforced by 32 Divisions from Russia he can still beat them although inferior in men and guns.[19]

By this stage of the war the C-in-C's positive outlook was viewed by some members of the government with more than a degree of cynicism, with his head of intelligence John Charteris fielding much of the criticism. Haig's optimism failed to convince the habitually pessimistic Lord Esher. His report was 'very sanguine about prospects on this Front. I did not care much for it.'[20] Haig's 'sanguine' approach to the threats facing his front coloured British strategy into the spring of 1918. According to Wilson, the Secretary of State for War, Lord Derby, agreed with him that Haig's staff was 'rotten and that all his forecasts are wrong and that Robertson endorses them. But Derby is a weak creature …'[21]

If Haig was 'sanguine' about the future, Robertson certainly was not. Close proximity to the Prime Minister and his supporters and attending the War Cabinet on a daily basis meant he was in no doubt at all of his political master's growing frustration with his advice. On 6 October Robertson complained to Haig about the 'Palestine rot' and of being labelled 'a hide-bound west fronter with no imagination.' He vowed to avoid being 'jockeyed by degrees into a wrong course', raising the prospect of 'a row'. Apparently Lloyd George had offered to fight French demands for the BEF taking over more front if the CIGS agreed to send extra divisions to the Middle East. Wully did not believe him.[22] Haig condemned the French demand for him to take over more line as 'unfair'; one which should be refused 'even to the point of answering threats by threats if necessary.'[23] Robertson attempted to mollify the Field Marshal, having heard from Lord Robert Cecil, a Tory grandee and ally, that 'perhaps you are a little disappointed with me in the way I have stood up for correct principles, but you must let me do my job in my own way.' Lloyd George was 'out for my blood very much these days', despite support from other War Cabinet members including Lord Curzon, Arthur Balfour and Lord Milner. The Prime Minister now had both his and

19   Imperial War Museum (IWM), (HHW 1) Henry Wilson diary, 10 October 1917.
20   Churchill Archive Centre (CAC), Cambridge, Viscount Esher Papers, Esher Journal (2/20), 15 October 1917, original emphasis. Esher was a long-standing and influential fixture in British politics, operating at a rarefied level without portfolio and no formal responsibilities.
21   Wilson diary, 16 October 1917.
22   *MCWR*, Robertson to Haig, 6 October 1917, p.233; see also CAC, Hankey Diary, HNKY, 6 October 1917.
23   NLS, Haig Diary 8 October 1917.

Haig's memoranda: 'He will be furious, & probably matters will come to a head. I rather hope so. I am sick of this d – d life.'[24]

It is hardly surprising, given the seemingly intractable position of both his principal military adviser and his most senior commander in the field, that Lloyd George sought new advice. This would come from individuals he knew had less sympathy with the Robertson-Haig alliance, however problematic this might have become in private. Sir Maurice Hankey, the Secretary to the War Cabinet, recorded that the Prime Minister had recently played host to Field Marshal Lord French and Wilson. Both were critics of the Flanders offensive, and both favoured 'some kind of central Allied control' of war policy. The day after Robertson had expressed his frustration, at a War Cabinet meeting 'the view was clearly expressed' that Haig's report 'did not provide a convincing argument that we could inflict a decisive military defeat on Germany on the Western Front next year' even if Russia remained an effective participant.[25] As a result, the Prime Minister recalled that at the start of the war, when 'equally grave decisions' had to be taken, his predecessor had called a 'War Council' to hear the views of a range of military experts. That had not happened because of lack of confidence in the commanders, he said. Wilson and French would be invited to offer their views, regardless of possible objections:

> In reply to a suggestion that the Chief of the Imperial General Staff might resent this procedure, the Prime Minister pointed out that neither General Sir Charles Douglas, then Chief of the Imperial General Staff, nor Field Marshal Lord French, the Commander-in-Chief Designate of the British Expeditionary Force had resented the War Council held in August 1914, and he himself would undertake to explain the matter fully to General Robertson.[26]

Lloyd George's mendacity did not fool Esher who noted that the 1914 meeting '*was* called because *no confidence* was felt that Sir C. Douglas or Sir John French were capable of giving military advice upon such grave issues'.[27] Nor was Robertson appeased. He immediately offered his resignation to Derby, who refused it and, in the short-term at least, managed to defuse the situation.

The next day, 11 October, with the CIGS present, the War Cabinet asked French and Wilson to produce their own 'appreciations' of the Robertson and Haig papers, and to make suggestions as to future policy.[28] Wully was, according to Hankey, ' as sulky as a bear with a sore head'.[29] That afternoon Wilson and French set to work

24   *MCWR*, Robertson to Haig, 9 October 1917, pp.234-5.
25   TNA CAB 23/13/20: War Cabinet, 10 October 1917.
26   Ibid.
27   CAC, Esher papers, ESHR4, VII (1917), Esher journal, 17 October 1917, original emphasis.
28   TNA CAB 23/4/21: War Cabinet, 11 October 1917.
29   CAC, Hankey diary, HNKY 1/3, 10 October 1917.

in the latter's office at Horse Guards, Wilson sitting at Wellington's desk.[30] They conferred throughout the writing period. The resulting two papers were products of extensive collusion.[31]

Robertson told Haig that:

> I do not much care what advice is rendered by French and Wilson as I shall not budge an inch from my Paper and I do not suppose you will budge from yours … the fact is that it is a very weak-kneed craven-hearted Cabinet and L.G. hypnotises them and is allowed to run riot.[32]

According to Lloyd George 'a turning point in the war' had been reached.[33] He believed there were four 'alternative policies' facing Britain. In short, these were:

1. Concentration of 'the whole of our forces on the Western front' with all other theatres treated as not only subordinate but with forces sufficient for 'safety on the defensive'. This, Lloyd George said, was Haig's recommendation.
2. Concentrate mainly on the Western Front but maintain active operations in other theatres, such as Mesopotamia and Palestine, in the hope that by 'rough handling' the Turks might be induced to 'come to terms'.
3. Lloyd George ascribed the third option to the French C-in-C Pétain. This comprised of limited attacks while concentrating on economic warfare until Russia recovered and the USA could supply enough men to ensure superiority.
4. Option four was described by the Prime Minister as 'knocking the props from under Germany'. The underlying basis was to counter the loss of Russia by depriving Germany of her allies, 'with a view to an eventual great concentration against an isolated Germany. This might be achieved by a combination of military and diplomatic operations against Turkey.' First it would be necessary to deliver a major military blow against them.[34]

Wilson set to work only to be interrupted that afternoon by Lord Milner, a member of the War Cabinet and a critic of Haig's strategy, who said that 'relations between L.G. and Robertson are impossible. Faults on both sides and mutual dislike. L.G. often unfair and Robertson often special pleading of gross and offensive type.'[35]

---

30   Wilson diary, 11 October 1917.
31   Wilson's diary records him working alongside or discussing his paper with French on 11, 12, 14, 15, 16 and 17 October 1917, by which time he had begun sharing them with his political allies, Wilson diary, 11-20 October 1917.
32   *MCWR*, Robertson to Haig, 11 October 1917, p.236.
33   Wilson diary, 11 October 1917.
34   TNA CAB 23/13/21: War Cabinet, 11 October 1917, pp.7-8.
35   Wilson diary, 11 October 1917.

Wilson's paper asserted that Britain's war policy had been reactive rather than proactive. A review was needed because in three years Britain had moved 'from being the most "contemptible" to being the most formidable' of Germany's enemies.[36] Russia was effectively lost as an ally, to be replaced by the USA which might be of significant value in 'the somewhat distant and problematical future.'[37] Wilson was not, unlike Haig, convinced that the time was right or the resources available to strike a decisive blow in the west. Haig had said he was 'confident that if the course I have recommended be adopted whole-heartedly we shall gain far more than a limited success in the field next year.'[38] Wilson disagreed. It was 'no use throwing "decisive numbers at the decisive time at the decisive place" at my head if the decisive numbers do not exist, if the decisive hour has not struck or if the decisive plan is ill-chosen.'[39]

He asked if it were possible for the allies to 'enlarge our view' and draw up plans so that 'when the decisive moment arrives we can produce the decisive numbers at the decisive place?'[40] According to Wilson there were three, not necessarily mutually exclusive, routes towards this objective:

i)   By eliminating some of the smaller of our enemies and thus releasing all the troops and material we now have in such secondary theatres – and incidentally setting free a large amount of tonnage.

ii)   By recruiting the necessary number of men and placing them in the field where and when required.

iii) By an enormous and overwhelming increase in guns, munitions, aeroplanes, tanks and all engines of war.

Regardless of which course(s) the War Cabinet chose, and this was his principal theme, it was 'essential that a much closer and more effective co-operation' should be established between the Allies.[41]

It has been argued that British grand strategy from mid-1916 was characterised by a general feeling of 'pessimism' amounting to defeatism. Some of Britain's political and military leaders were focussed on concluding the war on acceptable terms; in contrast to their public utterances epitomised by Lloyd George's commitment to total victory thanks to a 'knockout blow' on the Western Front.[42] Wilson was more positive. He remained opposed to a compromise peace and was confident that, with changes to

36   TNA CAB 27/8: WP 61, p.3.
37   Ibid., pp. 3-4.
38   TNA CAB 27/8: GT 2243, pp.13-14.
39   TNA CAB 27/8: WP 61, p.4.
40   Ibid., p.7.
41   Ibid., p. 8.
42   Brock Millman, *Pessimism and British War Policy: 1916-1918* (London: Frank Cass, 2001), and idem, 'A Counsel of Despair: British Strategy and War Aims, 1917-18', *Journal of Contemporary History*, 2 (36), (2001), pp.252-54.

strategic decision-making, Britain could emerge from the war with her empire and prestige intact.[43]

Wilson was as opposed to a major strategic effort in the Middle East as Haig and Robertson. The latter had said that even if successful, the military effect of Lloyd George's Palestine scheme would be of no value to us'.[44] It was 'very desirable' to reduce the number of Britain's enemies, but since Russia's collapse he did not see an extensive offensive campaign in Palestine 'as a sound military measure'. In his view 'the right military course to pursue is to act on the defensive in Palestine and the east generally and continue to seek a decision in the West'.[45] Throughout the war Robertson consistently opposed any large-scale offensives that could hamper Britain's effort in the west. In 1915, he condemned the forthcoming Gallipoli offensive as a 'ridiculous farce'.[46] Once he became CIGS he was, from time to time, prepared to consider actions away from France and Flanders to exploit perceived enemy weaknesses or to boost morale at home. He would not, however, subjugate the BEF's needs for those of armies to other theatres.[47]

Wilson's paper reiterated his strategic belief in the primacy of the Western Front. On this point at least, he emphasised, he was in step with his colleagues:

> I have always been (even years before the war broke out) and I shall always remain, an ardent 'Westerner', for the simple reason that it is along the west front that the bulk of the forces of our principal enemy is disposed and the death-grapple must be engaged in at the time and place and in the manner best suited to our cause.[48]

Nonetheless, he questioned Haig's and Robertson's continuing optimism for decisive results in the west in 1918: 'We seem to be as confident of success when Russia and Roumania [sic] have collapsed and France is temporarily weakened as we were when all these three countries were capable of heavy offensive actions.'[49] Conversely, Germany, having failed to win in the west in 1914, had turned eastwards and had 'succeeded in the Balkans, in Roumania and now in Russia.' Germany's plan had been to gain territory and supplies 'and put himself in the position to mass a much larger number of troops in the decisive theatre (i.e. in the West) when the time for the

---

43   TNA CAB 27/8: WP 61, pp.5-6.
44   TNA CAB 24/28/42, GT 2242: 'Future Military Policy', CIGS to War Cabinet, 9 October 1917, p.3.
45   Ibid., p.4.
46   Liddell Hart Centre for Military Archives (LHCMA), Robertson papers, (7/2/15), Robertson to Callwell, 19 March 1915.
47   See esp. David R. Woodward, *Field Marshal Sir William Robertson: Chief of the Imperial General Staff in the Great War* (Westport, Connecticut: Praeger, 1998), pp. 114-23 and 157-68.
48   TNA CAB 27/8: WP 61, p.4.
49   Ibid.

death-grapple came.'[50] Wilson, therefore, was not confident of an allied victory in the west in 1918. But nor did he support a major effort elsewhere. This must have come as an unwelcome surprise to the Prime Minister. Three weeks earlier Wilson had told his old friend Henry Rawlinson that he favoured sending '10 or 12 D[i]vs to Egypt to make sure of beating the Turks this winter [and] bringing them back to France for the summer offensive of 1918.'[51] At a meeting with the Prime Minister Wilson had 'expressed the strong belief that if a really good scheme was thoroughly well worked out, we could chase the Turks out of Palestine and very likely knock them completely out *during the mud months*, without in any way interfering with Haig's operations next Spring and Summer'.[52]

Then Wilson changed his mind. On the day the War Cabinet asked for his views, and in the light of Robertson's and the Navy's negative reports, Wilson discussed the issue with his long-time friend Ferdinand Foch, the French army's Chief of Staff. Foch thought it was 'late for Syria [Palestine] and we must spend the winter in making guns, arms etc.'[53] By the following day Wilson concluded that 'we are late to plan and carry out an attack on the Turks this winter' and thus 'this confines us to Europe'.[54] Having garnered the facts, and heard the opposition of his friend and mentor, Wilson came 'very reluctantly, to the conclusion that we are too late'.[55] He explained that a successful offensive against the Turks would have had to have been carried out during the 'mud-months' in France, from November to the end of April, when weather in the region was 'admirably suited for campaigning. We are too late now — in the middle of October — to make plans for the coming winter, and we are too late for other reasons also.'[56] Robertson's study had claimed two German divisions were available to reinforce the Turks and, if it became clear Britain intended a major offensive, more would be sent.[57] Wilson agreed. The Germans had second-guessed the British and had 'taken a much firmer grip of the Turk'[58] There was also the perennial problem of a shortage of troops. Agreeing with Haig and Robertson, Wilson advised that there would be insufficient manpower to send the necessary force to campaign in the Middle East and to remain effective in the west.[59] Third, he reiterated the Admiralty view that 'dwindling tonnage and difficulties of escort would make the transportation, upkeep and return of the necessary force

50   TNA CAB 27/8: WP 61, p.4.
51   CAC, Sir Henry Rawlinson Papers, Rawlinson Journal, RWLN 1/9, 2 October 1917.
52   Wilson diary, 5 October 1917 (original emphasis).
53   Ibid., 11 October 1917.
54   Wilson, 12 October 1917
55   TNA CAB 27/8: WP 61, pp.8-9.
56   Ibid., p.9.
57   TNA CAB 27/8, GT 2242: 'Occupation of Jaffa-Jerusalem Line', CIGS to War Cabinet, 9 October 1917, p.4.
58   TNA CAB 27/8: WP 61, p.9.
59   Ibid.

impossible'.[60] Wilson then sounded the death-knell for future large-scale adventures against Turkey:

> For all these reasons, but not because the West is the decisive theatre in the winter, I am clearly of opinion that it is impossible to send an expedition against the Turks this winter *and wrong to send an expedition next spring or summer.*[61]

However, Wilson disagreed with Haig and opposed his plan for another offensive, bolstered by newly-arrived American troops, on the Western Front in 1918. British manpower was in a parlous state, and the imminent collapse of Russia would mean German divisions being transferred from the eastern to the western theatre. Therefore: 'until the Americans can be got over in sufficient force we cannot hope to beat the enemy by force of numbers'.[62]

Having dismissed both Haig's hopes for another offensive in 1918, and Lloyd George's dreams of a strategic victory in the Middle East, Wilson moved on to what was arguably his most significant intervention in British war policy to date: unity of command. He did not use the specific term, cleverly opting for the more ambiguous 'Superior Direction'. Since the war began the irregular Allied conferences of politicians and generals had been disorganised, lacking in structure, and light on specific strategic policy. Wilson, who had spent much of the war liaising with the French, knew they favoured a more co-ordinated approach. He also knew the Prime Minister was looking for a way to wrest control of strategy from Robertson and Haig. In his report Haig had taken a dim view of inter-Allied control. He recommended that in future, Britain should:

> Insist on occupying the predominant positions in the Councils of the Allies to which our strength entitles us. More than once already we have subordinated our judgement to that of our allies with highly unsatisfactory results. We cannot afford to make such mistakes again, and whatever they may threaten [,] our allies cannot afford to quarrel with us. [63]

Likewise, Robertson believed 'the principle of "unity of command" and "one front" must be cautiously applied. In theory it is attractive, in practice it has not been encouraging.' He reminded the War Cabinet that it was 'responsible for the Nivelle era and its consequences'. Allied co-operation had seen Britain and France obliged to send

---

60   TNA CAB 27/8: WP 61, p.9.
61   TNA CAB 27/8: WP 61, author's italics.
62   TNA CAB 27/8: WP 61, p.11.
63   For the placing of Haig under French orders and the subsequent Nivelle Offensive see esp. Gary Sheffield, *The Chief: Douglas Haig and the British Army* (London: Aurum Press, 2011), and David French, *British Strategy and War Aims: 1914-1916* (London: Allen & Unwin, 1986) pp. 52-61; TNA CAB 27/8: WP 61, p.12.

150 heavy guns to Italy, and another 550 to Russia. 'All are lost to us', Robertson said.[64] Despite this support, the Italians had cancelled a promised offensive and adopted a 'more passive attitude' on their front. General Luigi Cadorna, the Italian Army commander, thought this *volte-face* 'would not prejudice Allied operations elsewhere'.[65] In the light of this, Robertson was dismissive of Britain's allies' willingness to fight. In his view, the French had also 'failed us badly this year' and 'must be made to fight'. Therefore:

> As far as 'unity of command' is concerned, we should endeavour to acquire for ourselves the control of operations next year on the West front, as we are entitled to do by our successes this year, the efficiency and spirit of our Armies, and the stability of our Government as compared with that of practically all our European Allies.[66]

As a long-term advocate of closer Allied co-operation, Wilson disagreed. Lloyd George had discussed the notion of a form of superior direction with him in August and suggested a trio of senior officers to review Robertson's recommendations. Wilson counselled against this as unfair to Robertson, but maintained the view that an inter-Allied body, including senior political representatives, was needed.[67] In early October, when Lloyd George finally decided to act, he met Wilson and French and said that:

> Robertson simply 'thwarted' him in every scheme … I asked L.G. about a superior organisation & he said of course that was the best plan but the French (and Italian) governments were absolutely rotten … & therefore he was reverting to his former idea of calling me in to examine Robertson's plans. Johnnie fulminated against R.[obertson], & L.G. agreed but said that R had got so much of the Press (M.[orning] Post, Northcliffe, Leo Maxse, etc.) & Asquith that it was a difficult question to remove him… Johnnie said he felt very hopeless about the whole thing, for although L.G. *knew* that Robertson was not big enough for the post yet he funked kicking him out…the fact is that L.G. is profoundly dissatisfied … but does not know what to do, or how to get rid of Robertson. I saw no animus against Haig.[68]

Wilson avoided the implication that 'superior direction' of the war would inevitably mean 'unity of command' at the military level, offering assurances to the soldiers

---

64   TNA CAB 24/28/42, GT 2242: 'Future Military Policy', CIGS to War Cabinet, 9 October 1917, pp.6-7.
65   TNA CAB 23/4/12: War Cabinet, 24 September 1917.
66   TNA CAB 24/28/42, GT 2242: 'Future Military Policy', CIGS to War Cabinet, 9 October 1917, p.6.
67   Wilson diary, 23 August 1917.
68   Ibid., 5 October 1917.

about their future status *vis-a-vis* such an organisation. Instead, he suggested, this would bring order and co-operation to the political direction of the war. There seems little doubt, however, that this was his ultimate expectation.[69] After dining with Lloyd George and French on 17 October he wrote:

> It became very clear to me tonight that L.G. means to get Robertson out *and* means to curb the powers of the C-in-C in the field. This is what I have been advising the last 2 ½ years & this is what the whole of my paper is directed to. Not to getting R.[obertson] put out but to forming an [sic] Superior Direction over all the CGSs and C-in-Cs.[70]

He and Lloyd George had discussed the subject several times.[71] The Allies had tried 'many expedients but always with most disappointing, sometimes even with disastrous results.'[72]

Wilson reassured the politicians that there was 'no question' of overruling national Cabinets since the 'Supreme War Cabinet, or Superior Direction as I have called it' would represent them. He also attempted, unsuccessfully, to reassure the generals that there was not 'the least danger of any interference with the soldiers in the field, since the Chiefs of the Staff in each country will remain as today'.[73]

Field Marshal Lord French's paper followed similar lines to Wilson's, advocating a defensive position on the Western Front until the French and Americans were able to take part in a combined offensive. Where Wilson's

Lord Derby.

paper was free of personal criticism, French was unable to hide his hostility towards Wully and Haig. He saw both, rightly, as having been prime movers in his dismissal

69   The concept of 'unity of command' differed over the course of the war, and between soldiers and statesmen.
70   Wilson diary, 17 October 1917.
71   Wilson met Lloyd George and discussed this and related issues on 5, 10, 13 and 17 October 1917, Wilson diary.
72   Ibid., p.12.
73   TNA CAB 27/8: WP 61, p.14.

in late 1915 and wanted revenge.[74] He took a strong line with Robertson's paper, condemning it as 'chiefly a form of special pleading in favour of continuing the offensive in the West.'[75] The critical tone meant that Wilson delivered both papers to Hankey, not to the CIGS. Eventually Hankey passed them to Derby:

> The whole subject is so thorny and Robertson is in so prickly a state … The reports confirmed my worst anticipations. They both recommended a central council including a staff of generals, in Paris, to be independent of the national General Staffs. This, alone, is enough to drive Robertson into resignation. They both condemned the continuation of the Flanders offensive, next year, which is the course that Robertson and Haig recommend. In addition, Lord French's report hits out hard at Robertson and Haig whose views were challenged in principle and in detail.

Hankey then added, but perhaps understandably omitted from his memoirs:

> Incidentally I may remark that the whole thing is a clever plot on Ll G's part. Earlier in the year at Litchfield he sounded them both [Wilson and French] and ascertained this was their view, no doubt playing on their ambition and known jealousy and dislike of Robertson, by letting them see that he agreed, accompanying this no doubt with a good deal of suggestions. Then he lets Haig go on, and even encourages him to do so, knowing that the bad weather was preventing a big result, in order to strengthen the argument. Then he guilelessly proposes the War Council, knowing perfectly well that the jury is a packed one, which will only report in one direction. By these means he fortifies himself with apparently unbiased military opinion in the great struggle with Robertson and Haig, which he knows he cannot face without it.[76]

Wilson saw Derby on 24 October: 'He told me he had not yet shown our Papers (Johnnie's and mine) to Robertson. He said Johnnie's was too personal and mine too unanswerable and if they were shown to Haig and Robertson there would be a hell of a row which might mean resignation of Haig, R. and himself!'[77] At this point the

---

74   TNA CAB 27/8, WP 60: 'Lord French's paper on the Present State of the War, future prospects, and future action, 20 October 1917'. See also, Richard Holmes, *The Little Field Marshal: A Life of Sir John French*, (London: Jonathan Cape, 1981), p.332.

75   IWM, Lord French of Ypres Papers, JDPF 7/7, draft of Lord French's paper on the 'Present State of the War, future prospects, and future action', 20 October 1917, p.17.

76   CAC, Hankey diary, HNKY 1/3, 20 October 1917, and Lord Hankey, *The Supreme Command*, Vols. I & II, (London: George Allen & Unwin, 1961), Vol. II, pp.714-15.

77   Wilson diary, 24 October 1917.

Prime Minister ordered French to tone down his paper.[78] Robertson's supporters in the War Cabinet, and in the press, meant that simply getting an alternative opinion would not be enough. Robertson told Haig that French's paper was being amended and: 'It would all be rather amusing if it were not so serious and did not involve such a waste of time. But I have no intention of wasting much time over it myself.'[79] Unfortunately for Wully, the issue was going to dominate the rest of his time as CIGS. The most powerful newspaper owning cheerleader for Robertson and Haig was Lord Rothermere, proprietor of the *Daily Mail* and *The Times*. The former newspaper was particularly vociferous in its support of the War Office and Rothermere was treated with great circumspection by Lloyd George.[80] As we shall see, once Rothermere lost faith with the War Office, Wully's fate was sealed.

The Supreme War Council, with a secretariat based at the Palace of Versailles outside Paris, was the direct result of Wilson's strategy recommendations. It was officially constituted at a meeting of allied leaders in Rapallo, Italy, on 7 November 1917. They were there to offer support to that country in the face of a major offensive by the Central Powers. Disaster was only averted at the Battle of Caporetto by the diversion of French and British troops from the Western Front.[81] Minds were finally focussed on the essential need for more formal allied co-operation.[82] In fact Wilson, who was appointed Britain's Permanent Military Representative (PMR), and Lloyd George did not have things all their own way. Robertson and the War Office machine conducted a rearguard action to stymie the influence of the PMRs, and by extension the Council itself. As already noted, Lloyd George's main purpose in establishing the Supreme War Council was to weaken the stranglehold he felt Robertson and Haig held over British strategy by removing either man, or both.[83]

Robertson attended the Rapallo meeting, having been sent to Italy to assess the crisis 'the most disastrous reverse suffered by Italy in the First World War.'[84] Thanks to the transfer of four (later six) French and two (later four) British divisions the line was

78   CAC, Hankey diary, 24 October 1917; For a detailed discussion of French's paper (TNA CAB 27/8: WP 60) see John Spencer, *Wilson's War: Sir Henry Wilson's Influence on British Military Policy in the Great War and its Aftermath* (Warwick: Helion & Co., 2020), pp.91-96.

79   *MCWR*, Robertson to Haig, 27 October 1917, p.239.

80   J.M. McEwan, 'Northcliffe and Lloyd George at War, 1914-1918', *The Historical Journal*, Vol. 24 (3), 1981, pp. 651-672; see also A.J.A. Morris, *Reporting the First World War: Charles Repington, The Times and the Great War* (Cambridge: Cambridge University Press, 2015).

81   The Battle of Caporetto (11th Battle of the Isonzo), 24 October-19 November 1917; one of the Italian army's greatest defeats.

82   Meighen McCrae, *Coalition Strategy and the End of the First World War: The Supreme War Council and War Planning, 1917-1918* (Cambridge: Cambridge University Press, 2019), p.97.

83   See, for example, David R. Woodward, *Lloyd George and the Generals* (Newark: University of Delaware Press, 1983), p. 221; idem, *Robertson*, p. 191; French, *Strategy*, p. 164.

84   George H. Cassar, *The Forgotten Front: The British Campaign in Italy, 1917-1918* (London: Hambledon Press, 1998), p. 65, and and J.E. Edmonds & H.R. Davies, *Military Operations Italy, 1915-1919* (London: HMSO, 1949), p. xxvii.

stabilised. For Lloyd George the episode was further evidence of the need for a better co-ordinated allied strategy. He warned the War Cabinet that Painlevé was again demanding the British take over more line in France (in the region of 100 kilometres). Before a decision, he wanted a review of options for 1918.[85] The setbacks in Italy were 'due to the fact that the [strategic] situation was never considered as a whole. The Conferences we had with our Allies, which had lately increased in number, were not really Conferences. They were only meetings of people with preconceived ideas who desired to find a formula which would reconcile them.' He therefore felt that Wilson's advice for an 'Inter-Allied Staff' was 'sound'. Its functions would not be to give orders:

> ... but their duties would be to examine the military situation of the Allies ...
> No one was thinking out the whole plan as though he were responsible for the whole battle-front of the Allies. In order to achieve success the War ought to be conducted as though there were one man sitting in the centre with equal responsibility for all fronts.[86]

Lloyd George outlined the structure and function of what was soon to become the permanent military staff of the SWC, and that of the Council itself. What was needed was 'for the first time, a real Inter-Allied General Staff, to examine the situation as a whole and to advise, without divesting the Government or General Staffs of their responsibility.' Stressing the body's advisory status, he said it would receive plans from the Allied commands and then 'suggest' what action should be taken.

> It was essential that this Inter-Allied General Staff should be an entirely independent body, not consisting of representatives of the National General Staffs, as in that case each representative would simply fight for the views of his own General Staff.[87]

The Cabinet debate centred on the role and powers of the permanent 'Inter-Allied General Staff' which 'would make a continuous study of the Allied war plans just as the General Staff of the War Office made a continuous study of our own military plans.' The draft minutes recorded, 'It was pointed out that this was a change which might, to some extent, diminish the authority of the Chief of the Imperial General Staff, but it was suggested that in practice it would not do so very materially.' This sentence was later crossed out by Hankey, along with another concerning the sensitivities of Robertson and his War Office colleagues:

---

85   TNA CAB 23/13/27: War Cabinet, 30 October 1917, (draft), p.1.
86   Ibid., p.2; for the ineffectiveness of inter-Allied co-operation in 1917 see McCrae, *Coalition Strategy*, pp.8, 25 and *passim*.
87   TNA CAB 23/13/27: War Cabinet, 30 October 1917, (draft), pp.2-3.

Some doubts were expressed as to whether the scheme could be carried out without friction with the present Military Advisers of the Government, and as to whether in practical working this scheme would not involve great friction, and as to whether the new machinery would, in fact, cure the evils mentioned by the Prime Minister.[88]

The key question would be 'the nature of the offensives for next year, and whether the main effort of the Allies was to be made in 1918 or 1919.'[89] As for taking over more French line, there was no point discussing this until the campaign for 1918 was agreed and this was 'exactly the sort of question which would be referred to the Allied Council'. [90]

Lloyd George and Painlevé agreed to set up the SWC, with the issue of the BEF taking over more line to await advice from the PMRs.[91] The War Cabinet agreed the terms under which Britain's PMR would work. The Prime Minister had 'cleverly' manoeuvred Major-General Sir Frederick Maurice, the Director of Military Operations (DMO) and a close ally of Robertson, into this invidious task while Wully was visiting the Italian front.[92] Article 4 said the PMRs would receive proposals for future plans from their general staffs and 'in consultation' would then produce a 'coordinated statement of those plans together with proposals for the combined action of the Allies.' It then confirmed Wilson's future role in driving British strategic planning: 'Should the plans received from the Chiefs of General Staffs not be, in the opinion of the military representatives, the best for ensuring such combined action it will be within their functions to suggest other proposals.'[93] Lloyd George had shown Wilson the draft the night before:

> He [the PMR] is not to be *on* the council because Robertson is not on the War Cabinet. All plans to be submitted to him by CIGS, and he has the power to alter, or even to make fresh plans without reference to the CIGS. I asked this particularly for it was in a formal note in Maurice's handwriting at the dictation of L.G![94]

When the War Cabinet met on 2 November 1917, Wilson was formally confirmed as the British representative on the 'Permanent Inter-Allied Advisory General Staff'

---

88 TNA CAB 23/13/27: War Cabinet, 30 October 1917, (draft), pp.2-3.
89 Ibid., p.5.
90 TNA CAB 23/13/27: Appendix to War Cabinet minutes, 30 October 1917 (draft), 'Letter from Lloyd George to M Painlevé'.
91 TNA CAB 23/13/28: War Cabinet, 31 October 1917.
92 Woodward, *Lloyd George and the Generals*, p. 213.
93 TNA CAB 23/4/36: War Cabinet, minutes and Appendix III, 1 November 1917.
94 Wilson diary, 31 October 1917; CAC, Hankey diary, HNKY 1/3, 31 October, 1 November 1917.

of the 'Supreme Inter-Allied Council' (the working title of the SWC). The insertion of the word 'Advisory' into the title of this new 'General Staff' served as a fig leaf to Lloyd George's assertion that the initiative did not erode the authority of the Robertson-dominated Imperial General Staff at the War Office. Derby, who shared Robertson's concerns, eventually bowed to the inevitable and 'expressed his approval' of Wilson's appointment.[95] Wilson recorded in his diary: 'I went then to see Derby who is in the devil of a funk of what Robertson will say, and he [Derby] thinks he may have to resign.'[96] Derby regularly spoke of resignation, a threat which lost more of its power every time he did so.[97]

In the historiography, Robertson is often painted at this stage in the war as a hapless, even helpless, victim of the cunning and mendacious Lloyd George, ably assisted by the wily Wilson. According to David Woodward: 'Lloyd George marched under the banner of unity of command, but his primary objective was to diminish Robertson's influence over future British strategy.'[98] While this was clearly the Prime Minister's aim, the CIGS, with limited support from Haig, fought a rearguard action aimed, if not at derailing the SWC, certainly limiting the powers of the PMRs. Robertson received the terms of reference for the new organisation while touring the Italian front.[99] Haig told him 'the new Allied Council System & of our representative. It has all happened in my absence, & I think Derby has let the Army down badly, as I shall tell him.'[100] Lloyd George asked Haig for his views of the SWC:

> I told him that the proposal had been considered for three years and each time had been rejected as unworkable … The PM then said that the two Governments had decided to form it; so I said, there is no need to say any more then![101]

Haig's willingness to accept the rulings of his political masters, regardless of his personal views, was one reason why he prospered both before and during the war, especially at times when his position was under critical scrutiny. Robertson would not stay silent. He thought the government was wrong and that its actions would lead to confusion about where military authority lay, with potentially varied strategy advice leading to confusion and to defeat. When the Allied leaders met at Rapallo, Robertson received an amended version of Lloyd George's scheme which Wilson had

95   TNA CAB 23/4/37: War Cabinet, 2 November 1917.
96   Wilson diary, 2 November 1917; David Dutton, (ed.), *Paris 1918: The War Diary of the British Ambassador, the 17th Earl of Derby* (Liverpool: Liverpool University Press, 2001), p. xxii and *passim*.
97   Derby never did resign; in April 1918 Lloyd George eventually shunted him off to Paris as ambassador, his place being taken by Alfred Lord Milner, a Wilson supporter.
98   *MCWR*, p. 245.
99   LHCMA, Robertson papers, 'Foreign Office telegrams to Robertson', (4/8/2-3), November 1917.
100 *MCWR*, Haig to Robertson, 4 November 1917, p.251.
101 NLS, Haig (manuscript diary), 4 November 1917.

accepted on 1 November. The crucial paragraph which gave Wilson and his colleagues power to over-rule the General Staffs (Article 4), had been reworded, and toned down, by Lloyd George:

(4) The general war plans drawn up by the competent Military Authorities of the Allied countries are submitted to the Supreme War Council which, under the high authority of the Governments, ensures their concordance. If the plans submitted to the Supreme War Council do not appear to them to be the best for ensuring combined action, it will be within their functions to recommend other proposals.[102]

Although the wording was more diplomatic than in Maurice's original, Robertson was not mollified. He submitted an alternative, striking out the second sentence and replacing it with: 'and submits if needed any necessary changes.'[103] This minor alteration made little difference to the overall tenor of the clause, and the Prime Minister accepted it.[104] Henceforth the plans of the General Staffs would have to be submitted to the SWC (and thus its PMRs) for approval and/or amendment. Robertson 'persisted in his opposition to the last', Hankey wrote.[105]

Lloyd George had secured a major victory over what he saw as a wrongheaded, narrow, and myopic military adviser. But he had not won the war. Wully was as determined as the Prime Minister that he was in the right, and

Rapallo Conference, 5-7 November 1917: L to R: Cabinet Secretary Lieutenant-Colonel Maurice Hankey; Lloyd George private secretaries John T. Davies and Frances Stevenson; Imperial War Cabinet member Lieutenant-General Jan Smuts. General Henry Wilson is behind with hands in pockets. (*The Sketch*, 5 December 1917)

102 LHCMA, Robertson Papers, 'Scheme of Organisation of an Inter-Allied War Committee (Amended draft proposed by Mr. Lloyd George)', (4/8/5), 4 November 1917.
103 TNA CAB 21/91: War Cabinet, Formation of Supreme War Council, 'Scheme of Organisation of an Inter-Allied War Committee (Amended draft proposed by Mr Lloyd George, and amended by R 42, from the Chief of the Imperial General Staff')', 7 November 1917.
104 Ibid.
105 Hankey, *Supreme Command*, (Vol. II), p. 721; TNA CAB 28/2, War Cabinet, IC (Allied Conferences), Vol. II, IC 30c, '*Procès-verbal* of a Conference of the British, French and Italian Governments, held at the "New Casino Hotel", Rapallo', 7 November 1917.

he had influential support. Robertson and the military members of the Army Council immediately got to work undermining the SWC, or more specifically its staff. His principal, and understandable, argument against the role of the PMR was the risk that politicians would receive mixed and potentially contradictory advice: namely Robertson's opinion and Wilson's opinion. In this spirit Major-General Sir Thomas Furse, Master General of Ordnance (MGO), submitted a memorandum condemning the proposals as 'unpractical and dangerous to the best interests of the Allies'.[106] For the government to receive the best advice the General Staff needed to be in close, detailed and 'hourly' contact with government ministries and military departments. To suppose that the PMR could do so from Versailles was 'chimerical' and 'the inevitable result of the scheme will be that the Prime Minister of this country will have two official military advisers belonging to our army, the Army Council in the person of the CIGS and our Permanent Military Representative on the Supreme War Council'. Friction between the two would 'inevitably be mirrored in the relations between their respective staffs and will spread throughout the Army'.[107]

The Army Council informed the War Cabinet it 'presumed that the technical advice given by the British Military Representative will be given on behalf of the Army Council, and that he will be subject to the authority of, and receive his instructions from, the Army Council'.[108] Lieutenant-General Sir Nevil Macready, the Adjutant General (AG), weighed in: The details as to Wilson's powers and responsibilities were so slight that 'I can only draw upon my imagination to visualise that officer's functions'.[109] Condemning the proposals as 'nebulous' and 'half-baked' Macready reminded Derby that as a soldier Wilson must be appointed by the Army Council and receive orders from a branch of his department: 'In the event of the technical advice given by him to the Supreme War Council being at variance with the expressed views of the Army Council, it is legally in their power, so long as he is a soldier, to remove him from his post.' Macready said his understanding of the new system was that the PMR would only act in an advisory capacity providing information supplied by the Army Council. If the Representative was to have greater powers then the CIGS should have the role and 'in the event of him exceeding his powers there could be no question as to how to deal with the situation.'[110]

106 LHCMA, Robertson papers, Memorandum: 'The Scheme of Organisation of a Supreme War Council', Major-General W.T. Furse, Master General of Ordnance, (4/8/8), 11 November 1917.
107 LHCMA, Robertson papers, (4/8/8), 11 November 1917.
108 TNA WO 163/22: Army Council, Minutes and Précis, Proceedings of the Army Council, 12 November 1917.
109 LHCMA, Robertson papers, Adjutant General to Secretary of State, (4/8/10), 13 November 1917.
110 LHCMA, Robertson papers, Adjutant General to Secretary of State, (4/8/10), 13 November 1917.

Derby asked Robertson what he thought. The CIGS was in general agreement with Furse, but instead of an Inter-Allied Staff, 'a misnomer without an Inter-Allied C-in-C', he favoured a Military Secretariat for the SWC. This would co-ordinate information from the various Allied forces, point up contradictions and lack of co-ordination, and prepare agenda:

> Beyond this all military advice to the Supreme Council should remain in the hands of the responsible military advisers of the respective Governments. Dual advice can only lead to delay, friction, weakening of responsibility and lack of confidence amongst the troops.[111]

In other words, as far as Robertson, and Lloyd George for that matter, were concerned, nothing would really change. After taking legal advice Lloyd George acknowledged the Army Council's authority but appealed to their sense of duty, insisting on Wilson's independence.[112] The Army Council was not to be bought off by smooth political language. The best way of minimising confusing advice would be for the CIGS to attend SWC meetings. It was essential that Wilson should not tender any advice to the SWC 'without first informing the Army Council of the nature of that advice.'[113] Lloyd George finally agreed that Robertson could attend SWC meetings but sidestepped further discussion about Wilson's obligations by saying it was too early to be prescriptive.[114]

Unlike their Allies, there would also be French, Italian and American representatives at Versailles, the British lost no time setting up their new secretariat. Hankey, the Cabinet Secretary, 'determined that it must be linked up with the War Cabinet Secretariat'; in other words, he, and ultimately the Prime Minister, would control the functions of the British PMR's office.[115] Robertson took a sinister view of the Prime Minister's motives. Referring to the recent overthrow of the moderate 'Provisional' government in Russia by revolutionary Bolsheviks, he condemned Wilson's secretariat at Versailles as 'the new Soviet'.[116] The War Office did what it could to stymie the establishment of the Versailles secretariat. Wilson complained that the 'WO is blocking things, Eddie Derby terrified, Wully sulky, Maurice hostile. All this will

---

111 LHCMA, Robertson Papers, Robertson to Secretary of State for War, (4/8/11), 15 November 1917.
112 TNA CAB 21/91: War Cabinet, Formation of Supreme War Council, 14 November 1917, and CAB 21/91: War Cabinet, Formation of Supreme War Council, 'Relations between Army Council and British Military Representative: Draft reply to the Army Council', 15 November 1917; CAB 23/4/50: War Cabinet, 16 November 1917.
113 LHCMA, Robertson Papers, 'Proceedings (Draft) of the Army Council: response to War Cabinet' (4/8/12), 19 November 1917.
114 Woodward, *Lloyd George*, p.227.
115 Hankey, *Supreme Command*, (Vol. II), p. 718.
116 LHCMA, Robertson papers, Robertson to Haig, (7/7/66).

have to be straightened out.'[117] Esher urged Hankey to send Milner to support Wilson 'for heavens [sic] sake don't weaken in the face of opposition or we are done *here* ... Now that the PM has embarked upon this Allied G[eneral] S[taff] (whether wisely or not) he *must* go through with it to the bitter end with extreme boldness.'[118] Matters came to a head when Wilson saw Derby, who was 'terrified of Robertson', and who was blocking appointments to the secretariat: 'I got cross and said, "very well then LG can't have me." This startled poor Eddie and he did not know what to say and I am not sure that he is not more frightened of me than of Robertson.'[119] Robertson's professional concerns were entirely legitimate, and his irritation understandable. Yet this petty politicking did him no credit, and only served to antagonise Wilson, the consummate politician: 'It is quite clear to me that Robertson and his gang mean to obstruct all they can. Well we shall have a fight.'[120] It also irritated members of the War Cabinet, including Milner, one of Lloyd George's most steadfast Unionist allies. Haig, who had accepted the change with his usual pragmatism, was busy fighting the ultimately unsuccessful Battle of Cambrai, and had neither time nor inclination to bother himself with Wully's travails.

In the eight weeks that Wilson served as British PMR at Versailles, he and his colleagues produced 14 policy documents, or 'Joint Notes' on a range of largely non-controversial subjects. Two addressed future strategic priorities and recommended that the allies stood on the 'active defensive' in the west in the coming year while they awaited the arrival of the Americans in force. The chronic British manpower shortage meant that Haig and Robertson had little choice other than to accept that there would not be another major British-led offensive in 1918.[121] There were well-founded, and as it turned out completely correct, concerns of a major German offensive in the west in the first half of the coming year. A re-run of 1917 was not a realistic strategic proposition. So far, so unremarkable. What was controversial however, and fully justified Robertson's worries over 'the Versailles people' getting into 'mischief', was Joint Note 14.[122] This paper proposed the establishment of an allied 'General Reserve'.[123] The initiative was Wilson's response to the manpower crisis facing both the British and the French armies; a mobile force of sufficient size to be rushed to a point of weakness when the enemy attack came. Both Haig, and Pétain opposed the idea from the outset, even though it had the support of Lloyd George and Georges Clemenceau, the

---

117 Wilson diary, 19 November 1917.
118 CAC, Esher papers, Esher to Hankey, 15 November 1917.
119 Wilson diary, 21 November 1917.
120 Wilson diary, 27 November 1917.
121 TNA WO 158/57: Joint Note 1, 13 December 1917, and Joint Note 12, 21 January 1918.
122 LHCMA, Robertson Papers, 7/7/70, Robertson to Haig, 6 December 1917.
123 TNA CAB 25/120: 'Supreme War Council, Papers and Minutes', (enclosure 64), Minutes of a meeting of Permanent Military Representatives of the Supreme War Council, (hereafter SWC Minutes) 23 January 1918, 'Schedule B': Joint Note 14: The General Reserve; see also Elizabeth Greenhalgh, *Foch in Command: The Forging of a First World War General* (Cambridge: Cambridge University Press, 2011), p.287.

newly-appointed French Prime Minister. Where, they wanted to know, would the men come from for this new force? Robertson had no objections to the principle of a general reserve; it made good strategic sense. He agreed with his colleagues' concerns over manpower, but the sticking point for the CIGS was who commanded this body. Wilson, working in tandem with the Prime Minister, proposed that the new reserve should come under the command of an 'Executive war board' chaired by Foch and comprising the other PMRs. The obvious effect of this would be to remove the power of command of a large body of men from the British and French C-in-Cs and place it instead under a French general with no constitutional responsibility to the British government. This was something Robertson could not accept. In the first half of February 1918, he and the Prime Minister, with their attendant supporters amongst Parliament and press, fought a bitter battle involving 'tortuous and byzantine' negotiations.[124] Lloyd George was only ever likely to win such a 'political' rather than 'military' struggle. After much acrimony the Prime Minister won out and Robertson, boxed in and fast-losing support, resigned on 18 February, to be succeeded as CIGS by his nemesis, Sir Henry Wilson.[125]

As British Prime Minister David Lloyd George had every right to involve himself directly in the direction of his country's military strategy, no matter how wrong-headed his views might have seemed to his professional advisers. Robertson's unwillingness to work within the confines of this constitutional fact was his ultimate undoing. While he paid lip-service to the over-arching authority of democratic cabinet government he strove always to retain his (and Haig's) grip on strategy. As the government's principal military adviser, the first duty of the Chief of the Imperial General Staff was to offer independent professional advice to the politicians he served. Robertson was an ardent 'Westerner', yet he had a long-held difference of opinion with Sir Douglas Haig. Robertson favoured an attritional approach, slowly nibbling away at the enemy, wearing him down over time. This contrasted with the C-in-C who favoured the 'breakthrough and breakout' approach so familiar to students of the Great War on the Western Front. Despite his own misgivings Robertson never strayed from public support for Haig, wisely calculating that any sign of disharmony would provide a weakness for Lloyd George, the ultimate 'armchair strategist', to exploit. Ultimately, Wully was unable to reconcile his responsibility to his political masters with his loyalty to his fellow soldier. In many ways, he was the architect of his own fate.

---

124 *MCWR*, p. 247; the story of Robertson's downfall is best told in Woodward, *Robertson*, pp.187-201.
125 For an assessment of Wilson's role as CIGS in 1918, see Spencer, *Wilson's War*.

3

From OTC to OCB
The Professionalisation of the Selection and Training of Junior Temporary Officers During the Great War

Charles Fair

> *An officer's first duty is, and always has been so, to train the private soldiers under his command so that they may, without question, beat any force opposed to them in the field.*
> Arthur Wellesley, Duke of Wellington

Introduction

One of the British Army's most important achievements in developing the war winning force of 1918 was to find and train enough junior leaders with the flexibility to operate in the semi-mobile warfare of the Hundred Days. This chapter will look at the selection and development of temporary junior officers and argue that by mid-1917 a highly professionalised system of Officer Cadet Battalions (OCBs) had evolved, and that this sat within a broader framework for developing officers. This system produced officers of sufficient quality and quantity and made a vital contribution to the BEF's success in 1918. This chapter will focus primarily on infantry officers.[1] The pivotal change in the Army's officer development model – how it selected, trained, and commissioned officers – was from a model of awarding commissions *prior to* officer training, to one of commissioning *after* training.

The importance of officer training has been somewhat neglected in the historiography of the BEF. The focus of research into the British Army's 'learning process' in

---

1   Space precludes discussion in this chapter of the battlefield performance of OCB graduates and the changing class structure of junior officers, both topics which will form part of my forthcoming PhD thesis.

the Great War has often been on technology, tactics and operations.[2] However, as Changboo Kang has observed, 'the contribution of junior infantry officers has not really been situated in the historiography of the "learning curve."'[3]

There has been no examination as to *how* men were selected and trained in the leadership skills that were required for platoon commanders to be effective in the new conditions of trench warfare. The Official History has little to say about this subject and subsequent historians have not covered it in depth. The starting point for understanding the British junior officer of the Great War is Gary Sheffield's *Leadership in the Trenches*. As his focus is on officer-soldier relations, morale and discipline, the OCB system and its development is covered in only a few pages.[4] The same applies to John Lewis-Stempel's popular history, *Six Weeks*.[5] This is complemented by a broad overview of the officer corps by Ian Beckett, Timothy Bowman and Mark Connolly in *The British Army and the First World War*.[6] These works draw attention to the importance of the OTCs in providing ad hoc officer training in 1914-15, but do not explore it in depth.

To date, the best description of the chronology and evolution of officer training and selection is by Charles Messenger who gives a concise overview in his study of the administration of the British Army in the Great War, *A Call To Arms*.[7] Also of note is Magda Hentel's 2017 PhD thesis, which presents a sociological study of the masculinity of lower middle class junior officers.[8] It identifies a number of memoirs and papers written by such men and looks at how the OCB system helped shape their wartime experience. Notably, it includes the first systematic study of the various journals produced by the OCBs.

In his monograph *The Human Face of War*, Jim Storr argues that we should place much greater emphasis on human factors in our theories of war and understanding of the nature of combat. He notes that 'only about 40 per cent of a typical tactical decision comes from the information presented. The other 60 per cent is brought to the

---

2   Jonathan Boff, *Winning and Losing on the Western Front: The British Third Army and the Defeat of Germany in 1918* (Cambridge: Cambridge University Press, 2012), Chapter 2 'Manpower and Training'.

3   Changboo Kang, 'The British Infantry Officer on the Western Front in the First World War', unpublished PhD thesis, University of Birmingham, 2007, p.397.

4   Gary Sheffield, *Leadership in the Trenches: Officer-Man Relations, Morale and Discipline in the British Army in the Era of the First World War* (Basingstoke: Macmillan, 2000), pp.53-60

5   John Lewis-Stempel, *Six Weeks: The Short and Gallant Life of the British Officer in the First World War* (London: Weidenfeld & Nicholson, 2010). pp.53-61.

6   Ian Beckett, Tim Bowman and Mark Connolly, *The British Army and the First World War*, (Cambridge: Cambridge University Press, 2017), Chapter 2 'The Officer Corps', pp.47-85.

7   Charles Messenger, *Call To Arms* (London: Weidenfeld & Nicholson, 2005), Chapter 10 'Officer Selection and Training', pp.288-334.

8   Magdalena J. Hentel, '"Temporary Gentlemen": The Masculinity of Lower-Middle-Class Temporary British Officers in the First World War', unpublished PhD thesis, The University of Western Ontario, 2017.

decision by the decision-maker, primarily in terms of his personality and experience.'[9] Storr argues that an 'obvious inference is that officer training and education are more of a factor in operational effectiveness than is commonly suspected, not least, in units' and formations' ability to learn.'[10]

This chapter examines the training of officers in the context of the British Army of the First World War. In 1914 there was no comprehensive infrastructure for selecting and training junior officers of the New Armies and Territorial Force. This chapter will explain how such an infrastructure – the OCB system – evolved out of the ad hoc measures that were set up in 1914 and 1915. Much of the early impetus came from 'bottom up' innovation supported by evolving policy from the Staff Duties Department of the War Office. As the chapter will show, by mid-1917 the OCB system had evolved into a more centralised process and produced large numbers of effective officers.

The Purpose of Officer Selection and Training

An infantry platoon commander has two main functions. First, he needs to be able to build cohesion in his platoon by training and developing his NCOs and private soldiers so that the platoon fights as a single entity rather than a collection of individuals. Platoon cohesion also helps to build morale, which in turn establishes 'the baseline motivation' to fight.[11] Second, he needs to be able to make effective tactical decisions amidst the chaos of battle.

To fulfil the first of these functions, the training of platoon commanders must build their technical competence so they can train and lead their platoons. The selection and training process needs to identify and develop men who will demonstrate the appropriate behaviours. Demonstrated competence, supported by appropriate behaviour, builds confidence in the platoon commander and NCOs, and thereby develops cohesion.

In the context of the Edwardian Army, Gary Sheffield summarises the desired behaviours as the maintenance of the 'Paternalism-Deference Exchange'.[12] The February 1917 tactical manual, *SS143: Instructions for the Training of Platoons for Offensive Action* advised junior officers of some of the behaviours that they would need to display in order to gain the confidence of their men. It stressed paternalism – 'Looking after his men's comfort before his own and never sparing himself' – as well as the need to enforce a willing and just discipline. It advised that 'a word of praise when deserved produces better results than incessant fault-finding' and that officers should recognise good effort, 'even if it is not really successful.' The OCB system

---

9   Jim Storr, *The Human Face of War* (London: Continuum, 2009), pp.194-95.
10   Ibid., p.192.
11   The concept of 'baseline motivation' to engage in combat is discussed extensively in Leo Murray, *War Games* (London: Biteback Publishing, 2018).
12   Sheffield, *Leadership in the Trenches*, p.71

would explicitly develop these attitudes and behaviours in their cadets and test them on exercises and in classroom exams.

However, it is not enough to have a platoon that is cohesive: it must fight hard in combat. The platoon commander and his NCOs need to make the right decisions at the right time. This means more than slavishly following battle drills. It is the ability to read the battlefield and the local tactical situation, in the context of understanding the higher commanders' intentions, and being able to adapt the plan accordingly. Effective decision making requires the ability to think clearly in the dynamic, chaotic environment of the battlefield.

In this regard, the platoon commander of late 1917 had several advantages over the New Army and Territorial officers of the early war. First, he may well have had prior combat experience in the ranks. Second, there was a high probability that he would have attended tactical courses at Divisional, Corps or Army schools in an active theatre.[13] Kang has analysed the war diaries of three battalions of the Warwickshire Regiment to demonstrate the frequency with which junior officers attended such courses. Many attended at least one course, with a respectable minority attending two or more.[14] These courses supported learning in mission-specific rehearsals prior to operations. Finally, the officer would have benefitted from the OCB course itself. This sat at the bottom level of a hierarchy of UK based schools, with those for prospective company and battalion commanders sat above it. This hierarchy is described in more detail below.

Scale of the OCB System

Excluding commissions to the RAMC and chaplains, the British Army commissioned 229,316 officers during the First World War. Sandhurst and Woolwich continued to produce Regular officers throughout the war. However, with 5,013 and 1,928 graduates respectively, they provided just a 3 percent of wartime combatant commissions.[15] In contrast, the OCB system, from its gradual introduction in February 1916 onwards, commissioned 145,621 men from over 50 officer-producing units. This represents 64 percent of all wartime combatant commissions, divided by arm of service as shown in Figure 1 below. Including the Garrison OCB, the infantry accounts for almost exactly half of these commissions.

---

13   These schools are discussed in Simon Robbins, *British Generalship on the Western Front 1914-18* (Abingdon: Frank Cass, 2005), pp.90-95; Paddy Griffith, *Battle Tactics of the Western Front: The British Army's Art of Attack 1916-18* (New Haven, Connecticut: Yale University Press, 1994), pp.186-91; Aimée Fox, *Learning to Fight: Military Innovation and Change in the British Army, 1914-18* (Cambridge: Cambridge University Press, 2018).

14   Kang, 'The British Infantry Officer on the Western Front in the First World War', pp.219-38. Given the incompleteness of most war diaries this is almost certainly an understatement.

15   War Office, *Statistics of the Military Effort of the British Empire During the Great War, 1914-1920* (London: War Office, 1922), pp.234-35.

Figure 1. Cadets commissioned from Officer Cadet Training Units between February 1916 and 1 December 1918[16]

	No. of Officer Cadet Training Units	No. commissioned
Infantry (Nos. 1-21, 23 OCB and Household)	23	69,312
Garrison Battalion (22 OCB)	1	3,572
Tanks (24 OCB)	1	1,714
Royal Artillery	6	19,131
Cavalry	2	2,621
Royal Engineers	3	3,566
RASC	2	4,960
Machine-Gun Corps*	–	3,053
RFC and RAF (until 8 December 1918)	16	37,692
Total	**54**	**145,621**

* From 1st October 1917 candidates for commissions in the MGC were required to have three months' commissioned service with other units.

Precursors to the OCB System

The 'temporary officers' of 1914 and 1915 – over 70,000 – were expected to fill in any gaps in their military knowledge by learning on the job.[17] By December 1914, it had been recognised that thousands of potential officers were serving in the ranks, 'so it was decided that NCOs and other ranks who were recommended by their commanding officers would be given a short course of officer training for four weeks.'[18] This training was to be carried out by Territorial units such as the various university OTCs (which by then had few undergraduates to train) which set up the schools. A School of Instruction was also set up by the Royal Military College, Sandhurst, with the cadets being billeted in Staff College.[19] Other Schools were set up by several Territorial Force Reserve Infantry Brigades. Men were commissioned first, and then

16   War Office, *Statistics of the Military Effort of the British Empire During the Great War, 1914-1920* (London: HMSO, 1922), p.235.
17   Deducting the 146,621 OCB officers from the 229,316 gives 76,745 temporary commissions which were not granted after a course at an OCB. Most date from 1914 and 1915, but some men were commissioned in early and mid-1916 whilst the OCB system was being set up.
18   Keith Simpson, 'The Officers' in Ian FW Beckett & Keith Simpson (eds.), *A Nation in Arms: A Social Study of the British Army in the First World War* (Manchester: Manchester University Press, 1985), p.79.
19   Brian Bond, *The Victorian Army and the Staff College 1854-1914* (London: Eyre Methuen, 1972), p.303.

ordered to report to a course having taken a few days of leave to purchase their officer kit.

It is not known how many officers' schools of instruction were in existence as records are sparse. Consequently, there has been limited discussion of them in the historiography, and there has been no attempt to establish the scale and reach of the school.[20] The evidence suggests that although there were more than commonly supposed, only a minority of eligible officers benefited from them.

Schools run by the OTCs are best documented. Reports of the Boards of Military Studies, or annual reports by the Senates at the various universities, histories of University OTCs and a handful of memoirs all give clues. For example, Cambridge University OTC (CUOTC) set up the 'Cambridge University School of Instruction' at Pembroke College.

Artists' Rifles OTC instructor caricatures by celebrated cartoonist Bert Thomas. (*The Tatler*, 26 December 1917)

Eleven courses were held at this School between December 1914 and February 1916 and 'a total of 3,744 officers passed through, many of them having just obtained their commissions via the OTC.'[21] In Oxford the University OTC set up the 'Oxford University School of Instruction' at Keble College, and about 3,000 officers passed through.[22] The majority, and possibly all, of the Senior Division OTCs set up similar schools, though none was on the scale of those of Cambridge and Oxford. From the available information, it is likely that no more than about 15,000 officers attended a course run by a senior division OTC or Sandhurst.

20 Discussion of these schools can be found in: Sheffield, *Leadership in the Trenches*, pp.53-54; Messenger, *Call To Arms*, pp.302-03; Beckett, Bowman and Connolly, *The British Army and the First World War*, p.66.

21 Hew Strachan, *History of the Cambridge University Officer Training Corps* (Speldhurst: Midas Books, 1976), p.145.

22 Bodleian Library, Oxford University OTC archive, OT 1/1/1 to OT 1/1/11, Oxford University School of Instruction. This is an estimate based on the total number of registration forms in these files.

There is little evidence of the schools that were run by the Reserve Brigades, and the best source for these has been from local newspapers in the British Newspaper Archive (BNA) with occasional mentions in *The London Gazette*. For example, the Tenby School of Instruction was formed in June 1915 under the Commandant, Major G. Ward, with Captain A.G. Ford as second in command. The third instructor was Lieutenant M.C. Richards. The first course reported on 15 June.[23] Photographs of the second and third courses survive in the local newspaper and these show 67 and 72 attendees respectively.[24] Major R.T. Follett, Rifle Brigade, was appointed temporary commandant in January 1916 and he presumably closed the school down in March.[25] The dates this school was active allow a maximum of eight courses with up to about 500 cadets attending.

Ireland had at least three schools of instruction, of which two were run by Belfast and Dublin UOTCs. A third one was held at Victoria Barracks, Cork, and the dates given in the limited evidence suggest it held nine courses in 1915 and two or three more in 1916.[26] In Scotland, schools were run by Edinburgh and Glasgow OTCs, the South Scottish Infantry Brigade, Stirling, and the Lothian Infantry Brigade, Edinburgh. In England there is evidence for schools held at Tynemouth, Scarborough, Liverpool, Norwich, Bury St Edmunds, Chelmsford, Chatham and Harwich.[27]

The regional commands appear to have been responsible for posting of new subalterns to schools in their areas. Western Command detailed officers to the Mersey School of Instruction at Freshfields near Liverpool. A total of 42 'vacancies for Welsh officers' at the school were allocated as follows in April 1915: 'Milford Haven Garrison, 8; Severn Garrison, 6; No. 3 District, 3rd Royal Welsh Fusiliers, 4; 43rd (Welsh) Division [38th Division as of 29 April 1915]; and 2nd Line Welsh Division, 6.'[28] Lieutenant J.A. Mackey, writing in January 1916 to his former colleagues on Bray Council in Ireland, observed 'that a good proportion of the officers in the school were Irish.'[29]

However, the output of the schools of instruction was far below what was needed with perhaps less than half of temporary subalterns of 1914-15 attending a course.

---

23   A list of Special Reserve officers attending the Tenby School is in the *London Gazette*, 9 June 1915.

24   These can be seen in *The Western Mail*, Thursday 22 July and Thursday 19 August 1915 editions.

25   *Western Mail*, 28 January 1916, p.6.

26   In early October 1915, twelve officers 'were recorded as 'distinguished' at the examination held on termination of the seventh course.' (*Belfast News-Letter*, 1 October 1915.) The end of the eighth course was noted in mid-November. *(Northern Whig*, 17 November 1915 p.10.) Two new officers, Charles Davison, Royal Irish Fusiliers and Robert Neill, 6th Royal Inniskilling Fusiliers were reported in the Irish press as having arrived at this school in early March 1916. *Ballymena Observer*, 10 March 1916, p.5; *Northern Whig*, 7 March 1916, p.8.

27   *The London Gazette* editions of 4, 7 and 9 June 1915 list Special Reserve officers attending a number of these schools. Others have been identified from references in local newspapers.

28   *Western Mail*, Friday, 2 April 1915.

29   *Weekly Freeman's Journal*, 8 January 1916, p.10.

Apart from the larger courses run by Cambridge and Oxford UOTCs, they were not able to benefit from economies of scale. Most of those formed by the TF Reserve Brigades had about 50-60 officers per course, with two or three instructors who were often 'dug-outs'. The instructors were not able to specialise in a subject and were also overseeing the administration. Edinburgh had two organisations running schools simultaneously at different locations. Clearly, this was not an efficient way of providing instruction at scale.

A larger problem was that the schools were training officers *after* they had been commissioned. There was therefore no opportunity to use the training as a selection tool to weed out men who were not up to the role of an officer. Inefficient men were still being commissioned because they had the 'right' social and educational background and interviewed well. If found to be inefficient, and assuming that there was no possible employment for them as an officer, they had to be formally requested to resign their commissions. This process could take months if they appealed to higher authorities such as the Military Secretary or their Member of Parliament.

For example, James Skinner, a 21-year-old employee of the Mercantile Bank of India and old boy of Berkhamsted School, joined the Inns of Court OTC in August 1914. He was commissioned into 9th Oxfordshire & Buckinghamshire Light Infantry (O&BLI) in October before transferring into the Machine Gun Corps. He served as OC of 62nd MG Company, 21st Division from 2 March to 16 July 1916.[30] As an acting major he appears to have been out of his depth 'as considered too young and inexperienced and not possessing sufficient military qualifications for the responsibilities which such a command entails on active operations.' After much consideration by the War Office he was recommended 'for employment not entailing the command of troops' and was not wanted as an instructor at the MGC schools at Grantham. The War Office requested his resignation and he submitted his application to resign in mid-November 1916; this process was finally completed in early January.[31]

There were three minor exceptions to the 1915 model of post-commissioning training. The combined output of these routes accounted for, at best, around 10 percent of the commissions awarded prior to the introduction of the OCB system. First, the Inns of Court OTC directly commissioned men who had met its standards after completion of basic and advanced training. It accounted for 2,035 commissions between the outbreak of war and March 1915.[32] Approximately 3,600 more were commissioned between March 1915 and the introduction of the OCB system.[33] Second was the GHQ Cadet School which had been set up by the Artists' Rifles in

---

30   The National Archives (TNA) WO 95/2156/3/1: 62nd MG Company War Diary. Skinner signed the months from March to June, but not that for July which contains no reference to the change of command, though the change in handwriting is noticeable.
31   TNA WO 339/21688: Lieutenant James Hay McInnes Skinner personal file.
32   Alan R Haig-Brown, *The OTC and the Great War* (London: Country Life, 1915), p.106.
33   The remainder once the 2,035 early commissions and 5,900 OCB commissions are deducted from the total.

late November 1914.[34] In April 1915 it had moved to Blendeques near St Omer and provided a six-week course.[35] Establishing numbers commissioned via this route is difficult, but it was probably in the order of 500 to 1,000 men by March 1916. Third, the second battalion of the Artists' Rifles at Gidea Hall in Essex had been converted to an OTC in November 1915 and was able to commission men who had already received basic training.[36] It is not known how many commissions were awarded via this route, but it is unlikely to have been more than a few hundred before the OCBs became fully established in the autumn of 1916.

Establishing the OCB System 1916

The OCBs came into being with Army Council Instruction No. 357 of February 1916. It stipulated that temporary commissions would only be granted to those who had passed out from an OCB, unless they had had previous service as an officer.[37] This was a crucial change in the officer development model as men would now only be commissioned after training. Selection took place in two stages (Figure 2). The initial selection was the same as before: recommendation from one's commanding officer, completion of the application form and a short interview with the GOC of one's brigade. However, passing these none too rigorous steps was now no longer a guarantee of a commission. Continuous evaluation and final selection towards the end of the OCB course meant that inefficient men could either be filtered out, or else given the opportunity to pass the course with additional training.

The introduction of the OCB system did not represent a 'clean break' with prior practice, with at least five being converted directly from a school of instruction, and others drawing staff from schools in their region. The first 11 infantry OCBs were set up in February and March using existing and available infrastructure. Oxbridge Colleges had few resident students and had already been used for billeting troops. It was a simple matter to convert the existing schools into No. 2 and No. 4 OCBs. A second new OCB was established at each University with No. 5 in Cambridge and No. 6 in Oxford. It was a source of great pride in Bristol that the city was the only university town other than Oxford and Cambridge chosen to host an OCB, with the Bristol School of Instruction being expanded and converted into No. 3 OCB.[38] The Sandhurst School was similarly converted into No. 11 OCB.

34   TNA WO 95/128/4: 1/28th London Regt (Artists' Rifles) War Diary October 1914-May 1917.
35   Messenger, *Call To Arms*, pp.318-20.
36   Army Order No. 429 of 1915 cited in Major S. Stagoll Higham VD (ed.), *The Regimental Roll of Honour and War Record of the Artists' Rifles 1914-1919, Third Edition* (London: Howlett & Son, 1922), p. xv
37   TNA: WO 293/4: Army Council Instruction No. 357, 14 February 1916.
38   'University of Bristol. Its Numerous War Activities', *Western Daily Press*, 11 November 1916, p.3.

Figure 2. Evolution of the Officer Development Model

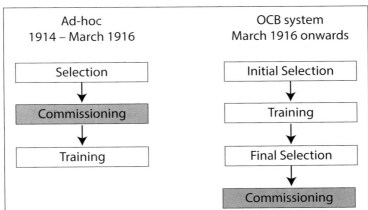

The two Scottish OCBs, No. 9 and No. 10, used an encampment at Gailes near Irvine in Ayrshire which had been used by Volunteers and TF since 1889. No. 1 OCB was initially established in a hutted camp beside the aerodrome at Denham in Buckinghamshire before being moved to a stately home in Devon.

Figure 3. Initial wave of infantry OCBs established in February-March 1916

OCB	Location	Notes on precursor unit(s) and subsequent moves
1	Denham, Bucks	*(Nov 1916 moved to Membland Hall, Newton Ferrers, Devon)*
2	Pembroke College, Cambridge	Cambridge UOTC and Cambridge U School of Instruction
3	70 Woodland Rd, Bristol	Bristol UOTC and Bristol U School of Instruction *(early 1918 moved to Parkhurst, Isle of Wight)*
4	Keble College, Oxford	Oxford UOTC and Oxford U School of Instruction
5	Trinity College, Cambridge	–
6	Balliol College, Oxford	–
7	Moore Park, Co. Cork	Some staff from Schools of Instruction in Cork, Belfast (run by Queens U of Belfast OTC) and Dublin (run by Dublin UOTC)
8	Whittington Barracks, Lichfield, Staffs	–
9 10	Gailes, Ayrshire	Drew some staff from Schools of Instruction in Scotland including those run by Edinburgh and Glasgow UOTCs
11	Sandhurst	Sandhurst School of Instruction *(early 1917 moved to Guards Lines, Pirbright)*

While the OCB system was becoming well established, the demand for replacement junior officers increased dramatically after 1 July 1916. This can be seen in the casualty data in *Statistics of the Military Effort of the British Empire* (henceforth SMEBE). Figure 4 below summarises the total officer casualties on a cumulative basis. If the trend line from August 1914 to 30 June 1916 was extrapolated, then the total officer casualties by the Armistice would have been in the order of 48,000. This is shown in the dotted line in the chart. The steep upturn in officer casualties that occurred from 1 July 1916 – nearly four times the prior rate – poses the question: to what extent was the British Army able to cope with this level of attrition of junior leaders?

Figure 4. Cumulative weekly officer casualties in the British Army 1914-18[39]

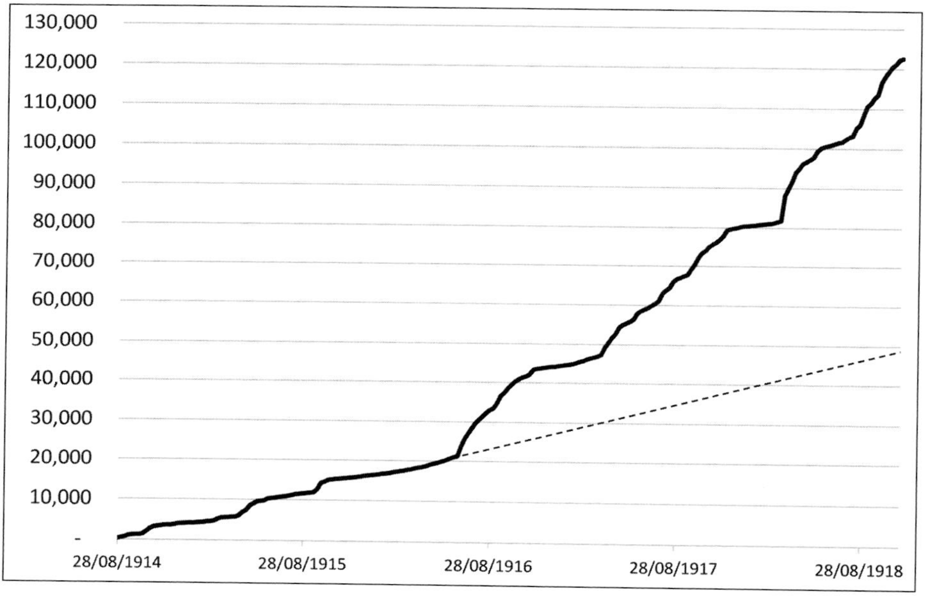

Although the length of the OCB course was initially four months, many of the earliest commissions in 1916 were awarded after only two or three months' training in order to meet demand. The first set of OCB exams was in May. In the spring and summer of 1916, the first wave of OCBs commissioned a minority of men into arms other than infantry, if those arms had not yet set up their officer cadet training units. These included the RFC and 51 MGC commissions which were awarded on 15 April

---

39   War Office, *Statistics of the Military Effort of the British Empire*, pp.252(i)-252(ii). This chart includes RND, Dominion Troops and Indian Native officers, but excludes RFC/RAF officers.

1916.[40] This latter group appear to have been mainly into the Heavy Branch of the Motor Machine Gun Service, including 20 of the first tank officers, who went into action on the Somme on 15 September, who were commissioned from Nos. 2, 4 and 5 OCBs after less than a month's OCB training.[41] The First E Company of No. 5 OCB which passed out in January 1917 included a 'Tanks Platoon' of 34 men.[42]

More OCBs were established from early autumn 1916 by which time their organisation 'had been perfected.'[43] The Inns of Court had continued to have four supernumerary cadet companies which provided training prior to commissioning. These were separated out, given a new commanding officer, and formed into No. 14 OCB.[44] Similarly, the supernumerary cadet companies of the Artists' Rifles OTC were formed into No. 15 OCB.[45]

Figure 5. Later infantry and MGC OCB establishments, August 1916–February 1917

OCB	Location	Date established	Notes
12	The Hutments,	Early Sept 1916	–
13	Newmarket	Early Oct 1916	–
14 (Inns of Court)	Berkhamsted, Herts	5 Sept 1916	*moved to Catterick 22 Jan 1918*
15 (Artists' Rifles)	Gidea Hall, Romford, Essex	Aug 1916	converted from Sch. of Instruction into cadet companies Mar 1916; converted to OCB Aug 1916
16	Kinmel Park, Rhyl	Oct 1916	–
17		15 Nov 1916	–
18	Prior Park, Bath	26 Nov 1916	–
19	Pirbright	Feb 1917	–
20	Twezeldown Camp,	Feb 1917	–
21	Crookham, Aldershot	Feb 1917	–

40   *London Gazette*, 24 April 1916, p.4240.
41   I am grateful to Stephen Pope for his assistance in identifying a number of these officers. Their lack of officer training is highlighted in their stories in his book *The First Tank Crews: The Lives of the Tankmen who Fought at the Battle of Flers-Courcelette, 15 September 1916* (Solihull: Helion & Co., 2016).
42   *ECoEcho: A Souvenir of the 1st 'E' Coy No. 5 Officer Cadet Battalion, St John's College* (Cambridge: Heffer & Sons Ltd, January 1917), pp.82-83.
43   Major S. Stagoll Higham VD (ed.), *The Regimental Roll of Honour and War Record of the Artists' Rifles 1914-1919, Third Edition* (London: Howlett & Son, 1922), p. xv.
44   Lieutenant-Colonel F.H.L. Errington, CB VD (ed.), *The Inns of Court Officers Training Corps During the Great War* (London: Printing Craft, 1920), p.31
45   Stagoll Higham VD (ed.), *The Regimental Roll of Honour and War Record of the Artists' Rifles*, p. xv.

OCB	Location	Date established	Notes
Garrison	Jesus College, Cambridge	12 Dec 1916	Renamed No. 22 (Garrison) OCB, Aug 1918
No. 1 MGC	Bisley	25 Sept 1916	Renamed No. 23 OCB late Sept 1917; *Moved to Hipswell Camp, Catterick, Jan 1918*
No. 2 MGC	Guards Camp, Pirbright	11 Nov 1916	Renamed No. 24 (Tank Corps) OCB Sept 1917; *Moved to Hazeley Down Camp, Winchester 8 Jan 1918*
Household Brigade	The Hall, Bushey, Herts	Feb 1917	–

These later establishments were typically in hutted camps, some of which may have been built for the purpose, and which would have been cheaper than renting universities or stately homes. Many of the later OCBs were co-located in pairs or set up near an existing OCB. This may have been in order to achieve economies of scale for sharing resources, as well as providing a ready-made opposition for exercises and sport. However, their setting up was no less chaotic than that of the first eleven OCBs in early 1916. Captain Neil Weir reported for duty as acting adjutant of No. 21 OCB on 7 February 1917 and described the first month:

> … the huts at our camp were still occupied by the RAMC depot who were leaving in drafts. Colonel Dickson had only four officers including the Quartermaster and about a dozen or so men to perform a permanent staff … I had to get down to it and try to form an orderly room with the aid of an ex-Lewis gun corporal. It was an uphill task and all the more so for me as I had no experience in this line before. There were no chairs, tables, stationery etc. In fact the whole thing was in a glorious muddle … I felt very miserable and the Mess was chaotic.
>
> On the 8th the 300 Cadets arrived and were formed into 'A' & 'B' Company … My time as Adjutant was spent in trying to get straight, writing out orders (as there were no typewriters), interviewing all sorts of people (chiefly tailors), and visiting Aldershot Command Headquarters with the Colonel trying to get men for the permanent staff …
>
> We gradually got rid of the RAMC and things began to settle down. The cadets had a rough time of it and instruction was very elementary but they made the best of it. Their feeding arrangements were none too good owing to a bad Administrative Officer and quarrels between the Army Canteens and Women's Legion. Everyone was pretty unhappy … Our training chiefly consisted of PT

and drill under the cadets themselves as we had no NCO instructors. Thus really the first month was wasted settling down…[46]

Refining and Scaling-Up: The OCB System in 1917

An underused source for understanding manpower issues is 'The Weekly Strengths of the British Army at Home'. Figure 6 shows the total recorded headcount of all the infantry Officer Cadet Battalions from May 1916 until the Spring of 1919.[47] The chart is notable for the monthly spikes and dips. These are explained by the monthly exams – held on the last Monday or Tuesday of the month – after which large numbers of men left their OCB, to be followed a few days later by a large intake of new cadets.

Figure 6. Total headcount of infantry OCBs, including permanent staff 1916–19[48]

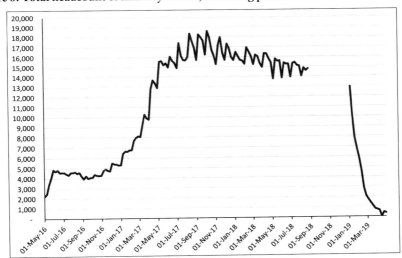

Note: Statistics are unavailable for the final four months of 1918.

46   Mike Burns, *Mud and Bodies: The War Diaries & Letters of Captain N A C Weir, 1914–1920* (Barnsley: Pen & Sword Books, 2013), Kindle edition, locations 2015 to 2032.

47   There is some underreporting in late 1916/early 1917 as a few OCBs took a few weeks after establishment to send in returns.

48   TNA WO 114/28 to 36. Data for No. 23 OCB is included from 24 September 1917 when it had been renamed from No. 1 MGC OCB. Units provided a weekly return to the War Office of their strengths, split by officers and other ranks. The returns often gave additional information such as the number of men in the various medical grades: however the exact information required by the War Office was subject to frequent change, so it is not always possible to follow some of the detailed information on a consistent basis. For example, for other ranks it is not always possible to separate the cadets from the permanent staff. Unfortunately TNA does not hold the volume with the returns from September to December 1918 inclusive.

The OCBs had been authorised to increase their headcount from 400 cadets to 600 on 31 May 1916 where the unit had enough accommodation to handle them.[49] Despite this, a comparison of the officer casualty chart and the headcount of the OCB system until March 1917 suggests that there is likely to have been a period in late 1916 and early 1917 when the demand for new officers as a result of the Somme exceeded the supply.

From Figure 6 for the thirteen-month period July 1917 until July 1918 inclusive we can calculate the 'peak to trough'. If we make the reasonable assumption that the number of officers and other permanent staff remained roughly unchanged from week to week, then this drop can be taken to be a fair estimate of the total 'production' of new infantry officers. Figure 7 depicts monthly output from the OCBs for this period, an average of just under 2,000 per month.

Figure 7. Estimated monthly output from the infantry OCBs July 1917-July 1918

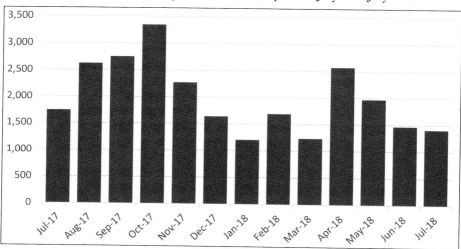

The peak of production was in August to November 1917. Whilst some of these new subalterns were posted to units in the UK, others would have been posted to the Western Front to replace losses suffered at Third Ypres. This output is evident in the large numbers of new subalterns that arrived in late 1917. For example, battalions in 48th Division saw large cohorts of new officers in September: 1/4th O&BLI received 14 officers and 1/5th Gloucesters 13 officers. The 1/1st Buckinghamshire Bn O&BLI 'accepted 12 new second lieutenants, all of whom came from the Essex and West Kent Regiments or the Artists' Rifles.'[50] In October the 1/4th O&BLI received 15

---

49   TNA WO 293/4: Army Council Instruction 1106, 31 May 1916.
50   K.W. Mitchinson, *The 48th (South Midland) Division 1908-1919* (Solihull: Helion & Co., 2017), p.179.

new officers causing its war diary to note 'the most unusual strength of officers', 1/5th Royal Warwickshire Regiment received 10 new officers and 1/1st Buckinghamshire Regiment eight new officers.[51]

However, the War Office had clearly been feeling confident in its source of supply – and that it had sufficient trained subalterns 'in stock' both in the UK and in theatre – that it could afford to extend the infantry OCB course to five months in late 1917, and again to six months in February 1918.[52] This explains the drop in production from December 1917 to March 1918. At No. 21 OCB the extension to six months was announced in the middle of February and 'it was decided that "A" & "B" Companies should pass out 50% at the end of that month.' The other 50 percent 'would stay on for an extra month under my supervision and that of my officers … This last month was amusing. I let the cadets run their own show and we spent our time in attending demonstrations etc.'[53]

The increase in production in April and May 1918 is probably due to a combination of the delayed passing out of that cohort as well as a call for OCBs to expedite commissions in order to make good the losses caused by the German Spring Offensive.

Depending on the arm of service, 1916 and early 1917 represents a transitional period when the OCB system was set up, tested and refined.[54] The spring and early summer of 1917 was, however, the time when the OCB system achieved scale. It also marks the point at which the War Office completed the standardisation of pre-commissioning officer training with the closing down of the GHQ Cadet School at Blendeques which was still providing a six-week course run by the Artists' Rifles. The GHQ School had commissioned at least 1,026 men, with the last recorded commissions on 21 April 1917.[55]

OCB Commanding Officers and Instructors

So far, 51 Commanding Officers of the infantry and MGC/Tank Corps OCBs have been identified.[56] Of these, at least 26 have been identified by Peter Hodgkinson as having commanded a battalion on a fighting front.[57] In almost all cases, this was

51 Ibid., p.192.
52 Burns, *Mud and Bodies*, Kindle edition, locations 2205 and 2367.
53 Ibid., location 2367.
54 For a summary of the changes made to the Officer Cadet Schools of the other arms see Messenger, *A Call To Arms*, pp.324-25.
55 TNA WO 95/128/4: 1/28th London Regt (Artist's Rifles) War Diary, October 1914-May 1917. This total is based on data given in this source, but it is not known whether all commissions were recorded.
56 That is COs of those OCBs listed in Figures 4 and 6 above. They have been identified from OCB journals, local newspapers, memoirs and service records of former cadets in TNA: WO339 and WO374. This is not a complete list of COs with perhaps another 15 or so to be identified.
57 Peter Hodgkinson, 'British Infantry Battalion Commanders in the First World War' unpublished PhD thesis, University of Birmingham, 2014, Appendix 1.

before they had command of an OCB. Of these 26, 16 had served in one or more colonial campaigns, 14 alone in South Africa.[58] In addition, another nine OCB COs had seen active service in one or more colonial campaigns (of which seven were in South Africa) but did not command a battalion on active service in the First World War. However, they may well have served as company commanders or as second-in-command of a battalion.

Almost all of the OCB COs had been either serving Regular soldiers in 1914 or had returned from recent retirement. Despite their roots in the TF, No. 14 and No. 15 OCBs were commanded by Regular officers from the start of their establishment.

One non-Regular CO was Lieutenant-Colonel Robert Raymer DSO who commanded No. 10 OCB from January to May 1918, after almost two years on the Western Front in command of the 1/5th South Staffordshires and 10th West Riding.[59] Raymer had served in South Africa and in 1914 was a major in the 2nd Jersey Militia.[60] He was a schoolmaster at Victoria College, Jersey, and the first CO on the establishment of its OTC in 1908.[61]

Two other exceptions were Lieutenant-Colonel Edwards and Lieutenant-Colonel Stenning, both senior academics, respectively COs of Cambridge and Oxford UOTCs, neither of whom had seen active service. Stenning was replaced as CO of No. 4 OCB by a Regular CO, Lieutenant-Colonel G.A.M. Buckley DSO, on 9 June 1918.[62] Buckley had been on the retired list with the Hampshire Regiment in 1914 and re-joined the army at the outbreak of war, commanding the 7th Leinster Regiment on the Western Front for two years. Edwards was also replaced as CO of No. 2 OCB in June 1918.[63] Perhaps anticipating the war extending into 1919, the War Office may have wanted to take firmer control of former OTC-led OCBs by replacing Stenning and Edwards with experienced Regular officers.

One example is known of an OCB instructor who was appointed to command an OCB. Major R.M. Tidmarsh had initially commanded A Coy of No. 4 OCB before being appointed second-in-command of that battalion in May 1916.[64] On promotion to lieutenant-colonel he commanded No. 13 OCB from 3 October 1916 until 1 August 1918.[65] Tidmarsh was a Regular officer of the West Riding Regiment who had served in South Africa but had not commanded a battalion on active service.[66]

58   *War Services Supplement, Quarterly Army List, quarter ending 31st December 1917* (London: HMSO, January 1918).
59   Hodgkinson, 'British Infantry Battalion Commanders in the First World War', Appendix 1.
60   *War Services Supplement, Quarterly Army List, quarter ending 31st December 1917*, p.3226.
61   Haig-Brown, *The OTC and the Great War*, p.106.
62   Keble College Archives (KCA): Part 1 Orders, No. 4 OCB, No. 47, 11 June 1918.
63   The identity of his successor has not been established, but a new signatory is seen on Army Form SD622s in the service records of No. 2 OCB cadets passing out in June 1918.
64   KCA: Part 1 Orders, No. 4 OCB, 4 March 1916 and 20 May 1916.
65   *London Gazette*, 27 October 1916, p.10424 and 6 September 1918 p.10611.
66   *War Services Supplement, Quarterly Army List, quarter ending 31st December 1917*, p.3425.

In contrast to the COs, company and platoon commanders were a mix of Territorial, New Army and Regular soldiers. Initially, many were drawn from the schools of instruction. Instructors at any one OCB at a given moment were drawn from a wide variety of regiments. However, some OCBs appear to have had a slight bias to instructors from a predecessor unit. For example, Nos. 14 and 15 OCBs both had significant minorities of their instructors drawn from the Inns of Court OTC and Artists' Rifles respectively.[67]

Similarly, Nos. 2 and 4 OCBs appear to have had a higher proportion of officer instructors from the OTCs than other OCBs, and this reflects their origins in the University OTCs and their Schools of Instruction. A photograph taken outside the library of Pembroke College shows the 20 officers of No. 2 OCB who formed the instructors as of October 1916. Seven officers including Lieutenant-Colonel Edwards were from Cambridge University OTC. One of these was Edward Vulliamy, a lecturer in French and modern languages as well as Honorary Keeper of the Pictures at the FitzWilliam Museum.[68] Another officer, Captain J.E. Mellor, was a schoolmaster at the Leys School and had been OC of that school's OTC. The remaining 12 officers represented a variety of regiments, and most were veterans of the Western Front, some of whom were in the latter stages of recovering from wounds. Captain Gordon Carey of the Rifle Brigade was Assistant Secretary at the Cambridge University Press and had been wounded during the flamethrower attack at Hooge on 30 July 1915. On discharge from hospital he was appointed to command a company of No. 2 OCB but returned to his battalion in France shortly after this picture was taken.[69]

The officer commanding B Company was Captain John Francis Carter. Carter had been educated at Haileybury before matriculating at Pembroke in October 1896. He was a scholar and took his BA in 1899 before becoming a schoolmaster. Carter was a keen part-time soldier and had joined a Volunteer Company of the Suffolk Regiment in January 1900 and served in South Africa until May 1901. In 1904 he took up a new post at Repton School where he served as a captain in the OTC.

---

67   Errington, *The Inns of Court Officers Training Corps During the Great War*, pp.66-68; Stagoll Higham VD (ed.), *The Regimental Roll of Honour and War Record of the Artists' Rifles*, pp.307-11.

68   Vulliamy had matriculated at King's College in 1895 and was a noted watercolourist. He served with No. 2 OCB for most of its existence, though in October 1918 was posted to the BEF in France as an Intelligence Officer. See *Alumni Cantabrigiensis* <http://venn.lib.cam.ac.uk/acad/intro.html> and *The Army List*.

69   *War Record of The Cambridge University Press 1914-1919*. Carey had been commissioned into 8th Bn Rifle Brigade in September 1914 and went to France in May 1915. Promoted Major in March 1917 and held acting rank of lieutenant-colonel for short periods during that year. In November 1917 he was attached as 'Staff Learner' to X Corps HQ; transferred to the Royal Flying Corps and appointed Adjutant of 2nd Wing RAF in May 1918. In November 1918 he returned home on appointment as Staff Officer at the Air Ministry. Mentioned in Despatches and awarded a Belgian Croix de Guerre.

No. 4 Platoon, 2nd OCB, Cambridge, December 1916-April 1917. Lieutenant E.A.
Mackintosh is seated sixth from right in the front row.

Carter was commissioned into the 6th (Reserve) Battalion of the Rifle Brigade on
14 September 1914. Given the losses on the Western Front, Carter was soon posted
to a Regular battalion, the 2nd Battalion Kings Royal Rifle Corps, and joined them
in the front line on 1 November 1914 during the First Battle of Ypres.[70] Carter was
admitted to hospital with pneumonia and tonsillitis on 8 November. He was invalided
back to England on 26 November and spent some weeks recuperating until he was
passed fit for light duty. By June 1915, Carter was back at Pembroke as an instructor
at the school of instruction.

Another B Company instructor was Peyton Hadley. Hadley had received a gunshot
wound to the left thigh at Guillemont on 18 August 1916. He was sent home to recu-
perate and was passed by a medical board as fit for light duty on 3 November. He had
already been helping No. 2 OCB in an unofficial capacity and was formally appointed
as an instructor on 11 November. Hadley served with 2 OCB until January 1918.

No. 4 OCB in Oxford similarly had a number of Oxford UOTC officers on its
instructional staff. In addition to Lieutenant-Colonel Stenning, C Company was
commanded by the Dean of Keble College, Captain F.W. Matheson. Other instructors were academics who had returned from active service with other regiments. These
included a lecturer in modern history at Hertford College, C.R.M.F. Cruttwell, who

---

70   Carter was in the highly unusual position of being a combatant officer who was also a
clergyman. In 1904 he had decided to seek Holy Orders and was appointed as a deacon.
He was ordained in 1906. Biographical information on Carter is taken from his personal
file (TNA WO 339/14003) and *Alumni Cantabrigiensis* database.

had served on the Western Front with 1/4th Berkshires.[71] Captain A.F. Becke, RFA, was instructor in Tactics and Organisation, giving his lectures in the debating hall of the Oxford Union.[72]

In Bristol the local press observed that 'no greater compliment could have been paid' to the University OTC, and 'no higher tribute' to its Commanding Officer Captain J.W. McBain who was appointed OC of A Company of No. 3 OCB.[73] Another instructor was the Winterstoke Professor of English, Arthur Skemp, who had joined Bristol UOTC after the outbreak of war, and who was commissioned in early 1916. Skemp was an outstanding instructor: his services were retained by No. 3 OCB and in January 1918 he was promoted to acting captain to command a company.[74]

As the war progressed, an increasing proportion of instructors had recent combat experience, marking a clear improvement from those at the schools of instruction in 1915. The large pool of wounded officers recuperating in the UK was an obvious source of instructors. Data from 'The Weekly Strengths of the British Army at Home' suggests that by late 1917 about two-thirds of the officer instructors in the infantry OCBs were not fit for General Service.[75] They were mainly men recovering from serious wounds and their service records attest to the frequency with which they attended medical boards.

However, obtaining a role as an instructor at an OCB was often a matter of luck and personal networks. Neil Weir was in hospital in Oxford in December 1916 when he received a visit from Captain Matheson, his former tutor at Keble:

> He asked me whether I felt keen on a job of instructing men to become officers and I must say that although I thought I should like the job I felt that I had no experience... Nevertheless he mentioned my name to Captain H.H. Hardy at the War Office, whose business it was to find suitable officers to act as instructors. [Hardy] wrote to me saying that I should go and see him personally when I came out of hospital.[76]

Weir visited Hardy who told him that he would be appointed to an OCB when sufficiently fit.

71   Cruttwell, later Principal of Hertford, is best known for being the butt of Evelyn Waugh and to military historians for his *A History of the Great War* (1934) and *The War Service of the 1/4th Royal Berkshire Regiment (T.F.)* (1922).

72   KCA: Part 1 Orders, No. 4 OCB, 23 March 1916. Becke is also well-known as part of the Official History team and compiler of the *Orders of Battle* volumes.

73   'Bristol & The War: The University as an Officers Training Centre', *Western Daily Press*, 27 March 1916, p.5.

74   I am grateful to Charles Harvey and other members of the Skemp family for the related information in this essay; *London Gazette*, 14 January 1918, p.813.

75   TNA WO 114/33 to 36: The Weekly Strengths of the British Army At Home. From 24 September 1917 officers were classified as to whether or not they are fit for General Service.

76   Burns, *Mud and Bodies*, Kindle edition, locations 2001-06.

Shortly after Colonel Stenning … wrote me suggesting that I should join [No. 4 OCB] for the purpose of looking round and getting into the run of things. Consequently I went up to Oxford on 24 January 1917 after I had had a medical board … I was still very lame and could only get about with the aid of a stick … And I soon found out what little I knew and how rusty I was.[77]

Weir was attached to C Company at Keble and found himself 'once more back in the old college, but this time living in the guest room and feeding with the dons in the SCR [Senior Common Room] as the other instructors did.' Weir found that four of the other instructors were Keble men, undoubtedly recruited by Matheson from the alumni network. 'On February 4th Captain Hardy came down to pay us a visit and asked me if I should like to go down to a newly formed OCB at Fleet, near Aldershot.'[78]

Captain Henry Hardy appears to have been an influential officer in the development of the OCB system. In 1917 he was a GSO3 in the SD3(a) department at the War Office which was responsible for the 'organization, training, curriculum and appointments to instructional establishments of Officer Cadet Units and Artists' Rifles and Inns of Court Officers Training Corps' and 'regulations and questions' relating to these.[79] Hardy was a schoolmaster and had been CO of Rugby School's OTC contingent before taking a Special Reserve commission in the Rifle Brigade and serving with the 8th Battalion from October 1914 to about May 1915.[80]

There is some evidence that schoolmasters, particularly those with experience in instructing in their school's OTC, were sought after as instructors in OCBs. This is perhaps not surprising given that Hardy was presumably well networked in the OTC world. The *Record of War Service* of the Junior Division OTC lists 38 public schoolmasters who were instructors in OCBs.[81] This is an understatement since a number of other school masters are known to have been OCB instructors but are not listed.[82]

In time, an instructor who was declared fit for General Service would be likely to return to an active theatre. Several former OCB instructors were wounded or killed. For example, Peyton Hadley was wounded again on 27 March 1918. He was invalided home and had largely recovered by August but was taken ill in the influenza

77   Ibid., locations 2009-11.
78   Ibid., locations 2013-16.
79   HC Perrot, BA, *The War Office List, 46th Edition*, (London: Harrison & Sons, 1917), p.73.
80   Major DH Steers RE, *Officers Training Corps (Junior Division) Record of War Service 1914-18 Public School Officers and Other Members of the Staffs* (Cambridge: W. Heffer & Sons Ltd, 1919), p.142. Hardy was headmaster of Cheltenham College 1919-32. I am grateful to Tim Halstead for this information and for bringing Hardy to my attention. Unfortunately the pandemic has prevented further research into his role and that of SD3.
81   Steers, *Officers Training Corps (Junior Division) Record of War Service 1914-18*.
82   For example there is no entry for the Perse School in Cambridge, a school with an OTC, and at least one of its masters is known to have been an OCB instructor.

pandemic and died in the Central Military Hospital, Eastbourne on 25 October 1918. The Master of Pembroke and his wife were at his bedside.[83]

Many OCB instructors actively sought to get back to the front. Even if they had already 'done their bit' they may have felt impelled by a mixture of emotions including loyalty to their units and comrades, and guilt at holding a safe job. Lieutenant E.A. Mackintosh had been wounded and gassed on the Somme on 30 July 1916. By November he had recovered sufficiently to be posted to No. 2 OCB as a bombing instructor. He returned to France in late September 1917. However, his biographers note 'the adequacy of his recovery … must remain in some doubt.'[84] At the height of the Third Ypres campaign 'it is easy to imagine him persuading a malleable Medical Officer to pass him as fit.'[85] He was killed at Cambrai on 21 November.

Other OCB instructors with no combat experience may have felt that their instruction was less credible as it did not come from hard-won experience. Some may have felt an element of shame that they had not shared the privations of their veteran students. Arthur Skemp of No. 3 OCB had been trying to go on active service since his enlistment but had been repeatedly held back because of his excellence as an instructor. He was eventually permitted to transfer his commission from the TF Unattached List to the Gloucestershire Regt on 16 August 1918 and arrived at the front with 1st Gloucesters on 23 October 1918. He was killed eight days later.[86]

OCB instructors without active service experience did have opportunities to visit the Western Front so that they could go into front line trenches and visit training establishments. The records of No. 4 OCB show that its OTC instructors visited units and schools in the BEF. For example, Lieutenant-Colonel Stenning went on attachment from 10–28 July 1916.[87] Arthur Skemp of No. 3 OCB also went on attachment that summer when he visited Fourth Army School.

An Instructors' School of Instruction was set up at Berkhamsted in January 1918 after No. 14 OCB had moved to Catterick. Little is known about this school beyond its remit to improve the quality of instruction. The course must have included instructional techniques but it is not known to what extent it included the latest doctrinal thinking. It had two commandants: Lieutenant-Colonel R.M. Williams MC followed by Lieutenant-Colonel H.S. Poyntz DSO. Both were Regular officers who had commanded battalions on the Western Front and had then commanded an OCB.[88]

---

83 Hadley is buried next to his parents in St Mary's churchyard, Heacham, North Norfolk and is one of the 305 members and three servants commemorated on Pembroke's war memorial.

84 Colin Campbell & Rosalind Green, *Can't shoot a man with a cold: Lt E Alan Mackintosh MC 1893-1917, Poet of the Highland Division* (Glasgow: Argyll Publishing, 2004), p.176.

85 Campbell and Green, *Can't shoot a man with a cold*, p.187.

86 Lieutenant A.R. Skemp was killed on 1 November 1918 and is buried in Highland Cemetery, Le Cateau, grave 2.C.18.

87 KCA: Part 1 Orders, No. 4 OCB, No. 50, 19 July 1916.

88 Hodgkinson, 'British Infantry Battalion Commanders in the First World War', Appendix 1. Williams had commanded No. 7 OCB from October 1916 to January 1918; Poyntz had

Lieutenant Bertram Peel of the Cameron Highlanders joined a month-long course at the Instructors' School on 13 May 1918 before being posted to No. 1 OCB. Peel had been a schoolmaster at Edinburgh Academy, and 2nd lieutenant in the Junior Division OTC before being appointed to a temporary commission in the Cameron Highlanders in June 1915. He was wounded in November 1915 and after six months of recuperation he was passed fit for light duty with a Training Reserve Battalion. Captain Hardy wrote from the War Office on 21 April 1918: 'May we please have him on May 13th? His CO has sent him to us with his blessing and he has experience of teaching, being a master at Edinburgh Academy. We should very much like him.'[89]

Compared with the schools of instruction in 1915 there is evidence for a marked improvement in the quality of instructors by the end of the war. Ernest Parker, a cadet at No. 16 OCB in 1917, considered he had 'first—rate instructors, some of whom had already won coveted decorations, including at least one VC.'[90]

OCB Training

The syllabus for the infantry OCB course in 1916 included training in map-reading, musketry, anti-gas measures, reconnaissance, open warfare, bombing, field engineering (including the siting and laying out of trenches and the construction of tunnels and dug-outs), 'interior economy' (which covered a variety of logistical and administrative topics) and military law.[91] A total of 540 hours of formal instruction was given over the course, or between 30 and 35 hours per week of formal instruction. This is shown below in Figure 8. This does not include the time cadets were expected to spend on preparing their kit for the next day, two or three afternoons per week of sport, book work and exam revision.

commanded No. 17 OCB for about six months in late 1917.

89   TNA WO 339/33069: Lieutenant Bertram Lennase Peel personal file; Steers, *Officers Training Corps (Junior Division) Record of War Service 1914–18*, p.47.

90   Ernest Parker, *Into Battle: A Seventeen-Year-Old Joins Kitchener's Army* (Barnsley: Pen & Sword, 2012) p. 66.

91   Cambridge University Library: OP.2100.8.5: 'B' Company, No. 2 Officer Cadet Battalion, *Summary of lectures, private study and practical work for the 4 months' course, exclusive of drill, bayonet fighting and physical training*, 1916.

Figure 8. Programme of Work (hours) in Infantry Officer Cadet Battalions c. late 1916[92]

Subject	1st month	2nd month	3rd month	4th month	Total
Physical Training	21	12	–	–	**33**
Bayonet Training	–	12	16	–	**28**
Drill	42	24	20	8	**94**
Musketry	18	27	14	19	**78**
Field Engineering & Trench Warfare	19	18	24	16	**77**
Bombing	–	6	14	–	**20**
Anti–Gas Training	2	2	4	–	8
Map Reading, Reconnaissance & Reports	8	20	6		**34**
Night Work *	–	–	–	–	–
Military Law	4	6	4	–	**14**
Military Administration, Interior Economy etc.	7	10	4	–	**21**
Tactical Exercises (Theoretical & Practical)	–	–	32	78	**110**
Special Lectures	5	7	6	5	**23**
Totals	**126**	**144**	**144**	**126**	**540**

* Instruction in night work will be included in the hours allotted to the various subjects above.

As one might expect, the emphasis in the first half of the course was in ensuring a high level of fitness and of individual skills. Members of the Army Gymnastic Staff gave instruction in PT and bayonet training. Musketry training ensured that the cadets themselves were at least competent shots, but, more importantly, were capable of running ranges safely and of instructing their platoons. Cadets at No. 4 OCB (Oxford) spent up to a week at a time at musketry camps on ranges near Warwick.[93]

At the start of the course, lectures were an important means of imparting knowledge, though their number diminished with the increased focus on practical instruction as the course progressed. An old boy of Worksop College described lectures at his OCB as 'a headlong race to accumulate vast stores of written notes in an absurdly small note book.'[94] In order to support delivery of lectures, No. 2 OCB constructed

92   TNA AIR 1 130 15 40 208: Officer Cadet Battalion RFC: syllabus and suggested extension of training course for cadets.
93   See for example KCA: Part 1 Orders, No. 4 OCB, No. 37, 14 June 1916.
94   'An Old Boy', *The Cuthbertian*, July 1918, p.112. The OCB was not identified.

a short length of trench in the grounds of the Leys School in Cambridge.[95] These trenches were used for instruction by the other OCBs as well as the schoolboys of The Leys OTC.

Field exercises became increasingly important in the third and fourth months of the course. It is likely that all OCBs had a training area within easy reach. The Oxford OCBs used a system of training trenches in Wytham Woods.[96] Nos. 16 and 17 OCBs at Kinmel Park Camp in North Wales had the use of two nearby trench systems in Kinmel Park and Bodelwyddan Castle Park.[97] No. 14 OCB used the 13,000 yards of trenches constructed by the Inns of Court on Berkhamsted Common.[98]

The Cambridge OCBs used a training area on the Gog Magog hills with an extensive trench system. Archaeological evidence of the trenches survives near Cherry Hinton.[99] The cadets marched there for instruction and practice in digging trenches, as well as lectures and practice in both attack and defence. They took part in exercises, the largest of which involved cadets from the other companies or other OCBs.

A major exercise on 13 April 1917 featured cadets from Nos. 2 and 5 OCBs and involved aircraft from the RFC as well as dummy tanks. Surviving photographs show that the 'tanks' consisted of a canvas-covered frame mounted on a small car or motorcycle and side-car combination. Metal tubes protruding from various points around the frame gave the appearance of guns.[100] This exercise was filmed as 'The Battle of the Gogs' by A.J. Pointer of the Victoria Cinema which exhibited the film a few days later. Other local cinemas were showing it until at least July.[101] The film included preparatory work such as filling bombs and the march to the training area before describing the battle:

> Aeroplanes were first reconnoitring, and then a thrilling trench raid took place, during which the aeroplanes were seen dropping bombs the enemy's trenches and swooping down to within a few yards of the ground sweep the trenches with

95   *The Leys Fortnightly*, Vol. 41, no. 731, 13 July 1917, p.299. I am grateful to Alison Lainchbury, Archivist at The Leys for this information and that relating to Captain JE Mellor.

96   *Wytham Woods* <https://www.wythamwoods.ox.ac.uk/history> (accessed 28 September 2020).

97   J Spencer, *CPAT Report No. 1255: Bodelwyddan Castle Park Trenches & Kimmel Park Camp Scoping Study*, (Welshpool: Clwyd-Powys Archaeological Trust, 2014).

98   Errington, *The Inns of Court Officers Training Corps During the Great War*, p.16.

99   These were identified by Historic England in their survey of First World War Training Trenches. See Martin Brown, *First World War Fieldworks in England* <https://historicengland.org.uk/whats-new/first-world-war-home-front/what-we-already-know/land/practice-trenches/>

100   Leeds University Library (LUL): Special Collections, Liddle Collection, H.L. Graham papers. Graham was an instructor at No. 5 OCB.

101   'Cambridge Picture Theatres – The Kinema, Mill-Road', *Cambridge Daily News*, 10 July 1917, p.4.

machine-gun fire. The spectacle of the bombing of the trenches was very striking, as was also that the gas attack, the deadly fumes being seen sweeping across the hillside in clouds. Through the smoke the soldiers could be seen wearing their gas masks. A 'tank' went lumbering by, making for the enemy's position, and then the infantry in the trenches were seen scrambling 'over the top' and rushing to the attack in extended order.[102]

The exercise included extensive use of pyrotechnics, with a local boy being injured after playing with some uncleared ordnance.[103]

The OCBs encouraged students to learn from each other. Major A.B. Pollak, Commanding Officer of No. 2 Cavalry Officer Cadet School in the Curragh urged cadets 'who have had practical experience in the field … to impart their experience to other cadets, not only in the lecture room by means of lectures, but in the field, and in the course of conversation in the Anteroom.'[104] This peer-to-peer learning would have been particularly important for young men going to an OCB direct from school or university OTCs.

OCB training was therefore more than a passive 'I will teach and you will listen' approach. It recognised that many cadets – some of whom had left school as early as 14 – may not have been suited to learning from books and lectures, so a variety of teaching methods was used. The OCBs encouraged active learning through discussion and sharing.

Exams and Passing Out

Robert Graves served as an instructor with Nos. 4 and 16 OCBs and estimated that 'we failed about a sixth of the candidates for commissions; the failures were sometimes public school boys without the necessary toughness, but usually men who had been recommended, from France, on compassionate grounds – rather stupid [NCOs] who had been out too long and were thought to need a rest.'[105] However, detailed analysis of surviving records suggests that pass rates were in the order of 90 per cent. 'Just over 1,000 cadets' passed through C Company of No. 4 OCB and 'of these just over 900 obtained commissions.'[106] A roll of No. 18 OCB (Bath) states that of 1,698 men who had entered the unit before the Armistice, 1,311 had been commissioned by then,

---

102 "Battle of the Gogs' Remarkable Military Pictures the Victoria Cinema', *Cambridge Daily News*, 19 April 1917, p.3.
103 'Explosive Found on Gogs', *Cambridge Daily News*, 18 April 1918.
104 National Army Museum (NAM): 9203-242: papers of 2/Lt. C. Huddlestone. Transcript of opening address No. 2 Cavalry Officer Cadet School 1918.
105 Robert Graves, *Goodbye To All That* (London: Jonathan Cape, 1929), p.305.
106 KCA: *'C' Company No. 4 OCB 1916-1919*, Keble College, February 1920.

with 387 more being commissioned before the unit was disbanded, or a pass rate of 91 per cent.[107]

Cadets were continuously assessed during the course. Command appointments during field exercises and drilling squads of fellow cadets were used to assess their capability in command roles. Cadets also had to pass three exams which covered subjects such as military law, field engineering and musketry. The exams were set centrally by the War Office each month and would be sat by all cadets passing out of all the OCBs in that particular month. The exams were held on the last Monday or Tuesday of the month with all three papers being sat on the same day. In Oxford the cadets of No. 4 OCB sat at rows of individual tables in the debating hall of the Union Society.[108]

Each cadet was allocated a number which indicated the table at which he should sit. The cadets were instructed to 'write their numbers but *not* their names' on the answer document 'Army Book A4'. Cadets could bring pens and pencils (black and coloured), an India rubber, a protractor and divider, but no paper or books of any kind.

An Examining Board – consisting of a president, a major, and another 5 to 8 officers – marked the papers with the results being published on Thursday. The examiners were therefore 'marking blind' without knowing the names of the cadets it would have been hard for the unconscious bias induced by prior knowledge of a cadet's education, class and service history to come into play. The first set of exam papers were published in May 1916 with a total of 5½ hours exam time. This rose to 6½ hours in May or June 1917.[109] Mid-term exam papers were introduced in September 1918 by which time the course had been extended to six months.

A Confidential Report (Army form SD 622) was completed – usually by the company instructors – for each cadet with the final recommendation, and this was signed by the commanding officer. Cadets were assessed on two key characteristics – 'Military Knowledge' and 'Power of Command and Leadership'. These were changed to the 'Ability to train a platoon' and the 'Ability to command a platoon' in late 1918.[110] Cadets appear to have been assessed on these measures on a rough scale from 'poor' through 'fair' (and sometimes 'very fair') and 'good' to 'excellent'.

However, character was arguably the important factor in deciding whether to award a commission, and this could over-ride a narrow failure to pass the final exam. Graves recounted that the final selection 'was made by watching them play games, principally rugger and soccer.' Those who played 'rough but not dirty and had quick

107 No. 18 Officer Cadet Battalion, November 26th 1916 to February 20th 1919, pub. *Bath Chronicle*, Bath, n.d. [1919?], p.7.
108 KCA: No. 4 OCB Part 1 Orders No. 89, 20 November 1916.
109 Based on surviving OCB exam papers held in LUL: Liddle Collection (File references GA/OCA; GS/0837 (Isherwood papers) and GS/0056 (Askew papers)), NAM: (Twist and Rees papers) and author's collection.
110 Analysis of completed Form SD 622s suggests this occurred in late 1918 with all the cadets commissioned after the Armistice showing this evaluation. The relevant instruction from the Staff Duties Department at the War Office has not yet been identified.

reactions' were selected.[111] Instructors at other OCBs may have applied similar criteria in making their final assessment.

For example, David Sadler, a 19-year-old cadet who had joined No. 2 OCB on 7 June 1918 had 'failed to qualify' at the final exam held on 26 November. However, on his confidential report he was assessed as 'good' in terms of his abilities to train and command a platoon and the instructors noted that he was 'Keen on all games. Is better at practical work than in theoretical. Smart and keen on his work. Will make an officer.'[112] Sadler was duly commissioned into the Gordon Highlanders. Cadets could be held back for a month for remedial training and exam retests if they were a little below the required standard. A cadet who failed to be recommended for a commission was returned to his unit with the rank he had held when he left it.

A question to be resolved is whether the OCB system became better at weeding out ineffective men. The evidence suggests that few inefficient men would get through the rigorous testing provided by the course, with most being screened out. One example is officer cadet Richard Leir who had left school in December 1913. On 9 September 1914 Leir enlisted in 19th Royal Fusiliers of the Universities and Public Schools Brigade. Given that he had attended Clifton College – one of the top public schools for producing Regular officers and Douglas Haig's alma mater – a commission in a New Army unit would have been a formality at that stage of the war.

However, Leir over-reached himself and applied for a Regular commission, starting a course at the Royal Military College, Sandhurst on 10 November 1914.[113] The Commandant of the RMC, Brigadier-General S.P. Rolt, wrote to Leir's mother on 10 May 1915: 'It is impossible for me to recommend him as likely to become an efficient officer.' Leir was duly returned to the ranks of the Universities and Public School Brigade. After a few months there he applied for a temporary commission and joined a course at No. 6 OCB, Oxford on 19 May 1916. However, the Commanding Officer wrote to his mother on 19 July: 'He is a gentlemanly cadet, and I think does his best, but he has apparently no capacity for learning and shows no initiative. He is not and, I think, will never be fitted to command a platoon.' His mother appealed for another month of evaluation, but this was to no avail with the CO writing on 19 August: 'It is even more clear to me now that this cadet will never make a leader of men.' Leir was returned to his unit.

However, the OCB system could give men a second chance. James Skinner, who, as discussed earlier in this chapter, had resigned his commission after criticism for 'inefficiency' in late 1916, re-joined the Inns of Court on 16 May 1917 and was sent to No. 5 OCB, joining a course on 7 September. By now 24, he was commissioned into the Cameron Highlanders on 30 October and was wounded on 7 June 1918 whilst serving with the 1st Battalion.[114] Other examples are known of cadets who failed an OCB

---

111 Graves, *Goodbye To All That*, p.305.
112 TNA WO 339/138820: 2/Lt David Wallace Sadler personal file.
113 TNA WO 339/63675: O/Cdt Richard Leir personal file.
114 TNA WO 339/21688: Lieutenant James Hay McInnes Skinner personal file; Roll of cadets, *The Blunderbuss*, No. 5, December 1917, p.67; casualty list *The Blunderbuss,* No. 7,

course at the first attempt but passed a second course a year or more later once they had had a chance to mature and gain experience. Other cadets were moved from a course at a cadet school in one arm to a course in another arm to which they were better suited, such as from an artillery or cavalry school to an ASC or infantry school. This suggests that the War Office was trying to give men a fair chance of gaining a commission.[115]

Continuation Training for Junior officers: Schools for Infantry Officers

The OCB system was, however, merely one part of a framework in which promising officers could be developed for more senior roles. The Senior Officers School at Aldershot, which equipped majors and newly appointed lieutenant-colonels with the skills to command a battalion, is well known. This school had been established in October 1916 with the intention of producing a reserve of commanding officers after a 10-week course.[116]

In between was an intermediate level set up by the regional commands. The three known examples are No. 1 School of Instruction for Infantry Officers at Brocton Camp, Staffordshires and the similarly named No. 2 School at Elstow Beds and No. 3 School at Tidworth.[117] No records survive for these schools but there are some clues from surviving orders, service records and memoirs.

These schools were set up from March 1916.[118] Basil Williams in *Raising and Training the New Armies* observed that they addressed the needs of two groups of subalterns. First were 'temporary officers of the 1914-15 period, who have never had regular training in anything but the most elementary duties' of whom 'a very small percentage … were up to the standard required.'[119] Second were the OCB graduates. Williams observed that 'at the end of their four months [they] are supposed to be fit to take up the ordinary duties of a subaltern in a platoon, they have not had time to learn the more advanced tactical work which is required of a company commander or even sometimes of a platoon commander.'[120]

The available evidence is that these schools provided at least two types of course. First, they ran two-month courses to train experienced subalterns who would be

October 1918, p.51.

115 This is the subject of ongoing research in my thesis: space precludes detailed discussion of these examples.
116 For a discussion of this school see Peter E Hodgkinson and William F. Westerman, '"Fit to Command a Battalion": The Senior Officers' School 1916-18', *Journal of the Society for Army Historical Research*, 93 (2015), pp.120-38.
117 Only these three are listed in 'The Weekly Strengths of the British Army At Home'. See TNA WO 114/28 to 36.
118 TNA WO 293/4: Army Council Instruction No. 592 17 March 1916; Captain Basil Williams, *Raising and Training the New Armies* (London: Constable & Co. Ltd, 1918), p.106.
119 Williams, *Raising and Training the New Armies*, pp.105-06.
120 Ibid., p.105.

'capable of commanding and administering a company in the field.'[121] Williams suggests that this was their main purpose and describes the programme as follows:

> The study of tactics absorbs the largest number of hours … and under that heading are included not only lectures and demonstrations on the ground, but actual practice by day and night of tactical work in the open and in trench warfare with troops. The commandant of the school … lays great store on tactical schemes in the open, so that the officers may not be misled into thinking that the present trench warfare on the western front is the only possible method of warfare. Other subjects of instruction are topography, musketry and field engineering. In order to give reality to the tactical schemes, some men are attached to the school for use in skeleton formation. Under the head of law and administration, a complete course is given in the duties of company commanders as to the discipline and internal arrangements of their companies, and their functions on a court-martial are clearly demonstrated by means of model court-martial proceedings conducted before all the students. The course is strenuous: the day's work in the field or the lecture room lasts from 8.30 to 5.45, with occasional night work in addition; leave is sparingly given …[122]

An officer could not go direct from an OCB to this course. He 'must have performed at least three months' regimental duty as a subaltern … in which to feel his feet as an officer and accustom himself to drilling men and acquiring self-confidence' and have been assessed 'as fit for higher training.' Officers 'who have already shown themselves to possess the power of leadership' were also sent to these schools from the BEF.[123] The syndicate structure of the course implies a lot of Tactical Exercises Without Training (TEWTs) and learning from the collective experience of the group.

For example, 2nd Lieutenant H.A. Gates had been commissioned from No. 19 OCB into the Rifle Brigade on 26 June 1917 before being wounded in late 1917. He attended No. 1 School between 12 January and 9 March 1918. His syndicate commander, a Major Wymer of the 2nd Hampshires, described his character as 'a conscientious and hardworking officer. He is reliable and self-confident.' His capabilities were described as 'good at drill and quick at learning new things. His military knowledge is good and he handles troops well in the field.' Lieutenant-Colonel L.W. Lucas, the commandant, summarised: 'a keen and capable officer who has taken great interest in his work. Fit to command a Company in the field.'[124]

Another officer who attended this course at No. 1 School between 18 May and 13 July 1918 was Lieutenant T.M. Weir of the Argyll & Sutherland Highlanders. Weir

121 Ibid., p.106.
122 Ibid., pp.106-07.
123 Ibid., pp.105-06.
124 TNA WO 339/93367: 2/Lt HA Gates personal file.

had been commissioned in November 1915, thereby missing the OCB system. His syndicate commander, Major Pilkington of the South Lancashire Regiment, described Weir as 'a steady, reliable, and well-balanced officer. He has energy and drive. He has a very good military knowledge and has been keen to acquire fresh knowledge during the course.' Lieutenant-Colonel Lucas added: 'I agree. A very sound and conscientious officer. Fit to command a Company in the field.'[125]

Gates and Weir exemplify the level of training and experience that many of the company commanders of the BEF would have had by the Hundred Days. Gates had served for five months and Weir for six months as platoon commanders in France before they had attended No. 1 School.

The schools also appear to have provided a number of short courses. Basil Williams observed that 'many officers are only too glad to get an occasional 'refresher' course.'[126] This is likely to have been particularly important for imparting new doctrine. For example, Norman Collins who had passed out from No. 8 OCB at the end of July 1916 was posted to 4th (Reserve) Seaforth Highlanders at Ripon. In over two months there before he was posted to France he was 'given refresher courses at the No. 1 School of Instruction in everything from tactical problem solving to advancing under artillery fire, from lectures on military law to the organisation of bombing parties.'[127]

The formation of these three schools was an early recognition that the OCBs would not produce a subaltern who was a 'finished article'. If the OCBs were contemporaneously thought of as 'mini-Sandhursts' imparting command and leadership skills, then these two schools can be thought of as analogues of the School of Infantry imparting technical infantry knowledge. The policy and thinking behind them almost certainly came from the Staff Duties Department at the War Office. It is clear that the OCBs were thought of as part of a more comprehensive, integrated system, and that much thought was put being put into the question of career development for subalterns over the winter of 1915–16.

Conclusion

This chapter has argued that the selection and training of junior officers itself went through a learning process, and as such there is evidence for both 'bottom up' innovation and more formal 'top down' dissemination of learning by the Staff Duties Department. This is consistent with Aimée Fox's model of innovation and change

---

125 TNA WO 374/72948: Lieutenant TMcC Weir personal file. It is possible Weir could have attended a month-long post-commissioning course at a School of Instruction in the UK before these were phased out, but there is no indication of this in his file.
126 Williams, *Raising and Training the New Armies*, p.105.
127 Norman Collins & Richard van Emden, *Last Man Standing: The Memoirs of a Seaforth Highlander During the Great War* (Barnsley: Pen & Sword, 2002), p.82.

in the British Army of the Great War.[128] There is also evidence for a greater degree of continuity from the OTCs to the OCB system than has been recognised to date. There was a marked improvement in the quality of instruction for junior officers, and this was partly the effect of having increasing numbers of OCB instructors with recent combat experience. Men not likely to make efficient officers were filtered out as the Army changed its officer development model with commissions only being awarded to men who had passed the OCB course.

Jim Storr observes that in peacetime 'the impact of changes to officer training policy are difficult to identify until years later, and so the linkage may not be obvious.'[129] However, in the learning laboratory that was the BEF of 1914-18 changes to officer training and selection policies were tested in combat mere months later. This provides an opportunity to try and identify such a linkage. The improved operational effectiveness of the BEF in 1918 was a result of a large number of interrelated factors, so further research is required to isolate the effects of improved officer selection and training.

However, OCB graduates were equal to the task of leadership in the BEF of 1918. In 1917 and 1918 they comprised an increasing proportion of platoon commanders and would have comprised the vast majority in the Hundred Days. Robert Graves' pithy observation that the OCB system 'saved the Army in France from becoming a mere rabble' has been extensively quoted, but not tested.[130] Further research will determine the extent to which OCB graduates filled the officer ranks and their contribution to the final victory.

Graves may have been exaggerating for effect, but the OCB system and the broader system of officer development into which it fitted undoubtedly played a part in the improved operational effectiveness of the BEF in 1918. It was the refinement and scaling up of that system in 1917 which set a consistent quality threshold, and which ensured that the BEF had a plentiful supply of junior officers for the following year. Ernest Parker considered of his fellow OCB graduates 'They were all men who had voluntarily joined Kitchener's Army ... When they finally returned to the battle fronts they brought an entirely new spirit into the ranks of the junior officers. Our lot were ready to lead the conscripts then training to fill the gaps in the units who would be fighting the Passchendaele battles of late summer 1917.'[131]

128 Fox, *Learning To Fight*, pp.5-7.
129 Storr, *The Human Face of War*, p.192.
130 Graves, *Goodbye To All That*, p.305.
131 Parker, *Into Battle*, p.66.

4

The Double-Edged Sword
Military Group Cohesion in British Infantry Battalions During 1917

Tom Thorpe

Introduction

Military group cohesion is a process of social integration within a small group or unit that is part of a military force. The degree of cohesion within the group or unit relates to the levels of trust between members. A cohesive unit is one which has high levels of trust between members and these relationships facilitate social solidarity, teamwork, cooperation and coordination of collective group tasks or functions.[1] For the previous 2,500 years, scholars, academics and military leaders have noted that cohesive groups of combatants in military units are critical for battlefield success.[2] For example, the Greek historian Xenophon wrote, 'no stronger phalanx than that which is composed of comrades that are close friends.'[3] Even today, cohesion is just as critical to military effectiveness; in the United Kingdom's defence doctrine (2014), it is essential to maintaining 'morale' and sustaining 'collective performance' of military forces.[4]

It was after the Second World War that the study of cohesion in military groups and units received attention. American social scientists were impressed by the effect close relationships (or cohesion) appeared to have on the morale and combat performance of

---

1   Guy L. Siebold, 'The Essence of Military Group Cohesion', *Armed Forces & Society* 33:2 (2007), p.288; Mikael Salo, 'United we Stand – Divided We Fall – A Standard Model of Unit Cohesion' (PhD Dissertation, University of Helsinki, 2011), p.3.

2   Nora Kinzer Stewart, *Mates and Muchachos: Unit Cohesion in the Falklands/Malvinas War* (New York: Brassey's Inc, 1991), p.12.

3   Cyropaedia of Xenophon, *The Life of Cyrus the Great*, para 7.1.30, Greek text and translations <http://perseus.uchicago.edu/perseus-cgi/citequery3.pl?dbname=GreekTexts&getid=1&query=Xen.%20Cyr.%207.1.34> (accessed 25 February 2020).

4   Ministry of Defence (UK), *UK Defence Doctrine, JDP-0-01*, 5th Ed. (London: Ministry of Defence, November 2014), pp.50, 38.

American and German soldiers.[5] US Air Force psychologists Roy Grinker and John Paul Spiegel observed that 'men seem to be fighting more for someone than against somebody.'[6] Combat historian S.L.A. Marshall, from his work studying US ground forces, believed that men were sustained in battle by the knowledge that others were around, as this made 'danger more endurable'.[7] Much of this post-war research on the relationships in small groups became known as primary group theory.

Modern studies by sociologists and social psychologists have further developed understanding of how close interpersonal relationships in teams can contribute to outcomes desired by military leaders. Cohesion can help promote support and caring between teammates, which, in turn, can act as a source of combat motivation, reduce battlefield stress, psychological breakdown and conditions like post-traumatic stress disorder.[8] Other commentators demonstrate that tightly knit groups help deliver higher levels of teamwork, interaction, communication and consensus-building, all of which lead to better cooperation between unit members and performance.[9] Cohesion is a critical factor in the outcome of modern conflicts, and is used in explaining Israeli victories over Arab armies, North Vietnamese success against US forces in Vietnam, and British triumph in the 1982 Falklands War.[10]

5   Samuel A Stouffer et al. *The American Soldier: Combat and Its Aftermath*, Vols.1&2 (Princeton: Princeton University Press, 1949). S.L.A. Marshall, *Men Against Fire* (New York: William Morrow & Co, 1947). For example, in interviews with German POWs, sociologists Edward Shills and Morris Janowitz wrote that solidarity between primary groups of men, namely small intimate groups of men who have close personal relationships, was the dominant motivator of Wehrmacht soldiers to fight on, often in hopeless situations. See Edward A. Shils & Morris. Janowitz, 'Cohesion and Disintegration in the Wehrmacht in World War II', *Public Opinion Quarterly* 12 (Summer 1948), pp.280-315.

6   Roy R. Grinker & John Paul Siegel, *Men Under* Stress (Philadelphia: Blakiston, 1945), p.32.

7   Marshall, *Men*, p.141.

8   Leonard Wong, Thomas A. Kolkditz, Raymond A Millen & Terrence M. Potter, *Why they Fight* (Carlisle: Strategic Studies Institute, U.S. Army War College, 2003), pp.10-11, 23-25; Gregory L. Belenky, Frank J. Sodetz & C. Frederick Tyner, Israeli Battle Shock Casualties: 1973 and 1982 (Washington DC: Walter Reed Army Institute of Research, 1983), p.17; Canby, Gudmundsson & Shay quoted in Brendan McBreen, 'Improving Unit Cohesion' (Thesis for The Commandant of the Marine Corps National Fellowship Program, 2002), p.8.

9   James Griffith, 'Multilevel analysis of cohesion's relation to stress, well-being identification, disintegration, and perceived combat readiness', *Military Psychology* 14:3 (2002), pp.217-39; Dorwin Cartwright, 'The nature of group cohesiveness' in Dorwin Cartwright & Alvin. Zander (eds.), *Group Dynamics: Research and Theory* (New York: Harper & Row, 1968), pp.91-109; Stephen J. Zaccaro & Charles A. Lowe, 'Cohesiveness and performance of an additive task: evidence for multidimensionality', *Journal of Social Psychology* 128:4 (1988), pp.547-58; Aharon Tziner & Yoav Vardi, 'Effects of command style on group cohesiveness on the effectiveness of self-selected tank crews', *Journal of Applied Psychology* 67:6 (1982), pp.769-75.

10   See Edward Luttwak & Daniel Horowitz, *The Israeli Army, 1948-1973* (Cambridge, Massachusetts: Abt Books, 1983 [1975]); William D. Henderson, *Why the Vietcong Fought* (Westport, Connecticut: Greenwood Press, 1979); Stewart, *Mates*.

Though cohesion within small groups or units may support the wider objectives of the military of which they are part, cohesive groups can also perform 'destructive' action which can be detrimental and obstructive to these goals. This behaviour takes many forms, such as cohesive groups deliberately deciding to maintain low levels of productivity, committing mutiny, refusing orders, initiating informal truces or committing serious crimes.[11] The example of the Canadian Airborne Regiment stands as an instance of the latter. The unit was disbanded in 1995 after an enquiry found that strong peer cohesion led to serious disciplinary problems such as 'extreme initiation rites' and the torture and death of a civilian while the regiment was on peacekeeping duties in Somalia two years previously.[12]

This study examines the nature, extent and impact of military group cohesion within the infantry battalions of 56th (London) Division during 1917. It will demonstrate that group cohesion was a strong, pervasive and robust force which contributed to soldier morale, motivation and resilience but also facilitated a series of protests, strikes and unrest in a number of units during the year.

It is pertinent to give a brief background on the 56th Division and its activities in 1917. The division was comprised of twelve first line Territorial battalions of the Middlesex and London Regiments in February 1916.[13] It fought through the Somme and saw considerable action in 1917. In January, the division held trenches near Laventie sector and became involved in fierce fights for a series of outposts they had constructed opposite Germans lines, known as the 'saga of the posts'.[14] During April, it was engaged in the opening days of the Battle of Arras, attacking German defenced at Neuville-Vitasse. Following this, the division fought in the Third Battle of Ypres, taking part in a failed attack against Inverness Copse, Glencourse and Nonne Bosschen woods on 16 August 1917.[15] Finally, in November 1917, 56th Division participated in the Battle of Cambrai.

---

11   Anthony King, *The Combat Soldier: Infantry Tactics and Cohesion in the Twentieth and Twenty-First Centuries* (Oxford: Oxford University Press, 2013), p.32; RAND, Sexual Orientation and U.S. Military Personnel Policy, an Update of RAND's 1993 Study (Santa Monica, California: Rand Corporation, 2010), p.296.

12   Donna Winslow, 'Rites of Passage and Group Bonding in the Canadian Airborne', *Armed Forces & Society* 25:3 (Spring 1999), p.445.

13   Infantry units of 56th Division TF were as follows: 167th Brigade: 1/7th Battalion, Middlesex Regiment, 1/8th Battalion, Middlesex Regiment, 1/1st Battalion, London Regiment (Royal Fusiliers), 1/3rd Battalion, London Regiment (Royal Fusiliers); 168th Brigade: 1/4th Battalion, London Regiment (Royal Fusiliers), 1/12th Battalion, London Regiment (Rangers), 1/13th Battalion, London Regiment (Kensingtons), 1/14th Battalion, London Regiment (London Scottish); 169th Brigade: 1/2nd Battalion, London Regiment (Royal Fusiliers), 1/5th Battalion, London Regiment (London Rifle Brigade), 1/9th Battalion, London Regiment (Queen Victoria's Rifles), 1/16th Battalion, London Regiment (Queen's Westminster Rifles).

14   W.H.A. Groom, *Poor Bloody Infantry* (London: William Kimber, 1976), pp.73-86.

15   Charles H. Dudley Ward, *The Fifty-Sixth Division* (London: John Murray, 1921), pp.144-64, 160.

1/1st Battalion London Regiment (Royal Fusiliers) orderly room, Guemappe,
29 April 1917. (Private collection)

Military group cohesion will be examined using the 'Standard Model for Military Group Cohesion', developed by sociologist Professor Guy Siebold.[16] The Standard Model appeared in 2007 as a model of interpersonal relationships a soldier has in a small military unit with groups of people around them, such as leaders or peers. The model is not without its critics, but is accepted by many historians and sociologists as a comprehensive approach to describe military cohesion.[17] It will be used in this historical study as a structural framework around which to examine cohesive relationships within units.

Within the model, cohesion occurs at two distinct levels; inside the primary group and outside it. Primary groups are small collections of people who have close regular personal social relations and treat one another as unique individuals. These can be families or sports teams. In this study, primary groups are based around the military structures in which men worked, fought and resided, primarily the infantry section of around seven to ten people or the platoon, which comprised of between 30 to 50 men.

16   Siebold, 'The Essence …', Salo, United We Stand, pp.51-54.
17   See Anthony King, 'The Existence of Group Cohesion in the Armed Forces: A Response to Guy Siebold', *Armed Forces & Society* 33:4 (2007). Salo, 'United We Stand; Robert Engen, *Strangers in Arms* (Montreal & Kingston: McGill-Queen's University Press, 2016), p.12.

In military settings, primary group relationships form between two sets of people; *horizontal cohesion* is between soldiers of equal military rank, and *vertical cohesion* is between leaders and their subordinates. Secondary group cohesion, on the other hand, is based on relationships with abstract entities outside the primary group. The focus for these secondary group relationships in the Standard Model is the broader organisation of which the soldier is a member. There are two areas of bonding in secondary group cohesion; *organisational cohesion* is the relationship between individuals and the levels of the military hierarchy above their primary group; for example, company, battalion or division. *Institutional cohesion* is the association between individuals and the service branch, such as the army, navy or air force.[18] The focus of this chapter will be on the primary groups level, examining horizontal cohesion relations between peers and the vertical cohesion between leaders and the led.

At both the primary and secondary group levels, cohesion is based on two types of motivation. The first is on a task basis (task cohesion), where people give commitment, reciprocity and allegiance to the group and/or the organisation collectively to complete shared tasks or jobs on behalf of the group, team or organisation through teamwork and a shared commitment to the task. The other is on a social basis (social cohesion), where group members give affection and emotional commitment to form mutually supportive relationships based on caring, interpersonal attraction, social support and intimacy among group members or personal attachment or duty to the organisation.[19]

The basis of these relationships is trust, which is the positive expectation that fellow group members will act in one another's best interest in situations involving risk. On a task basis, people give their trust to other team members with whom they share labour, risk and rewards for working on a joint project. On a social basis, trust rests on companionship and devotion between an emotionally committed group.[20]

The use of 'trust' as the basis of determining the existence of cohesion in the Standard Model means that a wide range of historical evidence may be used. Trust between people can be demonstrated through individual deeds and words as well as group actions and behaviour, such as high levels of confidence and loyalty to peers and leaders.[21] Historical records provide examples. For instance, it is possible to suggest that Rifleman Leslie Walkinton, serving in the 1/16th Battalion, London Regiment (Queen Westminster Rifles or QWR), had strong vertical cohesion with his platoon

---

18   Siebold, 'The Essence ...', pp.288-90.
19   Rand Corporation, *Sexual Orientation and US Military Personnel Policy: Options and Assessment* (Santa Monica, California: Rand Corporation, 1993), p.291.
20   Siebold, 'The Essence...', p.288. S.D. Boon & J.G. Holmes, 'The Dynamics of Interpersonal Trust: Resolving Uncertainty in the Face of Risk' in R.A. Hinde & J. Groebel (eds.), *Cooperation and Prosocial Behaviour* (Cambridge: Cambridge University Press, 1991), pp.190-212.
21   Frederick J. Manning, 'Morale and Cohesion' in *Military Psychiatry: Preparing in Peace for War* in Franklin D. Jones et al (eds.), *Textbook of Military Medicine, Part I* (Falls Church, Virginia: Office of The Surgeon General, United States Army, 1994), pp.11-12.

commander Second Lieutenant Harding, because he described him as the 'perfect example of a good officer' and 'an ideal leader in France' on whom he based his conduct when commissioned.[22] Language can be another indicator of trust; for example, if a soldier uses terms such as 'we', 'us' and 'our', this may suggest an affinity with their group or regiment.[23]

This chapter is structured into four sections. The first section outlines out the extent and nature of primary group cohesion by examining horizontal cohesion between men of the same military rank and vertical cohesion between leaders and subordinates. It will also assess how the publication of *SS 143* in February 1917 changed British platoon structure which in turn intensified cohesion within infantry platoons.[24] The second section explores how cohesion contributed to morale, resilience and leader influence. The third section considers how cohesion facilitated protests and strikes in 1917. The final section offers some conclusions.

Primary Group Cohesion

Horizontal cohesion is the positive interpersonal relationship between peers of the same rank and organisational status in a small (primary) group or unit based on an exchange of mutual trust and loyalty that can facilitate teamwork and caring between members.[25] Most men in the 56th Division bonded with the colleagues in their platoon or section on a task basis where their inter-personal relations were built around working collectively, interdependently and co-operatively around the work, tasks or function of their work group.[26]

An excellent example of how men worked together is set out in the account of Stuart Dolden. He was a cook in the 1/14th Battalion, London Regiment (London Scottish) for two years and worked with the other men in his section to supply hot food to their company. His memoir shows how the men had a shared commitment to their job and trusted each other. They co-operated to solve challenges: in one example they overslept one morning and then did not have enough time to light their cookers to boil water for the mess orderlies' tea. Their solution was to steal petrol from a nearby Army Service Corps (ASC) dump which heated the water rapidly, 'easily breaking the record'.[27]

22   M.L. Walkinton, *Twice in a Lifetime* (London: Samson Books, 1980), pp.14-15, 27, 41-42.
23   Frederick G. Wong, "A Formula for Building Cohesion," essay, Carlisle, Pennsylvania: U.S. Army War College, Carlisle Barracks, April 1985, pp.34-35.
24   *SS 143: Instructions for the Training of Platoons for Offensive Action* (BEF: GHQ, 1917). John Lee, 'Some Lessons of the Somme' in Brian Bond (ed.), '*Look to Your Front*' (Staplehurst: Spellmount, 1990), pp.79-89.
25   Siebold, 'The Essence …'; Kinzer Stewart, *Mates and Muchachos*, p.27; Manning, 'Morale and Cohesion', pp.11-12.
26   Salo, 'United We Stand', pp.22-26.
27   A. Stuart Dolden, *Cannon Fodder* (Poole: Blandford Press, 1980), pp.64-181,101-102, 127.

In platoon sections based around a team crewed weapon system, such as a Lewis gun or rifle grenade, the focus of task cohesion was organised around the deployment and maintenance of that weapon(s) in combat. For instance, the successful operation of the Lewis gun required the team to trust each other to work closely together to ensure it was kept supplied with ammunition and the weapon repaired in the event of mechanical problems such as stoppages, the latter being a well-known problem with the Lewis gun.[28] Consequently, the crew needed to be in close physical proximity and ensure constant communication when in action or training. During an attack, a Lewis gunner would run with his weapon and dive into a shell hole; then a man behind him, carrying spare 47-round 'bedpan' magazines, would take his place as he ran forward.[29] As a result of the nature of their work, Lewis gun teams could develop close relationships. Rifleman Archie Groom, who served in a Lewis gun section in the 1/5th Battalion, London Regiment (London Rifle Brigade or LRB), throughout 1917, recalled that his gun section was a 'team of good companions'.[30]

Why did men develop task cohesion? Men arriving at an infantry unit in France were frequently posted to a unit where they knew no-one. They were in an environment of potential death and injury, and many copied the actions of those around them to adapt and survive. They realised 'that the careful man probably outlived the careless' and sought to learn from their new comrades.[31] Men also learnt that collective action with their colleagues would probably increase their chances of individual survival.[32] Charles Moskos argued in his study of US soldiers in Vietnam that self-interest in self-preservation was a key driver for American soldiers to co-operate with each other.[33] It is highly probable that men in the First World War were motivated to a degree by similar egocentric interests and united in the 'face of common danger'.[34] Finally, men collaborated with others due to fear of punishment if they failed to follow orders.[35]

These task-based relationships were sustained by a variety of factors. Men would only establish task cohesion with others if they felt they could trust them to a sufficient degree. Those deemed to be untrustworthy through their unreliability, for whatever reason, could face exclusion. Sergeant Sam Lane of 1/13th Battalion, London

28   Groom, *Poor*, pp.105, 169.
29   Steve Roberts & Andrew Robertshaw (ed.) [written by Joseph Steward], *The Platoon, An Infantryman on the Western Front 1916-18* (Barnsley: Pen & Sword, 2012), p.176.
30   Groom, *Poor*, p.100.
31   Sam Sutcliffe (Phil Sutcliffe ed.), *Nobody of Any Importance: A Foot Soldier's Memoir of World War I* (London: Sutcliffe & Son, 2014), p.363.
32   Peter Hodgkinson, *Glum Heroes: Resilience and Coping in the British Army on the Western Front 1914-1918* (Solihull: Helion & Co., 2015), p.91.
33   Charles Moskos, *The American Enlisted Man* (New York: Russell Sage Foundation, 1970), pp.144-146.
34   Imperial War Museum (IWM), 75/36/1, G.E.V. Thompson, Account, p.5.
35   Dolden was read the *Army Act* on his arrival in his unit that listed the punishments for disobeying orders and made 'special note of the offences for which we could be shot.' See Dolden, *Cannon*, p.63.

Regiment (Kensingtons) noted this happened to a Suffolk farm labourer who joined his platoon in mid-1917. The 'man's movements were slow and threw the whole platoon out of gear.' Lane concluded he 'would never make a soldier'. As a result of his disruptive effects, the man 'did not mix with the other men.'[36]

Informal norms helped to sustain cohesion. These are group-held beliefs about how members of a group or unit should behave in a given context, and exert a powerful influence on behaviour.[37] In observational studies, it appears that collective behaviour is often directed towards a given task or situation which is dependent on how it benefits the group's security, comfort and well-being.[38] It is highly probable that similar informal norms existed in the units under study. For example, Groom learned early on that 'to survive, no unnecessary risk should be taken.'[39] Sam Sutcliffe, serving in the Kensingtons, observed that 'a dead soldier was of no use to his mates and most of us understood that.'[40] Men respected those who showed courage under fire but not those who embarked on risky 'devil may care behaviour', especially where this endangered the group unnecessarily.[41]

The process by which groups decided on collective action and setting informal norms is complex. Soldiers often found themselves in difficult situations where collective action was required, and agreement on the necessary action was achieved by debate and discussion amongst the group. For example, Smith and his colleagues in the LRB Transport Section held a 'hurried council of war' to carry out reprisals against a 'vitriolic' French farmer.[42] Some informal norms were set by unwritten rules of human co-operation which dictated that, if you wanted to share in the benefits of group action, then a shared effort was expected, such as working together to improve billets.[43] Fatalistic beliefs created some norms, where groups preferred 'ease and comfort to safety'.[44] Group rituals were passed down from veteran to newcomers, such as seemingly strange 'ancient trench superstitions' including 'it is bad luck to light three cigarettes with the same match' or look at a new moon through glass.[45]

36   Sam Lane, 'Scrap Book (continued) c. 1917', *Kensington* (Autumn 1974).
37   Daniel. C. Feldman, 'The Development and Enforcement of Group Norms', *Academy of Management Review*, 9:1 (1/1984), pp.47-53.
38   Knut Pipping, *Infantry Company as a Society* (Helsinki: National Defence University, No. 3/2008 [1947]), p.202.
39   Groom, *Poor*, p.155.
40   Sutcliffe, *Nobody*, p.363.
41   Walkinton, *Twice*, pp.21-22. Groom, *Poor*, p.155.
42   A. Rifleman (Aubrey Smith), *Four Years on the Western Front: Being the Experiences of a Ranker in the London Rifle Brigade, 4th, 3rd and 56th Divisions* (London: Odhams, 1922), p.202.
43   Ibid., p.182.
44   Thomas Tiplady, *The Soul of the Soldier: Sketches from the Western Battle-Front* (New York: Fleming H. Revell Co., 1918), p.121.
45   Douglas Pinkerton, *Ladies from Hell* (New York: The Century Co., 1918), p.73; Tiplady, *Soul*, p.195.

Task cohesion was also built by shared experience. Alexander Maclennan and his colleagues, serving in a Lewis gun team in the London Scottish, found the Battle of Cambrai to be a bonding experience. They called it the "'the Cambrai stunt" [and it] was … a marking point in our lives. We were to talk of events as being before or after "the Cambrai stunt"… [as] it had been a period of tremendous strain, weariness, thrill and the impress that it left … was one that endured.'[46] While battle was important, just living in a unit with other men socialised them into their unit's traditions and customs. Once in his Lewis gun section, Maclennan adopted the slang of the unit. He said, 'we had a language which would at first have bewildered a stranger … [for example,] Kip was bed.'[47]

Men frequently developed social relationships within their task groups. These relationships did not have the same emotional intensity and levels of caring of social cohesion-based relationships but they were still important. They were created because men were together with their colleagues for long stretches of time.[48] In the front line, one soldier reported that he and his colleagues 'never went outside the[ir] … platoon area' and 'out of the line we did not get much beyond our own circle for either training or recreation.'[49] Service life was characterised by large stretches of inactivity where there was a 'good deal of time was sitting about.' As a result, men formed relationships with their peers as there 'was always something or someone to laugh about; bits of letters to be read out … [and] cigarettes to smoke.'[50]

However, not all task group relations were characterised by the liking of colleagues. In 1918, T.H. Holmes was part of a company signals team in the Kensingtons. His colleague was Bill Steer, a former London Bridge Station porter. Holmes recalled that Steer was a 'very expert' signaller but he 'did not like Mr Steer' as he was a 'sly and mean … mischief maker'.[51] However, they worked together on the 'sacred duty … to keep contact with battalion HQ, and for this purpose to patrol the cable which was constantly being broken by shell splinters.'[52]

The evidence from the veteran testimony is that task-based relationships between men of the same rank were highly functional and resilient. Captain G.E.V. Thompson, in 1/9th Battalion, London Regiment (Queen Victoria Rifles or QVR), reported that there was 'a strong unbreakable bond of brotherhood' during his service.[53] Maclennan's memoir recalls how his interactions with his immediate colleagues were dominated by 'comradeship – a much used word but the correct one – always existed among us as a

46   London Scottish Archive (LSA), Alexander F.M. Maclennan, Military Memoirs, pp.114-16.
47   LSA, Maclennan, Memoirs, p.149.
48   Hodgkinson, Glum, p.79.
49   LSA, Maclennan, Memoirs, pp.46, 65.
50   Imperial War Museum Sound Archive (IWMSA), F.C. Higgins, 9884, Reel-9; IWM, Thomas H. Holmes, Account.
51   IWM, Holmes.
52   Ibid.
53   IWM, Thompson, Memoir, p.5.

team, and was also evident in the Platoon' [sic].[54] His comment here is significant as he is referring specifically to his work team rather than men with whom he developed social cohesion.

The other foundation upon which men formed horizontal cohesion was on a social basis. These relationships are mainly formed in groups rather than units as social cohesion was mostly a matter of choice rather than necessity and the boundaries of the group may, or may not coincide with the formal boundaries of that unit.[55] Social cohesion can be demonstrated between people by friendship, emotional attachment and solidarity.[56] While task cohesion relationships between men could be civil and have elements of friendship, social cohesion is about relationships which are not focused exclusively on the task, function or work of a unit but the people in the self-selected group.

The structure of these socially based cohesive relationships is complex and varied.[57] At the simplest level, many men developed strong relationships with a significant other. Roger Little's 1952 study of US infantry fighting in Korea described these as 'buddy relationships' and they were prevalent among the units under study.[58] These were probably the most common form of social cohesive relationship in the units under study. For example, Dolden was 'practically inseparable' from his friend Johnny.[59] Men could also form close relationships with a broader group of men, such as those with whom they messed. These were generally groups of up to five or six men. However, these groups often had a clear material motive for formation. For example, Aubrey Smith, in the transport section of the LRB, and his colleagues formed the closely-knit Devil's Mess to 'amalgamate their resources'.[60] In rare situations the group with whom men developed social cohesion was co-terminus with their unit and task group, most often their section. For, instance, John Tucker, working in the Kensingtons pioneer section of eight, had strong social and task cohesion with his comrades as they 'got on very well together'.[61]

These social cohesion relationships were reciprocal and caring and not governed by the same informal norms as task cohesion. Men found being close with other men in the 'immediate presence of death at the Front gives tone to every expression of life and makes it the kindest place in the world. No one feels he can do too much for you, and there is nothing you would not do for another' [sic].[62] Some had a 'love

---

54   LSA, Maclennan, Memoir, p.54.
55   Tamotsu Shibutani, *The Derelicts of Company K: A Sociological Study of Demoralization* (Berkeley: University of California Press, 1978), p.11.
56   Salo, PhD, pp.22-26.
57   John Bourne, 'The British Working Man in Arms' in Hugh Cecil & Peter H. Liddle (eds.), *Facing Armageddon, The First World War Experienced* (London: Leo Cooper, 1996), p.349.
58   Roger Little, 'Buddy Relations and Combat Performance' in Morris Janowitz (ed.), *The New Military* (New York: Russell Sage, 1964), p.198.
59   Dolden, *Cannon*, p.34.
60   Smith, *Four*, pp.95, 122.
61   John Tucker, *Johnny Get Your Gun* (London: William Kimber & Co., 1980), p.130.
62   Tiplady, *Soul*, p.43

passing the love of women.'[63] As a result, many men became emotionally close to their colleagues; Dolden remarked that he and Johnny 'shared everything, our joys and even our sorrows.'[64]

However, some men made calculated decisions not to get close to other men. Sutcliffe, who had served with the 2/1st Battalion London Regiment at Gallipoli, was posted to the Kensingtons in early 1916. He recalled that 'none of the men who had come from the old Battalion … with me ended up in my new Platoon. I even felt glad about that; a feeling of comradeship would have existed had any of them been with me, and I wanted no more of such attachments.'[65]

Sutcliffe was in the minority; many men found there were strong utilitarian reasons for having socially cohesive relationships with others. Being part of a group could also secure additional food and material comforts as it was common practice to share ones' parcels with others, and this was especially important when rations were short.[66] It also allowed men to share their resources to improve their collective quality of life, such as getting a primus stove to cook communal meals.[67] Close groups helped each other, Smith's Devil's Mess doing favours for each other and helping each other with their work.[68] Being with friends could help men cope with the strain and trauma of the trenches. Arthur Gristwood wrote that as a result of being with his chums in the LRB, he had 'other things to think of other than war.'[69] Some wondered whether there was 'anything to equal the happiness of the "camaraderie" and friendship of the life out here.'[70]

The development of social cohesion during the war often appears to have been dependent on task cohesion, which already had been established between relevant individuals. The accounts of Joseph Steward, Groom, Bob Brookes, Dolden, Tucker and Smith confirm that they all worked with their colleagues in task teams before developing friendships and emotional attachments.[71] By living in 'close acquaintanceship' with other soldiers, men 'got to know each other as men had never done before the War [sic]. Everyone's character, will-power, nerve, generosity, and general peculiarities came to be known little by little.'[72] However, this was not always the case. Many men developed close relationships with significant others based on going

63   Ibid., p.86.
64   Dolden, *Cannon*, p.34.
65   Sutcliffe, *Nobody*, p.354.
66   Anne Williamson, *Henry Williamson and the First World War* (Stroud: History Press, 2004), p.25; Smith, *Four*, p.209.
67   IWMSA, 9712, L.C. Furse, Reel-1.
68   Smith, *Four*, pp.103, 201.
69   Arthur D. Gristwood, *The Somme and The Coward* (Columbia, South Carolina: University of South Carolina Press, 2008 reprint of 1927 edition), p.123.
70   Julian. Bickersteth, *Bickersteth Diaries, 1914-1918* (Barnsley: Pen & Sword, 1995), p.183.
71   Steward, *Platoon;* Groom, *Poor;* Smith, *Four;* Bernard Joseph Brookes diary <http://www.bobbrookes.co.uk/index.htm> (accessed 26 February 2020); Dolden, *Cannon;* Tucker, *Johnny.*
72   Smith, *Four*, p.185.

through the same experience or needing social support at a particularly stressful time. An example of the former is Dolden and Johnny, who 'had joined up together and from that day were practically inseparable.'[73]

Trying to gauge the prevalence of social cohesion is difficult. One anecdotal way is to examine accounts of soldiers in the 56th Division. There are 17 accounts of privates who served across all units under study for nine months or more, and these include published accounts or diaries in archives.[74] Examination of these accounts provides a guide to the possible extent and nature of social cohesion in the units under study. Of these 17 accounts, 14 men record socially cohesive relationships with high levels of trust and friendships with other men at some point in their service. The accounts also suggest that once formed, social cohesion was only disrupted by personnel changes, caused either by casualties or transfers.

Running parallel with the relationships that men had with their colleagues of equal rank were vertical cohesion relationships between soldiers and their NCOs and officers. Vertical cohesion is defined as a positive primary group relationship between leaders and the led in a small unit; it is based on an interpersonal exchange of mutual trust, commitment and loyalty which results in the leader influencing his subordinates to actively co-operate, adopt and work towards the leader's goals and objectives.[75]

In theory, an officer or NCO could order his men to perform a given task or job and threaten formal disciplinary action if they failed to comply. Punishment for many was 'simply a means towards the end of maintaining discipline in a military force.'[76] The rationale is that man 'is not born obedient, he has to be trained from infancy, and the training is irksome, but the most spoiled child can be disciplined very quickly when properly instructed.'[77] The right of a leader to punish their subordinate was backed up in British Army's military penal code.[78] These set out a comparatively harsh regime:

---

73   Dolden, *Cannon*, p.34.
74   LSA, Maclennan, Military Memoirs; R. Gregory (ed.) [Tim Elliot], *Tim's War, The Psychology of War and Peace Through One Man's Eyes* (Sutton: Loaghtan Books, 2013); Pinkerton, *Ladies*; Tucker, *Johnny*; Steward, *Platoon*. Holmes, IWM. Douglas Bell, *Soldier's Diary of the Great War* (London: Faber & Gwyer, 1929). Groom, *Poor*; Elliot, *Tim's War*; Smith, *Four*; Bryan Latham, *A Territorial Soldier's War* (London: Gale & Polden, 1967); Dolden, *Cannon*; Frank Hawkings, *From Ypres to Cambrai* (Morley: Elmfield Press, 1974); T.H. Bisgood diary <https://www.greatwarforum.org/topic/29488-complete-diary-of-sergeant-th-bisgood-mm/> (accessed 26 February 2020); Brookes diary <http://www.bobbrookes.co.uk/index.htm> (accessed 26 February 2020); Walkinton, *Twice*; Bernard C. Stubbs, *Diary Kept by B.C. Stubbs* (Chicago: Private publication, 1915).
75   Siebold, 'The Essence …', p.289. Manning, 'Morale and Cohesion', p.13.
76   C.R.F. Legge, *Mainly About Discipline* (London: Gale & Polden, 1914), p.8.
77   Legge, *Mainly*, p.19.
78   This was made up of the *Army Act of 1881* <https://api.parliament.uk/historic-hansard/acts/army-act-1881> (accessed 26 February 2020); *The King's Regulations and Orders for the Army 1912* (London: HMSO, 1916) and *The Manual of Military Law* (London: War Office, 1914).

for example, the *1881 Army Act* listed 27 capital offences, more than were set out in the comparative French or German military codes.[79] The threat and use of formal disciplinary powers had an important deterrent effect in maintaining order in the 56th Division but leaders understood that they could get 'infinitely more out of the[ir men]' if they won their respect.[80] Whether an officer or NCO won the respect of his soldiers was dependent on whether he was trusted and accepted in the hearts and minds of his men.[81] Respect had to be earned and this was largely reliant on a leader's behaviour and conduct which was under constant scrutiny for any sign of 'weakness, inefficiency or indecision' as men's lives could depend on their leaders judgement and skill.[82] The evidence suggests that in the 56th Division during 1917 the vast majority of leaders were successful in building vertical cohesion by their conduct in battle and in the rear areas.

1/5th London Regiment Tommies, Flanders 1917.

79   Gerald Oram, *Military Executions During World War One* (London: Palgrave Macmillan, 2003), p.31.
80   Tom Thorpe, 'The extent, nature and impact of military group cohesion in London Regiment infantry battalions during the Great War' (PhD Dissertation, King's College London (KCL), 2017), pp.117-164. Anon. [Maj. Gen. T.D. Pilcher], *A General's Letters to His Son on Obtaining His Commission* (London: Cassell & Co., 1917), p.24; Gary Sheffield, *Leadership in the Trenches* (Basingstoke: Macmillan Press, 2000), p.64; Helen B. McCartney, *Citizen Soldiers: The Liverpool Territorials in the First World War I* (Cambridge: Cambridge University Press, 2005), pp.139-40.
81   John Adair, *Developing Leaders* (Maidenhead: Talbot Adair, 1988.) p.13.
82   Sheffield, *Trenches*, p.103. Tucker, *Johnny*, p.41.

In the trenches, where a leader was perceived as competent, brave and courageous, cohesion was built with their men. Second Lieutenant Conrad Wood had a 'good reputation' in the 1/4th Battalion, London Regiment (1/4th Londons) 'for being able to bring a patrol back to the same place as the start.'[83] In the QVR, Rifleman Stone disliked his RSM but respected him because 'he was a very brave man, he held a DCM.'[84] Soldiers in the Kensingtons respected their 26-year-old commanding officer, Lieutenant Colonel Robert Shaw, who led the unit from August 1917. He was a 'fine and gallant officer' and another wrote 'very cool under fire and a great leader.'[85] Finally, Corporal Bill Partridge, in the 1/7th Battalion, Middlesex Regiment (1/7th Middlesex), recalled that 'Captain Gillett was such a splendid [B] company commander. They called us 'Lucky B' ... because we had the least casualties of any company in the battalion. We put it all down to his ... uncanny ... leadership ... he ... [n]ever asked us to do anything he wouldn't do himself' [sic].[86]

Out of the trenches, other types of behaviour were important for building confidence and faith. Paternal care, especially an officer, was probably the most important behavioural trait that determined a soldier's attitudes towards their leaders.[87] The evidence suggests that officers and NCOs in the 56th Division actively sought to care for their men. For example, Padre Leighton Green, the 1/4th Londons chaplain, set up a 'Mag-Fag' fund based on subscriptions from his Norfolk based parishioners to supply magazines and cigarettes for his men.[88] The officers in the QWR set up a regimental canteen and their second in command obtained playing cards for his men.[89] NCOs also played a major role in caring for their men. For example, Private Hall in the 1/12th Battalion, London Regiment (Rangers), recorded in his diary that he and his colleagues were 'grateful to Corporals Kedgeley and Mortlake for their attention to our wants. It says a great deal for the good spirit which prevails together between NCOs and men.'[90]

The way in which officers interacted with their men was also important for establishing interpersonal relationships. An incident reported by T.H. Holmes, training with the QWR during 1917, demonstrates how varied leadership styles could generate different subordinate reactions. Holmes was recovering from inoculation and feeling ill after the injection and was visited by his commanding officer, Colonel Lambert

83   IWMSA, 11265, C. Wood, Reel-2.
84   IWMSA, 24883, H.V. Stone, Reel-2.
85   Tucker, *Johnny*, p.88; Personal archive, Fred Smith, I'll Always Remember, unpublished memoir, 1974, p.23.
86   IWMSA, William Partridge, Reel-2.
87   Sheffield, *Trenches*, p.104.
88   Stuart J. McLaren, *Somewhere in Flanders: The War Letters of the Revd Samuel Frederic Leighton Green* (Dereham: Larks Press. 2005), p.44.
89   J.Q. Henriques, *The War History of the First Battalion, Queen's Westminster Rifles 1914-1918* (London: Medici Society Ltd, 1923), p.164; NAM, 8901-105; J.Q. Henriques, Diary, 30 September 1917.
90   IWM, 67/13/1, F. Hall, Diary, 14 January 1916.

and the adjutant, Major Kelly. They had very different styles of communication. The 'colonel asked [Holmes] one or two sympathetic questions', but Kelly snarled sarcastic comments and 'poked [him] in the ribs with his … cane and said, "Pull yourself together man."' He assessed the former as a 'kind and clever soldier' but the latter, 'a bastard'. Holmes recalled that if he 'could have summoned the energy, I would have spat at him [Kelly]' and 'risked a court martial' [sic].[91]

Finally, officers and NCOs took a relaxed approach to discipline, rank and hierarchy compared to more formal practices in Regular army units.[92] NCOs and officers adopted this approach based on the pre-war traditions of the units; many of the NCOs and officers were pre-war territorials and served for much of the war.[93] Leaders generally resorted to formal disciplinary procedures and harsh penalties were only used *in extremis*. The number of courts martial by a unit is a useful indicator of unit leaders' reliance on the formal system of discipline and punishment. For example, the London Scottish had 17 courts-martial during the war which was dramatically lower than other units such as 119 in the 1st Battalion, Border Regiment (Regulars) and 93 in the 2nd Battalion, Royal Dublin Fusiliers (Regulars).[94] They also took a relaxed approach to inter-rank hierarchy and fraternisation. For instance, in November 1917, the LRB held a '1914 originals' dinner for men sent over with their first draft at which the 'distinctions of rank' disappeared.[95] In the Rangers at Christmas 1916, men and officers had festive company 'feasts', where they 'met together on terms of the utmost camaraderie and laughed and sang.'[96] Though leaders often eschewed the use of formal procedures of trial and punishment, they did not ignore disciplinary problems but instead sought informal and unofficial ways to resolve them. For example, in the Kensingtons, a subaltern Mr Thorn, was 'sporting' after he allowed his men to decorate their billet as they wanted 'insisting only that' rifles were kept clean.[97]

Broadly, leaders through their conduct developed positive relationships with their subordinates. In rare cases this relationship had a strong social-emotional component. A subaltern in the QVR recalled how he wrote home to tell how he 'mentioned in the hearing of two or three of the men that I had not received any letters for some time. Two days later I received this little lot (enclosed). All signed by their nicknames.'[98] There were some exceptions where leaders were regarded poorly by

91   IWM, Holmes.
92   See Thorpe, PhD, pp.139-60.
93   Ibid., pp.161-63.
94   Stephen Sandford, *Neither Unionist nor Nationalist* (Sallins: Irish Academic Press, 2013), p.260.
95   Smith, *Four*, p.285.
96   A.V. Wheeler-Holohan & G.M.G. Wyatt (eds.), *The Rangers' Historical Records From 1859 to the Conclusion of the Great War* (London: Harrison & Sons, 1922), p.88.
97   Steward, *Platoon*, p.129.
98   C.A.C. Keeson, *History and Records of Queen Victoria's Rifles 1792-1922*, Vol. 1 (London: Constable, 1923), p. xiv.

their men. For example, the London Scottish's D Company QMS was frequently drunk and failed to do his job. As a result his company often got the worst billets. It earned him little respect, and the company titled themselves the Poor Old Bastards of D Company.[99]

Overall, the reports in memoirs, diaries and interviews suggest positive vertical cohesion between leader and led in the 56th Division. For instance, in the LRB 'most of our officers were good' and men got on 'very well' with them and the NCOs.[100] In the QWR, the sergeants were a 'fine lot.'[101] In the Rangers, men 'got on well with sergeants' and in the 1/4th Londons, there were some 'decent blokes and some not so decent, but generally speaking they tried their best'.[102] In the Kensingtons, the D company platoon officers were 'very decent sort of fellows'.[103] Finally, Charles Ward, 1/7th Middlesex, said 'we like[d] our officers, they were all good men.'[104]

In 1917, horizontal and vertical cohesion were strengthened by unit and organisational change. The purpose, structure and function of military units influenced the building and development of cohesion inside them.[105] The BEF's experience on the Somme led to the development of new tactics set out in the February 1917 publication *SS 143: Instructions for the Training of Platoons for Offensive Action*.[106] It re-organised the platoon from four rifle platoons into four specialist sections of bombers, rifle grenadiers, riflemen and Lewis gunners. It also reduced the size of the platoon from 56 to 40 men with each section in a platoon being made up of nine men instead of 12.[107] The assault plan using these new sections was for the rifle grenadiers to give covering fire to the advancing rifle and bomber sections with the Lewis gun section engaging the 'main point of resistance' and working around a flank.[108]

These tactical reforms brought three significant changes to the way in which men fought in small units and this in turn affected cohesion. First, the introduction of specialist sections and crew-operated weapons, like Lewis guns and rifle grenades, meant that many men ceased to be independent riflemen but instead became increasingly interdependent co-operators in weapons systems and combat teams. The operation of these new arms and tactics required much higher teamwork, communication and co-operation on the battlefield, resulting in closer and more intense working

99   Dolden, *Cannon*, p.8.
100 IWMSA, 24878, H.G.R. Williams, Reel-3; IWMSA, 11043, C.F. Miller, Reel-1; Groom, *Poor*, p.45.
101 IWM, Holmes.
102 IWMSA, 8868, W.G. Holmes, Reel-1; IWMSA, 9884, F.C. Higgins, Reel-3.
103 The National Archives (TNA): RAIL 253/516, Frederick Woodhams, Letter.
104 IWMSA, 12026, C. Ward, Reel-8.
105 Salo, PhD, pp.63-70.
106 Lee, 'Some Lessons ...', pp.79-89.
107 *Infantry Training, 4-Company Organisation* (London: HMSO, 1914), pp. xiv-xv; *Field Service Manual, 1914: Infantry Battalion* (London: HMSO, 1914), p.7; *SS 143*, p.24.
108 *SS 143*, pp.6, 8.

relationships and greater cohesion. Modern research suggests that soldiers who operate crewed weapons report higher levels of cohesion than independent riflemen.[109]

The second change that occurred was that cohesion became increasingly focused on a smaller group of people as firepower replaced manpower. By February 1917, sections had been reduced to nine men, a 28 percent reduction on the 1914 establishment.[110] These size changes also increased cohesion as scholarship demonstrates that smaller groups have more significant interaction, shared decision making and better face-to-face collaboration.[111]

The third change was a major focus around keeping the unit together in training and on working parties. It stressed that 'working and carrying parties should be detailed by complete sections under their leaders.'[112] Training was also important as it aimed to develop a competitive *esprit des corps* with each section be encouraged to consider itself 'the best section in the platoon'.[113] This had the result of increasing the time that men spent together but also it sought to direct their loyalty and tribalism towards their leaders, section and platoon.

Morale, Resilience and Leader Influence

This section examines the contradictory impacts of the strong horizontal and vertical cohesion outlined above. Strong cohesion in platoons could help but also hinder the objectives of the wider military organisation of which they were part. The first part will explore how cohesion supported soldier resilience and morale and the second part will describe how cohesion shaped protest and 'mutiny'.

At its basic level, strong horizontal cohesion built endurance in the trenches. Being with other people that one knew well helped men cope with fear. Company was a distraction from the anxiety; Rifleman Polhill, in the LRB, said that an attack during 1917 Battle of Arras would have been 'very frightening' had he not had his 'friends' with him.[114] For others, it was the social surveillance of other group or unit members that pressured them to carry on. Marshall argued that in groups, where men were known to others, they had a 'social identity', and as a result, they would rather risk death than their 'reputation with other men'.[115] Douglas Pinkerton, serving in the

---

109   Morris Janowitz, *Sociology and Military Establishment* (New York: Russell Sage Foundation, 1959), pp. 66-67. Francis B. Kish, *Cohesion, The Vital Ingredient for Successful Army Units* (Carlisle, Pennsylvania: Army War College, 1982), p.21; Salo, PhD, p.76.
110   *SS 143*, p.24.
111   Salo, PhD, p.64.
112   *SS 143*, p.8.
113   Ibid., p.11.
114   K.W. Mitchinson, *Gentlemen and Officers: The Impact and Experience of War on a Territorial Regiment, 1914-1918* ((London: Imperial War Museum, 1995), p.159.
115   Marshall, *Men*, p.153.

London Scottish, described this phenomenon as 'a species of auto-intoxication' where 'men are dying all about you, and in the face of death … *but the fact that others are sticking it out* … must have an unconscious reaction that draws upon unsuspected wells of nervous and physical strength' to carry on [italics added].[116] He believed that '*the fear of what other men will think holds more men to their duty in the face of danger than does any firing squad in Flanders*' [italics added].[117]

Developing emotion-caring relationships with other men helped individuals cope with the stress and anxiety of active service. For example, in August 1917, the 19-year-old A.F.M. Maclennan was at a base camp waiting to be posted to the London Scottish. He reflected in his memoir that these were his 'cub days' and he found the life at camp tedious, stressful and depressing. He said, 'I was not happy' and believed 'it is certain that without the warm friendship of Wilson [his chum] and the comforting comradely chat of the others, I would have given up.'[118]

Horizontal cohesion also fostered morale. Strong socially cohesive relationships welded groups into resilient entities which would voluntarily remain and share the dangers of the battlefield. There are numerous accounts of men refusing legal exits from the frontline to take up safe jobs in the rear but choosing instead to share the danger of the front with their comrades. Aubrey Smith refused a job as a base hospital pianist saying he would be a 'fish out of water' until he was back with the section; he decided to 'sink or swim' with them.[119] Dolden refused a commission to remain a ranker cook with his mates in the London Scottish.[120]

The strength of these social relationships could be so powerful that men would choose to fight with their mates even when they had official permission to avoid combat. Ranker Frank Hawkings, fighting with the QVR, was sent back by the RSM as battle surplus before the 1916 attack on Gommecourt but he volunteered to join his company in the assault.[121] Private Frane, also in the Kensingtons, opted to go with his mates in the first infantry wave at the Battle of Arras despite being told that he could report sick.[122]

Strong vertical cohesion between commissioned and enlisted men could also generate the will to fight. For example, Second Lieutenant Ralph Larkin, a teenage subaltern in the 1/8th Battalion, Middlesex Regiment, during 1917 was 'loved by his men'.[123] His batman wrote to his parents saying 'I would go anywhere with him and I've been through hell and he proved himself a real good Officer' [sic].[124]

---

116 Pinkerton, *Ladies*, p.52.
117 Ibid., pp.149-50.
118 LSA, Maclennan, Memoirs, p.37.
119 Smith, *Four*, pp.251, 144.
120 Dolden, *Cannon*, pp.91-92.
121 Hawkings, *From Ypres*, p.94.
122 Steward, *Platoon*, p.111.
123 IWM, 6/32/1, W.R.E. Larkin, 'A Young Subaltern in Flanders, Letters Home' (unpublished memoir), p.13.
124 IWM, Larkin, p.36.

Trust in leaders could also ease mental strain in soldiers. Maclennan describes the influence of Captain Blackie, in the London Scottish during one incident in 1917, had on his nerves that had been 'rather gargled by that uneasy period under the minnies [German trench mortars].' Blackie's 'cool voice and the academically correct phrase was a tonic … one of those very fine men who officered us and whose example and leadership kept us going when normally our exhausted bodies – and shaken minds too – would have laid down and died.'[125]

Finally, high levels of vertical cohesion could motivate men to put discretionary effort into their jobs, so as not to let the leader down.[126] Smith and the LRB transport section always maintained a 'fair standard in their turn-outs' at Brigade inspections because of their affection for their section leader Second Lieutenant Sergeant Chrisp, whom they had known for years.[127]

Protest, Strikes and Mutiny

Strong primary cohesion could generate outcomes that were 'deviant'. The first area for consideration is the role of group loyalty and solidarity in initiating and sustaining 'rule-breaking' activity. Groups which had high levels of task and/or social cohesion often sought, where possible, to protect and further their group's or unit's security, comfort or welfare. How cohesive groups acted depended on the issue of concern and the context in which they found themselves. Cohesive entities did not often intend to break military laws or regulations but would do so, if they deemed it necessary on a particular issue and, importantly, if they could get away with it.

This decision-making process can be demonstrated in relation to food. The supply of fresh produce to soldiers was erratic, and they frequently had to eat iron rations. These were hated; bully beef was 'so nauseating over time that hunger became more preferable' and 'dog' biscuits cracked teeth.[128] The result was that many a young soldier 'ate very meagerly for a growing lad … a really full belly a rarity.'[129] Food was important for morale as nothing changed one's spirits from 'buoyancy to utter despondency or vice-versa quicker than a shortage or surfeit of rations.'[130] Maclennan said soldiers 'had the habit of relating our welfare to the size of the trench [bread] ration and shortage of this commodity was considered a genuine hardship.'[131]

125　LSA, Maclennan, Memoirs, p.107.
126　Gary Sheffield, 'Officer-Man Relations: Morale and Discipline in the British Army, 1902-22' (PhD Dissertation, KCL, 1994), p.286.
127　Smith, *Four*, p.340.
128　Smith, *Four*, pp, 226, 234; Groom, *Poor*, p.147; Tucker, *Johnny*, p.174.
129　Sutcliffe, *Nobody*, p.396.
130　Smith, *Four*, p.100.
131　LSA, Maclennan, Memoirs, pp.79-80.

Spurred on by intermittent hunger, food had a centrality in men's lives; it is not surprising that it became a topic of frequent discussion and a commonly held grievance. Smith recalled being hungry, stuck in the rain at night on the Somme in 1916 with no rations, and he and his friends were so outraged by their plight, that their 'conversations' would have made a 'Bolshevist see red'.[132] It appears that across the army, food was a frequent subject of discussion and anger; it was the top source of 'discontent' in the LRB.[133] In early 1917, Third Army Censor Captain Hardie reported that food remained the 'primary grouse' of the soldiers in his quarterly morale reports compiled from the analysis of soldiers' letters.[134] Nearly all groups and units would have had a collective view on the poor quality of army food and grumbled about with their comrades and colleagues.

Given this shared view held in multiple small groups and units, finding additional food, from whatever source, became a focus of horizontal cohesion and collective action. Some of this activity was 'legal' and involved men sharing resources; Dolden and mates formed the League of the Red Triangle to pool their food.[135] However, much of it was 'illegal', with men exploiting opportunities that arose to obtain more or better food. For example, W.G. Holmes and friends in the Rangers 'helped themselves' to stores when they got a chance.[136] Even future film actor Ronald Colman in the London Scottish resorted to 'stealing eggs from the nearby farms' because 'bully beef and tinned butter [were] coming out their ears.'[137]

Groups and units used similar decision-making processes to resolve other problems which they agreed collectively required action. For instance, Smith and colleagues posted to a railhead on a short-term assignment as part of the LRB's deployment on lines of communications duty in 1915, planned and worked communally against their NCO. He was considered to be a 'bullying, self-assertive RAMC lance-corporal' against whom they carried out a 'campaign of passive resistance'. The group cleverly challenged his orders; he would instruct men to find fuel to boil the kettle for the Rail Transport Officer's tea but they refused. They argued there was no fuel lying about readily available to collect; they had not been issued with fuel for this purpose, they would not 'stoop to beg for coal from a train driver' and 'stealing was out of the question'. This tactic was 'successful' as the lance corporal spent 'an hour a day hunting for wood and coal.'[138]

132 Smith, *Four*, p.162.
133 Groom, *Poor*, pp.147-148.
134 IWM, 84/46/1: R. Hardie, 'Report on Morale in Third Army, January 1917', p.4 and 'Report on Morale in Third Army, May 1917', p.4.
135 Dolden, *Cannon*, p.124.
136 IWMSA, 8868, William G. Holmes, Reel-4.
137 Juliet B. Colman, *Ronald Colman: A Very Private Person* (New York: William Morrow & Co., 1975), p.10.
138 Smith, *Four*, pp.79-80.

Groups also took similar action in other situations which threatened their wellbeing or collective comfort. Working fatigues were avoided, especially if they were tiring and dangerous like wiring parties, or they were burying details, deemed 'most distasteful [task] of all'.[139] F.J. Hall, serving in the Rangers, noted in his diary on 18 December 1916, that he and his mates 'cleared off after tea' to avoid being 'clicked' for a wiring party.[140]

In many cases, 'deviant behaviour' actively involved NCOs and officers, sometimes the very leadership of a battalion itself. For instance, in mid-1915, officers of the 1/2nd Londons deceived Brigadier-General George 'Uncle' Harper into believing that they were carrying out his orders for vigorous counter sniping by leaving empty cartridge cases 'specially arranged for his benefit' around sniper posts.[141] However, this was rare and more often NCOs and subalterns were complicit in theft or work avoidance. In 1917, Tucker's corporal 'Charlie' led the theft of pork chops from a French farmer; these were 'devoured with relish'.[142]

Most of this deviant activity by cohesive groups and units was covert and avoided any direct challenge to authority. In 1917, this changed with unrest and protest reported in several units in the 56th Division. The incidents reported in the division started in April 1917 when men in the LRB men instituted a 'small strike' because they had been contracted to work for a French farmer whilst behind the lines.[143] In August, after the LRB's participation at Third Ypres, problems were again evident. Men were close to a mutiny over the apparent bungling of the operation by staff and the 'rank and file' felt 'that the Passchendaele Ridge was not worth the sacrifice involved.'[144] This feeling of discontent prompted the CO, Lieutenant Colonel Wallis, to organise an open-air meeting with the unit to address their concerns.[145] Other incidents occurred during the fighting at Cambrai in late November. QVR soldiers went on 'strike' against 'working with the Hun' [sic] to build a POW 'cage'.[146] There was further trouble in the LRB when one company held a 'mutiny', 'downing tools' and complaining they had eaten iron rations for eight days, living in the cold without greatcoats and wanted hot food as they were as 'mad as hell' when they heard that a unit on their flank had received hot 'bread and soup'.[147] In all four incidents, the officers in each particular battalion appeared to have conceded to the demands and no formal disciplinary action against the perpetrators is recorded in the official records. The protests did not appear to escalate in any noticeable way.

139 Groom, *Poor*, p.59; Steward, *Platoon*, p.76.
140 IWM, Hall, Diary, 18 December 1916.
141 W.E. Grey, *2nd City of London Regiment (Royal Fusiliers) in the Great War* (London: London Regiment, 1929), p.35.
142 Tucker, *Johnny*, p.164.
143 Groom, *Poor*, pp.103-104.
144 Smith, *Four*, p.274.
145 IWM, F.H. Wallis, London Rifle Brigade Collection, account, no page numbers.
146 Elliot, *Tim's War*, p.93.
147 Groom, *Poor*, pp.147-48.

Why did men protest in an overt way in 1917? There is a clear sense of an 'inequality of sacrifice' in troops' recollections and writings. In 1917 soldiers often felt they were fighting at the front while people on the home front indulged in strikes to get paid more than the Tommy who was doing the most dangerous job.[148] For example, Sergeant H.V. Holmes, in the London Scottish, wrote a pamphlet in which he said striking for extra pay was unacceptable when the soldier 'received a shilling a day for the work he did for you.'[149] Others grumbled about their conditions; QVR Rifleman Tim Elliott's diary also contains gripes not reflected in entries for the other years, for example, about the short amount of leave British soldiers got compared to the French *poilu*.[150]

It is possible that this elevated feeling of grievance was a background cause of men collectively taking protest action. Due to only limited sources for these events, it is difficult to ascertain what exactly happened, but a sense of injustice was the dominant justification reported for taking these actions. The LRB's April strike was caused in part by the soldiers' belief that it was 'a damned disgrace' to make soldiers work during their 'hard earned rest'. The November 'mutiny' was triggered when men heard a nearby unit received hot food while they were on their eighth day on iron rations and they were 'mad as hell' at this unfairness.[151]

There was also considerable dissatisfaction with the 'staff' and this may have provoked men to public protest. Padre Julian Bickersteth, then senior 56th Division chaplain, wrote in September 1917 'how the soldier (i.e. the man doing the real job) hates the brass hat or staff officer' suggesting that the opinion was widespread across the division.[152] Men were frequently annoyed by the preparation they had to do for visits by staff officers. Smith gives many accounts of preparing for the visits of dignitaries, with 'spit and polish' to clean dirty kit on top of their normal duties. All too often, these visits were cancelled after the unit had been standing around, frequently in the rain, for a considerable length of time. Men became united in their 'grousing and cursing' and 'spluttering with wrath' against the 'red hats'.[153]

Catastrophes and heavy losses were, rightly or wrongly, widely blamed on the 'staff'. For example, the 'saga of the posts', where battalions of 169th Brigade were ordered to occupy outposts opposite the German frontline in January and February 1917, were levelled at the staff. Battalions 'were not very clear' what the 'higher authorities' sought to achieve by holding the posts which they thought was 'folly' that failed to achieve 'a

148 Adrian Gregory, *The Last Great War* (Cambridge: Cambridge University Press, 2008), p.112.
149 H.V. Holmes, *An Infantryman on Strikes: An Appeal to the Workers of Great Britain* (n.d.), pp.10, 18; Tucker, *Johnny*, p.135.
150 Elliot, *Tim's War*, pp, 84, 95.
151 Groom, *Poor*, pp. 103-04, 147-48.
152 Bickersteth, *Diaries*, p.214.
153 Smith, *Four*, p.122.

useful purpose'.[154] Many of the soldiers involved believed they were treated as 'expendable units' and could 'anyone wonder at the changed attitude [of soldiers] … when faced with so much indifference to casualties and hardships?'[155] The overt protests in 1917 were linked to 'staff policy'. Groom observed that the LRB strike in April was because of staff policy for the 'utilisation of troops for farm work'. Though not explicit, Groom also implies that the LRB 'mutiny' in November was also the staff's fault as 'someone was very much to blame for our treatment.'[156] Nevertheless, the operation for which the staff received the greatest castigation was the 56th Division's unsuccessful and costly assault on 16 August 1917. The staff were criticised by many regiments involved and blamed them for it being 'badly handled', having 'inherent weakness' and the LRB believed those responsible should have been sacked.[157] This perception was discussed by the men in their small groups and units. Groom observed, 'never before had any battle affected our nerves so badly.'[158] Smith recalled that men were 'stupefied by the losses', adding, there was 'disgust with British tactics' and a feeling by the 'rank and file' that the operation was 'not worth the sacrifice involved'. It appears that the discussion was widespread and groups and units were beginning to express their discontent. Smith made a cryptic comment that the discontent was making 'itself felt' in the unit.[159] An NCO, Orderly Sergeant Munday, reported the situation to the CO. In response, Wallis paraded the battalion and spoke to them about the attack. He agreed with the men's views that the attack had been pointless and with their wholly negative 'opinion of General Gough and his staff'. Wallis wrote afterwards that this meeting was so important that it needed to be held 'regardless of discipline or Field Service Regulations' so that the 'feeling of distrust' could be 'nipped in the bud'. His action, and the fact he believed that the LRB 'owe[d] a great debt of gratitude to … [Orderly Sergeant] Munday', suggests a severe threat to morale and discipline.[160] However, questions remain about why soldiers risked potential disciplinary action, what sustained the protests, why the incidents fizzled out and why officers took no formal action.

What made men publicly protest and risk potential disciplinary action? It appears in both incidents mentioned above that soldiers took time to reach to a position where they instigated overt action and risked potential punishment. In the April 'strike' soldiers only protested on their third day of working for the French farmer. Groom

---

154 Henriques, *Westminster*, p.137; Grey, *2nd London*, p.157; Keeson, *Victoria's*, Vol. 2, p.214; Mitchinson, *Gentlemen*, p.152.
155 Groom, *Poor*, p.82.
156 Ibid., pp.103-04,
157 Frederick Maude, *The History of the London Rifle Brigade 1859-1919* (London: Constable, 1921), p.205; F. Clive Grimwade, *The War History of the 4th Battalion, The London Regiment (Royal Fusiliers), 1914-1919* (London: London Regiment, 1923), p.305; Grey, *2nd*, p.232.
158 Groom, *Poor*, p.128.
159 Smith, *Four*, pp.273-74.
160 IWM, F.H. Wallis.

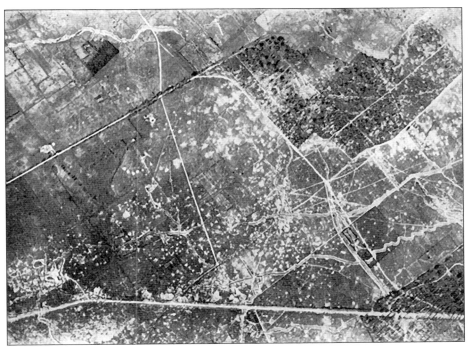

Inverness Copse and environs from the air, August 1917. (Dudley-Ward, *The 56th Division*)

Aftermath of the failed Inverness Copse, Glencourse and Nonne Bosschen woods assault:
London Regiment prisoners pose with their German captors, August 1917. (Private collection)

described that 'we were absolutely fuming at being asked to work a twelve hour day after what we had been through [Battle of Arras]' [sic].[161] This suggests it may have taken time for them to work themselves up to a fit of anger where they became impulsive and did not care about potential disciplinary repercussions.

In both the April and November incidents, fatigue could have been an issue. Groom noted that the work for the French farmer before the April 'strike' was very tiring and consisted of twelve hour shifts of back aching work in scorching weather, coming soon after they had been in battle.[162] In November, men were probably exhausted, hungry and cold having worked and lived for eight days outdoors in mid-winter.[163] Soldiers could have reached such a point of exhaustion that they did not care what happened or were not thinking of the possible repercussions. Studies have shown that where troops were famished and cold this could cause a breakdown in the social order of small groups, leading to 'bitching' and 'less satisfaction' and causing men to have 'less humour … and more irritability'.[164]

The second question is how these incidents were triggered and sustained? This is very difficult to determine given the paucity of evidence. It appears that in all situations, men were working or with their colleagues with whom they lived, fought and survived on a daily basis. In other words, they were with those friends and colleagues with whom they had task and social cohesion. As a result, many men, working with their small unit or group, would have followed their colleagues or comrades out of solidarity. They may well have also copied men outside their immediate primary group circle based on their 'social identity' with them as soldiers, as they wore the same uniform or were part of the same company or battalion. Soldiers probably welcomed the opportunity to show their protest on a commonly held view, such as the poor quality of the food, outlined above. Some may have perceived it safe to protest in the anonymity of the mass, where the chances of individual disciplinary consequences were low. Another factor that could have initiated and sustained the protests was that NCOs, including Groom, had experience of the LRB April and November protests.[165]

Some of the incidents could have mirrored a protest described by Aubrey Smith when he was returning from leave in 1918. He was at the dockside with other men, unknown to him, returning to their units. The Royal Military Police tried to organise the men into fours to march them away. The collected men refused and 'struck', refusing to comply and began 'calling the police all sorts of … names and asking them when they had last heard a shell.'[166] This act was impulsive, initiated by some random spark. The only thing the collected soldiery had in common was probably their shared

161 Groom, *Poor*, pp.103.
162 Ibid., p.103.
163 Ibid, p.147.
164 R.W. Seaton, 'Deterioration of Military Work Groups under Deprivation Stress' in Morris Janowitz (ed.), *The New Military* (New York: Norton, 1964), pp.245-46.
165 Groom, *Poor*, p. 147.
166 Smith, *Four*, p.308.

dislike of MPs. The MPs prevailed and the event was forgotten, but it demonstrates how collectively held views could shape spontaneous group behaviour.

However, Groom's account of the April protest reveals that it lasted for at least 24 hours. The men had protested on their third day of work but were sent back for a fourth day. He said they went to the farm 'and just wouldn't work'. They 'went through the motions and we won because the farmer wouldn't have us [back].'[167] It suggests that men could choose to and were willing to sustain their protest but not overtly defy orders. They went to the farm as ordered but just 'swung the lead'; the annoyed farmer refused to have them there.

The third question is: why did the incidents dissolve? The answer appears to be mainly that the men, through their protests, achieved their objectives. In the April protest, the farmer capitulated.[168] In the November 'mutiny', officers gave in to their demands, and by midday the following day, the men got their bread and hot soup.[169] Elliot and his mates who went on 'strike' about building a 'cage' with the 'Hun' also appear to have had their demand met as they got off duty at 3pm.[170] The officers had the power to resolve many of these issues as most protests revolved around working conditions.

Importantly, none of the demands made by the groups was political in any way, or a direct protest against the conduct of the war, unlike the French 1917 mutinies.[171] The evidence suggests that most men supported the war, and despite their disenchantment with strikers on the Home Front, many still believed in the cause.[172] After the Battle of Arras in spring 1917, Tucker commented that 'there seemed no likelihood of peace, the war being a deadlock … In spite of this … we were grimly determined to stick it out to the end, and in fact I never heard anyone suggesting that we should do otherwise.'[173]

Lastly, men also had strong vertical cohesion with their leaders and many were trusted and respected. For example, Wallis was regarded as a paternal and popular officer who had been with the LRB from the beginning of the war.[174] The fact that men during the November 'mutiny' went back to work around an hour later, even if they 'were going through the motions' this suggests that they had good vertical cohesion with their officers and trusted them to deliver on their promise.

---

167 Groom, *Poor*, p.104.
168 Ibid., p.104.
169 Ibid., p.147.
170 Elliot, *Tim's War*, p.93.
171 See J.G. Fuller, *Troop Morale and Popular Culture in the British and Dominion Armies 1914–1918* (Oxford: Oxford University Press, 1990), p.26; Leonard Smith, *Between Mutiny and Obedience* (Princeton: Princeton University Press, 1994).
172 Thorpe, PhD, pp.208-14.
173 Tucker, *Johnny*, p.136.
174 Smith, *Four*, p.55.

The final question is why did the officers take no formal action? These incidents were potentially severe, being clear examples of mutiny and direct challenges to military discipline. Leaders had two options; either to prosecute the offenders under the official procedures or directly bargain with the offenders. Concern was caused to officers by the two LRB incidents. The April strike 'stirred up a hornet's nest' and after the November protest 'there was fat on the fire' but there was no disciplinary action in either case.[175] Instead, officers in all cases appeared to concede to their men's demands.

Due to the lack of evidence, it is difficult to fully explain why officers chose to concede and not take any disciplinary action. Groom surmises that leaders took no action and hushed up the event to save the unit's reputation. It could also offer part of the explanation as to why none of the above incidents were recorded in official sources.[176] Moreover, formal punishments allocated would have been severe and difficult to mitigate. Leaders most likely realised that all the demands were very limited, spontaneous and could have been easily granted. Added to this, officers may have seen the protests in the context of bargaining and negotiation that dominated the vertical cohesion relationship that so many officers practised with their men on a daily basis.[177] Lastly, it is probable that many officers had sympathy with their men's protests. For example, many regimental officers and soldiers were united in their hatred of the staff. In February 1917, a 56th Division order dictated that soldiers salute senior officers [those at divisional, corps, and staff officers] or their cars [carrying their flags of rank] and threatened that if men did not obey and were caught for 'such slackness' it '*will tend to a confiscation of all leave allotments for units reported* [italics added]'.[178] In September the notice was reissued stating 'there is again a distinct slackness in saluting ... *some officers are especially bad at saluting and returning salute ... if they do, it is ... half–hearted*' [italics added].[179]

Conclusion

Cohesion was widespread, strong and durable within the 56th Division during 1917. Men of equal rank built solid horizontal interpersonal relationships based on trust, founded on mutual survival focused round the work, nature or function of their unit or platoon. These relationships were maintained and sustained through shared experience and informal norms. Some men went on to form strong emotion-caring relationships based on close friendship and social support. NCOs and officers were able to form strong vertical relationships with their subordinates based on trust developed by demonstrating professional competence, paternal care and courageous personal

175   Groom, *Poor*, pp.104-05, 147.
176   Ibid., p.147.
177   Thorpe, PhD, pp.157-60.
178   TNA WO 95/2946: 167th Brigade War Diary, Order No. 41, 13 February 1917.
179   TNA WO 95/2947: 167th Brigade War Diary, Order No. 152, 5 September 1917.

leadership in the trenches. Changes to platoon structures, tactics and weaponry introduced in 1917 enhanced cohesion in groups by reducing the social milieu in groups, forcing greater co-operation and interdependence and ensuring groups and units spent greater time together while working, fighting or training. Strong primary group cohesion within units led to outcomes that both furthered and frustrated the wider military objectives of the organisation of which sections and platoons were a part. On the one hand cohesion contributed to morale, resilience and leader influence; on the other hand, it facilitated covert 'crime' and a wave of overt protests and strikes amongst soldiers in the 56th Division throughout 1917. On balance, strong primary group cohesion largely helped the aims of the army more than it hindered them. The scale of the unrest recorded within the division was relatively limited, sporadic and spontaneous in scope and aims. The protests were also aimed at working conditions and were not political. Men had solid vertical cohesion with their leaders which enabled officers to defuse potential problems, such as in the LRB unrest after the disastrous 16 August attack and they were able to persuade men to return to work following the November 'mutiny'.

5

Intelligence Analysis
Major James Cuffe at GHQ

Jim Beach

James Cuffe served as an intelligence officer throughout the First World War.[1] Thus far, he has appeared within intelligence histories of that conflict only as a minor figure, and mostly in connection with his collection and liaison work in 1914.[2] More recently, using material held by the family, his daughter summarised Cuffe's military career in a magazine article.[3] Significantly, those papers, now deposited in the Imperial War Museum (IWM), contain intelligence memoranda written by Cuffe when, in modern parlance, he was a senior analyst at British General Headquarters (GHQ) on the Western Front between September 1916 and June 1918. This chapter subjects those documents to close examination. By comparing them with better-known primary and secondary sources, it offers a fresh perspective on GHQ's analytical practices and opens a new window upon British interpretations of German intentions, especially during the infamous Third Ypres offensive.

---

1 Unless indicated, all biographical information comes from Cuffe's *Who Was Who* entry, his naval service record in National Archives (TNA) ADM 196/62 or the copy of his service file supplied by the Army Personnel Centre (APC) to Patricia Spencer-Silver, 25 April 2008.

2 Christopher Andrew, *Secret Service: The Making of the British Intelligence Community* (London: Heinemann, 1985), p.83; Alan Judd, *The Quest for C: Mansfield Cumming and the Founding of the Secret Service* (London: Harper Collins, 1999), pp.244-48, 253-54, 264, 270, 277-78, 281-82; Janet Morgan, *The Secrets of the Rue St Roch: Intelligence Operations behind Enemy Lines in the First World War* (London: Allen Lane, 2004), p.223; Keith Jeffery, *MI6: The History of the Secret Intelligence Service, 1909-1949* (London: Bloomsbury, 2010), p.35; Michael Smith, *Six: A History of Britain's Secret Intelligence Service* (London: Dialogue, 2010), pp.39, 44, 48; Jim Beach, 'Doctrine Manuals and Car Crashes: British Espionage on the Western Front in 1914' in Gill Bennett (ed.), *Secret Intelligence and the Armed Services*, *RUSI Occasional Paper* (2012), pp.43-49; Jim Beach, *Haig's Intelligence: GHQ and the German Army, 1916-1918* (Cambridge: Cambridge University Press, 2013), pp.117-19, 182, 185, 229, 293.

3 Patricia Silver, 'A Dubliner in British Military Intelligence', *History Ireland*, July/August 2014, pp.36-39.

When the First World War broke out, James Cuffe was in his late thirties. A Dublin-born Irishman from a Roman Catholic family, his father had been a magistrate in Dublin and Wicklow. Cuffe commissioned into the Royal Marine Light Infantry in 1897, serving subsequently with the fleet and on secondment to the King's African Rifles. In 1908 he qualified as a French interpreter and, after six months of language leave in the summer of 1911, achieved the same level in German. Then, in July 1912, Cuffe's career took an unusual turn when he began a three-year detachment to the War Office's Directorate of Military Operations (DMO). In this period he was actually working for Britain's nascent Secret Service.[4] It also seems fairly certain that he had been recruited by his second cousin Lieutenant-Colonel George Macdonogh, then head of MO5 which was the DMO's special intelligence section.[5] Unsurprisingly, details of Cuffe's secret work are sketchy, but he does appear as AC in the diaries of Commander Mansfield Cumming, then head of the Secret Service.[6] Sadly, because this document remains classified we must rely upon inconsistent précis and quotations from two authors who have had privileged access. Cross-referencing these with other sources and ephemera from the Cuffe papers, a partial picture can be discerned.

During this pre-war period Cuffe seems to have been based sometimes in Charleroi and, at some point in 1913, was provided with a motorcycle to facilitate his work.[7] At the beginning of that year he had proposed a system of 'agents and scouts' to be

4   In 1909 both Britain's overseas espionage and domestic counter-espionage organisations were originally designated as forming a Secret Service Bureau. During the First World War the espionage organisation used MI1(c) as a cover-name while the counter-espionage organisation evolved into MI5. After the conflict the espionage organisation became known as the Secret Intelligence Service and during the Second World War it used the now-famous cover-name of MI6. Secret Service has been used for simplicity.

5   Thomas Fergusson, *British Military Intelligence, 1870-1914: The Development of a Modern Intelligence Organization* (Frederick, Maryland: University Publications of America, 1984), pp.181-82, 252; *War Office List*, 1910. Many thanks to Tony Comer for the genealogical research that connected them precisely.

6   It has sometimes been assumed that AC was Cecil Aylmer Cameron, who later ran espionage networks for the army. Judd, *Quest for C*, p.294; Smith, *Six*, p.38. But this interpretation is undermined by Cumming's 31 July 1914 meeting with both Cameron and AC. They cannot, therefore, be the same person. In other instances, Cumming used people's names and initials to create their codenames. In AC's case, the letters match one of Cuffe's forenames (James Aloysius Francis) and his surname. Furthermore, in early 1914, AC was introduced to another operative as 'Captain Francis', which matches both his rank and another of his forenames. Judd, *Quest for C*, p.254; Jeffery, *MI6*, p.35. Cameron's belated appearance is also consistent with MO5's plan to augment the 'scheme for secret service' with two additional officers during the 'precautionary stage' of a crisis. TNA WO33/642: A1663, 'A War Book for the War Office: An account of the special duties to be undertaken, and the arrangements to be made, by the branches of the War Office if war be threatened or declared', 1913.

7   Triumph number 218563: IWM, Cuffe Papers: *Touring Club de Belgique* membership card, 1914; Judd, *Quest for C*, 245. Triumph (3½ and 4 hp) frames manufactured in 1913 run from serial number 196101 to 219730: <veterantriumph.co.uk> (accessed 20 April 2020).

employed within Belgium in the event of war. By early 1914 further arrangements had been made, with Macdonogh telling Cumming that, in wartime, Cuffe would 'have nothing to do with [Secret Service]' but would run sources recruited by another operative until such time as the Germans had 'passed over their line.' At that point the scouts/agents would be handed off to another operative based in Brussels. To communicate with the I(b) section of the GHQ British Expeditionary Force (BEF), Cuffe would use a post office box in Lille. In the meantime, his priorities for 1914 were to reconnoitre Belgium's western frontier in the Ardennes and the river crossings near the fortress of Liège.[8] Assuming Cuffe had conducted similar activities in late 1912 and across 1913, he probably contributed information that was consolidated by the army into intelligence and geographical handbooks.[9] Indeed, in March 1913 Cumming noted material supplied by AC that was favourably received.[10] Although the evidence is limited, the general impression is that Cuffe was operating at the interface between the world of espionage and more conventional military reconnaissance.[11] Also, overshadowing Cuffe's activities in this period is an allegation that he somehow 'double-crossed' his colleagues.[12] This suggestion, however, can be dismissed as a case of mistaken identity because, by coincidence, Cumming's representative in Brussels was a former marine. Any suggestion of impropriety is far more consistent with that man's role, previous behaviour, and unexplained departure from the Secret Service.[13]

On 31 July 1914, four days before Britain declared war on Germany, Cuffe and other Secret Service operatives met Cumming in London before crossing the Channel.[14] He appears to have travelled immediately to Brussels, where his activities

---

8   Judd, *Quest for C*, p.244, 253-4; Jeffery, *MI6*, p.33.
9   TNA WO 33/615: General Staff, 'Intelligence Series: Belgium', 1914, WO 33/613; General Staff, 'Belgium: Road, River and Billeting Reports', Vol. 2, 1913.
10   Judd, *Quest for C*, p.248
11   This also consistent with the doctrinal paradigm prevailing at that time: Beach, *Haig's Intelligence*, pp.15-16.
12   'Rear Admiral Sir Henry Oliver [former Director of Naval Intelligence …] later concluded that the "head agent" in Brussels, Captain James Cuffe of the Royal Marines, had "double-crossed us."' Andrew, *Secret Service*, 83. Referring to an instance where a letter was opened without authority and a visit made to Rome to meet a potential agent, Oliver wrote 'we kept a head agent at Brussels a retired Royal Marine Officer and he once double crossed us badly but got paid out.' National Maritime Museum, OLV/12, unpublished memoire, p.97. Thanks to David Morgan-Owen for providing a copy of this source.
13   'Roy' Regnart had worked closely with Cumming while serving with the Naval Intelligence Division of the Admiralty. He retired in July 1913 and, despite misgivings expressed to Cumming by senior military officers, became the Secret Service's representative in Brussels. Linguistically talented, but a mistrusted and troublesome subordinate, Regnart was recalled to the fleet on 31 July 1914. TNA ADM 196/62, Regnart naval service record; Judd, *Quest for C*, pp.163, 185, 187-9, 202-5, 251-2, 261-2; Jeffery, *MI6*, pp.21, 23-5, 27-8, 33.
14   Cuffe service file supplied by the Army Personnel Centre to Patricia Spencer-Silver, 25 April 2008: Officers' Records Section to HQ British Military Representative, C-in-C Allied Forces, 20 February 1919; Jeffery, *MI6*, p.35.

included the recruitment of interpreters, guides, and scouts until 19 August when he headed south-west and linked up with the BEF.[15] One of the intelligence officers who met him recorded that Cuffe 'arrived from Belgium, where he has been organising [an] Intelligence Service.' The two of them then travelled to Mons and Charleroi, before Cuffe pushed on alone to Namur.[16] According to Macdonogh's later testimony, confirmed by a contemporaneous document, Cuffe was on a mission to deliver messages from GHQ just as the Germans began to surround that fortress.[17] On his return, Cuffe provided important corroboration for an air reconnaissance report of enemy cavalry at Nivelles.[18] He then travelled to Dinant, which appears to have been envisaged as a rendezvous point for Secret Service operatives, and again according to Macdonogh was 'probably the first British officer to come under fire.'[19] Cuffe's activities in September are less clear-cut. Although there is a vague reference to plans for him to return to Brussels undercover, he also appears to have been taken on administratively

15   TNA FO 371/2169/37734: Villiers (Brussels) to Foreign Office, 10 August 1914. This telegram relayed a message from Cuffe to 'Verbloski London'. The latter was the telegraphic address for the Secret Service: Cambridge University Library, Templewood Papers, III/2/7, Telegram, 8 January 1918. Thanks are offered to Colin Kauntze for alerting me, many years ago, to the Brussels telegram. Cuffe service file supplied by the Army Personnel Centre to Patricia Spencer-Silver, 25 April 2008: Pass issued by Belgian Ministry of War, 1 August 1914, Belgian army pass issued at Louvain, 17 August 1914. The last address noted on his *Touring Club de Belgique* membership card (9, Rue Bosquet) is the same as that notified by the British government to the Belgians: FO371/2163/36776: War Office to Foreign Office, 7 August 1914. AC also met Cumming in Brussels on 16 August. Judd, *Quest for C*, p.278.

16   University of Aberdeen Special Collections (UASC), John Baird Papers: Diary, 19-20 August 1914.

17   IWM, Cuffe Papers: Pass stamped General Staff Intelligence Section, signed by Macdonogh, 19 August 1914, Macdonogh testimonial, 20 May 1922. The Germans reached Namur on 19 August and began their bombardment two days later. James Edmonds, *Military Operations, France & Belgium 1914*, Vol. 1 (London: HMSO, 1933), pp.36-37.

18   TNA CAB 45/141: Macdonogh to Edmonds, 22 November 1922; Edmonds, *Military Operations 1914*, Vol. 1, p.52.

19   IWM, Cuffe Papers: Macdonogh testimonial, 20 May 1922. The British official history records the BEF's 'first contact with the enemy' on the morning of 22 August. Edmonds, *Military Operations 1914*, Vol. 1, p.62. The Germans first probed the French defences of Dinant on 15 August and again on the night of 21-22 August, before launching main assault on 23 August: John Horne & Alan Kramer, *German Atrocities, 1914: A History of Denial* (London: Yale University Press, 2001), pp.42-53. Demetrius Boulger, a British journalist and writer in his sixties, was declared to the Belgian government as an intelligence officer and his address was given as 14, Quai de la Meuse, Dinant: TNA FO 371/2163/36776: War Office to Foreign Office, 7 August 1914. In Cumming's diaries DB appears, from early 1913, as a collector within Belgium and the Netherlands as well as the controller of a small network of sub-agents. His identity is corroborated by a reference to him working on a history of Belgium alongside his Secret Service work. Judd, *Quest for C*, pp.244-45, 253-54, 269-70, 277-78, 281-82; Jeffery, *MI6*, p.33. When in Brussels, Cuffe also made arrangements to procure stores and transport for delivery to Dinant. FO371/2169/37734: Villiers (Brussels) to Foreign Office, 10 August 1914.

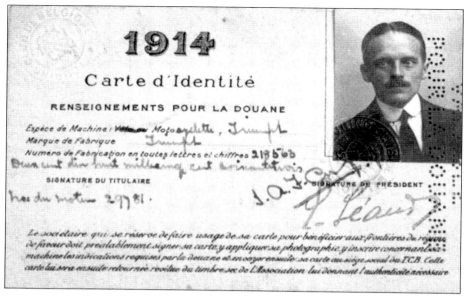

James Cuffe's Belgian Touring Club membership card, 1914.

by GHQ.[20] Cuffe was then sent as an intelligence liaison officer to the French army and, based in Compiègne for at least a month, he seems to have become involved in some sort of espionage management.[21]

In early December 1914 Cuffe began the process of transferring from the navy to the army. This took three months and was delayed by his superiors' desire for him to be promoted, combined with a lack of vacancies for regular majors within Irish infantry regiments.[22] Eventually he joined the Royal Munster Fusiliers, whose second battalion had sustained very heavy officer casualties in 1914.[23] In August 1915 Cuffe

20   Judd, *Quest for C*, pp.281-82; 'To be an intelligence officer in the field' (backdated to 15 August): TNA WO 123/199: BEF Routine Orders, 10 September 1914. Thanks are owed to Jock Bruce for his assistance here and in tracing other aspects of Cuffe's career.

21   IWM, Cuffe Papers: Diary, 6, 25 September 1914, John Baird Papers, UASC; Sub-CGS BEF to Colonel Huguet, 23 September 1914. During this period and through to the spring of 1915, Cuffe was probably subordinated to the I(b) section of GHQ because its head made enquiries about his pay. IWM, Kirke Papers, 82/28/1: Diary, 22 November, 16 December 1914, 27 March 1915.

22   Cuffe service file supplied by the Army Personnel Centre to Patricia Spencer-Silver, 25 April 2008: War Office to Admiralty, 10 December, Admiralty to War Office, 18 December 1914, MS1 War Office to MS BEF, 5 February, AMS BEF to War Office, 8 February, War Office to Admiralty, 8 March 1915.

23   Stouppe McCance, *History of the Royal Munster Fusiliers, 1861 to 1922*, Vol. 2 (Aldershot: Gale & Polden, 1927), pp.113-21. Many thanks to Tim Bowman for providing a copy

left GHQ to become the counter-espionage officer at Third Army headquarters.[24] Then, in the mid-winter of 1915–16 he attended a staff course and later augmented Fourth Army's intelligence section during the first part of the Somme offensive.[25] In September he rejoined GHQ as a GSO2, where he undertook the analytical work that is the focus of this chapter. Cuffe remained in that role until June 1918, when he joined the British team at Ferdinand Foch's headquarters.[26] From that position, his move in November to the International Armistice Commission was a fairly logical one. In May 1919, Cuffe assumed command of 1/Royal Munster Fusiliers, a post he held until their disbandment in the summer of 1922.[27] On half-pay from 1923 then retired pay in 1926, Cuffe settled near Winchester; becoming a city and later county councillor, as well as commanding 5/Hampshire Home Guard during the Second World War. He died in 1957.

Sources on Cuffe's personality are sparse. In 1917, Macdonogh's assessment was that 'he really is a very good chap, & thinks more than he says', and in 1922 described him as 'tactful & gets on well with his superiors & subordinates.'[28] By way of contrast, in 1918 Valentine Vivian, head of intelligence at Fourth Army, was reported to have judged Cuffe to be a 'most tactless man' and therefore unsuitable for a possible role with the British headquarters in Italy.[29] One of his subordinates at GHQ, remembered 'Cuffey' as an 'amiable fellow.' But also a man who 'never seemed to be quite at ease with anyone' and with 'a peculiarly withdrawn looking expression – as if he

of this book and contextual information on Irish infantry regiments. With an eye to his future career, at the time of Cuffe's transfer to the Munsters, Macdonogh had noted that two other newly-promoted majors were '4 or 5 years older than he is so won't stand in his way when he comes up for command.' IWM, Cuffe Papers: Macdonogh to Jane Cuffe, 17 March 1915.

24   Letter to Beatrice, 28 March 1918, Jim Beach (ed.), *The Military Papers of Lieutenant-Colonel Sir Cuthbert Headlam, 1910-1942* (Stroud: History Press for the Army Records Society, 2010), p.193.

25   IWM, Cuffe Papers: 'List of officers who attended the first course of instruction in Staff Duties at St Omer, December 1915-January 1916'; TNA WO 158/897: Charteris to Macdonogh, 9 July, 7 August 1916.

26   For the context of their work, see Elizabeth Greenhalgh, *Foch in Command: The Forging of a First World War General* (Cambridge: Cambridge University Press, 2011), pp.310-494

27   He also married Gertrude Jackson. Patricia Spencer-Silver, *Tower Bridge to Babylon: The Life and Work of Sir John Jackson, Civil Engineer* (Sudbury: Six Martlets, 2005), p.197. Between September 1921 and April 1922, Cuffe took his battalion to Upper Silesia to reinforce the British peacekeepers. For the army's operations in that region, see James Edmonds, *The Occupation of the Rhineland* (London: HMSO, 1987), pp.230-41; Peter Leśniewski, 'Britain and Upper Silesia, 1919-1922', PhD, Dundee (2000); Alun Thomas, 'The British Upper Silesia Force ('UPSI' Force): May 1921-July 1922', *Journal of Army Historical Research*, 95:384 (2017), pp.338-64.

28   Macdonogh to Charteris, 30 April 1917, TNA WO 158/898, Macdonogh testimonial, 20 May 1922, IWM, Cuffe Papers.

29   Letter to Beatrice, 29 March 1918, Beach, *Headlam*, p.194.

had suddenly thrown up a barrier and hastily retreated behind it.'[30] These sources also highlighted Cuffe's familial connection to Macdonogh. The always-acerbic Cuthbert Headlam, who had recorded Vivian's assessment, went further; 'I know Cuffe, the man in question. He is second rate to a degree – indeed a laughing stock outside GHQ – but, and here is the big *but*, he is a protégé of Macdonogh the head of all 'I' and so his career is being strictly looked after.'[31] The existence of familial and friendship networks within the army's officer corps is not a revelation.[32] Indeed, Headlam himself was fairly adept at using them to his own advantage.[33] But the charge of nepotism still needs to be explored in Cuffe's case. Macdonogh's hand in his 1912 move to the Secret Service is fairly obvious. Similarly, as the head of intelligence at GHQ, he presumably instigated Cuffe's transfer from the navy and arranged the Third Army posting. In December 1915 Macdonogh returned to London and became Director of Military Intelligence (DMI). But we can still discern an indirect influence. In July 1916, shortly before Cuffe was shunted to the Somme, John Charteris, the new Brigadier-General (Intelligence) (BGI) at GHQ, wrote to Macdonogh as follows:

> About Cuffe, I will do the best I can [...] but it is rather difficult. There is no GSO2 going at GHQ. We have no GSO2s in Corps or Armies for Intelligence, and Operations will not have Cuffe. I can, of course, always give him an administrative job, but I doubt very much whether he would like it or whether he would be able to do it. I will, however, take the matter up and will let you know in the course of a week what we have done.[34]

The DMI's influence therefore seems clear in this case. But in March 1918 the mooted appointment to Italy did not happen even though Macdonogh had apparently pressed Cuffe's case with the British commander there. Post-war, with Macdonogh then the army's Adjutant-General it is also tempting to assume that he influenced Cuffe's command appointment. However, the *Army Lists* for 1919 show that he was the third most senior major in the Munsters and, by the end of the year, its two battalions were commanded by Cuffe and the officer previously in second place. Finally, it should be noted that, like Macdonogh, Cuffe's Catholicism may have been a factor in how he was perceived within GHQ. Infamously, both Charteris and the commander-in-chief, Douglas Haig, recorded prejudiced generalisations about Catholics at the end of 1917.[35]

---

30   National Library of Scotland (NLS), Acc.5415: James Roy, 'Recollections of an Intelligence Officer, 1914-1919', p.126.
31   Letter to Beatrice, 28 March 1918, Beach, *Headlam*, p.193.
32   Aimée Fox, *Learning to Fight: Military Innovation and Change in the British Army, 1914-1918* (Cambridge: Cambridge University Press, 2018), pp.37-43.
33   Beach, *Headlam*, pp.9, 82, 86.
34   TNA WO 158/897: Charteris to Macdonogh, 5 July 1916.
35   Beach, *Haig's Intelligence*, p.47.

Memoranda

Cuffe's intelligence memoranda were written during his time with the I(a) section at GHQ. As suggested by its nomenclature, this was the leading part of the headquarters' intelligence staff because, as a 1917 document explained, it dealt with 'information regarding the enemy.'[36] Cuffe spent twenty-one months with I(a). Such a lengthy tenure was not remarkable. During the war, James Cornwall and John Dunnington-Jefferson – his two GSO2 peers – spent twenty-four and thirty-one months respectively in their GHQ posts.[37] During Cuffe's time, I(a) was divided into five or six sub-sections.[38] The smaller of these, headed by GSO3s, dealt with artillery, engineering, and what would later become known as technical intelligence. Another sub-section, headed by Dunnington-Jefferson, dealt primarily with the dissemination of intelligence. This left two main analytical sub-sections that were, in 1917, headed by Cornwall and Cuffe. Contemporaneous descriptions of their duties are summarised in Table 1.

Table 1. Duties of I(a) analytical sub-sections

Date	Cornwall's sub-section	Cuffe's sub-section
March 1917	Enemy's order of battle. Enemy's organization. Preparation of diagrams & statements showing distribution of German forces.	Daily situation map from all sources. Information of theatre of war and enemy's defences. Strategic movements of the enemy Enemy's plan of operations & probable movements in given contingencies.
July 1917	Enemy's order of battle. Enemy's organization. Preparation of diagrams & statements showing distribution of German forces. German recruiting & classes. Examination of German documents.	Situation maps from all sources. Information of theatre of war immediately behind the enemy's front. German lines of defence. Strategic movements of the enemy Enemy's plan of operations & probable movements.

36   TNA WO 158/961: OB/2010, GHQ to War Office, 7 April 1917.
37   Cornwall (January 1916 to January 1918); Dunnington-Jefferson (February 1916 to Armistice): *Quarterly Army Lists*, December 1918 and December 1919.
38   Unless otherwise indicated, organisational information is taken from: Privately held, Bowdler Papers: 'Organisation of Intelligence Section, General Staff, General Headquarters' [12 March 1917]; Library and Archives Canada, MG30-E61, Mitchell Papers, Vol. 14: I/Org/24, 'Organization of Intelligence Section, General Staff, GHQ', 23 July 1917. The former document is dated by the inclusion of Walter Kirke as head of I(b) before his move to 4th Division.

A fair amount of historical attention has already been directed towards the work done by Cornwall's section. This can be explained in two ways. First, perceptions of German manpower and morale are critical in understanding the BEF's offensive operations in 1916, 1917 and late 1918. Second, in his historical and memoir writings, Cornwall highlighted instances in which Charteris misjudged the decline of the enemy's army.[39] This chapter will hopefully redress the balance.

Fortunately, an American visitor in mid-December 1917 provided his superiors with a detailed explanation of the work of Cuffe's sub-section. In addition to the maintenance of dossiers on all 'town[s] in rear of the [German] line', he wrote that:

> Major [Cuffe] is in charge of the terrain immediately in the rear of the German army [...] He has supervision of collection of and rendering final opinion on statements of repatriates, spies, prisoners, army reports and airplane photographs of the works behind the lines. He pays attention to the general lines rather than to the smaller details [...] He also periodically publishes, for the Chief of the Intelligence Section, a review of the intentions of the enemy.[40]

This remit for predictive analysis is significant. In January 1918 Edgar Cox became head of intelligence at GHQ and, with the BEF now stood on the defensive, instituted the dissemination of a weekly appreciation of German intentions.[41] Cox also re-organised his staff. Within I(a), Cuffe's role was then described as 'Enemy Plans', with two GSO3s working under him focused on 'Enemy Communications & Rear Organisations' and 'Enemy Defences & Activity.'[42] Additionally, across 1917 and 1918, Cuffe's team also included a small number of Intelligence Corps officers who supported the work of the staff officers.[43] One of them, James Roy, was a literature academic who spent most of 1918 with I(a).[44] Although his memoir is silent with regard to the sub-section's analytical processes, Roy does tell us that he was responsible for the situation maps and worked alongside three other Intelligence Corps officers.[45] He shared an office with two of them; George Line, a director of a wallpaper

39 Beach, *Haig's Intelligence*, pp.1-5, 263-64.
40 National Archives and Records Administration (NARA), RG120/129/5866: 'Report on trip [18-22 December 1917] to British General Headquarters', 1 January 1918.
41 Beach, *Haig's Intelligence*, pp.185, 279.
42 TNA WO 106/359: 'Organization of Intelligence Section, General Staff GHQ', 3 May 1918.
43 For the evolution of this division of labour within the BEF, see Beach, *Haig's Intelligence*, pp.66-7, 82-85.
44 January to September: James Roy service file supplied by APC to Ian Dalziel, 4 November 2016: Application to transfer to the Territorial Force Reserve, 10 June 1921.
45 NLS, Acc.5415: James Roy, 'Recollections of an Intelligence Officer, 1914-1919', 123-24, 126.

company, and Alan D'Egville, a cartoonist.[46] In a neighbouring room was another junior officer with responsibility for the interpretation of air photographs.[47]

Because of his analytical responsibilities, Cuffe's memoranda offer a fresh opportunity to understand the creation of GHQ's intelligence picture. Before Cox's aforementioned weekly pieces, the only documentary evidence of the intelligence staff's predictive assessment function comes from occasional pieces preserved in the GHQ operational files.[48] For example, in early June 1917 Charteris wrote a 'Note on the Strategical Situation' to bolster the case for the Third Ypres offensive that Haig was then debating with London.[49] In contrast, Cuffe's memoranda are internal correspondence. Many are addressed directly to Charteris, while others have I(a) reference numbers indicating they were formal documents placed on file by the clerks.[50] The latter may have been circulated within the intelligence staff, or even more widely within GHQ, but, in the absence of distribution lists or the original files, this is conjecture. Similarly, we can only speculate on Cuffe's motives for retaining them. One explanation is that, even at the time, he recognised the potential historical significance of his work and wished for them to be preserved.[51] But even by the time of his death in 1957, military documents from the First World War had not been released to the Public Record Office.[52] And, as they were intelligence documents, Cuffe's cache would have been perceived as still-secret, even though the overwhelming majority of

46   TNA WO 374/42253: Protection Certificate, 2 June 1919; Alan D'Egville, *Adventures in Safety* (London: Sampson Low, Marston, 1937), pp.64-80.
47   In January 1918 this post was filled by John Bruce Lockhart, a schoolmaster who had recently arrived in France: TNA WO 374/42664: Intelligence Corps casualty form, IC7591, Fenn to MI6c, 5 November 1917. His more-famous brother, Robert, was a diplomat in Russia who, later in 1918, was imprisoned by the Bolsheviks. RH Bruce Lockhart, *Memoirs of a British Agent* (London: Putnam, 1932); Laura Engelstein, *Russia in Flames: War, Revolution, Civil War, 1914-1921* (Oxford: Oxford University Press, 2018), pp.254, 266, 383, 385, 387-89, 399, 416.
48   Even Cox's weekly assessments are not preserved in GHQ's operational files. Beach, *Haig's Intelligence*, pp.279-80. TNA also holds a voluminous amount of GHQ I(a) material within the WO 157 series, but these files contain only the daily intelligence summaries, their annexes, and summaries of Allied communiqués. They provide a useful compilation of raw intelligence and some snippets of assessment but, because of their wide dissemination, they do not include predictive assessments of German intentions.
49   TNA WO 158/24: Ia/35273, 11 June 1917; Beach, *Haig's Intelligence*, pp.243-44.
50   The serial numbers and dates match the filing reference sequence of other documents that were issued as annexes to the GHQ daily intelligence summaries. For the numbering of GHQ I(a)'s documents, see Beach, *Haig's Intelligence*, p.10.
51   This hypothesis is supported by an annotation, 'written before the operations of the 16/8/17', on one of the memoranda. IWM, Cuffe Papers: Cuffe to Charteris, 'Notes on the 'Probable moves of enemy troops to meet our operations' as foreseen by Fifth Army', 15 August 1917.
52   For the historiographical significance of the Public Records Act (1967), see Alex Danchev, 'Bunking' and Debunking: The Controversies of the 1960s' in Brian Bond (ed.), *The First World War and British Military History* (Oxford: Clarendon Press, 1991), p.270.

the documents lack the protective markings later appended to classified government materials.[53] Another explanation is that Cuffe had originally retained the documents as a sort of insurance policy. Across 1917 his superior, Charteris, became embroiled in an increasingly bitter dispute with Macdonogh, his cousin and mentor, over the extent to which the German army was close to collapse. And, at the end of that year, Charteris' officially-recorded optimism was a significant factor in him being replaced as head of intelligence at GHQ.[54] Although German manpower and morale did not fall within his analytical remit, it is a reasonable assumption that Cuffe was aware of this bureaucratic battle. He may, therefore, have decided to retain copies of his own assessments in case he became drawn into the conflict and found his analytical track-record being challenged?

Forty-five documents survive; the earliest dating from December 1916 and the latest from May 1918.[55] Their periodicity is inconsistent, with noticeable clusters in the first four months of 1917 and also from June to August of that year. Cuffe's average analytical output was presumably greater than a couple of assessments per month, so he seems to have preserved only those reports that he deemed important. Two-thirds of the reports date from 1917 and, overall, almost half of them are assessments of German intentions. The others include analyses of German defences, artillery, and targets for Royal Flying Corps (RFC) bombing missions. The latter consist of two reports, in March and July 1917, which suggested attacks upon specified ammunition depots, railway locomotives, and bridges over the River Scheldt.[56] The significance of those bridges had been highlighted by Cuffe in an earlier analysis of the railway system noting the interdiction vulnerability of German logistics into the Ypres sector.[57] However, such precision attacks were beyond the RFC's bombing capability at that time.[58]

The most unusual memorandum in the collection is 'Notes for the Press', dated 3 April 1918.[59] Presumably drafted for the correspondents at GHQ, it has a very clear

---

53   For government attempts, in the early 1960s, to suppress classified materials within collections of private papers, see Richard Aldrich, 'Policing the Past: Official History, Secrecy and British Intelligence since 1945', *English Historical Review*, 119:483 (2004), pp.933-34.

54   Beach, *Haig's Intelligence*, pp.245, 258-59, 266-71.

55   Four documents are undated, although their position in the sequence can be guessed, and two documents are duplicated within the collection. IWM, Cuffe Papers: Ia/26902, 'Note on the grouping of the enemy's artillery on the Somme front', 15 January 1917, 'Earliest date when the Germans can make an offensive on the Ypres Salient', 1 March 1917.

56   IWM, Cuffe Papers: Ia/29965, Cuffe to RFC, 10 March 1917, Ia/36361, Cuffe to Charteris, 'Bombing Scheme', 16 July 1917.

57   IWM, Cuffe Papers: Cuffe to Charteris, 29 December 1916, Ia/26255, 30 December 1916.

58   David Jordan, 'The Army Co-operation Missions of the Royal Flying Corps/Royal Air Force, 1914-1918', PhD, Birmingham (1997), pp.216-23.

59   The memorandum has the same formatting as the others, so Cuffe's authorship is a fair assumption. Thanks are offered to Stephen Badsey for his contextual advice regarding this document.

propagandist purpose. Positing that the German offensive had been a failure because of the absence of a breakthrough, it suggested, very patriotically, that 'a calm survey of the present situation ought to inspire the Allies with confidence, and the British Nation with pride, in the great deeds accomplished by Sir Douglas Haig and his splendid Army.' Although the document conceded that 'the Fifth Army has withdrawn (and is being reformed)', it argued that the Third Army had 'stood firm' against 'repeated blows.' After musings on the likelihood of a French counter-offensive, the document concluded with a prediction that:

> When operations in Flanders are again possible, Haig can again resume the battle of the Ridges. Last year, if it had not been for the intervention of the fifth element, 'Mud', the coast would have been ours. Haig in 1917 started too late. If it is possible to start again in Flanders at the end of April or early in May, with the advantage we gained last year, with our improved railway system, with a larger supply of men and assisted by the Belgians and the Americans, the reconquest of Belgium ought to be a certainty for the near future.

This end piece was very wishful thinking, given the BEF was a long way from being able to resume offensive operations and was, in fact, about to receive a second major blow from the Germans. But most oddly, it includes a criticism of the timing of Haig's operations in 1917. One can perhaps surmise that, in the somewhat chaotic atmosphere of March/April 1918, Cuffe was asked to step beyond his normal remit and draft this piece? There is a second anomalous item, also dating from April 1918, which is a contingency plan for naval support, including the landing of Royal Marines, to cover the withdrawal of the Belgian army.[60] Given Cuffe's prior service with the marines, his authorship is more explicable in this case.

German Retreat

Cuffe's first surviving memoranda addressing German intentions were written on 28 February and 1 March 1917. Because of their timing and content, they offer additional evidence for understanding a turbulent moment at GHQ. In January and early February, the Germans had sought to deceive the Allies with false rumours of an attack in Flanders. Although the British were initially taken in, by 20 February Charteris was telling Haig that the indications were a deliberate deception.[61] Five days later the German army began a withdrawal.[62] This new fluidity caused some

---

60   IWM, Cuffe Papers: [untitled, unsigned memorandum], 24 April 1918. For Allied withdrawal planning, see Beach, *Haig's Intelligence*, p.294.

61   Beach, *Haig's Intelligence*, pp.224-25.

62   For a succinct summary of the strategic and operational context of the withdrawal, see Jonathan Boff, *Haig's Enemy: Crown Prince Rupprecht and Germany's War on the Western*

consternation, but within a few days the BEF's intelligence staffs concurred that the Germans would execute a phased retreat and then resume a defensive posture on the recently-constructed Hindenburg Line.[63] At this point the French and British also took an important step towards co-ordinating their plans for a spring offensive. On 27 February, Haig attended an inter-allied conference in Calais at which it was decided, to his surprise and annoyance, that the BEF would be subordinated to the French commander-in-chief during the coming offensive.[64]

The following day, four connected events occurred: Haig was briefed by Charteris, Haig discussed the situation with his chief of staff, Cuffe wrote an assessment of the German army's intentions, and Charteris wrote to Macdonogh.[65] Haig's record of Charteris' briefing focused upon the strong indications that the Germans would cease their phased retreat on the Hindenburg Line. It did not mention any offensive intentions. In contrast, Haig noted that Lancelot Kiggell, his chief of staff, agreed with him 'that indications are mounting up that the enemy is preparing for a big decisive stroke.' Haig then suggested that the Germans would stand on the defensive on 'between Cambrai and Laon', draw in Allied resources when they attacked, before launching 'at a favourable moment' their own offensive against Ypres that would seize the Channel ports, 'cut our communications with England & end the war' in a German victory. He therefore resolved to submit a paper to the War Cabinet, alerting them to this danger. That document was duly produced and despatched four days later.[66] Given the rancour within British civil-military relations at this point, a question mark hangs over the intelligence foundations for Haig's arguments.[67] There are echoes here of Haig correctly interpreting German strategy as he had done a year earlier, but there is also a strong possibility he deliberately overplayed the threat to Flanders as a way of pushing back against the command arrangements that had been imposed upon him by the Calais conference.[68] Cuffe's memorandum therefore permits a better understanding of any intelligence perceptions that may have justified Haig's arguments.

Front (Oxford: Oxford University Press, 2018), pp.144-52.

63   Beach, *Haig's Intelligence*, 230. See also, Vallières to Nivelle, 2 March 1917 in Elizabeth Greenhalgh (ed.), *Liaison: General Pierre des Vallières at British General Headquarters, 1916-1917* (Stroud: History Press for the Army Records Society, 2016), pp.236-37.

64   For a comprehensive analysis of this planning process, see Elizabeth Greenhalgh, *Victory through Coalition: Britain and France during the First World War* (Cambridge: Cambridge University Press, 2005), pp.138-48.

65   In Haig's diary, the briefing preceded the discussion. Moreover, in Charteris' letter, the phrase 'I am writing tonight another note', suggests it was written in the evening. NLS, Haig Papers, Acc.3155: Diary, 28 February 1917; TNA WO 158/898: Charteris to Macdonogh, 28 February 1917.

66   TNA WO 158/22: OAD324, Haig to Robertson, 3 March 1917.

67   Beach, *Haig's Intelligence*, pp.230-31.

68   For the February 1916 situation, see Jim Beach, 'British Intelligence and the Battle of Verdun' in Spencer Jones (ed.), *At All Costs: The British Army on the Western Front, 1916* (Solihull: Helion, 2018), p.104.

On 28 February Charteris told Macdonogh that 'I cannot get rid of the feeling that there is something brewing on the pretty big scale in Flanders. It is difficult to lay one's hand on anything definite, but I feel sure it is the danger point for us.'[69] The same day Cuffe wrote to Charteris outlining his assessment of the enemy's intentions.[70] He began by noting the 'variety' of places and dates for a German offensive within 'the information received.' Cuffe pointed out that:

> The obvious conclusion is that all these rumours have been purposely started by the enemy. Another point of interest is the frequency with which Ypres or Flanders is coupled with Alsace, Belfort or some other point in the southern French area as possible points for the German attack. This may possibly be the object to separate as far as possible the British and French reserves.

He went on to suggest that the Germans would seek to 'regain the initiative' with an attack out of the Hindenburg Line. Cuffe's logic was that recent and substantive improvements to the railway system would allow them 'to concentrate large masses of troops in the Cambrai area in a much shorter period than was possible in 1916.' Arguing that 'the lessons of the war have shown that an actual break through is impossible', he suggested that it would be very difficult for the Allies to maintain their logistics – presumably in an attritional battle – within the devastated zone that had been created by the German retreat. It is interesting to note here the prominence of infrastructure development as predictive indicator. Presumably derived from air photography, this was a source that would grow in significance over the coming year.[71]

But, as Charteris' comment to Macdonogh indicates, there is no evidence of Cuffe's assessment gaining traction with his superiors. Indeed, the following day Cuffe appears to have been tasked with estimating when environmental conditions would allow for the putative German attack against Ypres.[72] The paper for the War Cabinet, which was probably being drafted the same day, contains no elements of Cuffe's assessment. Indeed it contains very little in the way of intelligence evidence beyond the following statement:

> We have no certain indications as yet on this point: but there can be no doubt that an attack between Lille and the sea presents many and great attractions to the enemy, and rumours and warnings of an intended German offensive, on a great scale, in that area, continue to reach [GHQ].[73]

---

69   TNA WO 158/898: Charteris to Macdonogh, 28 February 1917.
70   IWM, Cuffe Papers: Cuffe to Charteris, 'German Intentions', 28 February 1917.
71   Beach, *Haig's Intelligence*, pp.152-54.
72   IWM, Cuffe Papers. He estimated mid-April, due to the normal frequency of heavy rain early in that month: 'Earliest date when the Germans can make an offensive on the Ypres Salient', 1 March 1917.
73   TNA WO 158/22: OAD323, 'Review of present situation on the Western Front, with special reference to the German withdrawal on the Ancre', 2 March 1917.

Instead, the document contains numerous generalisations regarding German methods of war and speculative deductions about their most likely courses of action. Additionally, on the following day when it was sent to London, Charteris changed his position dramatically, writing to Macdonogh that 'I went most carefully to-day through all evidence with regard to Ypres, and there is very little positive evidence to support any theory of an attack in that direction.'[74] This perhaps suggests Charteris was privately signalling his dissent from the paper's evidential basis? Overall, the unavoidable conclusions from this episode are two-fold. First, the officer at GHQ who was responsible for assessing German intentions from intelligence evidence appears to have had no impact upon the process. Second, the paper for the War Cabinet recycled a questionable picture of the enemy's plans to try and undermine the arrangements put in place by the Calais conference.[75] Indeed, the French liaison officer told his superiors that, in order to trigger a get-out clause in the agreement, GHQ was pretending to be concerned about the threat to the Channel ports so as to 'avoid having to comply with the demands of the French.'[76]

Arras

On 9 April the BEF launched a month-long offensive at Arras. Like other instances in 1917, previous examinations of the intelligence surrounding this attack have focused primarily upon German manpower and morale.[77] Cuffe's memoranda include three assessments from April; two written before the first infantry attack and another just before the second phase of the battle. Like their predecessors, they provide additional evidence that revises and enhances our understanding of GHQ's perceptions. In this case we see Cuffe pushing back against prevailing opinion within headquarters and then, rather curiously, advancing an odd hypothesis first floated by Macdonogh.

Towards the end of March, with preparations for the offensive well-advanced, GHQ's French liaison officer reported that unnamed 'British staff officers' were concerned that Germans might pull back before the blow fell.[78] A few days later he followed up with further details:

---

74   TNA WO 158/898: Charteris to Macdonogh, 2 March 1917.
75   For the prolongation of concerns about an attack at Ypres, see Beach, *Haig's Intelligence*, pp.231-32.
76   Vallières to Nivelle, 5 March 1917 in Greenhalgh (ed.), *Liaison*, pp.238-39. The content of the letter suggests very strongly that Vallières had seen the paper sent to the War Cabinet.
77   Beach, *Haig's Intelligence*, pp.232-38.
78   Vallières to Nivelle, 26 March 1917 in Greenhalgh (ed.), *Liaison*, p.245. For British preparations, see Cyril Falls, *Military Operations, France & Belgium, 1917*, Vol. 1 (London: HMSO, 1940), pp.171-200, 300-20.

I undertook an investigation amongst the most competent officers of the [intelligence & operations sections] and I noticed that *all* are persuaded that the Germans will retire, avoiding battle, to the east of their current positions [...] Yet they have no certain proof to support this hypothesis beyond the fires and explosions noted yesterday [...] They remain ignorant of the *date* on which the enemy will begin this retreat; but most of these officers believe that it will occur *before* the date chosen [for the attack, 8 April].[79]

Charteris' letters to Macdonogh during this period offer some indications of the rationale that underpinned this perception.[80] He wondered whether the Germans were 'trying to lure us on into open warfare', observing that 'these fires are precisely the same symptoms' that preceded the earlier withdrawal to the Hindenburg Line. Charteris also highlighted the existence of a new defensive position, the Drocourt–Quéant Line, which was four miles behind the German positions at Arras.[81] On 31 March Charteris told Macdonogh that a prisoner, captured by Third Army, had indicated a retirement to that position was intended.[82] Although Charteris was sceptical about this evidence, he concluded that the Germans would 'withdraw in the course of the next four or five days.' Third Army recorded that:

Evidence therefore points to no further withdrawal except under pressure. Whether this means the enemy will stand to fight on his present positions or will withdraw to the Drocourt–Quéant line destroying all communications as he does so is uncertain. Indications seem to favour the latter view.[83]

At this point, and presumably tasked by Charteris to investigate the conflicting evidence, Cuffe wrote up the first of his assessments.

His short memorandum began with a clear statement: 'The balance of the evidence at present at our disposal indicates, I think, that the Germans do not intend to withdraw from the Vimy Ridge till they are compelled to.'[84] It then listed seven pieces of information that underpinned this conclusion. Prominence was given to the Kaiser's recent 'congratulatory messages to his troops on the successful strategic withdrawal.' Cuffe argued that further withdrawals would damage the otherwise good morale of the German army. But his strongest thread, presumably derived from air photography, focused on German defences. Cuffe pointed out that work was continuing on forward positions and, significantly, these fresh lines had first appeared after the now-known point at which the German high command had decided to retreat to

79   Vallières to Nivelle, 29 March 1917 in Greenhalgh (ed.), *Liaison*, p.246.
80   TNA WO 158/898: Charteris to Macdonogh, 25, 29 March 1917.
81   Falls, *Military Operations 1917*, Vol. 1, p.176.
82   TNA WO 158/898: Charteris to Macdonogh, 31 March 1917.
83   TNA WO 157/150: Third Army fortnightly intelligence summary 16-31 March 1917.
84   IWM, Cuffe Papers: Cuffe to Charteris, 'Intentions of the enemy', 1 April 1917.

the Hindenburg Line. Therefore a withdrawal from the Arras positions cannot have been part of a greater, premeditated scheme. Second, he noted air reconnaissance showing that 'work on the Drocourt–Quéant Line is not far advanced.'[85] Finally, he pointed out that German possession of Vimy Ridge, north of Arras, allowed the location of BEF battery positions – presumably by flash-spotting – and that the new technology of sound-ranging could not, 'in the din of battle', provide an effective substitute.[86] Cuffe's conclusion was essentially correct. Although the Germans were aware of the imminent offensive, they were also confident in their capacity to withstand the assault.[87]

On 4 April the British began their bombardment, preceded by a large-scale gas attack.[88] The next day Cuffe's second Arras memorandum was written.[89] From its content, he seems to have been tasked with re-visiting the question of whether the Germans would withdraw. Cuffe began by noting captured documents that set out their process for conducting a withdrawal. He highlighted the fact that rear guards would attempt 'to conceal the withdrawal by making a display as if his trenches were strongly held [...] The artillery left behind were to increase rate of fire.' Furthermore, he observed that previously the Germans had carried out demolitions 'in the early stages of [their] retirement.' Cuffe then tested this template against the available evidence. He pointed out that the enemy was essentially inactive, and there was 'no artillery retaliation when [the] gas was let off.'[90] Although he conceded that 'a number of fires and explosions have been reported in the area [east] of Arras', he countered it with the absence of 'craters at any cross-roads or points of tactical importance.' But Cuffe's strongest point was that 'recent photographs show that the Drocourt–Quéant line is not yet completed. The new work [...] shows no dug-outs, and very little wire [...] and everything points to this line not being nearly ready for occupation.' His overall conclusion was that 'judging by [their] former tactics', the Germans were displaying false indicators of a withdrawal. This second assessment was successful in shifting Charteris' outlook to some extent. Although still 'doubtful' about what was happening, the next

---

85   In mid-March air photography had revealed that the line was 'not in an advanced state of construction. The trenches do not appear to be much more than a trace at present.' Just before Cuffe wrote the assessment, it was noted that in one sector the line did 'not appear [to be] strong and has only one row of wire.' TNA WO 157/18: GHQ intelligence summaries, 19, 31 March 1917.

86   For flash-spotting and sound-ranging developments, see Beach, *Haig's Intelligence*, pp.91-97.

87   Boff, *Haig's Enemy*, p.152.

88   Falls, *Military Operations 1917*, Vol. 1, p.185. For additional context on the gas attacks, see Donald Richter, *Chemical Soldiers: British Gas Warfare in World War I* (Lawrence, Kansas: University Press of Kansas, 1992), pp.177-79; Albert Palazzo, *Seeking Victory on the Western Front: The British Army & Chemical Warfare in World War I* (Lincoln, Nebraska: University of Nebraska Press, 2000), p.115.

89   IWM, Cuffe Papers: Cuffe to Charteris, 'Notes on the present situation', 5 April 1917.

90   'The gas discharge of [4 April] temporarily silenced the greater proportion of the German artillery.' Falls, *Military Operations 1917*, Vol. 1, p.199.

day he told Macdonogh that 'it seems to me quite clear that [the enemy] wants to go back to the Drocourt–Quéant Line, the only point being that that line is not yet fully finished, and he may have to try and hold on another week to improve it.'[91] This subtle change in expectation may have gained currency within GHQ. The French liaison officer reported that 'the British high command is afraid of falling into partly abandoned positions. This explains the caution used in engaging forces [...] and they foresee a series of successive operations, at short intervals, rather than a rapid exploitation.'[92]

The initial attacks at Arras were successful, most famously at Vimy Ridge, but over the following week the offensive slowed to a halt.[93] Haig therefore decided re-set his forces and, after postponements due to bad weather, the offensive was scheduled to resume on 23 April.[94] Two days before its resumption, Cuffe produced his third memorandum.[95] This one took a much broader view of the situation; assessing that the Germans would take no offensive action on any front and that 'the enemy is still

James Cuffe at Advanced GHQ, 1917.
(Charteris Papers Acc.633, Military
Intelligence Museum)

relying on submarine warfare and possible dissensions amongst the Allies to assist him in obtaining a favourable decision on the Western front.'[96] With regard to the BEF's 'successful offensive at Arras', Cuffe suggested this had 'upset the enemy's plans' and,

91   TNA WO 158/898: Charteris to Macdonogh, 6 April 1917.
92   Vallières to Nivelle, 6 April 1917 in Greenhalgh (ed.), *Liaison*, p.248.
93   Boff, *Haig's Enemy*, pp.156-57.
94   Falls, *Military Operations 1917*, Vol. 1, p.379.
95   IWM, Cuffe Papers: Ia/32733, Cuffe to Charteris, 'Notes on the Present Situation',
     21 April 1917.
96   The Germans had resumed unrestricted U-boat warfare on 1 February 1917. For the
     disconnect between ends and means in this policy choice, see Holger Herwig, 'Total
     Rhetoric, Limited War: Germany's U-boat Campaign, 1917' in Roger Chickering & Stig
     Förster, *Great War, Total War: Combat and Mobilization on the Western Front, 1914-1918*
     (Cambridge: Cambridge University Press, 2000), pp.189-206.

drawing upon agents' reports, that it had prompted the Germans to develop fresh 'rear lines of defence' on a north-west to south-east axis, running along the French side of the Belgian border. In the north, he noted these also connected with the River Scheldt, which ran south-west to north-east.[97] Furthermore, Cuffe pointed out work on other rear defence lines in Flanders. His conclusion regarding the latter, presumably because of the aforementioned importance of the U-boat campaign, was that the Germans intended to 'hold the coast owing to the importance of Zeebrugge as a naval base.' And, overall, he suggested that an offensive 'north of Lille […] would interfere much more with the enemy's plans than any offensive west of the River Meuse.'

Given its content, this memorandum is rather odd compared to the earlier assessments focused more narrowly on the Arras offensive. However, its potential significance can be discerned from snippets within his superiors' correspondence. Back in early April, before the Battle of Arras had begun, Macdonogh floated the idea that:

> The Germans are going to remain on the defensive on the west, & that they are prepared to pivot on Lille & withdraw from French territory whenever a big attack has been mounted against them until they occupy a position covering the Lille – Valenciennes – Hirson – Mézières – Longwyon [railway]. I think they will hang on to Belgium & to the iron districts of French Lorraine until forced out of them by a military defeat.[98]

Therefore Cuffe's highlighting of potential defensive lines along the Franco-Belgian border aligned closely with Macdonogh's thesis of a withdrawal to roughly that position. Furthermore, on 23 April, as the British resumed their attack at Arras, Charteris suggested that the Germans 'are on a big movement of retirement, that they would like to get off with very little fighting, but that as we are pressing them they are turning at bay – practically an enormous rear-guard show from one end of the line to another.'[99] But, as they had already done further south against the French, the Germans held off the British attack and no large-scale withdrawal occurred.[100] However, these internal exchanges, now corroborated by Cuffe's memorandum, point towards an underlying assumption held by the intelligence staffs at both the War Office and GHQ; that, if pressed hard enough, the Germans might carry out another large-scale, strategic withdrawal. Such an evacuation of most French territory, but retention of Belgium would have created a diplomatically-complex situation.[101]

---

97   TNA WO 157/18 and 19: GHQ intelligence summaries, 27 March, 6 April 1917.
98   TNA WO 158/898: Macdonogh to Charteris, 5 April 1917.
99   TNA WO 158/898: Charteris to Macdonogh, 23 April 1917.
100   Boff, *Haig's Enemy*, pp.163-64. For the failure of the French offensive, see Robert Doughty, *Pyrrhic Victory: French Strategy and Operations in the Great War* (Cambridge: Belknap Harvard, 2005), pp.344-52.
101   For the German desire to retain political and economic control of Belgium and their nurturing of Flemish separatism, see Martin Kitchen, *The Silent Dictatorship: The Politics*

From this angle, Haig's communications with London a week later can perhaps be seen in a new light. On 1 May, at the start of the decision-making process that resulted in the Third Ypres offensive, Haig submitted a paper to the War Cabinet. It argued that the Germans had been 'weakened appreciably' by recent operations; however, 'the situation is not yet ripe for the decisive blow.'[102] Haig repeated these arguments in his diary, but also advocated preparations for 'clearing the [Flanders] coast this summer.' He suggested that an offensive at Ypres would mean 'attacking the enemy on a front where he cannot refuse to fight.'[103] Political prestige and protection of the naval bases would be significant motives for a German defence of Flanders, although the U-boats could have been re-located to the German coast.[104] But also, as Cuffe's memorandum had indicated, GHQ may have also believed that British territorial gains in Flanders would, by outflanking the pivot point of Lille, undermine the German option of a withdrawal to a defensive line along the Franco-Belgian border. This perception – if it did gain currency – cannot have lasted beyond mid-July, when Cuffe reported that air photography had been unable to confirm the existence of these new defences.[105] He told Charteris that the error had been caused by agents and refugees exaggerating their observations and the wider context of German misinformation about the extent of their rearward defensive systems.

Overall, Cuffe's work during the Arras offensive seems to have pleased Charteris, with Macdonogh stating that he was 'very glad to hear such good accounts' of him.[106]

of the German High Command under Hindenburg and Ludendorff, 1916-1918 (London: Croom Helm, 1976), pp.95-98, 148-49; Alexander Watson, *Ring of Steel: Germany and Austria-Hungary at War, 1914-1918* (London: Allen Lane, 2014), pp.260, 462; Sophie De Schaepdrijver, *Belgium* <encyclopedia.1914-1918-online.net> (accessed 18 July 2018).

102 TNA WO 158/23: OAD428, 'The Present Situation and Future Plans', 1 May 1917.

103 NLS, Haig Papers, Acc.3155: Diary, 1 May 1917. For Haig's enthusiasm for an offensive at Ypres, and previously-prepared plans, see James Edmonds, *Military Operations France and Belgium 1917*, Vol. 2 (London: HMSO, 1948), pp.1-6, 11-21; David French, 'Who Knew What and When? The French Army Mutinies and the British Decision to launch the Third Battle of Ypres' in Lawrence Freedman, Paul Hayes & Robert O'Neill (eds.), *War, Strategy and International Politics* (Oxford: Clarendon Press, 1992), pp.140-41; David French, *The Strategy of the Lloyd George Coalition, 1916-1918* (Oxford: Clarendon Press, 1995), pp.94-5; Robin Prior & Trevor Wilson, *Passchendaele: The Untold Story* (New Haven, Connecticut: Yale University Press, 1996), pp.32-33; Ian Beckett, 'Operational Command: The Plans and the Conduct of Battle' in Peter Liddle (ed.), *Passchendaele in Perspective: The Third Battle of Ypres* (London: Leo Cooper, 1997), pp.103-04; Nick Lloyd, *Passchendaele: The Lost Victory of World War I* (New York: Basic, 2017), pp.37-45.

104 Boff, *Haig's Enemy*, p.168. For the maritime dimension, see Paul Halpern, *A Naval History of World War I* (Annapolis: Naval Institute Press, 1994), pp.350-51; Andrew Wiest, *Passchendaele and the Royal Navy* (Westport, Connecticut: Greenwood, 1995), pp.65-90; Geoffrey Till, 'Passchendaele; The Maritime Dimension' in Liddle (ed.), *Passchendaele*, pp.73-87.

105 IWM, Cuffe Papers: Cuffe to Charteris, 'German defensive back lines', 19 July 1917. For deep air reconnaissance, see Beach, *Haig's Intelligence*, pp.144-46.

106 TNA WO 158/898: Macdonogh to Charteris, 30 April 1917.

Later, in July, Macdonogh tried to get Cuffe moved to the War Office. But Charteris resisted on the grounds that 'he is doing excellent work here and it would cause a very great dislocation if he were removed [...] I think also that he himself, apart from the wish to work under you, would really prefer to see the thing out in France.' Macdonogh therefore rescinded his request.[107]

Third Ypres

Cuffe's assessments related to the Third Ypres offensive can be broken into two groups; three memoranda written ahead of the first infantry assault and four written in August. The former were focused primarily on the strength of the German defences, while the latter were produced during a series of mostly unsuccessful attacks carried out by Fifth Army.[108] The August ones also include arguments for switching the axis of the offensive. An absence of similar documents from the later stages of the offensive is unfortunate.[109] Presumably Cuffe continued to make assessments in September and October but, for whatever reason, did not preserve them.

On 7 June Second Army captured the Messines Ridge, south of Ypres. Although some sporadic fighting continued over the following week, the success of the operation was apparent immediately.[110] Four days after the attack, Cuffe analysed German defensive positions in the southern part of the Ypres Salient.[111] He drew attention to the withdrawal of heavy guns and, from air photography, the underdevelopment of their rearward lines. Cuffe concluded that a German withdrawal was 'improbable [...] as he has no line to go back to.' Although this raises an interesting counter-factual question about what might have happened if Second Army had pressed its temporary advantage after Messines, there appears to be no linkage between Cuffe's musings and the machinations of GHQ.[112]

Cuffe's second memorandum is much weightier.[113] It was written in late June during a period which, in hindsight, was pivotal in the planning for the opening assault of the

107 TNA WO 158/898: Charteris to Macdonogh, 28 July 1917, Macdonogh to Charteris, 2 August 1917.
108 Prior & Wilson, *Passchendaele*, pp.104-10; J.P. Harris, *Douglas Haig and the First World War* (Cambridge: Cambridge University Press, 2008), p.369.
109 The only surviving memoranda from this period discusses the coastal sector. IWM, Cuffe Papers: 'Valley of the Handzaeme Canal and the possibilities of an attack in the Dixmude area', 9 October 1917, Ia/40660, BGI to Fifth Army (Intelligence), 9 October 1917.
110 Edmonds, *Military Operations 1917*, Vol. 2, pp.85-87.
111 IWM, Cuffe Papers: Ia/35275, Cuffe to Charteris, 'The sector between the Ypres–Menin Road and the River Lys', 11 June 1917.
112 For German perspective on Messines and Crown Prince Rupprecht's assessment that the British failed consistently to exploit their successes, see Boff, *Haig's Enemy*, pp.169-72.
113 IWM, Cuffe Papers: Ia/36146, Cuffe to Charteris, 'Notes on an offensive in the Ypres area', 28 June 1917.

First section of James Cuffe's intelligence assessment, 28 June 1917.

Third Ypres offensive. A core question within this process was whether the Fifth Army should attempt to break through the German defences or conduct a series of more modest, bite-and-hold attacks. This has been a constant focus for the historiography and discussion has centred upon the distances between the British front-line and the attackers' objectives.[114] Fifth Army had set a sequence of lines that culminated three miles into the German positions. This

Ia./36146.

SECRET

B. G. I.

NOTES ON AN OFFENSIVE IN THE YPRES AREA.

Distances (in the area under consideration).

(a) From the German front line to the STÜTZPUNKT Line — INVERNESS COPSE - SOUTH STATION Building — is 1,500ˣ roughly.

(b) From the front line to the LANGEMARCK - GHELUVELT Line varies from 2,600ˣ to 3,000ˣ.

Conditions of Defence Lines.

From recent photographs:

(a) The STÜTZPUNKT Line shows signs of recent bombardments and in several places the wire does not appear to be very strong.

(b) The GHELUVELT - LANGEMARCK Line in this area is for the most part strongly wired, but is not a strong line. At present it would best be described as a series of strong posts behind a wide belt of wire.

Although the actual defences in front of POLYGONE Wood do not appear very strong, it would probably prove a formidable obstacle to the attack.

prompted Brigadier-General John Davidson, the chief operations officer at GHQ, to question them in a memorandum that advocated advances of no more than 3,000 yards at a time. However, after further discussion, Fifth Army's plan was allowed to stand, with Haig giving mixed messages about whether he sought a breakthrough or not. This policy debate is rather opaque and Cuffe's memorandum offers some fresh insight.

114 Edmonds, *Military Operations 1917*, Vol. 2, pp.126–31, 436-39; John Davidson, *Haig: Master of the Field* (London: Peter Nevill, 1953), p.33; Tim Travers, *How the War was Won: Command and Technology in the British Army on the Western Front, 1917-1918* (London: Routledge, 1992), pp.14-15; Prior & Wilson, *Passchendaele*, pp.76–77; Andrew Wiest, 'Haig, Gough and Passchendaele' in Gary Sheffield (ed.), *Leadership and Command: The Anglo-American Military Experience since 1861* (London: Brassey's, 1997), pp.83-86; Andrew Green, *Writing the Great War: Sir James Edmonds and the Official Histories, 1915–1948* (London: Frank Cass, 2003), pp.168-73; Gary Sheffield & Helen McCartney, 'Hubert Gough' in Ian Beckett & Steven Corvi (eds.), *Haig's Generals* (Barnsley: Pen & Sword, 2006), p.86; Andy Simpson, *Directing Operations: British Corps Command on the Western Front, 1914-18* (Stroud: Spellmount, 2006), pp.93-94; Harris, *Douglas Haig*, pp.357-60; Paul Harris & Sanders Marble, 'The 'Step-by-Step' Approach: British Military Thought and Operational Method on the Western Front, 1915–1917', *War in History* 15:1 (2008), p.39; Gary Sheffield, *The Chief: Douglas Haig and the British Army* (London: Aurum, 2011), pp.227-28; Jim Beach, 'Issued by the General Staff: Doctrine Writing at British GHQ, 1917-1918', *War in History*, 19:4 (2012), pp.474-82; Lloyd, *Passchendaele*, pp.75-79.

Cuffe began by summarising the distances between the British front and German defensive lines. He noted that their first substantive position was 1,500 yards away, and a second, the 'Gheluvelt–Langemarck Line', was at a depth of between 2,600 and 3,000 yards. He assessed the latter as being 'for the most part strongly wired, but it is not a strong line. At present it would best be described as a series of strong posts behind a belt of wire.' He also highlighted the defensive potential of Polygon Wood. Cuffe then surveyed artillery positions, suggesting that while only a third of the German guns were east of the Gheluvelt–Langemarck Line, 'they have acquired a certain amount of practice in withdrawing batteries.' After noting a number of unoccupied battery positions in the rear, Cuffe argued that:

> There is no question as to the beneficial effect on the moral[e] of troops of an easy objective. On the other hand, the effect on the enemy's moral[e] of the lost of from five to ten batteries must not be lost sight of. If the frontage of the objective admits an advance of 3,000 [yards], does not form too pronounced a salient, and provides for good defensive flanks, the advantages of including the Gheluvelt–Langemarck Line in the first day's objective seems to outweigh the disadvantages of increased length of communications.

Davidson's memorandum contained a paragraph on morale that advocated shallow objectives because 'there is nothing [British] troops themselves dislike so much as great depth in the attack.'[115] Cuffe's first comment therefore indicates he had seen Davidson's paper or, at the very least, was aware of its contents. But he had countered Davidson's morale argument by suggesting that the potential capture of German guns should be factored in. Cuffe's concluding point was that:

> The enemy has no organized line in rear of the Gheluvelt–Langemarck Line. Work on the Staden–Zonnebeke Line is being actively pushed forward, but the line is far from completion. Therefore, the fresh [German] divisions brought up to oppose our advance, or to carry out a counterattack, would find themselves not only deprived of a portion of their artillery, but without any prepared defensive position. A slower methodical advance would give the enemy time to withdraw his guns east of the Staden–Zonnebeke Line, and to a great extent eliminate the factor of surprise.

In summary, although his analysis did not explicitly advocate objectives beyond the 3,000-yard maximum suggested by Davidson, the memorandum does indicate that the GHQ intelligence staff put their weight behind Fifth Army's more ambitious conceptualisation of the attack. It is difficult to argue that Cuffe's memorandum was decisive given that, on the day it was written, Haig was already meeting with his army

---

115 Edmonds, *Military Operations 1917*, Vol. 2, p.438.

commanders to discuss the issue.[116] That said, Charteris had briefed Haig earlier that day, and, assuming the BGI was aware of his subordinate's work, the picture painted by Cuffe would not have compelled a more cautious perspective.[117] His analysis had indicated that if the British were able to pierce the Gheluvelt–Langemarck Line, they would then encounter much weaker defences. But, given the infantry attack was still a month away, the Germans would, of course, have some time to rectify this shortcoming.[118]

Cuffe's next assessment was a brief one and was written a week into the fortnight-long bombardment that preceded the first infantry attack of 31 July.[119] Drawing upon evidence derived from prisoners and air photographs, he summarised the damage caused by British shelling and improvements made to German defences, particularly additional wiring and farms having 'been made into centres of resistance.' Noting that the Gheluvelt–Langemarck Line was 'still far from completion' and 'not strong', Cuffe assessed the 'main line of [German] resistance' would be at a depth of 1,500 yards.[120] This assessment, along with contemporaneous reporting from the Fifth Army's intelligence staffs, indicates some understanding of German defensive intentions and congruence between their views and those of GHQ.[121] Similarly, the latter's intelligence summaries also contain overt references to the German shift to using shell holes rather than trench lines for infantry positions, as well as the observation that the configuration of units at Ypres conformed to their new defensive doctrine.[122]

In August, while Fifth Army pressed repeatedly against the German defences with limited gains, Cuffe wrote another four memoranda. They have a recurring theme; the potential gains that could be accrued by shifting the focus of the offensive so as to outflank, from the south, the German position on the Gheluvelt Plateau and Passchendaele Ridge. The first, which was sent to Charteris a week after the first infantry attack, began by stressing that the BEF only had a six-week window to prosecute meaningful operations in Flanders.[123] This was based on the logic that fighting

---

116   Davidson, *Haig*, pp.31-32; Peter Simkins, 'Herbert Plumer' in Beckett & Corvi (eds.), *Haig's Generals*, p.154.
117   NLS, Haig Papers, Acc.3155: Diary, 28 June 1917.
118   For German defensive preparations, see Boff, *Haig's Enemy*, p.173.
119   IWM, Cuffe Papers: Ia/37422, 'Probable intentions of the enemy in the event of a British attack in the Boesinghe – Hooge sector', 24 July 1917.
120   IWM, Cuffe Papers: Position of Stützpunkt Line given previously in Ia/36146, Cuffe to Charteris, 'Notes on an offensive in the Ypres area', 28 June 1917.
121   TNA WO 157/211 and 212: Fifth Army intelligence summaries, 30 June, 7, 12, 20, 27 July 1917.
122   TNA WO 157/21 and 22: GHQ intelligence summaries, 16 June, 8 July 1917; Beach, *Haig's Intelligence*, p.247. For the development of German defensive tactics, see Boff, *Haig's Enemy*, pp.146-47, 166-67; Tony Cowan, 'The Introduction of New German Defensive Tactics in 1916–1917', *British Journal for Military History*, 5:2 (2019), pp.81-99.
123   IWM, Cuffe Papers: Cuffe to Charteris, 'The importance of Zandvoorde and the present military situation on the Western Front', 7 August 1917.

would cease on the Eastern Front at the beginning of October and this would provide the Germans with an opportunity to shift resources to the west. Dismissing any suggestion of the enemy making a voluntary withdrawal, Cuffe pointed out that:

> The enemy is carrying out in Flanders similar tactics to [… the Battle of the] Somme. He has constructed lines at regular intervals and well sited, which will enable him to withdraw his guns to safety when forced back, and besides gives him the selection of each battlefield.

His suggestion, therefore, was for the British to stand defensively on the positions they held on the Gheluvelt Plateau and, from Second Army's front in the south, push south-east to capture the village of Zandvoorde. This, Cuffe anticipated, would force a withdrawal of German forces in this southern sector.

A week later, Fifth Army launched the attack that captured Langemarck in the north but made little headway against the German positions on the Gheluvelt Plateau. Just before that operation Cuffe appears to have been tasked with critiquing a Fifth Army assessment of likely German reactions to the attack. As well as noting a good pool of divisions ready for counter-attack, he repeated his earlier point that the Germans were imitating their 1916 methods by 'narrow[ing] the front of our offensive by the construction of a series of defensive lines in rear, in which he can maintain [his] reserve divisions.'[124] On 18 August, two days after the Battle of Langemarck, Cuffe submitted another memorandum to Charteris to 'repeat my suggestion […] regarding the advisability of switching' the axis of the offensive.[125] Arguing that the Germans would be expecting a repeat of earlier attacks, he observed that:

> One of the lessons learnt in this war is that the value of the offensive varies at least inversely with the length of its duration. It is almost questionable whether, after the element of surprise has been eliminated […] the advantage does not favour the defensive. By the construction of carefully sited rear lines of defence the defender in a way regains what might be called the initiative of the defence. To continue the advance, the capture of each line necessitates a fresh artillery preparation, and the infantry encounter must take place on the battle-field selected by the defender.

Cuffe's remedy, therefore, was an initial 'advance in a south-easterly direction.' This, he argued, would be more promising, in part, because German defences in this sector were not configured to meet this sort of attack. Then, having pushed forward

---

124 IWM, Cuffe Papers: Cuffe to Charteris, 'Notes on the 'Probable moves of enemy troops to meet our operations' as foreseen by Fifth Army', 15 August 1917.
125 IWM, Cuffe Papers: Cuffe to Charteris, 'Notes on the present situation and the advisability of a change of objective', 18 August 1917.

successfully in the south, the British would 'force the enemy to withdraw south of the River Lys, [and] place us in a position to threaten' German defences upon the Passchendaele Ridge.

Cuffe's arguments for shifting the focus of British operations were followed by further setbacks for Fifth Army. On 24 August these prompted Haig to give Second Army primary responsibility for the offensive.[126] The following day Cuffe produced a detailed assessment of the terrain in the Zandvoorde area.[127] Unlike his earlier August pieces, which were memoranda addressed to Charteris, this document had an I(a) file reference number which may suggest a broader circulation. It is also clear, from the diary of Neill Malcolm, Fifth Army's chief of staff, that GHQ wished to include Zandvoorde within the next attack but this was not embraced by Herbert Plumer, Second Army's commander.[128] Therefore when they submitted their plans any attack on this sector was to be postponed because the 'state of the ground' west of Zandvoorde would hinder any attack.[129] So, although Cuffe's lobbying seems to have got his ideas on the planning table, their execution remains an intriguing what-if.

German Offensives

During the winter of 1917-18 it could be argued that Cuffe was the most important intelligence officer in the British army. With the BEF standing on the defensive, accurate predictions of their enemy's intentions became a must-have rather than a nice-to-have.[130] For the period between October 1917 and May 1918, eleven of Cuffe's assessments have survived, six of which pre-date the opening of the German offensives. Their focus varies, with some surveying the enemy's strategic intentions, while others analyse the threat to specific parts of the British line. Taken together, they provide a significant additional layer of evidence regarding what the BEF thought would happen. And, more importantly, they were written by the man with responsibility for addressing that very question.

Cuffe's first musings on German strategy came at the end of October.[131] In a short and fairly speculative piece, he pondered the possibility of their forces being used

---

126 Edmonds, *Military Operations 1917*, Vol. 2, p.206; Harris, *Douglas Haig*, p.371; Sheffield, *The Chief*, pp.235-36; Lloyd, *Passchendaele*, pp.144-45, 156.
127 IWM, Cuffe Papers: Ia/38796, 'Report on the country affecting the extension of our offensive southwards so as to include the capture of Zandvoorde', 25 August 1917.
128 Beckett, 'Plans', p.109. Many thanks to Ian Beckett for confirmation of the diary entries' exact phrasing.
129 Edmonds, *Military Operations 1917*, Vol. 2, pp.237-38.
130 For the planning and execution of German operations in this period, see David Zabecki, *The German 1918 Offensives: A Case Study in the Operational Level of War* (London: Routledge, 2006), 82-216; Boff, *Haig's Enemy*, pp.201-28.
131 IWM, Cuffe Papers: Cuffe to Charteris, 'Notes on the present situation and German intentions for the 1918 campaign', 31 October 1917.

in the Mediterranean or Middle East but argued that 'forc[ing] a decision on the Western Front' was the most probable course of action. At this stage, he suggested the Germans would attack the French because they were perceived as the weaker ally.[132] Cuffe re-visited the question at the beginning of December.[133] This memorandum was lengthier and gives greater insight into his methods and perceptions. First, Cuffe was dismissive of 'rumours', presumably derived from agent reporting, which he noted were 'very prolific [...] as usual.' He therefore focused upon 'actual indications on the British front of German intentions.' But, in reviewing evidence from artillery and wireless activity, plus defensive works, he was unable to point to anything specific. He therefore surveyed the 'principal factors affecting the German 1918 campaign' and, proceeding from an assumption that the Germans could move eight divisions per month from the east, he reiterated an earlier judgement that the enemy would attack the French, probably in Champagne, in March. A fortnight later, these conclusions with regard to divisional transfers and timing of the 'enemy's big blow' were included in Charteris' briefings to Haig.[134]

The next surviving memoranda are a cluster of four, all dating from late February.[135] By this stage, Cox had taken over as BGI and the GHQ intelligence staff had refined their expectations. In short, the offensive was still expected in March and the main threat to the British front was thought to be against Third Army's frontage southwards from Arras, plus the northern part of Fifth Army's.[136] One of Cuffe's memoranda, dated 24 February, unpacks some of the evidence which may have led to these conclusions.[137] North of Arras, although an increase in artillery strength had been observed, German prisoner statements and the 'state of the ground' in Flanders indicated no imminent threat. But to the south:

> Wireless evidence seems to point to a possible offensive between the [River] Scarpe and Bellicourt [...] and this assumption is confirmed by the captured document [...] ordering photographic reconnaissance of the [Cambrai] front. There are also indications that a new German army may have appeared north of Cambrai.

132 Ludendorff actually viewed the British as 'less formidable'. Boff, *Haig's Enemy*, p.203.
133 IWM, Cuffe Papers: Ia/42756, 'Notes on German Intentions', 6 December 1917.
134 NLS, Haig Papers, Acc.3155: Diary, 19, 20 December 1917; Beach, *Haig's Intelligence*, p.275.
135 The St Quentin memorandum is undated but was filed within these papers. Its remit seems similar to the Cambrai one, so they can be seen as a pair. Their sequencing was presumably established by Cuffe himself, but subsequent, accidental shuffling cannot be discounted.
136 Beach, *Haig's Intelligence*, pp.278-79.
137 IWM, Cuffe Papers: Untitled memorandum, 24 February 1918.

Given that 'captured document' was also used as a cover for signals intelligence, this might suggest that intercepted wireless messages were a more significant indicator of German intent in this period than has been previously thought.[138] Furthermore, prisoners reported 'that it is common talk that an offensive would take place in the Cambrai area early in March.' The other documents adopted a narrower focus; one looked at the threat to the Cambrai sector and another critiqued a paper submitted by Fifth Army.[139] The third explored something that became a significant blind-spot for BEF intelligence; the danger of a German attack against that army's frontage south of St Quentin.[140] But, containing mostly terrain analysis, it downplayed the danger because of the 'marshy ground.'

With regard to Cambrai, inferring from the aforementioned air photography target area, Cuffe suggested a narrow, and fairly shallow, push towards Bapaume, with the River Sensée and the Canal du Nord providing the Germans with defensible flanks. However, the short critique of the Fifth Army paper is more significant. Perhaps connected with the limited attack he envisaged toward Bapaume, Cuffe posited German operations with 'limited objectives [… which] must be considered probable on the British front.' He also set out two significant assumptions:

> The lessons of this war tend to prove that a break-through on the Western front is almost impossible. With the present elaborate trench system, the sectors not attacked can be weakly held, or be taken over by divisions withdrawn from the fight. Therefore as long as our railway communications are intact, there will be nothing to interfere with the 'roulement' of the Allied divisions.

Cuffe went on to point out that 'a German attack at the point of junction', presumably the one between the British and French armies, 'would not imperil the Allied lateral communications' because they ran at a depth of thirty miles behind the front. Although the Fifth Army paper has not survived, a similar phrase to one quoted by Cuffe does appear in a mid-January document issued by that headquarters.[141] In it, they suggested:

138 Beach, *Haig's Intelligence*, pp.162-67. However, it is also possible that the document came from a downed aircraft.
139 IWM, Cuffe Papers: 'Probability of hostile offensive in the Cambrai sector', 22 February 1918, 'Criticism of "Note on a possible German offensive on the Western front in relation to Fifth Army"', 25 February 1918.
140 IWM, Cuffe Papers: 'Note on the possibility of a German attack south of St Quentin', [n.d]. For the blind-spot, the paucity of contemporaneous evidence related to Fifth Army intelligence, and the subsequent doctoring of documents by their commander, see Beach, *Haig's Intelligence*, pp.281-85.
141 Service historique de la défense (Département terre), 17N 361: SG675/13, Fifth Army to Corps, 12 January 1918.

A great offensive [...] with Amiens as its objective, the German left resting on the Somme. The capture of Amiens, apart from its moral effect, would give the enemy a favourable base for continuing his operations, either northwestwards against the British, or southwards against the French, and would probably be conceived with the ultimate idea of driving a wedge between the Allied Armies.

Cuffe gave this notion short shrift, pointing out that Amiens was another ten miles on from the lines of communication and that if the Germans did reach there, the war would be lost anyway:

There would be no necessity for them to strike '[north-west] or towards Paris'; the attendant dislocation of the Allied railway system, and the cutting off of the Paris coal supply, with its consequent effect on production of war material, would necessitate the cessation of hostilities.

But he found it 'difficult to imagine the Germans risking such an extension of their communications before the armies of the Allies have been defeated in the field.'[142] In many respects Cuffe was anticipating the crisis that would actually unfold in late March but was a prisoner of an assumption that the fighting of 1918 would be similar to the slow-moving, attritional struggles of earlier years. And in being unable to make a mental leap, he was not alone at GHQ.[143]

Cuffe's next assessment, written a week after the first German attack on 21 March, suggests he had adjusted swiftly to the new realities.[144] In reviewing the enemy's options after their impressive territorial gains, he posited three possible axes of advance; westwards to capture Amiens, south-west to threaten Paris and engage the French, or north-west towards Doullens. Cuffe considered the latter to be the most dangerous because, having lost lateral rail communications through Montdidier, it would be more difficult for their allies to reinforce the BEF. He also felt it was the 'safest' choice because it 'only exposes one flank', whereas attempting to capture Amiens would over-extend the German lines of communication and expose both flanks. Operationally, and with benefit of hindsight, Cuffe's memorandum was wholly

---

142   In addition to Amiens, Cuffe also highlighted the fact that Hazebrouck was fourteen miles from the German front. For the argument that these railway hubs constituted the 'key vulnerabilities in the British logistic system', see Zabecki, *German 1918 Offensives*, pp.315-16. See also, Christopher Phillips, *Civilian Specialists at War: Britain's Transport Experts and the First World War* (London: University of London Press, 2020), pp.345-50.

143   Beach, *Haig's Intelligence*, pp.287-88.

144   IWM, Cuffe Papers: Ia/47797, 'Note on the present situation', 28 March 1918. Although it discusses the possibility of an attack 'north of the [River] Scarpe', the memorandum makes no mention of the German attack on Arras, so it was presumably written late on 27 March, then typed and disseminated the following day.

correct. But just before it was written, and flushed with the scale of his army's early successes, Ludendorff made the decision to go after Amiens.[145]

There is then a three-week gap before we see Cuffe again committing his thoughts to a surviving paper. Given the fluidity of the situation, this seems rather odd. The key developments during this period were an abortive German attack against Arras (28 March) and a far more successful one on the Lys front (9 April).[146] It is also clear that, with regard to the latter, Cuffe misjudged its seriousness. Two days after the opening of that offensive, the American liaison officer at GHQ recorded 'Col[onel] Cuffe's opinion that this present attack is not an attempt to break through but is still of the opinion that the next attempt to break through will be astride the [River] Scarpe to the north and south of Arras.'[147] The implication, therefore, is that Cuffe chose not to preserve his incorrect assessments from that period. However, his last three memoranda do offer a useful perspective on GHQ's thinking at the moment when the Germans decided to switch their focus, temporarily in the first instance, towards the French.[148]

On 19 April Cuffe reviewed the deployment of German divisions and drawing upon a retrospective analysis of their dispositions at the time of the first offensive, concluded they still had sufficient reserves 'to carry out a formidable blow on a two-army front.' He envisaged that they would continue to press in Flanders, probably with an accompanying attack against British Third Army around Arras.[149] In early May Cuffe reviewed multiple indications from prisoner statements and, from their phrasing, air photography. He pointed to danger in Flanders and, again, against Third Army.[150] Over the following fortnight, the American liaison officer provided a running commentary of GHQ's assessments, citing 'high intelligence authority' and 'some of the best intelligence officers.'[151] Although not named in these reports, Cuffe's role made him a prime candidate to have been the source of this information. Taken together with his final memorandum, which reviewed offensive indicators across the whole British front, a consistent picture emerges of a definite threat to Arras.[152] However, on 28 May the Germans actually attacked the French on the Aisne.

145 Zabecki, *German 1918 Offensives*, pp.152-57, 167-73; Boff, *Haig's Enemy*, p.215.
146 Zabecki, *German 1918 Offensives*, pp.155, 174-205; Boff, *Haig's Enemy*, pp.216, 220-25.
147 NARA, RG120/135/5815 and 5816: Quekemeyer to Nolan, 11 April 1918; Beach, *Haig's Intelligence*, 293-94. Cuffe had been promoted to Brevet Lieutenant-Colonel in January.
148 Zabecki, *German 1918 Offensives*, pp.206-12; Boff, *Haig's Enemy*, pp.225-28.
149 IWM, Cuffe Papers: Ia/48680, 'Note on the present situation', 19 April 1918.
150 IWM, Cuffe Papers: Ia/49421, 'Notes on the present situation', 9 May 1918.
151 NARA, RG120/135/5815 and 5816: Bacon to Nolan, 16, 20, 25, 26 May 1918.
152 IWM, Cuffe Papers: 'Note on the enemy's offensive preparations', 25 May 1918.

Conclusion

Cuffe's memoranda are important jigsaw pieces that can be inserted, often very neatly, into parts of the historiography that have recently lacked fresh evidence. On one level, his perspective is fairly parochial, in that he helps to redress the balance of attention given to different parts of GHQ's intelligence structure, with the story related here indicating that the I(a) Intentions sub-section was much more influential than had previously been imagined. Cuffe's analytical techniques and his consistent indication of sources also tells us that although evidence from traditional, human sources (prisoners, agents) was integrated into his work, it was cutting-edge technological sources (wireless interception, air photography) that provided the critical inputs. Similarly, the episodes that have been unpacked show that GHQ's operations section, and other army-level headquarters, reserved their right to interpret the intelligence picture in the ways they saw fit. Even if, as was the case in late February 1917, that was based on unsubstantiated speculation and a wider political agenda. The absence of German tactical doctrine analyses within Cuffe's output is also curious. The implication being that the operations staff, with responsibility for British doctrine, took the lead on interpreting any German developments and assessing their implications.[153]

Looking at the individual battles, Cuffe's performance as an analyst was mixed. Before Arras he provided nuanced, evidence-based assessments that guessed correctly that the Germans would stand and fight. And in so doing, he swam against the tide at GHQ. This success was followed by endorsement of Macdonogh's quixotic thesis of another German strategic withdrawal to the Franco-Belgian border, but this suggestion fell apart when corroboration was sought from air reconnaissance. One therefore wonders whether Cuffe's professional and familial fealty to Macdonogh overcame his previously cautious instincts? Third Ypres was the most important period of Cuffe's time at GHQ. Although we cannot prove him having a direct influence upon the key decision to seek a breakthrough, it is clear that the picture he painted – of weak rear defences – could have, indirectly, encouraged GHQ to allow Fifth Army to set deep objectives. However, once the offensive had stalled, to his great credit, Cuffe sought to find a weakness within the German defensive configuration. We shall, of course, never know if his idea of changing the axis of advance to capture Zandvoorde would have led to greater success, but it is a clear instance of intelligence analysis affecting GHQ's choices.

In the first half of 1918, Cuffe's work would have gained much greater prominence within the headquarters due to the new strategic situation. Here we see considerable rigour in his assessments of where the German blow would fall but, along with everyone else, he failed to think beyond the attritional battle template that had been laid down in previous years. That said, in February, Cuffe did point out correctly that if the Germans pushed forward too far without defeating the Allied armies, they

---

153   For additional context, see Beach, 'Issued by the General Staff', pp.473-88.

would over-extend their communications and expose their flanks. He was also very prescient in stressing the vital importance of retaining control of the railway junctions at Amiens and Hazebrouck and, after their initial success, of the danger of the Germans pushing north-west towards Doullens. In April and May his predictions were less successful and there is, perhaps, a sense of him playing it safe by stressing an ongoing threat to Arras?

Taking the long view of his First World War, James Cuffe had begun the conflict in a rather exciting role that involved secret agents and special missions. But, like so many others, his work became office-bound as the scale and complexity of the intelligence world grew beyond anything that might have been imagined in 1914. By late 1916 he had become a key cog in this vast machinery. We are therefore fortunate that, for whatever reason, he chose to preserve at least part of the record of his involvement in seismic military events. Cuffe's memoranda may not have transformed our understanding of the BEF's operations in 1917 and early 1918, but they have provided fresh insight and useful nuance.

6

'Discredit on Those Concerned'
The German Trench Raid Near Loos, 5 January 1917 and the
'Duty of Lying'

Michael LoCicero

Truth-loving Persians do not dwell upon
The trivial skirmish fought near Marathon[1]

During the extraordinarily harsh winter of 1916-17 a minor German trench raid occurred near Loos. This daring and meticulously planned enterprise, the origins, execution, and consequences thereof comprising most of this chapter, achieved complete surprise and resulted in enemy penetration as far as the village defences. Having overcome almost all resistance, the raiders managed to seize a large haul of prisoners much to the embarrassment of the British high command. Erroneously determined to have been ad hoc in nature and composition,[2] a subsequent court of enquiry determined that the unfortunate battalion involved was, despite some extenuating circumstances, primarily to blame for the reverse and the battalion commander and infantry brigadier concerned were sent home. Deemed a 'cleverly planned and courageously executed operation', the veteran German regiment involved proposed a subsequent 'multi-attack' operation whereby similar infiltration tactics would be employed on a large scale as a means of achieving a local breakthrough. Rejected by the high command, the scheme was indicative of the defensive/offensive strategic, operational, and tactical discussions occurring at all *Westheer* command levels during this time.[3] Moreover,

---

1   Robert Graves, 'The Persian Version' (1945).
2   See TNA WO 95/168: Hostile Raid Against Our Trenches M.1.B.6.y – H.31.C.5.2 on Morning of 5th January [1917] File, First Army General Staff War Diary and F.C. Hitchcock, *"Stand To": A Diary of the Trenches 1915-1918* (Uckfield: Naval & Military Press reprint of 1937 edition), p.231.
3   Ernst Schmidt Oswald, *Das Altenburger Regiment (8. Thüringisches Infanterie-Regiment Nr. 153) im Weltkriege* (Berlin: Oldenburg, 1927), pp.254, 257. Special thanks to Dr

certain aspects of the shelved plan anticipated the celebrated 'storm troop tactics' employed during the great German offensives of 1918.[4]

Duly reported by the British and German press at the time, the seemingly positive spin placed on the event by the official BEF communique was waspishly recollected in a brief passage by prominent journalist, author, and staff officer C.E. Montague in his culturally significant *Disenchantment* (1922):

C.E. Montague (seated left) as GHQ press censor.
(O. Elton, *C.E. Montague: A Memoir*)

Most of the fibs that we used in the war were mere nothings, and clumsy at that. When the enemy raided our trenches in the dead winter season, took fifty prisoners, and did as he liked for a while – so much as he liked that a court of enquiry was afterwards held and a colonel deprived of his command – we said in our official *communiqué* that a hostile raiding party had 'entered our trenches' but was 'speedily driven out, leaving a number of dead.'[5]

Derek Clayton for translation assistance. I should also like to thank the following friends and colleagues for their whole-hearted support and guidance with the research for this chapter: Andrew Arnold; Professor Stephen Badsey; Chris Baker; Stephen Barker; Dr Jim Beach; Professor John Bourne; Dr Tony Cowan; Lieutenant-Colonel Gareth Davies (Ret.); Alexander A. Falbo-Wild; Guy Gormley; Dr Peter Hodgkinson; Paul Humphriss; Dr Spencer Jones; Michael Mills; Professor Gary Sheffield; Professor Peter Simkins; Steve Smith; Jim Smithson; Dr Michael Taylor; Rob Thompson and Dr Christopher Wyatt.

4   Storm troop tactics as applied to overcome the position warfare deadlock during 1914-18, concerned deployment of small groups of specially trained assault infantry armed with innovative weapons and equipment to achieve break-ins or breakthroughs of the enemy trench system. This would be accomplished by careful prior reconnaissance to identify weak points followed by limited artillery preparation and employment of a firepower and shock action combination by infiltrating *Stosstrupp* sub-units. See Bruce Gudmundsson, *Stormtroop Tactics: Innovation in the German Army 1914-1918* (New York: Praeger, 1989); Ralf Raths, *Vom Massensturm zur Stoßtrupptaktik: Die deutsche Landkriegtaktik im Spiegel von Dienstvorschriften und Publizistik 1906-1918* (Freiburg: Rombach, 2009) and Stephen Bull, *Stosstrupptaktik. German Assault Troops of the First World War: The First Stormtroopers* (Stroud: Spellmount, 2014).

5   C.E. Montague, *Disenchantment* (London: Evergreen Books, [1922] 1940), p.130. Despite his age, Montague (1867-1928) volunteered for active service. Embarking for France

As noted later in this chapter, Montague's shared perception of how the raid was first reported to the public was rooted in Victorian/Edwardian class distinctions. Furthermore, his expressed disdain for a perceived cynical and lying wartime propaganda machine in what was the first English prose work to strongly criticize the way Great Britain waged the First World War, left no room for personal reflection upon what part of the population this propaganda was aimed at or the relatively benign official boilerplate content that more often than not conveyed essential truths about the numerous trench raiding operations conducted by both sides on the Western Front.

Loos Salient

It was on that deadlocked front extending from the Swiss frontier to the English Channel that the wet weather which first appeared during October 1916, gave way to bitter frosts succeeded by snowfalls in January 1917.[6] The Somme campaign having been terminated the previous November, stark conditions experienced on and in the devastated Picardy uplands and valleys defied the descriptive capabilities of the British official historian:

> The state of the ground of the Somme battlefield during December was such as was probably never surpassed on the Western Front – hardly even in the Ypres Salient. And if any part of that front were worse than another, it was the valley of the Ancre. Here, in a wilderness of mud, holding water-logged trenches or shell hole posts, accessible only by night, the infantry abode in conditions which might be likened to those of earthworms rather than humankind. Our vocabulary is not adapted to describe such an existence, because it is outside experience for which words are normally required.[7]

Approximately 75 kilometres to the north, a consequence of the autumn 1915 push by British First Army, was the dreaded Loos Salient extending from Fosse Cité de Loos to Cambrin inclusive on a front of approximately 6.5 kilometres.[8] Under the aegis of I

---

in late 1915, he was subsequently commissioned and employed as a GHQ intelligence officer responsible for press censorship. Acting in this capacity, Montague also conducted distinguished visitors such as David Lloyd George, Georges Clemenceau, J.M. Barrie, George Bernard Shaw, and H.G. Wells about the British sector of the front as an armed escort. See Oliver Elton, *C.E. Montague: A Memoir* (London: Chatto & Windus, 1929).

6   C.E.W. Bean, *The Australian Imperial Force in France 1917*, Vol. IV (Sydney: Angus & Robertson, 1943), p.21.

7   Cyril Falls, *Military Operations France and Belgium 1917*, Vol. I (London: Macmillan, 1940), p.65.

8   TNA WO 95/2190: 24th Division General Staff War Diary.

Corps (GOC Lieutenant-General C.A. Anderson),[9] the eastward protruding salient was held by its subordinate 6th (Regular), 21st (New Army) and 24th (New Army) divisions:

> Loos ... was part of the rich Lens coalfield, innumerable rows of dwellings laid out by set-square, each house with the same window over the same doorway, unending similarity, dull and utilitarian emblems of modern industrialism. The landscape was also desecrated by many pitheads and the long black crassiers – huge mammoths of waste substances often of great height and sometimes nearly a mile long.[10]

Finding himself situated in the bleak Hauts-de-France *mise en scène* often associated with Émile Zola's uncompromisingly grim and realistic novel *Germinal* (1885), battalion medical officer Captain George Pirie was unimpressed with his new surroundings: 'This is a wretched looking country, flat and nothing but dirty coal mining villages with crowds of huge slag heaps and chimney stacks.' In contrast to this negative reaction, men hailing from Lancashire, Yorkshire and other coal-producing regions found the French black country to be a source of comfort that reminded them of home.[11] Surveying the forward area landscape, Captain F.C. Hitchcock of 2nd Leinster Regiment observed:

> One could liken the Loos Salient to half a plate, with the enemy trenches looking down into ours from its outer edge. Hulluch on the extreme left, then the shambles of Loos and the Tower Bridge, now reduced to a wreckage of twisted girders and the Loos Crassier shooting out towards the Boche lines ... The trenches then curved down to Hill 70, coming to an abrupt turn at the famous Triangle to straighten themselves out towards the Double Crassier ... which started at the top of Hill 70 to run for some 1000 yards through the German and British lines – on the extreme right and neck of the salient.[12]

---

9   Lieutenant-General Sir Charles Alexander Anderson (1857-1940). Commissioned Royal Horse Artillery 1876; Jowaki-Afridi Expedition 1877; Second Afghan War 1878; Burma 1885; Northwest Frontier 1897; Bazaar Valley Expedition and Mohmand Field Force 1908; GOC South China 1910-13; GOC 7th (Meerut) Division 1913-15; GOC Indian Corps September-December 1915: GOC XVII Corps 1915-16; GOC XI Corps August-September 1916; GOC I Corps September 1916-February 1917. Note: Officers are described by the rank they held during winter 1916-17.

10   Frederick Ernest Whitton CMG, *The History of the Prince of Wales's Leinster Regiment (Royal Canadians) Part II: The Great War and the Disbandment of the Regiment* (Aldershot: Gale & Polden, 1924), pp.341-42.

11   Michael Lucas (ed.), *Frontline Medic. Gallipoli, Somme, Ypres: The Diary of Captain George Pirie RAMC 1914-17* (Solihull: Helion & Co., 2014), p.149 and Rob Thompson chapter correspondence, 4 January 2021.

12   Hitchcock, "*Stand To*", p.200.

Whilst tours of be duty there hardly compared with the myriad horrors of the Somme front, the salient was notorious for its almost constant sniping, trench mortar, mining and raiding activities.[13] Conditions in this 'putrid boneyard' and 'giant memorial' to the British high command's failed 1915 offensive and subsequent local fighting during spring 1916 had transformed the area into a labyrinth of shell holes, smaller salients, re-entrants, fortified mine craters and trenches, the latter often revetted with corpses amongst the rotting sandbag emplacements.[14] As Major James Jack observed during summer 1916, 'Part of our lines are in the famous Hohenzollern Redoubt [;] it is a disgusting sector with the parapets full of bodies, debris and rats.'[15] Corpses in various states also abounded in no man's land, Captain Hitchcock encountering 'a rusty Webley revolver lying beside a skeleton (probably that of one of our officers killed in the great Loos offensive of September 1915)' during an impromptu strengthening of barbed wire defences under cover of an early morning mist.[16] On another occasion, a three-man night patrol stealthily making its way through the frozen and desolate wasteland between the opposing lines encountered '5 or 6 bodies; no clothing was found and it was at first thought that they were our own troops as they were lying on our side of the mound. Further investigation discovered a leg with a jack-boot on the foot, which was German.'[17]

Deployment to a sector, as described in an interwar memoir, reeking of 'an atmosphere of putrification, amid the continual nerve-wracking strain of "Minenwerfers", of raid and counter-raid, mine and counter-mine', came as a rude shock to 2nd Leinster Regiment.[18] Occurring in the immediate aftermath of a gruelling Somme experience and active trench warfare at Vimy Ridge, the battalion was assigned to a particularly nasty subsector due north of the Double Crassier which dominated the area:

> During the battalion's stay in the Loos sector, these crassiers were a constant source of annoyance. They provided outlets for all kinds of Boche 'hate'. They were under-tunnelled, so that trench mortars could be pushed out on rails to fire and return under cover, and there were numerous and perfectly concealed machine-gun and snipers' nests along the sides.[19]

---

13   For example, casualties sustained in the Loos Salient by 24th Division during January 1917 amounted to 503 officers and men killed, wounded, and missing. See TNA WO 95/2194: 'Appendix C. 24th DIVISION. CASUALTIES FOR THE MONTH OF JANUARY 1917', 24th Division Adjutant and Quartermaster General War Diary.
14   Sidney Rogerson, *Twelve Days* (London: Arthur Barker, 1933), p.5.
15   John Terraine (ed.) *General Jack's Diary 1914-1918: The Trench Diary of Brigadier-General J.L. Jack DSO* (London: Eyre & Spottiswoode, 1964), p.156.
16   Hitchcock, *"Stand To"*, p.257.
17   'INTELLIGENCE SUMMARY, 73rd Infantry Brigade. From 12 noon 1/12/16 to 12 noon 2/12/1916' reproduced in Hitchcock, p.341.
18   Rogerson, *Twelve Days*, p.7.
19   Hitchcock, *"Stand To"*, pp.204-05.

Subsequent encounters with deadly *Minenwerfers*, 'aerial darts' routinely discharged from *Granatenwerfer* light trench mortars,[20] rifle grenades and other death-dealing devices inherent to position warfare, inflicted more Leinster commissioned officer fatalities than those sustained during the 'Big Push' of the

Loos miner cottages, 'dull and utilitarian emblems of modern industrialism.' (Private collection)

previous summer. According to Hitchcock, 'Officers had simply poured through the battalion since July 1916. This period covered the actions on the Somme, but our death-rate was never so high amongst officers in proportion to other ranks killed as it was for two months at Loos.'[21] As a component infantry battalion of 24th Division[22] (GOC Major-General J.E. Capper),[23] the 2nd Leinster Regiment marched to the Loos sector during its parent formation's relief of 40th (Bantam) Division in late October 1916.[24]

---

20   For *Granatenwerfer* Model F 1916 particulars, see Major James E. Hicks, *German Weapons – Uniforms – Insignia 1841-1918* (La Canada, California: James E. Hicks & Sons, 1963), pp.88-96.

21   Hitchcock was referring to the seven 2nd Leinster Regiment officers killed between 5 December 1916 and 3 February 1917. Three of the seven perished as a result of *Granatenwerfer* projectiles. Hitchcock, *"Stand To"*, pp.199-227, 258.

22   The 24th Division was raised in September 1914. Dispatched to France in late August 1915, it went on to suffer heavy losses during the Battle of Loos and was engaged on the Somme during August and September 1916. Its component infantry by January 1917 was as follows: 17th Brigade – 8th Buffs; 1st Royal Fusiliers; 12th Royal Fusiliers; 3rd Rifle Brigade, 72nd Brigade – 8th Queens Regiment; 9th East Surrey Regiment; 8th Royal West Kent Regiment; 1st North Staffordshire Regiment, 73rd Brigade – 9th Royal Sussex Regiment; 7th Northamptonshire Regiment; 13th Middlesex Regiment; 2nd Leinster Regiment. See Major A.F. Becke, *Order of Battle of Divisions, Part 3A – New Army Divisions (9-26)* (London: HMSO, 1945), pp.127-33.

23   Major-General Sir John Edward Capper (1861-1955). Commissioned Royal Engineers 1880; India and Burma 1880-97; Tirah Expedition 1897-98; South Africa 1899-1902; Commandant Balloon School and Factory 1906-09; Commandant Balloon School 1909-10; Commandant School of Military Engineering and Royal Engineer Depot 1911-14; Deputy Inspector General of Communications September 1914-May 1915; III Corps Chief Engineer May-October 1915; GOC 24th Division October 1915-May 1917.

24   Originally formed with undersized recruits, the 40th Division disembarked in France during early June 1916. On examining a sector log book previously filled out by a battalion

GHQ's declared general
policy for the 'British Armies
in France' throughout the
forthcoming winter was as
follows:

Granatenwerfer Model F 1916.

a) To improve our defences
    ...
b) To train troops
c) To harass the enemy by
    active   patrolling   and
    raids,[25] gas discharges
    and   concentrated
    bombardments.
d) To continue the present
    [Somme] offensive to a limited degree on the front of the Fourth and Fifth
    Armies ... [26]

Considering (a), First Army (GOC General Sir H.S. Horne)[27] headquarters at
Château Philomel, Lillers duly compiled a report. It observed that the 'general state
of the defences' was satisfactory. 'Owing, however, to recent bad weather and heavy
trench mortar fire, combined with a shortage of labour, portions of the defence lines
have fallen temporarily into disrepair. Whatever damage has occurred owing to the

officer from this formation, Hitchcock noted the following amusing passage: 'Wiring:
during the tour my company have placed out a number of knife rests in the vicinity of
Russian Sap, but they have always disappeared immediately, and I am forced to believe
the enemy takes them away.' Thus the inexperienced Bantam company commander was
unaware that *Chevaux de Frise* obstacles had to be secured in place with stakes and wire.
See Hitchcock, *"Stand To"*, p.209.

25   Raiding as practiced by the BEF during this period, had four objectives: 'I. To gain
     prisoners and, therefore, to obtain information by identification. II. To inflict loss and
     lower the opponent's morale, a form of terrorism, and to kill as many of the enemy as
     possible, before beating a retreat; also to destroy his dugouts and mine-shafts. III. To get
     junior regimental officers accustomed to handling men in the open and give them scope
     for using their initiative. IV. To blood all ranks into the offensive spirit and quicken their
     wits after months of stagnant trench warfare.' Hitchcock, *"Stand To"*, p.229. See also
     Stephen Badsey, 'The Raid on Narrow Trench' in Stephen Badsey, *The British Army in
     Battle and its Image 1914-18* (London: Bloomsbury, 2009), pp.137-38.
26   TNA WO 158/187: [GHQ] 'OAD 211', 17 November 1916, First Army Operations File.
27   General Sir Henry Horne (1861-1929). Commissioned Royal Artillery 1880; South
     Africa 1899-1902; Inspector of Artillery 1912; BGRA I Corps 1914; GOC 2nd Division
     1915; GOC XV Corps April 1916; GOC First Army September 1916. First Army
     consisted of three corps (Canadian Corps, I Corps and IX Corps on the right, centre and
     left respectively) in January 1917.

above causes will be made good as rapidly as available labour permits.'[28] Specifically, with regard to the Calonne – La Bassée Road area Loos village and vicinity inclusive, the document also observed:

Front and Support Trenches

These trenches, owing to recent bad weather and shortage of labour, are in poor condition and the dugout accommodation for the garrison is inadequate. Sandbag revetments built during the summer have been collapsing and the clearing of trenches employs most of the labour available.[29]

Machine-gun emplacements in the frontline are nearly all open but are combined with deep dugouts for guns and detachments.

Wire entanglements of this system have been considerably strengthened but cannot be considered as forming satisfactory obstacles until the work which is being carried out on them is completed.

Reserve Line

The condition of this line is, on the whole, good …[30]

Clearly, I Corps had much to do in order to strengthen and secure its front and support positions. Concurrently, with regard to (c), the Loos Salient would become a hotbed of raid and counter-raid activity engendered by somewhat questionable competition amongst corps/divisions. As Captain Hitchcock later observed:

Information [obtained from raid enterprises] regarding the identification of the opposite troops, their strength, how they held their line, and the exact locations of trench mortars, machine-guns, and their emplacements, and the position of sapheads in order to anticipate mining activity, was always being called for by corps and army headquarters. Rivalry between formations is excellent, but when overdone, can be most dangerous. The rivalry that existed in France in 1916 and 1917 over raiding operations had, indeed, been carried to an extreme limit.[31]

Indeed, trench raids – as instituted in a centralized and systematic policy throughout the BEF from early 1916 – were in such demand by I Corps and attached division headquarters that one 21st Division brigade staff officer anticipated orders by setting to work 'from the moment we returned to the trenches to examine every possibility,

---

28 TNA WO 158/187: 'First Army No. GS.474', 22 November 1916, First Army Operations File.

29 The subsequent freezes and thaws of January wreaked havoc on sector defences What was deemed marginal in late November 1916 was almost untenable by early 1917.

30 TNA WO 158/187: 'First Army No. GS.474', 22 November 1916, First Army Operations File.

31 Hitchcock, "*Stand To*", p.30.

and was able to suggest in broad outline a scheme, which was already under prepara-tion when the orders came and which was eventually carried out.'[32] Major-General Capper being an ardent proponent of raiding on his divisional front, battalion level response to such orders was, more often than not, unreflective when contemplating the perceived necessity for raids and unenthusiastic about the planning and execution thereof. Thus the hapless OC 1st Royal Fusiliers lamented to his battalion medical officer Captain Wilson[33] about an unwelcome I Corps arranged show: 'It's damned silly I know, but we've got to do it Doc. And what can I do?'[34] Enemy reaction to this calculated aggression was predictable, the Germans responding in kind, although they raided less frequently than their British and Dominion opponents.[35]

Patrouillenangriff and the '153er Methode'

For the German Army in France and Belgium, the winter of 1916-17 was a period of strategic, operational, and tactical re-evaluation. Concurrent with the failure of peace negotiations; impending re-introduction of unrestricted U-boat warfare (1 February 1917) and the 'ruthless mobilization' of civil society as a whole, the *Westheer* prepared to face further Anglo-French offensives in what had become a titanic matériel and attritional struggle that 'could only end when one side or the other toppled into the abyss.' To this end, an extensive revision of the current defensive doctrine resulted in the 'Collected Instructions for Trench Warfare'. The cornerstone of this institutional-wide disseminated document was Part 8, 'Principles for Command of the Defensive Battle in Trench Warfare' (1 December 1916). Its primary focus was the develop-ment and organisation of the defence-in-depth as a means of repelling large-scale enemy attacks that were certain to follow during the coming spring. Adherence to

---

32   See Tony Ashworth, *Trench Warfare 1914-1918: The Live and Let Live System* (London: Pan Books, 2000), p.177; Robert Blake (ed.), *The Private Papers of Douglas Haig 1914-1919* (London: Eyre & Spottiswoode, 1952), p. 125 and D.V. Kelly, *39 Months With the "Tigers", 1915-18* (London: Ernest Benn, 1930), p.55.

33   Captain Charles McMoran Wilson MC (1882-1977). Controversial personal physician to Winston Churchill 1940-65; knighted 1938; Baron Moran of Manton 1943. See Richard Lovell, *Churchill's Doctor: A Biography of Lord Moran* (London: Royal Society of Medicine Services Ltd, 1994).

34   Lord Moran, *The Anatomy of Courage* (London: Constable, 1945), p.142. For rationale and imposition of raids by BEF high command authorities and subordinate responses, see Ashworth, *Trench Warfare 1914-1918*, Chapter 8, and Kenneth Radley, *On the Dangerous Edge: British and Canadian Trench Raiding on the Western Front 1914-1918* (Warwick: Helion & Co., 2018), chapters 4, 5 and 17.

35   For example, 17 British and Dominion raids occurred on First Army front during January 1917, as opposed to nine German raids, patrols, and probes over the same period. See TNA WO 157/71: First Army weekly summaries of operations January 1917, First Army Intelligence File and Andrew B. Godefroy, 'A Lesson in Success: The Calonne Trench Raid, 17 January 1917', *Canadian Military History*, Vol. 8, No. 2, Spring 1999.

Infanterie Regiment Nr. 153 pre-war centenary commemorative postcard.

Infanterie Regiment Nr. 153 squad, December 1916. (Private collection)

the defensive did not mean that the western armies should adopt a passive stance. Rather, they were 'to remain active and not allow the enemy the initiative', the general expectation being to 'keep the other side off-balance by aggressive raids, patrols and local attacks.'[36] For the veteran *Altenburger Infanterie Regiment Nr. 153* (*IR 153*), this strident call for raid, patrol and local assault enterprises was in keeping with standard unit practice.[37]

A pre-war Regular army unit with antecedents dating back to 1807, *IR 153* was one of three infantry regiments attached to *8th Infanterie Division* (*Generalmajor* A. Hamann)[38] With recruiting grounds in Prussian Saxony and Thüringen, this formation – subsequently rated a 'first-class division' by enemy intelligence estimates – had been serving on the *Westfront* since August 1914.[39] Assigned to *IV Corps* (*Generalleutnant* F. Sixt von Armin) of *Sixth Army* (*Generaloberst* L. Freiherr von Falkenhausen), *8th*

36   Philip Zelikow, *The Road Less Travelled: The Secret Battle to End the Great War, 1916-1917* (New York: PublicAffairs, 2021); David Stevenson, *1917: War, Peace & Revolution* (Oxford: Oxford University Press, 2017), Chapter 1 and Jonathan Boff, *Haig's Enemy: Crown Prince Rupprecht and Germany's War on the Western Front* (Oxford: Oxford University Press, 2018), pp.144-46. See also Captain G.C. Wynne, *If Germany Attacks: The Battle in Depth in the West* (Brighton: Tom Donovan unexpurgated edition, 2008); Timothy T. Lupfer, *The Dynamics of Doctrine: The Changes in German Tactical Doctrine During the First World War* (Leavenworth, Kansas: US Army Command and Staff College, 1981); Robert T. Foley, 'The Other Side of the Wire: The German Army in 1917' in Peter Dennis & Jeffery Grey (eds.), *1917: Tactics, Training and Technology* (Commonwealth of Australia: Australian History Military Publications, 2007), pp.155-78 and Christian Stachlebeck, 'Strategy "in a microcosm": Processes of Tactical Learning in a WWI German Infantry Division', *Journal of Military and Strategic Studies*, Vol. 13, Issue 4, Summer 2011.
37   *Patrouille, Patrouillenangriff, Patrouillengang* and *Patrouillenunternehmung* were contemporary German terms for raid. 'In many instances there was little to distinguish early "raids" from rather more innocuous-sounding "patrols", and both had begun before the end of 1914.' See General Staff, *Vocabulary of German Military Terms and Abbreviations (Second Edition)* (Nashville, Tennessee: Battery Press 1995 reprint of 1918 edition), p.11 and Bull, *Stosstrupptaktik*, p.88.
38   *Generalmajor* Arthur Hamann (1857-1933). Commander *8th Division* from 14 September 1916. *IR 153* was commanded by *Oberst* Koenemann from 1 January 1915.
39   The *8th Division* had participated in the invasion of Belgium, Battle of the Marne and fighting south of Arras during 1914. Responsible for the Monchy sector during the early months of 1915, it opposed French assaults near Souchez in June before assignment to *Sixth Army* reserve. With the opening of the Loos offensive on 25 September, the division was subsequently deployed to launch a series of costly counter-attacks. Established in the Loos sector until early July 1916, the division went on to sustain heavy casualties on the front Poziéres–Longueval–Delville Wood. Relieved and dispatched north, a short period of line holding near Arras was followed by a return to the Somme in mid-September where hard fighting in the Thiepval–Courcelette area inflicted further heavy losses. Returning to the Loos sector, *8th Division* had been in situ there from 1 October. Its component infantry regiments as of January 1917 were *IR 72, IR 93* and *IR 153*. See Intelligence Section of the General Staff, American Expeditionary Forces, *Histories of Two Hundred and Fifty-One Divisions of the German Army Which Participated in the War 1914-1918* (London: London Stamp Exchange, 1989 reprint of 1920 edition), pp.158-59.

Division was responsible for the front Loos village to Cité St Elie from early October 1916. Taking up positions in the southern part of this line directly opposite and due north of Loos, *IR 153* continued to tactically apply with favourable results what its post-war regimental history referred to as the '153er methode' of raiding. Given that any supporting artillery fire would alert the targeted hostile garrison, the regiment determined that 'the enemy should be taken by surprise in his trenches – that means dispensing with the artillery bombardment altogether.' The 'logical development' of this idea had its roots in a modest raid near Loos on the night of 2/3 May 1916 when a *Leutnant* Hoyers led a small party against an 'inadequately and poorly defended' section of 16th (Irish) Division's line.[40] Dubiously deemed a 'partial success' by the regimental historian, the following tactical lesson was nonetheless learned:

> [T]he attack should go in on a wider front and positions in two places captured, so that nothing between them can escape.[41]

Application of this principle soon bore fruit when a succeeding operation against the 16th Division trenches on the night of 8/9 May resulted in three prisoners with no loss to the raiding party.[42] As the regimental history retrospectively observed:

> Apart from this tangible return, the morale success must be regarded as equally important. We had been in the enemy trench system twice with no losses at all! That gave us a feeling of confidence that meant a great deal for future operations.[43]

Following its first Somme tour, *IR 153* was deployed to the relatively quiet Arras front where orders for a large-scale raid in the Roclincourt sector were issued by superior headquarters. Operational fulfillment would be 'considerably more difficult in this sector, as the enemy wire was in very good condition and would have to be destroyed before any surprise break-in was possible.'[44] Launched on the night of 30/31 August, its planning process was a basic template for application of the 153er Methode. First, relevant aerial photographs were carefully studied to identify 'two flanking locations' for a potential break-in. Second, 'the chosen locations were closely reconnoitered by particularly intelligent and cold-blooded individuals who, having been carefully

40 Oswald, *Das Altenburger Regiment (8. Thüringisches Infanterie-Regiment Nr. 153) im Weltkriege*, p.248 and TNA WO 95/1955: 16th Division General Staff War Diary.
41 Oswald, p.248.
42 Ibid and TNA WO 95/1955: 16th Division General Staff War Diary.
43 Oswald., p.249
44 Ibid., p.249. 'In positional warfare in which "break-in" could often be successfully achieved, but "breakthrough" and "breakout" were condemned to failure, the trench raid was the ideal vehicle for practicing "break-in" tactics. It was one that both sides used.' Peter Hodgkinson, *A Complete Orchestra of War: A History of 6th Division on the Western Front 1914-1919* (Warwick: Helion & Co., 2019), p.171.

instructed by the high command, and who were already earmarked to take part in the operation, examined the condition of the enemy wire and other obstacles, its layout and possible approach routes.' Third, designated raid leaders were selected, strengths and assignments for each individual 'patrol' section determined whilst the attached pioneer company was employed to excavate 'a narrow and only knee-deep representation of the trench system in the back area ... which replicated exactly alignments and distances in the area designated for the break-in.' Thereafter, the chosen raiders practiced under the watchful eyes of instructors and representatives of the high command, the 'break-in and deeper penetrations, down to the smallest detail: slowly at first, and then at full speed initially in daylight, and then in the pitch-black, until the whole operation, every twist and turn of the trench system, was familiar to every man.'[45]

Other pre-raid preparations included substituting the tell-tale artillery bombardment with trench mortars tasked with eliminating barbed wire obstacles opposite pre-determined points of entry without revealing anything to the enemy:

> This was ensured by their carefully calculated and controlled fall of shot. Equally important was the fact that it had to appear unobtrusive/ inconspicuous, as they disguised the relatively few decisive shots amidst days of supposedly erratic shooting along various sectors of the enemy front as retaliatory fire. It was then the task of the machine-gunners, firing apparently nervous and irregular, yet frequent bursts, to force the enemy to suspend any nightly attempts to repair breaks in the wire, and to employ their working parties further back repairing damage done during the day by our heavy artillery fire. This intermittent MG fire had a second purpose: to feign nervousness and fear on our part, so that the enemy would not suspect an attack from the German trenches, but moreover to mask any noise made by our scouting patrols in No Man's Land who were tight up against the enemy lines.[46]

Meanwhile, keen night patrols prowled no man's land to complete essential preparations and familiarised themselves with forthcoming raid particulars; 'others behind the scenes were, with reference to weather readings, determining the day and hour of the operation. Most suitable were the early hours of the morning, say between 2 and 4 o'clock, when everything had quietened down in the enemy trenches, when many were actually asleep, and the alertness of the tired look-outs was waning.' The time just prior to or just after moonrise or when the sky was low were other viable alternatives.[47]

For their part, formations/units on *IR 153*'s flanks were requested to avoid any noticeable activity on the night of the raid and 'for several nights before that might alert or alarm our opponents.' The divisional pioneers were tasked with cutting narrow

45   Oswald, p.251.
46   Ibid., p.251.
47   Ibid., pp.252-53.

paths with oblique exits through the German wire entanglements, so that these avenues of approach remained unnoticed. Medical arrangements, although always provided for, 'were very rarely needed by our own men – more often than not they were only used for captured and wounded Englishmen.' Finally, just prior to Zero, two 'tape layers' were dispatched into no man's land to lay out white engineer tape as a means of delineating exact line of approach and assault direction. As an added precaution, the artillery were requested to immediately respond 'to any SOS signal on our part for a defensive barrage, but this scenario was never played out.' Carried out by two officers, 16 NCOs and 98 men, the final outcome of this painstakingly planned and organised operation was 14 prisoners, one Lewis Gun and one Stokes Mortar seized from 64th Brigade, 21st Division for the raiders' loss of one man mortally wounded and two men lightly wounded.[48] A second raid, following *8th Division's* autumn re-deployment to the Loos sector, was executed on the night of 23/24 October 1916. Seventeen prisoners and one Lewis Gun were obtained from 20th Middlesex, 121st Brigade, 40th Division at a cost of two men lightly wounded one of which returned to duty after cursory medical treatment.[49]

Neujahr 1917

The New Year found *IR 153* and the other regiments of *8th Division* in somewhat challenging sector occupation circumstances:

> The longer the war lasted, the more noticeable our manpower shortage and the enemy's numerical superiority became, and the more urgent the necessity for greater economy of forces for our high command. Only the threatened sectors of the front were allowed to have a proportionately narrow, strong and deeply-echeloned garrison, the so-called quiet sectors having to make do with the absolute bare essentials: and that was for the most part very little. As for which sectors of the front were 'threatened' and which were 'quiet', this could only be discerned with any certainty by knowing the strength of the enemy garrison: the only

48   Observed whilst crossing no man's land, the raiders were not bombarded by the British artillery until withdrawal with captives and booty. The 64th Brigade diarist confirmed the material loss. Casualties amounted to 10th KOYLI: six men killed; six men wounded and 11 men missing; 9th KOYLI: three men killed; four men wounded; 1st East Yorkshire Regiment: one man wounded and 15th Durham LI: one man wounded. See TNA WO 95/2159: 64th Brigade War Diary.

49   Oswald, *Das Altenburger Regiment (8. Thüringisches Infanterie-Regiment Nr. 153) im Weltkriege*, pp.251, 253-54. This raid occurred in the Puits 14 Bis subsector of which there is more below. 20th Middlesex casualties amounted to 4 men killed; 10 men wounded and 17 men missing. 'The alarm was never given until the Germans had left our trenches, so that no counter-stroke was organised.' See TNA WO 95/2613: 121st Brigade Headquarters War Diary and WO 95/2615: 20th Middlesex War Diary.

way that reasonably accurate conclusions could be drawn as to the intentions of the enemy high command was through observing any narrowing of enemy subsectors, any massing of large numbers of troops in restricted areas, and by recognising the quality (or lack of it) of any newly-arrived enemy formations.[50]

All of this was dependent on discerning which enemy formations/units were opposite. Already stretched thin in what was, as opposed to the Somme, an appraised quiet sector, the regiment was called upon to execute further raids which were 'for the most part very difficult tasks and therefore a real headache for the planners – and were demanded more and more frequently from on high.'[51] With operational antecedents in the offensive aspects of the recently introduced 'Principles for Command of the Defensive Battle in Trench Warfare', the local high command's specific desire to sabotage British dugouts and mineshafts and general expectation of 'live prisoners, weapons and other pieces of equipment, from which may be deduced the identity of the enemy garrison', *IR 153* received orders to execute a large-scale raid during the first week of January 1917.[52]

In the shadow of Loos Crassier, the targeted area was situated just beyond the eastern environs of Loos village. Exiting trenches on the western slope of Hill 70, an 'unremarkable' and 'barely discernible' height; 'yet it had sufficient elevation to overlook the landscape to the west', *IR 153*'s raiding force had to form-up in and traverse a gentle no man's land gradient of approximately 150 yards prior to entering the enemy frontline.[53] The consequent raid scheme embodied all of the hallmark 153er Methode organisation and details. More ambitious in scope than the Arras raid of the previous August, 202 men of *IR 153*[54] and *297th Pionier Mineur Kompanie* were tasked with breaching the British position at two designated entry points before penetrating as far as the enemy Support Line.[55] As a means of facilitating surprise, seven underground mines were to be detonated beneath the British frontline just prior to Zero:

---

50   Ibid., p.247.
51   Ibid., p.247. 'On high' likely refers to *Sixth Army*, *IV Corps* or *8th Division* headquarters.
52   Ibid., p.248.
53   Damien Finlayson, *Crumps and Camouflets: Australian Tunnelling Companies on the Western Front* (Newport, NSW: Big Sky Publications, 2010), p.142.
54   According to *IR 153* captives seized during the retribution raid on 26 January 1917 (see below), 'volunteers were always called on for fighting patrols, but that the men were told off for the ordinary reconnaissance patrols consisting of an NCO and 2 or 3 men. It was said that volunteers received better pay and food. A prisoner stated 120 men [sic] took part in a successful raid against our trenches at the beginning of January [5 January] and received 180 marks.' See TNA WO 157/71: 'SUPPLEMENT TO FIRST ARMY INTELLIGENCE SUMMARY – No. 748, Further examination of 16 unwounded prisoners of the 153rd Regiment, 8th Division captured E. of LOOS on 26th Jan. 1917', 29 January 1917, First Army Intelligence File.
55   Oswald, *Das Altenburger Regiment (8. Thüringisches Infanterie-Regiment Nr. 153) im Weltkriege*, Lehrskizze 24.

If the break-in into the enemy trenches was to go unnoticed, all of the men manning the enemy observation posts would need to be forced to keep their heads down for a short time. Studies had shown that it was psychologically probable that this could be done by detonating a mine: the day after – and this can be confirmed by personal observation of the place where the mortar shells habitually land – those in listening/observation posts, as soon as they hear the familiar noise of the shell approaching through the air, instantly abandoned the parapet and then remained under cover, not only until the whizzing projectile finally landed somewhere, but until the abundance of nice big rocks and lumps of chalk thrown up by the shell finally stopped raining down. A number of seconds would then pass by before the first look-outs would be back in position. Just as we ourselves would do when light mortar fire came down, but the English more so for in-coming heavy German shells, and especially when they came to expect that the first shell would be quickly followed by a second or a third – something that would not happen prior to an actual attack. This generously sufficient time lag between the detonation, which served as the signal for the commencement of the attack, and the first tentative re-emergence of the look-outs on the English parapet was enough for the storm troops to cover the 30-50 metres to the enemy trenches, the similarly-sounding impacts of the falling earth and stone debris disguising their running footsteps. The impact point of the 'signal shell' had to be chosen carefully, so as to have the most effective psychological effect on those manning the target sector, but also not to endanger our waiting storm troops.[56]

Therefore, the sequential amalgam of heavy *Minenwerfer*[57] fire on 'signal impact' points – the designated tocsin to assault – and shallow mine detonations was employed as a clever ploy to prevent otherwise alert enemy sentries from detecting *IR 153* raiders bearing down on them. Further to this, light *Minenwerfers*[58] were tasked with placing

---

56   Ibid., pp.250-52. British expectations with regard to enemy raids were articulated in 24th Division's defence scheme as follows: 'Raid with a view of causing damage, but with no intention on the part of the enemy of staying in our trenches … This form of raid will usually be a surprise. If the enemy gets into our trenches it will be difficult to prevent him from doing a certain amount of damage, and probably getting out again … The enemy has recently adopted a plan of slow systematic bombardment with trench mortars for perhaps two days, followed by a short intense bombardment followed immediately by a raid with a barrage isolating the assaulted area. His object is to kill men in the dugouts and to take prisoners.' See TNA WO 95/2190: 'Report on Raids' appendix, December 1916 and '24th DIVN DEFENCE SCHEME, COPY NO. 17. DEC 16, Part III., IV. ACTION TO BE TAKEN IN CASE OF ATTACK', 24th Division General Staff War Diary.

57   With an effective range of 585 yards, 25cm *Schwerer Minenwerfers* were employed for the signal impact bombardment.

58   With an effective range of 328 yards, 7.58 cm *Minenwerfers* were employed for the box barrage bombardment.

a 'box barrage' on five key trench junctions immediately after Zero in order to isolate the raid area from enemy troops attempting to intervene from the flanks and rear.[59]

Available moonlight, always useful once a break-in had been affected, would also facilitate 'orientation without our people being visible as they approached above ground.' In addition, the 'time just before or just after moonrise, or when it was low in the sky, were viable. Actually, it was not always that easy to find a suitable time, particularly when urgency came into the equation: on 5 January 1917, the very bright moonlight forced us into moving zero hour for the attack to the extraordinarily late time of six o'clock in the morning' German time or 5:00 a.m. British time.[60]

Winter Relief

Accustomed to routine inter-unit reliefs throughout the autumn and winter, the battalions of 17th Brigade (GOC Brigadier-General J.W.V. Carroll)[61] again exchanged places NE of Loos Crassier – centre brigade front – on the evening of 3 January.[62] Thus under a hostile artillery and trench mortar bombardment during which fire by the latter was implemented as per *IR 153's* ploy to force enemy sentries to take cover prior to the

---

59   Oswald, *Das Altenburger Regiment (8. Thüringisches Infanterie-Regiment Nr. 153) im Weltkriege*, Lehrskizze 24.

60   Ibid., p.253. The moon, in Waxing Gibbous phase, set at 6:41 a.m. Greenwich Mean Time on 5 January. British meteorological officers also noted that during the period 1-14 January, 'the moon sets on the day following that on which it rises.' British, French and Belgian armies operated in the Greenwich time zone; the *Westheer* was one hour ahead. First introduced in 1916, Daylight Savings Time was applied by all Western Front combatants, though not necessarily on the same start date. See TNA WO 157/71: 'JANUARY 1917, Times of Sunrise and Sunset/Times of Moonrise and Moonset', 31 December 1916, First Army Intelligence File and *Moon Phases January 1917* <https://www.calendar-12.com/moon_calendar/1917/january>

61   Brigadier-General John William Vincent Carroll CMG (1869-1927). Commissioned Norfolk Regiment 1891; West Africa and North Nigeria 1895-99; South Africa 1899-1901; Commandant Mounted Infantry Egypt 1909; OC Mounted Infantry South Africa 1910; OC 7th Norfolk Regiment 1914-15; GOC 17th Brigade September 1915.

62   In the British system, two infantry brigades normally held a divisional frontage of approximately 3,000 yards with one brigade in reserve. The four battalions per brigade rotated between frontline, support line, brigade reserve and rest 'seldom spending more than four days in each position. Within the battalions also, companies were rotated between frontline duty and rest, so that the ordinary soldier was unlikely to spend more than a night or two in a frontline trench accept in unusual circumstances.' Interestingly, 24th Division was defending the line on a three-brigade front from south of Loos to the Hulluch sector inclusive. Two-thirds of the garrison were situated in the front and support lines, the remainder in the reserve line. See Badsey, 'The Raid on Narrow Trench' in Badsey, *The British Army in Battle and its Image 1914-18*, pp.141, 143 and TNA WO 95/2190: '24th DIVN DEFENCE SCHEME, COPY NO. 17. DEC 16, PART II., I. THE DEFENSIVE SYSTEM' and 'PART III., II. HOW THE LINE IS HELD', 24th Division General Staff War Diary.

projected raid, the 8th Buffs relieved 3rd Rifle Brigade on the right front. At the same time, 1st Royal Fusiliers relieved 12th Royal Fusiliers on the left front, the departing battalions taking up brigade and divisional reserve positions in the rear respectively.[63] Defence of this sector was as per 24th Division's recently implemented general scheme:

a)   The frontline must be held at all costs.
b)   If any part of the line is broken and occupied by the enemy, the remainder of the line will still be held.
c)   If any part of the line is broken, a local counter-stroke will be at once delivered to recapture the lost trenches. This will be made by the troops on the spot.
d)   If the local counter-stroke fails, a comprehensive counter-attack by the brigade or divisional reserve, with artillery cooperation, will be prepared and launched.[64]

The now familiar frontline sector included positions consolidated on the near edge of Shoreditch, Carrot, Seaforth, Green Mound and Gordon craters. A consequence of earlier below ground fighting, permanently established bombing posts on western crater lips prevented the enemy from exploiting the yawning cavities below as cover to threaten the British trenches opposite. Ensconced in bombing posts on the eastern crater lips, vigilant German sentries also kept watch to prevent the enemy from gaining identical advantage.

    An undistinguished service battalion raised in Canterbury during September 1914, the 8th Buffs (OC Lieutenant-Colonel L.W. Lucas)[65] settled into the '14 Bis Right Sub-section'[66] encompassing front and second lines,[67] the aforementioned

63   TNA WO 95/2204: '17th INFANTRY BRIGADE OPERATION ORDER No. 11', 2 January 1917 and relevant brigade war diary entry, 17th Brigade War Diary. Relief confirmation was transmitted with the newly introduced 'BAB' trench code. The brigade scheme for holding this subsector was '2 battalions holding the Defended Localities, and Reserve Line, each finding their supports and local reserve. 1 battalion in brigade reserve.' See TNA WO 95/2190: '24th DIVN DEFENCE SCHEME, COPY NO. 17. DEC 16, 'Part III., II. HOW THE LINE IS HELD', 24th Division General Staff War Diary.
64   TNA WO 95/2190: '24th DIVN DEFENCE SCHEME, COPY NO. 17. DEC 16, 'I. GENERAL PRINCIPLES ON WHICH THE DEFENCE IS TO BE CONDUCTED', 24th Division General Staff War Diary.
65   Lieutenant-Colonel Leonard Wainwright Lucas DSO MC (1879-1963). Commissioned East Kent Regiment (Buffs) from Militia 1900; Aden 1903; Gordon Highlanders regimental adjutant 1907; 1st Buffs regimental adjutant 1912-15; temporary lieutenant-colonel and OC 8th Buffs March 1916. Lucas was a Trinity Hall, Cambridge administrator prior to Regular commissioning. See John Venn & J.A. Venn (eds.), *Alumni Cantabrigienses: A Biographical List of All Known Students, Graduates and Holders of Office at the University of Cambridge, From the Earliest Times to 1900*, Vol. 2 (Cambridge: Cambridge University Press, 1951), p.228.
66   TNA WO 95/2207: 8th Buffs War Diary. In German hands, Puits 14 Bis was a pre-war Lens Mining Company colliery installation situated north of Hill 70.
67   The second line was known as 'Engineer Trench' on British maps.

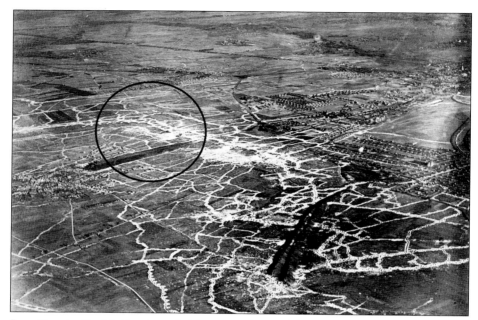

Loos Crassier, Double Crassier and vicinity in early 1917. The 5 January raid site (within circle) is just north of Loos Crassier. To the right are the 'innumerable' miners' dwellings of Cité St Laurent, Cité St Edouard and Cité St Emile. (Paul Humphriss)

mine craters and four communications trenches (Black Watch Alley, Seaforth Alley, Gordon Alley, Cameron Alley) which extended back to the Support Line and eastern extremity of Loos.[68] Conditions were wet and muddy, the deficient state of the trenches resulting from inclement weather and the necessity to rebuild them after a devastating *Minenwerfer* strafe during the Buffs previous tour.[69] The result was three reported cases of trench foot in the battalion shortly after the 3 January takeover.[70]

68   The 8th Buffs manpower strength on 1 January was 29 officers and 1,101 men. The battalion had recently been reinforced with one officer and a draft of 100 men on 31 December 1916. This was a result of an official decision to increase infantry battalion manpower strength by 100 men above establishment. See TNA WO 95/2194: 'Appendix A. 24th DIVISION. EFFECTIVE STRENGTHS – JANUARY 1917', 24th Division Adjutant and Quartermaster General War Diary; WO 95/2077: 8th Buffs War Diary and Alison Hine, *Refilling Haig's Army: The Replacement of British Infantry Casualties on the Western Front, 1916-1918* (Warwick: Helion & Co., 2018), p.181.

69   On 23 December 1916, the 8th Buffs diarist observed: 'Enemy minnied us all day, doing considerable damage. The frontline hardly exists & the C[ommunication] T[renche]s are bad.' TNA WO 95/2077: 8th Buffs War Diary.

70   TNA WO 95/2196: 24th Division Royal Army Medical Corps Assistant Director of Medical Services (ADMS) War Diary.

The sector defence scheme, as 'handed over' by 3rd Rifle Brigade, called for the front-line trench to be held by a series of sentry posts whilst supporting troops sheltered in deep dugouts situated in the Support Line.[71] Commenting on the relief, company commander Captain Eric Foster Hall[72] remarked in his pocket diary: 'On Wed, we relieved B Co[mpan]y. 3rd RB [Rifle Brigade] in support in cellars of houses on outskirts of Loos. For the first time we held the front with two companies and consequently A & C were in support – we supported D Coy. and had to lend them several men & an officer – [2nd Lieutenant W.H.] Darling' who had recently been assigned to the battalion.[73] One of the borrowed other ranks was 22-year-old former brick-layer G12573 Private Frank Winterbottom of Mossley, Manchester who, having originally enlisted with the Royal Fusiliers, was posted to 8th Buffs shortly after disembarkation in France in August 1916. An otherwise clean active service record was somewhat marred by a self-inflicted minor hand injury resulting from the accidental discharge of a service revolver. Charged with 'neglect to the prejudice of good order and military discipline', he was sentenced to 14 days field punishment. The ordeal was almost over when Winterbottom was ordered to the frontline in support of D Company.[74]

Operating in subterranean galleries beneath the Buffs' trench system was the 3rd Australian Tunnelling Company[75] (OC Major L.J. Coulter).[76] Ordered to extend

71   TNA WO 95/168: 'REPORT ON ENEMY RAID ON 24th DIVISION FRONT ON 5th JANUARY 1917', 5 January 1917, Hostile Raid Against Our Trenches M.1.B.6.y – H.31.C.5.2 on Morning of 5th January [1917] File, First Army General Staff War Diary and WO 95/2204: '17th INFANTRY BRIGADE OPERATION ORDER NO. 11', 2 January 1917, 17th Brigade War Diary.

72   Later Brigadier E. Foster Hall MC (1896-1988). Educated at Blundell's School where he was a member of the OTC, Foster Hall's pending City career was interrupted by the outbreak of war in August 1914. Enlisting as a Pte. in the Seaforth Highlanders, he was commissioned into the Buffs thereafter.

73   IWM Doc. 22414: Private Papers of Brigadier E. Foster Hall, January 1917 diary entry. Commissioned from the ranks in January 1916, 2nd Lieutenant William Henry Darling hailed from Bideford, North Devon.

74   *Private Frank Winterbottom* <https://www.findagrave.com/memorial/24374486/frank-winterbottom>

75   Deployed to Egypt in early 1915, the battalion-sized 'Australian Mining Corps' was assembled from men with professional backgrounds in civilian mining. The original intention was to dispatch the approximately 1,000-man strong unit to Gallipoli. Instead, the corps was shipped to France in May 1916 where it was re-designated 'Australian Mining Battalion'. Shortly after disembarkation, the battalion was divided into three (1st, 2nd, 3rd) tunnelling companies and one repairs company. Thus organised, the 3rd Australian Tunnelling Company operated in the Laventie–Fauquissart sector prior to taking responsibility for the Hill 70 sector.

76   Major Leslie J. Coulter DSO (1889-1917). Studied chemistry and mine management at Ballarat School of Mines 1907-08; employed Catherine Reef Mine, Bendigo and Mt Lyell Mine, Tasmania; commissioned Royal Australian Engineers 1915; OC 3rd Australian Tunnelling Company 1916.

activities southwards to include Hill 70 in November 1916, the rough and tumble Antipodean excavators were tasked with confronting active and aggressive offensive mining through the local white chalk rock by their German counterparts. Marked initial setbacks, including the loss of 20 sappers killed and one officer and eight sappers injured by an enemy camouflet on 27 November, initiated a fierce underground struggle whereby the Australians struck back 'with a maximum camouflet in the deep workings', steadily persevering with their counter-mining efforts despite heavy losses.[77] By early January five frontline mineshafts were in situ. Two mineshafts and a mine rescue station[78] were located in the Support Line. Unfortunately, the deepest level shafts had flooded by this time, a later report observing that 'Water is giving much trouble in this sector, and new galleries are being driven to take the place of those flooded out. Enemy is active on this front.'[79]

Thursday 4 January was overcast with rain and drizzle, I Corps' diarist remarking, 'A quiet day except for considerable hostile trench mortar activity in the CAMBRIN section during the morning. Heavy artillery responded to these trench mortars and also dispersed the working parties.' The 24th Division diarist recorded, 'Situation quiet. Indications of possible hostile relief observed opposite LOOS section. 173rd Tunnelling Coy. RE blew a camouflet at 3.0 p.m. SW of CAMERON CRATER.' The 8th Buffs diarist laconically observed, 'the enemy became rather active with their

---

77   Underground offensive/defensive mining in the Loos Salient had reached its apogee by early summer 1916. No mines were discharged by either side during the succeeding August, after which such activity declined. It was the increased *Minenwerfer* and *Granatenwerfer* activity and consequent mounting casualties that induced Brigadier-General R.N. Harvey (GHQ Inspector of Mines) to embrace a new subterranean defence scheme on 1 November 1916. With a primary focus on preservation of the trench garrison, it called for the linking of key fighting sectors; construction of uninterrupted defensive laterals beneath the frontline; improved rear to front communications, and the steady flow of ammunition and material to the forward area. Harvey's programme now underway, intense below ground fighting as experienced by 3rd Australian Tunnelling Company, continued intermittently into the New Year. See Andy Prada, *WWI Engineering: The Loos Salient* <https://www.youtube.com/watch?v=BKszzj-UMUs>

78   Mine rescue stations sites 'were chosen after examination of the mine system by the OC Mine Rescue School in consultation with the [Tunnelling] Company Commander. Where convenient one station served a group of mines but when possible, they were never placed more than 200 yards away from any mineshaft.' Specified quantities of rescue apparatus and stores (Proto pattern breathing sets, oxygen reviving devices, goggles, hoods, electric lamps, stretchers, etc., etc.) were gathered there for ready access. See Secretary, Institute of Royal Engineers, *The Work of the Royal Engineers in the European War 1914-1919: Military Mining* (Uckfield: Naval & Military Press reprint of 1922 edition), pp.80-81, Plate IV.

79   Bean, *The Australian Imperial Force in France 1917*, Vol. IV, pp.965-66; TNA WO 95/168: 'MINING SYNOPSIS FIRST ARMY FROM 13.1.17 to 19.1.1917', First Army General Staff War Diary and Australian War Memorial (AWM) 4 16/4/11: 3rd Australian Tunnelling Company January 1917 War Diary.

T[rench] [M]ortars. This activity continued throughout the night' without realising what it portended.[80]

A Most Successful Boche Ruse?

Friday 5 January: Divided into two separate assault groups, the raiders silently debouched from the German frontline trench to form-up in the waning pre-dawn darkness shrouding no man's land. Wearing steel helmets, gasmasks at the ready position, and armed with automatic pistols, rifles, bombs and mobile demolition charges, 160 NCOs and men of *IR 153,* accompanied by *Leutnant* Ullrich and 37 NCOs and men of *297th Pionier Mineur Kompanie,* were led forward by *Leutnant* Frotscher and *Leutnants d. R.* Reichardt, Plietzsch and Driedger.[81] Seeking available cover in shell holes and mine craters, the 202-man party, subdivided into 24 patrols of between three and 20 men each with codenames such as Annamaria, Bertha, Clara, Dora and so on, awaited the prearranged bombardment of signal impact points as the indicator to assault.[82]

As recounted in Captain Hitchcock's classic published diary, the German trench raid of 5 January 1917 was later determined to be an ad hoc affair instead of the 'cleverly planned and courageously executed' operation it actually was.[83] With regard to the tactical genesis of what *IR 153's* regimental history later claimed was a minimally prepared enterprise,[84] certain aspects of his vivid albeit discrepant second-hand account of complete surprise achieved with humiliating consequences for the battalion concerned appears to have been based on speculation and rumour propagated by divisional gossip:

> Shortly afterwards the following facts came to light about this raid. A German patrol crept up to an advanced post of the regiment concerned and caught the occupants unawares. These they snaffled quietly and returned to their line.

---

80 The method by which war diaries were maintained varied amongst BEF formations and units. Thus it remains uncertain, as Dr Jim Beach has pointed out in an email correspondence with the author, whether or not the 8th Buffs 4 January diary entry 'was written up on the day' or after the raid. Be that as it may, it is my contention that the battalion's diarist would have deduced the connection between the enemy's active trench mortar fire and subsequent incursion had the entry been made after 5 January. See TNA WO 157/1: FIRST ARMY INTELLIGENCE SUMMARY – No. 723, 4 January 1917; WO 95/594: I Corps War General Staff Diary; WO 95/2190: 24th Division General Staff War Diary and WO 95/2207: 8th Buffs War Diary.

81 *Leutnant d. R.*: Lieutenant of the Reserve.

82 Oswald, *Das Altenburger Regiment (8. Thüringisches Infanterie-Regiment Nr. 153) im Weltkriege,* p.254 and Lehrskizze 24.

83 Ibid.

84 Ibid.

The Boche commander sent out a large raiding party on the spot. This party proceeded into the frontline via the advanced sap-head and walked boldly down the main fire trench mopping up every sentry quietly.[85]

Nonplussed as to how the enemy achieved the audacious coup de main, I Corps headquarters remarked the day after, 'no serious bombardment took place immediately prior to the raid.'[86] So it was that the crucial part played by trench mortar fire upon signal impact points and the discharge of seven shallow mines to neutralize sentries before forcing an entry remained unknown in subsequent British accounts. Commenting on the raid break-in phase, the *IR 153* history observed:

> Gradually, it became common practice for our people to make little use of pistols or grenades, but to act as silently as possible, and as far as possible to take prisoners alive. The fact is, that the enemy never noticed – during the operation and for half an hour afterwards – that anything was awry, not to mention the fact that it seemed they remained blissfully unaware until daybreak that anything had happened at all.[87]

Therefore, it can be surmised that Hitchcock's embellished account of the successful enemy infiltration ruse had its origin in animated tales of the raiders sudden appearance amongst the unsuspecting trench garrison.

Zero hour 5:00 a.m.: The abrupt flash *of Minenwerfer* projectiles exploding simultaneously on signal impact points (junction of front and second lines with Gordon Alley and section of frontline trench west of Black Watch Alley) directly opposite the two assembly positions succeeded by mine eruptions was the moment the raiders, officers and NCOs beckoning them forward in the now smoky half-light, rose to their feet and

---

85   Hitchcock, *"Stand To"*, p.231. As part of the neighbouring 73rd Brigade, Captain Hitchcock's unit, 2nd Leinster Regiment, relieved 7th Northamptonshire Regiment in the sector – Loos Crassier exclusive – to the immediate right of 8th Buffs on 5 January. No reference to the German raid can be found in either of the battalion war diaries. Excused from frontline duty during the period 3-8 January, Hitchcock participated in behind the lines training for a daylight raid, scheduled for 10 January, against the formidable Triangle position. See TNA WO 95/2218: 2nd Leinster Regiment and 7th Northamptonshire Regiment war diaries and Hitchcock, pp.231-36.

86   TNA WO 95/168: '6th Division No. 1085 (C.b).', 6 January 1917, Hostile Raid Against Our Trenches M.1.B.6.y – H.31.C.5.2 on Morning of 5th January [1917] File, First Army General Staff War Diary. Conversely, a First Army intelligence summary noted that the raid 'was preceded by heavy artillery and trench mortar fire.' This observation may have been based on information gathered later than that found in the relevant formation war diary. See TNA WO 157/71: 'Summary of Intelligence, First Army, 1st to 16th JANUARY 1917', First Army Intelligence File.

87   Oswald, *Das Altenburger Regiment (8. Thüringisches Infanterie-Regiment Nr. 153) im Weltkriege*, p.257.

rushed forward.[88] Damaged by subtle preparatory bombardments and still not attended to because of seemingly sporadic machine-gun fire that prevented repairs during the nights prior to Zero, barbed wire obstacles were easily negotiated as plummeting mine debris masked approaching hostile footfalls from crouching Buffs sentries.[89]

Evading bombing posts situated on the western crater lips, the raiders surged into the British frontline at the chosen entry points. The corporal responsible for Seaforth Crater post managed to defend his position despite being 'completely surrounded & cut-off. Only three enemy got into the post & these were killed.'[90] Nearby Shoreditch Crater post also held out.[91] The fate of the Gordon Crater post is not recorded but it must be assumed the position was bypassed or overrun. A frontline trench post, an ex post facto report noted, 'near the head of SEAFORTH ALLEY fired on the enemy as he approached our line and a man was sent back to the support line to give the alarm, but this man was unfortunately wounded and returned to his post.'[92] The failure of this only attempt to alert those behind ensured that the enemy, as C.E. Montague later observed, did 'so much as he liked' on reaching the Support Line.[93]

Guided by repeated practice attack experience over a spit-locked facsimile, the 25 patrols boldly probed the intricate British defences whilst the box barrage sealed off the five key trench junctions through which enemy reinforcements would have to pass. Overcoming all resistance in the frontline trench, the right and left flanks were secured by trench block barricades constructed of appropriated sandbags and timber. Meantime, patrols converging from opposite directions occupied the second line.[94] Pioneers immediately set to work demolishing mineshaft entrances in both trenches, No. 21 Shaft in the frontline being completely wrecked by a mobile charge. Further along, No. 22 and No. 2 shafts appear to have been overlooked. 'Unconscious that a raid was in progress', four off-duty Australian tunnelling company listeners,[95] 'who

---

88   Henceforth, all times will be in Greenwich Mean Time.

89   A *153rd Regiment* prisoner taken during the retribution raid of 26 January remarked to his captors that he 'was surprised at the bad condition of our [British] trenches. They could see from their own lines the weak state of our wire.' See TNA WO 157/71: 'SUPPLEMENT TO FIRST ARMY INTELLIGENCE SUMMARY No. 748, Further examination of 16 unwounded prisoners of the 153rd Regiment, 8th Division captured E. of LOOS on 26th Jan. 1917', 29 January 1917, First Army Intelligence File.

90   TNA WO 95/2077: 8th Buffs War Diary.

91   TNA WO 95/168: 'REPORT ON ENEMY RAID ON 24th DIVISION FRONT ON 5th JANUARY 1917', 5 January 1917, Hostile Raid Against Our Trenches M.1.B.6.y – H.31.C.5.2 on Morning of 5th January [1917] File, First Army General Staff War Diary

92   Ibid.

93   Montague, *Disenchantment*, p.130.

94   Oswald, *Das Altenburger Regiment (8. Thüringisches Infanterie-Regiment Nr. 153) im Weltkriege*, Lehrskizze 24. I am grateful to Paul Humphriss who provided specially annotated British trench map abstracts depicting paths taken by the raiders as reproduced in Oswald's regimental history and contemporary archival documents.

95   Tunnelling company listeners were tasked with monitoring enemy underground activity from mineshaft faces. Their primary instruments were the Geophone, Western Electric

were going back to the billets in pairs', also appear to have been apprehended near the junction of the frontline with Gordon Alley at this time. In the second line, a demolition party encountered two tunnellers at 'Seaforth Incline'. Startled, they 'did not light the four heavy mobile charges that had been placed in the shaft.'[96]

With a third barricade established halfway up Black Watch Alley, the remaining patrols, bombing dugouts on their way up Seaforth Alley and Gordon Alley, pushed on to the Support Line where the bulk of the Buffs' D Company garrison sheltered in numerous deep dugouts.[97] Assigned night fatigue duties now finished as of the remaining period before dawn 'Stand To' observance,[98] men were dozing in the frowsty candle-lit depths below when the raiders, joining forces in the now secured trench, turned their attention to the vault-like entrances that sporadically appeared amongst its sandbagged and corrugated iron revetments. Hitchcock described what happened next:

> In English they yelled down the shafts of the deep dugouts the word 'GAS'. The sleepers, startled, donned their box respirators and came out of their dugouts to man the fire bays, only to be grabbed at and dragged across the 150 yards of No Man's Land without being able to fire a shot. When their shouts were not heard, the artful Boches fired Véry light pistols down the entrances which had the desired effect.[99]

Detector and Seismomicrophone. See Secretary, Institute of Royal Engineers, *The Work of the Royal Engineers in the European War 1914-1919: Military Mining*, pp.122-34.

96   AWM 4 16/4/11: 'REPORT ON ENEMY RAID AT LOOS ON 5/1/17' and 'Sketch Plan, Hill 70, Loos Salient, Scale 1 inch = 125 yds., Showing probable route taken by Enemy raiding party on 5/1/17', n.d., 3rd Australian Tunnelling Company War Diary and Bean, *The Australian Imperial Force in France 1917*, Vol. IV, p.966, fn. 9.

97   Oswald, *Das Altenburger Regiment (8. Thüringisches Infanterie-Regiment Nr. 153) im Weltkriege*, Lehrskizze 24. A somewhat ambiguous notation on this map ('M.W. Std. mit 15 flasch') appears to denote an assault on a Stokes mortar position containing 15 3-inch component projectiles whilst the raiders moved NE along Seaforth Alley. No mention of this is made in contemporary British documents.

98   Stand To: Shortened definition for 'Stand-to-Arms'. As enemy attacks were routinely mounted either before dawn or shortly after dusk, both sides took precautions to ensure the fire step was manned an hour before daybreak and nightfall.

99   Hitchcock, *"Stand To"*, p.231. The dugouts within the support line were the result of the 24th Division defence scheme of December 1916 which noted that the 'only means of preventing the garrisons being annihilated is to give them cover in deep dugouts. We must therefore aim at having deep dugouts for two thirds of the garrison of the Front and Support lines, and sufficient for the whole garrison in the Reserve Line ... Steps must be taken to minimize the danger of deep dugouts which is that the enemy may rush our trenches under cover of his gunfire before our men have had time to get out of the dugouts. There must be at least two exits from each dugout and be so arranged that men can quickly come out of them.' See TNA WO 95/2190: 24th DIVN DEFENCE SCHEME, COPY NO. 17. DEC 16, Part III., IV. ACTION TO BE TAKEN IN CASE OF ATTACK, 24th Division General Staff War Diary.

Some of this is corroborated by a First Army intelligence summary which stated that the Germans 'fired several Very lights down the dugouts.'[100] Hitchcock's story is contradicted by contemporary battalion and division reports, the 8th Buffs war diarist noting that raiders 'got into our support line, bombing dugouts & capturing prisoners.' The 24th Division report concluded, 'The enemy appears to have thrown bombs down one of the entrances to each dugout which he found and to have had men waiting at the other entrance for our men when they came out.'[101]

The Mine Rescue Station entrance in the same vicinity was, following the seizure of three 'Proto men', blown up 'with a mobile charge forming a small crater.' Situated just beyond the junction of the Support Line with Gordon Alley, the raiders also paused in front of Gordon Incline Shaft. Calling upon a sapper within to surrender in English, they proceeded to bomb the entrance after their intended prisoner retreated further into the shaft to avoid capture.[102] Farther on, two barricades had been constructed north and east of the same junction. The raiders, however, did not have it entirely their own way, for G/5456 Private J.E. Setterfield, acting as the D company commander's messenger, was at company headquarters in Cameron Alley 'when a signal came through that the enemy were making a raid on the line.'[103] Immediately dispatched to the Support Line with a 'Stand To' order, he 'had only gone a few yards from his dugout when he saw a soldier making flashes with an electric torch.' Setterfield 'was not three yards away and I asked him who he was. He answered something which I could not understand, and it was too dark to see whether it was one of our chaps, so I rushed up to him and found out it was a German officer [sic].' Reacting in an instant, he 'did not stop to argue with him; my rifle spoke first and down he went.'[104] On encountering a second man, Setterfield 'asked him who he was. He said 'Buff', so I passed on; but he fired at me, and then I got him also. I saw a third hopping over the parapet, but he was not quite quick enough, and I managed to bring him down.'[105] Doubling back to company headquarters, Setterfield joined a hastily assembled

---

100   TNA WO 157/71: 'FIRST ARMY INTELLIGENCE SUMMARY – No. 725', 6 January 1917, First Army Intelligence File. For the importance of intelligence about the German Army originating from the British frontline, see Jim Beach, *Haig's Intelligence: GHQ and the German Army 1916-18* (Cambridge: Cambridge University Press, 2013), Chapter 4.
101   TNA WO 95/ 2207: 8th Buffs War Diary and WO 95/168: 'REPORT ON ENEMY RAID ON 24th DIVISION FRONT ON 5th JANUARY 1917', 5 January 1917, Hostile Raid Against Our Trenches M.1.B.6.y – H.31.C.5.2 on Morning of 5th January [1917] File, First Army General Staff War Diary.
102   AWM 4 16/4/11: 'REPORT ON ENEMY RAID AT LOOS ON 5/1/17', 3rd Australian Tunnelling Company War Diary.
103   Having enlisted in January 1915, 25-year-old Private John Edwin Setterfield hailed from the Isle of Thanet.
104   No German officers were killed during the raid. Setterfield also recollected that his first kill was 'wearing the ribbon of the Iron Cross.'
105   Setterfield to sister correspondence quoted in *Thanet Advertiser & Echo*, 28 April 1917, p.5.

party 'composed of officers' servants which, led by 2nd Lieutenant Darling, counter-attacked near the 'Old Coy. Headquarters about 15 yards from Cameron Alley …' This provisional onslaught, the sole concerted Buffs effort to evict the raiders, stalled in front of the established eastern barricade after a spirited bombing fight.[106] To the west, dozens of bewildered prisoners, having been rounded up in the occupied section of Support Line, were sent down Seaforth Alley and Gordon Alley accompanied by escorts with fixed bayonets.

It was to the north and northeast that the deepest penetrations were made. The latter, carried out by eight Germans of Wally Patrol, exited Gordon Alley to probe the open area in the direction of Cameron Alley whilst the former (11 men of Martha Patrol under the leadership of *Leutnant* Reichardt) hurriedly pressed on from the junction of the Support Line with Seaforth Alley as far as the environs of Loos.[107] Whether or not these incursions were part of the original plan or taken wholly on the initiative of patrol leaders is not addressed in the post-war regimental account. Circumstance and doctrine point to both patrols taking advantage of a favourable albeit short-lived opportunity. Thus the alleged uninterrupted 40 minutes spent in the enemy trenches once the targeted area had been isolated and, as per the 1906[108] and subsequent infantry drill regulations, the German Army's general adherence to *Auftragstaktik* (mission command) which allowed junior officers and NCOs to operate with a certain amount of independence when confronted by the inherent unpredictability of combat, more than likely explain the actions of Reichardt and the Wally Patrol leader.[109]

It is not known exactly what time the raiders withdrew from the British line. *IR 153's* published history is silent on the subject whilst the 8th Buffs war diarist observed, 'all was quiet soon after 6:15 a.m.', so it can be speculated that the Germans began to retire at approximately 5:40 a.m. This is further substantiated by a First Army intelligence summary which noted, 'The enemy stayed in our trenches about 40 minutes', although it appears to be the only relevant contemporary document that specifically

106 Oswald, *Das Altenburger Regiment (8. Thüringisches Infanterie-Regiment Nr. 153) im Weltkriege,* Lehrskizze 24; TNA WO 95/168: 'REPORT ON ENEMY RAID ON 24th DIVISION FRONT ON 5th JANUARY 1917', 5 January 1917, Hostile Raid Against Our Trenches M.1.B.6.y – H.31.C.5.2 on Morning of 5th January [1917] File, First Army General Staff War Diary and AWM 4 16/4/11: 'REPORT ON ENEMY RAID AT LOOS ON 5/1/17' and 'Sketch Plan, Hill 70, Loos Salient, Scale 1 inch = 125 yds., Showing probable route taken by Enemy raiding party on 5/1/17', n.d., 3rd Australian Tunnelling Company War Diary.
107 Oswald, *Das Altenburger Regiment (8. Thüringisches Infanterie-Regiment Nr. 153) im Weltkriege,* Lehrskizze 24.
108 Frhrn v. Freytag-Loringhoven, *Das Exerzier=Reglement für die Infanterie vom 29. Mai 1906* (Berlin: Ernst Mittler & Sohn, 1907).
109 See Stachlebeck, 'Strategy "in a microcosm": Processes of Tactical Learning in a WWI German Infantry Division', *Journal of Military and Strategic Studies*, Vol. 13, Issue 4, Summer 2011, p.5.

validates post-war claims that he did so.[110] Elated by their success, the raiders were overheard 'going over the parapet singing at junction of Gordon Alley and frontline' by an Australian NCO stationed at L.G. 13[111] which was on the immediate left of the enemy break-in. The ongoing box barrage ceased once it was determined the raiding force had returned to the German line.[112]

SAY What about those 50 rations?

An oft-repeated yarn associated with the 5 January 1917 raid recounts the revelatory process by which 24th Division GOC Major-General Capper first became aware of the enemy coup de main.[113] 'Unique in itself', this enduring anecdote first appeared in Captain Hitchcock's published diary:

> The G.O.C. was sitting in his headquarters when his galloper[114] rushed in to tell him that the German wireless had been heard reporting 'a brilliant minor operation near Loos and the capture of 50 English prisoners.'[115] The General immediately detailed brigades to repeat situation reports for all their units, and he got the following returns from all:
>
> X Battalion
> Wind S.E. Situation normal A.A.A.[116]
>
> Having scrutinised all the situation reports, the G.O.C. was non-plussed, so he decided to tour his frontline sectors accompanied by his staff. They toured the 17th Brigade sector, which was northeast of Loos, and immediately discovered an unoccupied frontline which terminated at a newly erected barricade, and

---

110 TNA WO 95/2207: 8th Buffs War Diary and WO 157/1: 'FIRST INTELLIGENCE SUMMARY No. 725, 6 January 1917, First Army Intelligence File.
111 Listening Gallery 13.
112 AWM 4 16/4/11: 'REPORT ON ENEMY RAID AT LOOS ON 5/1/17', 3rd Australian Tunnelling Company War Diary.
113 See Moran, *The Anatomy of Courage*, p.73; Ashworth, *Trench Warfare*, pp.200-01; Michael Lucas, *The Journey's End Battalion: The 9th East Surrey in the Great War* (Barnsley: Pen & Sword, 2012), Chapter 7 and Radley, *On the Dangerous Edge*, p.64.
114 Galloper: Pre-war British Army slang for officer employed by a commander to carry messages.
115 In a 12 January 2020 email correspondence with the author, Dr Jim Beach observed that German wireless transmission 'reporting of the raid just doesn't ring true. My instinct would be [British] IToc [listening sets] picking up traffic and making an immediate report would be a more plausible explanation.' See also fn. 168 below.
116 'N.B. – Situation reports were a daily routine in trench warfare. At "Stand To" morning and evening, frontline companies had to render these reports. The direction of the wind had to be given as an anti-gas measure.'

farther on, a dead man. The G.O.C. then went off down the C.T. to find the battalion headquarters in this sector. The C.O. was very surprised; as far as he knew everything was normal in his frontline. The G.O.C., now reinforced by the battalion headquarters, returned to the frontline for further investigations. At the head of the C.T. he paused to peer across No-Man's-Land, and the following large notice in English stuck up in the wire entanglements met his gaze:

'SAY
What about those
50 rations?'[117]

Passage of time and a dearth of corroborating sources make it difficult to determine the veracity of this account. Thorough review of relevant war diaries and intelligence reports did not produce a single reference to the event. Its absence from available official records may have something to do with the aversion of contemporary diarists to record particulars 'damaging to reputations, personal or institutional …'[118] Nevertheless, the post-war German claim that the British 'remained blissfully unaware until daybreak'; the unsatisfactory state of 8th Buffs communications (see below) and the fact that Capper penned the preface for Hitchcock's volume, lend some credence to the tale.[119]

Major-General J.E. Capper, GOC 24th Division. (Author)

Captain Foster Hall was in a Loos village line redoubt before word came of the German raid, 'I didn't know what was on & slept on in bed.' Donning steel helmet, box respirator, revolver and webbing, he set off for the frontline that afternoon to 'relieve Overy while he went to orderly room.'[120] Trudging through a now re-occupied trench

---

117   Hitchcock, *"Stand To"*, p.230.
118   Radley, *On the Dangerous Edge*, p. xxvii.
119   Oswald, *Das Altenburger Regiment (8. Thüringisches Infanterie-Regiment Nr. 153) im Weltkriege,* p.257 and Hitchcock, *"Stand To"*, pp.7-8.
120   IWM Doc. 22414: Private Papers of Brigadier E. Foster Hall, 28 December 1916 to 8 January 1917 diary entry.

system permeated with the stench of cordite, Foster Hall managed to secure the only German prisoner resulting from the hostile trench raid:

> I heard a yell & a corporal shewed me a Hun crawling from shell hole to shell hole behind our frontline. He threw a bomb – a rotten shot. I threw one which was far better & wounded him which I later found out. We then had pot shots at him as he rolled over and over. I went right round the support line and up Cameron Alley & he had just come to rest near the top. He was badly-wounded & surrendered at once. I got several interesting souvenirs off him – knife, tooter & afterwards purse & identity disc. He could not talk English, but a little French. Stretcher-bearers got him & took him down & incidentally stole his watch & torch, which was gotten back as he was only wounded. However, he died twelve hours later & afterwards I got his identity disc & purse returned. He was a fine man, brave & clean & aged 29.[121]

Identification of the enemy unit that executed the raid was also readily affirmed by examination of corpses left behind 'close to our parapets and wire; two of these have since been brought in, and their identifications show them to have belonged to the 153rd Regiment, 8th Division, IV Corps.' This demonstrated 'no change in the distribution of the German forces opposite the Loos Salient, except that the position of the 153rd Regiment is slightly further S. than had hitherto been supposed.'[122]

Assuming that Major-General Capper returned to his headquarters shortly after the taunting enemy placard episode, it appears that – in addition to telephoning I Corps headquarters – the GOC 24th Division promptly compiled a full incident report for corps and army edification.[123] After chronicling what was known thus far, Capper

---

121 Ibid. The prisoner's pocket journal also appears to have been confiscated, a First Army intelligence summary remarking, 'from information obtained from a diary found on the wounded prisoner captured on the 5th inst. belonging to the 153rd Regiment, a local relief should have taken place yesterday.' His death from injuries was recorded in the intelligence summary for 7 January. Assuming that the prisoner's body was interred in a nearby cemetery, a search of the CWGC website, where eight German captives are recorded as having passed away between 5-11 January, failed to identify him. The equivalent *Volksbund* site does not allow for similar searches. See TNA WO 157/71: 'FIRST ARMY INTELLIGENCE SUMMARY – No. 726' and 'FIRST ARMY INTELLIGENCE SUMMARY – 727', 6 and 7 January 1917, First Army Intelligence File.
122 TNA WO 157/71: 'FIRST ARMY INTELLIGENCE SUMMARY – No. 724', 5 January 1917, First Army Intelligence File.
123 'Just how troublesome a successful enemy raid could be shows in the extensive paper trail surrounding an enemy raid ...' This is clearly demonstrated by the contents of TNA WO 95/168: Hostile Raid Against Our Trenches M.1.B.6.y – H.31.C.5.2 on Morning of 5th January [1917] File within the First Army General Staff War Diary. See Radley, *On the Dangerous Edge*, p.66.

went on to assure his immediate superiors that 'A Court of Enquiry[124] is being held by the O.C. 8th Bn. the Buffs which will no doubt clear up many points.' Unwilling to rely solely on its findings, Capper also advocated that a second court of enquiry should be 'assembled composed of officers outside the unit concerned', after which he asked I Corps to 'say whether a [court] president will be appointed from outside the Division or whether I should appoint a Brigadier from one of the other two brigades which were not concerned in the raid.'[125] An ensuing report observed:

> In forwarding a report on the raid made early this morning by the enemy on a portion of the front, I regret to state that it appears that the arrangements for communication between the front and support line were quite inadequate, but I prefer not to make any criticisms until the Court of Enquiry has been held.

Failure to inform I Corps about the number of prisoners taken was a serious oversight for which Capper made immediate amends:

> I also regret that no earlier information as to a number of our men being missing was given, but the earlier reports conveyed no intimation that such was the case; it was sent to corps headquarters by telephone as soon as received. I am taking action to ascertain the reasons for this failure to report losses.[126]

Sources slightly vary as to the number of killed, wounded, and missing. The 8th Buffs diarist recorded three killed; six wounded and 42 missing in addition to two men of 3rd Rifle Brigade missing and one man of 17th Brigade Machine-gun Company

124 A military court of enquiry had special and limited jurisdiction to investigate specific matters. Such courts, however, were not judicial tribunals. According to the *Manual of Military Law* (1914), p.637, it should constitute 'an assembly of officers directed to collect evidence, and, if so required, to report with regard to any matter which may be referred to them … A court of enquiry may be assembled by the Army Council or by the officer in command of any body of troops whether belonging to one or more corps … The court may be composed of any number of officers of any rank, and of any branch or department of the service, according to the nature of the investigation … The court will be guided by the written instructions of the authority who assembled the court. The instructions will be full and specific and will state the general character of the information required. They will also state whether a report is required or not.'
125 TNA WO 95/168: 'REPORT ON ENEMY RAID ON 24th DIVISION FRONT ON 5th JANUARY 1917', 5 January 1917, Hostile Raid Against Our Trenches M.1.B.6.y – H.31.C.5.2 on Morning of 5th January [1917] File, First Army General Staff War Diary.
126 TNA WO 95/168: 'I Corps G.X./283/13', 5 January 1917, Hostile Raid Against Our Trenches M.1.B.6.y – H.31.C.5.2 on Morning of 5th January [1917] File, First Army General Staff War Diary.

wounded.[127] Capper's first written report listed total manpower losses as 8th Buffs – two killed, six wounded, 42 missing; 3rd Rifle Brigade – two missing and 3rd Australian Tunnelling Company – seven missing as confirmed by OC Major Coulter.[128] It was not until the following day (6 January) that I Corps acknowledged with certainty that 'the enemy took away 51 prisoners.' This number – 44 infantrymen and seven tunnellers – is confirmed by *IR 153*'s regimental history.[129] Perusal of *Soldiers Died in the Great War* during research for this chapter finally determined that 8th Buffs, the only BEF unit involved to sustain fatal casualties, lost four men killed and one man died of wounds. One of these was Private Frank Winterbottom.[130] With two days remaining in the Puits 14 Bis subsector, the situation remained relatively quiet prior to the Buffs' relief on 7 January.[131]

An undoubted master-stroke

Remarking on the recurrent 'raid warfare' which his battalion was involved with during winter 1916-17, Captain Hitchcock noted that throughout this period 'the Germans had intermittently been harassing battalions in the Loos sector with their "Travelling Circus"', an appellation bestowed upon an imagined phantom 'sturmtruppen' unit, the sole function of which was to carry out manifold raiding operations up and down the British line at the behest of enemy headquarters.[132] As we

---

127 TNA WO 95/ 2207: 8th Buffs War Diary. I Corps manpower losses for the week 29 December 1916 to 5 January 1917 amounted to 32 men killed; five officers and 109 men wounded and 53 men missing, the majority of the latter captured during the 5 January raid. See WO 95/168: 'First Army. Weekly Report on Operations for period: 6 p.m. 29/12/16 to 6 p.m. 5/1/17', 6 January 1917, First Army General Staff War Diary.

128 See TNA WO 95/168: 'REPORT ON ENEMY RAID ON 24th DIVISION FRONT ON 5th JANUARY 1917', 5 January 1917, Hostile Raid Against Our Trenches M.1.B.6.y – H.31.C.5.2 on Morning of 5th January [1917] File, First Army General Staff War Diary and AWM 4 16/4/11: 'REPORT ON ENEMY RAID AT LOOS ON 5/1/17', 3rd Australian Tunnelling Company War Diary.

129 I Corps notified and updated First Army about the recent raid at 5:10 and 8:10 p.m. on 5 January. The latter message included early casualty and prisoner estimates. See TNA WO 95/168: 'C2121' pink message proformas, 5 January 1917 and '6th Division No. 1085 (G.b).', 6 January 1917, Hostile Raid Against Our Trenches M.1.B.6.y – H.31.C.5.2 on Morning of 5th January [1917] File, First Army General Staff War Diary and Oswald, *Das Altenburger Regiment (8. Thüringisches Infanterie-Regiment Nr. 153) im Weltkriege*, p.254.

130 The 8th Buffs fatalities were as follows: G/4710 Pte. E.J. Bingham; G/11740 Pte. A. Savill; G/2890 Pte. G. Stone; G/12573 Pte. F. Winterbottom killed, and G/12647 Pte. E.H. Hawkins died of wounds. Bingham, Savill, Stone and Winterbottom are interred at Philosophe British Cemetery, Mazingarbe; Hawkins is interred at Bethune Town Cemetery. See *Soldiers Died in the Great War 1914-19* CD Rom, Version 2.5, Naval & Military Press, 1998 and *Commonwealth War Graves Commission* <https://www.cwgc.org/>

131 TNA WO 95/2207: 8th Buffs War Diary.

132 Hitchcock, *"Stand To"*, p.245.

have seen, the raid of 5 January was planned and executed at the regimental level, the participants – thoroughly inculcated in the 153er Methode – recruited from within *IR 153's* available officer and other ranks manpower strength.

Conflation of the Altenburger regiment's vaunted tactical methodology with the *Sturmtrupp* tactics introduced in 1916 confirm certain similarities of approach notwithstanding the former's independent procedural development during a time of widespread military transition. This is reflected in the tactical transformation that 'took place as a simultaneous bottom-up and top-down process within which traditional and innovative doctrine and procedures were connected with each other in a kind of compromise.' The succeeding 'transformation began when Erich von Falkenhayn was the Chief of the General Staff and it was considerably intensified in late 1916 by the third *Oberste Heeresleitung* (OHL – the German Supreme Command) under Paul von Hindenburg and Erich Ludendorff.'[133] Thus *IR 153's* deployment of squad-like sub-units – 24 designated patrols of between three to 20 men each vis-a-vis the six to eight-man squads stipulated by the 1916 tactics – was implemented by the regiment as a basic tactical core. Other comparable aspects with regard to the raid prepara- tions phase were sophisticated reconnaissance, careful planning, and repeated prac- tice over trench system facsimiles. The ensuing assault phase was characterised as per *Sturmtrupp* modus operandi by fire suppression support from artillery/trench mortars; the rapid passage of no man's land; no hesitation when breaking into the enemy trench system; initial penetration at several points; by width rolling up (*Aufrollen*) of lateral trench lines; focus on close combat; hand grenades employed as the primary combat weapon; select patrols tasked with the defence of captured trenches and barricade construction, and a simultaneous and coherent withdrawal from the objective.[134]

With captives, appropriated enemy weapons, equipment and documents in tow, the exultant raiders marched to the rear for debriefing and a short but well-earned respite:

---

133 See Stachlebeck, 'Strategy "in a microcosm": Processes of Tactical Learning in a WWI German Infantry Division', *Journal of Military and Strategic Studies*, Vol. 13, Issue 4, Summer 2011, pp.4-5. It was in May 1916 that the second *Oberste Heeresleitung* decreed that all of the Western Front armies should dispatch small cadres of officers and NCOs to the recently established (1 April 1916) *Sturmbattaillon* for special instruction. 'Thereafter, these personnel were to return to their own formations where they would train more units in the new tactics. Progress was uneven owing to the pressures of active service, the difficulties of supplying enough new equipment, and the time taken to train the trainers, but soon dozens of new *Sturm* units were beginning to appear.' Simultaneous with this, each field army was to raise its own *Sturmbattaillon* to provide further theoretical instruction. By November 1916 most, if not all infantry divisions had at least one component *Sturmabteilung* of company strength whilst others had one on regimental strengths. Thus it can be presumed that the still ongoing *Sturmtrupp* tactics training initiative had some influence on the coinciding development and application of the 153er Methode. See Bull, *Stosstrupptaktik*, pp.83-84.

134 Raths, *Vom Massensturm zur Stoßtrupptaktik*, pp.166-67.

Fifty-one English, three of whom were wounded, were brought back: moreover, the enemy lost an estimated 20-30 men killed [sic]. On our side the losses were greater this time: five men dead; one severely wounded, three lightly wounded, and from the Mining Coy., two men dead. These losses, however, were caused mainly by an accidental explosion in the enemy mine workings rather than by enemy action.[135]

The cleverly-planned and courageously executed operation attracted the highest praise and recognition for not only the participants, but the whole regiment. During their interrogation by the German AOK 6,[136] even the English prisoners were unanimous in saying that 'the assault, which took place with minimal preparation, was an undoubted master-stroke. No one had noticed the approach of the Germans until they, as if springing from the ground, suddenly appeared in front of our dug outs.'[137]

Accolades from division,[138] corps and army headquarters were followed by recognition in the daily *Heersbericht* (Army bulletin):

In Army Group Prince Rupprecht of Bavaria, units of the Altenburger Regiment Nr. 153 earlier today penetrated as far as the fourth enemy trench line on the eastern edge of Loos, and by the clearing and blowing up of several galleries, inflicted sanguinary losses on the English and returned with 51 prisoners.[139]

Retrospective commentary in the regimental history documented the raid as the catalyst for larger scale enterprises:

The patrol on 5.1.1917 was of particular significance. Previously, all patrols undertaken using the 'I.R. 153 method' had run successfully and according to plan: the 5.1.1917 patrol proved beyond doubt that relatively large attacks (in

---

135 I was unable to determine at which mine the deadly accidental explosion occurred.

136 AOK 6: *Armee-Oberkommando 6* or *Sixth Army* headquarters.

137 Oswald, *Das Altenburger Regiment (8. Thüringisches Infanterie-Regiment Nr. 153) im Weltkriege*, p.254.

138 The *8th Division* order of the day noted that the raiders 'broke into the enemy position south-east of Loos, achieving complete surprise, mopped up the shell-torn ground and the three front trench lines, whilst one party pushed on as far as the fourth trench line on the north-eastern outskirts of Loos. On this occasion, seven tunnel entrances were completely destroyed using explosive charges by the miners, and the patrol brought in 51 English prisoners, three of them wounded. Our own losses – one dead, four missing and four wounded – were negligible in relation to the level of success achieved. The excellent and reliable contribution to the planning and execution by Lt. Blume, 8.MWK [*8th Minenwerfer Kompagnie*], must also be recognised.' See 'Divisions-Tages-Befehl', 6 January 1917 reproduced in Oswald, p.400.

139 Oswald, p.256.

this case 202 men!) could break into the enemy lines quickly and largely unnoticed, and then push deep into the trench systems (Patrol [led by] Lt. Reichardt penetrated over 400 metres – 300 metres as the crow flies – as far as the outskirts of Loos!) without encountering serious opposition.[140]

Wanting to expand on the success of this and previous raids, *IR 153* headquarters formulated an offensive proposal to achieve a complete and total breakthrough of the British line:

> After four such patrols that had gone exactly to plan, it was realised that one could attack a large number of locations simultaneously. Since 1915, both armies have tried to break through enemy lines in such a way as to achieve their total and irrevocable destruction – but in vain. The often days-long heavy artillery bombardment removed any chance of surprise, instead invariably resulting in the timely bringing forward of enemy reserves.[141]

The regimental proposition, 'most comprehensively drawn up', was to launch an attack against, 'on average, 10 to 12 locations, approximately one kilometre apart from each other; the enemy front should be attacked silently, using the "IR 153 Methode".' Consequently:

> The 'storm troops' should not then pull back, but should push on, backed up by a continual stream of reinforcements, through the enemy trench system into their rear areas and artillery lines: simultaneously – exactly as per our previous encounters – substantial attached units should then roll up the enemy trenches to the right and left of the original break-in, prior to gaining touch with similarly-tasked neighbouring units. Therefore, where one or more of the 10-12 attacks did not get forward, the troops on either side could open a way through for them.[142]

Conceding that 'despite painstaking preparation of the combined operation, the actual course of said operation can be disrupted by any number of setbacks, obstructions etc.', *IR 153's* history endorsed the advantages of the contemplated 'parallel multi-attack method, that, properly executed, only a few need to succeed in order to open the way to neighbouring units.' *Sixth Army* headquarters, however, 'considered the unquestionably severe difficulties often encountered as so significant, that it could not trust in this method's chances of success.' A boastful passage in the regimental history

---

140 Ibid. Similar tactical methods are employed by the hero of Bernard Newman's counter-factual war novel *The Cavalry Went Through* (1930), pp.40-47 whereby Hill 70 is captured in late 1915!
141 Oswald, p.256.
142 Ibid., p.257.

claimed the primary reason for rejection by the high command had more to do with conspicuous unit fighting skills:

> 'We don't have IR 153 along our whole front line' – was nevertheless recognition for our courageous Altenburgers. Our people always had an unshakable belief in the success of our operations; volunteers always came forward in more than ample numbers: yes, on one occasion even regimental, battalion and assistant clerks and orderlies helped storm the enemy trenches.[143]

Befittingly shelved at a time when the *Westheer* was focusing on the defence, *IR 153's* scheme was, with its envisaged infiltrating *sturmtruppen* trailed by reinforcements, evocative of tactics employed during the offensives of spring and summer 1918.[144] One obviously deliberate omission was the absence of conventional artillery support not to mention a short and centrally-controlled fire mission bombardment of the type conceived by innovative gunner Georg Bruchmüller.[145] Hence, it is understandable why the infantry regiment inspired breakthrough plan was not entertained beyond army level command.

Courts of Enquiry

Reading through Capper's second report, I Corps GOC Lieutenant-General Anderson added a declarative annotation in exquisite long-hand prior to forwarding this and other related documents to First Army:

> The incident has been the subject of a court of enquiry within the battalion today [5 January] and another court of enquiry under the presidency of a brigade commander of another division will be held on the 7th. Until the evidence taken has been seen, it is better not to comment on what appears undoubtably to have been a very unsatisfactory episode calling for considerable explanation. Meanwhile, both divisions [6th and 24th] on the line have been requested to consider means to block & watch the points where communication trenches from the frontline enter the support line.[146]

---

143 Ibid.
144 See Bull, *Stosstrupptaktik*, Chapter 8.
145 *Colonel* Georg Bruchmüller (1863-1948) was a German artillery officer who greatly influenced the development of modern artillery tactics during 1916-18. See David T. Zabecki, *Steel Wind: Colonel Georg Bruchmüller and the Birth of Modern Artillery* (Santa Barbara, California: Praeger, 1999).
146 See TNA WO 95/168: 'I Corps. G.X./283/13', 5 January 1917, Hostile Raid Against Our Trenches M.1.B.6.y – H.31.C.5.2 on Morning of 5th January [1917] File, First Army General Staff War Diary.

Review of the I Corps reports prompted First Army MGGS Major-General G. de S. Barrow[147] to observe, 'If the facts as stated in the attached report of O.C. No. 3 Australian Tunnelling Company are correct,[148] there must be something very wrong with the system of defence on the front of 24th Division.' To this he added, 'The Army Commander directs that steps be taken without delay to ensure that the line is held by such a system of posts, obstacles and blocks, with adequate intercommunication, as will render impossible the unopposed circulation of a party of the enemy through a section of trenches containing important mining shafts, and the surprise of supporting troops in their dugouts.' Barrow concluded with a sharp rebuke: 'The G.O.C. 24th Division states, "The arrangements for communication between front and support line were quite inadequate but I prefer not to make any criticisms until a Court of Enquiry is held." It is presumed that he is taking active steps to make certain that what appears to have been a very inadequate defence is reorganized where necessary.'[149] The I Corps response was that First Army's instructions had been 'communicated personally to the G.S.O. 1 24th Division[150] last night.' Furthermore, 'The G.O.C. 6th and 24th divisions have further been instructed to take steps to ensure that the precautionary

147 Major-General Sir George de Symons Barrow (1864-1959). Commissioned Connaught Rangers 1884; transferred 35th Scinde Horse 1886; Waziristan and North-West Frontier 1895; Staff College 1898; ADC GOC East Indies 1899; China 1900; ADC C-in-C India 1901; Interpreter C-in-C India 1902; DAQMG India 1903; DAAG Staff College Camberley 1908; GSO Staff College Quetta 1911; BGGS Cavalry Corps 1914; BGGS X Corps July 1915; GOC 1st Indian Cavalry Division August 1915 and MGGS First Army December 1915.

148 The after-action report and accompanying sketch plan provided by the OC 3rd Australian Tunneling Company was incorrect with regard to the determination that the raiders sole entry point was the vicinity of Seaforth Crater. Nevertheless, the accompanying sketch map accurately depicts mine positions and the location of particular incidents that occurred during the raid. See AWM 4 16/4/11: 'REPORT ON ENEMY RAID AT LOOS ON 5/1/17' and 'Sketch Plan, Hill 70, Loos Salient, Scale 1 inch = 125 yds., Showing probable route taken by Enemy raiding party on 5/1/17', n.d., 3rd Australian Tunnelling Company War Diary.

149 TNA WO 95/168: 'First Army No. 802/20 (G)', 6 January 1917, Hostile Raid Against Our Trenches M.1.B.6.y – H.31.C.5.2 on Morning of 5th January [1917] File, First Army General Staff War Diary. Also within this file were four untitled and undated sheets of foolscap with rough handwritten notes likely drafted by Barrow during a meeting with First Army GOC General Horne. The latter, having been recently appointed to army command in September 1916, was no doubt sensitive about the local reverse hence, the general tone of the document: '1. What are the dispositions of the 8th Buffs at the portion of the front raided? 2. What system of communication in [???] sentry post and their supports? 3. Where was the support? 4. Was there no SOS signal …? What is the system? 5. Was no alarm given by the posts or Seaforth & Shoreditch Craters? Have they any means of firing alarm? 6. What steps had they taken to deal with the portion of the line obliterated on Dec. 22. 17 [sic 1916]. Are there no [trench] blocks to prevent the enemy circulating so freely as he appears to have done? … What is wanted is immediate action, not to await [???] any court of enquiry.'

150 Lieutenant-Colonel Sir W.A.I. Kay DSO, GSO 1 24th Division 1 December 1916.

measures detailed in the attached letters are carried out today.'[151] Army headquarters was then assured that 'the G.O.C. 24th Division was communicated with, and [a] report on the measures he has adopted to carry out the requirements contained will be forwarded when received.'[152] Further to this, the I Corps staff major who drafted the reply on behalf of Lieutenant-General Anderson, informed First Army that he would be paying a personal visit to Major-General Capper at 24th Division headquarters.[153]

No transcript or outline document imparting the results of 8th Buffs peremptory court of enquiry was found amongst consulted archives. The verdict, however, appears to have been recorded in the battalion war diary:

Lieutenant-General C.A. Anderson, GOC I Corps.

The disaster seems to be almost entirely due to the fact that higher authorities order us to send our N.C.O.s to all corners of the earth. The result is that we have to leave inexperienced N.C.O.s in charge of important posts, & these failed to show the leadership that is necessary in case of emergency.[154]

One NCO, G/8777 Corporal P. Mordey of B Company, rose to the occasion whilst defending Seaforth Crater post despite being surrounded.[155] Second Lieutenant

151 See TNA WO 95/168: '24th Division No. 1085/1', 6 January 1917; '6th Division No. 1085 (G.b.).', 6 January 1917, Hostile Raid Against Our Trenches M.1.B.6.y – H.31.C.5.2 on Morning of 5th January [1917] File, First Army General Staff War Diary.
152 This document is not in the relevant First Army, I Corps or 24th Division TNA files.
153 TNA WO 95/168: 'First Army No. 1085/2 (G.b.).', 6 January 1917, Hostile Raid Against Our Trenches M.1.B.6.y – H.31.C.5.2 on Morning of 5th January [1917] File, First Army General Staff War Diary.
154 TNA WO 95/ 2207: 8th Buffs War Diary.
155 Cpl. Percy Mordey (1896-1975) of Peckham, South London.

Darling and Private Setterfield of D Company were also praised for their 'particularly fine work'.[156] What the higher authorities would make of the Buffs enquiry conclusion was now a matter for the second court of enquiry scheduled for 7 January.

Regrettably, the appointed brigadier-general president and officers composing the second court of enquiry remain unknown despite rigorous examination of the relevant formation and unit war diaries.[157] The only pertinent reference found was an entry noting that the brigade major of 73rd Brigade had attended the proceedings on 7 and 8 January.[158] Bearing the signature of Major-General Barrow, the court's findings were outlined in a First Army report of 22 January:

> The investigation of the Court of Enquiry makes it clear that –
> i)   The dispositions for the defence of the front were inadequate and faulty.
> ii)   There was a want of supervision by battalion H.Q.
> iii) The battalion defence scheme was not well thought out or drawn up.

As regards (i), the different points have been pointed out and commented on upon by the G.O.C. 24th Division and G.O.C. I Corps.[159]

The want of a proper system of communication between posts and supporting troops is particularly conspicuous and may, in some measure, account for want of confidence and consequent panic on the part of some of the garrison.

As regards (ii), the fact that the majority of the officers are very young and inexperienced, and that a proportion of the men were in the trenches for the first time, would call for more than ordinary control and supervision on the part of battalion H.Q. Although both the battalion commander and second in command are regular and experienced officers, this appears to have been particularly wanting.

As regards (iii), it is the immediate duty of the Brigade Commander to ensure that battalion defence schemes are suitable and well-drawn up, and of the Divisional Staff to satisfy itself that such is the case.

---

156 TNA WO 95/2207: 8th Buffs War Diary,

157 As per Lieutenant-General Anderson's statement that the appointed court president would be a 'brigade commander of another division', the brigade war diaries of 6th and 21st divisions, I Corps component formations at the time, were examined without result. See TNA WO 95/168: 'I Corps. G.X./283/13', 5 January 1917, Hostile Raid Against Our Trenches M.1.B.6.y – H.31.C.5.2 on Morning of 5th January [1917] File, First Army General Staff War Diary.

158 TNA WO 95/2217: 73rd Brigade War Diary.

159 Other than Capper's early critique (5 January) of 8th Buffs 'quite inadequate' communications between front and support lines, subsequent documents outlining the GOC 24th Division and GOC I Corps' defence disposition points were not found in the relevant TNA files. See TNA WO 95/168: 'I Corps G.X./283/13', 5 January 1917, Hostile Raid Against Our Trenches M.1.B.6.y – H.31.C.5.2 on Morning of 5th January [1917] File, First Army General Staff War Diary.

Whilst in full sympathy with, and making full allowance for, the severe conditions and many difficulties as represented by the G.O.C. 24th Division, the Army Commander cannot but express his grave disapprobation and point out that, with the exception of certain officers, N.C.O.s and men who did their duty in a gallant manner, the incident reflects discredit on those concerned.[160]

On balance, mitigating circumstances did not apply to 24th Division headquarters which, having issued a general sector defence scheme in December 1916, was deemed remiss in ensuring brigade level command provided component battalion defence scheme oversight. Likewise, if, as Peter Simkins notes in a seminal chapter, an infantry brigadier's primary non-combat responsibilities were 'training and administration',

then 17th Brigade headquarters was also justifiably presumed lacking with regard to subordinate unit supervision and guidance.[161]

Sympathetic to 8th Buffs' plight the second court of enquiry may have been, however, it did not accept the first court's determination that inexperienced NCOs were solely to blame. Nevertheless, it was an undeniable wartime fact that infantry battalions often experienced personnel 'turbulence' whereby officers and men were dispatched, in the words of the incensed battalion diarist, 'to all corners of the earth' on attached duties or courses.[162] As the OC 2nd West Yorkshire Regiment observed: 'The "paper strength" of the Battalion is 35 officers

Major-General G. de S. Barrow, MGGS First Army. (Author)

160 TNA WO 95/168: 'First Army No. 802/20 (G)., 22 January 1917, Hostile Raid Against Our Trenches M.1.B.6.y – H.31.C.5.2 on Morning of 5th January [1917] File, First Army General Staff War Diary.

161 Peter Simkins, '"Building Blocks": Aspects of Command and Control at Brigade Level in the BEF's Offensive Operations, 1916-1918' in Gary Sheffield & Dan Todman (eds.), *Command and Control on the Western Front: The British Army's Experience 1914-18* (Staplehurst: Spellmount, 2004), p.145. For the work and development of GHQ, army, corps, division and brigade 'G' (General) staffs, see Paul Harris, *The Men Who Planned the War: A Study of the Staff of the British Army on the Western Front, 1914-1918* (Farnham: Ashgate, 2016).

162 Chris McCarthy, 'British Infantry Battalion in the Great War' in Sheffield & Todman (eds.), *Command and Control on the Western Front*, p.174 and TNA WO 95/2207: 8th Buffs War Diary.

and 717 other ranks, but the "real" or "ration" strength is only 22 and 205, the remainder being casualties, sick, absent on duties and courses of instruction, with a few on leave.'[163]

Recognition that the Buffs, although well above strength at 1,130 officers and men, required more than the usual supervision resulted in the court placing the principal onus on to battalion headquarters. Its conclusion that 'a proportion of the men were in the trenches for the first time' points to many of the recently arrived draft, 100 in all, being assigned to D Company. The determination that most of the Buffs commissioned leadership was young and lacking in experience begs the question, where were the company officers during the raid? None was killed, wounded, or taken prisoner in the front, second or support lines, and only one of their number – 2nd Lieutenant Darling – organised a counter-attack.[164] Thus a portion of the trench garrison, with no officers present and reliant on inexperienced NCOs to tell them what to do, panicked in the face of the unexpected enemy incursion. Relative to this was the inadequate state of the defence and communications disconnect between crater posts and those behind. With regard to the former, the court was well aware of the poor trench conditions, meagre barbed wire defences and dearth of available labour for improvements as articulated in the First Army report of November 1916.[165] All the more reason then for battalion headquarters to meet, in its estimation, 24th Division's defence scheme expectations and make the best of a bad job by doing everything in its power to render the assigned subsector as impregnable as possible.[166] Concerning the latter, defensive scheme communication arrangements for the Puits 14 Bis subsector called for 17th Brigade to be connected with its two frontline battalions (8th Buffs on the right and 1st Royal Fusiliers on the left) by cable buried from four to eight feet in depth. The right subsection cables, buried from three to six feet in depth, were connected to the right, centre and left company headquarters. 'From there cables were extended by trench lines', although whether or not these links were connected to power buzzers

163 Terraine (ed.) *General Jack's Diary 1914-1918*, p.213. The 8th Buffs addressed gaps in its NCO ranks by confirmation of all acting and substantive ranks on 21 February 1917. See Mark Connelly, *Steady the Buffs! A Regiment, A Region and the Great War* (Oxford: Oxford University Press, 2006), p.133.

164 For the junior infantry officer experience from commissioning to active service, see Christopher Moore-Bick, *Playing the Game: The British Junior Infantry Officer on the Western Front 1914-18* (Solihull: Helion & Co., 2012), chapters 2 and 3.

165 TNA WO 158/187: 'First Army No. GS.474', 22 November 1916, First Army Operations File.

166 See TNA WO 95/2190: '24th DIVN DEFENCE SCHEME, COPY NO. 17. DEC 16, I. GENERAL PRINCIPLES ON WHICH THE DEFENCE IS TO BE CONDUCTED', 24th Division General Staff War Diary. Consideration of inter-battalion reliefs vis-à-vis maintenance of the frontline makes one wonder what the state of the Puits 14 Bis subsector was prior to 8th Buffs relief of 3rd Rifle Brigade on 3 January. Whatever the circumstances, it was the former unit that was successfully raided, division, brigade and component battalion headquarters now put on notice by the court's findings.

and/or vibrator telegraphs, then in the process of being phased out for use beyond brigade headquarters, is not recorded.[167] Fullerphones were installed at all three company headquarters in the line.[168]

Supplementing this vanguard technology were more conventional methods of communication, the employment thereof specifically emphasised in the divisional defence scheme: 'Every endeavour must be made to keep in constant touch by visual signalling [SOS Very lights, Lucas lamps, etc.] or orderly with our own troops on either flank and with those to the front and rear.'[169] Employed forward of brigade headquarters, the Fullerphone remained in short supply throughout 1916, 'but by early 1917 they had become a familiar and popular means of intercommunication, although restrictions as to their use as a means of voice communications had been firmly established' to prevent the enemy from listening in. For its main drawback 'was that, while telegraphic messages could not be intercepted, speech transmissions could be overheard.'[170] Assuming, based on Private Setterfield's account, that D Company

---

167 R.E. Priestley, *The Work of the Royal Engineers in the European War 1914-19: The Signal Service in France* (Chatham: W & J Mackay, 1921), p.178. The Power Buzzer Earth Induction set utilised a 150 to 200-yard baseline for earth transmission of electrical impulses that were picked up by a receiving amplifier situated between 2,000 to 5,000 yards distance. The Vibrator Telegraph was a military line telegraph device. It consisted of telegraph components mounted onto a rectangular wooden base. See Brian N. Hall, *Communications and British Operations on the Western Front, 1914-1918* (Cambridge: Cambridge University Press, 2017), pp.101-02 and *RCsigs.ca* <http://www.rcsigs.ca/index.php/Vibrator_Telegraph>

168 The Fullerphone was a portable DC line telephonic and Morse telegraph combination utilised in response to concerns about widespread German telephone tapping. Devised in 1915 by Captain Algernon C. Fuller of the Royal Engineer Signal Service, its most important feature was that all transmissions were immune to enemy *Moritz* telephone intercept devices which made the system suitable for employment in forward areas. Moreover, the device was sensitive with a sufficient for purpose line current of only 0.5 microampere. In practice, however, two microamperes were required for comfortable readings and it could be operated over ordinary army field lines of 25-33 kilometres distance. When superimposed on to existing telephone lines, Fullerphone and telephone signal messages could be transmitted simultaneously without mutual interference. See Hall, *Communications and British Operations on the Western Front, 1914-1918*, pp.176-77 and Jim Beach & James Bruce, 'British Signals Intelligence in the Trenches, 1915-1918, Part 1: Listening Sets', *Journal of Intelligence History*, (2019), DOI, 10.1080/16161262.2019.1659580, pp.5, 6, 9-10, 12, 14, 16, 22.

169 TNA WO 95/2190: '24th DIVN DEFENCE SCHEME, COPY NO. 17. DEC 16, I. GENERAL PRINCIPLES ON WHICH THE DEFENCE IS TO BE CONDUCTED', 24th Division General Staff War Diary. How it was that the outposts atop Loos Crassier on the right flank and 1st Royal Fusiliers on the left flank remained unaware of the raid is not addressed in the relevant documents.

170 Hall, *Communications and British Operations on the Western Front, 1914-1918*, pp.176-77. A January 1917 pamphlet (SS537 *Summary of Recent Information Regarding the German Army and its Methods*) observed that the *Moritz* device was 'responsible for providing the Germans with more identifications of British units then all their other intelligence sources

headquarters – where the sole company Fullerphone had been installed – was just outside the raided area, it can be hypothesized that signals security precautions and consequent imposed dependence on a doubtful visual signalling and message orderly configuration sealed 8th Buffs fate once the enemy raiders had achieved tactical surprise.[171]

Consequences

The second court of enquiry's damning conclusions did not bode well for Lieutenant-Colonel Lucas who was relieved for lack of organizational and leadership abilities in a quintessential competency-based dismissal.[172] Unwilling to blame the D Company commander who was 'the real culprit according to many battalion officers', he accepted full responsibility before relinquishing battalion command on 26 January.[173]

combined.' In October 1916 First Army GOC General Horne railed against 'abuse of the telephone.' It was from the following November that officially proscribed telephone conversations were monitored with positive effect by IToc (Intelligence/Interceptor/ Intercepting Telephone) listening stations which, in addition to monitoring German telephone traffic, policed internal communications in the forward area. Security lapse reports emanating from them could result in court martial proceedings. See Beach & Bruce, 'British Signals Intelligence in the Trenches, 1915-1918, Part 1: Listening Sets', *Journal of Intelligence History*, (2019), DOI, 10.1080/16161262.2019.1659580, pp.6, 13-15.

171 According to Brian N. Hall, '[V]isual signalling on the Western Front remained a very hazardous, slow and unreliable means of communication. As well as topographical constraints, fog, dust and smoke obscured flag and lamp signals, while lack of sunlight in winter rendered heliographs impotent. Moreover, as one signaller observed after the war, although each division established a comprehensive system of visual stations in the forward area, 'they had necessarily to be one way working, that is from front to rear, since signals from a station facing the enemy might be observed by him.' Subsequently, each passage from a forward signalling station had to be signalled through at least twice in what was became known as the D.D.D.D. procedure, and written confirmation of it sent by runner.' Hall, *Communications and British Operations on the Western Front, 1914-1918*, pp.104-05.

172 For battalion commander firing, see Peter E. Hodgkinson, *British Infantry Battalion Commanders in the First World War* (Farnham: Ashgate, 2015), pp.115-21. Lucas's successor, Major F.C.R. Studd (1881-1918), appears to have assumed command by 29 January, although the official succession date is recorded as 20 February. See TNA WO 95/2207: 8th Buffs War Diary; War Office, *The Monthly Army List for April 1917* (London: HMSO, 1917), col. 924e and War Office, *The Quarterly Army List for the Quarter Ending 31st December 1917*, Vol. 1 (London: HMSO, 1918), p.512a,

173 Connelly, *Steady the Buffs!*, p.133. The Buffs multi-battalion history is somewhat reticent about raid particulars, simply remarking that the Germans 'started the New Year with a heavy dose of gas and lachrimatory [sic] shells, and on 5th January an extensive raid.' The actions of 2nd Lieutenant Darling and Pte. Setterfield are also chronicled. Seaforth Crater post defender Cpl. Mordey is mistakenly identified as 'Captain Morley' but is noted as a DCM recipient in a related volume appendix. See Colonel R.S.H. Moody, *Historical*

Divisional headquarters first response to the setback was recorded by Captain Foster Hall following an unwelcome parade during which Major-General Capper addressed 8th Buffs:

> In the morning, the GOC inspected us & told us off slightly for let[ting] the Boche raid us. He did it very nicely, but it was snowing the whole time & very cold.[174]

This would not be all. High command expectations that officers and men redeem themselves and the tit for tat nature of raid warfare as practiced in the Loos Salient during winter 1916-17, assured that the battalion would be called upon to carry out an elaborate retribution raid sometime in the near future.[175] Launched the same day as Lucas's departure, 120 men of 8th Buffs; 113 men of 12th Royal Fusiliers and eight men of 104th Field Company Royal Engineers, supported by artillery, machine-guns and trench mortars, successfully stormed the German line 'dressed in white smocks and had their helmets painted white, owing to the snow on the ground' at 6:45 a.m.[176] Divisional and brigade headquarters appear to have had a hand in assigning capable officers from other battalions to provide operational oversight. Thus Lieutenant-Colonel R. Pigot, OC 3rd Rifle Brigade,[177] was tasked with planning and execution whilst Major S.H. Dix of 2nd Leinster Regiment oversaw the intensive training.[178] Some 15 or 16 of the *IR 153* garrison were reported killed by 'bullet, bayonet or bomb' and 17 prisoners brought back at a cost to the Buffs of one officer and one man killed and 15 men wounded. The Royal Fusiliers lost four officers and 10 men wounded and six men missing. Fulsome praise from division and corps headquarters

---

Record of the Buffs East Kent Regiment (3rd Foot) Formerly Designated the Holland Regiment and Prince George of Denmark's Regiment 1914-1919 (London: Medici Society, 1922), p.231 and Appendix III.

174 IWM Doc. 22414: Private Papers of Brigadier E. Foster Hall, 11 January 1917 diary entry.

175 For the frequency of retribution motivated trench raids, see Ashworth, *Trench Warfare 1914-1918*, pp.201-02. Further to this, Captain Hitchcock claimed that his battalion's successful raid on the Triangle was motivated by the 5 January raid, although the former enterprise had been in the planning stage from 2 January. See Hitchcock, "*Stand To*", pp.228-30.

176 TNA WO 95/2190: 'Report on a raid carried out by 120 men of the 8th Buffs and a 113 men of the 12th Royal Fusiliers and 8 men of the 104th Field Company', 27 January 1917, 24th Division General Staff War Diary.

177 Lieutenant-Colonel Robert Pigot DSO MC. Commissioned Rifle Brigade from Militia 1901; South Africa 1902; RFC 1913-14; 3rd Rifle Brigade September 1914; OC 3rd Rifle Brigade 1916; OC 11th Tank Battalion 1917-18 and 6th Tank Brigade 1918.

178 Major Stephen Hamilton Dix MC (1878-1917). Militia commission; ASC South Africa 1899-1902; Leinster Regiment 1901; Adjutant Militia and Special Reserve 1908-12; Army Cyclist Corps 1914; MID 1915; APM 1916. Detached from staff duties to take on the special raid training assignment, Dix would assume battalion command the following March only to be killed seven months later during the Third Battle of Ypres.

was forwarded to the units concerned – brigade and battalion honour had been preserved.[179]

One of three trench raids launched by 24th Division during the week of 21-26 January,[180] the operation of the 26th did not atone for the perceived shortcomings of Brigadier-General Carroll who relinquished command of 17th Brigade 'as, in the opinion of his divisional and corps commander, he was not fitted for command.'[181] With two ostensibly ineffective commanding officers sacked *pour encourager les autres* and new defensive arrangements consisting of posts, obstacles and blocks recommended by First Army in place, the Germans found it more difficult to penetrate the British line. Commenting on the 153er Methode, *IR 153's* regimental history declared, 'And so developed, one could say, a sort

Lieutenant-Colonel L.W. Lucas, OC 8th Buffs. (IWM HU 124381)

of formula for these operations which was invariably successful, until the enemy, as a

---

179   The German trenches raided were to the immediate left of the 5 January raid site. TNA WO 95/2190: 'Report on a raid carried out by 120 men of the 8th Buffs and a 113 men of the 12th Royal Fusiliers and 8 men of the 104th Field Company', 27 January 1917; 'C2121' pink message proformas, 26 January 1917, 24th Division General Staff War Diary and Radley, *On the Dangerous Edge*, pp.331-33. This raid is not mentioned in Oswald, *Das Altenburger Regiment (8. Thüringisches Infanterie-Regiment Nr. 153) im Weltkriege*.

180   TNA WO 95/2190: 24th Division General Staff War Diary. Two German raids occurred during the same period.

181   TNA WO 374/12561: BEF General Headquarters to War Office correspondence, 18 October 1917, CARROLL, Brig Gen J W V, Officers' Long Service File. There is a contradiction with regard to when Carroll departed 17th Brigade. The Buffs and Royal Fusiliers raid of 26 January after-action report was composed by the unfortunate brigadier-general on 27 January, whilst the relevant post-war orders of battle volume records his command tenure as ending on 16 January due to sickness, after which two lieutenant-colonels, one of which was Pigot, successively assumed temporary command. Considering that the former document is signed 'J.W. Carroll, Brig. Gen. Commanding 17th Brigade', it appears that Carroll's departure occurred shortly after the retribution raid. See TNA WO 95/2190: 'Report on a raid carried out by 120 men of the 8th Buffs and a 113 men of the 12th Royal Fusiliers and 8 men of the 104th Field Company', 27 January 1917, 24th Division General Staff War Diary and Becke, *Order of Battle of Divisions, Part 3A*, p.128.

result of his painful experiences, finally grasped the ruse and developed new methods to counter it, with varying degrees of success.'[182]

The Nemesis of Deception

Taking up the woeful tale of official wartime deceit first promulgated by C.E. Montague, Lord Moran, the aforementioned 1st Royal Fusiliers Medical Officer Captain Charles McMoran Wilson, expanded on the 5 January trench raid story in *The Anatomy of Courage* (1945), his acclaimed account of the psychological effects of war based on first-hand experience and anecdote. Warming to this theme, Moran claimed that this 'little incident' was 'such a perfect specimen of its kind that Charles Montague lifted it bodily from a letter I had written to *The Times* and dumped it in his *Disenchantment* in a chapter on the "Duty of Lying".' Reflecting back to the winter of 1916-17, he observed that it 'was a time of doubt and disillusionment' throughout the BEF. 'Men were weary, less certain of things. There was a feeling abroad that it was necessary to believe in someone or something to carry on at all.' This doleful state of morale, he continued, was further undermined by the 'garbled accounts the correspondents in France' which had 'done incalculable harm. Men, knowing the facts, rose up against that fancy literature' – the 'nemesis of deception'. Remarking on the trench raiding enterprises of the period, Moran postulated that success 'was no longer measured by statements of dugouts blown up and Huns destroyed, only prisoners counted; no journalism could bring in prisoners.' Evidence for this assertion followed with the reproduction of a First Army Intelligence Summary No. 724 entry which, blandly stating what was known at the time, observed that the enemy had 'attempted a raid' but was 'driven off' with losses on the morning of 5 January. Rankled by the perceived duplicity, Moran observed, 'We were told how the enemy attempting a raid on our line after severe fighting only succeeded in leaving identifications behind, which confirmed the disposition of the 153rd Regiment as elucidated by our intelligence department.'[183] The continuing thread of presumed disinformation appeared in *The Times* the next day:

182 Oswald, *Das Altenburger Regiment (8. Thüringisches Infanterie-Regiment Nr. 153) im Weltkriege*, p.249. For a singular contribution to these defensive arrangements, see Hitchcock, *"Stand To"*, pp.249-50 for the author's 'original' Lewis Gun post plan. For a personal account of First Army's c. 1915-17 developmental approach to frontline intelligence gathering for raids and the repelling thereof by observation, scouting and patrolling, see Major H. Hesketh-Prichard DSO MC, *Sniping in France: With Notes on the Scientific Training of Scouts, Observers, and Snipers* (Mt Ida, Arkansas: Lancer Militaria 1993 reprint of 1920 edition).
183 Moran, *The Anatomy of Courage*, pp.72-73.

GERMAN TRENCH RAIDERS NEAR LOOS
HEAVY TRENCH FIGHTING

The following telegraphic dispatch was received from General Headquarters in France: –

8:36 p.m.: – Early this morning a hostile raiding party succeeded in entering our lines south of Loos. Heavy fighting ensued, and the enemy was speedily driven out, leaving a number of dead in our trenches. Some of our men are missing.[184]

Mindful of the actual raid particulars, Moran refuted the official GHQ communique:

Readers of *The Times* would scarcely deduce from this that the Boche stayed forty minutes in our trenches extracting fifty-one prisoners from the deep dugouts in the support line of the battalion on our right, that a corporal and two men stuck to a machine-gun otherwise there was little fight shown, and that subsequently after a court of enquiry the officer commanding this battalion was removed from his command … The censor may have to draw his blue pencil through the truth for more reasons than one. Those who are compelled to be spectators might take hardly the tale of what actually happens in war. Stories like Loos are only tolerable because the same thing may befall the listener at any time. It made all the difference when a man could not share the fruits of incompetence.[185]

Such 'cooking of news before it was served up to the public in England', Moran concluded, was 'a prime factor in unsettling opinion in France. Men could not help seeing that this news was altered not because it gave information to the enemy for he already knew it; they were left to speculate in whose interest such editing was carried out.'[186]

From a socio-literary perspective Montague, who was the first to consider the Loos trench raid in a post-war disillusionment literature context, and Moran's views are heavy with hindsight and reflective of their class.[187] Replete with broad and patronizing Victorian/Edwardian generalisations about 'the people' (lower-middle and working classes), *Disenchantment* and *The Anatomy of Courage* are erudite testaments

---

184 *The Times*, 6 January 1917, Issue 41369, p.8, col. B.
185 Moran, *The Anatomy of Courage*, p.73.
186 Ibid., pp.73-74.
187 From this point on, the majority of my conclusions with regard to the German raid vis-à-vis Montague and Moran's perspectives on its contemporary reportage, are based on an informative email exchange (5 March 2012) with Professor Stephen Badsey, a noted scholar of modern conflict, propaganda, and military media matters. See also Stephen Badsey, *The German Corpse Factory: A Study in First World War Propaganda* (Warwick: Helion & Co., 2019), pp.32, 69, 272.

to upper and middle class senti-ments which failed to grasp that most British domestic propaganda, official announce-ments or otherwise, was primarily aimed at the lower orders and mass society. Thus both ex-servicemen authors, in addition to a litany of war poets, railed against the presumed gross deception with an air of intellectual and moral superiority. Behaving like 'people with hangovers after a party', these literati oracles of the 'truth about the war' were influenced by the pervasive anti-war and anti-government propaganda of the 1920s and

Charles MacMoran Wilson, later Lord Moran c. 1910.

30s.[188] Certain that Great Britain had been subjected to a lying and cynical propa-ganda machine of which war correspondents became the hated symbol, 'they were just believing a new set of propaganda falsehoods, and most (like Moran), continued to believe them.'[189] Paradoxically, modern scholars of First World War era politics and culture view the interwar disenchantment version of events as much more perni-cious and inaccurate in raw propaganda terms than the official wartime version.[190] So, what effect did the latter have on working class opinion at home and in France and how influential was it? Analysis of Moran's jaundiced perspective reveals an unsound dichotomy of thought: 'this was a big government and newspaper propaganda effort; but no one in the lower classes believed it was true; but at the same time all these lies meant greater lower-class support for the war ... If the propaganda campaign was as ineffective and counterproductive as Moran claims, do you think someone might have noticed?'[191] All things considered, it is impossible to determine its impact and there is no way of finding out. 'What is true is that the government and the establishment (including the newspapers) believed that this was the way the lower class wanted them to behave, and they were probably right. The relentlessly positive tone was a signal that

188 Badsey email correspondence, 5 March 2012.
189 Ibid.
190 See Correlli Barnett, *The Collapse of British Power* (London: Eyre Methuen, 1972); Dan Todman, *The Great War: Myth and Memory* (London: Continuum, 2002); Adrian Gregory, *The Last Great War: British Society and the First World War* (Cambridge: Cambridge University Press, 2008) and Badsey, *The German Corpse Factory*.
191 Badsey email correspondence, 5 March 2012.

their leaders had faith in them, and faith in victory, the equivalent of a kind word or a pat on the back.'[192]

What can be made of Moran's specific allegations about the Loos raid reporting and its impact on morale in France? His criticism of the First Army intelligence summary ignored the fact that a more comprehensive account of the event appeared in next day's summary i.e., after additional details had been gathered and passed up the chain of command. In point of fact, it was in this document that German presence in the British line for 40 minutes was recorded.[193] The GHQ communique deception claim also fails to withstand scrutiny to the extent that the relevant German *Heersbericht* entry appeared, as was common *The Times* editorial practice of the day, translated into English on the same page as the seemingly questionable communique. This deliberate juxtaposition of official BEF and enemy communiques provided readers with alternative narratives from which conclusions could be drawn.[194] In citing the GHQ communique, Moran appears to have been unaware that *The Times* sub-editor responsible 'used it effectively unaltered; but somehow this becomes the fault and responsibility of the war reporters with GHQ.'[195] The very nature of raids, their outcome, how they were recorded in intelligence summaries and reported by the press also eluded him. Couched in formulaic exposition such as 'the enemy attempted a raid' and 'the enemy was speedily driven out' was standard practice when there was nothing else to say, 'and strictly speaking correct since a trench raid was not intended to hold ground but to retreat afterwards. It puts the best possible "spin" on an event, like saying "everybody did their best."'[196] Such phraseology, redolent of Robert Graves's satirical poem 'The Persian Version', had a 'slightly desperate cheerfulness to it' that was commonplace in short official pronouncements amounting to boilerplate.[197] Therefore, it remains doubtful that 'anyone paid the slightest attention or would do so now if it were not that memoirs like those of Moran and Montague had not mentioned them.'[198] For its part, GHQ recognised that it had to comment; 'it would never deny that a real event had taken place or put itself in a position of responding late to a German claim; so

---

192 Ibid.
193 TNA WO 157/1: 'FIRST ARMY INTELLIGENCE SUMMARY No. 725, 6 January 1917, First Army Intelligence File.
194 *The Times*, 6 January 1917, Issue 41369, p.8, col. B.
195 Badsey email correspondence, 5 March 2012. For insight into the complex relationship between British GHQ and Fleet Street, see Stephen Badsey, 'Douglas Haig and the Press' in Badsey, *The British Army in Battle and its Image 1914-18*, pp.13-35. See also, Neville Stephen Lytton, *The Press and the General Staff* (London: W. Collins Sons & Co. LTD, 1920) for an entertaining personal account of BEF general staff and press corps interaction. The author was a GHQ press censor contemporary of C.E. Montague.
196 Badsey, 5 March 2012.
197 Ibid. See also Stephen Badsey, 'The Raid on Narrow Trench' in Badsey, *The British Army in Battle and its Image 1914-18*, pp.157-58.
198 Badsey, 5 March 2012.

if there was nothing to say these were the phrases that it used.'[199] Indeed, the fundamental reason for the existence of war correspondents and official communiques was the alarming political power of a London press that refused to be ignored. Added to this was a reasoned determination shared by Kitchener, Haig and Robertson amongst others that, broadly speaking, the opposing armies were equal, 'and that the country that won would be the one that outlasted its enemies in a contest of determination and sacrifice. This meant that public opinions and attitudes were critical to the war effort.'[200] It was during the next world-wide conflict – the uncertain spring of 1942 – that public opinion and the official process by which the nation was kept informed of events was once again taken into consideration, this time by the unknown author of a War Office memorandum prepared for the Churchill War Cabinet. Remarking on 'explanations of service matters, operations and occurrences', he observed: 'In these circumstances it is difficult to be candid and objective in all our reports to the public. We have to balance carefully the advantages arising from the maintenance of public confidence, or from complete secrecy and the enemy's ignorance.'[201]

Legacies

Chiefly remembered in two works of post-war literature and a published active service journal, the Loos raid of 5 January 1917 was not without its tragic human consequences. One familial repercussion concerned Private Frank Winterbottom whose widowed mother Florence, a resident of Anthony Street, Mossley, received a condolence letter from his company commander, Captain Foster Hall, in the post:

January 10th, 1917

Dear Mrs Winterbottom,
I am sorry to have to break such very bad news to you. Your son Private Frank Winterbottom was killed in action on the 5th last. The enemy made an attempt to raid our trenches and during the fighting that ensued your son was shot and killed. He died instantly and is a very great loss to us. We buried him in a small village behind the lines. I offer you the very sincere sympathy of the whole company in your very sad loss, and I know I am speaking for them all when I say we have lost a good friend and comrade.[202]

---

199 Ibid.
200 Ibid.
201 TNA WO 193/423: 'Misc. 7A. War Cabinet. Meeting to be held on __ April 1942', 11 April 1942, British Morale P. 1939-42 File.
202 *Private Frank Winterbottom* <https://www.findagrave.com/memorial/24374486/frank-winterbottom> Winterbottom is also commemorated on the St George's Church, Mossley 1914-18 war memorial.

Assurances of sudden death resulting from a hostile raiding 'attempt' was customary language employed by officers when composing commiseration correspondence. None of this, however, would comfort Mrs Winterbottom with regard to the financial consequences of her eldest son's loss, for her second son, a boy confined to a sanatorium, and a daughter were unable to provide a sustainable means of income 'and the soldier who so gallantly met his death was her chief support.'[203]

Intense raiding activity within the Loos Salient continued well into the following spring.[204] It was not until the opening of the Arras offensive on 9 April 1917 and consequent capture of Vimy Ridge that *Sixth Army* was compelled to sanction a strategic withdrawal as far as the western outskirts of Lens. Pivoting on Hill 70, this retirement led to the collateral abandonment of forward defences in the Double Crassier and Puits 14 Bis subsectors. Followed up by patrols of 6th and 24th divisions, the retreating *8th Division* succeeded in maintaining a hold on Hill 70 following stabilization of the line by 15 April. The key eminence remained in German hands until seized by the Canadian Corps in August 1917.[205]

The 8th Buffs went on to participate in the Vimy Ridge, Messines Ridge, Third Ypres, and Cambrai offensives. It was during the early 1918 general reorganisation of the BEF when British infantry brigades were reduced from four to three battalions each that the Buffs, along with 12th Royal Fusiliers, were disbanded, the remaining officers and men assigned to other units.[206] Reminiscing about 24th Division's slow recovery after its harrowing baptism of fire at Loos in September 1915, Lord Moran observed:

> Nearly a year passed before the 24th Division was thrown into the Somme, and by that time most of the battalions of the two brigades which were hammered at Loos had recovered. But two battalions never got over that battle – probably their officers were to blame. Six months before the Somme that was common knowledge, but General Capper, whose energy had done much for the division, could not bring himself to acknowledge that he had failed with these battalions.

---

203 Ibid.
204 For example, eight British and two German raids occurred in the Loos Salient from 6 January to 2 February 1917. See TNA WO/158/193: First Army weekly summaries of operations, First Army Operations File; Radley, *On the Dangerous Edge*, pp.328-33 and Hodgkinson, *A Complete Orchestra of War*, pp.171-77.
205 See Major-General T.O. Marden (ed.), A *Short History of the Sixth Division Aug. 1914–March 1919* (London: Hugh Rees, 1920), pp.28-31; Hodgkinson, *A Complete Orchestra of War,* pp.178-91 and Douglas Delany & Serge Marc Durflinger (eds.), *Capturing Hill 70: Canada's Forgotten Battle of the First World War* (Vancouver-Toronto: HBC Press, 2016).
206 Infantry units slated for disbandment were obtained from a list of 145 battalions. The 8th Buffs and 12th Royal Fusiliers were replaced by 8th Queens from 72nd Brigade. See Becke, *Order of Battle of Divisions, Part 3A*, pp.130-31. For the 1918 reorganisation, see Hine, *Refilling Haig's Armies*, pp.222-25.

When in the Somme fighting they crumpled up leaving the units on their flank
in the air, division paid in full the price of his failure to cut losses.[207]

The fact that the Buffs, who appear to have given a good account of themselves during
the intense Somme fighting of August–September 1916, and Royal Fusiliers served
in the same brigade as Moran's unit provokes speculation that these were the battalions captiously referred to, the 'common knowledge' allegations of poor morale and
commissioned officer incompetence contributing factors to their eventual dissolution.
Notwithstanding, a general War Office policy that last formed Service battalions
(both units were designated 'K3' or 'Third New Army') should be disbanded first
unless there was good reason for not doing so appears to disprove this.[208]

Major-General Barrow, after a short spell in command of 7th Division, went on to
serve in Palestine and the Third Afghan War. A number of Indian Army command
positions followed before his retirement in 1929.[209] Lieutenant-General Anderson
relinquished command of I Corps in early February 1917 in order to assume leadership of the Indian Army's Southern Command. He retired in 1920.[210] Major-General
Capper left 24th Division to take up the post of Director General Tank Corps in May
1917. A sapper officer, his keen interest in emerging military technologies almost
certainly influenced the appointment decision making process. Commenting on his
departure, The Wipers Times (1 [2] Wednesday, 15 August 1917) remarked that his
successor would be taking up the mantle of '"The Professor" ... who, through nearly
two strenuous years, had led us from greenness to understanding.' Representing
pre-war army authority, control and process, Capper's conservative approach to tank
development was unpopular with his immediate subordinates who privately referred
to him as 'Stone Age'. Subsequent home division command in summer 1918 and a
variety of post-war appointments including that of Lieutenant-Governor of Guernsey,
continued until retirement in 1925.[211] Brigadier-General Carroll experienced varied
career fortunes after relinquishing brigade command. Appointed OC 1st Norfolk
Regiment, he was wounded on 4 October 1917 during a costly and operationally barren Third Ypres flank assault near Gheluvelt.[212] His consequent evacuation
provided incentive for Carroll's immediate superior, Major-General R.B. Stephens

---

207 Moran, The Anatomy of Courage, pp.83-84.
208 Moody, Historical Record of the Buffs East Kent Regiment (3rd Foot) Formerly Designated
     the Holland Regiment and Prince George of Denmark's Regiment 1914-1919, pp.158-63 and
     Hine, Refilling Haig's Armies, p. 223.
209 General Sir George Barrow, The Fire of Life (London: Hutchinson & Co., 1942) and
     'Obituary: Gen. Sir George Barrow', The Times, 29 December 1959. p. 10.
210 John Bourne, forthcoming British 1914-18 generals reference volume.
211 Ibid.
212 See Sir J.E. Edmonds, Military Operations France and Belgium 1917, Vol. II (London:
     HMSO, 1948), p. 314. Norfolk Regiment contemporary Lieutenant-Colonel P.V.P. Stone
     was appointed GOC 17th Brigade on 12 February 1917. Fourteen years younger than
     Carroll, 33-year-old Stone relinquished command of 1st Norfolks after which the former

(GOC 5th Division),[213] to compose an adverse personal report in which he stated that the 1st Norfolk OC was 'efficient enough when he tries but I have no doubt that his losing his brigade has been a disappointment to him and I do not think he is now any good as a battalion commander.' Furthermore, Stephens 'had tried hard to inspire him with some energy – even to the extent of putting up his name for a brigade again but I am afraid he has not responded.' There was 'no doubt', he concluded, that 'the present condition of his battalion is thoroughly unsatisfactory. They are dirty and badly turned out and their marching is thoroughly bad.'[214] The report was passed on from corps to army and GHQ before Carroll's fate was conveyed by Major-General W.A. Peyton (Military Secretary to Field Marshal Sir Douglas Haig)[215] on behalf of the BEF C-in-C, the final recommendation being that 'in view of his long service Lieutenant Colonel CARROLL be considered for further employment.'[216] The next opportunity presented itself when Carroll was appointed commander of the White Russian 'Morjegorskaia Force', North Russia Expeditionary Force in 1919.[217] Retiring with almost three decades of military service after the Allied withdrawal from Archangel and Murmansk, his efforts there were rewarded with a DSO, St George's Cross and the St Vladimir Order 4th Class.[218] Lieutenant-Colonel Lucas took up an instructor's post at the Senior Officers School, Aldershot as a brigade major. He never served in France again.[219] Australian tunnelling OC Major Coulter was shot dead by a sniper

assumed battalion command. Becke, *Order of Battle of Divisions, Part 3A*, p. 128 and Bourne, forthcoming British 1914-18 generals reference volume.

213 Major-General Reginald Byng Stephens (1869-1955). Commissioned Rifle Brigade 1890; Second Matabele War 1897; Sudan 1898; South Africa 1899-1902; Staff College 1906; CO Cadet Company, Sandhurst 1907-11; OC 2nd Rifle Brigade 1914-15; GOC 25th Brigade 1915-16 and GOC 5th Division 1916.

214 TNA WO 374/12561: 'H.Q. 5th Division, A.Q. Branch, No. C.C./408.', 8 October 1917, CARROLL, Brig Gen J W V Officers' Long Service File.

215 Major-General William Eliot Peyton (1866-1931). Commissioned 7th Dragoon Guards 1887; Sudan 1896-98; South Africa 1900; Staff College 1901; OC 15th Hussars 1903-07; Quartermaster General India 1907; GOC Meerut Brigade 1908; Military Secretary C-in-C India 1912; Chief of Staff 1st Mounted Division (TF) 1914; GOC 2nd Mounted Division 1915; GOC Western Desert Force January 1916; Military Secretary BEF C-in-C May 1916-March 1918.

216 TNA WO 374/12561: Major-General Peyton to War Office, 18 October 1917, CARROLL, Brig Gen J W V Officers' Long Service File. The Military Secretary's post was central to the operation of the BEF's management of appointments, promotions and removals and its system of honours and awards.

217 The North Russia Relief Force (1918-19) was part of the Allied intervention in Russia following the Bolshevik Revolution. British, French, Italian and United States troops were deployed on the side of the counter-revolutionary White movement. See Damien Wright, *Churchill's Secret War with Lenin: British and Commonwealth Military Intervention in the Russian Civil War, 1918-20* (Solihull: Helion & Co., 2017).

218 TNA WO 374/12561: CARROLL, Brig Gen J W V Officers' Long Service File.

219 Venn & Venn (eds.), *Alumni Cantabrigienses*, Vol. 2, p. 228.

Loos 5 January 1917 raid site in 2017. Photographed from the approximate German frontline, what remains of Seaforth Crater can be found in the dense L-shaped thicket ahead. (Author)

on Hill 70 in June 1917.[220] Captain Foster Hall remained with the army after the Armistice and rose to the rank of brigadier.[221] Awarded the MC for his actions during the retribution raid of 26 January 1917, 2nd Lieutenant Darling was wounded during the Messines Ridge offensive. Wounded a second time during the March 1918 retreat, he was demobilised in 1919.[222] Corporal Mordey and Private Setterfield were awarded the DCM and MM respectively for their actions on 5 January 1917. The former went on to achieve the rank of colour sergeant; the latter was promoted to lance corporal. Setterfield, recovering from a third wound at the time of the April 1917 *Thanet & Echo Advertiser* article, proudly remarked, 'you should have seen me standing out in front of the Battalion shaking hands with the General. Some kid!'[223]

With the Puits 14 Bis subsector now behind British lines from April 1917, one recalls the penetrating observation of a British corps commander as the Third Battle of Ypres drew to a close. Commenting on enemy positions of 'intense interest' the

220 *Leslie J. Coulter* <http://www.miningmudmedals.org/Leslie_J._Coulter>
221 A.J. Smithers, *Cambrai: The First Great Tank Battle* (London: Leo Cooper, 1992), p. 186.
222 TNA WO 339/54979: DARLING, 2nd Lieut. W H File.
223 John Bourne email correspondence, 15 November 2019; *British Army WWI Medal Rolls Index Cards, 1914-1920* <https://www.ancestry.co.uk/search/collections/medalrolls/> and Setterfield to sister correspondence quoted in *Thanet Advertiser & Echo*, 28 April 1917, p. 5.

previous autumn, he wrote: 'Now they are in our possession they become less inter-esting day by day and are losing their battle characteristics so rapidly that I quite understand why no historian can ever produce any accurate description of anything but the broad lines of any battle.'[224] The validity of the final part of this statement open to question, the eastward advance up Hill 70 ensured that trenches previously defended with so much blood and effort rapidly became overgrown and fell into disre-pair. Postbellum clearance gradually erased the opposing lines, mine craters and shell holes about Loos as the land was reclaimed for cultivation, but vestiges both seen and unseen still remain. Extending from the centre of present-day Loos-en-Gohelle, the *Rue Louis Faidherbe* runs eastward and under an A21 autoroute overbridge as it ascends Hill 70. To the left and on the Loos side of that crossing lies the 5 January 1917 trench raid site. Motorway traffic now passes over the approximate German frontline designated 'Natal Trench' on period British maps. From there the crop-sown slope descends westward to a dense L-shaped thicket enclosing traces of Seaforth Crater. Farther west is a pleasant public footpath and recent housing development prosaically christened *La Cité des Oiseaux* both of which are situated on what was once a maze of British trenches, dugouts and mineworks. It was during home construction in 2012 that builders encountered 'saps dating from the 14-18 war. Underground cavi-ties weakened supporting structures making it impossible to establish the foundations of certain dwellings.' This unexpected inconvenience provided contractors with the opportunity to apply an innovative construction principle – employment of frames and wooden walls to obtain 'necessary lightness and excellent thermal performance.' Identified dugout and tunnel cavities were also utilised for the storage of bowel infilling pellets as a means of preventing foundation subsidence.[225]

---

224 John Baynes, *Far From a Donkey: The Life of General Sir Ivor Maxse* (London: Brassey's, 1995), p. 180.

225 Information with regard to *La Cité des Oiseaux* construction problems and solutions was gleaned from an all-weather information plaque erected just outside the neighbourhood entrance.

7

'I could not persuade myself it had been great fun'
The Operational Experience of III Corps During the German Retreat to the Hindenburg Line, Spring 1917

Nigel Dorrington

On the afternoon of 22 February 1917, a 7th Royal West Kents patrol, conducting a daylight reconnaissance near Miraumont in the Ancre valley, discovered, much to their surprise, that there was no enemy in the trenches opposite.[1] Over the next 24 hours it became clear that this was part of a general retreat on the part of the German Army, a move that simultaneously acknowledged and sought to frustrate the hard won Allied successes of the previous year. As early as September 1916 construction had begun on a new defensive line almost 20 miles behind the existing frontline. A withdrawal to this position would, *OHL* calculated, reduce the length of the front by some 30 miles, free up as many as 10 divisions to create a stronger reserve and buy more time to prepare the army to face the anticipated Allied spring offensive.[2] As part of withdrawal process the entire area between the old and new positions was to be razed: villages, bridges, roads, railways, farms and orchards were all to be destroyed, forcing the Allies to establish new lines of communication across the devastated area before they could begin the process of preparing the next offensive. Christened the *Siegfried Stellung*, the new defensive line became known to the Allies as the 'Hindenburg Line'.

The timing of the German withdrawal, between the offensive on the Somme in 1916 and that at Arras in April 1917, has led to a general neglect of this episode in the British historiography of the First World War. The overall impression is that the German army had succeeded at putting the BEF on the back foot, both operationally

---

1   C. Falls, *Military Operations, France and Belgium 1917*, Vol. 1 (Nashville, Tennessee: Battery Press, 1992), p.95. The 7th Royal West Kents were part of 55th Brigade, 18th (Eastern) Division.
2   J. Boff, *Haig's Enemy* (Oxford: Oxford University Press, 2018), pp.14, 8-150.

German cartoon commentary on the *Westheer's* withdrawal to the Hindenburg Line: A picture-puzzle on the Ancre – The German evacuation manoeuvres. Tommy: 'Where's that damned German?' (*Kladderadatsch*, 18 March 1917)

and tactically.[3] John Terraine's view may be considered a fair summary: 'Pursuit ... was hardly more than a pious hope ... When every tribute is paid to German skill, there remains a degree of Allied ineptitude to account for the missing of what might have been a great opportunity for inflicting damage.'[4]

The only detailed account of BEF operations is in the first volume of the Official History for 1917 which was published in 1940.[5] Relatively little attention has been paid to their impact on operational and tactical thinking except in the specialist fields of logistics and engineering.[6] However, there is much about the conduct of these operations that merits reconsideration. It was the only period of semi-open warfare that the BEF experienced between the late autumn of 1914 and spring of 1918. It also came at a time when the BEF was endeavouring to absorb the lessons of the Somme and implement them in its operational and tactical thinking through the publication of pamphlets such as *SS 135: The Training of Divisions for Offensive Action* and *SS 143: Instructions for the Training of Platoons for Offensive Action*.[7] Many of the same chal-

---

3   For example, see B. Liddell Hart, *History of the First World War* (London: Pan MacMillan, 1972), p.301.

4   J. Terraine, *Douglas Haig: The Educated Soldier* (London: Leo Cooper, 1990), pp.276-77.

5   Falls, *Military Operations 1917*, Vol. 1, pp.87-170, 525-34.

6   R. Thompson, 'Crossing the Devastated Zone, 1917: Lessons and Consequences for the British Expeditionary Force', *Bulletin of the Western Front Association*, 116 (2020), pp.13-17; M. Wedge, 'From the Hindenburg Line (1917) to the Hindenburg Line (1918): An Evaluation of the Developments in BEF logistical and engineering methodology based on the experience of open warfare gained during the German withdrawal to the Hindenburg Line (February-April 1917)', University of Birmingham BA dissertation, 2009.

7   General Staff, War Office, *SS 135: The Training of Divisions for Offensive Action* (Army Printing and Stationary Service, 1916) [*SS 135*]; General Staff, War Office, *SS 143:*

lenges encountered in the spring of 1917 would appear again in the late summer and autumn of 1918: the need for an increase in the tempo of operations, the need to maintain contact with a withdrawing enemy; the need to maintain supply lines across a devastated landscape; the need to find effective ways of co-ordinating different formations and arms in a fast changing situation and, above all, a realisation that a return to open warfare did not mean a reduction in casualties.

Falls' Official History account still remains the most detailed attempt to analyse the BEF's conduct of what became known as the 'German Retreat to the Hindenburg Line'.[8] Although highly critical of aspects of its initial stages, Falls, as both a former battalion officer and a divisional staff officer, was also well aware of the limitations that handicapped the British advance.[9] These included the reluctance of high command to press too hard on the heels of an enemy they knew to be retiring to a strong defensive position and from which they could launch a devastating counter-attack against any overextended pursuers.[10] This view was echoed by Robin Prior and Trevor Wilson in their study of General Sir Henry Rawlinson, GOC Fourth Army, under whose command III Corps, the object of this chapter, came.[11] Much of this caution was engendered by the success of German deception plans at the strategic level as demonstrated by the work of both David French and James Beach.[12] Consideration of the advance has been virtually absent in recent studies of the development of the BEF's operational art in favour of the 'set-piece' attack that came to dominate the British approach in 1917. Andy Simpson, in his study of corps level command, identified the emergence of the corps in this period as an effective operational formation rather than just an administrative one, but concentrated his analysis on Arras and Messines.[13] Paddy Griffith also saw the BEF in the advance as 'simply happy to rise from its muddy trenches and shake itself down ... The serious business of taking the next

Instructions for the Training of Platoons for Offensive Action (Army Printing and Stationary Service, 1917) [*SS 143*]. For their importance see P. Griffith, *Battle Tactics of the Western Front: The British Army's Art of Attack 1916-18* (New Haven, Connecticut: Yale University Press, 1994), pp.76-79; A. Simpson, *Directing Operations: British Corps Command on the Western Front 1914-18* (Stroud: Spellmount, 2006), pp.63-65: G. Sheffield, *Forgotten Victory: The First World War, Myths and Realities* (London: Headline, 2001), p.151.

8   E.A James, *A Record of the Battles and Engagements of the British Armies in France and Flanders, 1914-18* (Dallington: Naval & Military Press 1998 reprint of 1923 edition), p.16.

9   Falls, *Military Operations 1917*, Vol. I, pp.161-62.

10   Falls, p.169.

11   Robert Prior & Trevor Wilson, *Command on the Western Front: The Military Career of Sir Henry Rawlinson* (Oxford: Blackwell, 1992), pp.265-67.

12   D. French, 'Failures of Intelligence: The retreat to the Hindenburg Line and the March 1918 Offensive' in M. Dockerill & D. French (eds.), *Strategy and Intelligence: British Policy During the First World War*, (1996), pp.67-95, pp.77-84; J. Beach, *Haig's Intelligence: GHQ and the German Army 1916-1918* (Cambridge: Cambridge University Press, 2013), pp.223-32.

13   Simpson, *Directing Operations*, pp.61-82.

swing at the Germans was postponed until the big push in April.'[14] Only in some specific studies of the development of artillery, cavalry, engineering and logistics has the BEF experience been seen in a more positive light.[15]

This chapter seeks to shed light on the operational and tactical performance of the BEF through a case study of III Corps, part of Rawlinson's Fourth Army. In the course of this study particular attention has been paid to the observations made by Falls in the conclusion to his analysis of BEF operations during the retreat:

> When the Germans fell back the British divisions were for the most part bewildered and helpless until they had accustomed themselves to a new form [of warfare] … More local advantages might have been gained had there been more alertness and initiative … [However] several of the operations for the reduction of the German rear-guard locations and subsequently of the outposts to the Hindenburg Line were conducted with a skill which would have done credit to the most highly trained troops.[16]

In order to assess the validity of these observations the study will seek to examine the three key points raised above: the extent to which III Corps was caught unawares by the German withdrawal; whether or not it acted promptly enough to stand a chance of striking a heavy blow against its opponents; and how effectively its constituent forces were able to deal with the German rearguard once they had caught up with them.

Formed in August 1914, III Corps was to remain under its original commander, Lieutenant-General Sir William Pulteney, until February 1918.[17] For a general officer with such a lengthy tenure of command, Pulteney has been curiously overlooked by historians with only one recent biography.[18] Commissioned from the militia in 1878 with subsequent service in Egypt and South Africa, Pulteney had held brigade and divisional commands before the war, despite not having attended Sandhurst or Staff

---

14   Griffith, *Battle Tactics on the Western Front*, p.85.

15   M. Farndale, *History of the Royal Regiment of Artillery: Western Front 1914-18* (Woolwich: The Royal Artillery Institution, 1986), p.164; D. Kenyon, *Horsemen in No Man's Land: British Cavalry and Trench Warfare 1914-18* (Barnsley: Pen & Sword, 2011), pp.92-104; Thompson, 'Crossing the Devastated Zone', pp.13-17; Wedge, 'From the Hindenburg Line (1917) to the Hindenburg Line (1918)', pp.15-33; C. Phillips, 'A Modern Industrial Organisation: A Case Study of Fourth Army during the Battles of the "Hundred Days"', University of Birmingham M.A. Dissertation, 2009, pp.18-22.

16   Falls, *Military Operations 1917*, Vol. 1, pp.543-44.

17   A.F. Becke, *Order of Battle, Part 4, The Army Council, G.H.Q.s, Armies and Corps 1914-1918* (Newport: Ray Westlake, 1990), p.147. Corps Headquarters was established in August 1914 with the intention of taking 4th and 6th divisions under its command. However, it was not fully constituted until the beginning of October 1914.

18   A. Leask, *Putty from Tel-El-Kebir to Cambrai: The Life and Letters of Lieutenant General Sir William Pulteney 1861-1941* (Solihull: Helion & Co., 2015).

College.[19] That this command experience appeared to be the main grounds for his appointment as a corps commander in 1914 points to the problems that the expanding British Army already faced in finding suitable candidates for senior commands.[20] It has been wryly observed that the best staff officers were subsequently sent to III Corps to compensate for its commander's deficiencies.[21] One of those staff officers, Charles Bonham Carter, GSO1 III Corps from April to October 1917, later wrote in his unpublished autobiography that Pulteney was 'the most completely ignorant general I served under during the war and that is saying a lot.'[22] Yet, it is also clear from other comments such as those of Major-General R. Fanshawe, GOC 48th Division which was part of III Corps at this time, that 'Putty' was not

Lieutenant-General Sir William Pulteney.

entirely despised by his subordinates. When asked for his opinion as to the best corps commander he had served under during the war, Fanshawe replied without hesitation, 'Pulteney. He let me do exactly what I liked.'[23]

Despite its length of service on the Western Front, III Corps' experience of major offensive action prior to the Somme was limited and Pulteney emerged from that battle with a mixed record as a commander.[24] The fact that III Corps was one of only four British corps to take part in six or more battles in 1916 would imply that he was regarded by his superiors as reliable, but his degree of success varied.[25] On 1 July 1916, two divisions of III Corps suffered over 11,000 casualties for little territorial

19   Leask, pp.169-85.
20   J. M. Bourne, *Who's Who in World War One* (London: Routledge, 2001), p.239. See Leask, *Putty*, pp.729-30 for an examination of the role patronage may have played in Pulteney's appointment.
21   Bourne, *Who's Who in World War One*, p.239
22   Leask, *Putty*, p.730
23   C.E. Carrington, *Soldier from the Wars Returning* (London: Hutchinson, 1965), p.104
24   Simpson, *Directing Operations,* p.27. The only major offensive action that III Corps undertook after 1914 was a brigade-level assault, a diversion for the Loos offensive, near Bois Grenier on 25 September 1915. See J.E. Edmonds, *Military Operations, France and Belgium, 1915,* Vol. 2 (Nashville, Tennessee: Battery Press, 1995), pp.262-63.
25   Simpson, *Directing Operations,* pp.26-27. The remaining three formations were II Corps (Lt-Gen Jacobs), XIV Corps (Lt-Gen. Lord Cavan), and XV Corps (Lt-Gen. Horne).

gain, although over the following days the corps was able to secure both La Boisselle and Contalmaison.[26] On 15 September 1916, the 47th (London) Division, a subordinate formation of III Corps, suffered over 4,500 casualties during the capture of High Wood.[27] Pulteney overruled the wishes of the divisional commander, Major-General C. Barter, with regard to the use of tanks assigned to support the assault.[28] Although High Wood was captured, all the tanks were lost and the operation took much longer than Pulteney had anticipated.[29] He placed the blame on Barter who was sent home.[30] Pulteney's willingness to sack a subordinate he perceived as having failed would also become evident during the operations considered in this chapter. However, Fanshawe's comment on Pulteney may indicate that the latter had learned something from his experiences on the Somme and became more willing to take account of the views of his subordinates.[31]

On 16 January 1917 III Corps, then consisting of 1st, 48th and 50th divisions, received orders to proceed south of the River Somme to take over part of the line previously held by the French.[32] This was part of an agreement between Field Marshal Sir Douglas Haig and French C-in-C General Robert Nivelle for the BEF to extend its front south to free up French divisions for the intended spring offensive.[33] The relief of the French began on the night of 1/2 February and by 26 February III Corps held a line running south from the Somme opposite Péronne to Genermont with IV Corps

26   J.E. Edmonds, *Military Operations, France and Belgium, 1916*, Vol. I (Nashville, Tennessee: Battery Press, 1993), pp.371-91.
27   T. Norman, *The Hell They Called High Wood* (London: William Kimber, 1984), p.233.
28   Norman, pp.216-17. Pulteney expected the tanks to rapidly move through High Wood whereas Barter had wanted the tanks to work around the flanks of the wood. Simpson describes the judgement of the official historian that it was a 'tactical blunder' as 'strong words for the Official History.' See W. Miles, (ed.), *Military Operations, France and Belgium, 1916*, Vol. 2 (Nashville, Tennessee: Battery Press, 1992), p.364; Simpson, *Directing Operations*, pp.54-55, fn. 14.
29   Norman, *The Hell They Called High Wood*, pp.219-21, 223-24.
30   Norman, p.233. Haig recorded on 5 October 1916 that 'I had to send home General Barter (Commander 47th London Division) on Pulteney's recommendation. He mishandled his division so on the 15th and 16th at High Wood.' See G. Sheffield & J.M. Bourne (eds.), *Douglas Haig: War Diaries and Letters 1914-1918*, (London: Weidenfeld & Nicholson, 2005), p.238.
31   It must also be noted that the importance of the 'man on the spot' in decision making was now more explicitly stated in *SS 135* than it had been in *Field Service Regulations*. *SS 135* clearly states in two places that 'The decision must be left to the man on the spot' as he was 'the best man to judge when the situation is favourable for pushing on', though he was more likely to make the correct decision if he knew the intention of the higher commander. See *SS 135*, pp.22, 30.
32   The National Archives (TNA) WO 95/675: III Corps Summary of Operations January 1 to 31 1917, III Corps General Staff War Diary.
33   Falls, *Military Operations 1917*, Vol. 1, pp.38-40.

to the right and XV Corps across the river on the left.[34] The III Corps' front was now held by 48th (South Midland) Division on the left, 1st Division in the centre and 50th (Northumbrian) Division on the right.[35] Two new formations, 59th (2nd North Midland) and 42nd (East Lancashire) divisions, the former fresh from England and the latter from Egypt, were now attached to III Corps. 59th Division would start to relieve 50th Division in the line on 9 March.[36]

Once in place, III Corps immediately began planning for a series of minor operations in accordance with Fourth Army instructions to attack where success would improve observation over the German lines or deny observation over the British.[37] These would be the first operations that III Corps had planned since the publication of *SS 135* in December 1916. *SS 135* marked an important step in the dissemination of lessons that the BEF had absorbed from the fighting on the Somme during the previous summer and autumn.[38] Together with *SS 143*, issued in February 1917, *SS 135* laid out the new methodology to be used by the BEF in planning and executing future attacks.[39] It stressed the importance of effective co-operation between artillery and infantry in order to get the latter onto their objective.[40] One of the most important aspects of *SS 135* was how it now set out the relationship between corps and division in the planning process with the co-ordination of artillery at its heart.[41] An examination of the planning of operations by both III Corps and 48th Division demonstrates how quickly the new methodology contained in *SS 135* was being adopted. On 13 February Pulteney proposed an attack against La Maisonette, to be carried out by 48th Division.[42] This was one of three main vantage points that the Germans had over III Corps' lines, but the only one close enough to the front line to be vulnerable to attack. Pulteney's order, issued on 19 February, instructed Fanshawe to arrange the positions to be bombarded by heavy artillery with CRA III Corps, precisely as laid down in *SS 135*.[43] Additional artillery was allocated to 48th Division from other divisions within

34   TNA WO 95/675: III Corps Summary of Operations February 1 to 28 1917, III Corps General Staff War Diary; TNA WO 95/675: III Corps Operation Order No. 170, 21 February 1917, III Corps General Staff War Diary.

35   TNA WO 95/675: III Corps Summary of Operations February 1 to 28 1917, III Corps General Staff War Diary.

36   TNA WO 95/675: III Corps Summary of Operations March 1 to 31 1917, III Corps General Staff War Diary; TNA WO 95/675: III Corps Operation Order No. 175, 28 February 1917, III Corps General Staff War Diary.

37   TNA WO 95/432: Fourth Army Memorandum 305/2G, 13 January 1917, Fourth Army General Staff War Diary.

38   Simpson, *Directing Operations*, pp.63-64; Griffith, *Battle Tactics of the Western Front*, pp.76-77.

39   Simpson, *Directing Operations*, p.64; Griffith, *Battle Tactics of the Western Front*, p.77.

40   *SS 135*, p.9.

41   *SS 135*, Appendix A, p.61.

42   TNA WO 95/675: III Corps General Order 2034, 13 February 1917, III Corps General Staff War Diary

43   TNA WO 95/675: III Corps Operation Order No. 172, 19 February 1917, III Corps General Staff War Diary

the corps.[44] The 48th Division's own operation order even made specific reference to *SS 135* and the need for all those concerned with the attack to be aware of it.[45] The prominence of elements of *SS 135* in the planning for this operation demonstrates how quickly its utility had been recognised within III Corps. The changes contained in *SS 143* issued in February had been implemented equally quickly. The 1/5th Royal Warwickshires recorded the re-organisation of their platoons in March, before the start of the advance, and the new platoon structure would later be commented on favourably.[46]

The 48th Division's attack on La Maisonette, originally scheduled for 28 February, would eventually be postponed indefinitely, partly due to the poor state of the ground and its own trenches, caused by a sudden thaw, and partly due to the general logistical problems that were hampering Fourth Army as a whole.[47] Conditions in Fourth Army became so bad that on 23 February Rawlinson decided to postpone all but one of his army's proposed operations.[48] However, before the postponed operations could be re-scheduled events elsewhere on the BEF's front changed the situation entirely.

Part of the criticism levelled at the BEF was that it was not alert enough to the possibility of a German withdrawal to take even local advantage of it.[49] However, any examination of the activities of III Corps in late February and early March show it was taking active steps to try to discover when a withdrawal would take place. As soon as news reached III Corps about the developments on the Fifth Army front on 25 February, orders were issued for strong patrols to go out along the whole of the corps front to look for signs of impending withdrawal.[50] On 26 February divisions were instructed that: 'Patrolling will continue as active as possible along the whole front of the Army. Every opportunity will be taken of gaining ground. It is essential that any withdrawal on the enemy's part be discovered and followed up at one.'[51] The effect of these orders was recalled by Carrington:

---

44   These included three Army Artillery Brigades and 18-pdr, medium and heavy trench motor batteries and machine-gun companies from 1st and 50th divisions. See TNA WO 95/675: III Corps Operation Order No. 172, 19 February 1917, III Corps General Staff War Diary.

45   TNA WO 95/2746: 48th Division Operation Order No. 150, 21 February 1917, 48th Division General Staff War Diary.

46   C.E. Carrington, *War Record of the 1/5th Battalion, The Royal Warwickshire Regiment* (Birmingham: Cornish Brothers, 1922), p.43; TNA WO 95/2757: 'Operations of 144th Infantry Brigade from 29/3/17 to 5/4/17', 144th Brigade War Diary.

47   TNA WO 95/675: III Corps Summary of Operations February 1 to 28 1917, III Corps General Staff War Diary, pp.4-5; TNA WO 95/2746: 48th Division General Staff War Diary.

48   Falls, *Military Operations 1917*, Vol. 1, pp.117-18.

49   Falls, p.544.

50   TNA WO 95/675: III Corps Summary of Operations February 1 to 28 1917, III Corps General Staff War Diary.

51   TNA WO 95/675: III Corps Operation Order No. 174, 26 February 1917, III Corps General Staff War Diary.

When we were the front line company – three tours making seventeen days in all – one of the officers with a picked man went out on patrol every night for two or three hours to make sure there was no Boche activity in front of their wire and that they still held their line ... I noted seven such patrols in my diary.[52]

III Corps was almost entirely dependent on its infantry patrolling and artillery observation for information gathering. The last week in February was damp and misty, making it impossible for the RFC to make any meaningful contribution to the task.[53] The infantry, however, remained highly active, examining the enemy trenches and wire every night. The 1st Division kept a careful watch on its front as its intelligence summaries testify, but the continued reporting of hostile artillery activity, sniping, trench mortaring and the observation of work parties did not reveal any activity pointing to imminent withdrawal.[54] From every division the message was the same: the enemy continued to hold his line in normal strength along the whole length of the corps front.[55] Nor were this reconnaissance without risk. On 22 February, two officers from 1st Division entered the enemy line for half an hour without being challenged, but when a larger patrol later attempted to do the same they came under heavy fire and suffered severe casualties.[56]

On 2 March III Corps stated that, 'Reports received from prisoners and other sources still tend to show that the enemy means to retire to the Hindenburg Line.'[57] Every effort was now made through raiding and patrolling to find out if the enemy continued to hold his line in force. Between 4 and 9 March six raids were mounted along III Corps' front, two by each of the three divisions in the line. Raids carried out by 50th Division on 4-5 March brought back six prisoners.[58] Between 5 and 7 March two raids were mounted by 1st Division, but these failed to obtain any identifica-

52   Carrington, *Soldier From The Wars Returning*, p.137
53   TNA WO 95/675: III Corps Summary of Operations February 1 to 28 1917, III Corps General Staff War Diary.
54   TNA WO 95/1232: 1st Division Progress Summaries, 1st Division General Staff War Diary
55   For example, on 26 February 48th Division reported 'enemy still holding his trenches', 1st Division reported 'patrols went out in night and were fired on rifles and MG ... enemy very much on alert', whilst 50th Division reported that the 'enemy is holding his trenches in same strength as usual.' See TNA WO 95/675: III Corps General Staff War Diary.
56   TNA WO 95/675: III Corps Summary of Operations February 1 to 28 1917, III Corps General Staff War Diary. Only half of the party returned without their officer who had been badly wounded.
57   TNA WO 95/675: III Corps Operations Order No. 176, 2 March 1917, III Corps General Staff War Diary.
58   TNA WO 95/675: III Corps Summary of Operations March 1 to 31 1917, III Corps General Staff War. Diary. According to the divisional history these were 'the only incidents of more than ordinary interest which happened whilst the 50th Division was south of the Somme.' See E. Wyrall, *The Fiftieth Division 1914-1919* (London: Percy Lund, 1939), p.200. Neither raiding parties suffered casualties.

tion and suffered casualties.[59] Between 7 and 9 March, 48th Division also raided the enemy trenches twice. When the first raiding party found the enemy frontline to be empty, it was then decided to push further, extending the box barrage as far as the enemy's third line, though this attempt was halted by heavy enemy fire.[60] Both division and corps were very pleased with the initiative shown here, particularly the speed with which the artillery re-arranged the second barrage.[61] A second raid was also able to enter the enemy trenches, bringing back further prisoners and two machine-guns.[62] The conclusions drawn from these operations were that the enemy continued to hold his line in strength, though not where it was badly damaged by artillery fire, and was very much on the alert.[63] German artillery response had been slow and weak. This may have been a sign that the guns were being withdrawn.

Despite the success of these raids, III Corps was no nearer to discovering how soon the enemy intended to quit the positions in front of it. The Germans succeeded in maintaining the impression that their frontline would be held right up to the moment of their actual withdrawal: on 11 and 13 March the enemy's artillery was noted as being 'noticeably active' while as late as 15-16 March, only a day before the withdrawal took place, all three of III Corps' divisions reported that their patrols found the enemy trenches still held.[64] However, there were other signs of unusual German activity. From 1 March regular reports were received of large fires being seen in villages behind the German lines while on 13 March 1st Division reported that the enemy had started to register his artillery on his own frontline.[65] Far from being taken unawares by the German withdrawal, III Corps anticipated it and took active steps to detect it. It was to the credit of the Germans rather than any failure of effort on III Corps' part that the former were able to conceal the moment of withdrawal so successfully.

59   TNA WO 95/675: III Corps Summary of Operations March 1 to 31 [1917], III Corps General Staff War Diary.
60   TNA WO 95/2746: Report on Raid made by 1/4th Royal Berkshire Regiment on the Night of 7/8 March 1917, 48th Division General Staff War Diary.
61   TNA WO 95/2746: III Corps General Order 2916, 11 March 1917, 48th Division General Staff War Diary
62   TNA WO 95/2746: Report on Raid by the 6th R. Warwick Regt. on Night of 8 March 1917, 48th Division General Staff War Diary. This success was also credited to the 'careful preparation by Artillery and Infantry and the excellent shooting of the Artillery.' See TNA WO 95/2746: 48th Division General Order 3014, 15 March 1917, 48th Division General Staff War Diary.
63   TNA WO 95/1232: 1st Division G277/14/13, 7 March 1917 and G277/14/16, 9 March 1917, 1st Division General Staff War Diary; TNA WO 95/2746: 'Report on Raid made by 1/4 Royal Berkshire Regiment on the Night of 7/8 March 1917', 48th Division General Staff War Diary.
64   TNA WO 95/675: III Corps Summary of Operations March 1 to 31 1917, III Corps General Staff War Diary.
65   TNA WO 95/675: III Corps Summary of Operations March 1 to 31 1917, III Corps General Staff War Diary.

The intention of the French to start offensive operations to the right of Fourth Army from 17 March led to an order for both III and IV corps to simulate attacks of their own on that date.[66] The 48th Division was ordered to raid La Maisonette, the task being given to 145th Brigade which had successfully raided there previously.[67] Once again the influence of *SS 135* can be seen in instructions that the divisional commander would arrange the artillery plan with CRA, III Corps. However, demonstrating once again that initiative was not lacking in III Corps, provision was also made to extend the scope of the operation should the opportunity arise. Fourth Army had already issued instructions that, in the event of a German withdrawal, III Corps should be prepared to advance to the line of River Somme.[68] 48th Division was ordered to be ready to advance at short notice to secure a line south from La Maisonette and to push patrols forward to the river to look for suitable crossing points.[69] The soldiers were also warned to be on their guard against booby traps, a feature of the withdrawal already experienced by the Fifth Army, thus demonstrating the extent to which information was now being shared across armies within the BEF.

The 145th Brigade mounted their operation in the early hours of 17 March with instructions that if the enemy had withdrawn they were to consolidate the objective and send patrols forward to seek out the next line.[70] The attack met with very little opposition and patrols down to the river met no opposition at all.[71] In accordance with corps instructions 48th Division, (whose own commander, Major-General Fanshawe was acting as corps commander whilst Lieutenant-General Pulteney was on leave), then began to move forward to the line of the River Somme and sent patrols across to the far bank.[72] The prompt action of 48th Division to discover the extent of the German withdrawal and to prepare for further exploitation by crossing the river are a further demonstration that, far from being taken surprise, III Corps and its subordinate formations did indeed possess the flexibility to take advantage of opportunity that was characteristic of military effectiveness. Any caution in their subsequent movement was the result of the limits placed on them by Fourth Army and

66   TNA WO 95/675: III Corps Operation Order No. 180, 13 March 1917, III Corps General Staff War Diary.
67   TNA WO 95/2746: 48th Division Order No. 153, 15 March 1917, 48th Division General Staff War Diary.
68   TNA WO 95/675: III Corps Operation Order No. 181, 16 March 1917, III Corps General Staff War Diary; TNA WO 95/2746: 48th Division General Staff War Diary.
69   TNA WO 95/2746: 48th Division General Staff War Diary. This was based on information from a German deserter who informed his captors that the withdrawal had already begun.
70   TNA WO 95/2746: 48th Division General Staff War Diary.
71   TNA WO 95/2764: 'Active Operations of 1/4 Oxf. & Bucks. Lt. Inf., March 1917', 1/4th Oxfordshire & Buckinghamshire Light Infantry War Diary. Ten prisoners had been taken for the loss of one man killed and one officer and three men wounded.
72   TNA WO 95/2746: 48th Division Order No. 155, 17 March 1917, 48th Division General Staff War Diary

reflected the careful and methodical manner in which Rawlinson had already decided to conduct the Fourth Army advance.[73]

On 17 March, Haig held a conference of his Army Commanders to discuss the consequences of the German withdrawal for Allied operations.[74] His fear was that their intention was either to draw the Allies forward into a premature attack on the Hindenburg Line, the failure of which would lead to a devastating German counter-attack, or to create a reserve with which the Germans could mount their own offensive, possibly in Flanders.[75] The need to continue with preparations for the British offensive at Arras and his caution over any potential threat in Flanders meant Haig had little interest in encouraging a vigorous advance towards the Hindenburg Line. Instead, he instructed that advanced guards be sent forward in small groups and that, while no opportunity should be missed to inflict damage on the enemy, any attack in force should be avoided unless absolutely necessary for some special objective. Such attacks needed to be properly prepared for and supported by artillery.[76]

Rawlinson was also cautious. He too had feared a German trap, designed to lure the BEF out into the open on ground devoid of cover or communications as a result of the German demolitions.[77] Even if it was not a trap it offered the Germans, once they had reached the safety of the Hindenburg Line, the chance to turn on their pursuers who would be strung out, disorganised and short of supplies. As the Fourth Army analysis of operations later remarked: '[It] must be remembered that the enemy was unbroken and was making a long and carefully prepared and very deliberate retirement. There was no question of pursuing a demoralised enemy.'[78]

Neither did there appear to be any particular operational incentive for Fourth Army to force the pace, unlike Fifth Army which had to move forward to cover the flank of Third Army when the latter commenced the Arras offensive in April.[79] Rawlinson's plan, therefore, was to follow up the German withdrawal by advanced guards while the main body of the army moved forward in a series of bounds from one secure line to another.[80] The first of these would be his original front line. The second would be a line between the Canal du Nord and the Somme south of Péronne, on the high ground covering the crossing points. Only when adequate lines of communication had been constructed between them would Rawlinson risk moving closer to the Hindenburg Line.[81] There is no doubt that some officers found the cautious approach irksome. One

73   Falls, *Military Operations 1917*, Vol. 1, p.129.
74   Falls, p.127.
75   Beach, *Haig's Intelligence*, p.231.
76   Falls, *Military Operations 1917*, Vol. 1, pp.128-29.
77   Prior & Wilson, *Command on the Western Front*, p.265.
78   TNA WO 95/432: Fourth Army General Staff, *SS 156: Notes on Recent Operations compiled by G.S. Fourth Army*, April 1917, Fourth Army General Staff War Diary [*SS 156*].
79   Falls, *Military Operations 1917*, Vol. 1, p.138.
80   Falls, p.129.
81   Falls, p.129.

48th Division staff officer later described 'the feeling of general wonderment at the time produced by the limitations imposed by the higher command of the strangely formal, almost economical method of following up a retreating enemy.'[82]

A further factor that limited Rawlinson's aggression was the continuing withdrawal of divisions from his Army to reinforce Third and First Armies for the forthcoming offensive at Arras.[83] III Corps had already lost 50th Division at the start of March and four days into the advance, on 21 March, it lost 1st Division which was transferred to XIV Corps.[84] This last departure required considerable alteration in III Corps' front which was now divided between 48th and 59th divisions.[85] The latter had been in France for less than a month before it went into the line and even its own divisional history admitted it 'could be considered as only partially trained.'[86] Also just coming under III Corps' command at this time was 42nd Division which had arrived in France from Egypt that month and had yet to go into the line.[87] Thus III Corps lost two very experienced divisions within a month and had them replaced by two divisions with very little Western Front experience.[88]

The third constraint on pursuit was the logistical challenges that faced the BEF. During the advance in March the British had been forced to traverse a barren wilderness deliberately created by the retreating Germans. The prominence given to descriptions of the destruction in British accounts testifies to the profound sense of shock that observers felt at the scale of the devastation. 'The country was dead', wrote Carrington, 'laid waste with a destructive fervour worse than anything in the Thirty Years War, a devastation that had no parallel since the wars of the Mongols.'[89] The strain created the need to make immediate repairs to the transport infrastructure was revealed by III Corps' narrative of operations, which admitted that 1st Division, although officially transferred to XIV Corps, had to remain in the III Corps area to be employed in

82   TNA CAB 45/116: A.C. McLawford to Cyril Falls correspondence.
83   Falls, *Military Operations 1917*, Vol. 1, p.128.
84   TNA WO 95/675: III Corps Summary of Operations March 1 to 31 1917, III Corps General Staff War Diary. The 1st Division, however, did not immediately leave the III Corps area, so it was still available to assist in the repair of roads.
85   TNA WO 95/675: III Corps Operation Order No. 184, 20 March 1917, III Corps General Staff War Diary.
86   E.U. Bradbridge (ed.), *59th Division 1915-1918*, (Chesterfield: Wilfred Edmunds, 1928), p.13.
87   Falls, *Military Operations 1917*, Vol. 1, p.129
88   The 59th Division had only been employed in Ireland following the Easter Rising of April 1916 whilst 42nd Division had taken part in the defence of the Suez Canal and operations at Gallipoli in 1915. However, even the latter division was very much 'in the position of a new boy at a strange school ... much had to be learnt in the new school and much unlearnt.' See F. P. Gibbon, *The 42nd (East Lancashire) Division 1914-1918* (London: Country Life, 1920), p.88.
89   Carrington, *Soldier from the Wars Returning*, p.141.

'Laid waste with a destructive fervour worse than anything in the Thirty Years War':
Péronne *Mairie,* March 1917. The placard above the entrance states, 'Don't be angry,
just wonder!' Left behind by the withdrawing German garrison, it was widely reported
on in the Allied press as a prime example of Hun wickedness.

work on the roads.[90] Falls noted that 'The urgency of repairing and re-establishing the
Army's communications were now so great that each corps in the line was employing
at least a whole division, in addition to normal labour as working parties.'[91] Fourth
Army's operational analyses after the advance also drew attention to the importance
of rapid road repair and maintenance of roads.[92]

Three elements of the German policy of deliberate destruction put additional strain
on the troops. The first was the destruction of houses which prevented their use as
billets. It was noted that, 'The destruction of the majority of houses caused hardship to
our troops as the weather has been cold and wet.'[93] The second was the setting of booby
traps in anything that offered the slightest chance of shelter. This had already been
encountered by the men of Fifth Army in February and 48th Division had alerted its

90   TNA WO 95/675: III Corps Summary of Operations March 1 to 31 1917, III Corps
     General Staff War Diary.
91   Falls, *Military Operations 1917,* Vol. 1, p.135.
92   'Repair of roads and filling in craters ought to be put in hand at the earliest possible
     moment … The great dependence of our system of supply upon having roads and bridges
     good enough to take heavy lorries was very obvious.' See TNA WO 95/432: *SS 156,*
     Fourth Army General Staff War Diary.
93   TNA WO 95/675: III Corps Summary of Operations March 1 to 31 1917, III Corps
     General Staff War Diary.

own troops to the danger on 15 March.[94] Nonetheless, booby traps still took their toll, the worst incident being the destruction of a battalion headquarters in a cellar in Villers Faucon on 18 April.[95] The third element was the deliberate contamination of wells, usually by filling them with dung. Work recorded in 48th Division's area demonstrated that the main priority in April was the cleaning and refurbishment of wells.[96]

In order to mount and sustain an effective pursuit of the enemy it was evident that III Corps would need the ability to bridge the Somme as quickly as possible. The Somme, however, represented a formidable obstacle, with a canal on the left bank and marshy ground between that and the river.[97] Each bridge on III Corps' front was approached by a raised causeway up to half a mile long. On 27 February, Brigadier-General A.L. Schreiber, III Corps Chief Engineer, commenced an investigation into what the task would require, following it up with a meeting with the divisional CREs.[98] Lieutenant-Colonel H. Marshall, CRE 48th Division, had already made a reconnaissance of the approaches towards the Somme on 25 February.[99] In accordance with established practice it was decided that priority would be given to constructing light bridges capable of taking infantry and pack animals first, to be followed by medium pontoon and trestle bridges for divisional transport and field artillery, and finally heavy bridges capable of carrying mechanical transport and heavy artillery.[100]

An attempt to improve the efficiency of future bridging operations within the BEF as a whole had begun on 15 March with a conference of Chief Engineers chaired by Major-General R. Spring-Rice, Engineer-in-Chief, BEF.[101] Here it was agreed that each corps should appoint one officer to take charge of bridging and that an Army Troops company should be employed in each corps to build the heavy bridges required for the movement of motorised transport and heavy artillery.[102] First reconnaissance of potential crossing points, however, was left to the divisional engineers and the

---

94   TNA WO 95/2746: 48th Division Operation Order No. 153, 15 March 1917, 48th Division General Staff War Diary.
95   TNA WO 95/2758: 1/6th Gloucestershire Regiment War Diary. For an examination of the German use of booby traps during this period see I. Jones, 'The German use of Booby Traps and Long Delay Devices during the withdrawal to the Hindenburg Line in 1917', *Bulletin of the Western Front Association*, 116 (2020), pp.18-19
96   TNA WO 95/2748: 48th Division CRE War Diary. Between 17 and 31 March virtually all the entries concern work on bridges over the Somme, whereas from 1 April, wells are mentioned nearly every day.
97   Falls, *Military Operations 1917*, Vol. I, p.130.
98   TNA WO 95/697: III Corps CE War Diary.
99   TNA WO 95/2748: 48th Division CRE War Diary. Two days later, he was promoted to brigadier-general and became Chief Engineer of XV Corps. He was replaced by Lieutenant-Colonel Giles.
100   H.L. Pritchard (ed.), *History of the Corps of Royal Engineers*, Vol.5: *The Home Front, France, Flanders and Italy in the First World War* (Chatham: The Institution of Royal Engineers, 1952), p.278
101   Pritchard, pp.278-79.
102   Pritchard, p.279.

German withdrawal began before the other arrangements could be put in place.[103] The crossing of the Somme, therefore, was initially undertaken by the individual divisions within III Corps.

As the closest division to the Somme at the start of operations, 48th Division had already begun to prepare for a crossing on 15 March. Lieutenant-Colonel V. Giles, the newly appointed CRE, ordered that equipment for an infantry footbridge and medium bridge be made ready at once for a crossing opposite Halle.[104] Pontoons were launched and brought up on the night of 16-17 March. As a result, by dawn on 18 March, a company of the 1/8th Royal Warwickshires could be ferried across the river by pontoon rafts to Péronne, the first British troops to enter the town.[105] Additional rafts allowed a battery of field artillery to cross early the following morning.[106] Bridges were begun on 18 March and completed within six days, with a further six days to make one capable of taking motorised transport.[107] Throughout this time 48th Division's engineers and their infantry working parties had been completely self-sufficient, despite the fact that one of the field companies had been withdrawn to join the advanced guard. In 10 days they had built three horse transport bridges, six footbridges and a heavy timber bridge, all entirely from local material and without the help of a single army troop company. It was later described as 'a model of efficient planning and execution.'[108]

In contrast, although 1st Division had only two major crossing points in its sector, it suffered more problems with its bridging effort than 48th Division. The greatest of these was encountered at Brie where the physical difficulties created by German demolition were compounded by human error.[109] As it lay on the main road between Amiens and St Quentin, Brie should have been reserved for a heavy bridge, but the division failed to appreciate its importance and instead constructed a medium bridge to take only divisional transport and artillery. The situation was only rectified when it came under the direct supervision of Brigadier-General Schreiber, but it still took five days to complete, employing all three divisional field companies, a large infantry working party and, unlike 48th Division, additional assets in the form of two sections of engineers from another division and an Army Troop company.[110] In this case III Corps was held at fault for its failure 'to step in until the division had completed

---

103 Pritchard, p.279.
104 Pritchard, p.289.
105 Pritchard, p.290.
106 Falls, *Military Operations 1917*, Vol. I, p.132.
107 Pritchard, *History of the Corps of Royal Engineers*, Vol.5, pp.290-91.
108 Pritchard, p.291.
109 On the approaches to Brie, over a distance of 600 yards, the Germans had destroyed six bridges and blown a gap of 78 feet in the causeway. Three mines had also been laid under the causeway, though only one of these had exploded. See Pritchard, p.284.
110 H. L. Pritchard, *History of the Corps of Royal Engineers*, Vol. 5, p.288; TNA WO 95/697: III Corps CE War Diary. This was one example of where the thoroughness of the German demolitions actually worked against them as the British were able to use the rubble of the destroyed village to help repair the roadway, Falls, *Military Operations 1917*, Vol. I, p.133.

its own arrangements…had this been done, much time and labour would have been saved.'[111] If the arrangements made on 15 March could have been put in place in time, then the control of bridging would have been the corps' responsibility from the start, as it would become by the autumn of 1918.[112]

In general, however, the bridging operations carried out by III Corps are held up as good examples of their type by the Official History.[113] The speed with which the work was completed was a testament to the efforts of the field companies and their infantry work parties, though their task was made much easier by the absence of any active interference from the Germans.[114] The need for these operations had also been evident for a long time beforehand and both corps and divisional engineers had had ample time to prepare. However, the decision to leave the initial reconnaissance of bridging sites to divisions without proper oversight by corps exacerbated problems at Brie and required much extra effort to rectify the situation. Changes were made in May to the BEF's organisation of engineers at corps level to free Chief Engineers from administrative responsibilities and allow them to concentrate on engineering priorities by appointing additional CREs to administer all army troops assigned to corps.[115] Bridge construction in 48th Division's sector, however, had been a genuinely impressive effort, especially as it was achieved entirely with the division's own resources, and showed what was possible with careful planning and foresight.

Once crossings had been established across the Somme, mounting effective operations under conditions of semi-open warfare meant III Corps had to radically change its approach. Despite the importance that has been attached to *SS 135* in defining the BEF's new offensive methodology it was not intended to cover all operations, only methodical attacks on prepared positions.[116] Operations under conditions of open or semi-open warfare were still to be carried out according to the principles laid down by *Field Service Regulations*. These considered that pursuit was most likely after protracted action leaving both sides exhausted and even the victors would require time to re-organise and replenish their supplies. Pursuit, therefore, should be undertaken by 'as large a body of mounted troops as possible so that the enemy may be allowed no respite while this is being done.'[117]

111 Pritchard, *History of the Corps of Royal Engineers*, Vol. 5, p.285

112 Simpson, *Directing Operations*, p.173.

113 Falls dedicates over four pages to an account of these operations and describes the completion of the medium bridge at Brie within 24 hours as 'a remarkably fine achievement.' See Falls, *Military Operations 1917*, Vol. 1, pp.130-33.

114 For example Maj. Walker, 48th Division's Adjutant of Engineers, reported to III Corps on 18 March it would be safe to bridge by daylight as the Germans had evacuated Mont St Quentin that dominated the crossing points about Péronne. See TNA WO 95/697: III Corps CE War Diary.

115 Pritchard, *History of the Corps of Royal Engineers*, Vol. 5, p.301.

116 *SS 135*, p.3.

117 General Staff, *Field Service Regulations Part 1: Operations* (London: HMSO, 1909) [*FSR 1*], p. 158.

If pursuing an undefeated enemy, however, *FSR* warned that he would probably use his freshest troops to cover his withdrawal and that direct pursuit by the main body of the attacking force would rarely produce decisive results.[118] Only sufficient mounted troops to keep in touch with the enemy's movements were to pursue him directly, the greater part of the cavalry being aimed at his flanks.[119] 'Such infantry and artillery as are in hand should at once be despatched to assist that body of cavalry which is directed against the flank of the enemy's main force with a view to complete its overthrow' while the remainder were to press the enemy's covering force.[120] In all cases pursuing troops were urged to act with the greatest boldness and to be prepared to take risks unacceptable in other circumstances.[121]

The speed and skill with which the withdrawal had been conducted initially left III Corps struggling to regain contact. The first attempts were made by infantry patrols carried across the Somme by a combination of boats, rafts and hastily built infantry bridges.[122] The infantry's task, however, was to occupy and fortify a main line of resistance on the west bank of the Somme, to protect the crossing points in compliance with Fourth Army instructions.[123] It was the Corps Mounted Troops, the III Corps Cavalry Regiment and Cyclists, who were to re-establish contact with the enemy.[124] After a cavalry troop was assigned to each division to act as local protection, the corps advanced guard was organised into two columns, moving on parallel roads, and consisting each of a cavalry squadron and two platoons of cyclists.[125] A reserve was established of a cavalry squadron, a cyclist company and the III Corps Motor Machine Gun Battery. Late on the evening of 20 March, Fanshawe, still acting as temporary corps commander, ordered the establishment of a mobile column to act in their support. Dubbed 'Ward Force', it consisted of two battalions of infantry, two batteries of artillery, a machine-gun section and two sections of engineers, all drawn from 48th Division, and was to be commanded by Brigadier-General H.D.O. Ward, the divisional CRA. He was also to take the mounted troops under his command.[126]

---

118 *FSR 1*, p.159.
119 *FSR 1*, p.158.
120 *FSR 1*, p.159.
121 *FSR 1*, p.159. The phrase in bold is the original emphasis.
122 TNA WO 95/675: III Corps Summary of Operations March 1 to 31 1917, III Corps General Staff War Diary.
123 TNA WO 95/675: III Corps Operation Order No. 183, 18 March 1917, III Corps General Staff War Diary
124 TNA WO 95/675: III Corps General Order 2334/3, 19 March 1917, III Corps General Staff War Diary. The III Corps Cavalry Regiment at this time consisted of the RHQ; two squadrons of the Duke of Lancaster's Own Yeomanry and a squadron of the Surrey Yeomanry.
125 TNA WO 95/675: Report on the action of the III Corps MMG Battery during operations east of the Somme during March and April 1917, III Corps General Staff War Diary. These arrangements directly followed the principles laid down in *FSR 1*, p.98.
126 TNA WO 95/675: III Corps G.682, 20 March 1917, III Corps General Staff War Diary.

This creation of a combined arms advanced guard to act in concert with the Corps Mounted Troops was exactly in accordance with *FSR*.[127] The close co-operation between the different arms proved invaluable on those occasions when the Corps Mounted Troops ran into trouble. On 24 March, for example, it was the intervention of the Motor Machine Gun Battery, giving covering fire from the flank, that allowed a squadron of the Duke of Lancaster's Own Yeomanry to withdraw from a contact at Roisel.[128]

For four days, until they were relieved by 5th Cavalry Division, the Corps Mounted Troops ranged widely in advance of III Corps' outpost line, reaching as far as Vermand, seven miles beyond the line established on 20 March. As well as locating enemy rearguards and skirmishing with enemy patrols, they checked the state of bridges over the rivers Cologne and Omnigon and wherever a village was found vacant or lightly held they chased off the enemy and occupied it in a manner similar to what the Australians would later term 'peaceful penetration.'[129] Fourth Army's analysis of operations later drew attention to these successes:

> The value of Corps Mounted Troops in seizing and holding tactical points until the infantry could come up and relieve them was clearly shown…In those [Regiments] which had had the opportunity [for training in the winter] the results were very good; the reports received showed that the patrol officers had initiative and energy and that they developed good powers of observation … Once touch was obtained with the enemy it was maintained continuously.[130]

Yet the strain of these operations was considerable. Fourth Army's analysis highlighted the problem of wear on the horses, which had been on reduced rations for some months, and the numerous breakdowns among the bicycles of the cyclist battalions due to the poor state of the roads.[131] Conversely, the motorcycles of the Motor Machine Gun battery appeared to work well and experienced relatively little difficulty in moving around.[132] On 24 March all Corps Mounted Troops were replaced in the advanced line by 5th Cavalry Division, acting directly under the orders of Fourth

---

127 *FSR 1*, p.96.
128 TNA WO 95/675: Report on the action of the III Corps MMG Battery during operations east of the Somme during March and April 1917, III Corps General Staff War Diary.
129 C Squadron, Duke of Lancaster's Own Yeomanry took and held Brusle on 20 March and Tincourt on 21 March while D Squadron took Bernes and Poeuilly on 21 March 1917. See TNA WO 95/700: Duke of Lancaster's Own Yeomanry War Diary.
130 *SS 156*, p.3.
131 *SS 156*, p.3.
132 TNA WO 95/700: Report on the action of the III Corps MMG Battery during operations east of the Somme during March and April 1917, III Corps General Staff War Diary

Advanced scouts of 9th Hodson's Horse, 3rd (Ambala) Cavalry Brigade, 5th Cavalry Division on patrol near Vraignes during the advance to the Hindenburg Line. (Private collection)

Army.[133] The Corps Mounted Troops were now responsible for the immediate security of their corps and maintaining communications between them and 5th Cavalry Division.

Some of the actions of 'Ward Force' can be seen as part of the development of the combined-arms concept that would become a feature of the conduct of the 'Hundred Days campaign of 1918.[134] Although officially disbanded on 24 March, elements of the force continued to co-operate with 5th Cavalry Division, most notably in the capture of Roisel on 26 March.[135] Operating alongside two squadrons of lancers and three armoured cars, 'Ward Force' made a frontal attack on the village from the east while the cavalry attempted to envelope it from north and south simultaneously.[136] The infantry attack was greatly assisted by the armoured cars which knocked out

133 TNA WO 95/675: Fourth Army Order 540/17(G), 24 March 1917, III Corps General Staff War Diary.
134 Kenyon, *Horsemen in No Man's Land*, p.98.
135 TNA WO 95/675: III Corps Summary of Operations March 1 to 31 1917, III Corps General Staff War Diary.
136 TNA WO 95/2764: Active Operations of 1/4th Ox & Bucks Lt. Inf., March 1917, 1/4th Oxford & Buckinghamshire Light Infantry War Diary.

an enemy machine-gun holding up the advance.[137] Although not itself a particularly significant action, the role of 'Ward Force' at Roisel demonstrates a direct link with similar actions seen in the summer and early autumn of 1918.[138]

Throughout the initial mobile phase of the advance of III Corps had proceeded effectively and according to the principles laid down in *FSR*. Its mounted component had amply fulfilled the role of regaining and maintaining contact with the enemy as soon as it was able to get across the Somme. There had been no shortage of 'boldness' in their actions; indeed on one or two occasions they may have pushed boldness to the point of recklessness, but casualties throughout these operations had been remarkably light.[139] The use of a mobile combined arms column to support them, and later 5th Cavalry Division, again echoed the principles of *FSR* and allowed operations to continue while the bulk of the corps' strength was focused on securing the first line west of the Somme and establishing communications with the other side of the river. Once the infantry was released to continue the advance after 26 March the German rearguards were steadily pushed back by a combination of pressure to their front and the threat of envelopment on their flanks.[140] If III Corps' advance in March 1917 was cautious, it was not due to any lack of initiative by its own troops, nor any ignorance of *FSR* by its commanders, but rather reflected the caution imposed by Fourth Army.

At the beginning of April the character of operations undertaken began to change markedly. The French Third Army, to the right of the British Fourth Army, intended to attack the Hindenburg Line in the vicinity of St Quentin on 10 April.[141] Haig had already given Rawlinson verbal instructions on 31 March that he should be ready to

---

137 TNA WO 95/2764: Active Operations of 1/4th Ox & Bucks Lt. Inf., March 1917, 1/4th Oxford & Buckinghamshire Light Infantry War Diary; TNA WO 95/1164: Ambala Brigade War Diary. However, although the cavalry to the north of the village helped greatly by guarding the flank, that to the south was held up by flooded ground and the enemy were able to withdraw, leaving only a single prisoner behind.

138 For example, see the tactics and formations discussed in A. Thomas, 'Open Warfare during the "Hundred Days" 1918', *Stand To!: The Journal of the Western Front Association*, 96 (2013), pp.24-27.

139 C Squadron Surrey Yeomanry records six men wounded during the period 19-31 March, TNA WO 95/700: C Squadron Surrey Yeomanry War Diary; The Duke of Lancaster's Own Yeomanry lost one man killed, one died of wounds, one wounded and taken prisoner and one wounded during the same period, TNA WO 95/700: Duke of Lancaster's Own Yeomanry War Diary: III Corps Cyclist Battalion records three killed and six wounded between 19 and 31 March. See TNA WO 95/700: III Corps Cyclist Battalion War Diary. Total III Corps casualties for March 1917 amounted to 823, of which 191 were fatal and 22 were recorded as 'missing'. See TNA WO 95/675: Summaries of Casualties During the Month of March 1917, III Corps General Staff War Diary.

140 For example, see the actions at Longavesnes, Villers-Facon and Saulcourt (24 and 27 March) carried out by the Canadian Cavalry Brigade and supported by 143rd and 145th Brigades of 48th Division; TNA WO 95/675: III Corps Summary of Operations March 1 to 31 1917, III Corps General Staff War Diary, p.6; Carrington, *Soldiers from the Wars Returning*, pp.142-43; Kenyon, *Horsemen in No Man's Land*, pp.96-99.

141 Falls, *Military Operations 1917*, Vol. 1, p.152.

co-operate by providing additional artillery support and to exploit any success that might result from that attack.[142] These instructions were confirmed in writing on 2 April. Rawlinson was also instructed that he should support the advance of Fifth Army on his left.[143] These two operational goals are cited by Falls as the chief reason for the changed methods adopted by Fourth Army in its advance and the need to clear the outpost villages as quickly as possible.[144] Another reason for the hard fighting for the outpost villages was the renewed determination of the Germans to delay the British advance for as long as possible. This was in order to allow the completion of the southern portion of the Hindenburg Line which had been re-sited a mile and half in front of its original position in early February.[145] This resulted in the enemy offering 'considerably more resistance than in the first stage of the advance' and making much greater effort to regain lost positions, most notably at Gillemont Farm south east of Épehy, which was to change hands several times at the end of April in the last phase of active operations.[146]

However, once the bridges across the Somme were completed, and the RE field companies released for other tasks, the logistical situation quickly began to ease. No III Corps operation was disrupted by inadequate supplies, although heavy artillery support was limited by the problems of transporting guns and ammunition along cratered roads.[147] By the time active operations in the III Corps area effectively came to an end at the end of April, the logistical network had been greatly improved.[148]

By 1 April the outposts of III Corps had reached a line just four miles short of the Hindenburg Line itself.[149] Ahead, however, lay a cluster of hilltop villages and farm buildings that the Germans now held as their outpost line. The reduction of these positions was to occupy the attentions of III Corps for the next month. Orders had already been issued on 26 March to push the line forward by as far as Hargicourt and Épehy by 7 April so that observation over the Hindenberg Line could be obtained.[150]

142 Falls, *Military Operations 1917*, Vol. 1, pp.152-53.
143 Falls, pp.152-53.
144 Falls, p.153.
145 Falls, p.91.
146 TNA WO 95/675: III Corps Summary of Operations April 1 to 30 1917, III Corps General Staff War Diary.
147 Falls, *Military Operations 1917*, Vol. 1, p.161.
148 TNA WO 95/697: III Corps CE War Diary; Falls, *Military Operations 1917*, Vol. 1, p.532. The logistical situation was greatly helped by the repair of the main railway from Péronne and construction of a broad gauge line forward to Roisel.
149 TNA WO 95/675: III Corps Summary of Operations April 1 to 30 1917, III Corps General Staff War Diary.
150 TNA WO 95/675: III Corps, Operations Order 191, 28 March 1917, III Corps General Staff War Diary

The outpost attacks demonstrated that 48th Division had the eye for ground that both Fourth Army and their own corps commander believed was essential.[151] Although the villages themselves were formidable positions, the Germans had made the mistake of concentrating on their defence without considering the importance of surrounding terrain features. Not only did this give the attacking troops a clearly defined objective, but also the opportunity to capture them by first occupying positions that dominated them.[152] An attack by 144th Brigade against the village of St Emilie on 30 March deliberately avoided the southern face of the village which was overlooked by high ground held by the enemy, screening it instead by a series of platoon posts while the enemy were outflanked on the left and forced to retire.[153] The 48th Division would be able to make similar use of the open flanks of the German positions in attacks on four more of the outpost villages within a week. The most successful of these was against the twin villages of Épehy and Pezières on 1 April. This was a potentially difficult operation due to the considerable amount of open ground on the approach and the extended nature of the objectives.[154] The first was overcome by a night advance to a start line closer to the objective and the second by employing three battalions from two brigades, two against Épehy and one against Pezières. In order to achieve maximum surprise the attack was also carried out without a preliminary barrage, but with one already plotted to be used if the infantry called for it. Four days later the villages of Ronssoy and Lempire were captured in a similar attack by 145th Brigade, supported by 144th Brigade.[155] Once again a battalion from one brigade was used to support the other by securing the high ground that overlooked the objective. Fourth Army analysis later drew attention to the tendency of German garrisons to begin withdrawing as soon as their flanks came under threat.[156]

During the fighting for the outposts 48th Division had employed a variety of methods including night attacks and attacks made both with and without artillery support. Both the approach to the objective and the lines of consolidation were chosen with an eye to the ground and any source of cover.[157] Despite the novelty of attacking under conditions of open warfare the operations 'were very well carried out' although

151 TNA WO 95/432: *SS 156*, Fourth Army General Staff War Diary; TNA CAB 45/116: Lt.-Gen. W.P. Pulteney to Cyril Falls correspondence.
152 Falls, *Military Operations 1917*, Vol. 1, pp.154-55.
153 TNA WO 95/2757: Operations of 144th Infantry Brigade from 29/3/17 to 5/4/17, 144th Brigade War Diary. The failure of the centre company was blamed on its supporting artillery battery failing to receive its orders to fire in time.
154 TNA WO 95/2757: Operations of 144th Infantry Brigade from 29/3/17 to 5/4/17, 144th Brigade War Diary.
155 TNA WO 95/2746: 48th Division General Staff War Diary. The British official historian noted that Ronssoy was the last village of the *Somme Departement* remaining in German hands. See Falls, *Military Operations 1917*, Vol. 1, p.159.
156 TNA WO 95/432: *SS 156*, Fourth Army General Staff War Diary.
157 TNA WO 95/2757: Operations of 144th Infantry Brigade from 29/3/17 to 5/4/17, 144th Brigade War Diary.

Men of 48th Division and French Third Army in reserve positions near Le Verguier, 25 April 1917. (Private collection)

there was a tendency among the attacking troops to bunch when under fire.[158] The new organisation of the platoon for the attack was also found 'to work very well', an endorsement of the methodology to be found in *SS 143*.[159] The operation order and after action report for 144th Brigade's attack on 13 April around Hargicourt was circulated by III Corps as 'a good example of an operation successfully carried out under present conditions of warfare', whilst the capture of Tombois Farm on 16 April by 145th Brigade, achieved in heavy rain 'and most difficult circumstances', brought a congratulatory telegram from Rawlinson.[160]

However, not everything in these operations went according to plan. The attack on St Emile has been described as 'a rushed affair and one which cost more casualties than it should have done.'[161] The artillery barrage was inadequate to supress the enemy defenders and fell well beyond its intended target.[162] Carrington noted an incident

---

158 TNA WO 95/2757: Operations of 144th Infantry Brigade from 29/3/17 to 5/4/17, 144th Brigade War Diary.

159 TNA WO 95/2757: Operations of 144th Infantry Brigade from 29/3/17 to 5/4/17, 144th Brigade War Diary.

160 TNA WO 95/2746: III Corps General Order 3451, 14 April 1917, 48th Division General Staff War Diary; TNA WO 95/675: III Corps Summary of Operations April 1st to 30th 1917, III Corps General Staff War Diary.

161 K.W. Mitchinson, *The 48th (South Midland) Division 1908-1919* (Solihull: Helion & Co., 2017), p.144

162 Mitchinson, p.14

of 'friendly fire' during operations on 16 April when two companies of the 1/5th Royal Warwickshires blundered into each other in the darkness and opened fire.[163] On 24 April 144th Brigade suffered from the short shooting of 'a battery of another Division', which caused casualties and disorganisation.[164] The fighting at Gillemont Farm on 24-25 April cost 144th Brigade over 400 casualties and only the excellent support of the divisional artillery enabled it to beat off a series of determined enemy counterattacks.[165] A recent study of 48th Division has concluded that the attacks on Gillemont Farm at this time:

> Lacked flexibility, security and innovation and were usually characterised by insufficient concentration of force ... To have ordered it to proceed in such appalling conditions and with inadequate coordination between flanking units and the artillery was a grave misjudgement on the part of corps, divisional and brigade commanders.[166]

One of the most notable aspects of all the operations during this period was the increasing number of casualties that they generated. Official historian Falls noted of Fourth Army operations in general:

> Hardly any of these attacks had been made without fairly heavy losses, and in some cases, the losses, in proportion to the numbers engaged, had been higher than in the more fortunate of the trench warfare operations.[167]

This was borne out by III Corps casualties for April which were 3,588 of which 518 were fatal and a further 618 were listed as 'missing'.[168] This was three times the casualty rate for the preceding month. Mobile warfare was by no means less costly than trench warfare as the experience of the 'Hundred Days' campaign would reinforce.[169] The strain

---

163 Carrington, *Soldier from the Wars Returning*, p.144

164 TNA WO 95/2746: Report by Lt-Col. Tomkinson, 1/7th Worcestershires, 26 April 1917, 48th Division General Staff War Diary. The information about the fault lying with another division came from a covering note from Fanshawe when he forwarded the report to III Corps on 29 April.

165 TNA WO 95/2746: Report by Lt-Col. Tomkinson, 1/7th Worcestershires, 26 April 1917, 48th Division General Staff War Diary.

166 Mitchinson, *The 48th Division*, p.259.

167 Falls, *Military Operations 1917*, Vol. 1, p.161.

168 TNA WO 95/675: III Corps Summary of Casualties during the Month of April, 1917, III Corps General Staff War Diary.

169 Casualties for August 1918 would number over 116,000, in September nearly 109,000, in October over 115,000 and in November nearly 20,000 for a total of approximately 360,000 casualties in little over three months. Five of the BEF's 10 worst months in terms of casualties would occur during periods of open warfare. See War Office, *Statistics of the Military Effort of the British Empire During the Great War, 1914-1920* (London: HMSO, 1920), pp.253-65.

of mobile warfare on its participants was also considerable. Falls would later claim that despite the hardship, 'there was at least the partial compensation in the raised morale created by escape from water-logged trenches and in the exhilaration of pursuing the enemy across open country.'[170] Carrington, however, had a different recollection:

> Never had I been so exhausted and dispirited...Theoretically, as a keen young soldier I should have been delighted in this month of open fighting and should have been proud of our exploits. Chiefly I had been cold and frightened and I could not persuade myself it had been great fun.[171]

Whilst 48th Division's operations appeared to demonstrate a boldness and determination at odds with the impression of an army unused to the demands of open warfare, the performance of its neighbours on the right, 59th Division, was far more hesitant. In accordance with III Corps' instructions, 59th Division had advanced to the Somme on 18 March and had engaged in the building and fortification of a bridgehead at St Christ. When 1st Division was withdrawn into the corps reserve on 21 March, 59th Division had also taken on responsibility for the defence of the bridgehead at Brie. It was not until 27 March that the division moved forward to take up position on the new intermediate line as designated by Fourth Army.

Even the divisional history was forced to admit that, 'the Division now felt its lack of training for it was engaged in very difficult operations, necessitating ceaseless and bold patrolling, constant initiative on the part of subordinates and accurate judgement on the part of Brigade and Battalion Commanders.'[172] On 31 March it carried out its first major offensive operation, occupying the villages of Vendelles, Jeancourt and Hesbecourt, but 'without serious opposition', the whole task being made easier by the movement of IV Corps on the division's right which had turned the enemy's flank.[173] It was a different matter, however, when 178th Brigade attempted to take the enemy's outpost at Le Verguier on 4 and 6 April. The repulse of two attacks on this position was later attributed to the failure of the artillery to cut the wire in front of the German trenches, compounded by firing short during the withdrawal, and the lack of adequate reconnaissance beforehand to understand the ground and the precise location of the German positions.[174] The divisional commander, Major-General A. Sandbach,

170 Falls, *Military Operations 1917*, Vol. 1, p.162.
171 Carrington, *Soldier from the Wars Returning*, p.145.
172 Bradbridge (ed.), *59th Division, 1915-1918*, p.14.
173 TNA WO 95/675: III Corps Summary of Operations March 1 to 31 1917, III Corps General Staff War Diary. The 59th Division was able to benefit directly from this by dispatching a company from 178th Brigade to attack Jeancourt from the sector occupied by the neighbouring 61st Division. See TNA WO 95/3010: 59th Division General Order 202/5/1G, 30 March 1917, 59th Division General Staff War Diary.
174 Bradbridge (ed.), *59th Division, 1915-1918*, p.14; W. G. Hall, *The Green Triangle: Being the History of the 2/5th Battalion The Sherwood Foresters (Notts & Derby Regiment) in the Great European War, 1914-1918*, (Letchworth: Garden City Press, 1920), p.64; W.C. Oates, *The*

initially blamed the brigade commander, Brigadier-General E.W. Maconcy, relieving him of command, but for an officer of the 2/5th Sherwood Foresters it was clear that 'our army was still harnessed to a method of trench warfare useless in the open.'[175] Most of the brigade's officers had already expressed the opinion that a direct assault against the village was impracticable.[176]

The failure at Le Verguier was to have important repercussions for the senior officers of 59th Division. On 8 April, Sandbach was replaced by Major-General C.F. Romer, formerly BGGS III Corps. This was a conscious decision by Pulteney in response to 59th Division's perceived shortcomings. This was made clear in a post-war correspondence to Falls by a former III Corps staff officer: 'The 59th Division were new out from home and somewhat inexperienced so that we had some anxious times and disappointments at III Corps HQ; so that Lt.-General Pulteney ... sent down his Chief of Staff, Maj.-Gen. C. F. Romer, to take command of the division.'[177]

Sandbach was not the only commander to be removed from 59th Division. Within a week another brigade commander had been removed and two fresh brigadier-generals and a CRA were brought in.[178] However, these changes did not seem to cause much resentment among the men. A battalion commander in 178th Brigade wrote of Romer that 'all felt we were extremely lucky to get him' and the new divisional and brigade commanders were quick to reassure the men of the division that the failure at Le Verguier had not been down to them.[179]

Three days later, 59th Division finally captured Le Verguier after the Germans had withdrawn. On the night of 15/16 April the division carried what was described by the new divisional commander as 'a well-executed night operation' against Villeret by 176th Brigade.[180] On 27 April it was the turn of 178th Brigade to redeem itself in an attack on German positions around Hargicourt Quarry and Cologne Farm.[181] On this occasion, unlike at Le Verguier, 'the artillery support and liaison throughout, both in Battalions and the Brigade was excellent' and the wire 'well cut':

Sherwood Foresters in the Great War, 1914-1918: The 2/8th Battalion (Nottingham: J. and H. Bell, 1920), p.110.

175 Hall, *The Green Triangle*, p.75. Of the unfortunate Maconchy, Oates subsequently observed that 'His absence was much felt by those who had served longest with him. He was a soldier of the old school ... and he undoubtedly "made" the Sherwood Forester Brigade.' See Oates, *The Sherwood Foresters in the Great War*, p.104

176 Oates, p.107

177 TNA CAB 45/116: Lieutenant-Colonel L.W. Lever to Cyril Falls correspondence. Sandbach, Maconchy, whom Sandbach had relieved on 4 April, and a battalion commander previously relieved by Maconchy, allegedly all ended up travelling on the same boat back to Blighty. See S. Robbins, *British Generalship on the Western Front 1914-18* (London: Routledge, 2005), p.57.

178 Bradbridge (ed.), *59th Division, 1915-1918*, p.15.

179 Oates, *The Sherwood Foresters in the Great War: The 2/8th Battalion*, p.114.

180 Bradbridge (ed.), *59th Division, 1915-1918*, p.15.

181 TNA WO 95/675: III Corps Summary of Operations April 1 to 30 1917, III Corps General Staff War Diary.

> The arrangements made by Battalion Commanders for deploying and carrying out the assault were excellent and the greatest credit is due to these officers ... The morale of the troops was excellent and the success achieved has now put their tails at the right angle.[182]

After a shaky start 59th Division were now at last 'on their mettle'.[183]

The determination and level of tactical flexibility that 48th Division demonstrated during the fight for the outpost villages bears out one of Falls' observations in the Official History that it was 'the 'Somme' divisions that showed the greatest aptitude and most quickly learned the new lessons.'[184] In contrast, at the beginning of this phase of operations, 59th Division, lacking 48th Division's experience, found it much more difficult to co-ordinate its artillery support. This reflected the differing relationships between the two divisions and III Corps. The 48th Division was largely left alone, reports on its operations being circulated around the rest of the corps as exemplars of good practice. The treatment meted out to 59th Division was much more 'hands on', with a major shake-up of its senior leadership imposed by corps in order to improve its performance. Within a month, however, the division had shown great improvement, being able to mount effective operations with excellent artillery support that earned the praise of both the corps and Army commanders. *SS 135* may have promoted the idea of 'the man on the spot', but it had to be a man in whose judgement corps had sufficient faith for it to be effective.

Towards the end of April Fourth Army issued SS136, *Notes on Recent Operations*, covering the mobile phase of the advance and the initial operations against the outposts.[185] The main conclusion to be drawn from this was that the sudden change from trench warfare to open warfare had been 'the cause of some confusion and mistakes, especially among the younger officers and NCOs ... almost entirely due to ignorance ... of the principles laid down in *FSR*.'[186]

> These principles have been shown daily during these operations to be absolutely sound and no opportunity should be lost, either by tactical schemes or otherwise, of teaching open warfare tactics and especially the use of ground to all officers and NCOs.[187]

Other conclusions touched on the use of artillery during the advance, and the need for more flexibility in its employment under such conditions, the continuing effectiveness

---

182 TNA WO 95/3024: Operations against Cologne Farm on the Morning of the 27 April [1917] by 178th Infantry Brigade, 178th Brigade War Diary.
183 Falls, *Military Operations 1917*, Vol. 1, p.529, fn.1
184 Falls, *Military Operations 1917*, Vol. 1, p.162.
185 TNA WO 95/432: *SS 156*, Fourth Army General Staff War Diary.
186 TNA WO 95/432: *SS 156*, Fourth Army General Staff War Diary.
187 TNA WO 95/432: *SS 156*, Fourth Army General Staff War Diary.

of cavalry, how to manoeuvre the enemy out of fortified locations and the need for the rapid repair of roads. However, the main point that was reiterated again and again was that much of the necessary techniques already existed and just needed to be put into practice. At least one divisional commander heeded the advice not to lose any opportunity to teach the techniques of open warfare. As soon as his division had left the line, Fanshawe organised a divisional exercise based directly on the situation that they had faced on 18 March, but with the enemy holding positions on the main road leaving Péronne.[188] He was determined that whatever had been learned from the experience of the last month was to not to be wasted but made an integral part of his division's training regime.

In conclusion, any objective analysis of III Corps' operations must acknowledge that there is some truth in Falls' conclusions. Despite prior warning that its opponents might be on the verge of retiring, III Corps was still unable to take any major advantage of this and cause serious disruption to the German plan. In the first few hours of the advance the corps had completely lost touch with the enemy to its front and had to make strenuous efforts to regain contact. The advance during March was made at a steady pace, moving from one secure line to another. It was only as the corps advanced closer to the Hindenburg Line itself in April that real pressure was exerted on the enemy. The attacks made against the outpost villages, however, were conducted with determination and a high level of tactical flexibility, particularly by 48th Division.

The failure to discover the exact timing of the German withdrawal, however, was not down to any lack of alertness or initiative on the part of the divisions that comprised III Corps. It had kept the German lines under the closest observation throughout March and once the Germans had withdrawn it was quick to put into action the contingency plans that had been drawn up for the eventuality. The caution shown during the III Corps advance in March resulted more from external factors, especially Rawlinson's own caution and the deliberate demolition of the transport infrastructure, rather than a lack of initiative and aggression within the corps itself. Within the constraints of its orders III Corps acted as aggressively as it could, pushing the patrols of its mounted troops far out in front of its outpost line to establish contact with the enemy.

In terms of adapting to the transition from trench to semi-open warfare, III Corps and its divisions successfully demonstrated an ability to utilise both old and new methodologies. Planning within the corps showed understanding of the ideas contained within *SS 135*, especially the need to co-ordinate the artillery plan between the corps and the division. At same time, however, the manner in which mobile operations were conducted during the advance also demonstrated that the principles of *FSR* were still understood and applied. The formation of 'Ward Force' was completely in keeping

188 TNA WO 95/2746: 48th Division Order F.82, 6 May 1917, 48th Division General Staff War Diary.

with the principles contained in *FSR* and actions like the capture of Roisel on 26 March demonstrated an understanding of combined arms operations.

In terms of the relationship between corps and division, there was still some tension between the emergence of the corps as the highest operational formation, responsible for the co-ordination of the activities of its divisions, and the need for greater decentralisation of command in mobile operations. Deferring to the 'man on the spot' worked when that man was thought capable, but the temptation for higher authority to intervene remained, and indeed was sometimes necessary. In other areas, such as engineering and logistics, attempts to re-organise and redefine the roles and responsibilities between corps and division had started, but remained a 'work in progress'.

Progress itself was not always consistent at all levels of command, even in experienced formations like 48th Division, but it is important to realise that the BEF was never monolithic in its operational approach. Even as late as the Hundred Days campaign, variation could still be seen between different corps and divisions.[189] Different formations absorbed new ideas and lessons at different rates. The most important thing that they had in common was that they learned. An experienced division like 48th may have had past lessons reinforced rather than new lessons taught as in less experienced divisions like the 59th nevertheless, both formations benefitted from their experience and incorporated that learning into their training.

In the historiography of the First World War, Pulteney's III Corps does not have the reputation for operational innovation and effectiveness of Maxse's XVIII Corps or Congreve's XIII Corps. However, during the Advance to the Hindenburg Line in spring 1917 it demonstrated that, within the constraints imposed on them by strategic considerations and logistical difficulties, its formations could still absorb new techniques, mount effective operations and, most importantly, learn from the experience.

---

189 For example, see J. Boff, *Winning and Losing on the Western Front: The British Third Army and the Defeat of Germany in 1918* (Cambridge: Cambridge University Press, 2012), pp.153-59.

Patchy Progress & Powerful Performances
Tactical development in 8th British Division and 2nd Australian Division during the pursuit to the Hindenburg Line

Andy Lock

It is a welcome situation to engage in First World War literature with the notion of the BEF's learning process now largely accepted as fact. The last three decades of scholarship, driven by academics including Gary Sheffield, Peter Simkins, Paddy Griffith and William Philpott have established the Battle of the Somme in 1916 as a campaign in which considerable experimentation took place, and in which much was learnt about modern warfare. This bloody, and often error-fraught education played an integral role in the BEF's development into a tactically adept, technologically advanced and continental-sized army by the final year of the war.

First and Third armies assaults on 9 April 1917, at Vimy Ridge and east of Arras respectively, are usually cited as prime examples of improvements in the BEF's offensive capability, at least as far as large-scale set-piece offensives are concerned. Furthermore, attention is routinely drawn in modern historiography to the efforts across the BEF to adopt new formations down to platoon level. Two pamphlets issued during winter 1916-17, *SS 135: Instructions for the Training of Divisions for Offensive Action* and *SS 143: Instructions for the Training of Platoons for Offensive Action*, are held up as vital documents for the immensely expanded BEF. However, institution-wide issuance is no guarantee that said pamphlet will be read, let alone adhered to. In the BEF's case, most divisions would be involved in holding the line through what was an infamously harsh winter and would have little time to assimilate new doctrine prior to resumption of offensive action in the spring. Those divisions which went into action during the advance to the Hindenburg Line between February and April 1917 would have comparatively little time to incorporate the lessons of the Somme, and significant changes in fighting style would be required of them. This chapter will examine 8th Division and 2nd Australian Division in that period and assess the extent of their tactical progress from the previous year. In doing so, the uneven nature of the BEF's learning process in the wake of the Somme offensive will be demonstrated.

The advance to the Hindenburg Line often features in the relevant historiography as a preamble to the Battle of Arras, but with the exception of Third Army's southernmost divisions and Fifth Army's costly attacks at Bullecourt, the two operations took place quite independently of one another.[1] Operation *Alberich* and the ensuing pursuit are far more closely linked with the Somme campaign, both in terms of geography and formations involved. Despite significantly different experiences up to July 1916, the ordeal was superficially similar for 8th Division and 2nd Australian Division. Both had suffered heavy casualties in the early stages of the offensive; had had a lengthy spell away from subsequent Picardy fighting, then fought there again during October and November 1916 with mixed results. The 8th Division attacked towards Le Transloy on 23 October with all three of its brigades in line. Although able to advance on the flanks, the assault was held by machine-gun and concentrated rifle fire in the centre.[2] The 2nd Australian Division attacked near the infamous Butte de Warlencourt on 5 and 14 November; on both occasions the Australians achieved small break-ins that were subsequently driven out by German counter-attacks.[3] Following this, both divisions experienced changes at the top, with their divisional commanders replaced by high-performance brigadier-generals. In 8th Division, the Canadian-born Major-General William Heneker assumed command from Major-General Havelock Hudson, who was dispatched to India to take up the post of Adjutant-General. Heneker had commanded 190th Brigade in 63rd (Royal Naval) Division prior to assuming command on 10 December and had the good fortune to join the division during a spell of intensive training behind the lines.[4] On 28 December Major-General James Legge (GOC 2nd Australian Division) was replaced, albeit temporarily prior to permanent posting, by Major-General Nevill Smythe VC, formerly GOC 1st Australian Brigade. Smythe did not have the luxury of time away from the trenches with his new command; the demands of frontline service prevented intensive training except for two weeks in late January and early February. His division was also called into action sooner than most Fifth Army formations. The first German withdrawals to the Hindenburg Line occurred in late February, with 2nd Australian Division holding the line astride the Albert-Bapaume road at Le Sars.

1   The British official account, Cyril Falls, *Military Operations France and Belgium 1917*, Vol. 1 (London: Macmillan, 1940), covers early 1917 to the close of the Arras offensive. A non-exhaustive list of books covering Arras include works by Don Farr, Jim Smithson, Jonathan Nicholls and Andrew Rawson. All include at least one mention of the advance to the Hindenburg Line. Bean has written probably the most detailed description of operations during the pursuit, but his work is limited to Australian formations/units only.

2   TNA WO 95/1675/3: 'REPORT OF THE OPERATIONS CARRIED OUT BY THE 8th DIVISION WEST OF LE TRANSLOY FROM THE 23rd to 30th OCTOBER, 1916', 15 December 1916, 8th Division HQ War Diary.

3   W. Miles, *Military Operations, France and Belgium 1916* Vol. II (Uckfield: Naval & Military Press, 2019 reprint of 1938 edition), pp.470-73, 524-26.

4   For an able assessment of Heneker's military career, see John Bourne, 'Major-General W.C.G. Heneker: A Divisional Commander of the Great War' in Matthew Hughes & Matthew Seligmann (eds.) *Leadership in Conflict 1914-1918* (Barnsley: Leo Cooper, 2000).

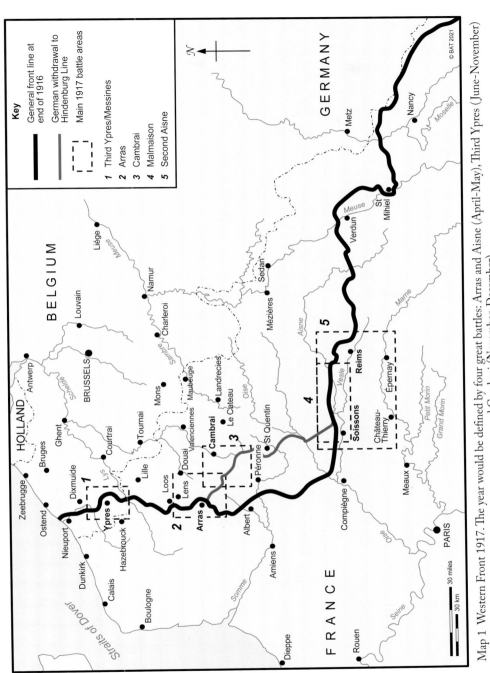

Map 1 Western Front 1917. The year would be defined by four great battles: Arras and Aisne (April–May), Third Ypres (June–November) and Cambrai (November–December).

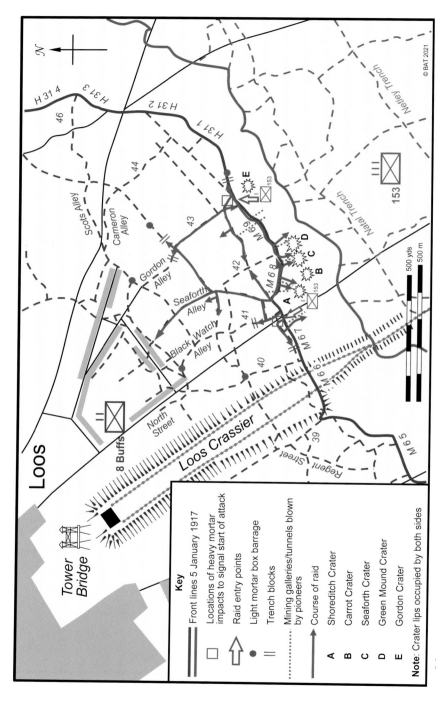

Key

	Front lines 5 January 1917
□	Locations of heavy mortar impacts to signal start of attack
⬆	Raid entry points
•	Light mortar box barrage
=	Trench blocks
⋯	Mining galleries/tunnels blown by pioneers
➤	Course of raid

A Shoreditch Crater
B Carrot Crater
C Seaforth Crater
D Green Mound Crater
E Gordon Crater

Note: Crater lips occupied by both sides

Map 2 Loos raid, 5 January 1917. During the extraordinarily harsh winter of 1916–17, a minor German trench raid occurred near Loos. This daring and meticulously planned enterprise achieved complete surprise and resulted in enemy penetration as far as the village defences much to the embarrassment of the British high command.

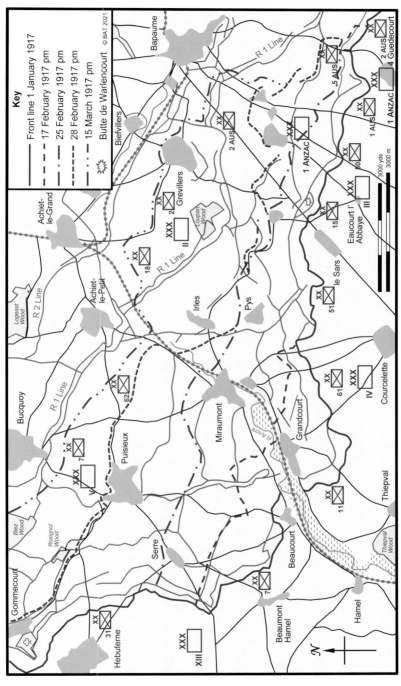

Map 3 Advance to the Hindenburg Line, February–March 1917. The German withdrawal to new defensive positions was conducted with tactical skill and ruthless efficiency. Anglo-French forces followed up as best they could but were wary of overcommitting against an unbroken foe.

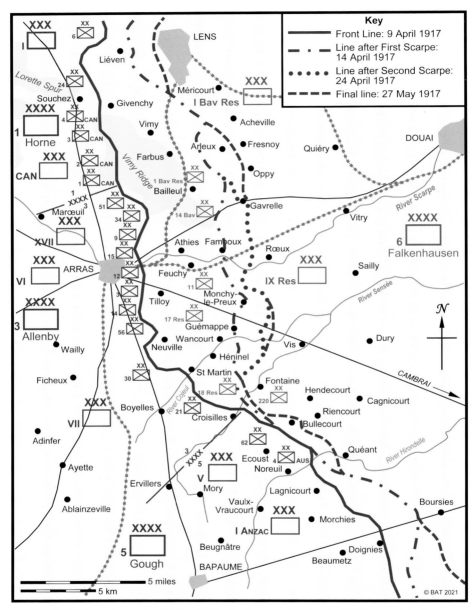

Key
- Front Line: 9 April 1917
- Line after First Scarpe: 14 April 1917
- Line after Second Scarpe: 24 April 1917
- Final line: 27 May 1917

LENS

Liéven

Lorette Spur

XXX
I

XX
6

XX
24

Souchez

Givenchy

Méricourt

XXX
I Bav Res

XXXX
1
Horne

XX
4 CAN

XX
3 CAN

Vimy

Acheville

Fresnoy

Quiéry

DOUAI

XXX
CAN

XX
2 CAN

XX
1 CAN

Vimy Ridge

Farbus

Arleux

Oppy

XX
1 Bav Res

Bailleul

River Scarpe

Marœuil

XXXX
1
3

XX
51

XX
34

XX
9

Gavrelle

XX
14 Bav

Vitry

XXXX
6
Falkenhausen

XXX
XVII

Athies

Fampoux

Rœux

Sailly

XXX
VI

ARRAS

XX
15

XX
12

Feuchy

XX
11

XXX
IX Res

River Sensée

XXXX
3
Allenby

XX
3

XX
14

XX
56

Tilloy

XX
17 Res

Monchy-le-Preux

Guémappe

Wancourt

Neuville

Vis

Dury

N

Wailly

Héninel

CAMBRAI

Ficheux

XX
30

St Martin

XX
18 Res

Fontaine

XX
220

Hendecourt

Cagnicourt

River Hirondelle

XXX
VII

Boyelles

XX
21

Croisilles

Riencourt

Bullecourt

Quéant

Adinfer

XX
62

Ayette

Ervillers

XXXX
3
5

XXX
V

Mory

Ecoust
Noreuil

XX
4 AUS

Lagnicourt

Boursies

Ablainzeville

Vaulx-Vraucourt

XXX
I Anzac

Morchies

XXXX
5
Gough

Beugnâtre

BAPAUME

Doignies

Beaumetz

5 miles

5 km

© BAT 2021

Map 4 Battle of Arras, April–May 1917. On the opening day the BEF secured its largest advance since the dawn of trench warfare. But the campaign soon bogged down into bitter attritional fighting resulting in the BEF's highest daily casualty rate of the war.

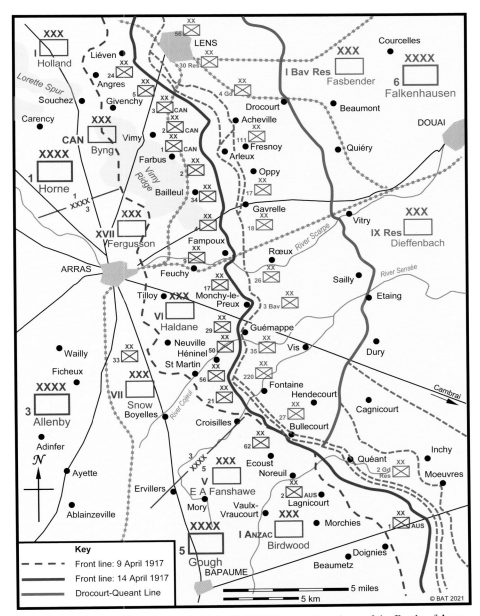

Map 5 First Battle of the Scarpe, 9-14 April 1917. The opening phase of the Battle of Arras was an impressive success born of thorough training and careful preparations.

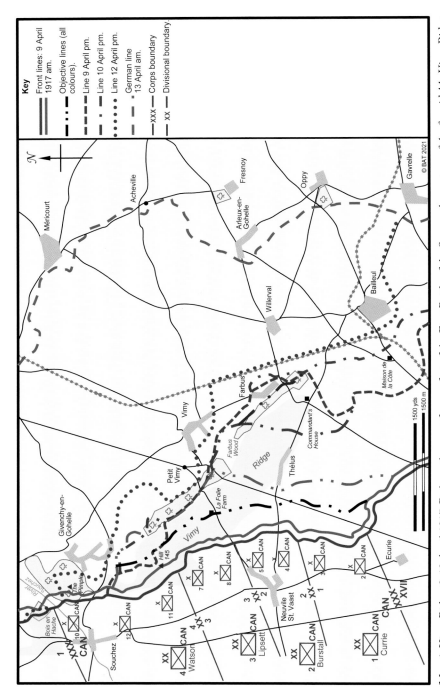

Map 6 Vimy Ridge, 9–13 April 1917. Perhaps the most famous feat of the First Battle of the Scarpe, the capture of the formidable Vimy Ridge position demonstrated how far the BEF had developed since 1 July 1916.

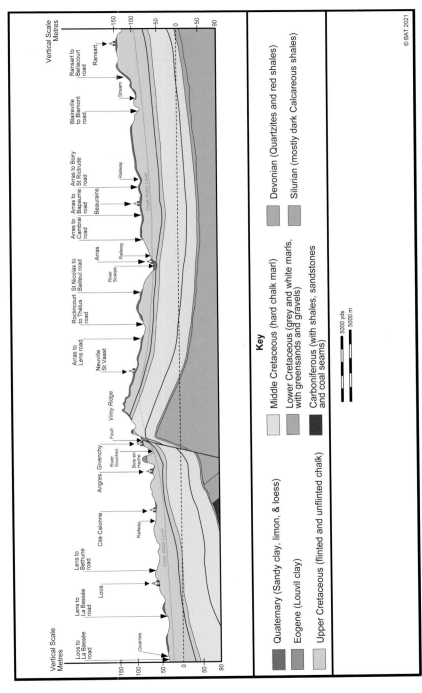

Map 7 Arras and vicinity geological survey. The ground beneath the city of Arras was distinctive and offered both help and hinderance to the Royal Engineers. It was ideal terrain for mining, but a high water table created problems with trench construction.

Key

- Quaternary (Sandy clay, limon, & loess)
- Eogene (Louvil clay)
- Upper Cretaceous (flinted and unflinted chalk)
- Middle Cretaceous (hard chalk marl)
- Lower Cretaceous (grey and white marls, with greensands and gravels)
- Carboniferous (with shales, sandstones and coal seams)
- Devonian (Quartzites and red shales)
- Silurian (mostly dark Calcareous shales)

5000 yds
5000 m

© BAT 2021

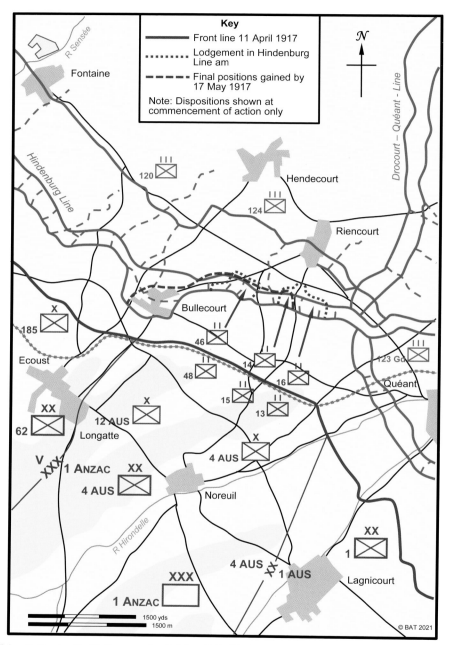

Map 8 Battles for Bullecourt, April-May 1917. The hastily planned and poorly implemented assault on 11 April resulted in severe Australian casualties and gave the Anzacs a lasting distrust of tanks.

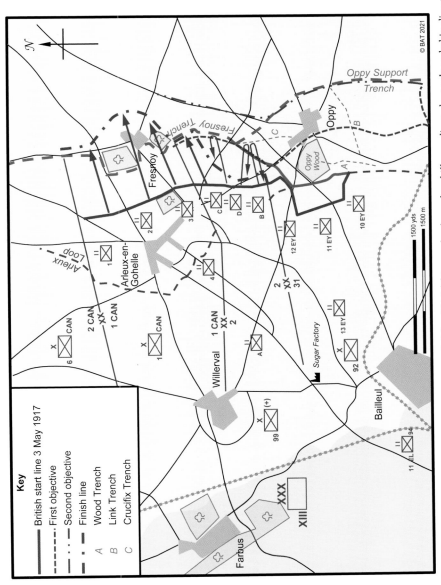

Key

———	British start line 3 May 1917
———	First objective
—·—·—	Second objective
— — —	Finish line
A	Wood Trench
B	Link Trench
C	Crucifix Trench

Map 9 Third Battle of the Scarpe, Oppy–Fresnoy sector, 3 May 1917. This poorly planned and ill-coordinated assault ended in disaster. The offensive demonstrated that, despite much improvement since 1916, that the BEF retained some serious operational weaknesses.

ix

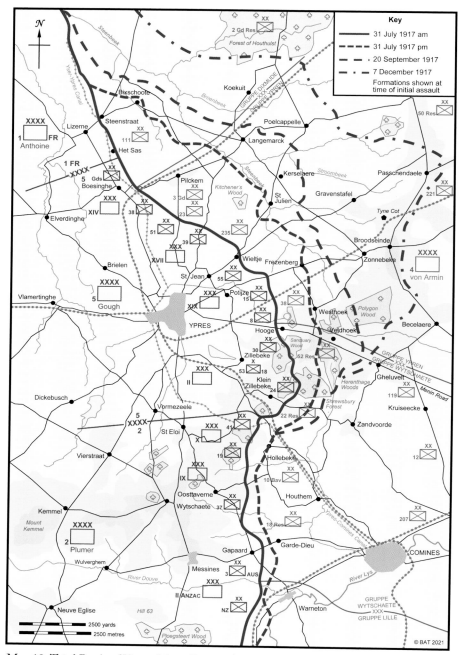

Key

——————	31 July 1917 am
– – – – –	31 July 1917 pm
– – – – –	20 September 1917
– · – · – ·	7 December 1917

Formations shown at
time of initial assault

Map 10 Third Battle of Ypres, July to December 1917. This gruelling, multi-phase campaign
would be the centrepiece of BEF operations for the year.

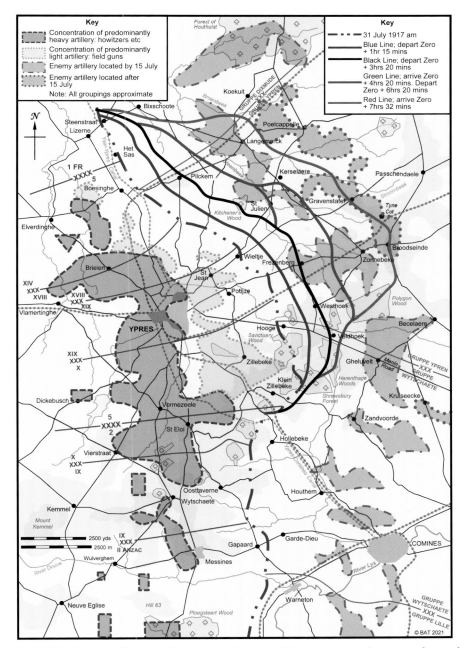

Map 11 Third Battle of Ypres artillery battle, 15-31 July 1917. Despite disadvantages of ground, the Royal Artillery mustered a staggering concentration of fire to crush the German Flanders defences. Particular attention was paid to identifying and silencing hostile artillery batteries.

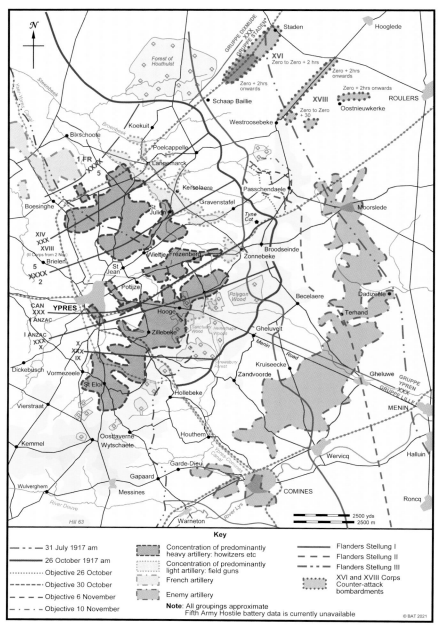

Map 12 Third Battle of Ypres artillery battle, October–November 1917. The British gunners continued their work in locating and neutralising German batteries but were hampered by wet weather and devastated, muddy ground which made forward movement an agonisingly slow process.

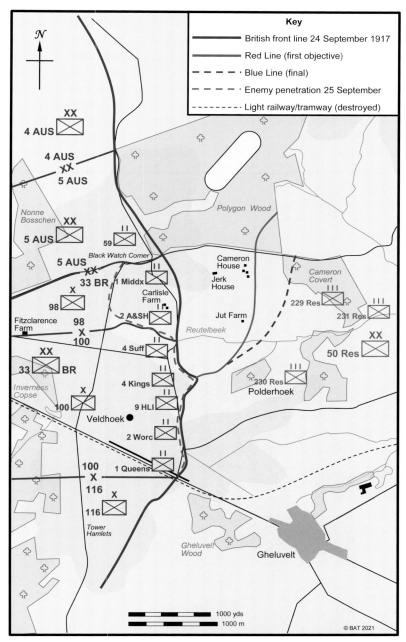

Map 13 33rd Division at Polygon Wood, 25-27 September 1917. Following a crippling German counter-attack, the division fought hard to hold its ground before joining in a general offensive the following day. The see-saw fighting would ultimately end in British victory.

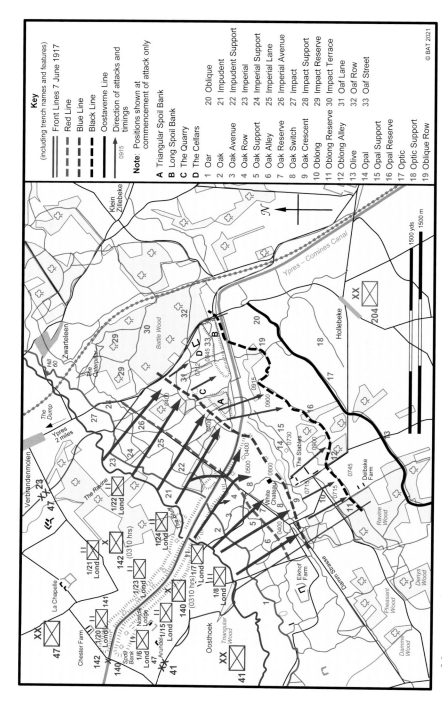

Map 14 47th (London) Division at Messines Ridge, 7 June 1917. Advancing against an unusually high density of German defenders, the Londoners faced numerous tactical difficulties which required skill and flexibility to overcome.

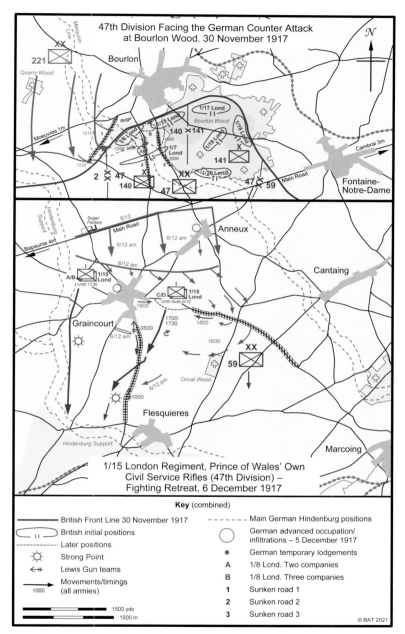

Map 15 47th (London) Division at Bourlon Wood and vicinity, November-December 1917. The division found itself defending an untenable position against the crack German *221st Division*. By 5 December, the Londoners were forced to withdraw with 1/15th London Regiment conducting a dangerous but ultimately successful fighting retreat.

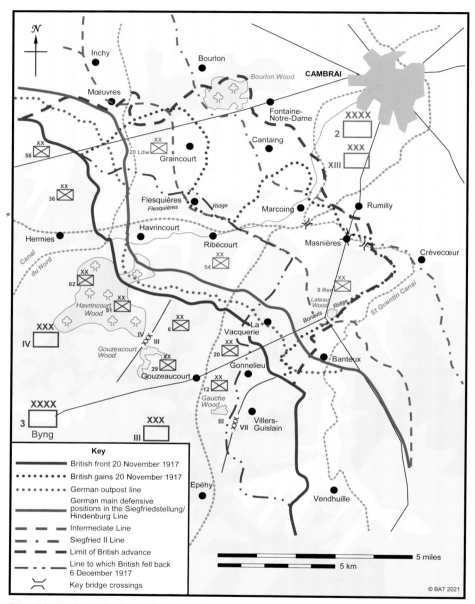

Map 16 Battle of Cambrai, November-December 1917. The combination of predicted artillery
bombardment and a massed tank assault allowed the BEF to make a notable first day advance.
The tide of battle soon turned when a large-scale German counter-attack wrestled back almost
all the ground they had lost.

The 2nd Australian Division's difficulties in November 1916 can largely be attributed to the weather, inadequacy of the artillery preparation (particularly on 5 November), and the strength of the defenders.[5] These circumstances exacerbated the problem of keeping assaulting troops supplied with bombs, ammunition, water and rations in the face of seemingly irresistible enemy counter-attacks. Over the next two months, efforts were made to enhance the division's ability to maintain territorial gains. In mid-December, prior to Legge's departure, all three component brigades participated in practice attack schemes with and without contact patrol aircraft. The proposed tactical premise in each case was enemy occupation of two lines of trenches (referred to as O.G.1 and O.G.2),[6] the first on a forward slope, the second on the reverse slope.[7] Trenches were marked with ploughed furrows, and

Major-General W.C.G. Heneker.
(IWM Q114834)

the advancing barrage designated by a line of horses, which stood on certain objectives prior to moving forward at prearranged times at 75 yards per minute.[8] While this all seems reasonable enough, an absence of uniformity with regard to practice attack formations suggests a lack of consensus as to which was strongest. For the exercises, 5th and 7th brigades opted to place all eight battalions in line, split into four (presumably company strength) waves, whilst 6th Brigade formed-up with 21st and 22nd battalions (21 and 22/Bn AI) in four assault waves, 23/Bn AI following in reserve and 24/Bn AI held as a 'garrison battalion'.[9] The divisional commander's response to

5   Australian War Memorial (AWM) AWM4 Subclass 23/7/15, 7th Australian Brigade HQ War Diary, November 1916, 'Report on the Operations of the 7th Australian Infantry Brigade between 3 and 7 November 16.'
6   O.G.1 and O.G. 2 were the names of two notorious trenches on I Anzac Corps front during the gruelling and costly Pozières fighting (July-August 1916) of the previous year.
7   AWM AWM4 Subclass 23/6/16, 6th Australian Brigade HQ War Diary, December 1916, '6th Australian Infantry Brigade Order No. 000', issued 13 December 1916.
8   AWM AWM4 Subclass 23/7/16, 7th Australian Brigade HQ War Diary, December 1916, 'Appendix 1, Training Order No. 8' issued 11 December 1916.
9   AWM AWM4 Subclass 23/5/18, 5th Australian Brigade HQ War Diary, December 1916, 'Appendix; Training Order No. 3', issued 12 December 1916; AWM4 Subclass 23/6/16,

the exercises was muted; the 2nd Australian Division headquarters war diary simply stating, 'The practice was, on the whole, satisfactory'.[10]

After Smythe assumed command, there is evidence of greater attention to detail during training and some effort to explore lessons beyond 2nd Australian Division's Somme experience. Brigadier-General Robert Smith (GOC 5th Brigade) attended a demonstration at I Anzac Corps School on the 'French system of Drill for the attack' on 20 January. Although the content and nature of the demonstration is not recorded, it resulted in subsequent attack formation alterations during the next series of division-wide practice attacks, which took place on 26 January.[11] On this occasion, all three brigades placed two battalions in line. Designated objectives were not simply the capture of trench lines, but also seizure of strong points beyond the second objective, and the pushing of forward outposts.[12] Smythe also took the trouble to have the lessons and recommended improvements of the 26 January exercise disseminated to subordinates concerned:

1   Barrage: Followed well initially, then infantry fell behind after capture of first objective. Following the barrage lifting off an objective, men should rush the trench cheering and shouting in order to reach the parapet first, to 'give impetus to attack for hand to hand fighting', and to 'rouse men's ardour'.

2   Scouts: Greater flexibility in formation and a better understanding of their role were needed. 'Require more training'.

3   Shallow columns used for advance on strong points; more easily handled, especially over larger distances, can more easily take cover and better for avoiding losses to enemy artillery.

4   Aforementioned columns should break to lines before the assault on the strong point.

5   Communication between battalions: Setting off from one objective to the next without coordinating with neighbouring battalion will leave a unit vulnerable to enfilade fire.

6   Lewis Guns: Should be placed at least 50 yards ahead of newly captured positions, forming the basis of a new line. Captured lines will be known to hostile artillery, any strong points therein are liable to be knocked out.

6th Australian Brigade HQ War Diary, December 1916, '6th Australian Infantry Brigade Order No. 000', issued 13 December 1916.

10   AWM AWM4 Subclass 1/44/17, 2nd Australian Division HQ War Diary, 14 December 1916.

11   AWM AWM4 Subclass 23/5/19, 5th Australian Brigade HQ War Diary, 20 January 1917. Smith was the only brigade commander able to attend the demonstration of 20 January, as John Gellibrand (6th Brigade) was away sick and Evan Wisdom (7th Brigade) was on leave.

12   AWM AWM4 Subclass 23/7/17, 7th Australian Brigade HQ War Diary, Appendix 9: 'Training Order No. 3'.

7   Old German lines not to be held for same reason. Digging a new line 100 yards distant will leave the enemy uncertain of the position taken until they can acquire aerial photographs.[13]

While these points were all valuable, and the practice itself more realistic and relevant than that carried out the previous December, 2nd Australian Division would have little time to assimilate the report's contents. Three days later (29 January 1917) they moved back to the frontline near Martinpuich. On 24 February, 5th and 6th brigades were in line when the first German withdrawal was detected. This took the enemy main line of resistance from the Butte de Warlencourt to a position known as Malt Trench in front of Le Barque, after which the enemy defences extended across the Albert-Bapaume Road to just of south of Loupart Wood where they joined Gamp Trench due north of Warlencourt. This movement, clearly not anticipated by I Anzac Corps headquarters, came at an inopportune moment for 2nd Australian Division. Major-General Smythe was on leave, an unfortunate circumstance that resulted in a chain of temporary promotions, with Brigadier-General John Gellibrand (GOC 6th Brigade) assuming divisional command; Lieutenant-Colonel F.W.D. Forbes (CO 21/ Bn AI) filling in as brigade commander and Major H.A. Crowther taking over as battalion commander.[14] On the evening of 24 February, the enemy's front and immediate support lines were occupied and the Butte de Warlencourt was, at last, in British hands.

By dawn on 25 February, outposts had been established about Warlencourt–Eaucourt, but ground conditions slowed the flow of information to Gellibrand (especially so from his own brigade) which, according to Charles Bean, was 'almost intolerable' to the temporary major-general.[15] No serious resistance had been encountered during the occupation of Gird and Gallwitz trenches, and it was unclear where the next enemy line would be established. Patrols continued to press forward throughout the morning and early afternoon. At 2.30 p.m. Gellibrand ordered 5th and 6th brigades to occupy Malt and Gamp trenches by 5.30 p.m. 'unless [they] proved to be strongly held by the enemy'. Following this, operations were mounted against Grévillers Trench.[16] Coordination was absent between 5th and 6th brigades, the former moving to the assault at 5:00 p.m. The 5th Brigade's entire frontage was visible from Malt Trench on the left. With 6th Brigade's attack delayed by a later jumping-off time and 21/ Bn AI's delay in taking up position, 5th Brigade was halted by sustained rifle and

13   AWM AWM4 Subclass 23/5/19, 5th Australian Brigade HQ War Diary, Appendix 8: 'Notes on Attack Practice carried out by 17th and 20th battalions on 26 January 1917'.
14   AWM AWM4 Subclass 23/6/18, 6th Australian Brigade War Diary, February 1917.
15   C.E.W. Bean, *The Australian Imperial Force in France 1917* (Sydney: Halstead, 1941) p.72.
16   AWM AWM4 Subclass 1/44/19 PART 3, 2nd Australian Division HQ War Diary, Appendix XXXV, Message 51.

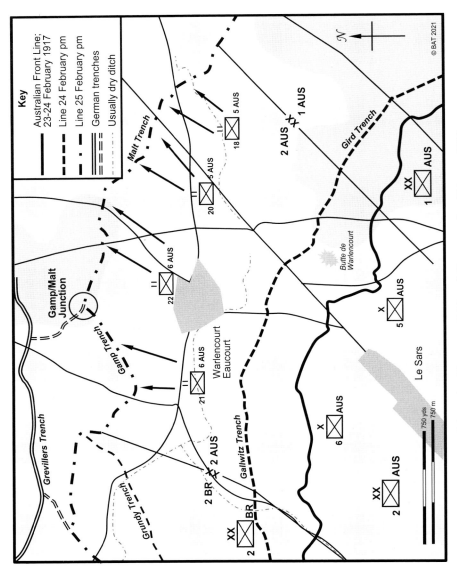

2nd Australian Division at Malt and Gamp trenches, February 1917.

machine-gun fire.[17] On the left, 20/Bn AI's advance stalled, whilst 18/AI, persevering for a time, attempted to negotiate shell holes before its left company sustained heavy casualties. For its part, 6th Brigade left the jumping-off line at 5.30 p.m. Two hours passed before brigade headquarters received word of the attack's progress. It was not until 7.16 p.m. that a message arrived from 22/Bn AI stating that 'occupation of objective held up by M.G. fire and heavy wire'. The 21/Bn AI did not get a message back until after 10:00 p.m. but managed to enter Gamp Trench at its most southerly point.[18] Further progress was impossible due to machine-gun fire from the junction of Gamp and Malt trenches, however, 21/Bn AI did manage to establish a post in Gamp Trench where the break-in had occurred. The division sustained 174 casualties for this small gain.[19]

Overnight efforts to bomb into Malt Trench and bring Stokes mortars to bear against the enemy garrison were unsuccessful. Confusion was common during this period. An officer of 14th Heavy Artillery Group had climbed the Butte in the afternoon of 25th, observed enemy artillery fire dropping on Malt Trench north of the Albert-Bapaume road and had incorrectly declared it to be unoccupied.[20] On the 26th, with friendly artillery fire finally being directed upon the 15-foot thick barbed wire belts front the objective, 5th Brigade managed to make some headway against Malt Trench just south of the Albert–Bapaume Road. However, 6th Brigade added to the prevailing confusion when a patrol of 24/Bn AI returned at 8.45 p.m. to report that they had been through Malt Trench and its junction with Gamp Trench. Moving some 200 yards along, they did not encounter the enemy.[21] The 6th Brigade was scheduled to be relieved that evening by 7th Brigade. This was well under way by the time an order to establish a post at the junction of Malt and Gamp trenches was received from divisional headquarters. Three parties of 28/Bn AI were immediately dispatched to carry out the order. The inter-brigade relief complete, a second patrol of 24/Bn AI came in, claiming they had been fired on by machine-guns situated at the Malt and Gamp trenches junction. Unaware of this, Gellibrand dispatched a note to 6th Brigade in which he enquired why Malt Trench had not been occupied. His puzzlement gave way to consternation, as early morning reports from 7th Brigade stated a patrol had attempted to enter the position. Held up by machine-gun and rifle fire, the patrol determined the position was held in some strength. At 9.40 a.m. on 27 February, Lieutenant-Colonel A.H. Bridges (2nd Australian Division GSO1) sent

17 AWM AWM4 Subclass 23/5/21, 5th Australian Brigade HQ War Diary, 'Report on Operations; 24th/25th February to 2nd March 17', 14 March 1917.
18 AWM AWM4 Subclass 23/6/18, 6th Australian Brigade War Diary, February 1917, 'Summary of Events; 24/27th February 1917'.
19 Falls, *Military Operations 1917*, Vol. I, p.98.
20 AWM AWM4 Subclass 1/44/19 PART 1, 2nd Australian Division HQ War Diary, 25 February 1917, 6.30pm.
21 AWM AWM4 Subclass 23/6/18, 6th Australian Brigade War Diary, February 1917, 'Summary of Events; 24/27th February 1917'.

a message to 6th Brigade demanding a copy of the Malt Trench patrol instructions. On threat of a 'full enquiry into the matter', Lieutenant-Colonel Forbes revealed that it was unlikely the patrol had entered Malt Trench.[22] Adding further weight to the myriad sources of disinformation was a contact patrol aircraft report, received on the morning of 27th, which stated that the lower portion of Malt Trench was unoccupied. Simultaneous with this, reports claiming that fighting was raging at the same location arrived from 5th Brigade.[23]

The 27 and 28 February were dominated by intense bomb fights, particularly on the right where 5th Brigade endeavoured to force a way up Malt Trench from the south-east. The 7th Brigade was more patient in their approach. Having established that the wire was too thick to be overcome without artillery support, Malt Trench was bombarded throughout 28 February. This was approved by General Sir Hubert Gough (GOC Fifth Army) who visited 2nd Australian Division headquarters at 11:00 a.m.[24] Artillery and trench mortar fire continued the wire-cutting bombardment until 7:00 p.m. on 1 March, when scouts determined the wire passable. The consequent 7th Brigade assault opened at 3:00 a.m. on 2 March, a sharp bombing contest occurring as German reinforcements entered the fight from the direction of Loupart Wood. Nevertheless, a link between 5th and 7th brigades was established and the attackers' territorial gains consolidated. Throughout this period of fighting, 2nd Australian Division had fought well, but without much innovation. Its approach relied on the methods employed throughout 1916. Clearly, elements of their performance, particularly with regard to communications, were unsatisfactory.

In the immediate wake of the Malt Trench fighting, 7th Brigade's staff compiled a 'lessons learned' document which centred around the value of attack preparations and the dangers of engaging in deadly bombing contests. Concerning the first point, 'that attacks hastily launched and without proper preparation against an entrenched enemy, frequently fail, and are costly', appears obvious, but in need of explicit statement. With regard to bombing attacks, 'it is invariably the side which can throw in the last reinforcement of bombers that seems to win', and 'that a prepared frontal attack is less costly, more successful, and more quickly accomplished than bombing attacks'. These pronouncements indicate growing scepticism amongst senior officers on the value of unsupported bombing.[25] No doubt established trench fighting techniques required

22   AWM AWM4 Subclass 1/44/19 PART 1, 2nd Australian Division HQ War Diary, 27 February 1917, 9.40am and Bean, *AIF in France 1917*, pp.96-97. Bean states that Malt Trench certainly WAS entered, but between two outposts.

23   AWM AWM4 Subclass 1/44/19 PART 1, 2nd Australian Division HQ War Diary, 27 February 1917, 11.50am. Pilot had flown over between 8 and 9 am.

24   AWM AWM4 Subclass 1/44/19 PART 1, 2nd Australian Division HQ War Diary, 28 February 1917, 11.15am.

25   AWM AWM4 Subclass 23/7/19, 7th Australian Brigade War Diary, March 1917, 'Appendix A: 'Report on Offensive Operations carried out by 7th Australian Brigade from 27 February 1917 to March 2nd 1917, inclusive', 7 March 1917.

revision and modification as a degree of movement characterised the actions of early 1917. One reoccurring problem, however, would be the relative lack of time away from the trenches for training and assimilation of lessons learned during previous operations. The 2nd Australian Division's only significant period for this had been in early December 1916, and while a divisional school was established and practice attacks occurred, there is no evidence of significant tactical innovation during this time. This was in contrast to the British 8th Division, in which a degree of creativity and adaptability was amply demonstrated.

The 8th Division, despite experiencing extensive changes to its command structure, enjoyed more stability during winter 1916-17 than 2nd Australian Division. The former's Somme experience was beset with practical difficulties, not the least on the offensive's tragic opening day at Ovillers (where the division suffered a staggering 5,121 men killed, wounded and missing), but more recently on 23 October between Gueudecourt and Le Transloy. Traversing very bad ground, small inroads were made on the division's flanks, but 25th Brigade was halted in the centre. This setback was attributed to 2nd Battalion Lincolnshire Regiment (2/Lincs) coming under heavy rifle fire directed by a 'very gallant German officer' who stood atop the enemy parapet.[26] However, tired battalions sent into action across a treacherous shell hole-ridden mudflat in the wake of a creeping barrage that advanced too quickly and was duly lost was the likely cause of the reverse. Lacking the necessary artillery cover and without the means to call for its adjustment, the assault was repulsed with heavy losses. A long-term result of this reverse was Major-General Heneker's assumption of command on 10 December. A harsh taskmaster and notorious disciplinarian, he wasted no time in relieving the GSO1, CRA and two brigade commanders (24th and 25th brigades) during what remained of December and January. There was also the challenge of integrating fresh drafts. The 2nd Battalion East Lancashire Regiment (2/E Lancs), one of the most depleted battalions, lamented the difficulty in organising 278 men from 26 different battalions, amongst which there were only two NCOs. Morale was not improved when a further 132 drafts arrived, '129 of which [were] marked "untrained."'[27] The need to incorporate the new arrivals into units depleted during the previous October meant that the focus of training through November and December would be on what may be termed 'soldiering basics'.

The 8th Division benefitted from its time out of the line. From the third week of November through to the end of the third week of January, the division embarked on a lengthy training programme at establishments already in place from early 1916. At various levels, a multitude of active service skills were already available for instruction. For example, the 2nd Middlesex Regiment (2/Mddlsx) war diary records small numbers of men periodically dispatched to a Lewis Gun school from September 1916

---

26   TNA WO 95/1730/1: 2nd Lincolnshire Regiment War Diary, 23 October 1916 entry.
27   TNA WO 95/1720/1: 2nd East Lancashire Regiment War Diary, 2 November 1916 entry.

through early 1917. This would typically involve two specialists, occasionally accompanied by an officer, being sent off for 5 or 6 days training.[28] The Brigade Grenade School would typically take seven other ranks for a similar period.[29] Divisional Schools of Instruction would accept single officers or entire companies for drill and instruction.[30]

Following a short spell in the line during mid-November, divisional training resumed under battalion arrangements whilst a divisional scheme was devised. The experience of the 2nd Battalion Northamptonshire Regiment (2/Northants) was representative of this period. With one day's training lost to bad weather (during which lectures were carried out under available cover by company commanders) and routine church services convened on Sunday 26 November, the remaining days were spent alternating between bombing practice, platoon drill and musketry on a 30 yard range. This daily regimen was proceeded by 30 minutes physical training. Sports events were scheduled for the late afternoon.[31] Junior officers from the recent drafts were dispatched to the divisional school of instruction. Bayonet training and trench mortar schools were also established at this time.[32]

Throughout December, 8th Division's training focused on physical fitness, wiring and Bangalore torpedo employment. Assaults were rehearsed by day and night. Meantime, the Fourth Army musketry school periodically accepted groups ranging in size from 53 in the case of 2nd Battalion Devonshire Regiment (2/Devons) to 190 from 2/E Lancs.[33] From 6 December, practice trenches and wooded areas were available for attack and defence exercises.[34] Brigade-level practice assaults were also arranged for with multiple battalions honing overland communications and attack coordination skills. This varied training programme's emphasis appears to indicate a change in offensive tactics whereby units with recent experience of the January and February operations disseminated acquired knowledge of the advancement of forward outposts and dispatch of aggressive night patrols to seize enemy outposts opposite.

28   TNA WO 95/1713/1: 2nd Middlesex Regiment War Diary, 5-8 September 1916 entries.
29   Ibid.
30   TNA WO 95/1723/1: 1st Worcestershire Regiment War Diary, 9 September 1916 entry.
31   TNA WO 95/1722/2: 2nd Northamptonshire Regiment War Diary, 25-30 November 1916 entries.
32   TNA WO 95/1713/1: 2nd Middlesex Regiment War Diary. The 26 November 1916 entry lists a number of courses.
33   TNA WO 95/1712/1, 2nd Devonshire Regiment War Diary. On 23 December, one officer and 52 ORs proceeded to Army musketry school, and C Company returned from the Divisional School of instruction. Additionally that day, 190 men of 2/E Lancs proceeded to the Army musketry school, while the rest of the battalion practiced wiring and destruction of wire with Bangalore torpedoes (WO 95/1720/1). The Final of the Divisional Football match also took place on 23 December, with 2/Northants beating 23rd Machine Gun Company.
34   TNA WO 95/1714/2: 2nd West Yorkshire Regiment War Diary, 6 and 12 December 1916 entries.

This has significance beyond 8th Division, as it demonstrates a concerted effort to counter the German outpost defence scheme. All of this suggests elements of tactical innovation and shared learning. With regard to the December training schemes, there is no evidence that *SS 135: Instructions for the Training of Divisions in Offensive Action*, published that same month, was consulted by either 8th Division or 2nd Australian Division.

Tactical innovation in 8th Division was demonstrated early in 1917 with new ideas on attack formations proposed at brigade conferences in mid-January. Among the plethora of suggestions and topics for discussion, the idea of 'Battle Patrol Platoons' (BPP) was suggested.[35] BPP were 'patrols of 10 or 12 men with a proportion of tools [who were to be] pushed forward as far as possible, and until close touch with the enemy is gained. These parties should be about 75 yards apart and should dig themselves in strongly. When this is complete, some Lewis guns should be sent forward.'[36] The concept was not an original one, having been proposed in 63 (Royal Naval) Division in November. Heneker's arrival from 63rd Division in December and subsequent adoption of BPPs, demonstrates an inter-division transfer of ideas and one method of learning dissemination across the entire BEF. Over the following weeks, previously designated 'special patrol' units had been raised to platoon strength in each battalion. By the final week of the month, 8th Division BPPs were ready for the GOC's inspection. On 19 February, General Sir Henry Rawlinson (GOC Fourth Army) paid a visit and observed 2nd Battalion Rifle Brigade (2/RB) and 2nd Battalion Royal Berkshire Regiment (2/R Berks) BPPs practice their novel battle drills.[37]

The 8th Division was in and out of the line during February. It was not earmarked for the forthcoming Arras offensive. Instead, the division took over the line at St Pierre Vaast Wood, XV Corps sector, where, maintaining pressure on the enemy, it would attack due east of Bouchavesnes. Originally scheduled for the end of February, the operation was rescheduled for 4 March.[38] Preparations were extensive and detailed; spit-locked practice trenches were dug near Chipilly, then altered after they were found to be incorrectly cut.[39] A week in mid-February was set aside for training there by battalions and brigades culminating in full-scale divisional rehearsals including a practice attack with no officer or sergeant-major participants.[40] The actual assault plan would involve three battalions, as opposed to five on 23 October 1916, advancing on

35   TNA WO 95/1726/5: 25th Brigade Conference, 25th Brigade War Diary.
36   TNA WO 95/3093/4: 'Tactical Notes by the Divisional Commander', Major-General C.D. Shute, 23 October 1916, 63rd Division HQ War Diary.
37   WO 95/1731/3: 2nd Rifle Brigade War Diary, 21 January and 19 February 1917 entries.
38   TNA WO 95/1676/2: 'Attack on German Trenches in C.16.c, C.16.a and C.10.c, NE of Bouchavesnes, carried out by 8th Division on 4th March, 1917', 8th Division HQ War Diary.
39   TNA WO 95/1726/5: 25th Brigade War Diary, 14 February 1917.
40   TNA WO 95/1729/1: 'Appendix 1: Report on operations 4-5 March carried out by the 2nd Battalion Royal Berkshire Regiment', March 1917, 2nd Royal Berkshire Regiment War Diary.

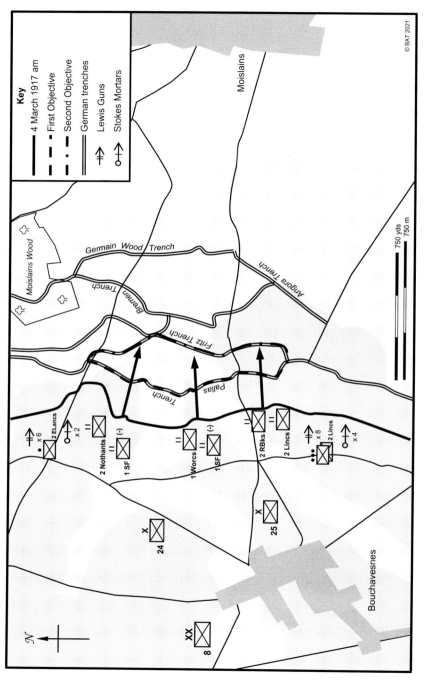

8th Division assault at Bouchavesnes, 4 March 1917.

a slightly wider front with increased depth of the assault waves. Reserves were to be kept close at hand and flank protection, carrying and 'mopping-up' party arrangements formalised.[41]

The winter of 1916-17 was notoriously harsh. In late February the temperature dropped, transforming previously muddy terrain into ground that was firm and easy to traverse. However, it was also impossible to dig saps or jumping-off trenches within the narrow no-man's land without detection. This forced the attackers to form-up in no man's land after nightfall. Wire-cutting was carried out by XV Corps heavy artillery in the days previous and patrols identified at least one large gap near the right flank of the attack.[42] In addition, an indirect machine-gun barrage was to be fired at intervals in the hours leading up to the assault and during the assault itself. Known strong points were targeted, but not the trench system as pulverised trenches were deemed difficult to hold against counter-attacks.[43] The divisional artillery had fire plans drawn up covering enemy approach trenches. Very lights and signal flags would be employed to signal targeting requests and barrage adjustments to the gunners.[44] The divisional engineers were tasked with removing the British wire immediately after dark on 3 March. Assault troops, moppers-up, support, flank guard and carrying parties were assembled by 4.35 a.m., 40 minutes prior to Zero.[45]

Strict noise and light discipline was necessary when forming-up in freezing conditions. The divisional staff, however, were cognisant of the fact that coughing might reveal the impending assault. Lozenges were ordered to prevent this and when they failed arrive, a supply of chewing gum was issued instead with 'extraordinary effective' results.[46] At zero hour (5:15 a.m.), the leading assault waves rushed forward to storm the second objective, leaving clearance of the first objective to the moppers-up following close behind. The latter performed their work well, the only significant resistance coming from a pocket of the enemy who clung to the centre of the line before it was overwhelmed by BPP of 2/Northants, which arrived in one of the supporting waves.[47] The official historian drew attention to the carrying parties of 1st Battalion Sherwood Foresters (1/ S For) for delivering bombs as supplies ran low, and

---

41   TNA WO 95/1717/2: '24th Infantry Brigade Operational Order No. 131', 24th Brigade War Diary.
42   TNA WO 95/1726/6: '25th Brigade Intelligence Summary for 24 hours ending 6am 2nd March, 1917', 25th Brigade War Diary.
43   TNA WO 95/1676/1: 8th Division HQ War Diary.
44   TNA WO 95/1717/2: 'Account of Operations 4th to 6th March', 24th Brigade War Diary.
45   TNA WO 95/1676/1: 8th Division HQ War Diary. The Assaulting troops of 24 Brigade had signalled their readiness earlier than those of 25th Brigade, at 3.20am. See WO 95/1717/2, 'Account of Operations 4th to 6th March', 24th Brigade War Diary.
46   TNA WO 95/1676/2: '8th Division No. G.12/14', 2 March 1917 and 'Report on Operations by the 24th Infantry Brigade, 4th March 1917', 9 March 1917, 8th Division HQ War Diary.
47   TNA WO 95/1717/2: 'Account of Operations 4th to 6th March', 24th Brigade War Diary.

the 22nd Battalion Durham Light Infantry (divisional pioneers) for excavating two communication trenches under fire by the early afternoon.[48]

The fighting for Fritz Trench was bitter. The position exchanged hands twice as German counter-attacks broke in only to be driven out again. Nevertheless, 8th Division ended the day with all objectives secured. Some 217 prisoners, four trench mortars and seven machine-guns were taken. British casualties amounted to 56 officers and 1,069 men killed, wounded and missing.[49] In terms of preparation, Bouchavesnes demonstrated a marked increase in attention to operational detail when compared to the previous October assault. This was no mean feat when considering that the division had little time to absorb recent reinforcement drafts and experienced officers were in short supply. The brigade major of 25th Brigade only had the rank of lieutenant but performed very creditably.[50] Broadly speaking, the operation was comparable to what First and Third armies would come to recognise during the forthcoming Arras offensive: that by early 1917, BEF formations were capable of planning and executing successful set-piece assaults provided they were given the time, manpower and resources. The next challenge, however, would involve an altogether different style of warfare, as within two weeks of the Bouchavesnes attack, the German Army commenced Operation *Alberich* – the planned withdrawal to the Hindenburg Line. The 23rd and 25th brigades were holding the line opposite Rancourt in mid-March when news arrived of the general enemy retirement.[51] Further north, 5th and 6th brigades of 2nd Australian Division were responsible for the line opposite Grévillers when the retreat was first detected. So began the first test of open warfare for both formations.[52]

Although the German withdrawal across much of the front was discovered on 17 March, opposite I Anzac Corps the enemy trenches were vacated five days earlier. This retirement to a second defensive system known as the R. II Line was a necessary preliminary to a general retreat. The German high command deemed this necessary as a means of avoiding an imminent offensive that they rightly suspected would open on 13 March. So it was that the enemy retreat went unnoticed until the early morning of 17 March. The 2nd Australian Division's experience is thoroughly recounted in Charles Bean's *The Australian Imperial Force in France 1917* and does not require full reiteration here, but some salient points are worthy of consideration:

48   Falls, *Military Operations 1917*, Vol. 1, pp.121-22

49   Ibid, 122-23.

50   TNA WO 95/1676/2: 'Report on Operations Carried out by the 25th Infantry Brigade on March 4th, 1917', 10 March 1917, 8th Division HQ War Diary.

51   TNA WO 95/1676/1: '8th Division Order No. 159', 27 February 1917, 8th Division HQ War Diary and WO 95/1717/2: '24th Infantry Brigade Operation Order No. 135', 2 March 1917, 24th Brigade War Diary.

52   The 8th Division and 2nd Australian Division arrived on the Western Front in early November 1914 and March 1916 respectively. Both disembarked after the strategic deadlock had set in.

rather than commit the entire division to pursuit of the enemy, and bearing supply difficulties over broken ground and damaged roads in mind, an ad hoc advanced guard force was formed on 18 March.[53] This consisted of 6th Australian Brigade, 12th Battery Australian Field Artillery, a squadron of 13th Australian Light Horse and two engineer sections. Brigadier-General Gellibrand, now reunited with his brigade after Major-General Smythe's return, was in command.[54] Pressing forward, the advanced guard force reached Vaulx-Vraucourt that same day. Ahead lay Écoust, Longatte, Noreuil and Lagnicourt with the formidable Hindenburg Line defences beyond. Gellibrand's attempt to enter this line of villages came after a confusing exchange of messages on 19 March during which he was informed that relief should be expected the following day. This was followed by a second message which stated that General Gough had visited divisional headquarters where he expressed expectations that Noreuil and Lagnicourt would be secured. Thus Gellibrand was under the impression that a direct assault on the villages had been sanctioned by the Fifth Army commander.[55]

The result was a rushed operation and consequent failure, as two advanced guard force battalions pushed along spurs on either side of the Hirondelle Valley in an attempt to rush Noreuil at dawn on 20 March. Bean and Falls both describe Gellibrand's move as ingenious. No doubt such boldness would have been encouraged during the open warfare of the following year, but the fact was that the attackers were exhausted and unfamiliar with this style of combat. Unable to form-up in a timely fashion, 21/ Bn AI, traversing the northern spur, was exposed at daylight, after which German artillery and machine-gun fire from Noreuil and Longatte took its toll. The 23/Bn AI, traversing the southern spur, was unable deploy in force, so lacked the necessary manpower strength to penetrate the village.[56] Australian casualties (13 officers and 318 men) were relatively heavy given the circumstances. One post-assault cause for concern was communications between the advanced guard force and divisional headquarters. Indeed, Smythe was never truly aware of Gellibrand's intentions until hours after the latter's force had withdrawn. This is confirmed in a message sent by 2nd Australian Division headquarters at 10.15 that morning: 'Your T1 and T2 not clear. Did you carry out reconnaissances and then attack? What information did reconnaissance give you? Why are you going back from Vraucourt to Bapaume? Beugnâtre indicated on orders as your headquarters.'[57] The question about reconnaissance was a valid one. It exposed a willingness to take unnecessary risks that appears reckless. Whilst Gellibrand's impressive leap forward had been of benefit during the pursuit

53   AWM AWM4 Subclass 23/6/19, 6th Australian Brigade HQ War Diary, 18 March 1917.
54   AWM AWM4 Subclass 1/44/20 PART 3, 2nd Australian Division HQ War Diary, Appendix XXIII, 'Second Australian Division Order No.102', 17 March 1917.
55   Bean, *AIF in France 1917*, p.179.
56   Ibid., pp.176-86.
57   AWM AWM4 Subclass 1/44/20 PART 1, 2nd Australian Division HQ War Diary, 20 March 1917.

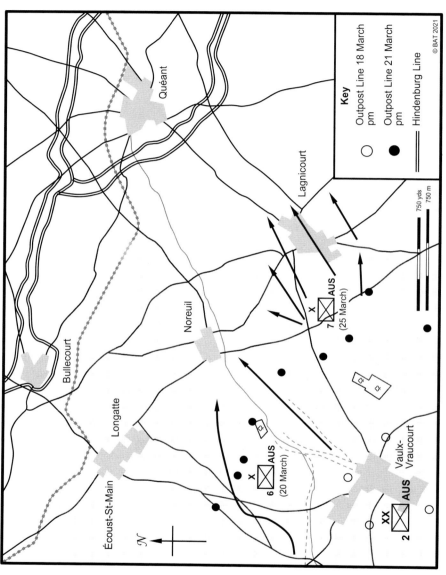

2nd Australian Division at Noreuil and Lagnicourt, 20–26 March 1917.

stage, a more circumspect approach would be required when dealing with defended villages. Brigadier-General Wisdom's 7th Brigade was brought up for that purpose.

The 7th Brigade, following Wisdom's decision to strike at Lagnicourt rather than Noreuil, attacked on 26 March. The days prior to this were spent on reconnaissance whilst awaiting reinforcements to arrive. Supporting this assault here would be two full brigades of field artillery, two batteries of 60-pdrs and a battery of 6-inch howitzers, as well as the 7th Australian Machine Gun Company. During the initial planning, an attack by British 7th Division on Écoust and Longatte was to have taken place simultaneously, but thick wire in front of those villages required artillery preparation, for which Lieutenant-General William Birdwood (GOC I Anzac Corps) was unwilling to wait. In the end, only Lagnicourt was attacked.[58] Flank protection was not forgotten, and each of the two attacking battalions (26 and 27/Bns AI) provided a company to carry out that role, as well as coordinating with 5th Australian Division on the right flank. There were, however, difficulties encountered during the forming-up: 'B' Company, 26/Bn AI, failed to reach the jumping-off line on time, and a late change in 5th Division's plan meant the projected right flank protection was not present on the jumping-off line either. Rather than delay the attack, two platoons of 26/Bn's D company (assigned the 'mopping-up' role) went into the assault line instead. Meantime, 'A' Company on the right flank extended its line and attacked in one wave rather than two. These last minute modifications sorted, the attackers rushed forward, B Company managing to catch up and assist with the clearance of Lagnicourt and establishment of posts on the far side of the village. Strong counter-attacks were repulsed. Thus 2nd Australian Division became the first BEF division to break into the Hindenburg Line's outpost villages. Following on this success, 7th Brigade's staff once again compiled a 'lessons learned' document. Despite there being no evidence that they had made use of the *SS 143* pamphlet, the conclusions reached relative to the latter are striking:

> The value of the training of platoon and section commanders in the independent handling of their units – most of the fighting, particularly during the enemy counter attack being done by these small units.
> The necessity to hold suitable bodies in reserve for counter-attack.
> The advisability of always providing for the protection of one's own flanks, irrespective of what units are operating there in conjunction…the impression that troops were protecting our right certainly delayed the launching of [the enemy counter] attack.

58   AWM AWM4 Subclass 23/7/19, 7th Australian Brigade HQ War Diary, Appendix C, 'Report on offensive operations carried out by the Advanced Guard, 2nd Australian Division, against the village of Lagnicourt – 26th March 1917'.

The value of Lewis guns used from the hip in attack. These were successfully used in dealing with hostile machine-gun positions and strong points.[59]

There was an excellent example of the cooperation of Lewis gun, rifle grenades, and bayonet, in the attack of a machine-gun position.

It is suggested that rifle grenades have a place in the echelon.[60]

In his recounting of the 20 March failure, Bean observed:

> [T]o Birdwood and Smythe the unexpected news of this engagement and of the casualties suffered – which were eventually found to be more than twice as severe as Gellibrand at first believed … came as a shock, especially as 50 men were missing … Gellibrand never regained with Birdwood the high opinion and confidence which his vigour in previous stages of the pursuit had won … The true blame appears to lie mainly with Gellibrand, who, reading into the order an imaginary implication, undertook a hazardous operation with insufficient time for its performance, but partly with the staff of the 2nd Division, which, knowing Gellibrand's inclination, had forwarded Gough's order in a manner that left an opening for misinterpretation as to the manner of its performance.[61]

Smythe's enquiry into Gellibrand's failed assault on Noreuil was certainly valid, but the case for the latter's defence is strong, especially given that his instructions originated from Gough. Gellibrand, having been entrusted with the advanced guard, briefed to maintain pressure on the enemy and with no definite knowledge of where the next line of resistance would be, it is unlikely that anything other than a repulse would have been sufficient to indicate where the enemy was. A conference of Fifth Army corps commanders was held on 20 March, at which it was stated 'it is evident that we cannot "rush" the defence any further than we have now done.'[62] The 2nd Australian Division's advanced guard had indicated to Fifth Army where the new enemy line was, and although the casualties sustained by 21/ and 23/Bns AI were no doubt excessive and regrettable, the need for a more cautious approach had been aptly demonstrated. The fact that this was accomplished with two battalions almost certainly saved lives. Clearly, there was a growing sense of offensive prowess in the division at this time, even if uniformity of progress eluded it.

59   The notes detail the improvised slings used for carrying the Lewis guns in this role and make recommendations for wooden handles and metal fastenings to radiators.

60   AWM AWM4 Subclass 23/7/19, 7th Australian Brigade HQ War Diary, Appendix C, 'Report on offensive operations carried out by the Advanced Guard, 2nd Australian Division, against the village of Lagnicourt – 26th March 1917'.

61   Bean, *AIF in France 1917*, p.186.

62   TNA WO 95/519/3: 'Appendix 11. Proceedings of Conference at Fifth Army Headquarters, 20-3-17', 21 March 1917, Fifth Army General Staff War Diary.

The 2nd Australian Division was promptly relieved by 4th Australian Division after Lagnicourt. A divisional conference was held on 31 March during which lessons of the previous weeks' actions formed the basis of discussion. Various training aspects were to receive special attention. Amongst these were night work and instructions for the use of captured German machine-guns, trench mortars and hand grenades, as well as British rifle grenades and Lewis guns. Rocket and visual signalling including Very pistols, would also receive attention. Moreover, the basic platoon structure was reorganised to better incorporate these weapons and devices.[63] As a final postscript to the division's Hindenburg Line operations, on its return to the line three weeks later, 5th Brigade was urgently rushed forward to repel a German attack on

Brigadier-General John Gellibrand.

Lagnicourt. In a swift and decisive blow that demonstrated an undeniable increase in tactical skills learned on the Somme and subsequent winter actions, not to mention a growing aptitude for mobile warfare, the brigade recaptured the village and inflicted over 2,300 casualties upon the enemy.[64]

Meantime, 8th Division, situated farther south, was on the march towards the Hindenburg Line. The first serious contact with the enemy came in the vicinity of Heudicourt on 30 March. A subsequent assault cleared Heudicourt, the nearby villages of Fins and Sorel-le-Grand, hamlet of Revelon, Dessart Wood, three copses and a dominating area of high ground. This advanced the XV Corps line some 6,000 yards, killing approximately 800 of the enemy for 68 casualties.[65] The captured villages

---

63   AWM AWM4 Subclass 1/44/20 PART 4, 2nd Australian Division HQ War Diary, Appendix 49, 'Proceedings of a Conference held at D.H.Q. on 31st March 1917'. One point mentioned at the conference, which was not crucial to aptitude in offensive actions, but of interest, was point 18: 'Prisoners of War – Men are to be warned that they are not allowed to take the private possessions of a prisoner such as money, small trinkets etc. By so doing, prisoners have become sulky and have not given information as freely as they otherwise might have done.'

64   Bean, *AIF in France 1917*, p.399.

65   TNA WO 95/432/2: 'XV Corps No. 57 G.X 3/4/17, Report on Operations Carried out by the 23rd Inf. Bde and 25th Inf. Bde, 8th Division, on 30th March 1917', Fourth Army HQ War Diary. Total casualties for the operation numbered 12 killed and 56 wounded.

were overlooked by a horseshoe of high ground to the north and east. Their retention would be impossible without possession of the high ground beyond, a fact not lost on Heneker and his staff. However, as the official historian observed, rapid seizure of the villages would facilitate the projected high ground assault.[66]

Having closely picketed Sorel and Fins the previous evening, the villages were secured by fighting patrols of 2/RB and 2/R Berks at daybreak on 30 March. For the assault on Heudicourt and the high ground around it, 23rd and 25th brigades would each be allotted four sections of 18-pdr field guns under direct control of the respective infantry brigadier-generals. The remainder of the divisional artillery and an attached field artillery brigade would be under the divisional CRA's command. The routine creeping barrage would not be followed as such. Instead, direct liaison between the infantry and field artillery would be maintained with Very pistols, lifting signals to be fired when and where required. Only the corps heavy artillery would fire to a fixed timetable, the bombardment moving forward from Heudicourt and Dessart Wood; over and past Revelon prior to halting as a sustained protective barrage to the north and east.[67]

With Revelon and the high ground beyond presenting tactical difficulties, the decision was made by 25th Brigade's commander (Brigadier-General C. Coffin) to delay the attack until the projected assault on Dessart Wood had the enemy's full attention. B Coy and the BPP of 2/RB advanced from Fins at 4:00 p.m. as planned. Momentarily held by two machine-guns firing from the east, which were immediately engaged by Lewis guns, No. 5 Platoon, B Coy, 1st Battalion Royal Irish Rifles (1/R I Rif) rushed the guns capturing one, the crew of the second fleeing to the rear.[68] Following this, the 2/RB attack overran Dessart Wood, Very lights being discharged at intervals during the advance through the wood. Once it had been sufficiently cleared, B and C Coys 1/R I Rif were ordered to press on to the high ground north of Revelon. By 4.30 p.m., Coffin deemed the situation in the north sufficiently advanced for the assault on Heudecourt to occur. Elements of 2/Mddlsx and 2/Devons, discharging Very lights as a means of alerting the brigade artillery to engage the northern part of the village, advanced towards the objective. Additional lights were fired to signal the lift on to Revelon. Once the village was clear, 2/Mddlsx and 2/Devons immediately moved eastwards employing skirmishers and Lewis Guns to protect the advance towards Revelon and copses, whilst a cavalry squadron of the Royal Wiltshire Yeomanry attacked the second copse from the south. All objectives were secured by 7:00 p.m. and 8th Division dug-in and consolidated its gains.[69]

66 Falls, *Military Operations 1917*, Vol. 1, p.154.
67 TNA WO 95/1676/2: 8th Division HQ War Diary, '8th Division Order No. 172', 29 March 1917, 8th Division HQ War Diary.
68 TNA WO 95/1739/4: 1st Rifle Brigade War Diary, 30 March 1917.
69 TNA WO 95/432/2: 'XV Corps No. 57 G.X 3/4/17, Report on Operations Carried out by the 23rd Inf. Bde and 25th Inf. Bde, 8th Division, on 30th March 1917', Fourth Army HQ War Diary.

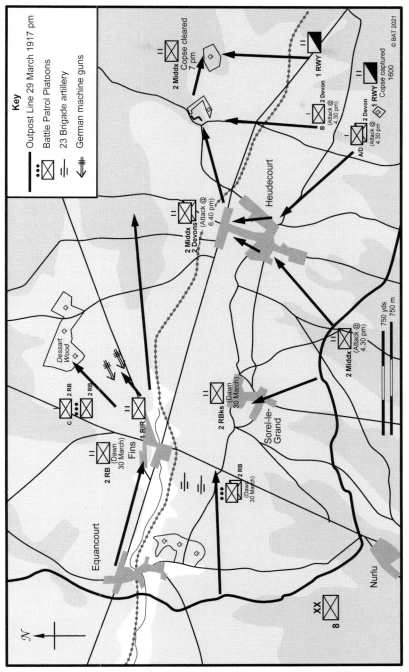

8th Division operations, 30 March 1917.

Key

- Outpost Line 29 March 1917 pm
- Battle Patrol Platoons
- 23 Brigade artillery
- German machine guns

2 Middx
Copse cleared
7 pm

1 RWY

B 2 Devon
(Attack @
4.30 pm)

A/D
(Attack @
4.30 pm)

2 Devon
Copse captured
1600

1 RWY

© BAT 2021

Heudecourt

2 Middx
2 Devons
(Attack @
6.40 pm)

Dessart
Wood

c 2 RB
2 RB

2 RB
(Dawn
30 March)

Fins

1 RIR

2 RBks

2 RB
(Dawn
30 March)

Sorel-le-
Grand

2 Middx
(Attack @
4.30 pm)

2 RB
(Dawn
30 March)

750 yds
750 m

Equancourt

Nurlu

XX
8

In his after-action report Heneker observed: 'Three weeks ago I really do not think that we could have, with success, carried out such an open warfare attack.' Praising the infantry for 'adapting themselves to circumstances', he also highlighted the value of pressing scouts and patrols forward regardless of the time of day. This aggressive policy of patrolling, maintenance of outposts and seizure of tactical vantage points had proved effective, the enemy having yet to develop a foil to this transformation in British tactics. Furthermore, the Germans had demonstrated their own tactical shortcomings in the defence of villages. In Heneker's view, 'The enemy's retirement is, I consider, badly carried out because he holds towns. As a result of this, we can concentrate our efforts on to something we can see. During the attack he barraged the villages but with no result, for we were not in them.' He also recommended that villages should be avoided. No mention was made of wooded areas.[70]

The tactical flexibility afforded by devolving command of artillery units to brigade commanders and allowing assault troops to determine barrage lifts demonstrated further tactical innovation. Creeping barrages had been widely employed and had undoubtedly proved of value. However, 8th Division's ability to construct a bespoke, flexible bombardment to suit the ground and current tactical requirements, was clearly the correct course of action. Discharge of Very lights to aid in communications was deemed to be successful to the point of rendering attached contact patrol aircraft redundant. Attention to operational and tactical detail extended to making certain that flanks were protected by 20th (Light) Division on the left and corps cavalry on the right.[71] The official historian observed that the 30 March operations were well-conducted with a level of creativity and flexibility well above that previously demonstrated by 8th Division. With no evidence that centrally-produced tactical training pamphlets were consulted, we must attribute this improvement in fighting ability to Heneker, his staff, and to senior officers who recognised military talent and promoted accordingly. The 2nd Australian Division's mixed performance during the advance to the Hindenburg Line is more difficult to assess. One factor which cannot be ignored is the change in divisional commanders, Smythe assuming command after Heneker. The former, therefore, was deprived of vital time to properly assess his new command's performance over the previous year and consider ways to improve its effectiveness. Unfortunately, 2nd Australian Division's first action of 1917 occurred at a time when its senior and junior leadership was disjointed. Indeed, the division's shaky performance at Malt and Gamp trenches exposed an inadequacy amongst battalion officers that only time and training would resolve. Measurable progress in this direction was made, as the 31 March divisional conference determinations and 7th Brigade's counter-attack at Lagnicourt appear to indicate.

Paddy Griffith, in his seminal *Battle Tactics on The Western Front*, observed, 'open warfare did in fact become a reality on four separate occasions – the retreat from Mons

70   Ibid.
71   Ibid.

in 1914, the advance to the Hindenburg Line in March 1917, the spring retreats of 1918, and then in the advances of the Hundred Days. In all four cases the BEF was essentially unprepared for the sudden shock to its system, and it would be only on the last occasion that it rose to the challenge at all convincingly.'[72] Moreover, Bean cites the historian of the *1st Guards Reserve FA Regiment*, 'Tommy was entirely strange to the war of movement; the result was heavy losses for him.'[73] These critical assessments do not stand scrutiny. Although advances through an apocalyptic scorched-earth landscape riddled with booby-traps caused serious logistical difficulties for both Fourth and Fifth armies (at which time there were no easy solutions), the infantry appears to have adjusted well, albeit imperfectly, to the transition from trench to open warfare. Indeed, it can be argued that on both Fourth and Fifth armies fronts, the BEF adapted more readily than the German Army, possibly due to the large numbers of senior commanders with experience of mobile operations during the South African War (1899-1902). The principles of fire and movement were unquestionably evident in 8th Division's actions, whilst 2nd Australian Division was swiftly adapting weapons and tactics for increased military effectiveness. Thus it is fair to observe that by late March 1917, 8th Division was more advanced than 2nd Australian Division in tactics and battlefield communications. Whilst it is possible to detect variations in performance between Australian infantry brigades, 8th Division's brigades appear to have operated in a more homogeneous manner. This can be put down to having more time out of the line for necessary training.

In summary, 8th Division and 2nd Australian Division demonstrated measurable progress in a several ways during the advance to the Hindenburg Line. Encouraged by new divisional commanders and staff, both formations endeavoured to learn and employ tactical techniques that had proved effective during previous operations. Research for this chapter points to the absence of consultation of centrally produced training pamphlets. Nevertheless, both divisions, based on past experiences, readily modified attack formations; took more care with flank protection arrangements, and held back reserves whilst the battle developed. Despite 2nd Australian Division's somewhat patchier performance during this period, it rose to the occasion by convening post-battle conferences and implementing their findings. Furthermore, when required to react in an unanticipated way – Lagnicourt on 15 April – the response was quick and decisive, thus demonstrating a marked improvement when compared with the division's performance in February and March. Reflecting more broadly, British and Dominion servicemen who fell during the advance to the Hindenburg Line and have no known grave are commemorated on the Thiepval Memorial to the Missing. The links between the Somme campaign of 1916 and the spring pursuit in 1917 are, therefore, not simply geographical. Entertaining the momentary thought

---

72   P. Griffith, *Battle Tactics on the Western Front: The British Army's Art of Attack* (New Haven, Connecticut: Yale University Press, 1994), p.160.

73   Bean, *AIF in France 1917*, p.78.

of ignoring the Battles Nomenclature Committee's determination that the Battle of the Somme terminated on 18 November 1916, and extending the campaign through April 1917, a conclusion is unavoidable; namely that there is a convincing case for refutation of the commonly held view that the Somme was a disappointing failure for Haig's armies. In addition, the organisation and tactics employed by Rawlinson and Gough's division's in early 1917 were a significant advancement from the previous year's campaigning. This, coupled with ever-increasing material strength and adoption of new technologies, resulted in a pervasive institutional confidence that sustained the British Army through its darkest year. The challenge would come in combining war-fighting augmentation, expanded industrial output, application of novel weapons and enhanced morale to achieve victory against an enemy who remained strong and far from beaten.

9

From Vimy Ridge to Hill 70
General Sir Henry Horne, First Army and the Development of British Operational Art During 1917

Simon Innes-Robbins

The recent anniversaries marking the First World War centenary offered an opportunity to re-examine the performance of the armies led by Field Marshal Sir Douglas Haig, arguably the most controversial era in the history of the British Army, and to place its performance in the context of military development in the 20th Century. The foremost problem for the British high command during the early years of the war was that of conducting a successful *strategic* offensive; this was the greatest 'learning curve' of all. It is still common to regard the German Army as an exemplar of military excellence and to disdain the British Army as exemplars of military incompetence and bumbling inefficiency. In reality, in sharp contrast to this perception, the British Army in 1918 was remarkably efficient, having undergone from August 1914 a profound, often painful, transformation from a small professional force organised for colonial policing to a mass army of volunteers and conscripts which fought a large-scale, high-intensity continental war against a first-class enemy. Between 1914 and 1916, the British Army grew to an unprecedented size, expanding in the 23 months following its deployment on the Western Front from four to 62 divisions. By 1918, the Royal Artillery was larger in personnel than the Royal Navy and, over several days during late October and early November 1918, the Canadian Corps alone discharged more shells than employed by both sides during the Second Anglo-Boer War of 1899-1902.[1]

One of the key aspects of the First World War was the way that the British Army's performance at the operational level improved dramatically between the Battle of

---

1   Paul Harris, '1918: Britain's Forgotten Victory: The British Expeditionary Force in the Hundred Days' Campaign: Tactics and Operational Art', *RUSI Journal*, Vol. 143, No. 6 (December 1998), p.73.

Loos (25 September-19 October 1915) and the final 'Hundred Days' offensive (8 August-11 November 1918). The latter campaign, which led to final victory, stands as one of the most brilliant offensives of the war. Success was achieved thanks to British operational techniques and artillery tactics which were in many respects superior and more sophisticated than those employed by the enemy. This clear success suggests that a 'learning process' had taken place and makes a compelling case for the development of British operational theory during 1914-18.

Yet, the development of British operational thought is a subject which has been comparatively neglected. The concept of the operational level of war is employed here in the sense of the 'area between strategy and tactics which denoted the fighting of battles in a given theatre of operations in pursuit of the political objective of the war',[2] and as the 'grey zone once called Grand Tactics, the tactics of large formations', such as army groups, armies and corps.[3] The 'operational level' was first articulated conceptually in 1923-24 by Aleksandr Svechin,[4] who summarised that 'tactics make the steps from which operational leaps are assembled; strategy points out the path.'[5] This approach was employed by the Soviets on the Eastern Front during 1943-45.

During 1914-16, the British high command lacked the operational level experience to control and manage the large battles it was fighting on the Western Front, but by the Armistice British generals were certainly thinking in operational terms. Lacking the formal doctrine beloved by French, German and Soviet armies until an army-wide doctrine was introduced in the 1980s,[6] the British Army failed to establish a theoretical model of operational thinking either during or after the war. As a learning organisation, the British Army preferred more informal and improvised means of learning to develop and disseminate new doctrine and did not leave a written body of operational doctrine despite some interest in 'grand tactics' by J.F.C. Fuller and Basil Liddell Hart in the post-war period.[7] Given inter-war developments in the German and Red armies, the operational level of war was an important military concept during

2   J.G.G. MacKenzie & Brian Holden Reid (eds.), *The British Army and the Operational Level of War* (London: Tri-Service Press, 1989), p. ix.
3   John English, *The Canadian Army and the Normandy Campaign* (New York: Praeger, 1991), p. xiii.
4   Foreword by Jacob W. Kipp for V.K. Triandafillov, *The Nature of Modern Operations of Modern Armies* (London: Routledge, 1994), p. xiv.
5   Quoted by David Glantz, *Soviet Military Operational Art* (Portland, Oregon: Frank Cass, 1991), p.23.
6   John Kiszely, 'Thinking about the Operational Level', *RUSI Journal* (December 2005), p.41; Hew Strachan, 'Operational Art and Britain, 1909-2009' in John Andreas & Martin van Creveld (eds.), *The Evolution of Operational Art: From Napoleon to the Present* (Oxford: Oxford University Press, 2011), pp.119-21.
7   Brian Bond, *Liddell Hart: A Study of his Military Thought* (London: Cassell, 1977), pp.21-61; Jay Luvaas, *The Education of an Army: British Military Thought, 1815-1940* (London: Cassell, 1965), pp.345-63, 379-410; Brian Hold Reid, *Studies in British Military Thought: Debates with Fuller and Liddell Hart* (Lincoln, Nebraska: University of Nebraska Press, 1998), pp.62-92.

the 1920s and 1930s. However, the contribution made by the British in 1917-18 has been largely ignored. It is thus ironic that the Anglo-Americans operated, notwithstanding success in two world wars, without a written operational theory. Conversely, the Germans were unsuccessful despite developing a sophisticated operational doctrine albeit with a number of alarming blind spots of which the absence of logistical and strategic-political factors within operational thinking is the most notable.[8]

The British Army's pre-war neglect of the operational aspects of modern war resulted in inexperience with the planning and staff work required for large-scale continental operations. Staff officers had little opportunity to hone their skills during peacetime. Neither army nor corps staff existed, a condition imposed by strict government budgets and the small size of the pre-war army. An antebellum divisional staff consisted of a General Staff Officer, DAAG, CRA and CRE with additional staff joining for manoeuvres, summer training and after the declaration of war in August 1914.[9] For example, 'the four additional staff officers who were, on mobilization, appointed to the 4th Division were strangers to it' and having little experience or training were unable to write operational orders.[10] Thus duties had to be learned 'on the job'. This was subsequently reflected in poor operational performance during 1915-17. One battalion commander noted that 'in the early stages of the war the Germans were better practised than were our staffs in the handling of large units.'[11] During the 1916 Somme campaign 'staff work (divisional, brigade & battalion) in the earlier stages of the battle was poor' as even 'the most competent officers were working on a scale and in conditions of which they had no experience, and they had to learn their job', but in the later stages 'the Staff, having had an opportunity to learn, were just beginning to take hold of their job.'[12]

Although provided with adequate technical training, staff officers had little theoretical knowledge of formations above divisional level. The primary task of a Staff College student 'was to learn the arts of lubrication' as they were 'to be greasers of the army machine, normal functionaries' and not 'as disciples of war and of wisdom.'[13] The then Brigadier-General William Robertson, as commandant (1910-13), bluntly informed his students that they 'were at the Staff College to learn staff duties and to qualify for Staff Captain, not to talk irresponsible trash' on 'subjects of policy or strategy.'[14] One of the most able trained staff officer, Major-General Sir Charles

---

8   Gerhard P. Gross, *The Myth and Reality of German Warfare: Operational Thinking from Moltke the Elder to Heusinger* (Lexington, Kentucky: University Press of Kentucky, 2016), pp.4, 89, 96, 117, 129, 131-32, 254-57, 301-03.

9   The National Archives (TNA) CAB 45/129: General Sir Thomas Snow, The Account of the Retreat of 1914, n.d.

10   LHCMA, Edmonds Papers III/8/5, Edmonds memoirs, Chapter XXIII.

11   TNA CAB 45/120: Lieutenant-Colonel R.R. Gibson to Edmonds, 10 August 1926.

12   TNA CAB 45/132: Pearson Choate to Edmonds, 6 April 1936 and 26 March 1926.

13   Colonel Sir Thomas Montgomery-Cuninghame, *Dusty Measure: A Record of Troubled Times* (London: John Murray, 1939), p.50.

14   Brigadier-General A.F.U. Green, *Evening Tattoo* (London: Stanley Paul, 1941), pp.32-33.

Harington (MGGS Second Army), admitted that he had not been prepared to 'think in "Armies"' having 'never even in theory' contemplated the problems of commanding a force larger than the original, six-division strong BEF. Nevertheless, in less than two years he found himself responsible for the staff work of an Army that 'two or three times in tenure exceeded thirty divisions.'[15] Harington blamed the British Army's many problems on the failure to develop 'a General Staff "doctrine"' in parallel to the large formations that had developed from nothing to standardise doctrine at army, corps and division level. The methods employed 'varied considerably' so that 'very divergent views are held and entirely different methods exist in the various armies, corps & divisions.'[16]

Despite this operational level inexperience, stunning displays of all-arms co-ordination at Vimy, Messines, Broodseinde and Cambrai showed how far the army had developed by 1917. Yet battlefield success created heightened expectations and local victories were often squandered as the BEF struggled to convert tactical achievements into operational and strategic victories. In the 1916-17 period the British Army was hobbled by a serious doctrinal controversy whereby the desire to obtain a quick and decisive 'Napoleonic' victory was adapted to the demands of modern warfare, notably the protracted length of operations that made a war-winning campaign or battle difficult to achieve.[17]

This led to a prolonged debate over whether to adopt breakthrough (an unlimited objectives attack) or siege operations (an attack for limited objectives only, often referred to as 'bite and hold' or the 'step-by-step' approach) in order to penetrate formidable German defences. With the decisive battle central to its outlook, the British Army in general and Haig in particular were ideologically opposed to the siege warfare approach stressing that 'since the object of war can only be attained by the destruction of the enemy's field armies, all fortress warfare must be considered as subsidiary to that end.' Moreover, it was advocated in *Field Service Regulations* that the army should seek to launch 'an attack without recourse to siege operations.'[18] When faced with the operational alternatives of either siege or breakthrough, army leadership was predisposed to the breakthrough whereas the trench stalemate increasingly necessitated commanders to focus on siege warfare methodology. The high command, notably Haig, insisted on pursuing the unrealistic aim of overrunning the German defences in one enormous blow in pursuit of a breakthrough. This would be the *modus operandi* during 1915-17 and the debate about the efficacy of limited and unlimited

15   General Sir Charles Harington, *'Tim' Harington Looks Back* (London: John Murray, 1940), p.53.
16   Imperial War Museum (IWM), Maxse Papers 69/57/11, DCIGS [Major-General C.H. Harington] to CIGS [Field Marshal Sir Henry Wilson], 11 July 1918.
17   Simon Robbins, *British Generalship on the Western Front 1914-18: Defeat into Victory* (London & New York: Frank Cass, 2005), pp.122-29.
18   General Staff, *Field Service Regulations, Part I, Operations, 1909* (London: War Office, Reprinted with Amendments, 1912), pp.127-128, 157, 162-63.

objectives continued, notably during planning for the Loos and the Somme offensives, when Haig refused to accept limited objectives and remained obstinately in favour of a dramatic breakthrough. The indecision over whether it was 'a problem of moving warfare, checked momentarily by field defences, as Haig thought' or a 'basic problem of siege warfare, the methodical approach and the blasting of a breach as Rawlinson [GOC Fourth Army] believed',[19] had a serious impact on the 1916-17 campaigns. This left a legacy of bitterness about British generalship during the war. The first day on the Somme represented the nadir for the British Army, but subsequent fighting on the Somme also witnessed the beginnings of a operational renaissance that resulted in victory in 1918.[20] This provided valuable tactical lessons, notably in employment of artillery and new weapons such as aircraft, machine-guns and tanks which in combination would overcome the German defences. The question in 1917 was not merely how to implement new methods and technology at a tactical level, but how to employ them at an operational level in order to resolve the strategic stalemate.

General Sir Henry Horne's career in 1917-18 sheds much light on this process. On assuming command of First Army on 30 September 1916,[21] Horne's primary task was, applying lessons learnt during the Somme offensive, to prepare for the Vimy Ridge assault. Major-General W.H. Anderson, his MGGS, noted later that 'the adverse comments of [French C-in-C General Robert] Nivelle's staff officers on his plan of attack had added to the strain before the battle' which was 'his first great offensive battle as an Army Commander.'[22] Horne was notified in January 1917 that Third Army would 'operate astride the River Scarpe' whilst the First Army offensive would be confined 'to the capture of the Vimy Ridge, including the high ground about Thélus.'[23] This was one of the most important tactical features on the entire Western Front. Considered impregnable by the Germans,[24] it would be 'a formidable undertaking.'[25]

The First Army's assault on Vimy Ridge 'was to some extent dependent on the success of the Third Army's major operation. Nevertheless, it was of vital importance to Third Army's success that the Vimy Ridge should fall at the first assault.'[26] The

19   Royal Artillery Institution (RAI), Anstey Papers, Brigadier E.C. Anstey, The History of the Royal Artillery, p.112.

20   Robbins, British Generalship on the Western Front 1914-18, pp.124-31.

21   IWM, Horne Papers, Horne, Diary, 30 September 1916.

22   Lieutenant-General Sir Hastings Anderson, 'Lord Horne as an Army Commander', p.409.

23   TNA WO 158/187: Lieutenant-General Sir Launcelot Kiggell to First Army, OAD 259, 2 January 1917.

24   Colonel G.W.L., Nicholson, Canadian Expeditionary Force, 1914-1919 (Ottawa: Queen's Printer, 1964), pp.244-47, 266.

25   Captain Cyril Falls, Military Operations France and Belgium 1917, Vol. I (London: Macmillan, 1940), p.300.

26   RAI, Rawlins Papers, Colonel S W H Rawlins, 'A History of the development of the British Artillery in France, 1914-18', p.110.

tactical importance of the ridge was that 'its possession would deprive the enemy of observation' over the British front whilst securing 'a commanding view of the plains' facilitating further operations.[27] In submitting his assault plan in late January, Horne noted that Thélus and Hill 140 'must be captured on the same day as the Third Army operation takes place' in order to complete First Army's allotted task, the formation of 'a strong defensive flank for the operations of the Third Army' whilst obtaining 'observation over the Douai plain.' This was 'vital to the Third Army operation, in order to deprive the enemy of observation into the valleys running southwest of Vimy Ridge.' Similarly, seizure of the 'Pimple' and Bois en Hache, which provided the enemy with 'good observation up the Carency and Ablain St Nazaire valleys', was 'essential to complete the Vimy Ridge operation.' The construction by the enemy of 'a new line on the reverse slope of Thélus Hill meant that its capture had to be undertaken 'as a separate operation, as soon as guns have been moved forward.'[28] As a result, Horne 'decided to attack and capture' the Pimple and Bois en Hache with I Corps and Canadian Corps following the operation against Vimy Ridge.[29]

Horne's planning was based not only on his own and subsequent British experience on the Somme, but also that of the French Army at Verdun. He took a personal interest in discovering what lessons had been learned. Following the recent success of General Sir Hubert Gough's Fifth Army on the Ancre (13-18 November 1916), Horne had visited that sector to 'find out as much as I can about the method employed etc.'[30] On 16 November Horne met Gough, who 'was in good form and great spirits' and 'very pleased with his success', his MGGS, Major-General Neill Malcolm, and his 'very old friend, [Lieutenant-General] Ted Fanshawe, the gunner' (GOC V Corps). He 'enjoyed a talk with them very much & heard all the latest about the fight' in which 'they had a splendid success and the Germans suffered very heavy loss.'[31] Convinced that 1917 was 'going to be a great year for the British Empire',[32] Horne's subsequent planning underlined the 'great importance' of 'complete preparation down to the smallest detail' to ensure that 'every man knows his job and has everything required to do it.' Above all, Horne emphasised 'the vital importance of really excellent artillery preparations.'[33]

GHQ stressed that 'the primary factors in the [recent] French success' at Verdun were careful staff work, thorough artillery preparation and support, the element of

27   TNA WO/106/402: Report on Operations against Vimy Ridge, April 9th to 16th, 1917, Canadian Corps.
28   TNA WO 158/199: General Sir Henry Horne, Plan of Operations for First Army, 'First Army No. GS 503/22 (a), 31', January 1917.
29   TNA WO 158/188: Lieutenant-Colonel J.E.S. Brind, First Army Order No. 103, 5 April 1917.
30   IWM, Horne Papers, Horne to wife, 14 November 1916.
31   IWM, Horne Papers, Horne to wife, 16 November 1916.
32   IWM, Horne Papers, Horne to wife, 1 January 1917.
33   TNA WO 95/168: 'Minutes of Conference of Corps Commanders held by GOC, First Army, at Chateau Philomel, 29th March 1917', 'First Army No. 1199(G)'.

surprise, and the high state of training in the infantry detailed for the assault.[34] The British were 'much impressed by the obvious efficiency and competence' of French staff work but felt that the their ally was 'in no way ahead of us in artillery thought, although they naturally excel in execution owing to a better supply of trained personnel.' The 'eminently successful' French preparatory bombardment had 'extended over a period of nearly a month', ebbing and flowing in intensity in order 'to mystify the enemy as to the date of the real attack … to make the enemy put down his barrages, and so disclose his artillery defensive programme' and 'to correct any faults in their own bombardments and barrages.' Moreover, during the French offensives of 24 October and 15 December 1916, the artillery operated according to time-tables which were laid down by the operational commander and 'rigidly adhered to.' Thus divisional commanders were unable to alter the bombardment. Counter-battery work was also of 'great importance.' During the attack of 15 December, 'the greater portion of the heavy artillery was employed on this task.' Therefore, the location and destruction of hostile batteries was 'the chief preoccupation of the artillery' throughout the preliminary bombardment. This required 'a greater proportion of long-range howitzers for counter-battery work.' There was no general movement of guns forward during the battle as the programme was carried out almost entirely from original battery positions. It was 'the universal opinion of Divisional Commanders that if it was desired to press forward, a new objective should be allotted, another attack prepared and carried out, and that the ground so gained should be held.'[35]

Horne drew his own conclusions from the Verdun report, noting that the preparatory bombardment had extended over a month following a rigid timetable and stressing the 'great importance' attached to counter-battery work and to a programme of protective barrages put down after the objective had been reached.'[36] Thus the success of

General H.S. Horne.

34   IWM, Horne Papers, [GHQ], 'Notes on a Visit of a Party of British Officers to Verdun, January 5th- 8th, 1917', n.d., unsigned.
35   IWM, Horne Papers 43/3, [GHQ], 'Notes on a Visit of a Party of British Officers to Verdun, January 5th-8th, 1917', n.d., unsigned.
36   IWM, Horne Papers 43/3, [Horne], pencil notes on the GHQ report on Verdun, n.d.

the First Army's pending assault would be dependent on artillery preparation, which was deemed 'all-important'.[37] The consequent artillery scheme,[38] a lengthy document of over 3,000 words issued by First Army on 8 February 1917, included a number of novel developments and concepts which became standard by 1918.[39] 'The most notable innovation' was the creation of the 'Double (Bombardment) Group Commander' to maintain close liaison between assault divisions and batteries undertaking destructive fire.[40] So it was that April 1917 witnessed 'the first marked improvement in liaison between infantry and heavy artillery.'[41]

Horne stressed that the destruction of the German intermediate line barbed wire and the capture of Thélus on the first day of operations depended 'on an adequate supply of the new [106] fuze for the 4.5" and 6" Howitzers' and that the First Army's scheme assumed that it would indeed be sufficient. Wire cutting on the Somme had been a lengthy process that consumed vast quantities of ammunition. Employment of the 106 instantaneous fuze and the wire destruction by heavier guns ensured wire cutting in 1917 could be done much more efficiently. Horne 'intended to commence destruction and wire cutting 3 or 4 weeks before Z Day, and to limit the bombardment proper to 48 hours at the outside.' There would be 'no intense bombardment prior to zero hour.' The field artillery was tasked with supporting the assault whilst heavy and siege guns, plus howitzers, were to be organized in groups for either counter-battery work or destruction of enemy defences.[42] Thus the artillery bombardment was 'divided into a preparatory period', which commenced on 20 March and an intensive bombardment, which commenced on 2 April.[43] The primary aim of the artillery plan was for batteries to fire 'continuously night and day' in order 'to prepare the way for the Infantry to advance to the final objective on the day of the assault, so that they may be able to reap the full benefit of a complete breakdown of the defence.'[44]

Horne made some effort to mislead the enemy as to his intentions. The Canadian Corps was supported by I Corps whose task was 'to deceive the enemy as to the exact limits of the operation' and by XI Corps which was 'to induce the enemy to believe'

37   Falls, *Military Operations 1917*, Vol. I, p.306.
38   TNA WO 95/168: Artillery Plan for the Capture of Vimy Ridge, First Army, GS 516/11(a), issued to I and Canadian Corps, 8 February 1917.
39   David T. Zabecki, *Steel Wind: Colonel General Bruchmüller and the Birth of Modern Artillery* (Westport, Connecticut: Praeger, 1994), p.115.
40   RAI, Rawlins Papers, Colonel S.W.H. Rawlins, A History of the development of the British Artillery in France, 1914-18, p.113.
41   RAI, Rawlins Papers, Colonel S.W.H. Rawlins, A History of the development of the British Artillery in France, 1914-18, p.114.
42   TNA WO 158/199: General Sir Henry Horne, Plan of Operations for First Army, First Army No. GS 503/22 (a), 31 January 1917.
43   TNA WO 158/187: Major-General W.H. Hastings, First Army Order No. 101, 26 March 1917.
44   TNA WO 95/168: Artillery Plan for the Capture of Vimy Ridge.

that an attack on the Aubers Ridge was intended.[45] Between 27 and 31 March, XI Corps was to carry out demonstrations, including a balloon concentration and artillery registration in conjunction with the right flank corps of the Second Army, whilst prior to 'Z' day, the I and XI Corps, would 'make every effort to deceive the enemy as to the exact limits of the operation, and would 'occupy his attention with artillery, rifle and machine-gun fire.'[46]

By 1917, the Royal Artillery 'was considerably ahead of the Germans' as the result of new techniques learned on the Somme and it was 'ludicrous to pretend' that the system employed by the Germans at Riga in late 1917 'was the equal in technique of the British counter-battery tactics, which even before the preliminary bombardment began at Arras, had destroyed much of the German artillery.'[47] That April, GIGS General Sir William Robertson informed Haig that he now had 'not only practically unlimited ammunition but also a far larger number of guns' than in 1916. These were 'being used in a most efficient manner.'[48] One of the 'important innovations' at Arras was that all of First Army's artillery[49] was placed under command of its General Officer Commanding Royal Artillery (GOCRA) who issued artillery instructions direct to corps subordinates. Moreover, the heaviest guns were placed directly under army GOCRA control for counter-battery work; bombardment of villages, and engagement with distant objectives.[50] Corps artillery, both field and heavy, was under the command of corps GOCRAs who also issued orders to subordinate divisional Brigadier General Royal Artillery (BGRA). Similarly, field artillery supporting divisional attacks was under the aforementioned BGRAs.[51]

On the opening day of the Somme offensive, each corps and division had experimented with support and counter-battery fire in pursuit of its own ideas which varied in method and result. Procedural differences with Arras were confined to minor details such as barrage pace, which was dependent on ground, anticipated opposition, and artillery methods that 'were generally uniform.' At Arras the artillery shared a common doctrine unavailable during the previous campaign. Indeed, on the Somme

45   TNA WO 95/168: Major-General W.H. Anderson, First Army No. GS 529/11(a), 6 March 1917 and TNA WO 95/168: Lieutenant-General R.C.B. Haking to First Army, XI Corps SS 1226/14, 17 March 1917 and Brigadier-General H.W. Studd, XI Corps SS 1226/22, 22 March 1917.

46   TNA WO 158/187, Major-General W.H. Hastings, First Army Order No. 101, 26 March 1917.

47   RAI, Brigadier E.C. Anstey Papers, Brigadier E.C. Anstey, The History of the Royal Artillery, p.141.

48   TNA Haig Papers, W.O.256/17, Field Marshal Sir William Robertson to Field Marshal Earl Haig, 14 April 1917.

49   RAI, Anstey Papers, Brigadier E.C. Anstey, The History of the Royal Artillery, p.144.

50   RAI, Rawlins Papers, Colonel S.W.H. Rawlins, A History of the development of the British Artillery in France, 1914-18, p.111.

51   RAI, Rawlins Papers, Colonel S.W.H. Rawlins, A History of the development of the British Artillery in France, 1914-18, p.111.

the artillery had 'either misunderstood or ignored the common doctrine which GHQ had laid down', whereas at Arras 'the artillery accepted and observed the principles contained in the pamphlets which, emanating from the office of the Major General Royal Artillery (MGRA), had been published by GHQ.'[52]

'Unprecedented importance' was given to counter-battery work.[53] The Vimy plan divided the Canadian Corps and I Corps artillery into counter-battery and siege groups for trench destruction. From the start, emphasis was placed on the counter-battery policy of shooting for destruction prior to zero hour, after which the aim was neutralization and elimination of hostile batteries 'with the greatest vigour' before commencement of the preliminary bombardment.[54] The successful destruction and neutralization of the enemy artillery required reorganization of the artillery information service to ensure that aircraft, balloon, flash-spotting, sound-ranging and ground observer intelligence was properly assimilated and passed on.[55] This was made possible by reforms implemented during winter 1916-17, a critical turning point when, drawing on lessons of the Somme, the BEF adapted corps-level centralisation of artillery firepower with formation of the Counter-Battery Staff Office (CBSO) in January 1917. From this point on the Royal Artillery slowly gained the upper hand on the battlefield.

Heavy and medium howitzers were not to be employed for any other task so long as destructive shoots against enemy batteries were required. Further to this, counter-battery work was given precedence over trench destruction. If the German artillery was unexpectedly reinforced, siege group batteries were to switch to counter-battery work. A distinction was also drawn between the nature of counter-battery work carried out during the first 10 days of bombardment prior to Zero, and on zero day itself. This was in sharp contrast to the German policy which confined counter-battery work to neutralization on the day of battle.[56] Thus the Battle of Arras 'was the first occasion on which systematic counter-battery work was carried out by British artillery.' The results were 'most satisfactory' and 'very little hostile artillery fire was encountered during the first day of attack and the next two or three days.'[57] Indeed, First Army subsequently reported, 'our counter-battery work had been entirely satisfactory, the enemy's barrage at the commencement of the attack being very spasmodic and finally being reduced to practically nothing.'[58]

52   RAI, Anstey Papers, Brigadier E.C. Anstey, The History of the Royal Artillery, pp.148-49.
53   Falls, *Military Operations 1917*, Vol. I, p.312.
54   TNA WO 95/168: Artillery Plan for the Capture of Vimy Ridge.
55   RAI, Anstey Papers, Brigadier E.C. Anstey, The History of the Royal Artillery, p.142.
56   RAI, Anstey Papers, Brigadier E.C. Anstey, The History of the Royal Artillery, p.141.
57   RAI., Rawlins Papers, Colonel S.W.H. Rawlins, A History of the development of the British Artillery in France, 1914-18, p.114.
58   TNA WO 95/169: Major-General W.H. Anderson, First Army Weekly Summary of Operations, 6 -13 April 1917, First Army No. 24(G), 16 April 1917.

The importance of RFC co-operation was also recognised,[59] two aircraft flights being allotted to each corps. Dividing the front into two sectors, there was one counter-battery group per sector. The third group was on standby for reinforcement of either sector. Counter-battery work was to be continuous, with the aim of destroying any identified hostile active batteries, 'ammunition not being stinted.'[60] In the 10 days before zero day, the aim was vigorous destruction of isolated active batteries and groups or nests of batteries. The identification and destruction of telephone exchanges was, preferably at the last moment, especially important. At zero hour, on the other hand, destruction would give way to neutralization. Every enemy position known to be occupied was fired on at this time, batteries of siege groups which had finished their tasks joining in with the counter-battery groups.

Following 15 minutes intense neutralizing fire, destructive fire was to resume as opportunity offered. Neutralization, so far as possible, was to be controlled by ground and air observation. Gas shells were to be employed, especially against guns which had not been entirely destroyed. The need for counter-battery fire after an advance was also foreseen, and large numbers of counter-battery group batteries were to redeploy forward.[61] First Army had been 'preparing to attack the Vimy Ridge all the winter' and for the last seven days had been shelling 'pretty hard', the ridge undergoing 'a very heavy bombardment.' In particular, British gunners put down 'a great deal of artillery fire' on roads and approaches, so that the enemy 'had not been able to effect their reliefs & so get their food up' with the result that 'they were in poor form ... had a bad time' and, 'except in a few cases', fought 'without much heart & surrendered freely.'[62] Lieutenant-General Sir Julian Byng (GOC Canadian Corps) reported that the Germans 'knew we were coming but they were demoralised.' The preliminary bombardment began in late February the British and Canadians keeping 'up a steady bombardment day & night, stopping the rations, reinforcements, reliefs etc. and making it as b----y as we could for them.'[63] The infantry were to advance behind a creeping barrage. There would also be a standing barrage in advance of the creeper which would 'occasionally search and sweep within narrow limits to prevent the occupants of the trenches on which the barrage is established from occupying shell holes in advance or in rear of them.'[64]

Owing to the great depth of the enemy defences, a simple 'rolling barrage' was no longer enough, and methodical long range heavy artillery fire in a 'run about barrage'

59 RAI, Rawlins Papers, Colonel S.W.H. Rawlins, A History of the development of the British Artillery in France, 1914-18, p.112.
60 RAI, Anstey Papers, Brigadier E.C. Anstey, The History of the Royal Artillery, p.141.
61 RAI, Brigadier E.C. Anstey Papers, Brigadier E.C. Anstey, The History of the Royal Artillery, p.142.
62 IWM, Horne Papers, Horne to wife, 9 and 10 April 1917.
63 IWM, Chetwode Papers, General J. Byng to Lieutenant-General General P.W. Chetwode, 30 May 1917.
64 TNA WO 95/168: Artillery Plan for the Capture of Vimy Ridge.

was required to deal with a hostile position 'organized in depth with many machine-guns.'[65] 'A similar lead in artillery matters' was established with development of the moving barrage. During the Arras offensive the British moving or deep barrage took its final form and was invariably employed thereafter. From the original thin line of shrapnel fire first employed on the Somme, it had expanded into a greater zone beaten by shrapnel, HE and smoke shells, which rolled over the enemy's position. Throughout this same period the German moving barrage (*Feuerwalze*) did not approach the same level of 'efficiency.' Thus, by April 1917, German artillery methods 'were well behind the British', the latter's artillery establishing 'a substantial lead in both technique and tactics' that 'the Official History not only ignores but seems to deny.'[66]

On 9 April 1917 Third and First armies attacked on 12 mile front. The First Army assault, launched at 5.30 a.m. on a front of 5,000 yards (approximately 3½ miles), was 'successful' except for a 'small portion' on the left: 65 officers, 3,280 men and 23 guns were captured. Third Army, attacking on a front three times as long, captured some 6,000 prisoners and 36 guns.[67] For its part, Horne felt his army had done 'more than our share', handling more guns than thought possible in the 'wildest' dreams of pre-war gunners.[68] Overall, the Canadian Corps assault was 'a great success' proceeding like clock-work to penetrate the Vimy defences to a depth of 4,000 yards, the Germans experiencing 'one of the hardest knocks' of the war. Artillery preparation and support 'had been excellent', the Canadians seizing the ridge despite considerable opposition, especially in the neighbourhood of Thélus. Having gained their final objectives by early afternoon and dug in, 'cavalry and infantry patrols' were sent out 'in the direction of Willerval and along the front of their position.' By the close of the day, the Canadians 'were established deeply in the enemy's positions on the whole front of attack … had gained a firm footing in the enemy's third line on both banks of the Scarpe' and had made 'an important breach in the enemy's last fully completed line of defence.'[69] It was 'a very famous day in the annals of the British Empire & of Canada in particular.'[70]

In short, 'in no previous British offensive had so little been left to chance.' Horne himself attributed the subsequent success to 'soundness of plan, thoroughness of preparation, dash and determination in execution, and devotion to duty on the part of all concerned.'[71] The brilliant capture of Vimy Ridge, 'a formidable undertaking' by

65   TNA WO 256/17: Field Marshal Earl Haig, Diary, 12 May 1917. See also Lieutenant-General Sir Launcelot Kiggell, Record of a Conference held at Noyelle Vion at 11 a.m. on the 30th April 1917, O.A.D. 426, 1 May 1917.
66   RAI, Anstey Papers, Brigadier E.C. Anstey, The History of the Royal Artillery, p.142.
67   IWM, Horne Papers, Horne Diary, 9 April 1917.
68   IWM, Horne Papers, Horne to wife, 11 April 1917.
69   IWM, Horne Papers 52/1, 'Despatch from Field Marshal Sir Douglas Haig KT GCB GCVO, Commander-in-Chief British Armies in France', 25 December 1917, p.8.
70   IWM, Horne Papers, Horne to wife, 13 April 1917.
71   Falls, *Military Operations 1917*, Vol. I, pp.318, 352.

Column of Canadian infantry advancing in the wake of a MK II Male tank, Vimy Ridge, 9 April 1917.

Men of the 28th Canadian Battalion establishing a signal station, Vimy Ridge, 9 April 1917.

Canadian Corps and I Corps, was 'vital to the success of the Third Army' and owed its success to 'the unprecedented completeness of the preparations' and destructive power of the artillery.[72] One of the most successful BEF operations of the war and Horne's first major operation as an Army commander, it demonstrated his rapid promotion was well deserved.[73]

First Army's artillery plan 'differed materially from that of the Third Army' because, although the preliminary bombardment was at first limited to 48 hours duration, the work of destruction commenced three to four weeks previously.[74] For its effort, Third Army proposed a short and intense barrage of 48 hours rather than a week's previous bombardment. This scheme was ultimately rejected by GHQ. Consulted for their opinions, the First, Fourth and Fifth army commanders 'stated that they preferred a longer bombardment' as a means of dealing with the enemy defences, most notably the barbed wire. Horne's plan for a lengthy preliminary bombardment was 'to destroy portions of the enemy's defences methodically for some time before the attack.'[75] On the Somme, he had favoured a slow and deliberate bombardment 'which was generally more accurate.'[76] Now, a bombardment of six days duration was being contemplated. This would ensure that 'the lanes through the backward lines of enemy wire have actually been cut, and that tactical points have been adequately dealt with by batteries of destruction.'[77] The First Army bombardment would require 30 times the amount of heavy artillery ammunition employed by the French two years previously and more than double, proportional to the extent of front, the quantity of all types of ammunition expended prior to 1 July 1916.[78]

Yet, in the final analysis First Army was correct with regard to wire-cutting difficulties because the obstacles fronting the Wancourt–Feuchy Line could not be reasonably cut in 10 days, let alone two or four. Having studied the ground, Horne observed that 'the work of our artillery was splendid, not a vestige of uncut wire & the trenches knocked to pieces'. He also noted that 'the whole ground however is churned up into a sea of muddy shell holes and it is very difficult to get our guns on.'[79] Moreover, Horne remarked that, whilst the 'impressive' bombardment had 'completely wiped out the German trenches & positions', leaving 'not a square yard that has not been

---

72   Falls, pp.300, 302, 312, 316.
73   RAI, Anstey Papers, Brigadier E.C. Anstey, The History of the Royal Artillery, p.152.
74   RAI, Rawlins Papers, Colonel S.W.H. Rawlins, A History of the development of the British Artillery in France, 1914-18, pp.110-111.
75   TNA WO 256/15: Haig Papers, Lieutenant-General Sir Launcelot Kiggell, Record of Army Commanders' Conference held at Rollencourt Chateau on Saturday, the 27th January 1917, at 11 a.m., O.A.D.291/22, 3 February 1917.
76   IWM, Fourth Army Papers, Notes of Conference held at Fourth Army Headqrs, 8th July 1916, Vol. 6 (Conferences and Various Somme Papers, 5 February-16 November 1916).
77   TNA WO 95/168, Major-General W.H. Anderson to Canadian Corps, First Army No. GS 529/12(G), 8 March 1917.
78   Falls, Military Operations 1917, Vol. I, p.316.
79   IWM, Horne Papers, Horne to wife, 11 April 1917.

hit with something', it had also left a landscape resembling 'the result of a volcano.'[80] This was inevitable when one considers that the artillery, employing 377 heavy guns and 520 field guns, fired more than 42,500 tons of ammunition each, a daily quota of nearly 2,500 tons with a total of 50,000 tons (over one million rounds) during the last week of systematic shelling. The result was a pock-marked wilderness of mud-filled craters[81] and serious traffic control difficulties when sending up ammunition supply columns.[82] Consequently, Horne reported to Haig that he 'thought he had used too many shells' which 'had broken up the soil so frightfully that all movement was now made most difficult' and that 'owing to the amount of artillery and ammunition available' the frontal attack had become 'the easiest' operation but that 'the difficult matter was to advance later on when the enemy had organized a defence with machine-guns.'[83] 'Subsequent examination of the ground covered by the attack demonstrated the remarkable effectiveness of the British artillery fire for destruction' but 'the First Army trench bombardment was somewhat overdone, for the defences on the western face of the Ridge were almost obliterated.'[84] The emphasis on a limited objective and the rigid time-table to co-ordinate the advance of the artillery and infantry had precluded exploitation of initial success.[85]

The failure to exploit was aggravated by Horne's emphasis on strictly limited objectives. Having been warned by GHQ that 'troops pushing forward in advance must be very much on the alert against counter-attack, he aimed to 'consolidate a line of defence on the ridge and push forward reconnoitring detachments, following up with advanced guards' but had 'specially warned commanders not to run large formations up against unbroken wire.' Horne made clear his own relatively limited ambitions, denying that he 'was preparing to push forward masses of troops' because 'if the fight for the Vimy proves to be a stiff one, neither the Canadian Corps nor the left of the XVII Corps might be fit to go much further.'[86] Having 'taken most of the famous Vimy Ridge', Horne was aware that he 'must now take care to *keep* it'[87] and, although keen to keep 'the Bosche at it & press as hard as we can', his main priority was to prevent the enemy from 'retaking the Vimy Ridge by a counter-attack.'[88] With 9th Cavalry Brigade at his disposal for exploitation, he believed there was 'no great chance

80 IWM, Horne Papers, Horne to wife, 5 June 1917.
81 Nicholson, *Canadian Expeditionary Force, 1914-1919*, pp.248-249, 251.
82 Nicholson, *Canadian Expeditionary Force, 1914-1919*, pp.248-249, 251 and Lieutenant-Colonel A.F. Brooke, The Evolution of Artillery in the Great War, Part VI, 243.
83 TNA WO 256/17: Haig Papers, Field Marshal Earl Haig Diary, 12 April 1917.
84 RAI, Rawlins Papers, Colonel S.W.H. Rawlins, A History of the development of the British Artillery in France, 1914-18, pp.114, 116.
85 Nicholson, *Canadian Expeditionary Force, 1914-1919*, p.258.
86 TNA WO 158/188: Lieutenant-General Sir Launcelot Kiggell to General Sir Henry Horne, 2 April 1917 and General Sir Henry Horne to Lieutenant-General Sir Launcelot Kiggell, 3 April 1917.
87 IWM, Horne Papers, Horne to wife, 9 April 1917.
88 IWM, Horne Papers, Horne to wife, 10 April 1917.

of using cavalry until we have defeated the German reserves & broken thro' the last line of wire … there was no opening for them.'[89]

Hampered by bad weather, 'including quite heavy snow' that interfered with road movement,[90] 10 and 11 April were thus spent in 'consolidating & moving guns forward.' However, 'great difficulty' was experienced 'in getting the guns through the broken up ground.' Thus road improvements became 'very necessary.' The subsequent storming of the 'Pimple' by 4th Canadian Division and the Bois en Hache by the 24th Division (I Corps) on the morning of 12 April denied all remaining observation to the enemy.[91] First Army had obtained 'command of the valley of the Souchez River',[92] capture of these positions forced the Germans to retreat to the Oppy Line on an 11-mile front to a maximum depth of 4½ miles. Withdrawing 'in some haste', they abandoned 'a lot of stores & equipment' whilst failing to destroy rolling stock, railway lines, roads, dug-outs, and cellars.[93]

After the initial Arras success and following some progress through the mining districts of Angres and Liévin towards Lens,[94] the offensive now became bogged down, Horne admitting on 16 April that First Army was 'at a standstill for the moment' owing to 'the wet weather & the state of the country' which 'made it difficult to repair roads & get guns etc. forward.' Indeed, the ground had been 'so much cut up by trenches & by shell fire' that it was 'extremely difficult to make or repair roads.'[95] Between 16-23 April, First Army continued the offensive west and north-west of Lens, but German resistance became increasingly stubborn and casualties mounted on both sides. It was clear that the enemy had no intention of withdrawing from Lens and its vicinity.[96] Subsequent heavy fighting, notably during the Second Battle of the Scarpe (23-24 April) and the disastrous Third Battle of the Scarpe (3-4 May) during which the Canadians seized Fresnoy, forced Horne to advise Haig that 'the divisions in the First Army are not equal to much offensive action at the present moment.'[97] A serious local reverse followed when the Germans recaptured Fresnoy on 9 May,

89   IWM, Horne Papers, Horne to wife, 19 April 1917.
90   IWM, Horne Papers, Horne to wife, 11 April 1917.
91   IWM, Horne Papers, Horne Diary 10 and 11 April 1917 and Lieutenant Colonel W.L.O. Twiss, 'Summary of Intelligence, First Army, 1st to 15th April, 1917', 17 April 1917.
92   IWM, Horne Papers, Horne to wife, 12 April 1917.
93   IWM, Horne Papers, Horne to wife, 14 April 1917and Lieutenant Colonel W.L.O. Twiss, 'Summary of Intelligence, First Army, 1st to 15th April, 1917', 17 April 1917.
94   IWM, Horne Papers, Horne to wife, 15 April 1917.
95   IWM, Horne Papers, Horne to wife, 16 April 1917.
96   IWM, Horne Papers 48/1, Lieutenant Colonel W.L.O. Twiss, 'Summary of Intelligence, First Army, 16th to 30th April, 1917', 2 May 1917.
97   IWM, Horne Papers 52/1, Horne to wife, 23 and 24 April 1917; 'Despatch from Field Marshal Sir Douglas Haig KT GCB GCVO, Commander-in-Chief British Armies in France', 25 December 1917, p.15 and TNA WO 256/18: Lieutenant-General Sir Launcelot Kiggell, Note of Proceedings at Army Commander's Conference, held at Doullens on Monday, the 7th May, 1917, at 11 a.m.

Horne notifying GHQ that 5th Division (XIII Corps), which was responsible for that sector, was 'exhausted' and that none of the four remaining divisions of XIII Corps were 'fit for offensive operations on a considerable scale.' This also made 'inadvisable the contemplated operations' to secure the Oppy–Mericourt–Vendin Line as 'such action would now result in a salient which would be dangerous in view of the prospective withdrawal of heavy artillery' for forthcoming operations in Flanders. Moreover, the withdrawal of 'a considerable portion of the artillery' from First Army and the unavailability of tanks 'for at least three weeks' precluded 'operations on any scale against Lens.'[98]

From mid-May, operations around Lens were essentially designed 'to draw pressure both off the Ypres sector and off the French Aisne front.'[99] Reduced to 'plenty of artillery & infantry scrapping' with the hope of giving the Germans 'a good hammering on a small scale' and 'keeping the Bosche busy' with the intention of inflicting 'very heavy' losses, Horne kept 'poking away' at the enemy whilst 'worrying him' as much as possible. The aim was also to force the defenders to launch counter-attacks that were 'good business for us as a rule, as they mean heavy losses to the Germans.' First Army could 'generally manage to get the guns on to them and knock over a lot of them.'[100] Such operations came at a cost owing to artillery shortages that forced the postponement of further large-scale operations until August. Horne was also 'anxious' about 46th (North Midland) Division, then conducting gruelling offensive operations about Liévin, which was 'very weak & tired' and unable to hold onto its gains. As Canadian Lieutenant-Colonel Andrew McNaughton recollected, the capture of Lens had become a personal obsession for Horne.[101]

It was at this time that the divide in British operational doctrine theory came to a head with the planning for the Third Battle of Ypres (31 July-10 November 1917). For this offensive, Haig and Gough proposed to smash through the German defences east of Ypres in one decisive blow. This ambitions scheme ignored the advice of Brigadier-General J.H. 'Tavish' Davidson (GHQ Director of Operations) who advocated 'a deliberate and sustained advance' divided into 'a succession of operations' to a depth of not less than 1,500 yards and not more than 3,000 yards in order to take advantage of offensive opening day success when the enemy was in 'a state of disorganisation.' Further to this, such an advance would bring the attackers into positions from which to 'deliver a second and well-organised attack.' Davidson concluded that if a series of

98   IWM, Horne Papers, Horne to wife, 9 May 1917; TNA WO 158/188, General Sir Henry Horne to GHQ, First Army No. GS 372/9 (a), 10 May 1917.
99   Brigadier-General Sir James Edmonds, *Military Operations France and Belgium 1917*, Vol. II (London: HMSO, 1948), p.219; Colonel G W L Nicholson, *Canadian Expeditionary Force, 1914-1919*, p.297.
100 IWM, Horne Papers, Horne to wife, 12, 11 and 15 May 1917.
101 IWM, Horne Papers, Horne Diary, 1 and 2 July 1917; Edmonds, *Military Operations France and Belgium, 1917*, Vol. II, pp.114-15; John Swettenham, *McNaughton, 1887-1939*, Vol. I (Toronto: Ryerson Press, 1968), p.98.

such advances were repeated every two or three days and momentum maintained, the cumulative effect of a sustained series of attacks would destroy enemy reserves without excessive demands being placed on the assault infantry. Believing that 'an 'all-out' attack' was only viable when the enemy was beaten and in disarray, Davidson questioned the feasibility of the decisive blow advocated by Haig and Gough. Instead, he supported a 'step-by-step' advance with limited objectives and overwhelming artillery support. This would inflict maximum damage to enemy manpower and morale whilst simultaneously reducing British losses.[102]

Previously, General Sir Henry Rawlinson (GOC Fourth Army) advocated limited objectives during 1915-16, once again outlining the choice between 'a decisive battle with an unlimited objective' and 'a battle of attrition', which was 'by far the most suitable at the present juncture.' He also noted that the British had failed 'to carry out a battle of attrition on absolutely definite lines, with successive objectives well within covering range of artillery and well within the physical capacity of the infantry.' He contrasted these attempts (Loos in September 1915 and the Somme in July and September 1916) with the limited operations at Longueval in mid-July 1916; Vimy in April 1917 and Messines the following June where 'the objectives given were well within the physical capacity of the troops' who 'reached their final objectives with their energies comparatively unimpaired, and consequently, in a state to throw back any counter-attacks that were likely to be put against them.' Rawlinson promoted delivery of 'a succession of carefully worked out hammer blows on the enemy at short intervals with the object of definitely beating him to his knees so that there is no question that his morale is finally broken.' Relying on his artillery assets, Rawlinson hoped to reduce the numbers of assaulting infantry 'thus economising troops and saving valuable time', so that greater reserves were available for the next assault phase.[103]

General Sir Herbert Plumer (GOC Second Army), who together with Rawlinson had submitted proposals for a limited offensive in Flanders the previous winter,[104] implemented Davidson's operational methods in September and October 1917 when Second Army conducted a series of offensives (Menin Road Ridge, 20-26 September; Polygon Wood 26 September-3 October; Broodseinde 4 October) which formed a succession of 'bite and hold' operations designed to wear down the enemy over many days. Consequent breakout and exploitation would occur during a hoped for final phase when the enemy was too weak to resist. Aware that current German tactics relied on defence in depth and staggered counter-attacks, operational objectives were

102 TNA WO 158/249, Major-General Sir John Davidson to the CGS, 'Operations by Second and Fifth Armies for the capture of the Passchendaele–Staden Ridge', 26 June 1917.
103 LHCMA, Montgomery-Massingberd Papers 94, General Sir Henry Rawlinson to GHQ, Fourth Army No.806 (G), 9 August 1917.
104 TNA WO158/38: Field Marshal Lord Plumer to GHQ, 30 January 1917; TNA WO158/214, General Sir Henry Rawlinson to GHQ, 9 February 1917.

selected to provide 'the greatest advantages to defeat the enemy counter-attack' when a 'real opportunity for inflicting loss on the enemy' presented itself. For its part, halted British infantry would be 'in condition to consolidate and hold the points gained.'[105] Plumer's tactics employed a methodical step-by-step advance with limited objectives. This entailed four steps of approximately 1,500 yards each with each division on a frontage of no more than 1,000 yards.' To support them 'he wanted his allotment of artillery doubled, asking for 1,339 guns and howitzers for the offensive front alone.' Buckling under the strain, German defensive measures 'failed with terrible losses against the systematic advances ...'[106]

The Menin Road Ridge, Polygon Wood and Broodseinde offensives demonstrated a scale of success comparable to that of Arras, Vimy Ridge and Messines not to mention Amiens later in 1918. Notable as one of the German Army's 'black days' whereby its entire frontline system was overrun with relatively light casualties sustained by the attacker, Broodseinde was 'by far the best thing the Second Army ever did.'[107] The success of Plumer's limited objective assaults, during which anticipated German counter-attacks 'suffered heavy losses' and were 'quite fruitless', forced the defenders to pack forward defences in force to their cost.[108] At last the British had come to grips with the enemy's defensive tactics. It was a downturn in the weather and consequent horrendous ground conditions that prevented Second Army from exploiting its September and early October pushes before the Third Ypres campaign was officially terminated on 20 November.[109]

Horne does not appear to have been involved in this crucial debate but was very much in agreement with Davidson, Rawlinson and Plumer, the latter experiencing recent success at the Battle of Messines (7-14 June 1917). Accompanied by Major-General H.F. Mercer (MGRA First Army) and Brigadier General P.G. Twining (DA&QMG First Army), Horne was 'shown round' Messines Ridge. 'Very anxious to see the position and the effect of the artillery fire etc.', Horne also observed that the bombardment 'had been most effective & combined with the mine explosions had reduced the German defences ... the work of nearly three years ... to nothing.'[110]

105 LHCMA, Montgomery-Massingberd Papers 95, Lieutenant-Colonel C.H. Mitchell, The Enemy's Tactical Methods East of Ypres, Second Army Intelligence, 16 September 1917 and Papers 94, Major-General C.H. Harington, Notes on Training and Preparations for Offensive Operations, Second Army, 31 August 1917.

106 RAI, Anstey Papers, Brigadier E.C. Anstey, The History of the Royal Artillery, pp.180, 169.

107 LHCMA, Maurice Papers 3/2/7, General Sir Charles Harington to Major-General Sir Frederick Maurice, 9 November 1934 and Edmonds, *Military Operations France and Belgium 1917*, Vol. II, pp. xi, 303.

108 LHCMA, Montgomery-Massingberd Papers 95, Translation of 5th [German] Guards Brigade Order I.Br.1125, General von Radowitz, 29 September 1917, GHQ Ia/40569, 7 October 1917.

109 See Heinz Hagenlücke, 'The German High Command' in Peter Liddle (ed.), *Passchendaele in Perspective: The Third Battle of Ypres* (London: Leo Cooper, 1997), pp. 52-53.

110 IWM, Horne Papers, Horne Diary, 17 June 1917 and Horne to wife, 17 June 1917.

King George V, Lieutenant-General Sir A. Currie and General Sir H. Horne
at Vimy Ridge, July 1917.

Following this, First Army discussions with I Corps concluded that 'the enemy attaches great importance to Hill 70' and that an operation to secure it would force him to react. Moreover, an operation to capture nearby Sallaumines Hill would offer the possibility of a two-prong advance onto high ground north and south of Lens. All would depend on receipt of additional troop and artillery reinforcements. None were to be had, so the I Corps attack was postponed.[111] Nevertheless, Haig was pleased that First Army's previous operations had forced the enemy not only to withdraw guns and reinforce 'his front about Lens with two divisions from the Ypres sector' but had also been 'very successful in misleading the Germans as to our intentions.' This no doubt influenced GHQ to provide First Army with additional heavy guns. Reinforced thus, Horne resumed discussions with regard to capturing Lens at an army conference on 10 July.[112]

Based on personal reconnaissance, Lieutenant-General Sir Arthur Currie (GOC Canadian Corps) believed that the First Army plan to break the German line south

111 TNA WO 95/171: Lieutenant-General A.E.A. Holland, I Corps No. 780, to First Army, 10 June 1917; First Army No.G.S.604/14, 14 June 1917 and Nicholson, *Canadian Expeditionary Force, 1914-1919*, p.279.
112 TNA WO 256/19 and 20: Field Marshal Earl Haig, Diary, 30 June and 3 July 1917; TNA WO 158/189: Henry Horne, First Army G.S.658/4, 10 July 1917.

of Lens and capture the city by stages, issued on 7 July before additional resources had been promised by GHQ, overlooked the fact that the ground over which the proposed advance would occur was dominated by Hill 70 and Sallaumines Hill. Expressing his reservations to Horne at the army conference on 10 July, Currie requested that the GOC First Army alter his plan and make Hill 70 the 'immediate main objective' and employ 'bite and hold' tactics whereby the Germans would dissipate available reserves in costly counter-attacks. Horne duly referred the matter to Haig, who paid a visit to Currie several days later and, commenting that the GOC Canadian Corps' plan was 'much better than previous suggestions', not only fully agreed with 'the desirability of attacking Hill 70 first' but also provided more artillery in addition to battery reinforcements previously promised on 10 July. Both Horne and Currie viewed the now sanctioned Hill 70 assault as the first in a series of carefully planned limited objective offensives. Supported by massive artillery firepower which would ultimately facilitate a 'step-by-step' occupation of Lens, Horne's double-envelopment scheme to advance onto the high ground north and south of Lens (Hill 70 and Sallaumines Hill respectively), as previously discussed with I Corps in June, appeared to offer every opportunity for success. As the Canadian Corps prepared for the offensive, the remainder of First Army (I, XI and XIII corps) orchestrated raids, increased wireless traffic, established dummy supply dumps, and ordered feint artillery registration and bombardments 'in order to mislead the enemy.'[113]

It was in early August that Horne, following a conference with Currie, 'postponed [the] Lens operation till better weather.' Nevertheless, the GOC First Army would continue 'raiding & pegging away' for a fortnight. Wishing 'to take no chances of failure', further postponements occurred due to continuing poor weather. Finally, on 15 August, under the umbrella of an impressive array of artillery employing one gun per 9.5 yards of front, the 1st and 2nd Canadian Divisions attacked on a front of nearly 4,000 yards in an 'entirely successful' offensive that reached 'a maximum depth of nearly a mile.'[114] Hill 70 was now in British hands and 'all objectives except a small portion' of 3rd Canadian Brigade's objective were secured.[115] First Army had 'had a

113 Daniel G. Dancocks, *Sir Arthur Currie: A Biography* (Toronto: Methuen, 1985), pp.105-7; A.M.J. Hyatt, *General Sir Arthur Currie: A Military Biography* (Toronto: University of Toronto Press, 1987), pp.76-7; Douglas E Delaney & Serge Marc Durflinger (eds.), *Capturing Hill 70: Canada's Forgotten Battle of the First World War* (Vancouver-Toronto: HBC Press, 2016), pp.11-13, 35-41, 63-5, 87-92, 97-8; Nicholson, *Canadian Expeditionary Force, 1914-1919*, p.285; Simon Robbins, *British Generalship During the Great War: The Military Career of Sir Henry Horne (1861-1929)* (Farnham: Ashgate, 2010), pp.181-83; Hugh M. Urquhart, *Arthur Currie: The Biography of a Great Canadian* (Toronto: J.M. Dent, 1950), pp.169-70.

114 RAI, Colonel S.W.H. Rawlins Papers Box 3, General Sir Noel Birch to Brigadier-General P.P. de B. Radcliffe, 9 July 1918; IWM, Horne Papers 48/1, Lieutenant Colonel W.L.O. Twiss, 'Summary of Intelligence, First Army, 1st to 16th August, 1917', 19 August 1917.

115 The 3rd Brigade managed to capture the remainder of its objective on the following day.

great day', holding 'throughout … against a number of counter-attacks' and inflicting 'very heavy losses' with artillery and rifle fire.[116]

Visiting that afternoon to congratulate Horne who had earlier reported that the attack had gone 'very well' with 'small' losses, Haig sanctioned the next operational 'step', the capture of Sallaumines Hill, which would take '3 weeks, perhaps longer.' The BEF C-in-C also ominously warned that he 'might want some of his [Horne's] guns' to support the ongoing offensive in Flanders.[117] On the 16th, Horne reported that the Canadians had defended their positions 'against many counter-attacks' taking 'over 900 prisoners' and that the enemy had 'lost *very heavily indeed* as they counter-attacked hard & across the open & our guns were hard at it knocking them over all day.' By 17 August First Army had captured 24 officers and 1,098 men and 'inflicted enormous losses on the Germans.'[118] Over the next week numerous enemy counter-attacks 'were swallowed up' by First Army's artillery fire. Isolated parties that made it through the barrage were mown down by machine-gun and rifle fire.[119]

In an after-action report analysis, First Army headquarters noted that 'the first of a series of counter-attacks', which were carried out by enemy frontline regiment support battalions 'were repulsed without difficulty', occurred between 8.00 and 9.00 a.m. and continued 'throughout the day at varying intervals.' Between 9.00 a.m. and noon the division in the line reserve battalions began to arrive and assemble. These were 'satisfactorily dealt with by artillery, machine-guns and rifle fire.' A weak and badly organised counter-attack finally developed between 1.00 and 2.00 p.m., and 'was easily crushed.' At 2.00 p.m. a succeeding counter-attack managed to re-occupy Chicory Trench but this was recaptured by British infantry at 6.00 p.m. Between 4.15 and 5.15 p.m. large parties of enemy troops, later identified as belonging to *4th Guards Division* from close reserve, were spotted assembling prior to engagement by artillery, machine-guns and rifle fire which inflicted 'heavy losses.' Launched across open ground at 5.30 p.m., the *Guards* counter-attack was repulsed with heavy losses. Further German efforts to regain lost ground occurred between 8.00 and 9.15 p.m. First Army subsequently noted that the morning German counter-attacks lacked co-ordination partly because the front selected included the junction of two divisions (*7th* and *11th Reserve*) and two *Gruppes* (*Loos* and *Souchez*). The midday, afternoon and evening assaults (hurriedly carried out by a reserve division) partly failed from lack of preparation, but close 1st RFC Brigade cooperation coupled with excellent

116 IWM, Horne Papers, Horne Diary, 15 and 16 August 1917; Horne to wife, 15 August 1917.
117 IWM, Horne Papers, Horne to wife, 15 August 1917; Gary Sheffield & John Bourne, *Douglas Haig: War Diaries and Letters, 1914-1918* (London: Weidenfeld & Nicholson, 2005), pp.316-17.
118 IWM, Horne Papers, Horne to wife, 16 August and [17] August 1917.
119 LHCMA, Alanbrooke Papers 1/1/10/41, Field Marshal Viscount Alanbrooke to mother, 18 August 1917.

German officer captured on Hill 70. (*The Sphere*, 25 August 1917)

German *Flammenwerfer* seized during one of the numerous counter-attacks to regain Hill 70.
(*Illustrated London News*, 15 September 1917)

observation ensured that Canadian artillery, machine-gun and, above all, rifle fire repulsed all German attempts to regain their lost positions with heavy losses.[120]

First Army also noted that special efforts had been made 'to obtain closer co-operation' between Canadian Corps and 1st RFC Brigade, with two-seater Sopwith 1½ Strutters of 43 Squadron continuously employed throughout 15 August to observe a 7,000 yards wide zone some 1,500 to 2,500 yards from the original frontline. It was through this territory that counter-attacking German reserves must pass. Engaging enemy aircraft and hostile infantry or artillery below, 43 Squadron strafed a plethora of available targets with machine-gun fire whilst maintaining regular contact with corps headquarters and corps heavy artillery. As a result, artillery observation aircraft were able to work unmolested throughout the day spotting hostile batteries and infantry concentrations 'most effectually.'[121] The Germans, a First Army intelligence report concluded, not only 'completely failed to stop our troops' but also delivered 'repeated counter-attacks throughout the day' which, apart from one sector where the line was 'completely re-established', were repulsed with 'very severe losses' by the artillery, and 'never succeeded in reaching our trenches' due to 'good ground observation and the perfect co-operation of our aeroplanes'. On the 16th, the Canadians made further progress, pushing up the eastern slopes of Hill 70 towards Cité St Auguste. Once again the enemy counter-attacked and, after a third attempt, succeeded in driving back some advanced outposts before being driven off with 'severe losses', after which the lost posts were regained.[122]

The following days were spent consolidating territorial gains and, as Horne observed, attempting 'to keep on the pressure' during subsequent hard fighting. The Germans had 'brought up a lot of fresh troops and were able to prevent our accomplishing all we wanted.'[123] The Canadian Corps attacked again on 21 August, this time securing the line of German trenches skirting Lens to the south-west and west.[124] However, inclement weather in late August acted 'very much against operations.'[125] Thus a promising operation closed with hastily planned assaults which were designed to maintain pressure on the enemy but merely resulted in disappointment and needlessly heavy casualties.[126] The notion of preventing 'operational exhaustion' to the point of diminishing returns would be an important aspect of the victorious Hundred Days

120 IWM, Horne Papers 43/3, Advanced First Army, 'Report on Capture of Hill 70 and Operations of August 15th and 16th, 1917', 17 August 1917, unsigned.
121 IWM, Horne Papers 43/3, Advanced First Army, 'Report on Capture of Hill 70 and Operations of August 15th and 16th, 1917', 17 August 1917, unsigned.
122 IWM, Horne Papers 48/1, Lieutenant Colonel W.L.O. Twiss, 'Summary of Intelligence, First Army, 1st to 16th August, 1917', 19 August 1917.
123 IWM, Horne Papers, Horne to wife, 22 August 1917.
124 IWM, Horne Papers 52/1, 'Despatch from Field Marshal Sir Douglas Haig KT GCB GCVO, Commander-in-Chief British Armies in France', 25 December 1917, p.31.
125 IWM, Horne Papers, Horne to wife, 29-31 August 1917.
126 Delaney & Durflinger (eds.), *Capturing Hill 70*, pp.22-24, 43-47, 73-74, 95-96.

offensives. Horne, having experienced his baptism of fire at army level during 1917, learned this lesson well.

Wanting to press on with the offensive, Horne proposed a combined operation during which I and XI Corps carried out a series of diversionary raids whilst the main attack, employing tanks, was carried out by three Canadian divisions tasked with seizing the Sallumines height in order to implement earlier plans to secure high ground north and south of Lens in an attempt to envelop the city and cut off the belea-guered garrison's withdrawal.[127] To accomplish this, Horne recommended a short and intense preliminary bombardment, reducing its length to a mere two days as a means of restoring the 'factor of surprise' and concluded that 'the work of destruction has, in the past, been carried too far' and that 'complete destruction on the scale carried out prior to the attack on Hill 70 cannot go hand in hand with surprise.'[128]

On 11 September GHQ approved the projected First Army offensive against Lens for 15 October or after.[129] However, on 2 October Horne was informed that all available troops would be made available for the Ypres offensive.[130] Horne's plans for the capture of Lens, hampered by postponements and limited resources, was finally abandoned when the Canadian Corps departed north to conduct operations against Passchendaele Ridge. Apart from 'a few raids' to keep the Germans busy and inflict 'very heavy casualties', so ended Horne's active participation in the offensives of 1917. First Army was placed on standby to support Third Army's offensive at Cambrai on 20 November. Commenting on this novel operation, Horne noted it had 'been done on new principles', employing 'a surprise attack by large numbers of tanks without any preliminary artillery bombardment or any warning.'[131] With the element of surprise re-established on the battlefield, Cambrai 'marked a fresh era in British artillery tactics of the war'.[132]

As Horne's military career aptly demonstrates, 1917 was a period of considerable debate within the British Army, as 'bite and hold' gained ascendancy over break-through as the preferred operational approach, the former providing a template for Field Marshal Bernard Montgomery among others to follow during the next world-wide conflict. The doctrinal divide within British operational planning came to a head, as the folly of the ambitious plans advocated by Haig, Gough and others was

127 TNA WO 158/189: General Sir Henry Horne to GHQ, 'Scheme for Operations against Lens', 2 September 1917.

128 TNA WO 158/189: General Sir Henry Horne to GHQ, General Artillery Plan, 2 September 1917; Palazzo, 'The British Army's Counter-Battery Staff Office and Control of the Enemy in World War I', p.70.

129 TNA WO 158/188: Lieutenant-General Sir Launcelot Kiggell to General Sir Henry Horne, OAD 617, 11 September 1917.

130 TNA WO 158/188: GHQ to the Five Armies, OAD 646, 2 October 1917.

131 IWM, Horne Papers, Horne to wife, 5, 8 and 22 November 1917.

132 RAI, Rawlins Papers, Colonel S.W.H. Rawlins, A History of the development of the British Artillery in France, 1914-18, p.166; Albert P. Palazzo, 'The British Army's Counter-Battery Staff Office and Control of the Enemy in World War I', p.70.

recognised. In stark contrast, the efficacy of limited operations such as Vimy Ridge, Messines Ridge, Hill 70 and Plumer's three offensives (Menin Road Ridge, Polygon Wood, Broodseinde) – whereby objectives were well within the physical capacity of the infantry to consolidate and repel inevitable enemy counter-attacks prior to preparations for the next offensive step – were duly noted.[133] The year also 'witnessed the turn of the tide' not only because 'those hammer blows were struck which led to the final victory in 1918'[134] but also because optimal operational methods had at last been adopted. Gradually, throughout 1917, the British developed an effective operational technique of launching a series of inter-linked set-piece offensives to break into and then dismantle or 'unlock' the formidable German defensive system. In short, each set-piece attack was dependant on securing observation points which allowed gunner observers to provide the best possible artillery support for the next limited advance.[135]

A number of serious tactical defeats had been inflicted on the German Army during 1917. This was the result of the development and acceptance of sensible and effective 'grand tactics', which had shown the validity of limited objective operations. Horne was at the forefront of this 'learning curve' with adoption of the step-by-step advance, a style of attack reliant on close co-ordination between artillery, infantry, tanks and aircraft in a series of inter-linked set-piece assaults. Nevertheless, the British Army had yet to convert tactical victory into a war-winning campaign. An equally important idea – a series of *simultaneous* offensives along several axis of advance rather than a single strategic thrust – had still to be fully formulated.[136] Unfortunately, this renaissance in British military thought has been overshadowed by the horrific manpower losses of the Somme, Arras and Third Ypres. Further to this, the apparent success of the limited approach has been somewhat overshadowed by Haig's stubborn refusal to cut his losses in October 1917 by halting the controversial latter stages of the Flanders offensive during which 'many thousand valuable lives' were lost in 'rather doubtful victories.'[137]

The lessons of 1917 were for all practical purposes enshrined in British doctrine by early 1918. By this time, Major-General Reginald Stephens (GOC 5th Division) proposed a strategy of 'many limited offensives carried out as quickly as possible one after the other – as fast as the guns can get there.' However, each offensive was 'to

---

133 LHCMA, Montgomery-Massingberd Papers 4, General Sir Henry Rawlinson to GHQ, Fourth Army No. 806 (G), 9 August 1917.

134 LHCMA, Alanbrooke Papers 3/1/85, Field Marshal Lord Alanbrooke, Notes for My Memoirs.

135 See Ian M Brown, 'Not Glamorous, But Effective: The Canadian Corps and the Set-piece Attack, 1917-1918', *Journal of Military History*, Vol. 58, No. 3 (July 1994), pp.421-44, and Paul Harris & Sanders Marble, 'The 'Step-by-Step' Approach: British Military Thought and Operational Method on the Western Front, 1915-1917', *War in History*, Vol. 15, No. 1 (January 2008), pp.17-42.

136 Harris, '1918: Britain's Forgotten Victory', p.74.

137 NLS, Haldane Papers, General Sir Aylmer Haldane, Autobiography, Vol. II, p.421 and Haldane, War Diary, 14 November 1917.

be sternly shut down after the first success' because 'we never lose many on the first day of a successful show, its afterwards [that] the losses come' and the 'first days can be so prepared nowadays that they are bound to succeed.'[138] GHQ observed that 'the development of active operations, whether undertaken by ourselves or the enemy, may normally be expected to take the form of a methodical and progressive battle, beginning with limited objectives and leading up by gradual stages to an attack on deep objectives in chosen portions of the front.' Each operation was one of 'successive steps in a continuous offensive' for carefully selected intermediate objectives that would 'best facilitate the reorganization of the infantry for the next stage of the attack.' Limited final objectives provided 'a good defensive line well within the physical capacity of our infantry and the zone of effective artillery support' yet with 'good observation over the enemy's defences' and suitable positions for the artillery, ready for 'the resumption of the attack at the earliest date possible.' It was emphasised that the offensive should 'be composed of several carefully prepared attacks' and carried out as 'a series of rapid blows, each delivered before the enemy has had time to reorganize after the previous one.'[139]

Large operations of this type were what the Red Army termed 'consecutive operations' or the conduct of successive attacks, each punctuated by brief pauses to rest and refurbish, in pursuit of a larger goal – the destruction of the enemy army. This solved the critical problem of devising successful offensives under modern conditions in which war had transformed into a protracted struggle with decisive victory resulting from a single campaign no longer attainable.[140] This was possible because the operational tempo of 1917-18 had substantially increased when compared with 1915-16 offensives owing to the greater experience of commanders, staff and troops. The greater availability of guns, ammunition and logistical support also contributed to the heightened momentum. During the Hundred Days, the *en masse* employment of tanks combined with the novel predicted artillery bombardment introduced at Cambrai in November 1917, was the tactical basis of a series of offensives that defeated the German Army in 1918. Indeed, First Army's most notable contributions to the final advance, Battle of Drocourt–Quéant Line (2-3 September) and Battle of the Canal du Nord (27 September-1 October), were, in planning, preparations and execution, evocative of Red Army 'consecutive operations' on the Eastern Front during 1943-45.[141]

---

138 LHCMA, Dill Papers I/8, General Sir Reginald Stephens to Field Marshal Sir John Dill, 6 March 1918.

139 LHCMA, Montgomery-Massingberd Papers 92, *SS135, The Training and Employment of Divisions, 1918*, GHQ OB 1635, January 1918.

140 Richard W. Harrison, *The Russian Way of War: Operational Art, 1904-1940* (Lawrence, Kansas: University Press of Kansas, 2001), pp.29, 106-7, 152-68.

141 Robbins, *British Generalship During the Great War*, pp.206-15.

10

Semper Ubique
The Royal Engineers at Arras, 1917

Alexander A. Falbo-Wild

> *Now the Line's but a man with a gun in his hand,*
> *An' Cavalry's only what horses can stand,*
> *When helped by His Majesty's Engineers,*
> *His Majesty's Royal Engineers,*
> *With the rank and pay of a Sapper!*
> Rudyard Kipling[1]

Hidden in Plain View

Easter Monday, 9 April 1917 greeted fraught sentries of German *Sixth Army* with a snow squall and the hellacious din of British *Trommelfeur*.[2] Within 10 minutes the shelling subsided, 'as if it had been switched off.' Scrambling out of dugout entrances to what remained of the parapet, the frontline garrison observed columns of enemy

---

1   Rudyard Kipling, *The Seven Seas* (London: Methuen & Co., 1896), pp.175-78. When first published, this poem featured 'Her Majesty' in reference to Queen Victoria. Recited or sung by sappers during 1914-18, its celebrated author had adjusted it to reflect the reign of King George V (1910-36).
2   Konrad Krafft von Dellmensingen & Friedrichfranz Feeser, *Das Bayernbuch vom Weltkriege: 1914-1918, Band 2* (Stuttgart: Belser, 1930), p.404. *Trommelfeur* was a ubiquitous German expression to describe the Royal Artillery's ability to fire with such dense rapidity that it sounded like a monstrous drum-roll. For a seminal study of its shattering psychological effect, see Scott Stephenson, *The Final Battle: Soldiers of the Western Front and the German Revolution of 1918* (Cambridge: Cambridge University Press, 2009), pp.21-25.

infantry appearing almost atop their defensive positions from Vimy to Fontaine.[3] Machine-guns chattered away prior to being overrun whilst desperate battalion and company commanders, requesting immediate artillery assistance, discharged coloured rockets into the sky to which there was no reply. Already crushed by a week-long preparatory bombardment, dubbed *Leidenswoche* ('Week of Suffering') by the over-wrought *Landsers*, supporting German batteries situated across the Douai Plain were smothered by a further 1.1 million projectiles. A bloody month of relentless reconnaissance sorties by the outclassed but undaunted Royal Flying Corps (RFC) continued to pay off, 80 percent of 533 enemy guns having been identified and engaged by British counter-batteries as of Z-Day.[4] The British and Canadian infantry's ghostly materialisation in no man's land, not to mention the mountains of shells available to the Royal Artillery (RA) and accurate fire mapping, were all courtesy of the illustrious Corps of Royal Engineers (RE).

Zero hour 05:30: 14 assault divisions of the British First and Third armies pressed forward to storm the enemy defences opposite. Their mission was to 'undertake the task of breaking through the enemy front between Givenchy and Quéant.' Once accomplished, 'a breakout of the reserves in the direction of Cambrai and Douai' would follow.[5] One of the *Westheer's* vital central rail networks lay just beyond. Following the breakthrough, a second phase of cavalry exploitation was designed to increase territorial gains as far as possible. This is contrary to the erroneous notion that the Arras offensive was a strictly *limited* diversion for the forthcoming French assault on the Aisne south. By the early afternoon of the 9th, the first two of four successive objective lines (black, blue, brown, and green) were reached. Over the next 48 hours, the vantages of the Vimy and Pont Du Jour ridges were seized. In addition, on reaching the western outskirts of Fampoux, situated astride the northern bank of the Scarpe River, the 9th (Scottish) and 4th divisions achieved the furthest advance (roughly 3 1/2 mi/5.6km) of any side in a Western Front operation since the opening battles of 1914.[6] Again, the RE were responsible for handling signals communications relaying critical information as quickly as possible. In no man's land, sappers industriously fortified the new frontline whilst the infantry provided cover. And, in many instances,

---

3   Jack Sheldon, *The German Army in the Spring Offensives 1917: Arras, Aisne and Champagne* (Barnsley: Pen & Sword, 2015), p.99.

4   Sheldon, p.85; C.G. Wynne, *If Germany Attacks: The Battle of Depth in the West* (Brighton: Tom Donovan unexpurgated edition, 2008), p. 115. For a detailed analysis of German versus British operational methods of air superiority at Arras see, Christopher J.M. Shaw, 'Between Barons and Wolves: British and German Tactical Command in the First Air War, 1914-1918', MA Massey University, 2012. For the most complete overview of the fierce aerial campaign over Artois, participant experience thereof and human cost see, Peter Hart, *Bloody April: Slaughter in the Skies Over Arras, 1917* (London: Weidenfeld & Nicolson, 2005).

5   French GQG Directive 2226, 4 April 1917.

6   A feat which was not bested until the German spring offensives of 1918. See Cyril Falls, *Military Operations: France & Belgium 1917*, Vol. 1 (London: Macmillan, 1940), p.231.

the engineers fought as well. One Territorial RE officer curiously observed, 'They are armed because their work may have to be carried out in the face of any enemy anywhere and everywhere, rather than for purely offensive purposes; though, even so, they are always infantry first and sappers afterwards.'[7]

Unfortunately, the offensive faltered. By 11 April, tactical cohesion was breaking down, the strategic window closed, and the German defence calcified with every wasted hour along the *Wotan* position of the Hindenburg Line. With the French catastrophe on the Aisne three days later, the Arras campaign devolved into a questionable slog prolonged into May. The strategic impasse also led to a horrific casualty rate of 4,000 men per day; the highest rate for any British battle of the war.[8] These harsh realities, combined with the Third Ypres and Cambrai campaigns later in the year, tend to consign Arras to historical footnote status.[9] Whilst understandable to some extent, Arras offers insight into the British Army's operational evolution in modern continental warfare. Nowhere was this truer than for the RE.

Wartime trench journals and magazines are replete with odes, humour and stories about these wizards of warfare. Post-war divisional histories and memoirs also pay tribute.[10] Although the efforts of some corps, formations and units have been the subject of detailed studies, the RE contribution generally tends to hide in plain sight within the subsequent historiography.[11] In the Artois, and in Arras proper, they found

7   Stuart Love, *History of the 520th Field Company, R.E., 1914-1918* (London: War Narratives Publishing Co., 1919), p.5.
8   Jonathan Nichols, *Cheerful Sacrifice: The Battle of Arras 1917* (Barnsley: Pen & Sword, 1995), p.211.
9   See, Jim Smithson, *A Taste of Success: The First Battle of the Scarpe* (Solihull: Helion & Co., 2017), pp. xiv, 210–11; David Stevenson, *With Our Backs to the Wall: Victory and Defeat in 1918* (Cambridge, Massachusetts: Belknap Press, 2011), p.11; Paddy Griffith, 'The Extent of Tactical Reform in the British Army' in Paddy Griffith (ed.), *British Fighting Methods in the Great War* (London: Frank Cass, 1998), p.12; Andy Simpson, 'British Corps Command on the Western Front' in Daniel Todman & Gary Sheffield (eds.), *Command and Control on the Western Front: The British Army's Experience 1914-1918* (Staplehurst: Spellmount, 2004), pp.107-08, 163-64; Jonathan Bailey, 'The First World War and the Birth of Modern Warfare' in Williamson Murray & MacGregor Knox (eds.), *The Dynamics of Military Revolution, 1300-2050* (Cambridge: Cambridge University Press, 2001), p.142.
10   E.G & K.O.D., 'The R.E. (Or More Professional Jealousy)' in T.E. Elias (ed.), *New Year Souvenir of the Welsh Division* (Cardiff: Western Mail, 1917), p.10; H.J.C. Piers, 'The Sapper', *The B.E.F. Times*, January 1918; J. Stewart & John Buchan, *The Fifteenth (Scottish) Division, 1914-1919* (London: William Blackwood & Sons, 1926), pp.16, 81; A.H. Hussey & D.S. Inam, *The Fifth Division in the Great War* (London: Nisbet & Co., 1921), pp.27, 252-53; Everard Wyrall, *The History of the Fiftieth Division, 1914-1919* (London: Percy Lund, Humphries & Co., 1939), pp.224–25.
11   Alexander Barrie, *War Underground: The Tunnellers of the Great War* (New York: Ballantine Books, 1961); Ian M. Brown, *British Logistics on the Western Front: 1914-1919* (Westport, Connecticut: Praeger, 1998); Brian N. Hall, *Communications and British Operations on the Western Front, 1914-1918* (Cambridge: Cambridge University Press, 2017); Donald

a sector of the Western Front well suited to their specialties. The 1917 spring offensive there offers the ability to survey the extent of RE involvement in sustaining a BEF campaign. It also illustrates the process of adaptation on the battlefield at an inflection point when the BEF mastered the breakthrough but not the breakout. The difficulties encountered when traversing the devastated ground at Passchendaele later that year were foreshadowed at Arras with the RE at the forefront of the operational and tactical dilemma.

From the concealment of whole divisions in electrically lit medieval labyrinths prior to the assault, to the rapid construction of shell hole strongpoints consolidating captured terrain, the RE were ubiquitous. Most importantly, especially for the BEF, 1917 was a year of sheer endurance and craft – the peak of the siege warfare phase on the Western Front. Despite occupying what Jim Smithson aptly describes as a 'Cinderella like position in the historiography of the First World War', Arras epitomises the grim intensity of 1914-18 battles in France and Flanders and the treacherous pendulum between attack and defence.[12] As a microcosm of the Western Front's static experience, it merits closer study. The works of Peter Doyle, Nigel Cave, Simon Jones, et. al. have notably addressed this omission. To their great credit, British official historian Cyril Falls and Jonathan Nichols devote some attention to military engineering at Arras. Much remains to be written however.[13] It is argued here that a deciding factor for success on 9 April 1917 was RE utilisation of Artois geography to offset the absence of strategic surprise, with BEF intentions revealed in advance by the preparatory bombardment and appalling operational security.[14]

Limited space warrants a focus on British Third Army area as specific studies of the First Army's Canadian Corps at Vimy Ridge abound.[15] It is hoped this chapter serves as a primer for further study of RE performance during 1914-18. To tell a tale of unsung heroes on a forgotten front – to make dubious use of those weary military

Richter, *Chemical Soldiers: British Gas Warfare in World War I* (Lawrence, Kansas: University Press of Kansas, 1992). See also Rob Thompson's seminal 'Mud, Blood, and Wood: BEF Operational and Combat Logistico-Engineering during the Battle of Third Ypres, 1917' in Peter Doyle & Matthew R. Bennett, *Fields of Battle: Terrain in Military History* (New York: Springer Science & Business Media, 2002).

12 Smithson, *A Taste of Success*, p. xiv.

13 Nigel Cave & Phillip Robinson, *The Underground War: Vimy Ridge to Arras* (Barnsley: Pen & Sword Military, 2011).

14 Jonathan Nichols, Foreword in Smithson, *A Taste of Success*, p. xvii; Sheldon, *The German Army in the Spring Offensives 1917*, pp.4-5. Four prisoners from 2nd Canadian Division, captured during a trench raid on *79th Reserve Division*, revealed astonishing levels of information about the forthcoming Arras offensive thereby confirming and refining German anticipations.

15 Bill Rawling, 'The Sappers of Vimy: Specialized Support for the Assault of 9 April 1917' in Geoffrey Hayes, Andrew Iraocci & Mike Bechthold (eds.), *Vimy Ridge: A Canadian Reassessment* (Ontario: Wilfred Laurier University Press, 2007); M.S. Rosenbaum, 'Geological Influence on Tunnelling Under the Western Front at Vimy Ridge', *Proceedings of the Geologist's Association* 100, No. 1 (1989).

history clichés – is less the point than to humbly essay how a set-piece offensive was exhaustively prepared and executed through the historically *vast* scope of British military engineering.[16]

Divisions of Labour: RE Organisation in Early 1917

The RE in 1917 consisted of three layers of service. The first was comprised of engineers employed at home or in the major theatre garrisons. Their array of vital infrastructure and support activities included large-scale construction missions such as forts, ports, and railyards alongside electrical, signal, and water management for military purposes.[17] They also focused on research and development projects including continuous wave (CW) wireless, trench water pumps, poison gases, grenades, anti-gas respirators and flame-throwers at RE HQ in Chatham. The RE were helmed in 1917 by Director of Fortifications and Works, Major-General Sir Kenneth Scott-Moncrieff who commissioned in the corps in 1873. Having held combat commands in Peking and Waziristan, he ultimately became a major reformer and ushered in doctrinal and organisational innovations.[18]

The next layer was the operational theatre where sappers served at army and corps level. This was the domain of the Army Troop and Siege companies which frequently required labour outsourced to available units and personnel. Much of this infrastructure work was focused on the construction of depots, bridges, railways, roads, and aerodromes. However, it also featured operational work such as cartography, tunnelling, camouflage, and forward artillery observation. It was at this level that critical Light Railway and Army Tramway companies were located, trafficking troops, provisions, and ammunition from railheads to the trenches. Their realm bridged the chasm between the port cranes of Boulogne to forward saps opposite Bapaume. Each army and corps was staffed with a Chief Royal Engineer (CRE) who was responsible for all engineering matters and coordination of operational activities and stores supply.

The final layer was the combat support element of sappers in the firing line with parent divisions or operational attachment as independent units. A divisional CRE was tasked with coordinating their actions and advising the division GOC. Their

16   For a brief discussion on Arras as a subject in Great War historiography, see Gary Sheffield, 'Vimy Ridge and the Battle of Arras: A British Perspective' in Hayes, Iraocci & Bechtold (eds.), *Vimy Ridge*; David Reynolds, *The Long Shadow: The Great War and the Twentieth Century* (London: Simon & Schuster UK, 2013), p.111.

17   For an exhaustive treatment of the vital non-RE logistical services which utilised RE built infrastructure to supply the British Army during the war see, Clem Maginniss, *An Unappreciated Field of Endeavour: Logistics and the British Expeditionary Force on the Western Front 1914-1918* (Warwick: Helion & Co., 2018).

18   The principle commander of the RE was originally titled 'Chief Royal Engineer' by Royal Warrant in 1716 with the post dating back to mercenary engineers employed since the time of William the Conqueror.

high standard was maintained throughout the war due to the requirement of passing a tradesman test prior to earning the rank of sapper. This both identified the essential intellectual qualities required for engineer work and appropriate assignment of the candidate based on individual skills. When the war settled down into trench stale-mate, the Western Front transformed into a kind of mega-city locked in perpetual combat, and the RE adjusted to siege warfare conditions with a growth of units and combat specialities. It is important to note that expansion in quantity did not corre-spond with a decrease in quality.

Pre-war discussions abounded in the *Royal Engineers Journal* and *Army Review* on the lessons of the various conflicts from 1898-1913. As Colonel S.A.E. Hickson DSO RE observed in a 1906 article, 'the immense size of modern armies, and the immense range of modern arms – as has now so often been proved – makes the fronts that the defender can protect, and the distances over which the assailants must march, so great that time is given to enable the defence to make the most formidable works and obstacles.'[19] His argument, to be explored further, was to call attention to the emerging necessity of sappers accompanying infantry to breach these lethal bastions. But the efficacy of the combined pioneer/sapper effort in providing infrastructure and mobility to British formations in India was perhaps the most persuasive argument as it had actually been put into practice. Many continental forces, including the French and German armies in comparison, employed pioneer units as the primary combat engineering element within a fighting division.[20]

Signal and survey services expanded their responsibilities and personnel whilst Tunnelling and Special (chemical) companies and a Camouflage Park were raised to greatly augment the BEF's operational surprise capability.[21] By spring 1917, BEF RE units increased by 23 percent from the previous year.[22] This expansion occurred across the entire establishment. But the core combat engineering element in the British Army lay within the division, the structure of which remained largely unchanged since the Haldane Reforms of 1906. Its component engineering units are described as 'the most mobile branch of the RE' where they 'go forward right up to the enemy's lines and beyond'[23]

In early 1917, divisional RE assets consisted of one signal company (289 men), three field companies (651 men), and one pioneer infantry battalion (800 men), roughly 1,740 men per division. Therefore, roughly 31,320 sappers and pioneers provided support for

19   S.A.E. Hickson, 'The Role of Engineers on the Field of Battle', *The Royal Engineers Journal*, III, No. 4 (April 1906), p.39.
20   Erich Schnee, 'The German Pionier: Case Study of the Combat Engineer's Deployment During Sustained Ground Combat', Fort Leavenworth, Kansas, US Army Command & Staff College, 2018, p.6.
21   G.H. Addison, *The Work of the Royal Engineers in the European War, 1914-1918: Miscellaneous* (Chatham: Institution of the Royal Engineers, 1927), pp.107, 109.
22   Addison, pp.61-71. Extrapolated from available annual growth figures.
23   Love, *History of the 520th Field Company*, p.5.

the 18 assault and reserve divisions at Arras. The five participant Dominion divisions increased this number. Namely, the Royal Canadian Engineers (RCE) of the four divisions of the Canadian Expeditionary Force (CEF) who were assigned to capture Vimy Ridge in the north and the Royal Australian Engineers (RAE) of 4th Australian Division operating in Fifth Army sector who were tasked with securing Bullecourt in the extreme south.[24] Organised along nearly identical lines to British divisions, there were only minor differences. A CEF division's complement numbered approximately 2,500 sappers and pioneers.[25] Divisional pioneer battalions also contained 1,000 men and 4th Canadian Division at this time received *two* pioneer battalions. The 4th Australian Division had 1,536 sappers and pioneers.[26] This Dominion complement amounted to a 23-division engineering spearhead for the Arras offensive, some 43,856 out of roughly 276,000 men or approximately 16 percent of the total assault formation manpower strength.[27]

Finally, it is important to consider the operational picture with future reference to geography and responsible RE units. The new Allied strategy for spring 1917, along with the German strategic withdrawal (Operation *Alberich*), meant an increase from the original 10 attacking divisions to 18 and a shift in focus northward away from Bapaume toward Arras. Offensive responsibilities thus gravitated from Fifth Army to Third Army. First Army was assigned a flank guard task by seizure of Vimy Ridge after Field Marshal Sir Douglas Haig persuaded his French counterpart, General Robert Nivelle that it should be an objective. The primary architect for the RE's contribution to the Arras offensive was Major-General Edward R. Kenyon, Third Army's CRE. As a pre-war theorist, historian and 20th (Light) Division's first CRE, he was experienced, capable and innovative with a clear focus across the tactical and strategic spectrum.[28]

To better understand the potential impact of this force – and as a primer for those less familiar with the RE – it is useful to consider the types of frontline RE units in early 1917 and how the year marked a critical moment in their development.

---

24   The RCE and RAE were established in 1902–03 when Canada and Australia's military engineering branches were permanently in the Imperial Defence scheme. This included the Royal New Zealand Engineers (RNZE).

25   Rawling, 'The Sappers of Vimy',126.

26   Anon., *History of the 11th Field Company Australian Engineers* (London: War Narratives Publishing Co., 1919), p.75.

27   The figure is based on the average British and Dominion division strength (approximately 12,000 men) in 1917.

28   Kenyon was later struck in the arm whilst observing bridging over the Scarpe on 2 May 1917. See also H.L. Pritchard, (ed.), *History of the Corps of Royal Engineers*, Vol. 5 (Chatham: Institution of the Royal Engineers, 1952), p.300; V.E. Inglefield, *The History of the Twentieth (Light) Division* (London: Nisbet & Co., 1921), p.4; E.R. Kenyon, *Notes on Land Fortification and Coast Fortification* (Chatham: W & J Mackay & Co., 1894); E.R. Kenyon, 'Gibraltar Under Moor, Spaniard, and Briton', *Royal Engineers Journal* XIII, No. 1 (June 1911).

Combat Engineering and Pioneering

At the centre of all RE efforts was the Field Company. Their remit was to provide shelter for a division and facilitate its mobility and accommodation during operations. Field companies were armed construction and demolition specialists. The War Office recognised their utility when they expanded the division's initial Field Company allotment from two to three in February 1915. By late 1916, there were roughly 56 BEF divisions in France and Flanders with approximately 168 field companies. With the paper strength of 217 all ranks, field companies were comprised of a mixture of skilled tradesmen, such as carpenters, masons,

Major-General E.R. Kenyon.

welders, smiths and draughtsmen. Issued with ordinary service rifles, they were able to serve as infantry in a crisis or as per mission requirements. The latter normally involved explosives and technical intelligence gathering during trench raids. However, following the rather reckless allocation of sappers to infantry assault waves during the Somme offensive, divisional commanders husbanded their Field Company assets during major offensives throughout 1917. This tactical revision also appeared in *SS 135: Instructions for Divisions in Combat*, which will be addressed further on.[29]

Supplying labour for less skilled but critical work in the frontline was a perennial problem, especially given the dim view the infantry took towards digging trenches under sapper supervision. According to Spencer Jones, the need for reform was clear following the Second Anglo-Boer War where 'poor equipment, limited training, and overreliance on the Royal Engineers had created a distinctly negative attitude toward the effort required to entrench properly.'[30]

---

29   *SS 135: Instructions for the Training of Divisions for Offensive Action* (London: HMSO, 1916), p.33.

30   Spencer Jones, *From Boer War to World War: Tactical Reform of the British Army, 1902–1914* (Norman, Oklahoma: University of Oklahoma Press, 2012), pp.106-07.

RE Field Company sapper poses inside an Arras Cathedral portico, spring 1917. As with similarly equipped comrades, his P08 web equipment including bayonet, prepared him for full contact with the enemy. (Author)

The answer lay in what in modern parlance is known as a 'force multiplier'; infantry battalions converted to pioneers for what K.W. Mitchinson dubbed 'organised and intelligent labour.'[31] Although technically not part of the Corps of Royal Engineers, such units directly supported its activities, employed RE plans and designs, and were subordinate to divisional CREs. Their mission was primarily to fight as infantry whilst providing semi-skilled labour for construction and maintenance of roads and entrenchments.[32] This vital addition to engineering manpower freed Field Company sappers for more specialised tasks such as construction of camouflaged observation posts and concrete pillboxes. As one Indian Army major observed, 'sappers and pioneers working in combination provide very effectively for all field work.'[33]

The lack of prestige in field work construction raises the question of how pioneer battalions were chosen and the corresponding effects on morale. Little scholarship has emerged since Mitchinson's work.[34] However, the 23rd Division's post-war history

31   K.W. Mitchinson, *Pioneer Battalions in the Great War: Organized and Intelligent Labour* (Barnsley: Pen & Sword, 1989), p. xi.
32   This included bridging by 1918. AEF pioneer infantry battalions served in a nearly identical capacity when they arrived on the Western Front with minor differences in formation attachment or allocation.
33   H.R. Stockley, 'The Technical Troops of an Indian Division', *The Army Review* 3, No. 1 (July 1912).
34   William Westerman, 'The Handy Man of the Division: Assessing the Effectiveness of the Pioneer Battalion Concept in the First Australian Imperial Force', *British Journal of*

RE 1916-17 Christmas card designed by W. Heath Robinson. (Author)

observed that a battalion census was taken for tradesmen's skills the one with the highest proportion for the task. The 17th and 20th divisions selected Durham Light Infantry battalions predominantly composed of miners.[35] In other cases, selection was arbitrary or done at the regimental depot prior to a battalion's departure for France. Conversely, selection could also be a source of *esprit de corps*. As 37th Division's first commander Major-General Lord Edward Gleichen recounted, 'the 6th Bedfords were the last to arrive, [and] told off as the Pioneer Battalion; but they didn't want to be pioneers and the [9th] North Staffords did, so I speedily effected [sic] the alteration – and have never regretted it, for two better battalions in their respective roles I could never expect to have.'[36]

Signalling

It could be argued that the solution to the riddle of the deadlocked Western Front lay in mastery of communications. Reliable relay of information, orders and updates – command and control (C2) – is an essential element to military success since before Herodotus. It found renewed importance in an advanced industrialised Europe where the qualitative increase in firepower and scale of armies dispersed soldiers per square metre from the eighteenth century's 1:10 to approximately 1:250 by the time of the Arras offensive.[37] To put battalion commanders in touch with superiors and neighbouring units was difficult enough. To provide divisional and corps commanders with a clear picture of an unfolding assault – much less the ability to meaningfully affect events in time – was a Herculean task verging at times on the Sisyphic. For the British Army of 1917, the mission of maintaining communications infrastructure fell to the Royal Engineers Signal Service (RESS).

The most rudimentary unit of the service was the Signal Company which served at army, corps and division levels with smaller sections attached to brigades and battalions. A Signal Company would often take the numerical designation of its parent formation (e.g. 30th Signal Company was attached to 30th Division). Manpower was recruited from the skilled ranks and offices of the civilian telecommunications industry, or those with an aptitude for signal/electronic work as defined by the RE tradesman test. This high standard was maintained despite the RESS's most significant expansion and reorganisation of the war taking place in 1917.

Myriad signalling demands, however, still outstripped the number of signallers provided. This occurred even though the average 1917 two-division per corps RESS

Military History 3, No. 2 (2017).
35   H.R. Sandilands, *The Twenty-Third Division, 1914-1919* (London: William Blackwood & Sons, 1925), p.13; A.H. Atteridge, *The History of the 17th (Northern) Division* (Glasgow: Robert MaClehose & Co., 1929), pp. 24-25 Inglefield, *The History of the Twentieth (Light) Division*, p.3.
36   *The Golden Horseshoe: The Journal of the 37th Division BEF* (London: Cassell, 1919), p.14.
37   Martin van Creveld, *Technology and War: From 2000 B.C. to the Present* (New York: The Free Press, 1989), p.173.

establishment had expanded by approximately 2,000 sappers since 1914.[38] As such, the situation required men to be trained in signalling whilst RESS personnel maintained the core strength of expertise within their Signal Company organisation. This education took place either at the RE Signal School in Chatham or various schools operating behind the front. Thus one might encounter along a snowy bit of communications trench near Neuville St Vaast in March 1917, a signaller of 15th Royal Warwickshire Regiment or 76th Siege Battery, sporting the standard issue white over blue signaller's brassard, labouring away with a 5th Signal Company linesman.[39]

Chemical Warfare

The rather vague sounding RE Special Brigade was the chemical warfare component of the BEF. Created in 1915, it originally consisted of four numbered companies of 10 sections each. Special Brigade organisation by 1917 evolved into its final configuration with five numbered battalions (1-5) comprised of five alphabetical companies each (A-Q). The 5th Battalion numbered sections 1-4 with its fifth section, lettered Z, specialising in trench mortar deployment. A Special Brigade battalion was led by a captain.[40] These units colloquially remained 'Special Company' assets and were one of the BEF's most closely guarded secrets. By 1917, Special Brigade operations became far more methodical and potent since its rather inauspicious debut at Loos in 1915.

Reasons for this development were accurately assessed by Major Victor Lefebure, British chemical warfare liaison with the French Army, as the crude yet effective Livens Projector and British industry's capacity for lavish gas shell production became available. In the case of the former, the preferred tactic of releasing gas clouds could be achieved with a maximum range of 1,500 metres, thus far exceeding static cylinder releases. With regard to the latter, selective employment of lachrymatory shells during the Somme proved relatively effective. For the Arras offensive, British manufacturers were able to manufacture large quantities of munitions containing pulmonary agents. Combined, these factors enabled the Special Brigade to discharge lethal gas with greater depth and concentration than ever before.[41] Batteries of 6-inch Newton and 3-inch Stokes mortars were also supplied with chemical rounds delivered for concentration fire against deeper targets.

Special companies also dispensed smoke and used flame projectors. The latter technology was cumbersome and difficult to move. The immense and elaborate Livens Large Gallery projectors employed on the Somme were locally successful but their overall effect was limited due to mobility issues. However, the Livens Projector (gas)

---

38   R.E. Priestley, *The Signal Service in the European War of 1914 to 1918 (France)* (Chatham: W. & J. Mackay & Co., 1921), pp.352–53. See also tables 1 and 5 in Appendix IV.

39   In support of the Vimy assault, the 76th Siege Battery RGA was attached to British 5th Division in Canadian Corps area.

40   Richter, *Chemical Soldiers*, p.236.

41   Victor Lefebure, *The Riddle of the Rhine: Chemical Strategy in Peace and War* (London: W. Collins Sons & Co., 1921), pp.57-58.

was simple to operate, cheap to construct and capable of firing smoke and flammable oil rounds. Flamethrower devices were not prominent amongst the BEF's varied arsenal. Smoke, in contrast, was ever present in British offensives and increasingly vital to success. Given the importance of the Arras offensive, more than half of the Special Brigade's battalions were concentrated, under the aegis of a Third Army Special Company headquarters, in Artois by early 1917.[42]

Tunnelling

Raised in February 1915 in response to nascent German mining operations, RE Tunnelling companies were not organic to divisions, nor any other command for that matter. Like their Special Brigade contemporaries, their allocation to fighting formations was based on operational necessity. This included, in earnest, BEF acquisition of the Arras frontage in March-April 1916. Around that time, Tunnelling Company activity centred on counter-mining and demolition work during the intense subterranean combat at Vimy Ridge. Yet, their most valuable effort arguably lay in their ability to construct underground systems for discretely ferrying supplies by foot or rail to reduce casualties and wastage resulting from enemy artillery fire. By January 1917, 32 British and Dominion Tunnelling companies had been organised.. An attempt to raise the Tunnelling Company establishment from 321 men to 548 was cancelled by 1917, with civilian mining firms and the Board of Trade warning of the unsustainable drain on home front manpower. Of the 32 Tunnelling companies operating within the BEF, eight were assigned to expand the existing cave network directly beneath, and extending east of, Arras.[43] These included the 172nd, 176th, 179th, 181st, 184th, 185th, 255th, 256th, and New Zealand Tunnelling companies. Many were veterans of the Somme, and some were thoroughly experienced with the fierce underground war which had raged around Artois since March 1916.[44]

Mapping and Forward Artillery Observation

The 20th century's military landscape was almost entirely altered by the power of artillery. Desolation brought dispersion. The result was a turn from line-of-sight target acquisition to indirect fire (firing blindly from a map grid) which emerged just before the war. This included pulverising enemy earthworks as well as locating and silencing his own artillery. These techniques were qualitatively enhanced by active service demands – particularly with regard to counter-battery skills. To this end, the

42   Falls, *Military Operations 1917,* Vol. I, p.310; TNA WO 95/95/401/1: HQ Special Companies RE War Diary, March 1917.
43   Addison, *The Work of the Royal Engineers*, pp.15, 61.
44   Paul Reed, *Walking Arras: A Guide to the 1917 Arras Battlefields* (Barnsley: Pen & Sword, 2007), pp.13-17 and, Smithson, *A Taste of Success*, pp.30-35; Alan H. Maude, (ed.), *The History of the 47th (London) Division, 1914-1919* (London: Amalgamated Press,1922), Chapter 5 and Everard Wyrall, *The History of the Second Division, 1914-1918*, Vol. 1 (London: Thomas Nelson & Sons, 1921), pp.244-64.

RE coordinated direct support through Field Survey companies. Despite assignment to army level command, they operated in shell holes and outposts opposite enemy lines whilst gathering intelligence for topographic map surveys.

The duties executed by a Field Survey Company (FSC) contingent are complex and predate the war. Both the RA and RE were responsible for their capabilities. However, by spring 1916 FSC were amalgamated into four single RE controlled companies of 80 men, each allotted to the four field armies, with 5th Field Survey Company raised following the creation of the Fifth Army later that year. Each company establishment consisted of Topographical, Map, Observation (colloquially 'flash-spotting') and Sound Ranging sections directed by a headquarters section.[45]

Observation and sound-ranging sections utilised techniques and technology that some regarded as esoteric if not occult. Yet, their methods can be summarised as corroborating visual and aural inputs (telescope and microphone placement) from German artillery activity into triangulated intelligence on map firing grids. Data was duly adjusted for weather and geographic variables. This allowed for silent registration of RA batteries thus enabling tactical surprise. For their part,1st, 3rd, and 5th Field Survey companies observed and charted the ground before Arras.

Forward Rail Transportation

Once delivered to French ports, the bulk of BEF manpower and materiel was transported by broad gauge railways to army areas from where the journey continued to divisional railheads. This duty was the responsibility of the RE Railway Operating Division (ROD) employing both British and French engines and rolling stock. However, as a concomitant of British unpreparedness for total war, the northern French rail network all but collapsed from exponential use *just* as artillery production finally deluged BEF batteries with ammunition. Illustrating the scale of the dilemma, average weekly ammunition consumption during the Somme rose from mere 82,000 to roughly 575,000 rounds during six months campaigning.[46] Arras only promised an increase in munitions traffic. A supply chain catastrophe was largely averted due to the appointment of Major-General Eric Geddes, who comprehensively restructured the entire BEF transport system as Director General of Transport.

The most important result of Geddes' reforms was the expansion and centralisation of tactical supply routes by Light Railway companies and the raising of nine new Army Tramway companies during January-March 1917. Both operated along narrow gauge

45   Addison, *The Work of the Royal Engineers* pp.17-18; John R. Innes, *Flash Spotters and Sound Rangers: How They Lived, Worked, and Fought in the Great War* (London: Allen Unwin Brothers, 1935), pp.51-53. See April 1917 war establishment figures in TNA WO 402/388: M.N. MacLeod, 'History of the Fourth Field Survey Battalion, Royal Engineers', June 1919.

46   War Office, *Statistics of the Military Effort of the British Empire during the Great War, 1914–1920* (London: HMSO, 1922), pp.408-09. See also Figure 4.7 in Brown, *British Logistics on the Western Front*, p.121.

Light Tramway Company operating near Arras, spring 1917. (US National Archives & Records Administration)

lines to transport men, shells, and stores to the front.[47] Light railway lines shunted shipments from divisional railheads to brigade dumps within enemy artillery range whilst Army tramways, largely improvised by Field Company sappers before the reforms, operated from brigade to battalion in forward zones. Narrow gauge railways critically lessened reliance on roads which required constant maintenance with large quantities of shingle, flint, and gravel thus squandering precious ROD cargo space. Moreover, Army Tramway Company, operating quieter petrol- driven and hand-powered engines, could transport rolling stock (including gas cylinders) right up to the trenches.

However, until autumn 1916 the entire transport system remained dangerously ad hoc.[48] Tramways companies, for example, were greatly hindered by a lack of coordination by divisional and corps CREs due to constant relocation of these units along the front. Divisions typically laid narrow gauge track systems that were then disregarded by incoming divisions, which laid out their own schemes. By March 1917, Geddes placed both light railway and army tramway companies under army level authority. Even so, divisional shipments still tended to be handled by corps CREs, albeit more efficiently.[49]

47   Addison, *The Work of the Royal Engineers*, p.201.
48   Addison, p.201; Brown, *British Logistics on the Western Front*, pp.125–27.
49   Addison, *The Work of the Royal Engineers*, pp.201–02; Brown, *British Logistics on the Western Front*, pp.145-46.

'A Unique Accommodation': Arras from the Engineering Perspective

Once Nivelle extended BEF offensive objectives to include Vimy Ridge, and the Germans completed Operation *Alberich*, the entire BEF offensive axis shifted northward away from the Somme front. The three corps, XVII, VI, VII, of General Sir Edmund Allenby's Third Army would spearhead the assault.[50] Corps planning for the Arras offensive can be distilled into four interdependent engineering factors – topographical features, geological suitability, construction resources and weather patterns.[51]

Topography considered overland activity – observation points, concealment and the flow, velocity and direction of lines of communication. It was also critical for artillery observation, fieldwork construction, and road building. Surveys for geological suitability involved assessing soil conditions for underground concealment and mining operations. This included pioneer and field company activity when consolidating captured positions. Construction resources referred to local acquisition of lumber, stone and freshwater to maintain operational tempo in both the preparatory and execution phases. Finally, weather and climate patterns could be all-deciding factors for the best-laid plans. The contrast between the subsequent Messines Ridge and Third Ypres offensives, for example, dramatically illustrate this point. Both were launched in West Flanders over ground just above sea level. However, prevailing temperatures and English Channel jet streams resulted in high-pressure weather for optimal visibility and terrain stability for Messines in early June. But by early autumn, the Third Ypres offensive was adversely affected by torrential downpours despite BEF meteorologist expectations of average weather.

For the 1917 Arras battlefield, overland topography was situated on the eastern Artois plateau averaging 348ft/106m above sea level with two layers of chalk soil.[52] The frontline began in the north with the most impressive vertical feature south of the Channel coast at Vimy Ridge which rested upon the Marqueffles fold and fault lines situated just south of Givenchy along the Souchez River. Cresting at 482ft/147m above sea level, French pre-war surveys (subsequently reconfirmed by RE surveys) determined displacement at 131ft/40m folding and 59ft/18m faulting.[53] As such, the southward escarpment across Thélus and Neuville St Vaast was gentler than a

---

50   Falls, *Military Operations 1917*, Vol. 1, pp.171-72.

51   Peter Doyle & Matthew R. Bennett, 'Military Geography: Terrain Evaluation and the British Western Front 1914-1918', *The Geographical Journal* 163, No. 1 (March 1997), pp.1, 3. This study, whilst thoroughly recommended for understanding the importance of terrain in war, still largely omits Arras (apart from a brief mention of Vimy) in favour of Somme and Flanders operations. The authors' methodology, however, proved useful when researching this chapter.

52   Edwin M. Bridges, *World Geomorphology* (Cambridge: Cambridge University Press, 1990), p.209.

53   C.E. Tilley, *Geological Work on the Western Front* (Chatham: W & J Mackay & Co., 1922), p.28.

sheer drop into the trough of the Scarpe River which flows west to east and derives its name from the tectonic feature. The escarpment to the north, however, sharply inclined. The Scarpe, sourcing from the groundswell about Tincques, flows for 93 kilometers in a deep and wide channel before veering north to the Scheldt near the Franco-Belgian border about Tournai. Along its winding course east of Arras are marshes and ponds and, in the vicinity of metropolitan areas, it is funnelled into man-made canals. This assisted RE waterway transport operations as will be seen following Z-Day. The Scarpe's lateral direction also reduced the necessity for bridging missions. Nevertheless, Third Army held two Army Troop bridging units in reserve as a contingency.[54]

The front continued to the Arras central sector, which is situated astride the southern bank of the Scarpe at 197ft/60m. above sea level. From there the ground is punctuated by a series of notable ridges and knolls (known to the British as Orange Hill, Telegraph Hill, Infantry Hill, Observation Ridge, Greenland Hill) including the most important objective of the forthcoming offensive's breakthrough phase, the Pont du Jour Ridge. Whilst less visually dramatic than Vimy, the village of Monchy-le-Preux, perched on the less discernible height, overlooked Arras from the west and the Douai plain from the east. As Jonathan Nichols observed, 'this great whale-backed ridge was destined to become the most powerful German fortress on the Western Front.'[55] Otherwise, the terrain gently descends back to 394ft/120m towards Bullecourt and is veined with two brooks, the Cojeul and Sensée. But it was the city of Arras itself which the official historian described as 'the chief feature' of the battlefield and what an RE official history called 'a unique accommodation.'[56]

On the bright, brisk morning of 17 March 1917, Sergeant Albert Simpkin and two DRs from his section motored through the ancient Baudimont Gate into the *Pas-de-Calais du Nord's* historic capitol with orders from the 37th Signal Company CO to memorise street layouts so they could navigate it 'blindfolded'.[57] In a few weeks' time, 37th Division, to which Simpkin belonged, would be bussed to the city in readiness to leapfrog the 12th (Eastern) Division onto the Pont du Jour Ridge. After parking their single-cylinder Triumphs, the trio scouted deserted streets 'blocked with fallen masonry' where 'only the main thoroughfares have been kept clear of debris.'[58] But what this 'city of the dead' hid was a hive of military activity below. Hurrying across the zeroed-in *Grand' Place*, Simpkin observed giant craters resulting from German siege howitzer bombardments buckling portions of the ancient quarry and tunnel

---

54   Pritchard, *History of the Corps of Royal Engineers*, Vol. 5, pp.299-300.
55   Nichols, *Cheerful Sacrifice*, 20.
56   Falls, *Military Operations 1917*, Vol. 1, p.175; Pritchard, *History of the Corps of Royal Engineers*, Vol. 5, p.292.
57   David Venner (ed.), *Despatch Rider on the Western Front 1915–18: The Diary of Sergeant Albert Simpkin MM* (Barnsley: Pen & Sword Military, 2015), p.89.
58   Venner, p.90.

system. The entrances to *Les Boves*, as they were known locally, lay beneath.[59] 'Dating from olden times', Simpkin subsequently reflected in his diary, 'they were made to protect the people from the cannon of the invader. History repeats itself. Few towns have a history exciting as that of Arras. From the time of the Romans, hardly a generation has passed without the town being besieged.'[60] Indeed, Arras experienced nine sieges since serving as Roman garrison town christened *Nemetacum* (Sacred Grove) in the fourth century.

Whilst tenth century Arras boomed from the international wool and tapestry trade, city planners and engineers burrowed beneath its streets to create a footbound subway system to facilitate traffic, maintain sewers, store merchant goods and protect against invaders. This latter use gained prominence when France sought to retake Arras and environs from Spanish Hapsburg possession in 1640. Cardinal Richelieu's forces besieged the citadel for 88 summer days until its Irish mercenary commander finally capitulated.[61] When the Germans arrived in 1914, their lack of similar success was substituted by an artillery siege. And like the British they took advantage of the available cave systems on their side of the line for concealment. As the Third Army CRE historical report observed, the entrances to *Les Boves* were located all over the city's cellars, alleyways and municipal structures. In addition to Arras's underworld, there were two capacious quarries situated in the eastern suburbs of St Sauver and Ronville. Excavated for chalk in the seventeenth century, the earliest underground passage or *souterrain* was established in 1602. [62]

The primary Arras tunnel arteries were quickly decluttered with only minor improvements required. However, the Ronville–St Sauver systems required more maintenance. Floor levels could be extremely uneven. Third Army noted that 'the levelling that was done probably increased their capacity by 20 percent in the case of the good caves by as much as 100 percent in the worst'[63] Subterranean traffic pace, the laying of tram lines for light rolling stock, and the ability to place wounded on flat surfaces were all considerations. Work to connect *Les Boves* to the *souterrains* and the city's Crichon sewer commenced on 10 October 1916, spearheaded by the 181st and New Zealand tunnelling companies, the latter unit, commanded by Major Jack Durgan, is perhaps the most renowned aspect of the Arras offensive apart from the Canadians Corps

---

59 The phrase is likely Gaulish for cellar, as its modern French equivalent is simply *les caves*. Though Gaulish largely perished by the sixth century, evidence suggests its use in provincial areas of France into the tenth century.

60 Venner, *Despatch Rider on the Western Front 1915–18*, p.90.

61 Owen Roe O'Neil returned to Ireland the following year to lead an attempt to restore Catholicism to Ulster.

62 TNA WO 95/383/3: 'Preparation and Use of the Caves', Third Army CRE War Diary, April 1917; Tilley, *Geological Work on the Western Front*, p.44.

63 TNA WO 95/383/3: 'CRE, Preparation and Use of the Caves', Third Army CRE War Diary, April 1917.

Entryway No. 3 to the St Sauver *souterrain*. (Brumwell, *The History of the Twelfth (Eastern) Division in the Great War, 1914-1918*)

at Vimy Ridge.[64] On consultation with his senior NCO, Durgan determined that his miners, having been fiercely engaged in the Vimy Ridge area weeks before, required reinforcements. To that end, the 35th Division lent an infantry battalion (17th West Yorkshires) for the job as its divisional sappers and pioneers laboured on roads, Nissen hut assembly and entrenchments. To identify qualified candidates, men with pre-war mining occupations were sought with double rations being offered in compensation. Their progress was remarkable. The New Zealand Tunnelling Company alone managed a BEF mining record of 1,742ft/531m in the first week of November 1916, doubling their weekly averages from the previous year.[65] By early 1917, the immediate Arras system work, Ronville tunnels inclusive, incorporated a field hospital, phone exchanges and tramway system. Tramways were laid in small gauge or monorail with much of the foremost line utilising wood track and trucks fitted with rubber wheels for sound suppression. By the first week of January, the 184th Tunnelling Company had also finished linking the St Sauver *souterrains* to the Ronville system.

64   This is also partly due to the fact that one of the surviving quarries, the Wellington Cave, was built and christened by the RNZE.
65   TNA WO 95/407/1: New Zealand Tunnelling Company War Diary, November 1916; Nichols, *Cheerful Sacrifice*, pp.28-29.

The 35th Division, since deployment to the Arras sector in August 1916, also made significant improvements prior to the pre-offensive work programme taking over. Labouring amidst frequent *Minenwerfer* bombardments, the trenches radiating from the Arras suburb of St Nicholas along the Baillieu–Douai Road were 'not only cleaned, revetted, and fully duck-boarded, but, by making use of the waterpower of the Scarpe, battalion headquarters, etc., were eventually lit by electric light.'[66] The divisional historian went on to observe that 'the soil of Arras lent itself to good trench-making, and similar results might not have been obtained in certain portions of the line without a prodigious amount of labour.'[67]

The primary reason for such progress was related to Artois geology. The region, as previously mentioned, is primarily composed of chalk. But there were two layers (quaternary and upper cretaceous) that greatly assisted mining operations whilst helping or hindering sapping and field work efforts. Quaternary (limon and loess) is porous and flinty. Easy to shift when dry, a rise in the water table over New Year 1916-17, however, caused concerns about moisture retention and consequent flooding by underground springs. Whilst this enabled well-digging, it also created entrenching difficulties as related below.[68] The cretaceous levels were more impervious to water with 'hard chalk' occupying levels around 360ft/110m above sea level. Given the cretaceous chalk strength, there was a limited need for lumber to maintain overhead gallery strength.

All told, the RE mining effort permitted 13,000 troops (at least one overstrength division) to reside within the Arras's tunnel system whilst the connected St Sauver–Ronville *souterrains* and quarries allowed a further 11,500 troops (one understrength division) to shelter and march to fire trenches, immune to German artillery.[69] Six of the original 10 tunnel exits – all south of the Cambrai Road – were affected by the German strategic withdrawal which denied Third Army the ability to detonate saps under the enemy's front trenches, especially in the Ronville sector. However, despite the St Sauver system's proximity to the front, the Ronville subway held twice as many troops. The former's tunnels held approximately 2,000 men with 13 exits whilst the Christchurch quarry in the Ronville system alone housed 4,000 troops with 10 exits.[70] Aside from the need to prepare cover and concealment, the primary problem facing the RE at Arras and for the remainder of 1917, was facilitating overland movement.

Upon receipt of Haig's orders for the offensive on 17 November 1916, Major-General Kenyon immediately replied with a list of RE necessities. As the Army and RE official histories observed, the key difficulty before and during any offensive, Arras included,

66   H.M. Davson, *The History of the 35th Division in the Great War* (London: Sifton Praed & Co., 1926), p.57.
67   Ibid.
68   Pritchard, *History of the Corps of Royal Engineers*, Vol. 5, pp.294-95; Tilley, *Geological Work on the Western Front*, 28.
69   Falls, *Military Operations 1917*, Vol. 1, p.192.
70   Ibid., p.191 and Sketch 6.

A scene likely along the Cambrai Road during the run-up to the Arras offensive. Note the road metal embedded into the earthen pavement. (US National Archives & Records Administration)

was road maintenance and construction.[71] This was exacerbated by Arras's proximity to the frontline (closer than Ypres) whilst acting as a major route hub for the offensive. Kenyon anticipated serious devastation resulting from artillery bombardments and underground mine discharges. He was, when considering the latter, certainly justified given the frenetic tunnelling operations at Vimy throughout 1916. Kenyon delegated the task of forward communications into no man's land as a divisional responsibility whilst marshalling Third Army's strategic assets for all-important road work. This employment of divisional RE and pioneers was as per *SS 135*.[72]

A major aspect of congestion and load inefficiency was the compounding effect of road maintenance supply. Prior to 1917, although the bulk of men and material were delivered to divisional railheads by broad gauge rail lines, a substantial number of tonnes were delivered by horse and lorry via roadways in the last mile to the front line. The natural wear and increased exposure to shelling required disproportionate space for broad gauge deliveries dedicated to flint and gravel for highway repairs. Road slab and road metal/stone or maintenance became the highest planning priority.

Kenyon aimed for 12 routes across the Third Army front with supply heads at the entrance of each road. These were able to store materials for an extension up to 5mi/8km into the newly captured ground. Some 50,000 tonnes of timber were required as well

71   Ibid., pp.189-90; Pritchard, *History of the Corps of Royal Engineers*, Vol. 5, p.293.
72   Pritchard, p.294; *SS 135*, Chapter IX.

as 1,000 tonnes of road stone each. But, whilst slab road was eminently sturdy, easily installed, and resistant up to the German 5.9-inch howitzer fire, it remained a temporary solution compared to road metal/ stone.[73] This demand came at a most inopportune moment.

Fledgling Transportation Directorate issues during the Geddes' reforms briefly (but critically) halted the majority of ROD rail traffic in March 1917. This slowed the material transport for road construction. With a premium on space for supplying various organisations in preparation for the offensive, Falls noted that if the RA and RE competed for ROD cargo space, RE needs were subordinated to the RA. This is illustrated by delivery figures between 17 March and 9 April. These indicate that whilst 100 percent of RA ammunition requests were met, only 61 percent of requested road stone deliveries were made. Likewise, demands for RE stores were only met by 63 percent. However, RE materials required for ROD maintenance were fulfilled at 98 percent.[74] Complaints over the lack of RE stores from corps and divisional CRE pale in comparison to absence of sufficient quantities of road metal. However, supplies of both would remain critically deficient until January 1918.[75]

Surprise, Strongpoints and Thoroughfares, 9-14 April

As Zero-hour approached, the Third Army around Arras was a compressed spring. Whilst its assault infantry discreetly massed in the front trenches and tunnel exits, FOOs directed artillery fire on enemy defences and batteries opposite. As G.C. Wynne observed in his study of German defensive practice, 'by the eve of the infantry assault the front trench system had become lines of mud-filled shell holes and [the] wire entanglement had been blown to shreds.'[76] The Transportation Directorate reforms and ROD efforts ensured that the RA had all the shells it required. Surprise was exchanged for exhausting the defenders and annihilating everything short of his concrete pillboxes.[77] With the RE preparatory phase mostly complete, the corps' spearhead element of 43,856 sappers stood ready to maintain offensive momentum. Tunnelling Company sappers created breaches into no man's land near exits of tunnel networks, whilst the Special Brigade fired final salvoes during the lead up to zero hour.

73   Pritchard, pp.189, 293; TNA WO 95/383/3: 'Preparation and Use of the Caves', Third Army CRE War Diary, April 1917. Road metal entered British civil engineering lexicon in the 1820s and it is still in use for driveway paving and commonly mistaken for gravel which is of a finer and lighter grade of stone.
74   Falls, *Military Operations 1917*, Vol. I, p.190, fn.1.
75   Thompson, 'Mud, Blood, and Wood', p.253.
76   Wynne, *If Germany Attacks*, p.121.
77   Sheldon, *The German Army in the Spring Offensives 1917*, p.85.

The gas programme simultaneously commenced with the opening bombardment on 4 April. This included 4.5-inch howitzers and 60-pdr guns concentrating lethal gas against identified enemy batteries, telephone exchanges, and command centres. Chemical barrages and cylinder releases also commenced at that time. In addition, XVII and VI corps Special companies also discharged Livens Projector batteries and 4-inch Stokes mortars to further saturate the target area with long- and short-range projectiles respectively. Another wave of gas was released from cylinders on the 6th.[78] With a pause to assess the RA barrage's efficacy in wire cutting, the original Z-Day of 8 April was delayed for 24 hours, as was the Special Brigade zero hour discharge plan.

For the first time, most of the Special Brigade's success was attributed to shell fire. Since its inception, the routine method of gas deployment had been with cylinders.[79] This required frequent trips up tramways, roads and communication trenches prior to reaching release positions. Exposure to German shellfire made these activities particularly dangerous. For example, a large-scale 4th Canadian Division trench raid in late March was compromised when sporadic German artillery penetrated RE gas cylinders with devastating results. A harsh CEF assessment resulted in a Canadian Corps general order to remove *all* cylinders from the Vimy front.[80] Despite trouble with cylindric release, this was more than compensated for by the Stokes, Newton and Livens Projector rounds which achieved depth, concentration and accuracy on Z-Day. Seventy-five minutes to Zero (05:30), all lethal gas discharged east of the Black Line objective lifted, whilst 60-pdr batteries maintained fire on German gun positions until Zero+1.

With the German front softened by a barrage which was twice as powerful as that of the Somme in an operational area half its size, the rested, fed, and well-prepared British assault troops burst from trenches, saps and tunnel galleries at 05:30. However, the hard lessons of 1915-16 precluded divisional engineering assets from prematurely entering the fray. A re-evaluation of the pre-war debate on sappers and pioneers forming-up in assault waves was settled in *SS 135*. Within the manual's nine points of recommended action, point seven advised 'they must be kept back till the situation permits of their proceeding straight to their task; they will arrive fresh and properly organised, and will be able to get to work at once.' It further advised that this timing should be in the hands of 'the man on the spot' – a brigadier-general or battalion commander.[81]

For 34th Division, attacking towards the Pont du Jour Ridge in the centre of XVII Corps sector, 'the three Field Companies [207th, 208th, 209th] and the Pioneers [18th Northumberland Fusiliers]', the divisional historian observed, 'were to be employed

78   Falls, *Military Operations 1917*, Vol. 1, p.185.
79   Lefebure, *The Riddle of the Rhine*, pp.57-58; Richter, *Chemical Soldiers*, p.177.
80   Richter, p.175 and Tim Cook, '"A Proper Slaughter": The March 1917 Gas Raid at Vimy', *Canadian Military History*, Vol. 8, Issue 2 (1999). Conversely, the Canadian Corps found gas projectile delivery useful.
81   *SS 135*, pp.33-34.

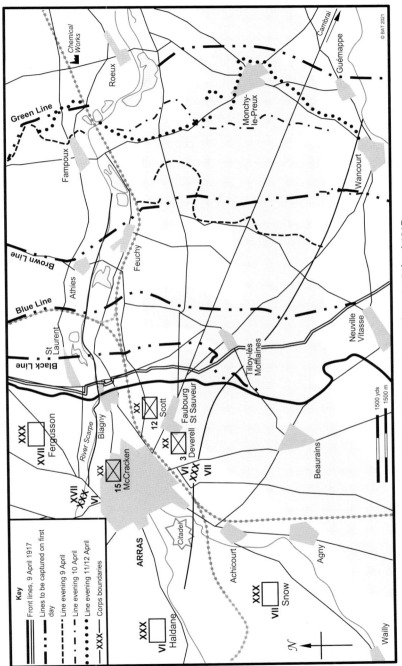

VI and VII corps advance, Arras 9-12 April 1917.

in opening up communications as the assault progressed, and elaborate arrangements were made for getting supplies and material forward by pack animals and on wheels.' The division also protected its combat engineering element by ordering it 'to remain in dug-outs in Roclincourt Valley' situated approximately 600yd/458m behind the fire trenches.[82] Further south near Héninel, between the Cojeul and Sensée objectives, the 56th (London) Division deployed its component 167th and 168th infantry brigades to the right and left respectively with 169th in immediate reserve. It assigned the 416th Field Company to the right flank whilst the 513th Field Company and 5th Cheshires (divisional pioneers) were situated on the left. Two sections per Field Company were withheld along with the 512th Field Company in divisional reserve.[83]

The RA/RE barrage was impressive. However, the consequences for such efficacy included an utterly devastated forward battle zone averaging approximately 2mi/3.2km in depth on 9-10 April. This prevented any transport except mules and carrying parties to cross terrain described by one source as 'the geography of hell.'[84] With regard to mules, they could only trek along what remained of shelled roadways. The official historian noted that main road damage extending from Arras was not as severe as Kenyon anticipated. However, congestion was a factor, especially after hostile batteries recovered. Thus a delay of two or three days was required before First Army's RE units could tend to the reconstruction and extension of critical roadways in support of the planned exploitation. This would harry the RESS mission to lay communications wire forward. Lines were constantly driven over, damaged by shellfire, or trampled by foot and hoof as signallers attempted to maintain them.

Artillery destruction of the German positions, however, left pockets of resistance to harass both forward movement and consolidation. As pioneers from 9th (Scottish) Division experienced when approaching Fampoux that evening, 'a machine-gun suddenly came to life' on a work detail of 9th Seaforth Highlanders. Their original assignment to dig a communication trench interrupted, the men 'dropped their shovels, picked up their rifles, and after killing its crew carried off the machine-gun as a trophy.'[85] Dozens of such incidents plagued sapper and pioneer work over the next 24-48 hours, yet the overall progress was maintained. By the evening of 9-10 April, the satisfaction of nearly reaching the Blue Line objectives was marred by misery as gusting rain transformed into heavy snowfall. In the 34th Division's sector, the Brown

82   J. Shakespear, *The Thirty-Fourth Division, 1915-1919: The Story of Its Career from Ripon to the Rhine* (London: H.F. & G. Witherby, 1921), p.99.

83   Dudley Ward, *The 56th Division (1st London Territorial Division)* (London: John Murray, 1921), p.120. The component Territorial Field companies were originally 1/Edinburgh (416th), 2/1st London (512th), and 2/2nd London (513th) before the January 1917 enumeration.

84   Michael Stephenson (ed.), *Battlegrounds: Geography and the History of Warfare* (Washington, DC: National Geographic Society, 2003), pp.9, 263.

85   John Ewing, *The History of the 9th (Scottish) Division, 1914-1919* (London: John Murray, 1921), p.195.

line was consolidated during the push to the Green line objective. Meantime, patrols went out, sappers and pioneers reinforced frontline positions and 'stocked a dump of S.A.A., bombs, food, and water close behind the Blue Line.'[86]

Critical to consolidating the advances was reinforcing cratered ground and villages. For example, the 15th (Scottish) Division's history notes that by the evening of Z-Day, as 37th Division passed through to advance on Monchy-le-Preux, 'the 44th Brigade, which had remained in the Blue Line, continued its work, and with the 74th Field Company, R.E., thoroughly consolidated that position. Strongpoints were erected, communication trenches commenced, dumps made and filled, etc.'[87] This activity had a basis in the *SS 112* manual which outlined five 'principles of consolidation of captured trenches'. These are abbreviated as follows:

a)   To establish a series of strongpoints or centres of resistance, wired all round and mutually supporting each other according to the ground. These points should be provided with machine or Lewis guns at once.

b)   To provide good communications to the rear from these points.

c)   To fill in all hostile trenches within bombing [grenade] distance of points occupied.

d)   To establish, if possible, simultaneously with the consolidation of strong points in the rear. These points should, if ground is favourable, be placed to cover the intervals between the works in the frontline.

e)   The strong points can later be connected to form a continuous frontline.[88]

Referring once more to the four military engineering considerations, topographical features and geological suitability particularly come into play when considering the enemy's fieldworks and subterranean systems. Upon taking up the defence of Monchy-le-Preux on the sleet-ridden evening of 11 April, 29th Division found, 'the village contained excellent deep dug-outs made by the Germans with some good cellars.'[89] German military engineering was legendary for employment of concrete and strengthening of natural features. For British infantry preparing to halt successive counter-attacks by the elite *3rd Bavarian Division*, these defences were welcome assets.[90] It was here that the problem of water table and quaternary chalk harried the

86   Shakespear, *The Thirty-Fourth Division*, pp.106-07.

87   Stewart & Buchan, *The Fifteenth (Scottish) Division*, p.121.

88   *SS 112: Consolidation of Trenches, Localities and Craters After Assault and Capture, With a Note on Rapid Wiring* (London: HMSO, 1916), p.1.

89   Stair Gillon, *The Story of the 29th Division: A Record of Gallant Deeds* (London: Thomas Nelson & Sons, 1925), p.98.

90   For *3rd Bavarian Division's* elite status, see Intelligence Section of the General Staff, American Expeditionary Forces, *Histories of Two Hundred and Fifty-One Divisions of the German Army Which Participated in the War 1914-1918* (London: London Stamp Exchange, 1989 reprint of 1920 edition), p.80.

sappers of 455th, 497th, and 510th Field companies and 2nd Monmouthshire Pioneer Battalion with 'the discovery of water levels hardly below the surface.' As haste was made to secure the position, they found 'the trenches in the north-eastern outskirts of Monchy were always water-logged, and 400yd/365m east of the village a likely site for trenches had on one occasion to be abandoned on account of the persistent oozing up of water in the most unlikely of places, due presumably to underground fissures.'[91] The artesian well difficulty was exacerbated by weather conditions which 5th Division described as 'vile'. Furthermore, it encountered roads in 'an appalling state, and it was with the utmost difficulty that the guns were pushed forward.'[92] Struggling to compensate for artillery damage, 'the R.E. worked indefatigably at making plank roads over the quagmire of shell-holes and bridging the larger craters.'[93] An RE officer subsequently observed, 'perhaps with a degree of self-interest' that road maintenance and repair were of the highest priority. This merely reflected the entire RE command structure's focus following the pre-offensive tunnelling and accommodation preparations. To prove his point, the same officer reported 40-50 large shell craters were bridged with 35mi/56.3km of road built.[94]

The importance of thoroughfare construction in 15th Division's sector alone from 9-11 April amounted to '1,200 yards [1,097m] of tramway laid, with 500 yards [450m] of trench-boards on either side and 700 yards [640m] of board down the centre.'[95] The engineers also made use of the Scarpe itself. As pontoons were constructed at Third Army RE workshops at St Pol, they were brought up whilst divisional sappers and pioneers cleared the river of debris and obstructions. Subsequent reliefs by the 17th, 9th, 4th, and 51st divisional sappers and pioneers contributed to its free flow and 'the waterway was welcomed by the medical staff.'

Ultimately, the RE spearhead at Arras mastered set-piece operations to the neglect of maintaining operational tempo.[96] No amount of preparation, however, could cope with the annihilating bombardments of 1917. It was not until RA doctrine adopted a predicted artillery fire scheme later that year at Cambrai that the RE, not to mention the infantry and armoured branches, were able to maintain said tempo over ground not rendered impassable by lengthy bombardments.[97]

91   Gillon, p.99.
92   Hussey & Inam, *The Fifth Division in the Great War*, p.155.
93   Ibid., p.156.
94   Mitchinson, *Pioneer Battalions in the Great War*, p.144.
95   Stewart & Buchan, *The Fifteenth (Scottish) Division*, p.128. Both the 9th and 15th divisional histories are unique amongst their pre-1940 publication contemporaries with regard to attention to RE and pioneer work.
96   This is a more lucid term expression describing an army's rate of advance.
97   Jonathan Bailey, 'British Artillery in the Great War' in Paddy Griffith (ed.), *British Fighting Methods in the Great War* (London: Frank Cass, 1996), pp.34-36; Bailey, 'The First World War and the Birth of Modern Warfare', p.142; Ewing, *The History of the 9th (Scottish) Division*, p.200; Priestley, *The Signal Service in the European War*, p.174; Thompson, 'Mud, Blood, and Wood', pp.242, 252.

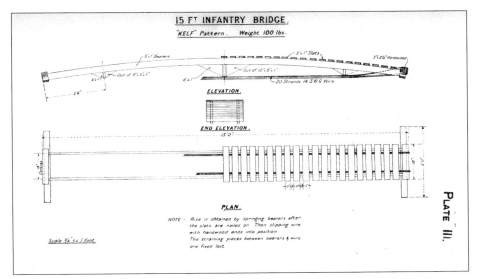

RE infantry footbridge schematic. Assembled by Army Troop companies in corps workshops or near the front by Field companies and Pioneer battalions, some 6,000 were assembled in one corps area alone as a means of traversing the devastated zone. (Addison, *The Work of the Royal Engineers in the European War: Forward Communications*)

Footbridge constructed over the Scarpe near Blangy, late April 1917. Note the arch built to allow riverine traffic to pass beneath. (US National Archives & Records Administration)

Conclusion: Engineering a 'Taste of Success'

Although not Haig's strategic preference for early 1917, healthy GHQ scepticism about Nivelle's overambitious plan for an Anglo-French lunge in Artois–Aisne-Champagne did not preclude an exhaustive attempt at securing a strategic breakthrough at Arras as evidenced in RE preparations. As Falls observed of the 9 April success:

> Many of the preparations for the offensive at Arras could be made in a compara-tively short period before it was launched; none required so early a start or so long a view as those of the Royal Engineers, including their Signals branch. It had been conclusively proven unless railways, roads, water supply, and tele-phonic communications worked efficiently and unless it could be insured that their systems could be rapidly pushed forward into the enemy's lines after the first attacks, opportunities presented by early successes would be lost, and, in fact, no great offensive effort could be continuously maintained.[98]

Placed in its proper perspective, the Arras campaign – especially its opening battles – is a clear marker on the rough road to victory. The seizure of the imposing Vimy Ridge by First Army's Canadian Corps is rightly acknowledged as a major tactical feat, but this success is all too frequently lauded at the expense of Third Army. This is understandable due to the campaign's ultimate strategic failure and horrendous daily casualty rate (especially for the infantry and RFC).

Arras was only the second major offensive the BEF undertook in France and Flanders. Nineteen-fifteen was fought with an improvised and underequipped (espe-cially in artillery) army. Of the four notable operations in that trying year, only Loos in September was on a scale of a grand offensive. Nineteen-sixteen, dictated by the agreement to participate in the Allied General Offensive and German pressure on the French at Verdun, challenged the British to finally wage war on a continental footing with the fourth and fifth waves of Kitchener recruits entering the line.[99] Contrary to Basil Liddell-Hart's view that surprise, 'this master key of all the great captains of history had been rusting since the spring of 1915', the BEF achieved just that at Arras two years later, even if it was incomplete due to employment of a protracted bombardment.[100]

The problems for maintaining offensive tempo were listed in priority order according to Third Army reports: road extension and signals. With road network issues previ-ously discussed in detail, it is worth summarising the complexities of the RESS situ-ation in April 1917. Its chief difficulties were arguably the development of reliable

---

98   Falls, *Military Operations 1917*, Vol. 1, pp.188-89.
99   Bruce Gudmundsson, *The British Army on the Western Front 1916* (Oxford: Osprey Publishing, 2007).
100   Basil Henry Liddell Hart, *A History of the World War, 1914-1918* (Boston: Little, Brown, 1935), p.410.

vocal telecommunications systems and operational security for them. Some historians have suggested that the neglect and subsequent slow evolution of wireless sets was catastrophic. They argue that 'the British Army's Signal Service singularly failed its parent organization by its inability to develop wireless communications to its fullest' thereby placing greater strain on its personnel to ensure delivery. It is further posited that the CW wireless and telegraphs available to the British Army in 1915 'could have been used on the Somme and certainly would have made a significant difference in the 1917-18 battles.'[101] However, closer inspection reveals that the matter was thoroughly explored by the War Office and RE. It was found that technology limitations, particularly with to regard overland conductivity, meant that research and development at RE HQ in Chatham would not be available in time. Wireless was often in demand as the continued reliance on visual communications (Lucas Lamps, rockets, Very lights, etc.) and vocal criticisms of telephonic communications right up to the Hundred Days in 1918 attest. Operational security matters in the latter case had been critically addressed after 1916, resulting in greatly enhanced surprise as to the *timing* and scale of the subsequent Arras offensive.[102]

The Arras offensive's success owed much to geography and pre-existing lines of communication. On the Somme, at Messines Ridge and at Third Ypres, mining operations were primarily demolition missions of limited tactical application. Arras, by contrast, fully utilised mining's greater value: concealment. Overall, chalky soil in the vicinity of Arras – despite a tendency for its upper strata to become waterlogged – was generally stable, particularly below the water table. This allowed for extensive mining and utilisation of ancient subterranean systems that only required minor maintenance. The most labour-intensive effort was in the connecting disparate subways and expanding them to shelter the manpower of over two divisions whilst new galleries, stocked with critical provisions, were extended to offensive jumping-off positions.

Although the barrage surrendered strategic surprise, the massive concealment operation did achieve tactical shock. British troops were rested and relatively impervious to almost all German guns and howitzers during the preparatory phase. It is interesting to contemplate what might have happened had Third Army executed a shorter 48-hour hurricane bombardment, which favoured a strategic surprise, supported by tunnelling and sapping efforts.[103] This is could have been worsened if the Germans had more competently executed their defence-in-depth concept. In essence, the British were able to take advantage of *OHL's* egregious error in defending every bit of

---

101 Mike Bullock & Laurence A. Lyons, *Missed Signals on the Western Front: How the Slow Adoption of Wireless Restricted British Strategy and Operations in World War I* (London: McFarland & Co., 2010), p.1.

102 Jonathan Boff, *Haig's Enemy: Crown Prince Rupprecht and Germany's War on the Western Front* (Oxford: Oxford University Press, 2018), p.156.

103 See Trevor Harvey, 'Arras, Allenby and Artillery: The Decision for a Four-Day Preliminary Bombardment', *Journal of the Society for Army Historical Research*, Vol. 94, No. 380, Winter 2016.

ground despite its push for mutually supportive dispersal of positions and occupying formations.[104]

But even if the level of tactical surprise at Arras is debatable, the consequences of the subterranean system and protective mining employment were substantial. The 12th Division which, having spent more time in the city and its environs during 1917 than any other BEF infantry formation, could aptly be described as the 'Arras division', offered this reflection on the efficacy of tunnels: 'The formation of the deep dugouts holding 50 men each lying down, in the front system to take two battalions, or 4 sitting, was fully justified, notwithstanding the immensity of work it entailed … one battalion which was in the line for five days, four of which were the bombardment, did not have a single casualty. The use of these and of the caves and the covered approaches gave the troops security, allowed them real rest and enabled the attack to be commenced with physically fresh men.'[105]

That the Arras offensive ultimately failed to achieve a strategic victory remains undisputed. The RE's shortcomings vis-à-vis obstacles created by the annihilating bombardment is evocative of Anglo-American success at Normandy followed by failure to prepare for painfully slow and costly hedgerow fighting. Considering RE unit expansion, increases in sapper employment specializations and the myriad logistical and doctrinal reforms put into practice within such a short period of time, the campaign marks a moment of greater importance than the Somme and equal to that of Messines Ridge. 'If Messines represented the greatest achievement of the war in offensive mining', Cyril Falls observed, '[then] the Battle of Arras marked the outstanding effort of protective tunnelling.'[106] Its victorious opening (9-14 April), nonetheless, offered what Jim Smithson has termed a 'taste of success' in a year of pronounced disappointments.

104 Christian Stachelbeck, '"Lessons Learned" in WWI: The German Army, Vimy Ridge and the Elastic Defence in Depth in 1917', *Journal of Military & Strategic Studies* 18, No. 2 (2017), p.122.

105 TNA WO 95/1824/4: 'VI Corps Report', 20 April 1917, 12th Division War Diary; P. Middleton Brumwell, *History of the 12th (Eastern) Division in the Great War, 1914-1918* (London: Nisbet & Co., 1923), pp.91-92. According to the 12th Division history, the mayor of Arras in 1917 heralded the division as 'the defenders and deliverers of Arras.'

106 Falls, *Military Operations 1917*, Vol. 1, p.309.

11

Especially Valuable?
The I Anzac Corps and the Battles of Bullecourt, April-May 1917

Meleah Hampton

In May 1917, the Melbourne illustrated humour magazine *Punch* celebrated a great victory by the Australian Imperial Force on the Western Front. Despite conceding that exactly what the Anzacs did at Bullecourt 'we do not yet know' in an article simply titled 'Bullecourt' *Punch* claimed that the battle would be 'a source of deeper gratification to Australians than Gallipoli; not because the fighting was more heroic, but because it was more successful – because there is a definite gain from it, and it sets the Allies a good stride nearer their goal.'[1] *Punch* was not alone. A wide-range of newspapers and broadsheets across Australia joyously proclaimed, 'the dogged manner in which the Australians are forcing victory at Bullecourt, and there penetrating the Hindenburg Line ... the forcing of Bullecourt was a task for which the Australian initiative and disregard of restraint if there was a chance of breaking through, were especially valuable.'[2] It is hard to imagine a description of events further from the truth.

Race to the Line

For the men of the I Anzac Corps (1st, 2nd and 4th Australian infantry divisions), the path to Bullecourt began early in the new year of 1917. The corps war diary described a gradual increase of German activity in the lines opposite, with increased aerial observation and reconnaissance reports describing various new works and increased enemy patrols. At the same time, however, the Germans demonstrated a reluctance to engage. As early as 14 February, an Australian raid on Sunray Trench near the Butte

---

1   'Bullecourt', *Punch* (Melbourne), 24 May 1917, p.5.
2   'Bullecourt', *Northern Times*, 14 May 1917, p.4.

de Warlencourt reported that the 'enemy did not show fight.' I Anzac Corps' divisions continued to patrol no man's land in the days that followed. Just over a week later, another raid, this time on Stormy Trench, reported that 'very little resistance was encountered and in all 32 prisoners were secured.' The following day, 23 February, a patrol headed for the Butte Quarry could discover no sign of the enemy despite it being the usual haunt of enemy snipers. Furthermore, the Germans seemed to be deliberately shelling their own frontline. [3]

It soon became clear that the Germans were slowly and silently withdrawing. To where, and why, was less clear to I Anzac Corps headquarters, and the men in the frontline continued patrolling to maintain touch with the enemy. Some patrols spent several hours in no man's land yet encountered no one; others encountered occupied and well-defended positions. I Anzac Corps was often wrong-footed, as with a planned attack by the 2nd Australian Division, which was disrupted when the German garrison defending the Warlencourt–Loupart Line were found to have voluntarily withdrawn. Operations were made more difficult by the weather. Snow and fog limited the ability of the Royal Flying Corps to undertake reconnaissance flights. This placed additional pressure on foot patrols that endured bitterly cold temperatures, punctuated by frequent sleet and snow storms, as they struggled to ascertain enemy intentions.

I Anzac Corps was witnessing the German withdrawal to the Hindenburg Line, the strong defensive position the enemy had spent the winter constructing. A shorter, more defensible line, it was situated in ideal tactical positions as far as possible, and strongly fortified with thick belts of barbed wire, deep trenches, dugouts and strong-points. The process of following up the withdrawal was complicated and stressful, as it was rarely possible to be sure if an objective was vacant, booby-trapped or occupied. Nevertheless, there was an unprecedented opportunity to occupy positions deemed unobtainable just weeks before.

As with the previous year, I Anzac Corps was operating as part of the BEF's Fifth Army (known as Reserve Army in 1916). Its GOC, General Sir Hubert Gough, was in his element during this strange and hectic period. An ambitious, aggressive and impetuous commander, he had previously demonstrated that perhaps the most important attribute his subordinates could show him was initiative. During summer 1916, in the midst of activity on the left flank on the Somme push, Gough issued a memorandum ordering corps commanders to push on. They were to 'impress upon their subordinate leaders the necessity for the energetic measures and offensive action which the present situation requires' by having 'Subordinate Commanders … think out and suggest enterprises instead of waiting for orders from above.' In Gough's estimation, territorial gains would facilitate further operations so long as formations/units would 'press

---

3   Australian War Memorial (AWM) 4/1/29/13: General Staff 1st Anzac Corps Headquarters War Diary, 14-23 February 1917.

General Sir Hubert
Gough (left) and King
Albert of Belgium, May
1917.

the enemy constantly
and … continue to gain
ground as rapidly as
possible.[4] Despite the
cost, nothing appears
to have changed with
regard to this stance,
and he was just as quick
to rush into operations
in 1917.

Here then, a little
over six months
later, was the perfect
example of what
Gough attempted to
accomplish on the
Somme. Pressing the
enemy as they with-
drew meant that
ground recently aban-
doned by the enemy
could be quickly occupied. But applying pressure on the Germans, retreating or not,
was not to the taste of the GOC I Anzac Corps, Lieutenant-General Sir William
Birdwood. During the Pozières and Mouquet Farm operations in July-September
1916, he had been reluctant to order a determined advance, and studiously avoided
conducting large, coordinated attacks wherever possible.[5] Birdwood was, however,
largely successful in masking his own lack of determination behind weak, non-specific
orders, received and carried out by subordinate commanders. Now, as the Germans
slowly melted away in front of I Anzac Corps lines, even he became enthusiastic as
vigorous Australian patrols seized undefended ground.

4   AWM 26/42/1: Memorandum SG.43/0/1 by Army Commander, Reserve Army, 3 August
    1916.
5   Meleah Hampton, *Attack on the Somme: 1st Anzac Corps and the Battle of Pozières Ridge,
    1916* (Solihull: Helion & Co., 2016), p.209.

By late March, operational tempo had built to such dimensions as to demand larger-scale operations usually involving one or two battalions attacking a garrisoned outpost village the Germans were slow to abandon. One of the many examples of this type of operation occurred on 20 March when the rush to advance as rapidly as possible had a negative impact on 6th Infantry Brigade, 2nd Australian Division.[6] Both Gough and Birdwood had suggested, largely through telephone conversations, that the line should be advanced to one encompassing the villages of Longatte, Noreuil and Lagnicourt. With little time to prepare – 6th Brigade GOC Brigadier-General John Gellibrand only received the phone order to advance at 11:00 p.m. the night before – the brigade was ordered to occupy Noreuil. There was little available intelligence as to how strongly the village was held or what force would be required – or even available – to capture it. Moreover, there would be no strong, coordinated artillery barrage – just one or two batteries bombarding roads leading from the objective and parts of the village itself during the attack. Two battalions, the 21st and 23rd, with support from the Light Horse, were allotted the task.

Mounted patrols were sent off to reconnoitre the approaches to Noreuil at 3:00 a.m. on 20 March, just four hours after the first orders were received at brigade headquarters. Gellibrand had hoped to send the infantry ahead of the Light Horse in order to provide support nearer to the village. Delayed by heavy rain and snow, they did not arrive until at least an hour after the mounted patrols had departed. Pressing forward, several companies of infantry made it to the edge of Noreuil but eventually, lacking flank protection, they were forced to withdraw in the face of heavy machine-gun fire from Longatte and Noreuil. Gellibrand subsequently observed that he thought flank support essential to any further advance, however, 'considering that the greater part of the action was fought at close range and that our troops broke off the action on receipt of orders, the total casualties, though I deplore the number, is not so high as I expected. Three officers and 28 men were killed; as many as 200 others wounded or missing.'[7] The failed attack on Noreuil was a clear warning that ad hoc operations with patchy artillery support were unlikely to succeed, and that there was a good chance that the villages ahead would be more strongly defended. Fifth Army's pursuit operations continued, but their nature would change.

Noreuil would remain an important objective with regard to Gough's future plans for I Anzac Corps. Patrols from the 6th Brigade indicated that there was one company of German infantry with at least four machine-guns occupying the village. Nearby Lagnicourt was supposed to have an entire battalion of infantry with another four machine-guns while Longatte had approximately two artillery companies and another four machine-guns, which could be effectively trained on Noreuil.[8]

6   For further details on Australian operations during the retreat to the Hindenburg Line, see Chapter 8 in this volume.

7   AWM 4 23/6/19: 6th Australian Infantry Brigade report, 22 March 1917, 6th Infantry Brigade War Diary.

8   Ibid.

Despite these reports, when the time came to attack again in early April, the first option was to investigate the area with strong infantry patrols in the hope that Noreuil could be occupied with little or no resistance. The patrols tasked with this reconnaissance came from 13th Infantry Brigade, 4th Australian Division which had recently entered the frontline. In what should have been no surprise, its patrols were unable to get to close to the village, being stopped short by machine-gun and rifle fire every time they got with 200 yards of it.[9] With stark evidence that a smaller operation than the one that had failed just days before would not be successful, plans for a comparatively larger operation were set in motion.

The assault, initially intended for 1 April 1917 but later delayed to the following day, was to be conducted by two battalions, the 50th and the 51st, but this time provisions were made for strong flank support. This would be provided by British V Corps on the left and 52nd Battalion on the right. The infantry would advance behind an artillery barrage that would provide crucial covering fire. With 50th Battalion on the left and the 51st on the right, both battalions would swing around to meet in a classic pincer movement. Following this, the routine 'strong patrols' would press forward and establish a line on the railway running due north of Noreuil.[10]

Accordingly, at 5.15 a.m. on the morning of 2 April 1917 – 'a most suitable hour', according to brigade headquarters – 13th Australian Infantry Brigade launched its assault on Noreuil. The assault battalions were familiar with the ground which ensured that they were able to depart the jumping-off line 'without the slightest hitch.' The barrage advanced 100 yards in two minutes and was reported by the 13th Brigade to be 'carefully made out and thoroughly executed ... [and] was not too quick.'[11] But whilst it covered the advance to the outskirts of the village, there its usefulness ended. There the attackers encountered a much larger garrison than expected, with 50th Battalion pinned down by numerous machine-guns unhampered by the thin barrage. Relying on their own firepower – Lewis guns fired from the hip, rifle grenades and bombs – its companies enveloped and silenced the hostile machine-gun positions. By nightfall Noreuil was in Australian hands, the new line largely continuous and in the process consolidation. The village would later house Australian infantry brigade, machine-gun company and trench mortar battery headquarters during the Bullecourt fighting.

After-action reports dealing with the capture of Noreuil almost completely omit one important factor on the battlefield – enemy barbed wire obstacles. The 13th Brigade's report mentioned wire once, remarking that on 50th Battalion's right flank, roughly

---

9   AWM 4 23/13/14: 13th Australian Infantry Brigade Summary of Intelligence to 8a.m. 28th March 1917, 13th Australian Infantry Brigade War Diary, March 1917, Appendix 13.

10   AWM4 23/13/14: 13th Aust. Infantry Bde. Order No. 58, 30 March 1917, Appendix 1, 13th Australian Infantry Brigade War Diary, March 1917.

11   AWM4 1/48/13 Part 1: Report of attack 13th Australian Infantry Brigade, Appendix 5, 4th Australian Division War Diary, April 1917.

where the two battalions met, the 'line was thinly wired.'[12] The 50th Battalion's own report states that 'the right company was temporarily held up by wire which it eventually got through,'[13] whilst an account from a participant who was there observed that the company's commander, Captain Harold Armitage, had to lead his men with revolver in hand into a 'long ding-dong struggle' to get through the wire at all.[14] The barrage, which reports at a higher level suggest was 'carefully made out', was reported by 50th Battalion to have not been thick enough, and to too slow for the troops to follow without walking in to it.[15] This tendency towards optimism that masked difficulties in reports making their way up the chain of command, had not been present the year before when the Australians were operating along Pozières Ridge. Reporting at that time had been characterised by frankness. And yet, only a short time later, even experienced brigades such as the 13th were watering down problems encountered in reports to division and corps.

The capture of Noreuil effectively ended the follow up operations to the Hindenburg Line. From the time patrols first encountered empty German trenches until early April 1917, the rush was on to keep up. Objectives were seized by mixed forces of cavalry, infantry and artillery deliberately kept as small as possible in order to maintain operational tempo. Noreuil, more than any other outpost village, had demonstrated that the time for pushing strong patrols forward in the hope they could capture the objective had gone. But the idea that the time had come to adopt a measured approach, i.e., to pause and meticulously plan attacks as part of an overarching strategy instead of rushing to advance as quickly as possible was, above all else, clouded by the success of recent hasty and somewhat haphazard operations. It would be some time before this situation changed.

Arras Offensive

The Allies had not been simply sitting idle and waiting for the Germans to withdraw to the Hindenburg Line. Senior commanders had been planning a major offensive for several months. Following the dismissal of French C-in-C General Joseph Joffre, his replacement, General Robert Nivelle planned a breakthrough offensive against the Chemin des Dames and in the Champagne. Ridge. In support of this grand assault, the BEF was to conduct a series of attacks about Arras, starting a week earlier, with the objective driving east before linking up with the projected French advance. Although the plan was disrupted by the German withdrawal, its essence remained. Of course,

12   Ibid.
13   AWM4 23/67/10: Report on Attack on Noreuil and Ground to North East, 50th Infantry Battalion War Diary, April 1917.
14   '50th Battalion at Noreuil', *Adelaide Register*, 6 April 1918, p.9.
15   AWM4 23/67/10: Report on Attack on Noreuil and Ground to North-West, 50th Australian Infantry Battalion War Diary, April 1917.

hindsight reveals sweeping infantry movements followed by a cavalry breakthrough was impossible at this stage of the war. Nevertheless, for the British the opening days of the campaign (9-14 April) resulted in some success, notably at Vimy Ridge. By the time offensive ended on 16 May, however, the battle had degenerated into a bloody stalemate.

The role Fifth Army was to play during Arras offensive, flank support for the main operation, was much the same as during the Battle of the Somme. During 1916 that meant activity on the left flank of Fourth Army. At Arras, Fifth Army was acting on the right flank of Third Army, which was conducting the main thrust towards Cambrai. However, this time Fifth Army would be attacking at right angles to the Third Army advance, moving north as Third Army drove east. It was hoped that this would protect the flank and enable a greater advance than otherwise envisaged. Situated in the middle section of this line was the fortified village of Bullecourt. It would have to be secured to enable Third Army to press on without coming under punishing enfilade fire.

Following the capture of Noreuil, I Anzac Corps was ordered to capture Bullecourt. Specifically, the Australians were to seize the village without a direct assault. Instead Bullecourt was to be 'pinched out' by outflanking it on the right, while the British 62nd (West Riding) Division, forming the left arm of the pincer movement, outflanked it on the left.[16] The 4th and 12th infantry brigades, 4th Australian Division were assigned the task, and wire-cutting barrages in front of the Australian line began in earnest on 8 April. The assault was to be launched on 10 April, the day after the Battle of Arras opened.

Once again, infantry preparations for this operation involved, as per 4th Australian Division orders of 6 April, 'a very vigorous offensive' to be immediately adopted. 'Strong fighting patrols will be sent out and the enemy cleared out of no man's land. It is essential that this should be done to enable our attacking force to form up unob-served.' Even if the important lesson of the Hindenburg Line pursuit operations had been that attacking with the smallest force possible in the first instance was not always the right approach, the belief that these 'strong patrols' would be able to effect an advance in place of a larger force was never entirely abandoned. In the lead up to Bullecourt, battalion commanders were informed that 'the fact that limited objectives are laid down is not intended absolutely to restrict subordinate commanders, if they see a chance of making a little more ground, for our chances of success are greater if we act boldly while the enemy is disorganised.' Nevertheless, with the next sentence they were advised that 'at the same time the isolated advance of detachments pushing forward beyond support must be avoided.'[17] A note of unrealistic optimism is charac-teristic of this period, no more so than within I Anzac Corps.

16   TNA WO 95/3079/2: 62nd Division Order No. 31, 8 April 1917, Appendix 9g, 185th Infantry Brigade War Diary, April 1917.
17   AWM4 1/48/13: Part 1: Preliminary Instructions No. 2, 6 April 1917, 4th Australian Division War Diary, Appendix 21, April 1917.

Pre-battle intelligence resulting from patrol work opposite the Australian line was added to on the morning of 8 April, when three men of 5th Dorsetshire Regiment (British 11th Division) appeared in 12th Brigade's trenches. Captured on 11 January near Beaumont Hamel, they managed to escape and were able to describe traversing four lines of sparsely occupied German trenches on the way back to the British lines.[18] While this would seem to be a positive, the escapees also recollected large amounts uncut wire, an unwelcome observation readily confirmed by Australian patrols. Moreover, it appeared that the heavy artillery, when firing high explosive shells, were creating large craters beneath the wire belts while the wire itself remained largely intact.[19] The escaped prisoners also observed that the 'wire was very thick and strong in front of the Hindenburg Line.' They had managed to 'walk straight over, [but] it did not appear to be cut about.'[20] Having digested these reports, Gough characteristically latched on to the idea that the enemy defences were lightly held and downplayed the possibility of uncut wire. In response, he ordered more patrols and advanced guards.

The line to be attacked was subjected to a heavy preliminary bombardment by the 4th Australian Division's artillery. From 6 April batteries were told that 'there are at present no limits on ammunition expenditure. It is governed purely by what the brigades can bring up and shoot.'[21] The gunners also prepared to provide infantry support. The latter were issued verbal attack orders on the morning of 8 April. Assault brigades were told that they would be attacking a series of three objectives under the cover of a modified lifting barrage. The barrage would fire onto each objective, then lift off to a point half way to the next objective, creeping back to this objective slowly as the captured one in front was consolidated.[22] That same day orders issued by 4th Australian Division artillery assigned battery groups to each infantry brigade. They stated that 'groups will adjust their barrage line in consultation with the Infantry Brigadier concerned, and in all ways will co-operate closely with the infantry brigades.'[23] Yet the following morning further instructions were issued stating that 'strong patrols are being sent out by the 4th and 12th Australian infantry brigades tonight … if reported unoccupied, the infantry will occupy [the enemy line] immediately … if the line is reported held, an attack – supported by Tanks – may take

18 Ibid.
19 AWM4 13/13/11: Left Sector First Anzac Artillery Daily Intelligence Report, 8 April 1917, 4th Australian Divisional Artillery War Diary, April 1917.
20 AWM4 23/12/14: 12th Australian Infantry Brigade Intelligence Summary No. 1, 8 April 1917, 12th Australian Infantry Brigade War Diary, Appendix 2, April 1917.
21 AWM4 13/13/11: Left Sector First Anzac Artillery Instructions No. 1, 6 April 1917, 4th Australian Divisional Artillery War Diary, April 1917.
22 AWM4 23/12/14: 12th Australian Infantry Brigade Memorandum, 8 April 1917, 12th Australian Infantry Brigade War Diary, Appendix 2a, April 1917.
23 AWM4 13/13/11: Left Sector First Anzac Artillery Order No. 2, 8 April 1917, 4th Australian Division Artillery War Diary, April 1917.

place.'[24] These last minute adjustments were not unusual for this period. Objectives were commonly lengthened and shortened while operational and tactical plans could be modified or entirely revised at short notice. However, there would be a very significant change prior to the imminent Bullecourt operation when, overnight, the lifting barrage, the overarching firepower the infantry hoped for, was cancelled and replaced by a tank spearhead. Therefore, the artillery, remaining alert to infantry SOS signals, would be relegated to providing flank support and fire on the village throughout the attack.

Sixty tanks had been made available for the Arras offensive. Forty were assigned to Third Army in the centre, whilst First Army on the left flank had eight, and Fifth Army twelve. The limited experience with tanks the previous year had demonstrated that 'the moral effect of the machine in motion is very great,' and it was thought that just their presence on the battlefield, even if stalled, could intimidate the German infantry and draw their fire.[25] At this stage of the war the new, more effective Mk IV models were still in production, and did not arrive in France until the end of April 1917. Instead, the tanks available for the early stages of the Arras offensive were Mk I and the slightly improved Mk II models. Both designs were mechanically unsound and suffered from myriad problems ranging from ditching to difficulties communicating with the infantry.

The inclusion of tanks had been part of the earliest plans for the British spring offensive. These underwent a series of revisions as the military situation changed, at least once resulting from the German withdrawal and again on 1 April. Tanks were to be 'subsidiary to the main attack,' taking out enemy strong points and other positions *after* the artillery and infantry had passed through. The sixty tanks were to be spread along a front of 32,000 yards or nearly 30 kilometres and, with the emphasis on parcelling out available vehicles along the front instead of concentrating them in deep echelons in one or two sectors, there was little the tank arm could do beyond operate in a supporting role.[26] They were, given their indifferent reliability and limited numbers, certainly not in a position to replace the artillery barrage entirely. Nevertheless, this is what Gough proposed to do before the Bullecourt attack.

Australian Official Historian Charles Bean ascribed the change from lifting barrage to tank support alone to a suggestion made by a Major W.H.L. Watson, CO of D Company, 11th Tank Battalion:

> [I]t was common knowledge that the Fifth Army was rather short of artillery for the heavy task confronting it, and on the night of April 8th Major Watson worked out, for his own satisfaction, a 'surprise concentration' in which his

---

24   AWM4 13/13/11: Left Sector First Anzac Artillery Instructions No. 2, 9 April 1917, 4th Australian Divisional Artillery War Diary, April 1917.

25   TNA WO 95/91/5: Preliminary Report on the Tank Operations at the 'Battle of Arras, 9-13 April 1917, Tank Corps HQ War Diary.

26   Ibid.

tanks, massed on a narrow front ahead of the infantry, should steal up to the Hindenburg line without a barrage. As they entered the German trenches, down would come the barrage, under cover of which, and assisted by the tanks, the infantry would 'sweep through'.[27]

Watson managed to present this scheme at a time when Gough was brimming with confidence after news of the Arras offensive's opening day. With characteristic impetuosity, Gough decided to adopt the proposal for a dawn attack the following morning. Watson, reportedly startled at orders to implement his scheme within 24 hours, rushed to get it done. Curiously, although it was 'common knowledge' that Fifth Army was short of artillery, the 4th Australian Division was able to supply its available batteries with unlimited amounts of ammunition for a preliminary bombardment. Even if there were not as many guns available as the attackers would have wished, there was no reason to do away with artillery support altogether except for total agreement with Watson's plan on the part of the commanding officers involved.

Hailing from the London suburb of Wandsworth, Major William Henry Lowe Watson had transferred to the tank arm from the infantry in late December 1916. By his own account the three months that followed lacked practical, intensive instruction, as 'painfully few real tanks were available for instruction.' Instead, he and his men trained with dummy tanks, laboriously transporting large, heavy canvas facsimiles across faux battlegrounds trailed by laughing children. It was not all heavy lifting:

> [W]e were allowed occasionally to play with real tanks. A sham attack was carried out before hilltops of generals and staff officers, who were much edified by the sight of tanks moving. The total effect was marred by an enthusiastic tank commander, who, in endeavouring to show off the paces of his tank, became badly ditched, and the tank was for a moment on fire. The spectators appeared interested.[28]

This farcical training produced the man who, weeks after completing it, was suddenly not only in charge of Fifth Army tank employment but, by extension, also in command of the primary firepower support for an impending two-brigade infantry assault. His scheme, presumably born of classroom experience in planning 'numerous attacks on the map', was adopted without question and with no more than 24 hours to implement it. Of all the hasty, last-minute, poorly thought out and dangerous of Gough's arrangements, this has the strongest claim for being the worst.

---

27   C.E.W. Bean, *The AIF in France 1917,* Vol. IV (Sydney: Angus & Robertson, 1941), p.272.
28   Major W.H.L. Watson, *A Company of Tanks* (London: William Blackwood & Sons, 1920), Chapter 2.

First Battle of Bullecourt, 11 April 1917

At 12.30 a.m. on 10 April 1917, I Anzac Corps messaged 4th Australian Division to say, 'under Army Orders action will be taken on 10th instant as verbally arranged tanks will precede advance.'[29] The operation was to commence at 4.30 a.m. It is unclear when the verbal orders were issued, but it was at some point on 10 April, leaving fewer than 24 hours to organise the attack. Nevertheless, the battalions of the 4th and 12th brigades were able to reach their jumping-off positions on time and, laying out in the snow, sleet and rain, awaited the arrival of the expected armoured support. They did not. Instead, the tanks became lost in the darkness of a heavy snowstorm. Once it was ascertained that they would reach the jumping-off position in broad daylight instead of during the pre-dawn hour as planned, the attack was called off. The men were fortunate in their journey back that they were concealed by a raging snowstorm and suffered fewer casualties than might otherwise have been expected during a daylight withdrawal. After having lain out in the inclement weather for hours they were 'considerably exhausted.'[30] Worse still, nobody had thought to inform the neighbouring 185th Brigade, 62nd Division, tasked with attacking on the left, that the operation was postponed. Held up by barbed wire and completely unsupported on the right flank, it was forced to withdraw.[31]

It was an ignominious start to a novel tactical experiment. There were other signs that the tanks would not be as effective as hoped. On 9 April 48 tanks were employed by First and Third armies. None of the eight assigned to First Army managed to keep up with the infantry and became ditched shortly afterwards. In Third Army, the eight tanks accompanying XVII Corps advanced at Zero, but at least four ditched and another two were knocked out by shellfire. Worse, of the 16 tanks assigned to VI Corps, five failed to reach the jumping-off line in time, one suffering from engine trouble before breaking down altogether after it was coaxed across the line. The remaining tanks became ditched or were disabled by hostile shelling. The fate of the VII Corps armour was similar. In fact, tanks were so ineffective that the after-action report compiled by the 'Heavy Branch Machine Gun Corps'/'Tank Corps'[32] was essentially a detailed list of ditched vehicles, mechanical failures and total destruction. Of those vehicles reported to have reached enemy lines there is almost no mention of subsequent activity except in the case of a few tanks with VII Corps, which reportedly caused the Germans to 'surrender freely' at the sight of them. 'The moral effect of the tanks', the report continued, 'was great, inspiring our infantry and demoralising

---

29   AWM4 1/29/15 Pt 1: 1st Anzac Corps War Diary, April 1917.
30   AWM4 1/48/13 Pt 2: Report on Attack against Hindenburg Line by 4th Australian Division – April 11th, 1917, 4th Australian Division War Diary, Appendix 39, April 1917.
31   TNA WO 95/3079/2: 185th Infantry Brigade War Diary, April 1917.
32   At this stage of the war the relatively new tank arm was titled Heavy Branch Machine Gun Corps (HBMGC). The name was officially changed to 'Tank Corps' on 27 July 1917. The latter will be employed throughout this chapter to avoid confusion.

the enemy.' Nevertheless, for Fifth Army, about to employ tanks as the spearhead element of the Bullecourt assault, the most important information gleaned from the report was that the total number of vehicles available to First and Third armies was reduced by 83 percent on the first day by *ditching alone*.[33] Thus even the most basic enquiry would have made it clear that tank performance during the recent operations was insignificant at best and would never succeed in the role Fifth Army headquarters had allotted them.

There was no question that Bullecourt assault would be launched again the day after the abortive attempt of 10 April. Furthermore, there would be little in the way of modifications to the plan. At least the 24 hour delay allowed for improvements in the artillery preparations. While tanks maintained their role as the only source of overarching firepower support to the infantry, there would also be additional artillery cooperation. Moreover, the delay allowed for more accurate artillery registration. The heavy artillery was to continue to shell enemy positions around Bullecourt, Riencourt and Quéant (albeit with no increase on their night time rate of fire) from the start of the operation. At 4.45 a.m., some 15 minutes after the operation was scheduled to start, the field artillery would place barrages on each flank. Infantry and tanks were allotted half an hour to reach Bullecourt, at which time the bombardment of the village would halt in order to allow four tanks to enter and mop up the hostile garrison. A further 15 minutes would be allowed to pass, after which the bombardment of Riencourt would stop, again, to allow one or two with infantry to enter. The infantry had the option to signal the artillery for fire on targets hindering the advance, but the overall plan almost completely divorced the artillery from the assaulting battalions. This was in no way reflective of the most recent applications of firepower in the advance.

Once determined, the projected role of tanks at Bullecourt never changed. Forging ahead at 4:30 a.m. on 11 April, they were to precede the infantry advance. Hopes for armour efficacy amongst junior infantry officers was great after they were told that 'on reaching the trenches, and as soon as they have occupied them, the tanks will display a green disc meaning "come on." As soon as the signal is given, the infantry will advance and seize their objective. Subsequently two tanks will deal with Bullecourt.'[34] How 12 tanks were to occupy successive trenches remains obscure, although it must be presumed that the orders meant to empty them of the enemy ready before the infantry arrived. There was also no contingency for what might happen if the infantry failed to distinguish the green discs from a distance in the pre-dawn light.

The GOC 4th Australian Division, Major-General William Holmes, had had enough warning of the impending attack on Bullecourt to personally carry out a

---

33 TNA WO 95/91/5: 'Preliminary Report on the Tank Operations at the 'Battle of Arras', 9-13 April 1917, Tank HQ Corps War Diary.
34 AWM4 23/12/14: 12th Australian Infantry Brigade Order No. 135, 10 April 1917, 12th Australian Infantry Brigade War Diary, Appendix 4, April 1917. See also AWM4 23/4/19: 'Fourth Australian Infantry Brigade Order No. 76,' 10 April 1917, War Diary 4th Australian Infantry Brigade War Diary, Appendix 4, April 1917.

thorough reconnaissance. Based on his findings, he decided to employ one brigade in a direct attack on the village itself while carrying out subsidiary operations on the flanks. However, on 6 April I Anzac Corps headquarters informed him that the village was to be 'squeezed out' by advances on its flanks alone. Deploying two battalions of 12th Brigade and all four battalions of the 4th Brigade, Holmes committed none to a direct assault on Bullecourt itself. Entry into the village would occur after the tanks had been through it. He subsequently observed that 'the infantry brigadiers made very thorough arrangements for the attack and in spite of the short time given them in which to complete their plans, all details were well thought out.'[35] What remained unclear, however, was the state of the enemy's barbed wire defences, and whether or not tanks would be enough to 'smash the wire' where required.[36]

Major-General W. Holmes.

At 3.05 a.m. on the morning of 11 April 1917, 11 of the 12 assigned tanks operating on 4th Australian Division's front were reported to be in position. At 4:00 a.m. the assault battalions confirmed they were in position as well. Zero hour having been set for 4.30 a.m., the operation would begin at the precise time. This undetected forming-up would be its only success.

Rumbling forward at Zero, the tanks made their way towards the enemy defences. Two were knocked out in Bullecourt. Another two returned damaged. Two reached the Hindenburg Line but were destroyed by shellfire while waiting for the infantry to catch up. Two tanks were reported to have cleared Riencourt with approximately 200 Australian infantry, but as a strong German counter-attack overwhelmed and captured everyone involved, this is likely an exaggeration. Holmes suggested that this party only got within 150 yards of the village before surrendering. He also suggested that 'only one [tank] reached the Hindenburg Line … where it was immediately put

35 AWM4 1/48/13 Pt 2: 'Report on Attack against Hindenburg Line by 4th Australian Division – April 11th, 1917', 4th Australian Division War Diary, Appendix 39, April 1917.

36 TNA WO 95/91/5: 'Preliminary Report on the Tank Operations at the 'Battle of Arras', 9-13th April 1917, Tank Corps HQ War Diary.

Derelict British
tank opposite the
Hindenburg Line
defences. (Private
collection)

out of action. It is doubtful whether any tank passed the Hindenburg Line, although one was reported being observed going towards Hendecourt.'[37] Despite disparities in the reporting, it is certain that shellfire accounted for at least six vehicles, with another two or three badly damaged by it. Only one tank is recorded to have returned safely. The tank plan had failed.

What then of the unprotected infantry? Battalions moved off the jumping-off line at 4.45 a.m. into fierce machine-gun and rifle fire that had not been diminished or suppressed by the preceding tanks. Within a short distance the attackers encountered swathes of uncut barbed wire along most of the attacking front, which again had not been 'smashed' by the tanks or indeed the artillery during the preparatory bombardments. Under intense fire and unable to negotiate the wire, 4th and 12th brigades separated, leaving a gap that would never be closed and which 'was a continual source of worry and danger to both brigades' throughout the assault. The flank bombardments were light and tentative at best due to conflicting information about where the infantry actually was. As a result, the Germans were able to deliver repeated counter-attacks against both flanks and through the gap as well.[38]

Somehow, in the face of determined resistance and mounting casualties, disparate groups of Australian infantry managed to enter and secure the first two trench objectives. The third remained beyond reach. Isolated and under constant attack, contemporary reports indicate 'fierce bomb fighting took place from the moment our men entered the captured position.'[39] Unceasing German machine-gun fire from Riencourt and Bullecourt cut down every attempt to supply the hard-pressed attackers with bombs and S.A.A. It was becoming increasingly difficult to hold on. Sometime after

37   AWM4 1/48/13 Pt 2: 'Report on Attack against Hindenburg Line by 4th Australian Division – April 11th, 1917, 4th Australian Division War Diary, Appendix 39, April 1917.
38   Ibid.
39   AWM4 23/4/19: 'Intelligence Summary – Attack,' 11 April 1917, 4th Australian Infantry Brigade War Diary, Appendix 4, April 1917.

11:00 a.m. yet another strong German counter-attack began to force the Australians back. At 11.20 a.m. Lieutenant D.S. Aarons of 16th Battalion risked his life by passing through a machine-gun barrage to relate first-hand information on the situation to headquarters. He reported that at least 25 percent of the brigade were casualties, bombs had run out and the enemy was threatening the weak Australian line from all sides. It was clear that the position was untenable. By noon a general retirement was in progress under cover of a light artillery barrage.

Holmes did not hold back his opinion on what caused the failure – the tanks, and the tanks alone. 'Owing to the tanks giving no assistance whatever to the infantry,' he observed:

> ... the latter had to advance under heavy machine-gun fire across open ground and clamber over wire which was in many places quite undamaged. This caused heavy casualties and the troops, when they reached their objectives, were in considerable confusion and very reduced in numbers.

Not only that but, he added, 'owing to the tanks failing to do their work, a large gap was left between the two brigades, which could never be closed, and whence the enemy delivered repeated counter-attacks.'[40] There was nowhere else to lay the blame. The performance of the infantry, Holmes wrote, 'who went forward unaided, against a strongly wired line and captured it and held it for seven hours, speaks for itself.' Even the artillery, in his estimation, deserved praise for answering all calls made upon them, and for quickly putting down a barrage to assist withdrawing troops when required, although the gunners were 'considerably handicapped by doubt as to the position of our troops.' Holmes felt, however, that 'if Bullecourt had [been] attacked as originally intended, and if our attack had been carried out under an artillery barrage – even with the wire only partially cut as it was – I am confident that the ground gained could have been held.'[41] Although there was no way of knowing if this would have been the case, based on previous fighting experience on Pozières Ridge, it is likely to have provided the best chance of success.

Holmes's vitriol was echoed in a report written by 4th Brigade battalion commanders, Lieutenant-Colonel Edmund Drake-Brockman of 16th Battalion and Lieutenant-Colonel John Peck of 14th Battalion. They wrote that the Bullecourt operation was 'one of the most heroic achievements by any body of troops.' Unlike Holmes, however, they did not view the artillery cooperation with sympathy:

> [U]naided by Artillery, forsaken by Tanks on which so much depended, the Brigade crossed formidable unbroken wire and secured both objectives which

40   AWM4 1/48/13 Pt 2: 'Report on Attack against Hindenburg Line by 4th Australian Division – April 11th, 1917, 4th Australian Division War Diary, Appendix 39, April 1917.
41   Ibid.

they held on to for 7 hours and only then forced to retire owing to overwhelming numbers of the enemy, numerous casualties, shortage of bombs with no immediate hope of getting more up; and hesitating co-operation from the Artillery. [42]

Tank cooperation, they observed, was 'useless, or worse than useless' and, in their fury, even attacked the tank crews themselves claiming that they had no idea what they were there to do, and that 'personal safety and comfort seemed their sole ambition … The whole outfit showed rank inefficiency' and, in some cases, crews appeared to lack 'British tenacity and pluck, and that determination to go forward at all costs, which is naturally looked for in Britishers.'[43]

Whilst Australian fury over the failed attack at Bullecourt was directly aimed at tanks, the Tank Corps itself was not happy with the course of events either. Initial plans had been for the tanks to work *behind* the infantry to assist with mopping up, with both arms working forward under cover of a lifting barrage. Fifth Army had turned this on its head by removing the artillery barrage altogether and putting the tanks *in front* of the infantry to overcome strongpoints first. The Tank Corps after-action report stated, 'the whole operation from a tank point of view was a makeshift; it possessed little or no power of endurance or co-ordination and no means was possible of turning to our advantage the accidents of battle once Tanks had been launched.'[44] There were too few tanks to effectively undertake the assigned role and there was no reserve available, factors which were very clear to tank commanders. Failure at Bullecourt demonstrated what many tankers already knew; that armour struggled to traverse heavily shelled ground, and that tanks should be deployed in depth rather than being strung out across the front in penny packets. Furthermore, tanks should never precede the infantry, which was borne out, and their lack of general mobility meant they should never operate outside of an artillery barrage. Bullecourt had reflected very badly on the Tank Corps inasmuch as the nascent unit had little to do with the decision-making process.

Watson, the architect of the Bullecourt tank scheme, later referred to it 'a minor disaster'. He also claimed that 'the Australians, in the bitterness of their losses, looked for scapegoats and found them in my tanks, but my tanks were not to blame.' He never really identified who was to blame and vaguely observed, 'I have heard a lecturer say that to attack the Hindenburg Line on a front of fifteen hundred yards without support on either flank was rash.'[45] Somehow the absolute failure of the tanks and the resultant shambolic infantry assault also escaped the upper echelons of command. Brigadier-General Hugh Elles, the Tank Corps commander, responded to the Bullecourt

42   AWM4 23/4/19: 'Special Operation on 'Tank' Co-operation in Attack Night of 10/11th April 1917, 4th Australian Infantry Brigade War Diary, Appendix 5, April 1917.

43   'Special Operation on 'Tank' Co-operation in Attack Night of 10/11th April 1917. AWM4 23/4/19, 4th Australian Infantry Brigade War Diary, Appendix 5, April 1917.

44   TNA WO 95/91/5: Preliminary Report on the Tank Operations at the 'Battle of Arras', 9-13 April 1917, Tank Corps HQ War Diary.

45   Watson, *A Company of Tanks*, p.71.

First Battle of Bullecourt: Australian prisoners under escort.

after-action reports that crossed his desk with the remark that 'this is the best thing that tanks have done yet.' Higher up the chain of command, Gough forwarded a message to Watson informing him that 'The Army Commander is very pleased with the gallantry and skill displayed by your company in the attack today, and the fact that the objectives were subsequently lost does not detract from the success of the tanks.'[46] Watson celebrated this success with a short holiday in Amiens.

The two Australian brigades at First Bullecourt suffered some 3,300 casualties killed, wounded and missing. Approximately 1,170 Australians were taken prisoner, the largest number captured in a single engagement during the war. No ground was retained, and the 4th Australian Division was withdrawn to Albert to recover. Further battles were on the horizon, but the Australian infantry had to undergo specialised intensive training in 1918 before they ever worked with the tank arm again.

German Counter-attack at Lagnicourt, 15 April 1917

Two days after the disastrous attempt to seize Bullecourt, the 4th Australian Division was relieved in the line by 2nd Australian Division. It was to immediately revert to the former programme of vigorous patrolling while being prepared to occupy the Hindenburg Line 'should the enemy defence at this point weaken under pressure of

46   Ibid.

the advance of the Army on our left.[47] This the 2nd Division was prepared to do, dispatching several patrols nightly to try and determine how strongly the trenches opposite were held, and what condition they were in.

This scheme was disrupted in the early hours of 15 April, when the 11th Battalion of 3rd Brigade reported the enemy massing on its front. Within five minutes of the report, the Germans attacked under intense artillery fire, and within half an hour were advancing 'in great strength' towards the recently captured town of Lagnicourt.[48] By 5.45 a.m., the attackers had passed through Lagnicourt. The 20th Battalion, having rapidly deployed to confront the enemy head-on, fiercely resisted all along the line whilst an effective artillery barrage materially assisted efforts to push the enemy back. Within three hours, the Germans were back in the Hindenburg Line, and the original Australian line re-established.[49]

That same day, three prisoners captured during the German riposte, were asked during interrogation what the counter-attack objective had been. They replied that it was a minor operation designed to seize field gun batteries and hold Lagnicourt for 24 hours or so before withdrawing to their own line. Moreover, the enemy opposite the Australians were considered 'dispirited,' their senior officers hoping to improve morale through the action. They also confirmed that the Germans had no intention of further withdrawals and that the Hindenburg Line was still being strengthened.[50]

Notwithstanding these prisoner assertions, the enemy spoiling attack demon-strated the relative weakness of the Australian defences. Having previously focused on offensive operations, this sudden reversal of fortune was a reminder that a proper defence had to be established and maintained. This is a prime example of just how far the German withdrawal removed commanders at all levels from the basic military principle of securing positions against counter-attack. Therefore, the possibility that the enemy could resort to offensive action was simply not taken into consideration and it showed. Even battalion and company commanders, who had previously neglected local defences, were shocked by the sudden attack.

Second Battle of Bullecourt, 3 May 1917

Regardless of the dismal failure at First Bullecourt, British GHQ's imperative for the ongoing Arras offensive was to push on as quickly as possible – nowhere more so than on Fifth Army front. In fact, the day after the fruitless assault, Gough's

47   TNA WO 95/519/5: Summary of Operations of Fifth Army for week ending 8p.m. 13th April 1917,' Fifth Army War Diary, April 1917.
48   AWM4 23/3/18: 3rd Australian Infantry Brigade War Diary, 15 April 1917.
49   AWM4 1/44/21 Pt. 2: Weekly Summary of Operations for period 12 noon 14th April to 8a.m, 20 April 1917, 2nd Australian Division War Diary, April 1917.
50   AWM4 1/44/21 Pt 1: Examination of Prisoners, 15 April 1917, 2nd Australian Division War Diary, April 1917.

headquarters issued orders to renew the attack on the Hindenburg Line. This time 62nd Division was to directly attack Bullecourt, while 2nd Australian Division attempted to establish a line in part of the Hindenburg defences known as the Drocourt–Quéant Line. The operation was to take place on 15 April, the same day as the German counter-attack, so was postponed. The preparations would take some time. Meantime, small attacks, strong patrols and other activities were the order of the day.

On 16 April, French C-in-C Nivelle launched his great offensive. Although demonstrating initial promise, it soon became apparent that it would not achieve the promised breakthrough in 48 hours and, like so many campaigns on the Western Front, it degenerated into a costly battle of attrition. Thus the British campaign around Arras, designed to support the French campaign in the first instance, became an important means of diverting German reserves away from Nivelle's stalled push. By early May BEF C-in-C, Field Marshal Sir Douglas Haig, certain of the capacity of his troops, remarked on 3 May that the BEF could 'at once advance to the attack, if the French have the means and the intention to continue their present plan. If they cannot the battle we must another plan.'[51]

As Haig was expressing this idea to General Philippe Pétain, Nivelle's successor, I Anzac Corps launched its second assault on Bullecourt. Theirs was not the lion's share of the operation, which was to be carried out by 62nd Division on the left. Further north Third and First armies launched an ambitious general assault that would prove to be one of the 'blackest' days of the war.[52] Australian bitterness over the outcome of First Bullecourt resulted in some concessions, the most important being the timing of the assault (3.45 a.m.) which suited the Anzacs far more than it suited Third and First armies which went on to experience disastrous operational consequences. As for the despised tanks, they would be kept a very long way from the Australian line.[53]

As with the previous assault plan, Bullecourt was to be 'pinched out'. For the second operation, 62nd Division was tasked with seizing the village and the Hindenburg Line defences that ran in front of it. The Australian objectives remained much the same. The first objective was the front and second line trenches of the Hindenburg Line. Further on, the Drocourt–Quéant Switch Line was the designated second objective; Riencourt village the third. With no question that the artillery barrage would be substituted for something else, the Australian infantry were to be supported by a creeping barrage lifting roughly 100 yards every three minutes. Additional protective barrages could be called for should the advance be held up, and allowances were made for counter-battery fire and flank bombardments when and where necessary. The 2nd Division left little to chance, issuing extensive orders with tailored instructions

---

51   Haig Diary entry, 3 May 1917 in Robert Blake (ed.), *The Private Papers of Douglas Haig 1914-1919* (London: Eyre & Spottiswoode, 1952), pp.226-27.

52   See Chapter 12 in this volume.

53   Jonathan Walker, *The Blood Tub: General Gough and the Battle of Bullecourt 1917* (London: Spellmount, 1998), pp.131-32.

for specialist machine-gun and engineer units. Primary emphasis was on firepower and cautious advance in order to maintain close contact with the neighbouring 62nd Division.

The delay had been of material benefit to the infantry of 2nd Division The 5th and 6th brigades had been allotted the task of attacking on 15 April, but once the operation was postponed, they were withdrawn from the line to rest. During this time they extensively practiced day and night attacks over ground marked out to represent designated objectives. In addition, operation orders and instructions, disseminated by division and brigade headquarters, were issued to assault battalions to ensure all ranks knew their role.

At 3.45 a.m. on 3 May, the infantry of 5th and 6th brigades passed over the jumping-off line on time and in good order. On the left, 6th Brigade found the wire largely cut. Despite some machine-gun and trench mortar fire from Bullecourt, its battalions were able to secure their assigned portion of the Hindenburg Line within 30 minutes. On the right, 5th Brigade encountered swathes of uncut wire and sustained heavy losses from machine-guns situated on the left. This part of the assault quickly fell into disarray. Severe officer casualties ensured that the attackers could not reorganise in time to engage the enemy effectively. Lacking junior leadership at the sharp end, stragglers made their way back instead of carrying on. To remedy this, available reserves consisting of replacement officers and 150 stragglers were duly sent forward. Another 200-400 stragglers of 5th Brigade were reorganised by officers of 6th Brigade. By this time the barrage had moved on, leaving both attacker and defender to engage in grisly, close-quarter trench fighting.

This muddled situation on the right began to act as an anchor to the advance on the left, as 6th Brigade struggled to maintain touch with 5th Brigade. The situation was little better on the left where 2/6th West Yorks of 185th Brigade was to maintain touch with 6th Brigade. Encountering heavy machine-gun fire – one enemy gun was spotted firing from a derelict tank – whilst making its way through the early morning darkness and dust raised by the barrage, the battalion became disoriented, and veered left away from 6th Brigade. Convinced that the attack on the whole was failing from as early as 4.50 a.m., 6th Brigade headquarters requested modifications to the artillery programme whereby the barrage was halted somewhere beyond the second objective in order to facilitate the infantry's reorganisation and consolidation efforts.

Over the succeeding days 1st, 2nd and 5th Australian divisions (I Anzac Corps) and 7th, 58th and 62nd divisions (V Corps) fought hard to effect an advance beyond the Bullecourt defences. On I Anzac Corps' front more and more infantry were drawn into the fight, with battalions of 1st Australian Division being drawn in. Small advances were made through bombing attacks, while repeated German counter-thrusts threatened to hurl the Australians back. It was subsequently reported that 'all ranks of the 2nd and 1st Australian Divisions, during their occupation of the Hindenburg Line, were continuously engaged with the enemy under heavy shellfire or in close combat, and they held on their positions with their usual tenacity and

Bullecourt and environs from the air, 25 May 1917. (Paul Humphriss)

determination.'[54] The fighting continued for days, with renewed offensive efforts on 7 May resulting in further gains. A final German counter-attack precluded their abandonment of Bullecourt and, on 12 May, after 9 days of relentless fighting, the shattered village passed into British hands. Brigade after brigade of Australians had been rotated in and out of the line during Second Bullecourt. Indeed, it was also deemed necessary to dispatch elements of 5th Australian Division to reinforce or relieve 1st and 2nd divisions, both of which were slowly being ground down. In costly display of tenacity and determination, hundreds of casualties were sustained by I Anzac

54   AWM4 1/44/22 Pt 2: 'Report on the Operations against the Hindenburg line by the 2nd Australian Division, between the 3rd and 10th May 1917.' 2nd Australian Division War Diary, Appendix 19, May 1917.

Corps for little or no territorial gain. After more than a week of vicious, unremitting fighting; after sustaining more than twice the casualties of First Bullecourt; after the capture of an obscure village that contributed almost nothing of strategic importance, the job was done and the Australians, exhausted by the ordeal, were withdrawn for rest, refitting and intake of reinforcements.

Conclusion

It takes very little in the way of hindsight to find the claims of Melbourne *Punch* that Bullecourt would become 'a source of deeper gratification to Australians than Gallipoli; not because the fighting was more heroic, but because it was more successful' laughable if not so tragically wrong.[55] The entire experience was an exercise in lost perspective, lost lessons and lost lives. As per official battle nomenclature, the 'German Retreat to the Hindenburg Line'[56] transformed into an exhilarating chase for commanders – at all levels – inured to static trench warfare. The fact that the unexpected enemy move was a *voluntary withdrawal* and not the result of offensive action appears to have been recognised only as an intellectual exercise. It felt like success and success must be exploited. This played into the hands of Fifth Army GOC Hubert Gough who, primarily due to an aggressive and impulsive approach to the conduct of war, had risen in rank far more rapidly than expected. Birdwood and the I Anzac Corps staff, having previously served under Gough during the Pozières operations, were fully aware of his nature. And yet they were equally at fault for falling under the spell of aggressive pursuit by constant patrolling and minor attacks as a means of expediting the enemy's retirement. While this may be a sound military approach – to maintain pressure on a retiring enemy in the hopes of forcing a rout – it should not have been the only approach. Up until First Bullecourt Fifth Army and its subordinate I Anzac Corps' operational modus operandi was to push forward strong patrols to seize abandoned posts. This approach was expanded to employment of strong patrols to *attack and* capture *defended* posts. It was only when these patrols were repulsed that a small-scale, set-piece attack, usually involving one or two battalions, was organised. This was, however, never the preferred option in that as often as these attacks succeeded they would also take more time thus derailing the all-important speed of the advance.

The early stages of the German withdrawal was a time of intoxicating pursuit with few ramifications for British and Australian commanders. By the time serious obstacles were encountered, Noreuil on 20 March for example, the failure to halt, take stock of the situation and prepare for the assault would, more often than not, result

---

55   'Bullecourt', *Northern Times*, 14 May 1917, p.4.
56   See Major A.F. Becke, *Order of Battle Part 4 – The Army Council, GHQs, Armies and Corps 1914-1918* (London: HMSO, 1945), pp.

in a repulse with heavy losses. It was prior to First Bullecourt when the questionable scheme of an arrogant and overreaching tank commander competed with more pressing matters for Gough's attention. In the end, the GOC Fifth Army's inclination for accelerated enterprises won and paved the way for the shambles. Second Bullecourt demonstrated that careful preparations and increased firepower could still result in a long and bloody slog for negligible gains. This loss of overall perspective becomes an important factor when judging events during the German withdrawal and subsequent Bullecourt operations, no more so than on I Anzac Corps front. There was no proper reassessment of whether the strategy and tactics were appropriate. Strong patrol after strong patrol was ordered forward to carry out increasingly risky enterprises while brigade after brigade suffered enormous losses in two deadly assaults that resulted in the capture of Bullecourt and for what? The overarching logic behind any need to occupy the village had long since departed even as the infantry fought on.

The senior command of I Anzac Corps, Lieutenant-General Sir William Birdwood and his senior staff officer Brigadier-General Cyril Brudenell White, appear to have learned very little under Gough. During the Pozières fighting of the previous year, operations deteriorated into rushed piecemeal attacks resulting in small-scale but reportable successes instead of measured, steady advances protected by well-planned artillery barrages. By early 1917 the situation took a tragically farcical turn when the nascent tank arm was deemed to be a magical instrument of breakthrough far beyond previously demonstrated capabilities before Birdwood and White would stand up to Gough instead of grumbling behind his back.

There were some positives to the Australian experience at Bullecourt, but they require closer scrutiny to uncover. Lower level commanders like Drake-Brockman and Peck found a voice, and a very strong sense of what would work and what would not. And somehow, despite Birdwood's vacillatory style of command, they were able to make their opinions stick in some cases, most notably the clear concessions made for 3 May. Therefore, this period demonstrated clear principles by which to conduct an offensive operation. While it was always clear that artillery was critical to success, the advance to the Hindenburg Line and subsequent Bullecourt operations also demonstrated why, and in what manner, this overarching firepower could contribute to (or more often, undo) a battle plan. Thus the harrowing Bullecourt experience materially contributed to Australian understanding of trench warfare on the Western Front. All of this, however, is presumed with a great deal of hindsight in order to identify small positives in the cumulative disaster that was Bullecourt. And while the Australian press hoped to find national glory in a grand contribution to the overall war effort, in no time Bullecourt had been relegated to a second-hand story. The 10th anniversary of the battle barely raised a stir in the press, and soon afterwards it was gone altogether.

12

Black Day of the British Army
The Third Battle of the Scarpe 3 May 1917

Harry Sanderson

Of all the battles fought by the British Army during the First World War, according to British official historian Cyril Falls, the Third Battle of the Scarpe stood out 'in the minds of many who witnessed it' as 'the blackest day of the war.'[1] One of these witnesses was veteran infantryman Private C.R. Smith who had served in France with the 7/Buffs (East Kent Regiment), 18th (Eastern) Division since July 1915. He had participated in and witnessed previous severe fighting including the opening day of the Somme offensive on 1 July 1916; 'Battle of Bazentin Ridge' (14-17 July); 'Battle of Thiepval Ridge' (26-28 September); 'Capture of the Schwaben Redoubt' (30 September-5 October); 'Capture of Regina Trench' (21 October); 'Battle of the Ancre' (13-18 November) and, in February and March 1917, 'Operations on the Ancre' and the 'Retreat to the Hindenburg Line'. Wounded during Third Scarpe, Smith remarked in his diary that 'we were far worse off in this attack than any the division had ever been in.'[2]

The Third Scarpe was fought on 3 May 1917 as part of the wider Battle of Arras and involved two British field armies, five corps and twelve divisions. What followed was disaster; in most places the attack was repulsed without any gains and with very heavy casualties. The only clear success was Canadian Corps' capture of Fresnoy village, but this was lost five 'days later. What made this all the more surprising was that it came less than one month after the BEF's greatest success of the war to that point: the opening of the Battle of Arras on 9 April. Despite being the black day of the

1   Cyril Falls, *Military Operations: France and Belgium,* Vol. 1 (London: Macmillan & Co., 1940), p.450.
2   IWM: Documents 8486: 'My Diary', Vol. 3, p.102, C.R. Smith Papers and Major A.F. Becke, *Order of Battle Divisions, Part 3A – New Army Divisions (9-26)* (London: HMSO, 1945), pp.85-86.

British Army, Third Scarpe remains relatively understudied with examination of its events largely restricted to brief excerpts from more comprehensive texts in which it is frequently cited as an example of a poorly conducted attack and evidence of weak British generalship. J.P. Harris repeated the official historian's remark and described it as a 'miserable mess' whilst Ian Beckett, Timothy Bowman and Mark Connelly viewed the offensive as a 'dismal epilogue on the battle [of Arras].'[3] This chapter expands on these observations by examining Third Scarpe in depth. It will demonstrate that 3 May was indeed a black day for the British Army and that the blame for the shambolic offensive lies squarely on the BEF high command who, in its planning, preparations and execution, were overambitious and hasty whilst simultaneously failing to recognise that the troops employed were inadequately trained and unsuited to the task.

Fundamental to Third Scarpe's failure was its timetable. The battle was conceptualised on 26 April, but other operations took precedence until 29 April, leaving just four days for planning and preparations. Yet, the battle need not have been fought on 3 May. The original justification behind the Battle of Arras had been distracting German attention away from a massive French offensive in Aisne–Champagne to the south. To achieve this the BEF's C-in-C, Field Marshal Sir Douglas Haig, agreed to a large-scale offensive at Arras on 9 April. On the left of the British front, First Army, under General Henry Horne, attacked Vimy Ridge with the Canadian Corps. On the right, Third Army, under General Edmund Allenby, attacked on a front nearly 10 miles wide during the First Battle of the Scarpe.[4] Months of planning and preparation preceded the offensive, and on 9 April it achieved some of the largest territorial gains of the war in the west to that date. Vimy Ridge was seized; Third Army advanced up to 3½ miles, and over 9,000 Germans were captured.[5] The offensive continued the following day, but with diminishing returns although one corps still managed to advance an additional mile.

At this point a long-standing weakness – excessive optimism – of the BEF's commanders began to take hold.[6] Haig and Allenby believed they had the German army on the run and the desire for decisive victory overrode support for the French assault. On 10 April Haig urged the importance of continuing the advance, after which Allenby messaged his corps commanders that 'Third Army is now pursuing a defeated enemy and that risks must be freely taken.'[7] Harris viewed this as 'grossly

3   J.P. Harris, *Douglas Haig and the First World War* (Cambridge: Cambridge University Press, 2008), p.327; Ian Beckett, Timothy Bowman & Mark Connelly, *The British Army and the First World War* (Cambridge: Cambridge University Press, 2017), p.320.

4   Beckett, Bowman & Connelly, *British Army*, pp.307-12. For a recent account of the First Battle of the Scarpe, see Jim Smithson, *A Taste of Success: The First Battle of the Scarpe: The Opening Phase of the Battle of Arras, 9-14 April 1917* (Solihull: Helion & Co., 2017).

5   Falls, *Military Operations 1917*, Vol. I, pp.236, 341.

6   Simon Robbins, *British Generalship on the Western Front 1914-1918: Defeat into Victory* (London: Frank Cass, 2005), pp.68-82.

7   Gary Sheffield & John Bourne (eds.), *Douglas Haig: War Diaries and Letters 1914-1918* (London: Phoenix, 2006), p.278; Gary Sheffield, *The Chief: Douglas Haig and the British*

unrealistic'.[8] German reinforcements were arriving whereas the attack impetus was reduced by growing exhaustion and increasing casualties. Poor weather with heavy snow and rain also hampered the British advance. By 11 April the balance of power had tilted towards the Germans and whilst the British had limited success, most of their assaults were repulsed with heavy losses. This did not dissuade Allenby. Third Army launched numerous small-scale attacks over the next three days for little gain. Similarly, in the south, General Hubert Gough's Fifth Army launched a disastrous attack at Bullecourt on 11 April where 2,258 out of 3,000 attacking infantrymen of 4th Brigade, 4th Australian Division became casualties.

General Sir Edmund Allenby.

Finally, from 15 April there was a week's pause ordered by Haig after three divisional commanders in Third Army registered their opposition to further attacks.[9] Dreams of a decisive victory had been shattered.

Respite was brief, as the BEF still had to support the French offensive. First and Third armies attacked again on 23 April at the Second Battle of the Scarpe, which resulted in limited success and heavy casualties. British GHQ recognised that major success was highly unlikely. So it was that on 26 April Haig's Chief of the General Staff, Lieutenant-General Launcelot Kiggell, informed Allenby and Horne that attacks were to continue only until French operations ceased. It was agreed that First Army was to attack Arleux on 28 April, after which both armies would launch a general offensive on 3 May. This latter assault, the Third Battle of the Scarpe, was to be fought in conjunction with a Fifth Army assault at Bullecourt.[10] Before the end of April Haig was informed that whilst the French were to attack on 5 May,

   Army (London: Aurum Press, 2011), p.216.
8   J.P. Harris, *Haig*, p.305.
9   Falls, *Military Operations 1917*, Vol. I, p.378.
10   Ibid., p.412.

their operations were certain to cease. According to what Allenby and Horne were told, there was now no need for Third Scarpe to be fought. However, Haig changed the justification from supporting the French to achieving a new defensive line. This was not an egregious aim, as haphazard advances throughout April had left the BEF in a vulnerable position. However, there was plenty of time to achieve this. On 30 April Haig informed Allenby and Horne that the advance 'should be deliberately and methodically made, without hurry' and set a deadline of 15 May.[11] Yet, in an obvious contradiction, the C-in-C decided Third Scarpe would proceed on 3 May because initial plans and preparations had commenced on 29 April. This questionable decision laid the foundations of Third Scarpe's failure. Responsibility for this rests with Haig.

The BEF high command was, however, unfazed by their planning. Between Haig, Allenby, Horne and their headquarters, it was decided that twelve British divisions would attack across a front roughly twelve miles wide, extending from modern day Fresnoy-en-Gohelle in the north to Fontaine-lès-Croisilles in the south. Attacking a wide front demonstrated an awareness of past mistakes, as the fighting of 11-14 April involved isolated attacks on narrow fronts that allowed the German defenders to rake the advancing infantry with enfilade fire causing heavy casualties. When the idea of capturing certain German positions with similar attacks before 3 May was postulated, Allenby ruled it out, arguing a large-scale attack had a 'better chance of success and would probably be less costly.'[12] In turn, when Allenby aimed to conduct a night advance on 3 May to pursue what he assumed would be retreating enemy, Haig, sensibly, vetoed it believing the British infantry were not sufficiently trained to carry it out.[13]

First and Third armies issued preliminary orders for the attack on 29 April. First Army's orders were vague, simply stating 'on a day "Z", to be notified later, First Army will continue operations by XIII and Canadian Corps, in co-operation with Third Army.'[14] Third Army's orders were more detailed, containing a definite date of 3 May, the objectives, and methods to be employed such as a creeping barrage.[15] By 1 May all details had been finalised. All divisions employed the same basic approach throughout the Arras offensive; the infantry would advance in waves behind a creeping barrage, whilst the heavy artillery would target enemy batteries, strongpoints and rear areas. Specifics such as creeping barrage pace were left to divisions. The objectives for each division were also fixed. From left to right across the British front, in First Army the Canadian Corps were to capture Fresnoy with the 1st and 2nd Canadian divisions

---

11   The National Archives, London (TNA) WO 95/170/3: 'Note for Conference on 30th April 1917', First Army War General Staff War Diary.

12   TNA WO 95/363/1: 'Third Army Narrative of Operations May 1917', Third Army War Diary General Staff.

13   Falls, *Military Operations 1917*, Vol. I, p.431

14   TNA WO 95/169/2: 'First Army Order No.114', First Army General Staff War Diary.

15   TNA WO 95/805/3: 'VII Corps GCR 604/439: Third Army Plan of Attack for May 3rd', VII Corps General Staff War Diary General.

whilst XIII Corps' 2nd and 31st divisions were to capture Oppy Wood and village and the area between them and Fresnoy exclusive. Third Army's XVII Corps was to capture Greenland Hill and the villages of Roeux and Plouvain with 9th and 4th divisions. The 12th, 3rd, and 56th divisions of VI Corps were to capture a general line from Pelves village to St Rohart Factory and VII Corps' 14th, 18th, and 21st divisions were to seize the villages of Chérisy and Fontaine. The 29th and 50th divisions were in army reserve and unavailable for the battle.[16] It took time for these orders to work their way down from corps to divisions, brigades and battalions. It was only on 2 May that the majority of units received final orders; For example, 54th Brigade, 18th Division, only issued them at 0600 on 2 May, after which they reached component battalions around lunchtime.[17] This negated the possibility of feedback, discussion or alterations. In many cases a single conference between senior officers was all that could be managed.[18] The overriding problem, however, was that these plans were fuelled by the over-optimism of the high command. They ignored the increasing strength of the German defenders and the declining power of British forces. Moreover, objectives were far in advance of what could realistically be achieved and the short timetable allowed no opportunity for this to be addressed.

The first problem was that the German defenders were stronger than when Arras began. On 9 April the British attack was opposed by six German divisions; at Third Scarpe it faced seven.[19] The Germans had also replaced divisions which had suffered heavy casualties with fresh ones. Immediately after 9 April the Germans sent nine new divisions to the Arras front, and on 11 April the British were facing a 'practically new army'.[20] Of the seven German divisions at Third Scarpe, three had fought in April but the remainder were fresh and newly arrived.[21] The German artillery was also better off, as lost guns were quickly replaced and the heavy artillery assets increased in number.[22] The official historian provides a figure of 881 enemy guns on 9 April versus 1,145 by 23 April.[23]

The Germans also addressed significant weaknesses in their defensive approach to defence. Over the winter of 1916-17, they implemented a new defence-in-depth system which replaced the traditional frontline with staggered defensive layers thousands

16   All these objectives are rough guides simplified for ease of understanding. For example, 18th Division's final objective was a line 200 yards east of Chérisy.
17   TNA WO 95/2041/5: '54th Infantry Brigade Order No. 65', 54th Brigade General Staff War Diary.
18   TNA WO 95/2041/5: 'Extracts from Diary of Brigadier-General C. Cunliffe Owen, Commanding 54th Infantry Brigade, 18/Division', 54th Brigade General Staff War Diary.
19   Jonathan Boff, *Haig's Enemy: Crown Prince Rupprecht and Germany's War on the Western Front* (Oxford: Oxford University Press, 2018), p.158.
20   Falls, *Military Operations 1917*, Vol. I, p.259.
21   Ibid., p.458
22   Jack Sheldon, *The German Army in the Spring Offensives 1917: Arras, Aisne & Champagne* (Barnsley: Pen & Sword, 2015, Kindle e-book), loc. 6572/9347.
23   Falls, *Military Operations 1917*, Vol. I, p.384.

of yards in depth, and with numerous divisions in reserve ready to counter-attack. However, on 9 April, despite three defence lines, each comprised of extensive trench systems and strongpoints, the German *Sixth Army* deployed far too many men in the forward zone. The German infantry lost one-third its manpower when these positions were rapidly overrun.[24] *Sixth Army* reserve divisions, situated too far back to counter-attack, were unable to provide assistance that day. Thus *Bavarian Infanterie Regiment Nr. 8's* reserve battalion was 22 kilometres from the frontline. It had six-and-a-half out of eight companies in the front line, with only 13 other ranks in the second line.[25] Thus the British faced next to no opposition once they had broken through the enemy first line.

The Germans responded by purging senior officers. Most importantly, *Colonel* Fritz von Loßberg was appointed Chief of Staff to *Sixth Army*, which was responsible for the Arras front. During the British pause between 15 and 23 April, Loßberg withdrew his forces to the still intact German third line. This was a formidable position. It largely occupied high ground allowing for clear observation and exploited hilly terrain by constructing defences on reverse slopes where they were difficult for the British to observe. Loßberg strengthened it further by implementing a new approach which abandoned rigidly holding a fixed defence line. Rather, there was an outpost zone between 1,500-2,000 yards deep, which was filled with a patchwork quilt of mutually supporting fortified villages, concrete dugouts, disconnected trenches, woods, shell holes and other defences all camouflaged and packed with machine-guns. Behind this was an even deeper battle zone, and even further back was a reserve line where counter-attack divisions were held ready. Whilst the individual positions were less formidable than those of 9 April, they worked more effectively. If the British succeeding in capturing one area, it did not compromise the remainder of the line. Instead the attackers became trapped as the remaining enemy positions, supported by artillery, inflicted heavy losses before counter-attack divisions were sent in to sweep back the latest enemy incursion.[26]

This was the defensive system First and Third armies faced at Third Scarpe. Overcoming it would be a more difficult task than that which had been faced on 9 April. British commanders do not appear to have realised this despite acquaintance with the new German defence during Second Scarpe and Arleux on 23 and 28 April respectively. In both cases the infantry had fought their way forward, but whilst some gains were held, German counter-attacks forced the attackers back to their original jumping-off line. On 30 April VI Corps reported, 'the enemy's defences consist of no regular system but of disconnected trenches' which were 'well sited and difficult to observe.' However, they were 'very incomplete' thus giving the impression they

24   Ibid., pp.175, 241.
25   Boff, *Haig's Enemy*, pp.161-62
26   See Falls, *Military Operations 1917*, Vol. I, p.402; Sheldon, *The German Army;* G.C. Wynne, *If Germany Attacks: The Battle in Depth in the West* (Westport, Connecticut: Greenwood, 1976).

German cartoon commentary on the battles of the Scarpe: The English
'breakthrough' cavalry in readiness at Arras – 'Hey Tommy, if our nags don't
get some exercise before pursuing the Germans, we shall have to give them
enemas!' (*Kladderadatsch*, 20 May 1917)

thought the enemy intended to build an extensive trench system similar to that faced
on 9 April.[27] Other formations were equally nonplussed, a brigade of 9th (Scottish)
Division noted, 'the exact line held by the German is uncertain.' Its staff only knew
the enemy opposite was holding a series of strongpoints.[28]

In contrast to this complex and deadly defence system, the attacking forces were a
blunted weapon. The Royal Artillery had been severely weakened by the end of April.
This was a major problem as the gunners were vital to success. When the Arras offensive began, the attackers possessed more guns than ever before, with nearly 2,000
more than in 1916, and these of better quality and heavier calibres.[29] There was more
ammunition and many shells benefitted from the new 106 Fuse, which cut barbed wire
far more effectively as it exploded immediately on contact. Increased attention was
also given to counter-battery fire and the means (sound-ranging, flash-spotting, aerial

27   TNA WO 95/2933/4: 'VI Corps No. G.X.1/H/140 [30 April]', 56th Division General
      Staff War Diary.
28   TNA WO 95/1762/3: 'Preliminary Instructions No.1 for Operations on May 3rd', 26th
      Brigade General Staff War Diary.
29   Sanders Marble, *British Artillery on the Western Front in the First World War: 'The Infantry
      cannot do with a Gun Less'* (Abingdon: Routledge, 2016), p.263.

photography) to carry it out. The preliminary bombardment opened on 20 March, increasing in intensity on 2 April. The German defences were devastated as trenches were blown in and batteries silenced or destroyed. At Vimy Ridge, 212 German guns had been identified with 83 percent of them being destroyed by counter-battery fire.[30] On 10 April Allenby remarked that 'the German guns were smothered from the start.[31] This rendered much of the German defence impotent. Combined with an effective creeping barrage, which preceded the British infantry advance at 0530 on 9 April, there was little in the way of opposition. The 9th Division found the 'ease' with which the attack proceeded 'almost miraculous' compared to previous experience.[32] In most instances the enemy 'surrendered freely' and within three hours over 2,000 Germans had been captured by the division.[33] The primary difficulty for the attackers was recognising heavily damaged German trenches that were almost unidentifiable.[34]

However, the British advance had forced the German defences and their artillery, back beyond the range of the British batteries. This necessitated construction of new artillery positions and moving the guns forward, a task hampered by poor weather and roads damaged by the preliminary bombardment. Many batteries including the heavy artillery, were still being shifted forward when Third Scarpe began. On 2 May the Canadian Corps was only able to confirm effective artillery fire on enemy rear areas 'within a very short period of time' due to the large number of heavy guns still moving forward.[35] Individual guns were also rendered inoperable due to wear and tear resulting from incessant use. Ammunition supply also became difficult and whilst roads were improved and additional lorries became available by the end of April, projectiles often had to be transported to batteries by pack mule.[36] This severely limited the quantity of fire and, combined with the short time frame prior to Third Scarpe, seriously undermined the effectiveness of the preliminary bombardment.

When the preliminary bombardment began on the night of 30 April, it had three days to neutralise the re-established German defences. This proved to be an impossible task. First, the quantity of shells the British could fire was far lower due to many heavy guns being unavailable and ammunition supply problems. This is clear in the case of Canadian Corps. Prior to its capture of Vimy Ridge its artillery, along with supplemental batteries from other corps, fired 279,100 rounds in the initial stage of the bombardment, and 777,400 rounds in the second stage (rounded to nearest

30   Ibid., p.178.
31   Liddell Hart Centre for Military Archives London: Allenby Papers, ALLENBY 1/8/2, Allenby to Lady Allenby correspondence, April 10 1917', Allenby Papers.
32   Captain J.H.F. McEwan, *The Fifth Camerons* (Edinburgh: David Macdonald, 1921), p.81.
33   TNA WO 95/1738/3: '7th Seaforth Highlanders Narrative of 9th April 1917', 9th Division General Staff War Diary.
34   John Ewing, *The History of the 9th (Scottish) Division 1914-1919* (London: John Murray, 1921), p.194.
35   TNA WO 95/1050/2: 'Canadian Corps Summary of Intelligence 2nd May', Canadian Corps General Staff War Diary.
36   Falls, *Military Operations 1917*, Vol. I, p.381.

hundred).[37] In total the German defences were pulverised by over one million artillery projectiles. Yet during Third Scarpe the Canadians were reliant on their component artillery and only managed to fire 101,200 rounds between 30 April and 3 May.[38] The Canadians were attacking a narrower frontage, roughly 2,100 yards compared to 4,900 yards on 9 April, but adjustments still demonstrate a remarkable decline. For every yard of frontage on 9 April, 216 artillery projectiles were fired. On 3 May, the figure was just 48. This was not merely a Canadian problem. The XIII Corps on the right similarly fired 113,000 rounds between 30 April and 3 May but had to attack on a frontage of 5,800 yards This meant the corps' artillery only fired 19 rounds for every yard of ground attacked. Thus 31st Division reported that Oppy Wood received only a 'very mild' bombardment from heavy guns, and it was only two days after Third Scarpe thar it received a 'really effective' bombardment.[39]

The artillery's quality was also limited as it struggled to identify the German defences in time. The effectiveness of counter-battery fire declined as most German batteries remained unidentified when the barrage opened. Valiant RFC efforts to carry out aerial photography did identify some enemy positions as did sound ranging, but the majority remained undetected.[40] There were also problems in targeting known German strongpoints due to the difficulties with observation. The bombardment's effect was minimal in many places. By the evening of 1 May VII Corps could only confirm two direct hits on one machine-gun emplacement.[41] Improvements were made, however, and on 2 May XVII Corps reported that it had 'dealt with' eleven hostile batteries.[42] But his was too little, too late, and most enemy defences and batteries remained intact. The 4th Division reported after the battle that their advance was held up by machine-gun fire from buildings which the artillery had not destroyed, and that an 'inadequate' preliminary bombardment was the main cause of failure.[43] It was clear that the British artillery was not going to neutralise the German defences as it did on 9 April.

The infantry were going to have to fight hard if victory was to be achieved, yet they were even weaker than the artillery. By 3 May many units were severely

---

37   Ibid., p.315.
38   Figures obtained from TNA WO 95/183/4 and WO 95/183/7: 'First Army Total Number of Rounds of Gun and Howitzer Ammunition Expanded: First Army General Staff War Diary.
39   TNA WO 95/2342/3: 'Account of Operations of the 31st Division on May 3rd, 1917', 31st Division General Staff War Diary.
40   TNA WO 95/782/1: 1-3 May diary entries, VI Corps Commander Royal Artillery War Diary.
41   TNA WO 95/811/5: 'Operation Report from 7.30 30/4/17 to 7.30 1/5/17', VII Corps Commander Royal Artillery War Diary.
42   TNA WO 95/363/9: 'Summary of Artillery Action 2/5/1917', Third Army General Staff War Diary.
43   TNA WO 95/1446/2: '4th Division Operations on the 3rd May 1917', 4th Division General Staff War Diary.

understrength. The main BEF doctrinal pamphlet, *SS 135: Training of Divisions for Offensive Action*, advocated a battalion should have a maximum 'assaulting strength' of 800 men.[44] Even before Arras began, battalions rarely achieved this for although their paper strength was in excess of 800 men, many were performing various non-combatant roles including signalling, running orders, managing transport, carrying munitions and equipment forward, as well as constructing and maintaining everything from trenches to latrines. Private A.W. Lewis remarked that the infantry were 'the REs [Royal Engineers] human transport … their pack mules.'[45] On 7 April the 2nd Division had 10,092 infantry or 909 men per battalion excluding officers. Some 1,239 men were lost to non-combatant roles and 398 were untrained replacements for casualties suffered during routine trench warfare. This lowered their assaulting strength to 8,455 men, or 705 per battalion.[46] As a matter of routine, battalions also left a contingent of officers and other ranks behind prior to attacks. This ensured a 'nucleus' survived after heavy casualties thus lowering manpower strength further. Those selected usually numbered at least three officers, 63 other ranks, and one-third of the battalion's Lewis gunners, scouts, snipers, signallers and runners.[47]

The situation only worsened when, during April, the BEF sustained 78,000 casualties with infantry losses predominant.[48] Most divisions suffered approximately 2,000 casualties with the 34th Division alone losing between 5,000 and 6,000, which rendered it unfit for action.[49] It was impossible to replace these losses in the time available, and whilst replacement drafts arrived they were not equal to the losses.[50] The British advance also increased demands for manual labour as large amounts of materiel had to be shifted forward, new trenches and additional overland routes constructed, and captured German fieldworks repaired and converted for use. All of this lowered battalions assault strength. By 27 April, 2nd Division had detached 2,438 men for non-combatant duties. In addition to this, the division had suffered nearly 1,000 casualties, yet only 513 reinforcements had arrived. The division's fighting strength was 6,820 men, or just 568 per battalion.[51] Whereas the Germans relieved their divisions

44   General Staff, *SS 135: Instructions for the Training of Divisions for Offensive Action* (London: Harrison & Sons, 1916), p.23.
45   Imperial War Museum, London (IWM): Documents 7765: 'Wanderers in a Strange Land: The Story of Alfred William Lewis in the 1914-1918 War', p.30, A.W. Lewis Papers.
46   TNA WO 95/1296/2: 'Strength Return Made up to 12 Noon Saturday 9 April', 2nd Division General Staff War Diary.
47   *SS 135*, p.78.
48   Falls, *Military Operations 1917*, Vol. I, p.458.
49   TNA WO 95/363/1: 'Third Army Narrative of Operations May 1917', Third Army War General Staff War Diary.
50   See TNA WO 95/1446/2: '4th Division Operations on the 3rd May 1917', 4th Division War General Staff War Diary for complaints.
51   TNA WO 95/1296/2: 'Strength Return made up to 12 Noon Saturday 27 April', 2nd Division General Staff War Diary.

following heavy casualties, First and Third armies remained reliant on those that started the offensive in early April.

For Third Scarpe, only the 18th and 31st divisions were fresh, having avoided the fighting in April. Most battalions were fortunate to have an assaulting strength of over 500 men on 3 May. The 14th (Light) Division was stronger than most with an average battalion strength of 571.[52] Other formations were worse off. The 4th Division averaged 440 men per battalion, This included stretcher bearers and those carrying munitions forward.[53] The 9th Division had lost the South African Brigade to heavy casualties.[54] The 2nd Division was the weakest of all. Already understrength, it suffered roughly 2,000 casualties at the Battle of Arleux on 28-29 April.[55] It was so weak that its three brigades were amalgamated into a single composite brigade which was still understrength with just 1,400 fighting men or 350 per battalion.[56] Even in the purportedly fresh 31st Division, three battalions took just 472 men each into action on 3 May.[57]

The Third Scarpe scheme demonstrated little awareness of this weakness. *SS 135* recommended a full-strength battalion should attack on a maximum frontage 350 yards. If there was a 'particularly strong fortified point, such as a village or a wood' this was reduced to 200-250 yards. Whilst these recommendations were somewhat exceeded in many places on 9 April, they were largely followed. In its attack on Vimy Ridge 1st Canadian Division's six assault battalions had a frontage of 350 yards each, whereas those of the 4th Canadian Division had a frontage of 500 yards each.[58] At Third Scarpe, however, despite reduced frontages, most formations far exceeded *SS 135*'s guidance. The 31st Division alone attacked on a frontage 3,600 yards wide. It also faced Oppy Wood and village, two particularly strong fortified points. According to *SS 135*, this required between 15-18 full-strength battalions, not including supports and reserves. The division had twelve understrength battalions in total and attacked with six, giving it an average frontage of 600 yards each. The division noted in its post-battle report that the frontage was 'much in excess' of what was 'suggested in our recent official instructions (Vide *S.S. 135*).' This was despite the fact that the scale of the task was well known as a previous attack by two divisions on the same

52   TNA WO 95/1870/1: 'Numbers going into Action 1-5-1917', 14th Division General Staff War Diary. This excluded officers and men kept back as per *SS 135* and men employed in transport lines.
53   TNA WO 95/1446/2: '4th Division Operations on the 3rd May 1917', 4th Division General Staff War Diary.
54   TNA WO 95/1777/2: South African Brigade War Diary.
55   The Division did not record a specific number. Everard Wyrall, *The History of the Second Division 1914-1918*, Vols. I & II (London: Thomas Nelson & Sons, 1921), Vol. 2, p.437.
56   TNA WO 95/1369/2: 'Report on the Attack by the 99th (Composite) Infantry Brigade on 3/5/1917', 99th Brigade War General Staff War Diary.
57   TNA WO 95/2342/3: 'Report on the Action of May 3rd 1917, 92nd Infantry Brigade', 31st Division General Staff War Diary.
58   Falls, *Military Operations 1917*, pp.322, 328

frontage had failed completely. In an example of over-optimism, the 31st Division was ordered to attack as 'it was hoped that the enemy's troops would have been shaken by the previous attack.' In reality, the Germans had relieved the original defenders with fresh troops who actually outnumbered the attackers.[59] When the division advanced its waves were deployed in a single line with ten paces between each infantryman, thinly spread even before the inevitable casualties.[60] How this formation was to deal with concentrated pockets of resistance or resist counter-attacks is unclear. The 31st Division was not unique; on their left the composite 99th Brigade, 2nd Division, had a front some 2,200 yards wide. This required nearly 5,000 men, but the brigade had just 1,400 available.[61] Whilst not as severe, to the south 21st Division's battalions attacked across frontages of between 800 and 500 yards.[62] Fortunately, not all of the attacking formations were stretched so thin. The 18th Division, despite being fresh and stronger than the other attacking divisions, only required its battalions to attack on frontages of 300 to 350 yards.[63]

This was not the only issue. The infantry were often exhausted after days of continuous fighting in poor weather. In mid-April, Major-General C.P.A. Hull, GOC 56th (London) Division, reported that his men were not 'as physically fit as they might be' and the weather was so poor that 24 hours in the trenches reduced them from fighting fit to unfit for active operations. Hull concluded, 'if it keeps wet, then this Division will be in no state to attack.'[64] There was little chance for men to recover, as preparation for Third Scarpe required extensive manual labour in the few days available. The 31st Division had two nights to construct 'several hundred yards' of assembly trenches, expand the 2,000 yards of existing trenches, dig cable and communication trenches, construct ammunition dumps and fill them.[65] It was a similar story elsewhere. The 167th Brigade, 56th Division, reported that improving their trench system took a severe amount of effort giving the infantry no chance to rest.[66] In many places these preparations remained unfinished on 3 May. The 55th Brigade, 18th Division, had

59   TNA WO 95/2342/3: 'Account of Operations of the 31st Division on May 3rd, 1917', 31st Division General Staff War Diary.
60   TNA WO 95/2359/4: Untitled report on 3 May 1917, 93rd Brigade General Staff War Diary.
61   TNA WO 95/1369/2: 'Report on the Attack by the 99th (Composite) Infantry Brigade on 3/5/1917', 99th Brigade General Staff War Diary.
62   TNA WO 95/2163/2: '110th Infantry Brigade Narrative of Operations – May 3rd, 1917', 110th Brigade General Staff War Diary.
63   TNA WO 95/2047/1: 'Distribution of 55th Infantry Brigade at Zero Hour', 55th Brigade General Staff War Diary.
64   TNA WO 95/1869/2: '56th Division No. GA 296', 14th Division General Staff War Diary.
65   TNA WO 95/2342/3: 'Account of Operations of the 31st Division on May 3rd, 1917', 31st Division General Staff War Diary,
66   TNA WO 95/2947/2: 'Report on the Action of 167th Inf Bde during the Period 27th April to 4th May', 167th Brigade General Staff War Diary.

no observation posts to monitor the infantry's progress. This made artillery support adjustment especially difficult once the offensive began. Similarly, command posts were situated in captured German dugouts that were too small to house battalion and brigade headquarters, not to mention their exact location was known to the enemy.[67] Similar problems were encountered by 3rd Division which was holding Monchy village where hostile artillery prevented the establishment of permanent observation posts.[68]

The quality of the infantry had also declined. Those that participated in the opening of the Arras offensive had reached a peak of excellence over the winter of 1916-17, as the quantity and quality of training increased dramatically. This was due to increasing BEF manpower, which allowed formations to be withdrawn from the frontline for training much more frequently and for longer periods. A sample of six divisions demonstrates that they were withdrawn for a minimum of one month's dedicated training between November 1916 and April 1917, whereas the previous year only three had had similar opportunities.[69] Falls observed that they 'reached their highest standard of training since the force had become a citizen army.'[70] However, this training was focused on attacks against static trenches such as those faced on 9 April. Thus the infantry were not extensively trained in open-warfare or against the new style German defences. Following fierce fighting in February 1917, the 18th Division reported that whilst their men were 'thoroughly conversant with trench warfare' there 'are very few who have even an elementary knowledge of open warfare.' When faced with the latter, the men became 'sticky' which was 'akin to the attitude of an individual without clothes being suddenly driven from the privacy of his boudoir into the limelight of the public gaze.'[71] A similar problem was encountered at Arras when, on 14 April, Allenby complained to Haig that his men were like 'blind puppies' in open warfare.[72] Heavy casualties only worsened the situation, as the new drafts often had very limited training in even basic skills. In one extreme example, on 23 April the 8/ Black Watch, 9th Division, received a draft of 97 men chiefly composed of transfers from the Army Service Corps who had had no previous infantry training and some

---

67   TNA WO 95/2050/3: 'Notes on the Operations at Chérisy', 8th East Surrey Regiment War Diary.
68   Falls, *Military Operations 1917*, Vol. I, p.439
69   The following TNA formation war diaries were consulted:
      WO 95/1733-1743, 9th Division General Staff War Diary
      WO 95/2015-2017: 18th Division General Staff War Diary
      WO 95/2128-2134: 21st Division General Staff War Diary
      WO 95/2341-2344: 31st Division General Staff War Diary
      WO 95/2765-2768: 49th Division General Staff War Diary
      WO 95/2844-2847: 51st Division General Staff War Diary
70   Falls, *Military Operations 1917*, Vol. I, p.198
71   TNA WO 95/2016/1: 'Report on Operations from 18th Feb-3rd March 1917', 18th Division General Staff War Diary.
72   Sheffield & Bourne, *Douglas Haig*, p.284

of whom could neither fix bayonets nor load rifles.[73] There was little chance to address this before Third Scarpe began. Whilst some formations, 3rd Division for example, had managed to conduct some rudimentary training when in reserve during mid-April, many others were unable to do so.[74] Nor did they understand the new German defensive system well enough to train men in how to overcome it. Rather than work with the tools at their disposal, Allenby and Horne continued to employ them in a task they were unprepared for.

Preparatory training was also absent prior to 3 May. This involved rehearsing battalions in the exact roles they were to perform in a forthcoming attack which had been utilised since late 1915.[75] This increased attack cohesion, as the infantry better understood assigned tasks and learned how to cooperate with other arms such as artillery and tanks It also increased infantry endurance in the face of heavy casualties by ensuring other ranks could identify objectives and take them without reliance on officers who often became casualties early on. This approach was enacted uniformly throughout First and Third armies prior to 9 April. The 9th Division spent February and March practising for the coming attack with model trenches, aerial photographs, and detailed maps to fully acquaint the men with objectives and roles. The enemy were even represented with real machine-guns firing blank cartridges and with artillery putting down smoke barrages to imitate the creeping barrage the men were to follow. Some infantry officers were taken into the air by Royal Flying Corps (RFC) to observe the effectiveness of air to groundsignalling.[76] Prior to Third Scarpe, there was neither the time nor intelligence on enemy positions to perform training remotely close to this. Private Smith of 18th Division, which was famous for extensive use of rehearsal attacks, had one officer briefly outline the general plan of attack on a map. There was little contingency planning. Smith remarked in his diary, 'it was quite easy to read if off on paper. Nothing was said [of] what was to be done if our right or left never reached the German front line.' Echoing the optimism of the British commanders, he observed that 'of course such a thing would never happen. The Germans would run away before we got to them.'[77] The 54th Brigade was able to 'carefully' drill its moppers up, who followed close behind the first advance to neutralise remaining pockets of enemy resistance. This training, however, lacked thoroughness inasmuch as there was neither time to identify all of the enemy positions or spit-lock them on

73   Falls, *Military Operations 1917*, Vol. I, p.444

74   TNA WO 95/1378/1: 'Report on Operations Carried out by 3rd Division Covering the Period 15th April to 15th May', 3 Division General Staff War Diary.

75   For examples of this training on the Somme, see Spencer Jones, 'XIII Corps and the Attack at Montauban, 1 July 1916' in Spencer Jones (ed.), *At All Costs: The British Army on the Western Front 1916* (Warwick: Helion & Co., 2018), pp.270-91 and Jonathan Porter, *Zero Hour Z Day: XIII Corps Operations Between Maricourt and Mametz* (Privately published, 2016).

76   Liddle Collection, University of Leeds (LC) Liddle/WW1/Air/024: 'Combat In and Over Delville Wood I', pp.81-87, Arthur H. Betteridge Papers.

77   IWM: Documents 8486: 'My Diary', Vol. 3, pp.97-98, C.R. Smith papers.

the training ground.[78] Against intact and unfamiliar German defences, the attackers, thinly stretched, exhausted and inadequately trained for the task, were unlikely to succeed.

The situation was bleak, but Haig managed to make the situation considerably worse when he decided that Third Scarpe was to be a night attack. There had been a debate over zero hour, the time the infantry assault began, between Gough and Fifth Army, who wanted to attack Bullecourt in the dark at 0330 because they knew the terrain well and wanted to achieve surprise. Allenby and Horne, however, wanted zero hour to be at dawn, 0405 because their men were unfamiliar with the ground. Haig convened a conference on 2 May between himself, Allenby and Gough to adjudicate the matter. This was controversial, as Allenby believed Haig was not impartial due to a long-standing enmity between the two whereas Gough was Haig's protégé.[79] Archibald Wavell, who served under Allenby, wrote in his biography of the latter that it was 'obvious that Allenby's opinion carried little weight' with Haig, 'especially if Gough … had a different view.' Haig 'often' interrupted Allenby when he was speaking by turning to a different commander and asking their opinion.'[80] Haig, however, was aware of both cases. He subsequently wrote in his diary how Gough's attack 'must cross some open ground in the dark', whereas Oppy Wood, opposite First Army, could 'only be passed conveniently by daylight.' His fear was that if Fifth Army attacked earlier, 'the enemy would become alarmed and barrage our front before the troops can get out of the trenches.'[81] He decided that the two attacks had to start simultaneously, and rather than siding with Allenby or Gough, he arbitrarily set zero hour halfway between the requested times. Thus the assault would commence at 0345 when not only was it still dark but the moon had also set. Third Scarpe was to open in pitch blackness. This had disastrous consequences. Orders only reached the attacking formations the afternoon before the attack began. Night operations were inadvisable in general, *SS 135* recommending that they 'should be avoided if possible' and only conducted in favourable circumstances.[82] Conducting one with less than twelve hours' notice was pure negligence. The entire nature of the attack had changed; infantry could not navigate by sight or easily identify friend from foe; visual signals were useless nor could observers track the attack's progress. Brigadier-General Henry Hugh Tudor, commanding 9th Division's artillery, wrote in his diary how he 'pleaded for an attack at dawn' because the method of attack was based on blinding the enemy by smoke-shell whilst the infantry

78   TNA WO 95/2041/5: 'Extracts from Diary of Brigadier-General C. Cunliffe Owen, Commanding 54th Infantry Brigade, 18/Division.', 54th Brigade General Staff War Diary.
79   Matthew Hughes, 'Edmund Allenby' in Ian F.W. Beckett & Steven J. Corvi (eds.) *Haig's Generals* (Barnsley: Pen & Sword, 2006), pp.12-32. Gary Sheffield & Helen McCartney, 'Hubert Gough' in Beckett & Corvi (eds.), *Haig's Generals*, pp.75-96.
80   Archibald Wavell, *Allenby: A Study in Greatness* (London: Harrap, 1940), p.170.
81   Sheffield & Bourne, *Douglas Haig*, p.290.
82   *SS 135*, p.28.

advanced in daylight.[83] Nor had the infantry received extensive training in night operations beyond initial recruit training in Great Britain. A select few might have experience from trench raids but had seen no action approaching the scale of Third Scarpe and, in any case, it was usual for trench raiders to spend days in preparatory rehearsals. For most this was to be the first, and last, major battle they were to carry out at night. Plans and preparations had to be adjusted in haste. Ideally, the attacking formations could have placed phosphorescent markers out in no

Brigadier-General H.H. Tudor.

man's land for orientation, but this did not occur. At most, attacking troops managed to take compass bearings for navigation, and in some cases tapes were laid out in no man's land to facilitate nocturnal alignment.[84] Harris adjudged Haig's decision a 'somewhat disastrous compromise', whereas Gary Sheffield described it as 'highly unfortunate'.[85] The latter reduces Haig's culpability too much. Having vetoed Allenby's plan for a night pursuit, he knew the infantry were not ready. Expecting them to then perform a major night assault was inexcusable. In making this choice, Haig cemented the fate of the attackers and ensured Third Scarpe was certain to be a black day.

On the night of 2/3 May the British infantry moved into jumping-off trenches in full view of alert German defenders, who immediately began to shell the British line and deploy machine-guns into no man's land in expectation of imminent assault. At 2100 hours, the 3rd Division's front faced a heavy barrage of gas and high explosive shells which caused 'considerable' casualties and disorganised and delayed the assembly.[86] The 2nd Division was a victim of an ill-advised decision by its artillery commander to fire a 'Chinese' barrage, a commonly employed ruse intended to distract enemy attention from where the actual attack was taking place. As the actual

---

83   IWM: Documents 2949: 'A Gallant Gunner General: The Life and Times of Sir H. Hugh Tudor K.C.B., C.M.G.', together with an edited version of his 1914-1918 War Diary, 'The Fog of War', p.167, General Henry Hugh Tudor papers.

84   TNA WO 95/2958/1: 'B.M. 126', 169th Brigade General Staff War Diary.

85   J.P. Harris, *Haig*, pp.324-25. Gary Sheffield, *The Chief*, p.221.

86   TNA WO 95/1378/1: 'Report on Operations Carried out by 3rd Division Covering the Period 15th April to 15th May', 3rd Division General Staff War Diary.

location was on 2nd Division's front, it drew 'heavy retaliation' from hostile artillery which caused 'delay and loss to the infantry ... seriously affected the bringing up of munitions and supplies, and undoubtedly caused the enemy to be very much on the alert.' Two companies were so delayed that they arrived at the jumping-off line a few minutes after the assault opened and the German defenders were ready and waiting.[87] At 0345 on 3 May, the moon had set and zero hour had arrived; the heavy artillery intensified its fire, the field artillery commenced the creeping barrage, and the infantry began the advance.

At the northern flank of the offensive the attack's one clear success was achieved as the Canadian Corps stormed Fresnoy. This was the one place where the German defenders were surprised by the early zero hour, and even then it was a hard fight. The 1st and 2nd Canadian divisions had to force their way through barbed wire obstacles under fire and demonstrated a high level of skill in outflanking numerous German positions to rapidly overcome enemy resistance. By 1030 they occupied Fresnoy and repulsed several counter-attacks with machine-gun, rifle and artillery fire throughout the late morning and afternoon. The official historian viewed this as 'the culminating point of the series of brilliant successes by the Canadian Corps during the Arras battles.' But the price had been high, with a casualty list of 64 officers and 1,410 other ranks.[88]

For the remainder of the offensive, a tragic story emerged as the deeply flawed nature of Third Scarpe became apparent. In the darkness, cohesion was almost immediately lost all along the line. The situation was worsened by heavy mist, not to mention smoke and dust resulting from the bombardment. Visibility was two to three yards and the attackers were rendered blind.[89] The only available guidance were the explosions of the creeping barrage. On unfamiliar ground and with no experience in night attacks, formations disintegrated and officers could do little to control their men; visual signals were useless and whistles were drowned out by the bombardment. Assault waves became ragged and intermixed, as those in the rear caught up with those in front, and men bunched up to the left and right.[90]

Disarray turned to disaster as the Germans mounted a fierce resistance. The preliminary bombardment had been ineffective and heavy machine-gun and rifle fire hit the advance almost immediately. Reports of intact strongpoints came in from up and down the line. The 4th Division was held up by machine-gun fire from buildings and the enemy artillery remained unsubdued, nor was it dealt with by heavy artillery due

87   TNA WO 95/1369/2: 'Report on the Attack by the 99th (Composite) Infantry Brigade on 3/5/1917', 99th Brigade General Staff War Diary.
88   Falls, *Military Operations 1917*, Vol. I, p.450.
89   J.H.F. McEwen, *The Fifth Camerons* (Edinburgh: David Macdonald, n.d.), p.83; TNA WO 95/2047/1: '55th Infantry Brigade Account of Operations Against the Village of Chérisy on May 3rd 1917', 55th Brigade General Staff War Diary.
90   TNA WO 95/2933/4: '56th Division Narrative of Operations from 28th April to 21st May 1917', 56th Division General Staff War Diary.

to the impossibility of effective observation in the dark.[91] To the south, 14th Division was faced by heavy machine-gun fire from St Rohart Factory and despite the infantry having marked it as a priority target, there was 'little or no fire by the heavy artillery' directed on it once the attack began.[92] Farther south on 18th Division's front, the 54th Brigade assault was halted by an impassable belt of intact barbed wire prior to encountering heavy shelling and enfilade machine-gun fire.[93]

Moreover, the Germans had deployed numerous machine-guns situated in trenches, outposts and shell holes throughout no man's land. Overlooked by the preliminary bombardment, an inconsistent creeping barrage failed to suppress them. Indeed, the 18th Division reported that two or three of its component field batteries opened fire too early and it was 'some minutes' before full intensity was reached.[94] Poor intelligence with regard to the enemy defences also proved critical in places where the creeping barrage actually opened beyond the first line of German defences. This inconsistency was exemplified by the advance of 56th Division's two brigades. On the right, 169th Brigade reported that the barrage 'was perfect' and the leading waves met little opposition advancing close behind it.[95] On the left, 167th Brigade's experience was the complete opposite, as both the preliminary bombardment and creeping barrage completely missed the first objective. Contrary to how the German defence was meant to operate, the defenders manned the trench in strength and, a prime target had the artillery performed as expected, stood shoulder-to-shoulder on the fire-step. Instead, as the assault waves crossed the crest separating attacker and defender, the former were greeted with heavy rifle and machine-gun fire before the advance was stopped in its tracks.[96] It was here that darkness was the saving grace for the British infantry, which fell back without suffering severe losses. A daylight attack in this sector would have resulted in a massacre.[97]

The 9th Division suffered worse than most. The notorious Roeux Chemical Works, despite being a select target for the heavy artillery, was almost untouched with German machine-gunners alert and waiting.[98] The creeping barrage was 'ragged' and inaccurate, hampered by uncertainty over precise targets, and troubled by the fact that the enemy occupied shell holes 'closer to our frontline than had been expected and which

91 TNA WO 95/1446/2: '4th Division Operations on the 3rd May 1917', 4th Division General Staff War Diary.
92 TNA WO 95/1870/1: 'S. 19/47 BM', 14th Division General Staff War Diary.
93 TNA WO 95/2041/5: 'Extracts from Diary of Brigadier-General C. Cunliffe Owen, Commanding 54th Infantry Brigade, 18/Division', 54th Brigade General Staff War Diary.
94 TNA WO 95/2047/1: '55th Infantry Brigade Account of Operations Against the Village of Chérisy on May 3rd 1917', 55th Brigade General Staff War Diary.
95 TNA WO 95/2958/1: 'B.M. 126', 169th Brigade General Staff War Diary.
96 TNA WO 95/2947/2: 'Report on the Action of 167th Inf Bde during the Period 27th April to 4th May 1917', 167th Brigade General Staff War Diary.
97 Falls, *Military Operations 1917*, Vol. I, p.438.
98 TNA WO 95/1767/1: 3 May 1917 diary entry, 5th Cameron Highlanders War Diary.

had consequently missed the barrage.'[99] Further misery was caused by an error in the artillery trench maps which resulted in some shells landing in friendly trenches.[100] The infantry, on leaving the jumping-off trenches, encountered withering fire. An experienced formation with a reputation as an effective fighting force, in the pitch dark and under galling fire, the 9th Division's attack quickly descended into chaos. The 5/Cameron Highlanders, attacking on the right, became confused by a series of enemy flares discharged on the right flank. Unable to orientate themselves on an available landmark, the infantry believed this was the objective. Pivoting towards this display, they crossed the front of the 2/Essex Regiment, 4th Division which mistook the shadowy figures in front for Germans and opened fire.[101] Two companies of the 10/Argyll & Sutherland Highlanders following close behind did not realise this had happened, and advanced straight past the Camerons. Thinking the latter battalion was in front of them, they unexpectedly stumbled into the German defences.[102] In the centre, the 9/Scottish Rifles were meant to attack at an oblique angle on the left. Despite having taken compass bearings and placing a lamp as a guide, they became hopelessly lost and mistook the frontline of a neighbouring battalion on the right for that of the enemy's before advancing on it whilst firing from the hip.[103] In most places this was enough to stop the attack dead with very heavy loss. By 0600 most of the attackers were back in the original jumping-off trenches. However, one battalion, 6/King's Own Scottish Borderers (KOSB) did manage to press on and made considerable progress.

It was a similar story all along the British line. Most of the assault was stopped in its tracks, although in some places infantry managed to press on. As they did, however, they were drawn further and further into the enemy trap. First, the attackers were cut off from reinforcements when, within minutes of Zero, the Germans called down an artillery barrage on British trenches and rear areas. The counter-battery fire had clearly been insufficient and the supporting artillery, with no chance of identifying enemy battery positions in the dark, was powerless once the offensive started. Brigadier-General F.A. Dudgeon, GOC 42nd Brigade, 14th Division, reported that the British counter-battery fire was 'very ineffective' and the enemy 'kept up for 15 hours the heaviest bombardment I have yet experienced.'[104] Whilst most of the British first wave avoided this fire, two delayed companies of 2nd Division were caught by the 'full force

99   TNA WO 95/1739: '9th Scottish Division Narrative of Events May 3rd 1917', 9th Division General Staff War Diary.
100 TNA WO 95/1739: 'Account of the Battle on May 3rd 1917, 26th Infantry Brigade', 9th Division General Staff War Diary.
101 McEwen, *The Fifth Camerons*, p.83;
102 TNA WO 95/1739: 'Account of the Battle on May 3rd 1917, 26th Infantry Brigade', 9th Division General Staff War Diary.
103 TNA WO 95/1739: '9th Scottish Division Narrative of Events May 3rd 1917', 9th Division General Staff War Diary.
104 TNA WO 95/1870/1: '42nd Inf Bde S. 19/47 B.M', 14th Division General Staff War Diary.

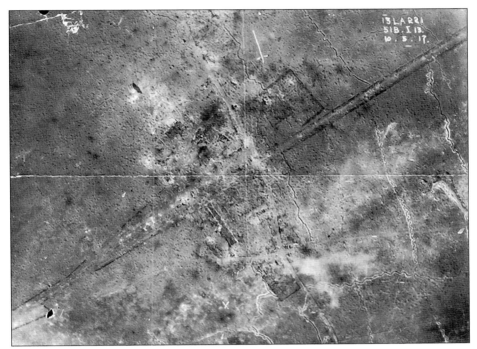

Roeux Chemical Works from the air, 10 May 1917. (TNA WO 95/1498: 1/East Lancs War Diary)

of the enemy artillery and machine-gun barrage' which inflicted crippling casualties that reduced them to 'shattered remnants'.[105] Hostile artillery fire also prevented reinforcements from being sent forward. Moreover, battalions that never exited the jumping-off trenches suffered heavy casualties, a battalion of 14th Division lost 15 percent of its strength, whilst two in 3rd Division lost 350 men between them.[106] At this stage the British gunners, lacking available observation posts and firing blindly in the darkness, had no idea where the infantry was. Having kept two batteries of field artillery back as a ready reserve, the 21st Division was unable to employ this asset because of the same uncertainty.[107]

A combination of darkness, thinly stretched infantry and disintegrating formations resulted in the attackers inadvertently bypassing numerous German positions. In most cases the defenders hid as attackers passed over them before re-manning their defences and opening fire from the rear. These ranged from isolated machine-guns in shell

105 TNA WO 95/1369/2: 'Report on the Attack by the 99th (composite) Infantry Brigade on 3/5/1917', 99th Brigade General Staff War Diary.
106 TNA WO 95/1870/1: 'General Remarks on German Artillery Fire on 3rd May 1917 on 14th Divisional Front', 14th Division General Staff War Diary.
107 TNA WO 95/2163/2: '110/S.45/52', 110th Brigade General Staff War Diary.

holes to large buildings, trench systems and dugouts. On 12th (Eastern) Division's front, the infantry managed to consolidate a section of enemy trench captured in the first advance. However, within 15 minutes they were counter-attacked and driven out by a hostile force previously missed in the darkness.[108] Having reoccupied the trench, the Germans opened rifle and machine-gun fire on the British infantry still waiting to advance and cut off from those who had advanced beyond them.[109] Unfamiliarity with the ground and the lack of rehearsal training contributed to this problem, as even designated moppers up often failed in their task. For example, despite assigning two platoons to mop up, 54th Brigade, 18th Division encountered a group of German dugouts large enough to hold an entire battalion had not been neutralised. As 'practically none' of the men returned, this was only surmised.

German resistance did not slacken. Rather than breaking through the enemy defence line, the attackers encountered a bristling belt of staggered defences. Seeking cover in captured trenches did not ensure safety because the Germans had preregistered these positions prior to the opening bombardment. One 31st Division private recalled, 'how easy it was to get into the German trenches and how big a mistake we all made, because the Germans had emptied their trenches and put their artillery within a yard or two.'[110] Whilst this distance was exaggerated, it was a stark testimony to the intensity of German shelling. One by one, the remaining British battalions were halted as the assault became increasingly disjointed. Rather than one broad wave, the offensive had been reduced to numerous isolated thrusts. Where these penetrated the German lines, the defenders took full advantage by working round the flanks of the British infantry which, on coming under fire from all sides, triggered a domino effect as one formation, on being forced back, exposed the flank of the next and so on. This finished the 4th Division attack. On its left, 10th Brigade suffered heavy losses whilst attacking Roeux and, in one notable incident, a German machine-gun lay hidden behind a wall perpendicular to the advance. As the assault wave came level with it, the machine-gun opened fire inflicting serious losses.[111] The brigade's moppers up also failed to neutralise a fortified chateau which had been bypassed. This allowed its garrison to open fire on the rear of the assault infantry and follow-up reserves. Forced to withdraw to their original jumping-off line which exposed 12th Brigade on the right. On approaching Plouvain, its designated final objective, the brigade's advance encountered heavy enfilade machine-gun fire from positions opposite 10th

108 TNA WO 95/1824/4: 'Operation of 3rd May 1917', 12th Division General Staff War Diary.
109 TNA WO 95/1858/5: 'Report on Operations Carried out by the 37th Infantry Brigade on May 3rd 1917', 37th Brigade General Staff War Diary.
110 Laurie Milner, *Leeds Pals: A History of the 15th (Service) Battalion (1st Leeds) The Prince of Wales's Own (West Yorkshire Regiment) 1914-1918* (Barnsley: Pen & Sword, 1990), p.248.
111 Falls, *Military Operations 1917*, Vol. I, p.443.

Brigade front. Heavy casualties, including all battalion officers, were sustained before the attackers fell back.[112]

In the south, the 18th Division made one notable gain when 55th Brigade stormed the village of Chérisy, its final objective, along with elements of 14th Division on the left and the 54th Brigade on its right. The 55th Brigade did, however, have several advantages. Its front was far narrower than other units, it was relatively fresh and the German defences were thinner than elsewhere. The defending *Infanterie Regiment Nr. 114* lacked dugouts for protection against hostile artillery fire, so even the weak preliminary bombardment had inflicted significant casualties. Closely following the creeping barrage, the 8/East Surreys and 7/Buffs drove back the remaining defenders with bayonets and hand grenades after advancing into the teeth of heavy fire.[113] C.R. Smith provided a vivid description of the fighting: men were 'falling like corn before a sickle' and were shot down as they ran 'in a circle' by enemy snipers. The ground was 'literally covered' with 'heaps of dead and wounded.' Smith gradually made his way forward moving shell hole to shell hole before entering a German trench where a group of Tommies were pinned down by enemy fire. On spotting a lone Lewis gunner, Smith attempted to assist him by bringing his weapon to bear on a sniper but as soon as he appeared, Smith was struck in the shoulder and the gunner through the forehead.[114] Chérisy having been secured, the position remained tenuous. Cut-off from reinforcements, with numbers dwindling and flanks completely exposed, 55th Brigade managed to repel several local counter-attacks. Nevertheless, by late morning the fresh III Battalion, *Reserve Infanterie Regiment Nr. 225* arrived and began manoeuvring around the brigade's left and right flanks. It was now a question of when, not if, they would be forced to withdraw. Continuous German artillery fire rendering the position untenable, and the hard-pressed battalions hurriedly withdrew.[115] Private R. Cude, 7/Buffs, was less diplomatic describing the precipitate retirement as a 'rout'.[116] At some points, the pursuing German infantry followed behind so closely that British units in occupation of the original frontline could not open fire for fear of striking their own men. Casualties mounted and those not shot down were overwhelmed and taken captive. In less than one hour the entire 18th Division was back in its jumping-off line.[117]

Except for the Canadian Corps, a similar fate befell the remainder of the assault infantry that managed to achieve some territorial gains. Last to withdraw was 169th Brigade, 56th Division, which, despite having its flanks exposed, was left unmolested

112 TNA WO 95/1446/2: '4th Division Operations on the 3rd May 1917', 4th Division General Staff War Diary.
113 Sheldon, *The German Army*, loc. 7235.
114 IWM: Documents 8486: 'My Diary', Vol. 3, pp.99-100, C.R. Smith papers.
115 Sheldon, *The German Army*, loc. 7268.
116 IWM: Documents 129: R. Cude Diary, Vol. 1, p.73, R. Cude papers.
117 TNA WO 95/2047/1: '55th Infantry Brigade Account of Operations Against the Village of Chérisy on May 3rd 1917', 55th Brigade General Staff War Diary.

before falling back at 0115 on 4 May.[118] Other battalions were not so fortunate. Three KOSB companies, having advanced some distance on 9th Division's front, found themselves isolated behind re-manned German defences. To assist their withdrawal, 1½ companies of 12/ Royal Scots was launched at 2000. Unfortunately, machine-gun fire cut them down with 120 out of 180 men lost. Nevertheless, the sacrifice did allow a 'considerable number' of KOSB remnants to return.[119] Hopelessly cut-off, other groups were taken prisoner. How far the 2/Essex had advanced remained unknown, a subsequent 4th

The aftermath of 18th Division's rout at Chérisy, 3 May 1917. (G. Seitz, et al, *Geschichte des 6. Badischen Infanterie-Regiments Kaiser Friedrich III. Nr. 114 im Weltkrieg 1914 bis 1918*)

Division report remarking that 'no one came back and no one could get forward to them.'[120] Similarly, the 37th Brigade, 12th Division, was uncertain how far its first wave had advanced. No survivors returned.[121] On 18th Division's front poor communication and observation resulted in the erroneous belief that Chérisy had been held. Two battalions, ordered forward to reinforce at 1915, met with heavy machine-gun fire and suffered heavy casualties for no gain.[122] One junior officer, recalling the unfortunate incident, described it as 'sheer murder'.[123]

By the morning of 4 May the only territorial gain made was the capture of Fresnoy in the north, and an advance roughly 500 yards in depth and 1,000 yards in width by 37th Brigade, 12th Division. Thus the offensive had not advanced the British position in any meaningful way, nor could it be claimed that German attention had been distracted away from French operations in the south, as the Germans did not call

118 Falls, *Military Operations 1917*, Vol. I, p.488
119 TNA WO 95/1770/3: '27th Brigade Report on the Attack on 3rd May 1917', 27th Brigade General Staff War Diary.
120 TNA WO 95/1446/2: '4th Division Operations on the 3rd May 1917', 4th Division General Staff War Diary.
121 TNA WO 95/1858/5: 'Report on Operations Carried out by the 37th Infantry Brigade on May 3rd 1917', 37th Brigade General Staff War Diary.
122 TNA WO 95/2047/1: '55th Infantry Brigade Account of Operations Against the Village of Chérisy on May 3rd 1917', 55th Brigade General Staff War Diary.
123 LC: WW1/WF/REC/01/H18: 'Fifty Years After: Memoirs of a Combatant Officer of the 18th Division 1914/18 on the Western Front', p.90, P.G. Heath Papers.

upon any reserve divisions to support the defence, Falls contemptuously stating in the Official History that 'there is no need to describe the operations in any detail from the German point of view, because the British failure in general was complete.'[124]

British losses had been exceptionally high. Officer casualties were so heavy amongst battalions of 26th Brigade, 9th Division, that it proved 'impossible to collect any accurate accounts of what really took place.' Brigadier-General Tudor observed, 'The day seems to have ended in defeat everywhere and the Division is finished for the time being as a fighting unit.'[125] Of the 46 officers and 1,416 other ranks of 92nd Brigade, 31st Division, who entered the battle, 34 and 758 became casualties respectively; a casualty rate of 74 percent for officers and 53 percent for other ranks.[126] The neighbouring 93rd Brigade suffered similarly, reporting over 1,100 casualties.[127] Further south, 42nd Brigade, 14th Division, reported that 5/Oxford Light Infantry lost 291 out of 523 men as casualties. Furthermore, the 9/Rifle Brigade lost 298 out of 477 men. This marked a casualty rate of 56 and 62 percent respectively.[128] In total the Commonwealth War Graves Commission's database of British soldiers fatalities during 1914-18 shows that First and Third armies lost 4,840 men killed on 3 May 1917. It is impossible to give a precise casualty figure, as recording methods varied in accuracy and time span.[129] By compiling the various records kept in war diaries, a rough figure of around 16,000 British casualties emerges.[130] Given that between 9 and

124 Falls, *Military Operations 1917*, Vol. I, p.273
125 TNA WO 95/1739: 'Account of the Battle on May 3rd 1917, 26th Infantry Brigade', 9th Division General Staff War Diary and Tudor, 'Fog of War', p.167.
126 TNA WO 95/2342/3: 'Report on the Action of May 3rd 1917, 92nd Infantry Brigade', 31st Division General Staff War Diary.
127 TNA WO 95/2359/4: 3 May 1917 diary entry, 93rd Brigade General Staff War Diary.
128 TNA WO 95/1870/1: '5/OLI Casualties by Companies' & '9 Rif Brig Casualties by Companies', 14th Division General Staff War Diary.
129 The Official History does not provide a total figure.
130 Alongside previous citations, the following publications and records were consulted: Falls, *Military Operations 1917*, Vol. I, pp.445, 450; TNA WO 95/1369/2: 'Report on the Attack by the 99th (Composite) Infantry Brigade on 3/5/1917', 99th Brigade General Staff War Diary; WO 95/1770/3: '27th Brigade Report on the Attack on 3rd May 1917', 27th Brigade General Staff War Diary; WO 95/1745/1: 5 May 1917 diary entry, 9th Division Adjutant and Quarter-Master General War Diary; WO 95/1446/2: '4th Division Operations on the 3rd May 1917', 4th Division General Staff War Diary; WO 95/2933/4: '56th Division Narrative of Operations from 28th April to 21st May 1917', 56th Division General Staff War Diary; WO 95/1858/5: 'Summary of 37th Infantry Brigade Casualties', 37th Brigade General Staff War Diary; WO 95/1857/1: 3 May 1917 diary entry, 8th Royal Fusiliers War Diary; WO 95/1857/2: 3 May 1917 diary entry, 9th Royal Fusiliers War Diary; WO 95/1427/4: 3 May 1917 diary entry, 9th Brigade War Diary General Staff; WO 95/1879/2: 3 May 1917 diary entry, 14th Division Adjutant and Quarter-Master General War Diary; WO 95/2047/1: '55th Infantry Brigade Account of Operations Against the Village of Chérisy on May 3rd 1917', 55th Brigade General Staff War Diary; WO 95/2016/1: 'Casualties 3rd May 1917 to 5th May 1917', 18th Division General Staff War Diary; WO 95/2132/1: 'Notes on Lessons Learnt During the

11 April First and Third armies suffered 13,000 casualties, this represented a horrific loss. German losses are also unclear, though some of the defending formations did suffer heavily. For example, *Reserve Infanterie Regiment Nr. 17* lost some 650 casualties at Fresnoy.[131] After the battle some commanders attempted to find solace with the conclusion that German losses were as severe as their own. For example, Brigadier-General A.B.E. Cator, GOC 37th Brigade, wrote to his sister on 6 May that whilst 'we lost heavily and gained no ground to speak of ... I think, though, the Germans lost very heavily, and it was a drawn battle.'[132] However, even if every German unit had sustained similar casualties, their losses would still have been under 14,000 and given that *17th Reserve Division* was defending against the most successful attack, this is highly improbable. Attempting to seek an element of justification for the battle, Brigadier-General Francis Maxwell VC, GOC 27th Brigade, 9th Division teetered on the edge of delusion when he reported:

> If, however, the attack was unsuccessful and casualties heavy I submit that an enemy which cannot take advantage of a successful defence by counter-attack is one that is either ignorant of war or has little stomach for it. The Germans were not ignorant of war; counter-attack, to their credit, was almost their religion. A satisfactory conclusion can therefore be drawn from their absolute failure to strike back on 3rd May.[133]

The final ignominy heaped on the attackers occurred when Fresnoy was lost to a German counter-attack on 9 May. It had been in British hands for five days. Third Scarpe was not just a defeat. It was a disaster. Numerous explanations were offered to explain the fiasco. Common to all was the confusion caused by the night attack but reports also cited other factors including thinly dispersed infantry waves, lack of knowledge of the ground, weak preliminary bombardment, ineffective counter-battery fire and the alert German defenders. It was clear all of these played a significant role in the failure. Complaints about the infantry's training are less convincing: 21st Division reported that the attack 'brought home to all how little reliance the infantry soldier placed in his rifle' as well as 'want of initiative on part of officers and NCOs [sic].'[134] The official historian lamented that 'the atmosphere of siege warfare hung about the British army when it passed to open or semi-open warfare' and that the musketry

Operations of 21st Division from 24 April to 12 May 1917', 21st Division General Staff War Diary.

131   Falls, *Military Operations 1917*, Vol. I, 454; Sheldon, *German Army*, loc. 7109.
132   Trevor Harvey, *An Army of Brigadiers: British Brigade Commanders at the Battle of Arras 1917* (Warwick: Helion & Co., 2017), p.281.
133   TNA WO 95/1770/3: '27th Brigade Report on the Attack on 3rd May 1917', 27th Brigade General Staff War Diary.
134   TNA WO 95/2132/1: 'Notes on Lessons Learnt During the Operations of 21st Division from 24 April to 12 May 1917', 21st Division General Staff War Diary.

Oppy Wood assault: 31st Division prisoners are escorted to the rear, 3 May 1917.

skills of 55th Brigade at Chérisy could have held back the Germans if they 'could really use their rifles.'[135] Whilst it was true that British infantry training at this stage was far more heavily focused on trench attacks rather than open warfare, this criticism overlooks the tactical situation faced during Third Scarpe. Confused by darkness and unfamiliar terrain, under fire from all sides and threatened by encirclement, the idea that improved musketry skills would have made much difference is questionable. Similarly, Brigadier-General J. Kennedy, GOC 26th Brigade, 9th Division, argued that whilst his men had 'perfected' the organised trench attack they did not know how to fight in the open and that once the creeping barrage was lost there was 'a tendency to think that nothing more can be done.' He claimed the Regular army of 1914 'would gain much ground' through alternative rushes supported by their own rifle fire. Yet, Kennedy undermined this argument by admitting, 'it is certainly no good launching a fresh attack or sacrificing more troops against machine-guns in position.' Such was the case on 3 May. In any case, the solution was more 'elasticity' in both training and attack formations.[136]

Culpability for Third Scarpe lies with the BEF high command which tried to achieve far more than was possible with the forces available. As C-in-C, Haig must

135 Falls, *Military Operations 1917*, Vol. I, pp.297, 454
136 TNA WO 95/1739: 'Account of the Battle on May 3rd 1917, 26th Infantry Brigade', 9th Division General Staff War Diary.

bear most of the responsibility for this. It was his decision to continue the offensive regardless of information that its primary justification, support for the French offensive farther south, was no longer relevant. Further to this, First and Third armies had been greatly reduced by manpower losses during April whilst the Germans had strengthened their forces opposite. Once the decision was made, failure was almost certain due to the limited time frame in which a large-scale offensive could be planned and prepared for as well as both Allenby and Horne stretching their weakened divisions much too thinly. Disaster was ensured by Haig's decision to transform the operation into a risky night assault. This was too much to ask of the infantry which, in addition to its parlous manpower state, remained relatively untrained for the task of surmounting a strong defensive system occupied by a tough, resourceful and vigilant enemy. They paid the price.

13

'Artillery Conquers, Infantry Occupies'
A Study in the Performance of the British Artillery at the Third Battle of Ypres

Simon Shephard

The BEF entered the First World War with *Field Service Regulations Part 1: Operations (1909) (FSR)* as its doctrine.[1] Whilst at the Staff College in 1912, J.F.C. Fuller sought to extract what he saw as the 'Principles of War' which he believed were hidden in the prose of *FSR*.[2] Fuller anonymously published his ideas in an article entitled 'The Principles of War with Reference to the Campaigns of 1914-15'.[3] He went on to teach them at the CO's Course in 1917 and subsequently contributed them to the 1924 re-write of *FSR*. In 1916 Fuller listed the 'Principles of War' as the Objective, the Offensive, Mass, Economy of Force, Movement, Surprise, Security and Cooperation. He further stated that the interplay and balance between the principles is affected by the following conditions, themselves part of Clausewitzian friction: Time, Space, Ground, Weather, Numbers, Morale, Communications, Supply and Armament. Fuller's work can be seen as representative of a commonly held British combat doctrine during the First World War.

By 1917 the conduct of the artillery battle had moved from 'Inadequacy' (1914) through 'Experimentation and Build up' (1915) and was now oscillating between 'Destruction' (1916) and 'Neutralisation'.[4] The army level of command provided

---

1   General Staff, *Field Service Regulations Part I: Operations* (London: HMSO, 1912 [1909]).
2   J.F.C. Fuller, *The Foundations of the Science of War* (London, Hutchinson & Co. Ltd, 1926) pp.14-16 and S. Mitchell, 'Learning from Defeat: 32nd Division and 1 July 1916' in S. Jones (ed.), *At All Costs: The British Army on the Western Front 1916* (Warwick: Helion & Co., 2018), pp.324-53.
3   J.F.C. Fuller, 'The Principles of War, With Reference to the Campaigns of 1914–1915', *The Journal of the Royal United Services Institution*, Vol. LXI, No. 441, February 1916, pp.1-40.
4   D. Thuell & T.G. Bradbeer, 'Fires and Combined Arms Maneuver: The Battle of Vimy Ridge, 9 April 1917' in T.G. Bradbeer (ed.), *Lethal and Non–Lethal Fires: Historical*

direction and allocated resources, with corps planning the battle, conducting the deep and counter-battery (CB) battles whilst directing the divisions in the conduct of the close battle. Using Fuller's principles this chapter will study the effectiveness of the British artillery during three of the nine battles which make up Third Ypres; Pilckem Ridge (31 July), Menin Road Ridge (20 September) and Second Battle of Passchendaele (26 October to 10 November).

Destruction and Movement: Pilckem Ridge

When Gough launched his attack on 31 July 1917 the artillery battle had already been raging for nearly a month. His artillery staff had been preparing for it since 17 June.[5] At the end of June GHQ redistributed the BEF's artillery so that Fifth Army had 65 brigades and Second Army had 18 brigades whilst also allocating Fifth Army nearly four times the quantity of shells and five times the number of 106 percussion fuzes (for wire-cutting) than Second Army.[6] In doing so GHQ ensured Fifth Army had sufficient numbers, namely one 18-pdr per 15 yards and one medium or heavy howitzer (excluding counter-battery guns) per 50 yards of front in order to deliver the massed firepower required.[7] Haig's senior artillery advisor, Major-General Noel Birch, met with Gough and Plumer's two General Officer's Commanding Royal Artillery (GOCRA) Major-Generals Sir Herbert Uniacke and Christopher Buckle on the 8 July, to coordinate the artillery requirements.[8] Buckle had been in post for one day although Second Army's Artillery Instruction No. 1 had already been issued and stressed the need for 'uniformity of method to be maintained between the two armies.'[9]

Case Studies of Converging Cross Domain Fires in Large-Scale Combat Operations (Fort Leavenworth, Kansas: Army University Press, 2018) pp.186-87.

5   RA Institute, Military Document 1160, (RAI/MD) Uniacke, Lieutenant General Sir Herbert, Papers, 'Part VII – Tactical Development', n.d., p.134.

6   RAI/MD 1160, Uniacke, 'Part VII – Tactical Development', p.134; R.J. Lewendon, 'The Cutting of Barbed Wire Entanglements by Artillery Fire in World War 1' in *The Journal of the Royal Artillery,* Vol. CXII, No. 2, Autumn 1984, pp. 115-17; TNA WO 158/249: Fifth Army, General Staff (GS) Folio 356, 17 June 1917; TNA WO 158/207: Second Army' GS' Folio 353, 30 June 1917 and TNA WO 95/951: XVIII Corps, GS, 'The Third Battle of Ypres – Operation of XVIII Corps 31st July', 1917.

7   RAI/MD 1160, Uniacke, 'Part VII – Tactical Development', p.140.

8   A.F. Becke, *Order of Battle of Divisions,* Parts 1A, 2A, 2B, 3A, 3B, 4 (London: HMSO, 1935-45).

9   TNA WO 158/207: Folio 357, 4 July 1917 and RAI/MD 1160 Uniacke, 'Lessons from the 1917 Battle Fighting of the Fifth Army from an Artillery Point of View', December 1917 – Draft Copy.

Fifth Army issued its artillery plan in late June and within days the corps GOCRAs were issuing their own orders.[10] Fifth Army's II Corps issued a comprehensive 76 page stand-alone plan including maps. In contrast XIV Corps' plan was a 15-page appendix to their GS Instruction No. 4 containing none of the details found in the II Corps scheme.[11] For its part X Corps, in Second Army, issued a Warning Order on the same day as II Corps issued its plan.[12] Haig informed all army commanders of 'the importance of overcoming the enemy's artillery by CB work before an attack was launched.'[13] Fifth Army introduced a new technique for this work, in which Uniacke directed that fire should:

Major-General C.R. Buckle.

[R]ender useless for further occupation the immediate ground round the gun positions by means of a fierce concentration bombardment by every medium and heavy howitzer battery that can be brought to bear.[14]

The GOCRAs also expected to support the attack by destroying the German front line defences, before providing the infantry with protection during the assault and consolidation phases. Yet Gough's direction that after the initial assault, commanders

10   RAI/MD 1160, Uniacke, 'Part VII – Tactical Development', p.135 and RAI/MD 183/31, J. Headlam, 'Second Army – Proceedings of Corps Commanders Conferences', 26 June 1917. The relevant orders relating to the artillery preparation phase of the battle are not held in TNA files for XVIII and XIX corps.
11   TNA WO 95/652-6: II Corps, GOCRA, 'Artillery Plan', 3 July 1917, and TNA WO 95/912–6: XIV Corps, GS, 'Instruction No. 4 Appendix A-C, Addendum', 11 July 1917 and associated maps.
12   TNA WO 95/865-1: X Corps, GOCRA, 'Artillery Instruction No. 24', 3 July 1917.
13   TNA WO 158/249: Folio 353, 14 June 1917 and Albert P. Palazzo, 'The British Army's Counter-Battery Staff Officer', *The Journal of Military History*, Vol. 3, Issue 1, January 1999, p.68.
14   RAI/MD 1160, Uniacke, 'Lessons from the 1917 Battle Fighting', p.135.

were to use their initiative to seize abandoned or lightly held ground, added uncertainty to their barrage plans.[15]

On 8 July the senior gunners discussed the need for Fifth Army to work with the French First Army which would be covering its left (northern) flank. Uniacke unsuccessfully requested additional support from French long range guns.[16] The commanders agreed to the 'the barrage in depth' technique for the attack and whilst practice barrages were to be arranged, particularly at the junctions of corps and armies, there was to be no front wide barrage so as not to disclose the flanks of the attack. Second Army was also asked to extend its practice barrages beyond X Corps' southern flank to aid deception.[17] Given the nature of the Ypres salient, it was impossible for the British to conceal their intentions from the Germans.[18] In his account of the battle, General von Kuhl, Chief of Staff of *Armee Gruppe Kronprinz Rupprecht*, stated that it was clear 'a big British offensive in Flanders must be reckoned with.'[19] By the beginning of July, the Germans had determined an attack was imminent and was likely to fall on both sides of Ypres in the sector held by their *Fourth Army*. The only unknown was the date.[20]

Command and control of the large number of field artillery brigades deployed in support of the assault divisions was vested across the available CRAs. As a result 38th (Welsh) Division's CRA took command of both his field artillery brigades behind the right side of his division (known as the Right Group) whilst the CRA 20th (Light) Division commanded his own artillery brigades and one army brigade in support of the left of 38th Division (Left Group).[21] The heavy artillery under the Brigadier-General Corps Heavy Artillery (BGCHA) formed the CB groups and the Bombardment Double Groups. The Double Groups consisted of two heavy artillery groups (HAGs) operating under a single nominated commander.[22] To ensure effective cooperation the divisional artilleries (DA) were to provide each attacking infantry brigade HQ with a

15   TNA WO 158/249: Folio 362, 7 June 1917.
16   TNA WO 158/249: Folio 357, 18 June 1917 (apparently no mention of the anniversary
     of Waterloo was made during this meeting); TNA WO 158/207: Folio 363, 9 July
     1917 and Folio 364, 'Response to a Fifth Army Request for Locations to be Engaged
     by French First Army's Artillery', 10 July 1917, in which its artillery commander,
     General F.D. Laboria, observed: 'In answer to the request that you addressed to me
     about the possibilities of action of the Artillery of the 1st French Army on the villages
     of LEEDEGHEM, DADIZEELE, MOORESLEDE, the camps of BECERLARE
     and the vicinity of ROULERS, I have the regret to know that these objectives cannot be
     counter-balanced by the French artillery because of their remoteness.'
17   TNA WO 158/207: Folio 363, 9 July 1917.
18   TNA WO 158/249: Folio 374, 4 July 1917 and Folio 353, 15 June 1917.
19   RAI/MD 1050/3, Colonel R. MacLeod Papers, General von Kuhl's account of 'The
     Battles in Flanders During the Summer and Autumn of 1917'.
20   RAI/MD 1050/3, MacLeod, 'The Battles in Flanders', p.15.
21   V.E. Inglefield, *The History of the Twentieth (Light) Division* (London: Nisbet, 1921),
     pp.143-145, 157.
22   TNA WO 95/652–6.

battery commander and an additional officer to each attacking battalion's HQ. They also provided a forward observation officer (FOO) from each field artillery brigade whilst the HAG provided an additional FOO for each attacking brigade front.[23]

Von Kuhl believed the British artillery preparations began on 22 July although they formally started on 16 July and were intended to last approximately nine days.[24] II Corps' plan makes clear that their CB work started on 1 July whilst XVIII Corps' machine-guns commenced night time harassing fire from 20/21 July onwards.[25] With the removal of ammunition restrictions on 4 July the tempo of artillery operations increased rapidly in advance of the official start date.[26] By holding the high ground around the salient the Germans had the advantage not only in terms of observation, but also in terms of covered approaches and artillery positions behind the Pilckem Ridge and Gheluvelt Plateau, as well as a reverse slope second line and opportunities for enfilade fire.[27] In contrast, the British held 'indifferent' positions with few features behind which their batteries could be concealed.[28]

To locate the German batteries the British artillery needed additional support. By now the BEF's ability to deliver accurate CB fire had improved significantly since the start of the war and was well supported by Royal Engineer (RE) Field Survey companies and Royal Flying Corps (RFC) observation squadrons and kite balloon sections.[29] The CB battle was now co-ordinated by the new corps level Counter-Battery Staff Officer (CBSO) and supported by increased intelligence capacity.[30] Despite the advances in locating techniques, the poor weather and the prevailing westerly winds meant that results from both sound ranging and flash spotting proved to be disappointing. To counter this the sections were pushed further forward, which only added

23   Ibid.
24   TNA WO 95/865-1: 'Artillery Instruction No. 25', 7 July 1917 and RAI/MD 1050/3, MacLeod, 'The Battles in Flanders',
25   RAI/MD 1050/3, MacLeod, 'The Battles in Flanders', p.14 and TNA WO 95/652–6.
26   TNA WO 95/912-6, 'Instruction No. 7', 4 July; TNA WO 158/249: Folio 353, 15 June 1917 and Peter Chasseaud, *Artillery's Astrologers: A History of British Survey and Mapping on the Western Front 1914-1918* (Lewes: Map Books, 1999), p.32.
27   RAI/MD 1160, Uniacke, 'Part VII – Tactical Development', pp.141-42; Chasseaud, p.325 and TNA WO 95/951: 'The Third Battle of Ypres – Operation of XVIII Corps 31st July, 1917'.
28   C.N.F. Broad, 'The Development of Artillery 1914-1918' in *The Journal of the Royal Artillery*, Vol. XLIX, No. 2 and 3, April 1922, pp.129-130; F.H. Mackay, 'Feeding the Guns' in *Stand To!*, No. 9, pp.7-9; TNA WO 95/951: 'The Third Battle of Ypres' and Palazzo, 'The British Army's Counter-Battery Staff Officer', p.66.
29   Broad, 'The Development of Artillery', p.129; Bailey, *Field Artillery and Firepower*, pp.127-41 and Palazzo, 'The British Army's Counter-Battery Staff Officer', pp.62–63
30   Andy Simpson, *Directing Operations: British Corps Command on the Western Front 1914-1918* (Stroud: Spellmount, 2006), p.81; General Sir Martin Farndale, *History of the Royal Regiment of Artillery: The Western Front 1914-1918* (London: Royal Artillery Institution Printing House, 1986), pp.344–45, 368 and Palazzo, 'The British Army's Counter-Battery Staff Officer', pp.61-62, 64-65, 67.

to the problems and resulted in their communication lines being frequently cut.[31] The ability to locate the German artillery positions through aerial photography and observation was also hampered by their changing tactics. In the past the heavily defended German positions were easy to spot in photographs. By July 1917 however, they often opted for concealment and the use of single and mobile guns to confuse the British.[32]

The corps artillery staff produced daily instructions for their heavy units covering the firing programme and details on shoots to be supported by the RFC.[33] At the end of each day, reports were produced on the CB and the bombardment groups' activities whilst RFC observed shoots generated short synopses. From these the CB staff would understand how successful the shoot had been. The observation of some shoots could be affected by debris and smoke from other engagements, so arrangements were made to ensure batteries did not spoil each other's observation.[34] Throughout July the weather also affected aerially observed shoots, although not always in the way imagined, with some shoots curtailed on fine days by haze.[35] In addition to the programmed shoots the CB batteries would respond to any opportunity targets identified by RFC observers. When visibility failed they fired 'rakes', subjecting an area to the undirected fire of a number of batteries. The Germans recognised that during the last third of July they were being subjected to a planned destructive bombardment.[36]

The artillery battle was fought 24-hours a day.[37] At night the DAs, supported by machine-guns, engaged those areas within range whilst the HAGs would complete similar tasks for those in depth.[38] By way of example, on the night of 16/17 the 92nd HAG fired 'isolation' or 'harassing shoots' against roads, railways and cross roads with short irregular bursts of fire including the extensive use of gas.[39] II Corps directed that 'every round must be a surprise to the enemy ...' This required haphazard and unexpected fire and needed the 'most carefully worked out schemes.'[40] For the week beginning 16 July Fifth Army reported 'photographs show that the shooting has been accurate' whilst going on to state that CB work 'was particularly successful' with 48 gun pits or positions destroyed and a further 184 damaged together with 88 fires and explosions. Second Army's reports lack the detail of the Fifth's but make clear that

31   Chasseaud, *Artillery's Astrologers*, p.326.
32   Ibid.
33   Palazzo, 'The British Army's Counter-Battery Staff Officer', p.66.
34   Broad, 'The Development of Artillery', p.131 and TNA WO 95/652–6.
35   TNA WO 95/917-2: 'Counter Batteries Work Done from 6.0.P.M. 19th to 6.0.P.M 20th July, 1917'.
36   RAI/MD 1050/3: MacLeod, 'The Battles in Flanders', p.16.
37   TNA WO 95/917-1: 'Daily Tactical Progress Reports', 6 pm 4 July – 6 pm 25 July [1917].
38   TNA WO 95/652-2, II Corps GOCRA.
39   RAI/MD 1050/3, MacLeod, 'The Battles in Flanders', p.17.
40   TNA WO 95/652-6.

all corps artilleries had been active whilst also noting that despite poor visibility, the RFC had carried out a large amount of work.[41]

The Army and DA field brigades were also actively employed during the preparatory period. From 16 July to the night of 22/23 July the field artillery brigades assigned to II Corps attacked 96 German defensive positions. Some tasks required them to block routes at set intervals or to cut communication wires. Additionally, the DAs were tasked with clearing the barbed wire in front of the German first defensive system whilst the HAGs were tasked with clearing the remainder. XIV Corps identified that the Germans were continuing to strengthen the depth of their position and that to create 20 yard gaps in every 100 yards of wire would require 20,500 6-inch howitzer shells in addition to significant quantities field artillery ammunition.[42] Flexibility was built into the programmes so that if, due to weather, some observed shoots could not be fired before 17:30 CRAs could order the balance of the day's ammunition to be fired against suitable registered targets.

Haig had originally set 25 July as the attack date. However, in mid-July Gough requested a postponement of three days (until 28 July). His request was supported by a short note prepared by his artillery staff.[43] Although Fifth Army believed the CB battle would be won by 25 July they wanted additional time to move guns forward to engage German batteries which had been withdrawn out of range, as well as reducing the volume of movement required on the day of the attack. The delay would also provide time for batteries still arriving to register and for the railway lines to be extended so that the 12-inch howitzers could carry out additional CB work.[44] Haig agreed to Gough's request, whilst also asking Second Army to address two concerns. First, 'whether [their] allotment of guns to bombardment was not too extravagant for the frontage of attack' and second, 'whether [they had] sufficient guns for … counter-battery' work beyond the Gheluvelt Plateau.[45] As a result, it was agreed to shorten the length of Second Army's bombardment to X Corps' attack frontage and to increase the number of batteries undertaking CB work.[46] On 21 July the French requested a further delay stating that poor visibility had affected their ability to conduct CB work.

41   TNA WO 158/217: 'Weekly Summary of Operations – Second Army, For the week ending 6 p.m. 19 July, 1917'.
42   TNA WO 95/912-6 'Instruction No. 4 Appendix A' and TNA WO 95/652-6.
43   J.E. Edmonds, *Military Operations France and Belgium 1917*, Vol. 2 (London: HMSO, 1948) and TNA WO 158/249: Folios 383 and 397, 'Notes from Conference', 12 July 1917. Although Edmonds suggests the conference took place on 7 July and that Haig agreed to a postponement from 25 to 30 July, the Fifth Army record of this conference is dated 12 July (Folio 383) and contains a manuscript comment in red stating the artillery paper was handed in on 12 July, at which time Haig agreed to postpone the arrack until 28 July in line with the three-day delay requested by Gough.
44   TNA WO 158/249: Folios 383 and 397, 'Notes from Conference', 12 July 1917.
45   TNA WO 158/207: Folio 367, 20 July 1917.
46   RAI/MD 1160, Uniacke, 'Part VII – Tactical Development' and TNA WO 95/642-4: 'Summary of Information Received up to 9 p.m. 31 July, 1917'.

Major-General H.C.C. Uniacke and General F.D. Laboria, the neighbouring French First Army artillery commander.

After consulting his staff and Gough, Haig agreed to postpone the attack until 31 July.[47]

II Corps used these delays to order as many German batteries as possible to be destroyed by the evening of 27/28 July. Thereafter, every available gun would be concentrated on the remaining active German batteries and on positions which the CBSO considered likely to become active. Additionally, on the nights of 28/29 and 30/31 July all German batteries in range were to be subjected to a bombardment using 25,000 gas shells.[48] As part of the bombardment programme the HAGs were tasked with employing their heavy guns against deep targets such as hutted encampments, stations, railway sidings, depots and ammunition dumps as well as various headquarters. On the night of 30/31 July, a sequential programme of intensive concentrations was fired by the HAG.[49] Taking advantage of the delay, Uniacke changed his mind and conducted a practice barrage along the whole front. Von Kuhl noted the effectiveness of the British deep fire describing it as a 'heavy and extensive harassing fire ... reached up to 20 km in the rear areas behind [our] front line.'[50]

47   Edmonds, *Military Operations 1917*, Vol. 2, pp.132-33 and TNA WO 158/249: Folio 388, 23 July 1917 and Folio 389, 28 July 1917.
48   TNA WO 95/652–6.
49   Ibid.
50   RAI/MD 1050/3, MacLeod, 'The Battles in Flanders', p.16

During the preparatory bombardment for the Somme, numerous guns had been unavailable due to technical issues and a lack of spare parts.[51] By Third Ypres the ASC had improved matters with Fifth Army routinely reporting no more than 5 percent of its guns in repair, and 99 percent of all guns available on 31 July.[52] To maintain an element of surprise II Corps directed the DAs not to disclose all of their 18-pdrs until 30 July.[53] In the case of 30th Division, tasks were allocated for these guns for 30/31 July when they were to support the overnight barrage before joining the creeping barrage. However, even with these unmasked batteries firing, the II Corps attack barrage was delivered by only 70 percent of the available 18-prdrs, supported by a further 225 howitzers and trench mortars.[54] The remainder were either preparing to move or had been made available to answer additional calls for fire.[55] In the first 10 minutes of the attack the available II Corps batteries fired approximately 22,000 rounds.[56] Even before this onslaught the British shelling had been so heavy and effective that the Germans, describing it as 'drum fire', had been forced to replace some front line divisions.[57]

Despite the effectiveness of the artillery preparations, Gough's decision to attack deep objectives meant that the final objective was beyond the range of most 4.5-in howitzers whilst the third objective was very near to, or in some cases beyond, the maximum range of his 18-pdrs.[58] Yet the battles of Vimy[59] and Arras[60] had identified a change in German tactics with them now using mutually supporting machine-guns emplaced in depth positions.[61] To address this Uniacke had identified the need to employ a 'barrage in depth' rather than the previous technique of 'piling up' the barrage on the trench line. Additionally, he set the protective barrage well beyond the objective to allow the infantry to reorganise securely.[62] At the same time all available medium and heavy guns were to be concentrated on the deep battle targeting the movement of reserve troops, convoys and bottlenecks on roads etc.[63]

51   B. MacCormick, 'Lessons Unlearned: The Somme Preparatory Bombardment, 24 June-1 July 1916' in Jones (ed.), *At All Costs*, p.139.
52   RAI/MD 1160, Uniacke, 'Report on the Behaviour of Artillery Equipment, Fifth Army, During Quarter Ending August 31, 1917'.
53   TNA WO 95/652-6.
54   Ibid.
55   Ibid.
56   Ibid.
57   RAI/MD 1050/3, MacLeod, 'The Battles in Flanders', p.16,
58   TNA WO 95/912-6: 'Instruction No. 4 Appendix A(ii)'.
59   From 9 April to 12 April 1917
60   From 9 April to 16 May 1917.
61   USA WO, NORO, 'Experience of the German First Army in the Somme Battle, June 24 to November 26, 1916', pp. 77–144. This German *Second Army* document (compiled by General Fritz Von Below) was captured and translated in January 1917.
62   RAI/MD 1160, Uniacke, 'Part VII – Tactical Development', p.136 and Broad, 'The Development of Artillery', pp.129-30.
63   TNA WO 95/652–6 and Broad, 'The Development of Artillery'.

Fifth Army's staff assumed the attack would achieve its objectives by 14:00. Planning accordingly, they directed all field artillery, and as much heavy artillery as possible, to be pushed forward on the afternoon of 31 July to prepare for the next phase. To meet this direction II Corps' artillery formed five echelons. The DAs provided the first and third echelons. The first echelon was to move forward two hours after the second objective had been secured, and the third echelon after the third objective had been taken. The fourth and fifth echelons consisted of heavy and siege batteries whilst the second echelon provided a mobile CB group.

When the assault commenced Von Kuhl credited the British with delivering a 'storm of fire … the like of which had never been experienced before', describing it 'as if Hell itself had opened.'[64] On the day, GHQ reported the results as being 'highly satisfactory' whilst II Corps reported '[their] artillery neutralising programme was very effective and …. the [Germans] defensive barrage was extremely feeble.'[65] Although the three northern corps made good progress, it was on the all-important southern flank, where II Corps was aimed at the Gheluvelt Plateau, that progress was difficult.[66] All three of their assault divisions successfully advanced behind the creeping barrage onto the first objective subsequently stating that the artillery work was effective and 'beyond praise'. Yet despite such comments they all failed to get *beyond* their first objectives.[67] In part this was due to the condition of the ground which slowed the infantry advance, and in the case of 8th Division hampered forward movement of artillery; meanwhile 30th Division noted delays at the first objective caused by machine-gun fire and as a result they lost the barrage.[68] Such machine-gun fire, delivered from depth positions beyond the protective barrage, was an important factor in halting the British.[69] These problems should not have been a surprise. The nature of the ground was well known, as it had been fought over for 2½ years, and it should have been expected that despite the protracted bombardment, some positions would inevitably survive.[70] In Uniacke's view the rate of advance, which was set by the

---

64   RAI/MD 1050/3, MacLeod, 'The Battles in Flanders', p.17.
65   TNA WO 158/207: Folio 372, 1 August 1917.
66   RAI/MD 1160, Uniacke, 'Part VII – Tactical Development', p. 144
67   TNA WO 95/1677: 8th Division GS 'Narrative of the Operations on 31 July-3 August 1917'; TNA WO 95/2312: 30th Division GS, 'Observations 30th Division 31 July to 4 August 1917' and TNA WO 95/2190: 24th Division GS, 'Account of Operations 24th Divisional Front 31 July 1917'.
68   TNA WO 95/1677: 'Narrative of the Operations'; TNA WO 95/2312, 'Operations 30th Division'.
69   TNA WO 2190: 'Operations 24th Divisional Front' and RAI/MD 1160, Uniacke, 'Part VII – Tactical Development'.
70   Lieutenant-Colonel Alan Brooke, 'The Evolution of Artillery in the Great War, Part VI', *The Journal of the Royal Artillery*, October 1925, pp. 369-87; P. Doyle, *Disputed Earth: Geology and Trench Warfare on the Western Front 1914-18* (London: Unicorn Publishing, 2017), pp.59-73 and USA WO, NORO, 'Armies', p.66.

GS, was fine for reasonable ground but not for the conditions in the salient which were further exacerbated by the day's torrential rain.[71]

On the XIX and XVIII corps front their lead brigades gained their third objectives by about 11.00, but shortly thereafter the protective barrage ceased and the British artillery remained unsure of the new front line. At 14.00 the Germans counter-attacked, supported by an intense enfilading barrage from behind Zonnebeke and the Gheluvelt Plateau, forcing back the British who lacked artillery support.[72] After several hours of hard fighting, the British were able to form a defensive front, under artillery protection, on the second objective at around 16:00.[73] The German counter-attacks were less successful against XVII, II corps and Second Army, where they were broken up by artillery and machine-gun barrages.[74] It should be noted though, that in these sectors the British had largely remained on either their first or second objectives and were therefore, within range of their own guns.[75] The attack had cost the nine assault divisions between 30–60 percent of their fighting strength for less than half of Gough's initial 6,000-yard minimum requirement.[76] The German defences had been underestimated, particularly their ability to still concentrate significant amounts of artillery, whilst their new techniques of dispersed machine-guns and the tactics of flexible defence supported by counter-attack or *Eingreif* divisions had not been anticipated.[77] The Germans, for their part, whilst recognising in many places that the infantry had broken through their lines congratulated themselves in breaking the 'violence of the assault'.[78]

Neutralisation: Menin Road Ridge

Gough's II Corps attack to seize Westhoek, 10 August, and his army's attack at Langemarck, 16 August, both failed, in part, due to effective German counter-attacks

71   RAI/MD 1160, Uniacke, 'Part VII – Tactical Development', p.144
72   TNA WO 95/1914: 15th Division, GS, 'Narrative of Operations of the 15th (Scottish) Division, 29 July-4 August 1917'; TNA WO 95/2093: 55th Division, GS, 'Report on Operations, Ypres 29 July-4 August 1917'and TNA WO 95/2566: 39th Division, GS, 'Operations of 31 July 1917'.
73   Edmonds, *Military Operations 1917*, Vol. 2, pp.170-74.
74   Ibid., pp.174-76.
75   TNA WO 95/1677: 'Narrative of the Operations'; TNA WO 95/2312: 'Operations 30th Division' and TNA WO 95/2617: 41st Division, GS, 'Report on Operations on 31 July & Subsequent Days', 6 August 1917.
76   Edmonds, *Military Operations 1917*, Vol. 2, p.179 and G. Sheffield, 'Haig and the British Expeditionary Force in 1917' in P. Dennis & J. Grey (eds.) *1917: Tactics, Training and Technology* (Canberra: Australian Military History Publications, 2007), p.8.
77   Edmonds, *Military Operations 1917*, Vol 2, p.179.
78   RAI/MD 1050/3, MacLeod, 'The Battles in Flanders', p.18.

supported by fresh artillery.[79] A combination of intelligence assessments and captured documents led the British to realise that the Germans were no longer holding their front line trenches in strength; instead their garrisons, armed with machine-guns, occupied mutually supporting shell holes. Conversely, the Germans had recognised that the further the British advanced the more disorganised they became and as a result the British artillery were unable to judge the exact position of their own troops.[80] This enabled the Germans to withdraw their counter-attacking troops, known as *Eingreif* divisions, and their supporting mobile artillery to relative safety some 3 to 5 miles to the rear.[81] Despite all of this by the end of August the Germans had been ejected from the forward positions and had 'used up' 17 divisions.[82]

During this period Second Army's artillery continued to engage the Germans whilst seeking to identify why the previous attacks were unsuccessful.[83] On 10 August Plumer sought the views of his corps commanders: IX Corps' GOC thought they were being asked to cover too much distance; X Corps' GOC focused on ensuring reserves were available, whilst GOC II Anzac Corps offered two solutions. He proposed to either penetrate to a depth which enabled the capture of the Germans' field artillery or alternatively 'to confine [the] attack to a strictly limited objective, well within the range of our own Field Artillery …' and then to attack again as soon as '…our Field Artillery [has] moved up to new positions to cover the next bound.'[84] They all agreed there was great value in developing the use of machine-gun barrages.[85] They also discussed the need to slow the artillery barrage, so the infantry could keep up with it, whilst they asked for it to be deepened and to include the use of 'searching and sweeping fires'.[86] Fifth Army was also grappling with the new German tactics and although Gough focused on the resolve of his infantry, he also explored proposals from GOC XVIII Corps to make greater use of smoke.[87] During this period Uniacke issued memoranda on both the new German defensive tactics and how the attack

79   TNA WO 158/254: Fifth Army, 'Summary of Operations of Fifth Army for the Week Ending 6 p.m. 10th August 17', and 'Summary of Operations, Week Ending 6 p.m. 17th August 17'.
80   Broad, 'The Development of Artillery', p.132.
81   RAI/MD 183, Headlam, 'Corps Commanders Conferences', 20 August 1917.
82   R. Foley, 'The Other Side of the Wire: The German Army in 1917' in Dennis & Grey, (eds.) *1917 Tactics, Training and Technology*, pp. 173–74.
83   RAI/MD 183, Headlam, 'Corps Commanders Conferences', 26 June 1917.
84   RAI/MD 183, Headlam, 'Corps Commanders Conferences – Annex A', 10 August 1917.
85   RAI/MD 183, Headlam, 'Corps Commanders Conferences', 10 August and 20 August 1917; G.S. Hutchison, *The Thirty-Third Division in France and Flanders'* (London: Waterlow & Sons, 1921), p.65 and C.E. Crutchley, (ed.), *Machine Gunner 1914–1918: Personal Experiences of the Machine Gun Corps* (London: Purnell Book Services, 1975), p.107.
86   RAI/MD 183, Headlam, 'Corps Commanders Conferences', 20 August 1917.
87   TNA WO 158/250: Folio 411, 'Notes on Army Commanders Conference at Lovie Chateau on 17th August 1917'; Folio 415 'Notes on Conference, 25th August 1917', and Folio 426 "Notes on Conference, 10th September 1917'.

barrage might be adjusted to overcome them.[88] He identified two issues: the infantry falling back when the Germans counter-attacked, in line with Gough's views; and the ability of the Germans to deliver machine-gun fire from depth onto the objective, which he believed could be countered by modifying the attack barrage.[89]

A key feature of Uniacke's new tactics was the need to 'recognise … that obliteration of the trench lines is of minor importance [compared] with anti-machine-gun work.' He also identified that German counter-attacks, which occurred as the British were still advancing, were only successful if the previous British CB work had been ineffective, whereas German machine-guns were only effective during the attack and before the infantry were able to consolidate their gains. Therefore, he proposed using CB guns and a portion of the howitzers to give the attack barrage the additional strength and depth needed to defeat the German machine-guns.[90] Uniacke proposed the attack barrage should now consist of four elements; a 'Creeping' barrage in front of the infantry, a 'Combing' barrage focused on strong points and communication trenches etc., which was to be organised in depth and planned in such a way that 'a hostile machine-gunner is unable to realise that a lift has taken place …', and a 'Neutralising' barrage to engage all distant machine-gunners, including on the flanks. These barrages were designed to ensure that at all times there was 2,000 yards of protective fire in front of the infantry.[91] Finally a 'Standing' barrage designed to break up the *Eingreif* divisions was to be fired well forward of the final objective and focused on areas 'likely to shelter formed bodies.' Accuracy and constant shelling of fixed points was to be discarded; rather fire should '"sweep" and "search"' areas. Believing the Germans were aiming their machine-gun fire to land just beyond the British side of the creeping barrage, Uniacke proposed dividing it into two with a 200-yard gap between each line. In this way he hoped that the Germans would mistake the first line as being the whole barrage, adjust their fire accordingly, and thus fall short of the still protected advancing infantry. He later considered the use of smoke rounds to help mark the protective barrage lines and to smother German observation posts. Gas was to be used on probable counter-attack routes.[92] Throughout this period Uniacke and Buckle were sharing their ideas with each other and with Birch at GHQ.[93]

88 RAI/MD 1160, Uniacke, 'Memorandum on the Enemy's Present System of Defence', 20 August 1917 and 'Attack Barrages, As Modified by the Enemy's latest Tactics', 25 August 1917 (later modified by an undated Addenda)
89 USA WO, NORO, 'Supplementary Instructions As to the Construction of Defences', pp.74-76 and RAI/MD 1160, Uniacke, 'Attack Barrages', p. 1.
90 RAI/MD 1160, Uniacke, 'Attack Barrages', p.3.
91 RAI/MD 1160, Uniacke, 'Attack Barrages', pp.3-5.
92 RAI/MD 1160, Uniacke, 'Addenda to Attack Barrages, As Modified by the Enemy's latest Tactics', n.d.
93 RAI/MD 1160, Uniacke, GHQ 'No. R.A./?/47', 2? August 1917.

Light railway ammunition train, Ypres front August 1917.

Having reviewed his options, Haig concluded that he needed to continue attacking east of Ypres and to focus on securing the Gheluvelt Plateau as the next step.[94] He now placed Plumer in overall command with Gough in a supporting role.[95] In line with Haig's direction that a series of limited objective or 'steps' be taken, Plumer submitted his plan to secure the first 'step' to GHQ on the 29 August. He estimated that he would need three weeks to prepare which, with the weather improving, would also allow the ground to dry.[96] Included with the plan was an outline of his artillery requirements. To support the proposed I Anzac and X corps attacks (across a frontage of 6,800 yards and to a depth of between 1,000 and 2,000 yards) Plumer asked for 1,339 artillery pieces to deal with deep targets, CB work and the cover the actual attack.[97] He also requested a further 491 artillery pieces to support the corps on his right flank. His staff calculated that during the seven-day preparatory barrage and

94   H.A. Jones, *The War in the Air, Being the Story of the part played in the Great War by the Royal Air Force*, Vol. 4 (Oxford: Clarendon Press, 1934), p.179 and Edmonds, *Military Operations 1917*, Vol. 2, pp. 231–36.

95   TNA WO 158/250, Folio 416, 26 August 1917 and Folio 418, 28 August 1917.

96   Edmonds, *Military Operations 1917*, Vol. 2, p. 236; TNA WO 158/208: Folio 377, "G. 140', 29 August 1917; RAI/MD 1160, Uniacke, 'Part VII – Tactical Development', p.151; G. Powell, *Plumer: The Soldier's General* (Barnsley: Pen & Sword, 1990 [2004]), p.210 and Jones, *The War in the Air*, p.180.

97   TNA WO 158/208: Folio 377, 'G. 140 – Table A', 29 August 1917; H.R. Sandilands, *The 23rd Division* (London: William Blackwood & Sons, 1925), pp.174-75 and Jones, *The War in the Air*, p.180.

the first 24 hours of the attack they would require 3,616,355 artillery rounds.[98] On 1 September Plumer gave planning direction to his corps commanders.[99] He made clear that he intended to conduct a series of limited attacks, in rapid succession, with each being in range of the full power of the artillery.[100]

With no formal training and only *SS 139/3: Artillery Notes, No. 3 Counter-battery Work* (March 1917) to help guide them, the newly appointed CBSOs devised many of their own solutions to CB staff work.[101] Some GOCRAs, such as Brigadier-General Hamilton Reed VC of X Corps, provided significant guidance on what he expected from them in terms of plans and programmes.[102] He also reinforced the need for close liaison with the infantry whilst he sought to improve liaison across the artillery groups by directing his Bombardment Group commanders to affiliate a battery, preferably whose arcs overlapped, to each of the field artillery brigades.[103] During this period artillery barrage and attack maps were becoming increasingly complex and were subject to scrutiny by the artillery staff up to and including GHQ level.[104] To improve aerial observation Second Army directed that every available RFC machine was to be used during the preparatory phase.[105] They also directed that each CHA was to provide a senior officer to their supporting RFC squadron whilst the RFC continued to attach their own signallers to their assigned RGA batteries.[106]

Second Army issued general principles for the artillery along with formal instructions.[107] These include techniques such as thickening barrages by superimposing guns from other parts of the corps front, the use of different starting points (front, middle or rear of an area), with the heavy artillery sometimes following rather than preceding

98   TNA WO 158/208: Folio 377, Enclosure to 'G. 140' entitled 'General Principles on Which the Artillery Plan will be Drawn', 29 August 1917.
99   TNA WO 158/208, Folio 385, 'Second Army Operation Order No. 4.', 1 September 1917.
100 Edmonds, *Military Operations 1917*, Vol. 2, pp. 240-242 and J. Boff, *Haig's Enemy* (Oxford: Oxford University Press, 2018), p.178 and TNA WO 158/208, Folio 389, 'Corps Commanders Conference, 4th September 1917'.
101 Smith, *Do Unto Others*, p.84 and Palazzo, 'The British Army's Counter-Battery Staff Officer', p.65.
102 RAI/MD 183, Headlam, 'Corps Commanders Conferences', 20 August 1917 and TNA WO 95/865-2: 'X Corps Artillery Instruction No. 39', 3 September 1917.
103 TNA WO 95/865: 'X Corps Artillery Instruction No. 39.', 3 September 1917.
104 RAI/MD 1160, Uniacke, 'Part VII – Tactical Development', pp.154-55.
105 T.G, Bradbeer, 'Gunners at Cambrai, 1917: How the Royal Artillery Set the Conditions for the Successful Armored Assault' in Bradbeer, (ed.), *Lethal and Non-Lethal Fires* and Spencer Jones, 'Air Observation and the Royal Flying Corps in the Great War', Larkhill lecture, 18 October 2019.
106 TNA WO 158/208, Folio 387: 'Second Army Artillery Instructions No. 2', 2 September 1917; Farndale, *History of the Royal Regiment of Artillery*, p.207 and Jones, 'Air Observation'.
107 Edmonds, *Military Operations 1917*, Vol. 2, Appendix XXIII and TNA WO 158/208: Folio 387, 'Second Army Artillery Instructions No. 2', 2 September 1917.

the field artillery. All barrages were to finish 'by jumping back in the opposite direction to which they [had] been moving.' A key difference from Pilckem Ridge was the tactical decision that three front wide practice barrages were to take place with the volume of fire approximating that of the actual attack barrage.[108] The aim was to attune the Germans to this level of fire without an attack taking place. The initial preparatory barrages were to isolate the German garrison and forward artillery positions, through the destruction of communication routes. Once done the Germans could be neutralised later. To lower German morale two thirds of the ammunition allocated to this task was expended at night. The previous tactic of destroying all German trenches was to be avoided as it simply created more shell holes for them to hide in.[109] On the 3 September X Corps issued their artillery orders and II Anzac Corps followed suit on 9 September.[110] The Australians had already positioned their Bombardment and CB batteries so that, without further forward movement, they could reach 2,000 yards beyond the final objective whilst X Corps ensured that all 18-pdrs were within 5,000 yards of it.[111] Concealing their artillery strength was a key requirement with only the batteries required for defensive duties allowed to fire, although CB work was to be carried out 'with the greatest vigour' whilst 'neutralization was to continue …'[112] Fifth Army approached the preparatory phase differently to both Second Army and their previous battles.[113] Gough believed that an assault after a 'really intense … hurricane bombardment for the last 24-hours' would surprise the Germans; Uniacke planned accordingly.[114] He directed that ammunition expenditure was to be reduced with the available ammunition focused on CB work, with only a small portion being used for other tasks.[115] Uniacke took this opportunity to rest his batteries.[116]

108   TNA WO 158/208: Folio 385, 'Barrages During Preliminary Bombardment', n.d. but enclosed within folio; Folio 390, 'G. 697', 7 September 1917 and Folio 392, 'G. 721', 8 September 1917.
109   Broad, 'The Development of Artillery', p.131; Palazzo, 'The British Army's Counter-Battery Staff Officer', pp.59–60; TNA WO 158/208: Folio 387, 'Second Army Artillery Instructions No. 2', 2 September 1917' and AWM4 13/4/5 Part 1 GOCRA 1st Anzac Corps and HQ Royal Artillery, Australian Corps, 'Artillery Instruction No. 118', 9 September 1917.
110   TNA WO 95/865-2: 'X Corps Artillery Instruction No. 39.', 3 September 1917and AWM4 13/4/5 Part 1 'Artillery Instruction No. 118', 9 September 1917.
111   AWM4 13/4/5 Part 1, 'Artillery Instruction No. 116', 8 September 1917 and 'Artillery Instruction No. 118', 9 September 1917.
112   AWM4 13/4/5 Part 1 'Artillery Instruction No. 118', 9 September 1917.
113   TNA WO 95/952-1: 'XVIII Corps Order No. 69', 13 September 1917; Royal Artillery Historical Trust (RAHT) 249, XVIII Corps, GOCRA War Diary, 'XVIII Corps Artillery Instruction No. 12', 12 September 1917 and 'Instructions for Heavy Artillery Barrages', 16 September 1917.
114   TNA WO 158/250: Folio 426, 'Notes on Conference, 10th September 1917' and RAHT 249, 'XVIII Corps Artillery Instruction No. 12.', 12 September 1917.
115   TNA WO 158/250: Folio 426, 'Notes on Conference, 10th September 1917' and RAHT 249, 'XVIII Corps Artillery Instruction No. 11', 10 September 1917.
116   RAI/MD 1160, Uniacke, 'Part VII – Tactical Development', p.156.

Second Army's seven-day preparatory bombardment was subsequently amended so that it was completed within the first five days. The focus for CB work was now on the neutralisation of the German artillery rather than its destruction. Between the end of August and the 19 September, Second Army fired 1,863 CB shoots of which approximately 73 percent were classified as neutralising.[117] In return the Germans only fired 131 destructive shoots. However, despite doing what they could to provide protection for their artillery, the congested nature of the salient meant that the British gunners suffered considerable casualties.[118] Second Army's X Corps experienced 239 casualties in the week prior to 20 September, whilst a single field brigade reported that they had 20 guns destroyed over a three-day period.[119] Fifth Army's XVIII Corps reported 34 officer and 795 other rank casualties, of which five officers and 148 were killed.[120] To help neutralise the German batteries immediately prior to the attack, Plumer had intended to use gas. However, his corps commanders persuaded him that, despite its effectiveness at Vimy, they did not want it used on the day, preferring it to be used early in the preparations.[121] Armed with a better understanding of the German counter-attack tactics, the British also identified ways to defeat them. They calculated that in the three hours it would take them to reach their final objectives the *Eingreif* divisions would be able to travel some four miles. They bombarded all the places at about this range which gave cover from aerial observation and might therefore, conceal German troops.[122] Concurrently they sought to control German counter-attack options by specifically bombarding some potential routes whilst leaving others untouched.[123]

The attack barrage was to consist of five lines of fire which would move in concert with each other. Immediately in front of the attacking infantry would be an 18-pdr barrage (called A), 200 yards ahead of this would be one made up of mixed 18-pdrs and 4.5-in howitzers (B). At 600 yards Second Army requested the inclusion of a massed machine-gun barrage (C), 200 yards beyond which was a 6-in howitzer barrage (D) and then a further 200 yards again was a barrage of 60-pdrs with 8-inch and 9.2-inch howitzers (E). Initially, all barrages were to move forward together in 100-yard lifts,

---

117 TNA WO 158/218: 'Summary of Operations', 6, 11, 20 September 1917. Fifth Army did not record such details in their weekly operational summaries.

118 AWM4 13/4/5 Part 1, 'Artillery Instruction No.113', 6 September 1917.

119 TNA WO 95/865 'Comparison of Casualty Figures', n.d. and Hutchison, *The Thirty-Third Division*, pp.68-69

120 Royal Artillery Historical Trust 249, XVIII Corps, GOCRA 'War Diary', 1-20 September 1917.

121 TNA WO 158/208: Folio 400, 'Corps Commanders Conference, 15 September 1917' and Thuell & Bradbeer, 'Fires and Combined Arms Maneuver', p.187.

122 Broad, 'The Development of Artillery', p.133.

123 TNA WO 158/208: Folio 387, 'Artillery Instructions No.2', 2 September 1917'; TNA WO 158/208: Folio 377, 29 August 1917; RAHT 250 'XIX Corps Artillery Instruction No.15', 1 September 1917, and AWM4 13/4/5 Part 1, 'Artillery Instruction No. 118', 9 September 1917.

to the first objective and then pause. Here the A barrage would remain in place to protect the infantry whilst barrage lines B-E would move forward a further 300 yards in three lifts before all falling back to their original line. After a 10-minute pause all barrages would move forward for five 100-yard lifts at roughly seven-minute intervals, by the end of which the infantry would have advanced 1,000 yards from their jumping off position. Once there they would pause for 30 minutes whilst the machine-guns, by now out of range, would be moved forward. The B, D and E barrages again searching ahead before returning ready for the next advance. The attack would then continue, supported by the A, B, D and E barrages until the infantry reached their final objectives whereupon all artillery barrages would pause before moving forward 400 yards where the A barrage was to remain whilst the B, D and E barrages advanced a further 900 yards. Once the machine-guns arrived they were to re-establish themselves in the barrage line thus creating a 2,000-yard protective barrage in front of the consolidating infantry.[124] Subordinate commanders were given latitude to adjust or mix the B and C barrages to best suit their need whilst they were also permitted to open the spacing between the barrages from 200 to 300 yards if greater depth was considered necessary.[125] Fifth Army, whilst conforming to the overall scheme, decided to reduce the lift distance to 50 yards after the first two 100 yard lifts.[126] Despite the improving weather and the ground, in places, starting to dry, the terrain remained extremely difficult to negotiate and was further churned up by the preparatory and attack barrages. Therefore, the proposed timings for the barrage were refined, halts on subordinate objectives were lengthened and the rate of advance of the barrage slowed.[127] Of note, and despite the increased timings, GOCRA I Anzac Corps made it clear that what was 'not required is to cover the whole country with more and more shell holes …'[128]

The Battle of Menin Road Ridge commenced at 05:40 on 20 September.[129] After overnight rain a thick mist clung to the battlefield and the cloud remained low.[130] A combination of the long delay since Gough's last major attack, Fifth Army's 24 hour hurricane bombardment and Second Army's repetitive barrages had lulled some Germans into believing that the British had closed down their Flanders offensive; Von

124 TNA WO 158/208: Folio 387, 'Appendix 1 to Artillery Instructions No. 2', 2 September 1917' and Folio 389, 'Corps Commanders Conference, General Questions, Artillery Plan', 4 September 1917.
125 RAI/MD 1160, Uniacke, 'Part VII – Tactical Development', p.155; TNA WO 158/208: Folio 387, 'Amendment 1 to Artillery Instructions No. 2', 2 September 1917' and AWM4 13/4/5 Part 1 'Artillery Instruction No. 118', 9 September 1917.
126 TNA WO 158/250: 'Notes on Conference, 10th September 1917'.
127 TNA WO 158/208: Folio 393, 'G. 796', 10 September 1917.
128 AWM4 13/4/5 Part 1 'Artillery Instruction No. 118', 9 September 1917.
129 TNA WO 158/208: Folio 404.
130 AWM4, 1/29/20 Part 6, I Anzac Corps, GS, 'Operations on 20th September – Second Army', 22 September 1917

Australian 18-pdr battery, September 1917.

British 15-inch howitzer, Menin Road 5 October 1917.

Kuhl, for one, was surprised to find a full-scale attack underway.[131] GHQ allocated 3,125 artillery pieces to this battle, including 222 dedicated only to fire should the German guns behind the Gheluvelt Plateau engage.[132] All known Germans observation posts were obscured by smoke.[133] Careful planning enabled up to a third of the field artillery to be made available to deal with zone calls and other fleeting opportunities without affecting the attack barrage.[134] Once the morning mist cleared seven RFC Corps squadrons played a significant part by providing continuous observation over the battlefield.[135] They called for 394 zone fires, of which about a third were actioned immediately, whilst they also called down destructive fire on 32 batteries and neutralising fire on a further 48. The Balloon Sections observed 128 active batteries and assisted the artillery in engaging 48 of them.[136]

Fifth Army attacked with XIV Corps as flank guard, XVIII Corps in the centre and V Corps on its southern flank. XVIII Corps secured their final objectives by 11:00. The Germans launched four counter-attacks but only one had limited success; the others were beaten back by combined machine-gun and artillery fire.[137] The V Corps found progress harder, with 55th (West Lancashire) Division subjected to considerable machine-gun fire and, held up by the Schuler Galleries strongpoint; they lost the barrage although they still made progress. The Germans launched three counter-attacks against them; all of which were stopped by artillery and machine-gun fire. To its south 9th (Scottish) Division successfully captured the Bremen Redoubt by 08:40 and their final objective, by 09:12. In doing so they reported suffering only limited casualties and that the '[o]ne or two feeble attempts … at counter-attacking were easily disposed of.'[138] With the exception of 55th Division, Fifth Army's other assault divisions all reported favourably on the new barrage techniques.[139] The effectiveness of its added depth in dealing with the German shell hole posts was praised whilst also being described as having 'perfectly timed bursts'.[140] The 9th Division noted that

131 Edmonds *Military Operations 1917,* Vol. 2, p.244, fn. and Boff, *Haig's Enemy,* p.179.
132 Farndale, *History of the Royal Regiment of Artillery,* p.205.
133 TNA WO 158/208: Folio 387, 'Second Army Artillery Instructions No. 2', 2 September 1917 and Folio 389, 'Corps Commanders Conference, General Questions, Artillery Plan', 4 September 1917.
134 TNA WO 158/208: Folio 387: Second Army Artillery Instructions No. 2', 2 September 1917.
135 Jones, *The War in the Air,* p.185; AWM4 1/29/20 Part 6, 'Operations on 20th September', 22 September 1917 and S. Jones, 'Air Observation and the Royal Flying Corps in the Great War', Shrapnel Lectures, Larkhill, 18 October 2019.
136 Jones, *The War in the Air,* p.184
137 TNA WO 158/255: 'Report on Operations on September 20th, 1917', 6 October 1917.
138 TNA WO 158/255: 'Operations on September 20th', 6 October 1917.
139 TNA WO 95/2903: 55th Division GS, 'Report on Operations East of Ypres 19th–24th September 1917' and 'Daily Summary, Noon 17th September to Noon 18th September 1917'.
140 TNA WO 95/WO95/2846: 51st Division, GS, 'The Battle, 20th September 1917'and TNA WO 95/2987, 58th (2nd/1st London) Division GS, 'Narrative of Operations, 18

the decision to slow the pace of the lifts, after each objective was passed, had worked well.[141] Whilst the new tactics helped to stop the German counter-attacks, Fifth Army's hurricane bombardment meant more German artillery had survived and as a result they lost nineteen 60-pdrs and forty-seven 18-pdrs to CB fire.[142]

Abutting V Corps was Second Army's I Anzac Corps, with X Corps to their right followed by IX Corps providing the southern flank guard. The attack went well, all corps had achieved their first objectives by 06:15 with their second objective captured between 09:45 and 10:00. By the close of the day, and with the exception of a strong-point at Tower Hamlets which remained in German hands, Second Army's divisions had secured all their final objectives. They were subjected to three major counter-attacks and a further eight local ones, all of which were stopped by artillery and machine-gun barrages.[143] Both Australian divisions and 23rd Division commented favourably on the attack barrage with 1st Australian Division citing the artillery as a prominent feature of the day's success. The 23rd Division noted that, as Uniacke had identified, the 'chief opposition to the attack came from machine-guns' with the German artillery fire being 'weak and ineffective.'[144] By comparison they described the British artillery as being 'faultless in covering the advance ...' with the standing barrage 'no less effective covering [the] consolidation ...'[145] The 41st Division, which had failed to capture Tower Hamlets, noted that its brigades had been held up by machine-gun fire from concrete emplacements and dug outs.[146] As in Fifth Army, Second Army's divisions all reported on the successful destruction of German counter-attacks. After the battle the Germans estimated that the British, attacking with nine divisions across a front of nine kilometres, were supported by three times the weight of firepower used on 31 July. Although they had been unable to launch effective counter-attacks, they nevertheless congratulated themselves on preventing the British from reaching their artillery position, whilst failing to understand the evolving nature of the British tactics.[147]

October 1917' and 'Summary of Intelligence No. 81 for period 8 a.m. 20th September to 8 a.m. 21st September 1917'.

141 TNA WO 95/1740: 9th Division, GS, 'Events Report Parts I-III'.

142 Farndale, *History of the Royal Regiment of Artillery*, p.207.

143 Broad, 'The Development of Artillery', p.133 and AWM4, 1/29/20 Part 6, 'Operations on 20th September', 22 September 1917.

144 Sandilands, *The 23rd Division 1914-1919*, p.189

145 TNA WO 95/2169: 23rd Division, GS 'Second Army Offensive, 20th September 1917'; 'Comments on Operations on 20th September 1917'; AWM4 1/42/32, 1st Australian Division, GS, 'Report on Operations of 20th September 1917'; AWM 1/44/26 2nd Australian Division, GS, 'Report on Operations, 17th to 22nd September 1917' and Sandilands, *The 23rd Division*, p.185.

146 TNA WO 95/2617: 41st Division, GS, 'War Diary', 20 September 1917.

147 Farndale, *History of the Royal Regiment of Artillery*, p.207 and J. Boff, *Haig's Enemy*, p.178.

Obstinacy: Fighting Fuller's Conditions at the Second Battle of Passchendaele

On 20 September Plumer issued the warning order for his second 'Step', the Battle of Polygon Wood, to take place on 26 September.[148] By this time the concentration of British artillery within the salient was described as 'guns of all calibres being locked almost wheel to wheel along the whole front, and in many lines ...'[149] However, Plumer was unable to gather the mass of artillery he desired so he narrowed the assault frontage to 8,000 yards whilst setting shallower objectives.[150] The new tactics of short bounds supported by prepared defensive barrages again worked well, although machine-gun fire from concrete pillboxes did cause some problems.[151] The Germans again altered their tactics: they would again occupy their forward trenches in strength, adding further depth through the employment of additional divisions whilst still holding back the *Eingreif* divisions.[152] Aware of these changes the British reverted to the tactics of the Somme by bombarding, sweeping and raking the whole area with fire although the net effect was to further destroy the already shattered ground.[153] The third 'Step' at Broodseinde went well with Rupprecht forced to note that his artillery had been overwhelmed by British firepower.[154] However, by the fourth 'Step' at Poelcappelle the British tried to operate beyond their artillery's capabilities. At Menin Road Ridge divisions had been supported by approximately 90 guns; now each had to make do with around 25. The attack was a failure: in many places it did not even reach the German front lines.[155] Plumer's attempt to conduct four attacks in quick succession had lost momentum, floundering for two reasons. First, the rains had returned and second, intact barbed wire covered by machine-guns went undetected.[156] Artillery tactics continued to evolve during this period including the use of 18-pdr smoke shells to help mark the arrival of the barrage at an objective, and the firing of a short intense burst to indicate the barrage was preparing to move forward.[157]

Despite these problems and believing he had gained a good 'jumping off point', Plumer believed there 'was every reason to hope that Passchendaele would be

148 Powell, *Plumer* p.218 and TNA WO 158/208: Folio 406, 'G.340', 20 September 1917.
149 TNA WO 158/208: Folio 403, 'Artillery Instruction No. 3', 17 September 1917; Folio 405, 'G. 360', 19 September 1917 and Crutchley (ed.), *Machine Gunner*, p.111.
150 Boff, *Haig's Enemy*, p.178.
151 Broad, 'The Development of Artillery', p.134 and C.E.W. Bean, *The AIF in France 1917*, Vol. IV (Sydney: Angus & Robertson, 1941), p.814.
152 Erich Ludendorff, *My War Memories*, Vol. 2 (Uckfield: Naval & Military Press 2005 reprint of 1919 edition), p.489; Boff, *Haig's Enemy*, pp.180-81 and Edmonds, *Military Operations 1917*, Vol. 2, pp.294-95, 318
153 Broad, 'The Development of Artillery', p.134.
154 Boff, *Haig's Enemy*, p.182 and Edmonds, *Military Operations 1917*, Vol. 2, pp.303-15.
155 Boff, p. 183
156 Edmonds, *Military Operations 1917*, Vol. 2, pp.325, 328-29.
157 Holland, 'Smoke', pp.372-80 and RAI/MD 1160, Uniacke, 'Part VII – Tactical Development', p.158

captured.' He prepared his fifth 'Step' for 12 October.[158] However, with only three days available, most of which was spent moving guns forward there was insufficient time to deal with the formidable German defences or conduct CB work.[159] As a result the First Battle of Passchendaele was a failure; the infantry struggled in the mud, and the attack barrage gave the impression 'of being no more than casual shelling.'[160] Second Army's II Anzac Corps led the attack. On the left the New Zealand Division was supported, despite the best efforts of their gunners, by 'weak and erratic' fire and it was consequently mauled trying to cross uncut wire, whilst on their right the 3rd Australian Division was forced back by German machine-gun and artillery fire.[161] Fifth Army fared no better, with many of its guns unable to get to their firing positions.[162] In the aftermath, Haig reinforced Second Army with the Canadian Corps and requested a plan for gaining Passchendaele Ridge.[163]

The Canadians replaced II Anzac Corps on 18 October and found that as well as the Germans they were also going to have to fight the conditions, most notably Napoleon's fifth element: 'mud'.[164] The GOCRA, Brigadier-General Edward Morrison, noted that whilst the artillery had not been able to destroy the German pillboxes, they had in places physically tipped them over. Plumer discussed the upcoming operations with his corps commanders on 16 October. They focused on the ability to bring forward sufficient guns and ammunition for the next attack.[165] Morrison had already conducted a reconnaissance of the area and received 'a rude awakening'. He could find only 10 of the 12 HAGs, which between them could only muster 60 percent of their allocated guns whilst large quantities of the field guns were either bunched together, completely

158 TNA WO 158/208: Folio 465, 'Operation Order No. 8',10 October 1917; Folio 646, 'Harrington D.O.', 12 October 1917; Folio 465, 'G. 669', 12 October 1917; J.R. Byrne, *New Zealand Artillery in the Field 1914–1918* (Auckland: Whitcombe & Tombs, 1920 [2004]), pp. 194-195; Bean, *The AIF in France 1917*, Vol. IV, pp. 921-23 and Edmonds, *Military Operations 1917*, Vol. 2, p.338.
159 Edmonds, *Military Operations 1917*, Vol. 2, pp. 339-40.
160 Powell, *Plumer*, p.225; P. Griffith, 'The Tactical Problem: Infantry, Artillery and the Salient' in P.H. Liddell (ed.) *Passchendaele in Perspective: The Third Battle of Ypres* (London: Leo Cooper, 1997), p.68 and L. Hughes, 'Command, Artillery and the Soldier: Mud and the Third Battle of Ypres 1917', MA, University of Birmingham, 2017, p.31.
161 Edmonds, *Military Operations 1917*, Vol. 2, pp.341-43.
162 Ibid., pp.343-45
163 TNA WO 158/251: Folio 1, 'Record of Conference', 13 October 1917; TNA WO 158/208: Folio 447, 'OAD. 654', 6 October 1917; Folio 455, 'Corps Commanders Conference on 7th October 1917', 8 October 1917; Folio 46, 'G. 511', 9 October 1917; T. Cook, 'Storm Troops: Combat effectiveness and the Canadian Corps in 1917' in Dennis & Grey (eds.), *1917 Tactics, Training and Technology*, pp. 43-44.
164 RAI/MD 1160, Uniacke, 'Part VII – Tactical Development', p. 161 and S. Raby-Dunne (ed.), *Morrison: The Long Lost Memoir of Canada's Artillery Commander in the Great War* (Toronto: Heritage House, 2017), p.150.
165 TNA WO 158/209, Folio 10, 'Proceedings of Conference', 16 October 1917.

isolated from their batteries or bogged into the mud.[166] Despite these findings it was agreed that if the weather remained favourable, the requested number of guns could be got forward by 22 October, in time to support Fifth Army's preliminary assault.[167]

Morrison was placed in charge of all the artillery allocated to the Canadians and he immediately set about 'reorganizing and readjusting' his command.[168] He strengthened the command and control of the DAs supporting each of the front two divisions, using previously surplus field artillery brigade HQs to create sub-groups under the DA HQs.[169] To improve control during the attack barrage, the corps front was divided into 200-yard wide strips with heavy batteries allocated to each.[170] To keep the roads free the Australians had prevented the recovery of damaged guns: the Canadians now returned 31 derelict 18-pdrs together with 19 4.5-inch howitzers to the workshops.[171] Due to the poor state of records left by the Australian CBSO the Canadians had to start afresh. However, with German fighter aircraft operating freely over the battlefield, photographs were taken from high level and were practically useless. Although the situation gradually improved it remained imperfect.[172] Many of the units Morrison took command of had been fighting for exceptionally long periods of time and he observed that they were suffering from the 'conditions' and physical exhaustion. Work was undertaken to relieve 12 field artillery brigades, two HAGs and 11 siege/heavy batteries whilst a further three 60-pdr batteries were withdrawn due to lack of guns.[173] Fifth Army was grappling with similar problems. The requirement to rest gunners was constantly referred to in orders but never in such a way that corps commanders were forced to action it.[174] Although DAs tended to arrive and leave corps areas roughly in line with their divisions, army field brigades were rotated much less frequently. Out of 12 DAs in Fifth Army during Second Passchendaele, 11 had spent less than 30 days in the line whereas nine of the 14 army field brigades had been in the line for over 90 days.[175]

The Canadians needed to improve their lines of communication and ammunition supply. The two forward divisions were each supported by just one road, which were

166 Raby-Dunne, (ed.), *Morrison*, p.151; TNA WO 95/1059/3, Canadian Corps, HQ RA, 'Canadian Corps Artillery Report on Passchendaele Operations Oct. 17 to Nov. 18th 1917'and Nicholson, *Canadian Expeditionary Force 1914-1918*, p.313.
167 TNA WO 158/251: Folio 4, 'Operation Order No. 30.', 18 October 1917 and TNA WO 158/209: Folio 13, 'Artillery Instruction No. 18', 20 October 1917.
168 Raby-Dunne (ed.), *Morrison*, pp.152-53.
169 TNA WO 95/1059/3: 'Artillery Report'.
170 Ibid.
171 Nicholson, *Canadian Expeditionary Force 1914-1918*, pp. 313-14 and TNA WO 95/1059/3: 'Artillery Report'.
172 Jones, *The War in the Air*, p.207 and TNA WO 95/1059/3: 'Artillery Report', p.12.
173 TNA WO 95/1059/3: 'Corps Artillery', p.3
174 RAI/MD 1160, Uniacke, 'Part VII – Tactical Development'.
175 RAI/MD 1160, 'Annex B to Appendix X, Ammunition Supply and Expenditure', n.d.

little more than mule tracks.[176] There were no lateral routes and as a result most of the batteries were bunched together, presenting 'excellent opportunities' for German CB fire.[177] Solutions for moving guns had to be improvised with a common one being the laying of long, six-inch-wide planks parallel to each other with the outside edges built up with corrugated iron to prevent the gun wheels from slipping off. The conditions were such that it took one hundred men a week to create a 900m route. They developed a mule based 'pack echelon' to bring ammunition forward once the roads ran out.[178] Given the state of the ground and the weather conditions, the storage of ammunition on battery positions also remained a problem throughout the battle.[179]

GHQ allocated the Canadians 587 guns. However, with the ground a 'sea of mud … the construction of platforms and the provision of cover' 'afforded serious difficulties.'[180] In one of the field brigades only seven guns were in action and these were firing from wherever they had bogged in.[181] Two methods of building gun platforms were used to address this problem. One was to drive piles into the ground with planks or sleepers placed on top of them and the gun wheels held in place by sandbags. The other was to level the ground and sandwich corrugated iron between two layers of sand bags. Personnel and communications had to make use of captured pillboxes or improvise shelter with whatever they could find.[182] The poor state of the ground prevented the Canadians from initially bringing forward any 9.2-inch howitzers although with the assistance of the light railways they were able to bring up their 6-inch howitzers. However, these also required considerable field engineering support to enable them to fire without the need to re-site their trails after every two to three rounds.[183] The expansion of the light railway network was slow and most heavy batteries could only be supplied by using push trucks. The Germans sought to hinder this time consuming and labour intensive work through harassing fire and gas.[184] Maintaining a supply of replacement guns was also critical. The Canadians refined the Australians' pool system and, by withdrawing guns from departing units, created a reserve of ninety 18-pdrs and twenty-four 4.5-in howitzers.[185] However,

176 Raby-Dunne (ed.), *Morrison*, p.152.
177 TNA WO 95/1059/3: 'Artillery Report'.
178 Ibid.
179 Ibid.
180 Nicholson, *Canadian Expeditionary Force 1914-1918*, p. 313 and TNA WO 95/1059/3: 'Artillery Report'.
181 Raby-Dunne (ed.), *Morrison*, p.151
182 TNA WO 95/1059/3: 'Artillery Report'.
183 Ibid.
184 TNA WO 95/1059/3: 'Artillery Report' and Edmonds, *Military Operations 1917*, Vol. 2, p. 347.
185 AWM4, 13/4/5, 2nd Australian Division, BGRA, 'Instruction No. 2.', 13 September 1917, AWM4 13/14/5, pp. 62-63 and AWM4, 13/10/36, 1st Australian Division, BGRA, Administrative Memorandum No. 2, n.d., pp.44-45 and TNA WO 95/1059/3: 'Artillery Report'.

even with these divisional pools it could still take two days or more for replacement guns to reach battery firing positions.[186] In some instances broken guns could not be repaired due to a lack of spares or tools.[187] Despite all their efforts the Canadians were never able to deploy all their allocated artillery.

To seize Passchendaele Ridge and village Plumer intended to use even shorter 'Steps' with just four days between each. The Canadians began to prepare to attack on 26 October.[188] The artillery instructions make clear that this work was not just focused on the sixth 'Step' but was to build cumulatively toward achieving the final objective.[189] They also introduced the use of burst fire barrages which were to be fired at a depth of 900 or 1,000 yards from the SOS line. All guns were to fire for six minutes after which there would be complete silence for 30 minutes and then a further six-minute burst was to be fired.[190] These shoots took place in the evening when the Germans were likely to be moving, with the silent period designed to assist in locating retaliating German guns although this proved to be relatively ineffective.[191]

The CB and bombardment groups allocated to the Canadians were predominantly based in two areas where their batteries were completely intermingled and 'so far back that only the nearest German guns could be reached.'[192] Therefore, work continued throughout to improve the effectiveness of both these groups. The CB work again focused on neutralization and harassment. Despite an average availability of only 57 percent of their guns the CB group still fired 281,293 shells. Of these only 3,021 (1 percent) were fired on destructive shoots whereas 217,964 (77.5 percent) were fired as part of neutralisation or harassment shoots. The remaining 60,947 were expended on other tasks.[193] Despite the weather having improved, at least at the start of the period, it remained difficult to conduct RFC observed shoots. Of the 204 programmed by the Canadians only 59 took place of which only 12 were classified as successful.[194]

Plumer's sixth 'Step' commended at 05:40 on the 26 October, with the Canadians the principal attacking force, supported by the artillery of both armies and by flank attacks by Fifth Army's XVIII Corps to the north and I Anzac to the south, whilst X

---

186 RG9-III-D-3, 2nd Canadian Division, Administrative Branches and Staff, 'War Diary', 23 October 9 November 1917
187 TNA WO 95/1059/3: 'Artillery Report'.
188 TNA WO 158/209: Folio 15, 'Artillery Instruction No. 15.', 15 October 1917; Folio 16, 'Operation Order No. 9.', 21 October 1917 and TNA WO 95/1059/3: 'Artillery Report'.
189 TNA WO 95/1059/3: 'Artillery Report' and TNA WO 95/1060/2: Canadian Corps, CHA, 'Operation Order No. 90', 23 October 1917.
190 TNA WO 158/209: Folio, 12, 'Artillery Instruction No. 16', 17 October 1917; Folio 14, 'Artillery Instruction No. 17', 18 October 1917 and TNA WO 95/1059/3: 'Artillery Report'.
191 TNA WO 95/1059/3: 'Artillery Report'.
192 Ibid.
193 Ibid., Appendix C.
194 Ibid., Appendix D.

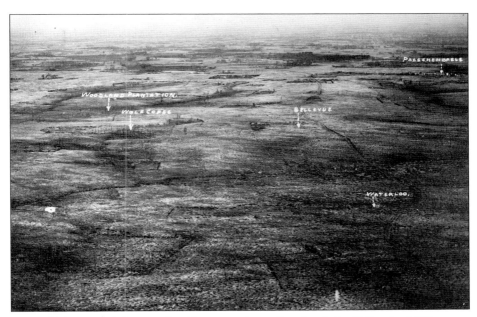

Oblique aerial photograph of the approaches to Passchendaele, 17 October 1917.
(Private collection)

Corps also sought to capture the Gheluvelt Plateau.[195] The attack went in under cover of mist, and then rain set in for the rest of the day.[196] The CB group fired a neutralisation shoot and then remained prepared to engage a known group of mobile German batteries which had come into operation during previous attacks.[197] The attack barrage was a variation on the five-layered version used since 20 September. The distance between barrage lines was reduced to 100 yards whilst the B and E barrages were now split into two elements with 1/3 of the available 18-pdrs forming the B.1 barrage whilst the 4.5-in howitzers now constituted the B.2 barrage. The E barrage was composed of the E.1 line fired by the 8-in and 9.2-in howitzers and the E.2 line delivered by the 60-pdrs. The barrage now had seven lines of fire but less depth (700 yards).[198] To enable the infantry to close up to, and adjust their attacking formations, the attack barrage was held in place for eight minutes before it started to move forward.[199] Lifts were notionally set at 100 yards every eight minutes although they actually lifted

---

195 TNA WO 95/1051-3: 'Instructions for the Offensive – Passchendaele No. 1', 23 October 1917 and Edmonds, *Military Operations 1917*, Vol. 2, p.349.
196 Nicholson, *Canadian Expeditionary Force 1914–1918*, p.319.
197 TNA WO 158/209: Folio 15, 'Artillery Instruction No. 18', 20 October 1917
198 TNA WO 95/1059/3: 'Artillery Report'.
199 Ibid.

50 yards every four minutes, with smoke shells marking the arrival of the barrage at an objectives and also used to prevent German observation.[200] Despite the efforts of the artillery, which were praised by the attacking divisions, and which included a direct hit on a pillbox by a 15-inch shell, the day proved a difficult one for the infantry.[201] Although the Canadians penetrated the German *Flanders Stellung II*, the 3rd Canadian Division was halted halfway to its final objective whilst 4th Canadian Division was forced back by counter-attacks.[202]

As the battle raged the attacking divisions were already being asked for information to enable the artillery to plan the seventh 'Step'. They were directed to note that the latest German defensive measures included leaving isolated pockets of resistance which could potentially be captured. These were deemed to be particularly vulnerable to artillery and machine-gun fire which was be 'employed without intermission and limited only by … ammunition supply and the physical endurance of the men.'[203] Prior to the next attack Plumer informed his corps commanders that 18-pdr and 60-pdr shrapnel shells should 'burst high on account of the soft ground in order to give the best effect.'[204] As a result the Canadians used between 50 and 75 percent of air bursts.[205] Seeking to gain a secure baseline for the assault on Passchendaele village, Plumer launched 'Step' seven on 30 October.[206] The artillery supported it in much the same way as they had the previous attack.[207] 'Step by Step' was working, albeit on an increasingly narrow front (2,300 yards), and with ever decreasing depth (1,000 yards).[208] Plumer then paused for seven days to allow the Canadians time to relieve their assault divisions and move forward more artillery.[209] During this pause Haig replaced Fifth Army's XVIII Corps with II Corps, whilst placing it and the entire attacking front under the command of Plumer.[210] II Corps' role was to support the Canadians with enfilading artillery fire.

200 Ibid. and TNA WO 95/1051-3: Canadian Corps, GS, 'Instructions for the Offensive No. 1', 23 October 1917.
201 TNA WO 95/1059/3: 'Artillery Report', p. 9; TNA WO 95/3839: 3rd Canadian Division, GS, 'Narrative of Operations for week ending 1 November 1917'; TNA WO 95/3881 4th Canadian Division, GS, 'Narrative of Operations 6 p.m. 25th October to 6 p.m. 1st November 1917' and Nicholson, *Canadian Expeditionary Force 1914-1918*, p.319.
202 TNA WO 158/425: Canadian Corps, GS, 'Phase 6. October 1917, Narrative of Operations', n.d. and Nicholson, *Canadian Expeditionary Force 1914-1918*, pp.318-20.
203 TNA WO 95/1051-3: 'Instructions for the Offensive No. 2.', 26 October 1917 and 'Preparatory Operation Order No. 160', 27 October 1917.
204 TNA WO 158/209: 'Corps Commanders Conference, 29th October 1917', 30 October 1917.
205 TNA WO 95/1059/3: 'Artillery Report'.
206 Nicholson, *Canadian Expeditionary Force 1914-1918*, pp.320-23.
207 TNA WO 158/209: Folio 24, 'Artillery Instructions No. 20', 26 October 1917; TNA WO 95/1051-3: 'Operating Instruction No. 161', 28 October 1917.
208 Nicholson, *Canadian Expeditionary Force 1914-1918*, p.323.
209 Nicholson,, p. 323 and TNA WO 95/1051-6: Canadian Corps, GS, "CHA unreferenced memo to 'R.A. Canadian Corps'", 4 November 1917.
210 TNA WO 158/209: 'G.771', 31 October 1917.

At around this time the Canadians changed their tactics for dealing with pillboxes; they had previously tried to lower German morale through heavy daytime bombardments combined with night-time harassing fire. However, they now realised that this 'increased the difficulties of attacking [them] by rendering the ground ... even more impassable.'[211] Other than this change the 1st and 2nd Canadian divisions, following the usual artillery preparations, attacked on the 6 November behind a powerful barrage and, for once, a clear sky.[212] The artillery of II Corps enfiladed the German positions while the rest of Second Army simulated a major attack.[213] For this eighth 'Step' the attack barrage was again adjusted with the initial delay reduced to two minutes, to prevent the Germans from bombarding the jumping off point, with 100 yard lifts every eight minutes thereafter.[214] By 11:00 both divisions had secured their objectives and whilst the Germans initiated six counter-attacks, five were broken up before they could be assembled and the sixth was defeated by machine-gun and artillery barrages.[215] For the first time a Continuous Wave (CW) Wireless station was used to call down fire between a FOO at Passchendaele and the CHA headquarters some 9,000 yards away.[216] A key moment occurred when an infantry battalion requested a barrage falling on its lines be lifted which was achieved within five minutes.[217] Finally the Canadians had captured ground from which they could observe into the depth of the German defensive position.[218] As a result, the Germans were forced to 'side-slip ... batteries to the north and south.'[219]

The ninth 'Step' on 10 November was designed to gain the remaining high ground to the north of the village.[220] Artillery preparations followed the normal pattern whilst the speed of CW wireless transmission was successfully tested against those of pigeons and signal lamps.[221] As a result the station was maintained.[222] The only change to the attack barrage was that the initial pause was increased to three minutes

211 TNA WO 95/1059/3: 'Artillery Report'.
212 Nicholson, *Canadian Expeditionary Force 1914-1918*, pp. 323-24.
213 TNA WO 158/209: Folio 30, 'G.771', 31 October 1917.
214 TNA WO 95/1051-6: 'Instruction for the Offensive No. 3.', 4 November 1917' and TNA WO 95/1059/3: 'Artillery Report'.
215 Nicholson, *Canadian Expeditionary Force 1914-1918*, pp.324-25 and TNA WO 158/427: '8th Phase – November 6th 1917 Narrative', n.d.
216 TNA WO 158/427: 'Operation Order No. 165', 4 November 1917.
217 Nicholson, *Canadian Expeditionary Force 1914-1918*, p.25; *General Report on Wireless Telegraph Communications in the Canadian Corps from February 1915 to December 1918* <http://www.rcsigs.ca/index.php/Wireless_Telegraph_Communications_in_the_Canadian_Corps>
218 TNA WO 95/1059/3: 'Artillery Report'.
219 Ibid.
220 TNA WO 158/209: Folio 41, 'Operation Order No. 12.', 7 November 1917 and TNA WO 158/427: 'Instructions for the Offensive.' 7 November 1917.
221 TNA WO 95/1059/3: 'Artillery Report', pp. 28-29 and G.S. Suriano (Se: Associazione culturale Se, 2017), pp.57-61.
222 *General Report* <http://www.rcsigs.ca/index.php/Wireless_Telegraph_Communications_in_the_Canadian_Corps>

whilst burst fire was to be used late in the day to help deter German counter-attacks.[223] All shells used the 106 fuzes, set for air-burst, throughout the first 70 minutes of the attack barrage.[224] The attack was launched at 06:05 and by 12:15 the Canadians were reporting that they had secured their objective. However, with the British 1st Division on their left held up they were forced to alter their line to create a defensive flank. Once more bad visibility hampered CB work and prevented the RFC from providing support.[225] Despite the calling down of a barrage onto the Germans as they formed up to counter-attack, the latter were able to advance to close range before they were beaten back.[226] The day ended with the Canadians holding onto their gains, consolidating their position and pushing patrols forward.[227] Although Second Army continued to plan for future operations, the capture of Passchendaele effectively concluded the Third Battle of Ypres.[228] Despite the problems the British had faced in these final 'Steps', Ludendorff described the combined might of the Second and Fifth Army's artilleries as having been able to hurl '[e]normous masses of ammunition, such as the mind had never imagined before the war …'[229] Nevertheless, the Canadian success at the Second battle of Passchendaele had, perhaps, as much to do with their obstinacy in the face of adversity as it did with the effectiveness of their artillery.

Conclusion

Prior to the start of Third Ypres Haig had articulated that the objective, Fuller's First Principle, for his artillery was the defeat of their German counterparts. To achieve this both Fifth and Second armies focused their efforts on the CB battle. Initially Fifth Army's aim was the complete destruction of German batteries. However, by the time Second Army took the lead for Menin Road Ridge the artillery technique changed from Fuller's required destruction to that of neutralisation. German batteries were now isolated to prevent resupply or replacement. The artillery's other offensive requirement was to destroy as much of the German defensive position as possible. The additional days before 31 July were therefore used to further reduce the German defences. This additional time (one of Fuller's conditions) proved to be counterproductive as it hindered the infantry's advance whilst also failing to destroy all the defensive positions.

---

223 TNA WO 158/209: Folio 43, 'Artillery Instructions No. 24', 7 November 1917.
224 TNA WO 95/1060/2: 'Corps Heavy Artillery Operation Order No. 93', 5 November 1917.
225 Nicholson, *Canadian Expeditionary Force 1914-1918*, p.326.
226 TNA WO 158/428: 'Phase 9: November 10th 1917. Narrative', n.d.
227 Nicholson, *Canadian Expeditionary Force 1914-1918*, p.326.
228 TNA WO 158/209: Folio 42: 'G 3/3', 7 November 197 and Folio 45, 'Artillery Instructions No. 25.', 9 November 1917.
229 Ludendorff, *My War Memories*, Vol. 2, p.491.

The BEF was more than able to deliver the numbers, supply and armaments (three of Fuller's conditions), in order to meet the Principle of Mass. Fifth Army's problem, on 31 July, was that their field artillery lacked the range to cover the entire depth of the attack and so it was unable to maintain sufficient mass throughout the duration of the attack. Uniacke's attack barrage for Pilckem Ridge advanced beyond rather than 'piling up' on the Germans trenches. However, this technique failed to prevent significant numbers of German machine-gunners from successfully engaging the assaulting infantry. By the September battles, the attack barrage consisted of the vast majority of available guns and machine-guns, firing a five-layered barrage, 1,000 yards wide, to provide security (Fuller's eighth principle) for the assaulting infantry. This technique continued to be successful up until Poelcappelle when, Fuller's conditions of ground, weather and time worked against Second Army's artillery's preparations and as a result the attack failed.

Despite having significant resources the British still had to husband them, in line with Fuller's Economy of Force principle. Improved techniques by the RFC, together with the new CBSO post, helped to ensure that targets were identified and systematically engaged with the appropriate allocation of guns and shells. In these areas the artillery performed effectively when not being adversely affected by the weather. Both artillery commanders sought to co-operate (another of Fuller's principles) with each other. Thus when Gough attacked Buckle sought to ensure his tactics and techniques conformed to Uniacke's and Fifth Army requirements. Their roles were reversed from September onwards, when Plumer became the lead commander, although it was not possible for Uniacke to completely conform to Buckle's plans as demonstrated at Menin Road Ridge.

In seeking to achieve the Principle of Movement, Gough chose to attack beyond the range of his field artillery and in so doing helped to set the conditions for failure at Pilckem Ridge. Fifth Army's artillery had to move forward whilst the infantry were still advancing towards their third and fourth objectives. As a result, when the Germans counter-attacked, the infantry was exposed and forced back until they were once more under the artillery's protection. Plumer's tactical decision to conduct a number of limited attacks meant that Second Army's artillery could pre-position their artillery in such a way as to ensure the infantry would always be fully protected. His artillery commanders, aware of the next 'Step', were able to plan ahead and thus increase the tempo at which Second Army could operate. However, when the pace was forced at Poelcapelle, Plumer's limited 'Steps' failed as badly as Gough's deep attacks.

Fuller's Principle of Surprise was almost impossible to achieve given the observed nature of the salient. One of the few areas in which Fifth and Second Armies deviated from each other was in how they tried to achieve surprise at Menin Road Ridge. Uniacke's intense 24-hour hurricane bombardment and Buckle's repetitive Army and corps preparatory bombardments did secure a measure of surprise. However, it can be argued that Fifth Army's tactical decision to forgo the usual artillery preparatory phase, and in particular the offensive requirement of winning the CB battle, meant that they suffered more from German retaliatory fire. It did, however, enable Uniacke to rest some of his batteries, thus going some small way to meeting Fuller's condition of maintaining morale.

The Principle of Security has already been discussed with regard to the use and development of the protective attack barrage. The artillery also sought to provide security for the consolidating infantry via their destruction of counter-attack routes and forming up points. Additionally, they also needed to provided tactical security, or protection to their own batteries. However, this was an almost impossible task given the nature of the salient. Both armies did what they could although, as has been noted, by the time the Canadians had arrived the ground conditions meant it was almost impossible to move away from the few roads that could be maintained.

When assessed against Fuller's Principles of War and taking due consideration of his conditions it is clear that whilst mistakes were made both Fifth and Second armies artilleries performed effectively. Where the infantry plans aligned with the artillery's tactical and technical abilities, and when enough time was allowed to prepare, the Gunners were more than able to effectively protect the infantry during the assault and as they consolidated. Throughout the campaign the British artillery never sought to conquer but, its performance, at its most effective, did allow the infantry to attack, secure and then occupy the ground under its protection. In the end it was the performance of the British artillery which drew the most admiring and envious comments from the Germans. Their official narrative states:

> The considered judgement of the frontline soldiers who had fought in Verdun and along the Somme, was that the artillery fire which the [British] used in Flanders during 1917, to prepare and to accompany his assaults, was much more severe than anything formerly met with.[230]

---

230 RAI/MD 1050/3, MacLeod, 'German Official History' translation, p.66.

14

Deserving of All Praise
The 33rd Division at Polygon Wood, 25-27 September 1917

James Taub

Within the many sub-battles comprising the Third Battle of Ypres, one in particular stands out as a noteworthy study of the BEF in defence and counter-attack. Whilst the majority of offensive activity in the Salient during the latter months of 1917 were British assaults, the reverse experienced by 33rd (New Army) Division just south of Polygon Wood in late September remains something of an anomaly. The fighting resulted in a rebuff of a German attempt to reverse the success of the Battle of the Menin Road Ridge, 20-25 September, during which General H. Plumer's Second Army had penetrated vaunted enemy defences. It is an episode intertwined with nationalistic sentiments due to it taking place on the flank of an Australian advance. Consequent historiography demonstrates that it was deeply meaningful to the Antipodean forces engaged. However, the German counter-stroke remains a footnote to British and Dominion success. Indeed, it receives scarce mention in prominent works about Third Ypres. Prior and Wilson's volume only devotes five paragraphs to the fighting.[1] Nick Lloyd's recent campaign history covers it in three sentences.[2] Nevertheless, the events south of Polygon Wood during 25-27 September offers excellent insight into the harrowing ordeal of a British infantry division when confronted by a surprise counter-attack, an experience all too common during the fighting around Ypres in summer and autumn 1917.

1   Robin Prior & Trevor Wilson, *Passchendaele: The Untold Story*, 3rd Ed. (New Haven: Yale University Press, 2016), pp.127-28.
2   Nick Lloyd, *Passchendaele: A New History* (London: Viking, 2017), p.194.

The 33rd Division, 1915-17

The 33rd New Army Division was an incredibly mixed formation with a rich history and fascinating personalities ranging from famed war poets such as Robert Graves, controversial political and religious personalities such as Reverend J. White,[3] other rank memoirists like Frank Richards,[4] regimental historians such as Captain J.C. Dunn,[5] and military leaders of the next world-wide conflict such as future Field Marshal Bernard Law Montgomery.[6] The 12 infantry battalions consisted of Regular, Territorial, and New Army personnel bolstered by conscript drafts arriving in 1917. Originally designated 40th Division, the 33rd had been re-designated as such with the breakup of the K4 divisions in April 1915. By November of that year, the reformed division deployed to France under the command of Major-General H. Landon. At this time it was composed solely of New Army battalions of the Royal Fusiliers, Essex Regiment, Middlesex Regiment, and King's Royal Rifle Corps (KRRC). In an effort to bolster newly arrived divisions with experienced units, veteran battalions were brought in to broaden formation capability. During late November and early December, 99th Brigade in its entirety was swapped with 2nd (Regular) Division's 19th Brigade, whilst three other veteran battalions of 5th Brigade were exchanged for three New Army battalions.[7] By New Year's Day 1916, 33rd Division contained troops with combat experience from Mons to Loos who were able to disseminate knowledge to neophyte Kitchener battalions. The division's structure remained the same (minus the addition of machine-gun and trench mortar companies), so that by the Third Battle of Ypres, the 33rd was veteran formation with more than a year and a half of training and experience behind it.

The 33rd Division first entered the line near Cambrin and Cuinchy where it carried out several trench raids favourably recognised as high up the chain of command to BEF C-in-C Sir Douglas Haig.[8] The first true test of the division's recently paired battalions came during the Battle of the Somme. On 15 July 1916, the 33rd's 100th Brigade, GOC Brigadier-General A.W.F. Baird, attacked the Switch Line and Martinpuich to the northwest of High Wood. The results were disastrous. Having

3   See John White, *With the Cameronians (Scottish Rifles) in France: Leaves from a Chaplains Diary* (Glasgow: John Smith & Son, 1917).

4   Frank Richards, *Old Soldiers Never Die* (Uckfield: Naval & Military Press 2003 reprint of 1933 edition).

5   J.C. Dunn. *The War the Infantry Knew 1914-1919: A Chronicle of Service in France and Belgium with the Second Battalion His Majesty's Twenty-Third Foot, the Royal Welch Fusiliers* (London: Abacus, 2004).

6   J.M. Bourne. *Who's Who in World War I* (London: Routledge, 2001), p.212.

7   *The Long, Long Trail* <https://www.longlongtrail.co.uk/army/order-of-battle-of-divisions/33rd-division/> (Accessed 10 July 2020).

8   Graham Seton Hutchison, *The Thirty-third Division in France and Flanders, 1915-1919* (London: Waterlow & Sons, 1921), p.9. Haig assumed the rank of field marshal on 1 January 1917.

little in the way of artillery support, no ground was gained as assault battalions attempted to advance through bullet-swept terrain that was supposedly cleared by 7th Division.[9] The 1/9th Highland Light Infantry (Glasgow Highlanders) bore the brunt of this tragic oversight:

> Superior authority did little or nothing to help — apparently it was not believed even yet that there were any Germans there — and at about half-past seven Col. Darling got a message from General Baird stating that it had been represented that the 7th Division should be asked to clear the wood preparatory to our attack and enquiring if anything was being done about it. Nothing was being done. The local commanding-officer had received no direct order to clear the wood, although 'it had been suggested' that he should do so. It was too big a job for him, however, so Col. Darling was left to tackle the problem himself.[10]

This was followed by a 20 July assault into High Wood itself by 19th Brigade. Confusion reigned according to CSM P. Docherty of 5/6th Scottish Rifles, 'The barrage lifted, and as soon as we got into the wood platoons, companies, sections, and battalions got inextricably mixed up.'[11] The fight ended with 33rd Division maintaining a tenuous hold within the wood at an extremely high cost. The Scottish Rifles sustained 407 casualties including 18 officers – the remaining 198 men withdrawing on relief under the leadership of a surviving lieutenant.[12]

The 33rd Division again returned to the High Wood sector in mid-August. Baird's 100th Brigade was again assigned to attack. The result was a relatively successful operation which assisted in the capture of the much-contested Delville Wood. The division was finally relieved for a period of rest and refitting in late September. It was at this time that Major-General R.J. Pinney, later the subject of Siegfried Sassoon's well-known poem 'The General', assumed command. A pre-war Regular with Indian and South African War experience, Pinney was a teetotaller who was lambasted throughout the division for almost immediately cancelling the daily rum ration. Private Frank Richards caustically remarked:

> Our Division was the worst in the whole of France for rum issues: if we got any at all we were issued with half a ration instead of a whole one. In lieu of the half ration of rum the Divisional General, Major-General Pinney, erected places a

---

9   Jan Chojecki & Michael LoCicero (eds.), *We Are All Flourishing: The Letters and Diary of Captain Walter J.J. Coats 1914-1919* (Solihull: Helion & Co., 2016), p.198.

10 A.K. Reid, 'Shoulder to Shoulder: The Glasgow Highlanders: 9th. Bn. Highland Light Infantry 1914-1918', Unpublished manuscript, 1988, p.53.

11 P. Docherty, '5th Battalion Reminiscences Part II', *The Covenantor, Regimental Magazine of the Cameronians (Scottish Rifles)*, January 1936.

12 The National Archives (TNA) WO 95/2422/3: 5th Battalion Cameronians (Scottish Rifles) War Diary, 20 July 1916.

couple of miles behind the frontline where men returning from the line could have a hot cup of tea and one small biscuit. In his comfortable quarters many miles behind the Front I expect he couldn't see what benefit rum was to any man. Because of this there were more prayers offered up for him than any general in France. He was called a bun-punching crank and more fitted to be in command of a Church Mission hut at the Base than a division of troops.[13]

CSM Docherty even went so far as to claim, 'Our divisional commander, Major-General Pinney, would not allow any troops of our division to be issued with the rum ration, and I attribute the heavy casualty list to this order.'[14] Pinney's temperance predilections may have been distasteful to those expectant of this popular army comfort, but his competent command style was an entirely different story. By late October, 33rd Division participated in the ongoing fighting near Le Transloy where it carried out assaults on the notorious Boritska, Rainy and Dewdrop trenches. Following these actions, it occupied the Guillemont–Ginchy Ridge and launched several raids that earned the praise of XIV Corps GOC Lord Cavan.[15] The division remained in the Somme sector throughout the winter of 1916-17 before entraining north for the Battle of Arras.

Whilst not part of the initial Arras assault on 9 April, 33rd Division first saw action when 19th Brigade was temporarily attached to 21st Division during the latter's 13 April operations against the Hindenburg Line near Fontaine-lès-Croisilles. The 98th and 100th brigades relieved 21st Division whilst 19th Brigade remained in the captured positions. Over the following week the division pushed out patrols and listening posts as far as the outskirts of Bullecourt to the south, whilst the divisional artillery provided flanking fire on Monchy-le-Preux.[16] This activity was followed by a large-scale assault on 23 April during which 98th and 100th Brigades, with 19th Brigade in immediate support, successfully advanced before repelling fierce German counter-attacks. Unfortunately, as 19th Brigade, 1st Cameronians and 5/6th Scottish Rifles in the forefront, leaped-frogged through the front brigades, it lost touch with 98th Brigade and failed to secure the formidable 'Tunnel Trench' objective.[17]

Assaults continued on 26 and 27 April. Carried out by 19th Brigade's 2nd Royal Welch Fusiliers and 5/6th Scottish Rifles, for the first time in 33rd Division's history the massed protective cover of a creeping barrage laid down by the 19th Machine-gun

---

13   Richards, *Old Soldiers*, p.217.
14   Docherty, '5th Battalion Reminiscences'. This accusation may have been based on casualties resulting from sickness.
15   Hutchison, *The Thirty-third Division*, p.23.
16   Ibid., p.35.
17   Whilst both the 1st and 5/6th Battalions of the Cameronians (Scottish Rifles) are of the same regiment, in all contemporary texts the 1st is referred to by the preferred title of Cameronians; the 5/6th preferred the Army's official nomenclature of Scottish Rifles.

5th Scottish Rifles 1916 Christmas card. (Author)

Company provided protection for the assault infantry.[18] The attack reached the German line but was repelled with heavy losses after bitter close-quarter fighting. Whilst small-scale operations continued throughout May, the major part of the 33rd's involvement with the Arras offensive was over. The division, which had sustained losses of 240 officers and 5,431 other ranks, was withdrawn to the rear where much of the month of June was spent refitting and taking part in an elaborate divisional horse show.[19]

The 31 July 1917, opening day of the Ypres offensive, found 33rd Division detraining at Dunkirk before spending August in the Nieuport sector. Trench raids and casualties by shelling occurred during the occupation of this peculiar seaside sector of the Western Front. On 27 August, orders were received for relief by 32nd Division. The exchange complete by 1 September, the 33rd commenced training in the Éperleques area. Battalion reinforcement drafts were also received at this time. Frank Richards later wrote, 'I re-joined the Battalion in a village near Ypres and guessed that we would soon be in a blood tub.'[20]

The 33rd Division's fighting experience up until its entry into the Third Ypres offensive had been one of the slow, methodical, yet proven learning curves experienced by the British Army on the Western Front. While this was by no means perfected by the time of its entry into the Third Battle of Ypres, there were demonstrable signs of operational and tactical development based, for example, on the searing experience of attacking with exposed flanks at High Wood and deployment of massed machine-gun barrages at Arras. These and other experiences were fine-tuned for application in the coming fight. Major-General Pinney, a competent and aggressive commander, had led what was considered a good combat division with a reputation for units operating closely together. Most recently, it had proven itself capable of piercing positions as strong as the Hindenburg Line defences. It was, therefore, unfortunate that two and a half weeks prior to participation in the Third Ypres offensive, he was admitted to hospital.

Into the Line

Pinney's departure came at an extremely inopportune time. Due to enter the fighting at Ypres, the 33rd Division might find itself led by a temporary GOC unfamiliar with subordinate units and their capabilities. Fortunately, divisional command was assigned to Brigadier-General Phillip R. Wood who had previously been GOC of 14th (Light) Division's 43rd Brigade during desperate fighting at Inverness Copse. This see-saw

---

18   Hutchinson, *The Thirty-third Division*, p. 44.
19   For an illustrated contemporary account of the divisional horse show, see 'Arras Spring Meeting', *Illustrated Sporting and Dramatic News*, 20 June 1917).
20   Richards. *Old Soldiers*, p. 245.

action in late August had resulted in the division capturing and then losing the much-contested woodland. The experience caused Wood to question concentrated force in British assaults. In a memorandum dated 29 August, he listed eight requirements for consideration prior to the launching of limited assaults against small but tactically vital objectives. Thus the necessity to deploy troops in 'worm' columns capable of overwhelming enemy defences prior to consolidating positions for repelling inevitable counter-attacks.[21] As Nick Lloyd notes, heavy casualties and war-weariness resulting from successive campaigns since January 1917 may have dissipated previously learned lessons of the Somme, hence Wood's desire to impart sound tactical advice to superiors and subordinates alike.

On 20 September, the 33rd Division was held in reserve eight miles west of Ypres by X Corps (GOC Lieutenant-General Sir T. Morland). However, its divisional artillery as well as component machine-gun companies supported 23rd Division's attack.[22] On that day, Second and Fifth armies joint offensive (Menin Road Ridge) succeeded in penetrating the German defences to an average depth of 1,250 yards.[23] This successful push on to the Gheluvelt Plateau, within reach of Polygon Wood and Broodseinde Ridge, was one of the great successes of the campaign. As was common at this point in the war, divisions, having reached their objectives, could anticipate relief by fresh formations. Thus the 33rd, under orders dated 21 September, marched forward to relieve 23rd Division on the 24th.

Offensive plans to push through Polygon Wood and onto the Broodseinde Ridge were already in development. On 20 September, British GHQ issued instructions to resume the attack at dawn on 26 September. This required Second Army (X Corps and 33rd Division inclusive) and Fifth Army to assault the Broodseinde and Gravenstafel ridges with four and two corps respectively. Divisional orders issued on the 24th determined boundaries and objectives. The 33rd would attack with Brigadier-General J.D. Heriot-Maitland's 98th Brigade, consisting of 1st Middlesex Regiment in front, 2nd Argyll & Sutherland Highlanders (A&SH) in support, and 1/4th Suffolk Regiment in reserve. This brigade held a line from Black Watch Corner, situated at the southwestern edge of Polygon Wood, to the Reutelbeek stream where its boundary with Baird's 100th Brigade was situated.[24] The latter brigade consisted, from right to left, of 1st Queen's (Royal West Surrey) Regiment which was responsible for the left flank/divisional boundary with the neighbouring 39th Division; 1/9th Highland Light Infantry (Glasgow Highlanders); 2nd Worcestershire Regiment, and 4th King's (Liverpool) Regiment (detached from 98th Brigade) with its left flank abutting 1st Middlesex. The 16th KRRC remained in brigade reserve.[25] Brigadier-General C.R.G.

21   TNA WO 95/1904/4: 'Lessons from the Attack', August 1917, 43rd Brigade War Diary.
22   J.E. Edmonds, *Military Operations France and Belgium 1917*, Vol. 2 (Nashville, Tennessee: Battery Press, 1991), p.242.
23   Prior & Wilson, *Passchendaele*, p.121.
24   TNA WO 95/2425/2: 98th Brigade War Diary, September 1917.
25   TNA WO 95/2429/1: 'Brigade Order No. 274', September 1917, 100th Brigade War Diary.

Glasgow Highlanders resting during the march forward, 24 September 1917.

Mayne's 19th Brigade remained in divisional reserve with two battalions to the west at Bedford House. The remaining two battalions were in reserve just outside Ypres.[26] To 33rd Division's north was 15th Brigade of 5th Australian Division (II Anzac Corps) under the charismatic leadership of Brigadier-General H.E.E. 'Pompey' Elliott, who was hell-bent on capturing Polygon Wood in its entirety.[27]

The relief of the 23rd Division was completed on the night of the 24/25 September. By 12:30 a.m. the 1st Queen's on the far right reported the line secured.[28] On the far left difficulties due to navigating the ground accounted for the 1st Middlesex not confirming all companies in position until 4:30 a.m.[29] The terrain posed serious challenges which 33rd Division would struggle to overcome throughout the subsequent fighting. The 1st Middlesex diarist remarked that 'The line taken over consisted mainly of short isolated lengths of trench dug amongst the shell holes with supporting lines in rear.'[30] The 2nd Worcesters diarist stated that 'Both on this and subsequent

26   TNA WO 95/2421/2: 19th Brigade War Diary, September 1917.
27   For a recent biography of this controversial Australian commander, see Ross McMullin, *Pompey Elliot* (Carlton North: Scribe Publications, 2002).
28   TNA WO 95/2430/1: 1st Queen's (Royal West Surrey) Regiment War Diary, September 1917
29   TNA WO 95/2426/1: 'Report on Operations on 24th, 25th, and 26th September, 1917', 1st Middlesex Regiment War Diary.
30   Ibid.

occasions, the difficulty of finding the war amid the mass of shell holes, especially by night, was very noticeable. It interfered not only with the communication by runner but also with the supply of stores and ammunition.'[31] The same diarist also observed that on his battalion's immediate right, the Glasgow Highlanders had become mixed up with neighbouring battalions and that much of its line was facing directly north instead of east.[32] Guides provided by 23rd Division routinely became lost, and the official handover to 33rd Division headquarters was delayed until 10:00 a.m. on the 25th, well after the last of 23rd Division's units had withdrawn.

In the midst of this confusion, further strain was added to ongoing line consolidation with the unexpected notification that Second Army gunners would be conducting a practice barrage on the German lines.[33] Report confirming individual companies had occupied allotted positions continued to flood in throughout the early hours of the morning. Meantime, British observers noted that the enemy opposite was not particularly active. This all changed at 5:15 a.m. when a screeching torrent of hostile shells deluged the 33rd Division line.[34]

Spoiled

The latest British advance on 20 September and the anticipated relief of 23rd Division provided the Germans with the opportunity to counter-attack with available *Eingreifdivision*.[35] *Kronprinz* Rupprecht of Bavaria, commanding the *Armee Gruppe* to which the defending German *Fourth Army* belonged, had recognised the immediate need to dislodge the British from recently won territory on Gheluvelt Plateau with a spoiling attack. His diary entries for 23 and 24 September observed:

> We cannot tolerate the idea of the enemy firmly in control of the Zonnebeke heights or the Geluveld [Gheluvelt]. They are now so close to achieving this that the fear must be that they will achieve it with their next attack. We must ensure

31   TNA WO 95/2430/2: 'The Action on the Menin Road, September 25th-27th, 1917', 2nd Worcestershire Regiment War Diary.
32   Ibid.
33   Ibid.
34   Several war diaries, the British Official History and German orders captured on 26 September reported the barrage as beginning at 5:15 a.m. Other reports state it was 5:30 or 5:45 a.m.
35   By summer 1917 German tactics dictated allowing the British to make small territorial gains before counter-attacking *Eingreifdivisions* were unleashed. See Captain G.C. Wynne, *If Germany Attacks: The Battle in Depth in the West* (Brighton: Tom Donovan unexpurgated edition, 2008), pp.199-226 and German Werth, 'Flanders 1917 and the German Soldier' in Peter Liddle (ed.), *Passchendaele in Perspective: The Third Battle of Ypres* (London: Leo Cooper, 1997), pp.324-42.

that our counter-strokes during the next enemy assaults are driven right up to their planned objectives.

It appears as though fresh attacks against Groups Ypres and Wijtschate are about to take place. It is to be hoped that they do not take place too soon because we currently lack reserves behind the main battle front.[36]

The task of assaulting the defences held by 33rd Division, a section of the *Wilhelm Stellung* in British hands since 20 September,[37] fell to *50th Reserve Division*.[38] Following a 30-minute preparatory bombardment, the 3rd Battalion, *Reserve-Infanterie-Regiment (RIR) 229*, was to attack on a line from the southern edge of Polygon Wood to the Reutelbeek. Beyond the latter feature, 3rd Battalion *RIR 230* would simultaneously assault southward to the Menin Road. For its part, 1st Battalion *RIR 230* was tasked with helping to secure the objective whilst companies of *RIR 229* would press the Australians on the western edge of the wood itself. The crack *Sturmbataillone No. 4* was also made available to the assault force. Its task was to provide support along the Menin Road with *Flammenwerfers*, *Minenwerfers* and *Infanterie-Geschütz* light assault guns. Furthermore, companies of *RIR 231* were tasked with occupying the jumping-off line in readiness to fill any unexpected gaps during the operation.[39]

The German bombardment caused complete chaos amongst the already jumbled ranks of 33rd Division. No less than 27 field guns, 17 howitzer, 15 high angle heavy and 5 flat trajectory heavy batteries, as well as the batteries of neighbouring division artillery, poured fire onto the 1,900 yard wide front.[40] The 1st Middlesex reported that, 'The shells used by the enemy were mostly heavy, and included gas and heavy shrapnel.'[41] The 2nd Worcestershire Regiment reported that the enemy effectively targeted their frontline trenches; the reserve trenches followed before the hostile

36   Jack Sheldon, *The German Army at Passchendaele* (Barnsley: Pen & Sword, 2007), p.166.
37   The German defences prior to the opening of Third Ypres 'consisted of three zones, each 2,000 to 3,000 yards deep: a forward zone, a battle zone and a rearward zone, the backs of which were marked by the second (*Albrecht*), the third (*Wilhelm*) and the Flanders Line, respectively.' See Edmonds, *Military Operations 1917*, Vol. 2, p.143.
38   Raised in 1914, the *50th Reserve Division* had served in Poland and on the Western Front during 1915-16. In January-April 1917 it fought on the Ancre and participated in the withdrawal to the Hindenburg Line. Following a period of uneventful line occupation near Arras during May and early June, the division entrained for the Ypres front where it sustained heavy casualties from 31 July to 2 August. Relieved on 10 August, it returned to line near Gheluvelt on 20 September. See Intelligence Section of the General Staff, American Expeditionary Forces, *Histories of Two Hundred and Fifty-One Divisions of the German Army Which Participated in the War 1914-1918* (London: London Stamp Exchange, 1989 reprint of 1920 edition), pp.493-96.
39   TNA WO 95/2429/1: 'Translation of Divisional and Regimental Orders for the Enemy's Attack on the 25th of September 1917', 100th Brigade War Diary.
40   Ibid.
41   TNA WO 95/2426/1: 'Report on Operations on 24th, 25th, and 26th September, September 1917', 1st Middlesex Regiment War Diary.

Unteroffiziers of *RIR 231* c.1916-17 (Author)

barrage shifted onto the rear area where battalion headquarters sustained direct hits once every 15 minutes.[42]

Men sought cover in the shattered trenches and numerous shell holes of previous fighting. Only the most fortunate were able to shelter within captured German pill-boxes that dotted the landscape. Command and control was lost by battalion and brigade commanders as communications were disrupted. Battalions subsequently reported in their war diaries that instructions from the rear and reports from the front had no chance of getting through due to the smoke and intense fire on all avenues of approach. The 2nd A&SH's diarist perhaps put it best with the blunt statement that 'All communications were at once severed.'[43] Captain C.C. Stormont Gibbs of 1/4th Suffolks recalled:

> The CO's revolver took one piece of shell that would have killed him and I got a clod in the back that knocked me down and that was all. In fifteen minutes one regrets to record there were only two officers left with their men. The rest had simply run away and were found at the transport lines two days later, some being court-martialled. Half the men had gone similarly and most of the rest

42   TNA WO 95/2430/2: The Action on the Menin Road, September 25th-27th, 1917', 2nd Worcestershire Regiment War Diary.
43   TNA WO 95/2426/2: Report on Operations 24th-26th Sept, 1917, 2nd Argyll & Sutherland Highlanders War Diary.

were dead. In one place where there was a short piece of unbroken trench I found six men leaning against the side in life-like positions but quite dead and quite untouched. The detonation of a shell had killed them simply by blast. The concussion in the air all round was almost maddening: one felt in torment.[44]

Closely following the bombardment, the German infantry, estimated to be 1,000 men strong, pressed forward. At 5:30 a.m. S.O.S. flares ascended across the 33rd Division front, but smoke from the bombardment contributed to an already thick ground mist which made it almost impossible to discern calls for help. 100th Brigade reported that no runners were able to break through, and that no wire communications were still connected to the divisional artillery. To the north, the neighbouring Australian 58th Battalion observed the enemy massing. Their communications similarly cut, a battalion signaller attempted to send a message by pigeon before discovering that almost all of the birds had been killed or rendered unconscious by the bombardment.[45]

As the German assault struck the British line between Polygon Wood and Menin Road, the marshy ground about the Reutelbeek – inundated and further disturbed by masses of artillery which pulverized the landscape over the preceding weeks – forced the attackers to siphon their thrusts to the extreme flanks of 33rd Division. Rifle and Lewis Gun fire from the Worcesters, King's and Glasgow Highlanders held the central assaulting companies of *RIR 229* and *RIR 230* in check. On 1st Middlesex's front, the brunt of the assault followed the trail along the southern edge of Polygon Wood. From there German troops fell upon the battalion's left flank where three platoons of B Company were isolated in individual shell holes. On encountering these outposts, the Germans worked their way to the flanks and rear, surrounding and even bypassing them in a textbook example of infiltration tactics. The Middlesex war diarist remarked that 'The defence was greatly handicapped by the fact that most companies had been but an hour or two in their position and had not seen the ground by daylight; moreover the outgoing unit had only held that sector for about 24 hours and were unable to furnish company commanders with very much information.'[46] A company situated on the battalion's right managed to hold off the attackers with defensive fire that pinned the them down behind a small ridge in front.

Fighting continued as the Germans consolidated their gains. However, the assaulting companies in Polygon Wood were halted by the Australians, who were

---

44   R. Devonald-Lewis (ed.), *From the Somme to the Armistice: The Memoirs of Captain Stormont Gibbs MC* (London: William Kimber, 1986), p.158.

45   AWM 111.52, 'REPORT ON OPERATIONS of 15th AUST. INF. BDE. AT POLYGON WOOD ON 24th, 25th, 26th & 27th SEPTEMBER 1917' and A.D. Ellis, *The Story of the Fifth Australian Division: Being an Authoritative Account of the Divisions Doings in Egypt, France and Belgium* (London: Hodder & Stoughton, 1919), p.240.

46   TNA WO 95/2426/1: Report on Operations on 24th, 25th, and 26th September, September 1917, 1st Middlesex Regiment War Diary.

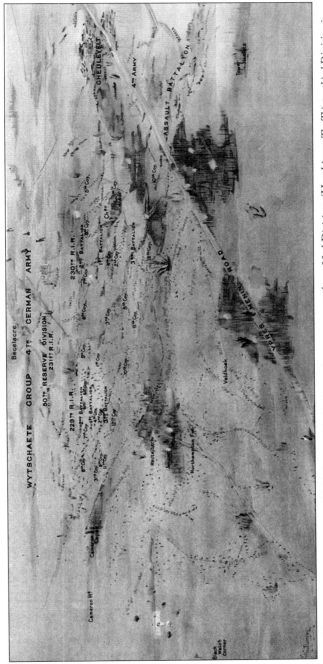

Oblique panorama rendering of *50th Reserve Division's* surprise counter-attack on 33rd Division. (Hutchison, *The Thirty-third Division in France and Flanders, 1915–1919*)

forced to turn a company of 58th Battalion southwards in response to infiltration of the 1st Middlesex defences.[47] By 6:30 a.m. the Middlesex observed a renewed German assault as at least five waves of hostile infantry approached from positions near Jerk House. These reinforcements entered a gap between A and B companies opened by previous attacks. Entering the Middlesex main line of resistance, the Germans methodically worked their way down the line with hand grenades. Resorting to bayonets and rifle butts, attacker and defender engaged in savage hand-to-hand combat. All of the Middlesex front company officers became casualties as the remainder of the battalion fell back 150 yards to where C and D companies, in reserve, were ensconced. The latter had remained unaware of the situation in front owing to mist, smoke and the sustained fire of enemy machine-guns. The Australians noticed these guns had been deployed along the road, but they remained unseen by the Middlesex.

A similar situation was developing farther south. The Germans, having managed to breach the 1st Queen's line, companies in occupation of the battalion support line remained unaware of this due to the communications breakdown. It was not until 7:30 a.m. that a 2nd Lieutenant Hughes of B Company stumbled into battalion headquarters to report on the situation. The enemy, employing a heavy *Minenwerfer*, almost annihilated the Queen's frontline B and D companies. Sixteen minutes later, CSM Tripper of D Company arrived gravely wounded to report that the line was broken, but D Company's headquarters was still holding out. With its two remaining companies, the Queen's organised an immediate counter-attack. However, sustained enemy artillery and trench mortar fire ensured it 'was practically impossible to get a company thro' the barrage.'[48]

Perhaps the unit which had the best grasp of the situation was 2nd Worcesters, which had traversed these same fields during a legendary counter-attack almost three years earlier. Now it faced a drastically different situation as isolated groups of Tommies were observed surrendering to right and left. The Worcesters' primary focus, however, remained on the right flank. In the frontline, B Company reported that it had no contact with the Glasgow Highlanders on the immediate right but were holding the Germans back with accurate rifle fire. A request for reinforcements and more ammunition was received at battalion headquarters. A Company, on receipt of orders to dash forward, made its way to the occupied German pillbox serving as HQ where boxes of S.A.A. (small arms ammunition) were torn open and bandoleers handed out to the passing column. Captain Brooks, A Company's CO, had his leg broken by a shell. Two subalterns were also wounded, leaving only one junior officer to extend the battalion line southwards.[49]

47   Australian War Memorial (AWM) 4 23/75/20, 58th Infantry Battalion War Diary, 25 September 1917.

48   TNA WO 95/2430/1: 1st Queen's (Royal West Surrey) Regiment War Diary, 25 September 1917.

49   TNA WO 95/2430/2: 'The Action on the Menin Road, September 25th-27th, 1917', 2nd Worcestershire Regiment War Diary,

The desperate need for S.A.A. across the entire front led to extraordinary feats of bravery. Out of 61 VCs awarded for Third Ypres, over 40 were for assaulting pillboxes. However, the one 33rd Division recipient, Lance Corporal John Brown Hamilton of the Glasgow Highlanders, earned his for bringing much-needed ammunition forward under fire.[50]

The Germans, having broken 1st Queen's front, went on to overrun two companies. Gun teams of 100th Machine-gun Company were also silenced, two guns being destroyed by *Flammenwerfers,* the surviving crewmen killed or captured by follow-up troops.[51] As the post-war history of the Glasgow Highlanders observed, 'As far as the forward companies were concerned, it was a case of each man for himself, but the support companies by sending forward part of C and a few men of B to reinforce and counter-attack, prevented the line from being broken.'[52] By 9:30 a.m. this counter-attack proceeded with the support of a 16th KRRC company. The precipitate assault managed to recover the support line before it was halted by German fire. To the north, the 2nd A&SH's rushed to the aid of 1st Middlesex whilst dispatching platoons to cover the gap between 33rd and 5th Australian divisions. Along the former's front, the situation began to stabilize as both sides consolidated and awaited reinforcements.

As remnants of 33rd Division's shattered battalions consolidated, plans were drawn up to retake the lost ground. Confusion engendered by the enemy assault resulted in junior officers and NCOs seizing the initiative by deploying reserves and preparing local counter-attacks. Meantime, Lieutenant-Colonel L.L. Wheatley, CO 2nd A&SH's, dispatched one company to Major H.A. Hanley, CO 1st Middlesex, as soon as the German attack opened. No further word from Hanley received, Wheatley took the added precaution of dispatching two more companies with orders to press forward with an offensive posture.[53]

At midday, 33rd Division headquarters called on 19th Brigade to enter the fight. To that end, the 5/6th Scottish Rifles were subordinated to 98th Brigade north of the Reutelbeek. Of the perilous journey there, the battalion history observed: 'The approach was none too pleasant, for many of those who had gone up the previous night were lying dead all over the place.'[54] Across no man's land, the *50th Reserve Division* sent in its last uncommitted regiment, *RIR 23*. A *Leutnant* Heider recalled:

50   Lloyd, *Passchendaele*, p.108 and *Supplement to The London Gazette November 26th, 1917* (Accessed 20 July 2020).

51   Graham Seton Hutchison, *History and Memoir of the 33rd Battalion, Machine-gun Corps: And the 19th, 98th, 100th and 248th M.G. Companies* (London: Waterloo Bros. & Layton, 1919), p.32.

52   Reid, *Shoulder to Shoulder*, p.77.

53   TNA WO 95/2426/2: 'Report on Operations 24th-26th Sept, 1917', 2nd Argyll & Sutherland Highlanders War Diary.

54   David Martin (ed.), *The Fifth Battalion: The Cameronians (Scottish Rifles) 1914-1919* (Glasgow: Jackson & Son, 1936), p.127.

On 25 September 1st Company Reserve Infantry Regiment 231 ... was on stand-by located near Geluveld to the right of the Ypres–Menin road. We had already suffered several casualties due to the artillery fire. At midday I was ordered by *Hauptmann* Burger to advance and occupy the line of the *Wilhelm Stellung* to the right [north] of the road. It was one of the most difficult missions that I was ever given during the war. It meant that I had to get forward several hundred metres through the heaviest imaginable artillery defensive fire – and in broad daylight. I gave my orders to my men, adding: *The hour has come when I have to trust each and every one of you implicitly. I shall go first and you must follow me, well spread out. We shall meet up again in the frontline. Go forward with God!* Moving with me were my two young runners, Joachim Algermissen from Hildesheim and Gefreiter Wilhelm Koch from Konigsdahlum, near Hanover. With total disre-gard for their lives and completely calm, they rushed with me from shell hole to shell hole. On one occasion I was almost buried by a shell. Just as we reached the frontline and were pleased to have reached it unscathed, Algermissen was shot through the chest. Shouting, *Praised be the Lord Jesus Christ!* he collapsed, mortally wounded ... It was uplifting to see my men arriving one by one in the frontline, but one third of the company had fallen victim to the ferocious fire on the way. I was later able to establish that none had faltered. Those missing were all reported killed or wounded. [55]

Bolstering the hard-pressed defenders' small arms fire, some 16 machine-guns poured deadly fire into the oncoming mass before the German assault was halted.[56] For its part, the divisional artillery, maintaining supporting fire throughout the day, was also able to carry out the X Corps practice barrage previously scheduled for 2:30 p.m.[57] Simultaneously, the 1st Middlesex, 2nd A&SH's and the newly arrived 1/4th Suffolk reinforcements launched a counter-attack north of the Reutelbeek. Just ahead, surviving British troops were still visible holding out in pockets about the original frontline, and for a time relief was thought to have broken through to them. However, at 5:30 p.m., 98th Brigade confirmed that the operation had failed.[58] Taking stock of the situation, Lieutenant-General Morland, GOC X Corps, observed, '6:20 a.m. German attack on 33rd Division, penetrates their trenches in several places. Various other attacks during day. Nearly all ground lost gained back in counter-attacks.'[59]

55   Sheldon, *The German Army at Passchendaele*, pp. 167-68.
56   Hutchison, *33rd Battalion Machine-gun Corps*, p. 27.
57   TNA WO 95/2410/1: Commander Royal Artillery 33rd Division War Diary, 25 September 1917.
58   TNA WO 95 2406/3: 33rd Division War Diary, 25 September 1917.
59   Bill Thompson (ed.), *General Sir Thomas Morland KCB KCMG DSO: War Diaries & Letters 1914-1918* (Kibworth Beauchamp: Matador, 2015), p.230.

Counter-stroke

The aforementioned practice barrage provided the first intimation that Second Army still expected 33rd Division to attack at dawn on 26 September. By this time 19th Brigade was moving forward, with 1st Cameronians subordinated to 100th Brigade and 20th Royal Fusiliers and 2nd Royal Welch Fusiliers moving into nearby Sanctuary Wood where they would report directly to Brigadier-General Wood at divisional headquarters. Arriving at sundown, the shattered terrain and continuous bombardments proved a massive challenge to the advancing battalions. The 5/6th Scottish Rifles war diarist observed, 'The positions of the frontlines of both the 98th Brigade and the enemy was uncertain. Guides were supplied but owing to the extremely difficult ground and lack of knowledge of the route by the guides, the companies got lost.'[60]

At 9:00 p.m. orders from X Corps were received at divisional headquarters. The 33rd Division was to assault on the morning of 26 September. Considering the local reverse, consequent disorganisation and casualties – 1st Queens had been reduced to approximately 150 men – assigned objectives were less optimistic than before.[61] The revised objective was to push the enemy back from recently captured positions whilst providing flank protection for 5th Australian Division's advance through Polygon Wood. Further to this, the 33rd was to obtain observation over the Reutelbeek valley. The offensive was scheduled to open at 5:50 a.m. Heriot-Maitland's 98th Brigade with three support battalions of 19th Brigade, would attack alongside the Australians, the main burden falling on 1/4th Suffolk, and 5/6th Scottish Rifles. The 100th Brigade, which had been badly mauled on the 25th, was tasked with regaining its former front whilst simultaneously supporting 98th Brigade's assault. The jumping-off line extended from Black Watch Corner south to the eastern edge of Carlisle Farm. From there it continued across the Reutelbeek to the Menin Road. The first objective (Red Line) ran well to the east of the original British line where the line centred

Brigadier-General J.D. Heriot-Maitland. (Hutchison, *The Thirty-third Division in France and Flanders, 1915-1919*)

60   TNA WO 95/2422/3: 5th Battalion Cameronians (Scottish Rifles) War Diary, 26 September 1917.
61   TNA WO 95/2406/3: 33rd Division War Diary, 26 September 1917.

around Cameron House. The next objective (Blue Line) ran along the eastern edge of Polygon Wood from Joist Farm through Cameron Covert at a south-westerly angle before extending back to Jut Farm and the Menin Road.[62]

Throughout the night of 25/26 September, British gunners laid down barrages at the specific requests of individual battalions in order to interrupt enemy defensive preparations. Confusion continued to reign as units struggled to get into position before zero hour. For the Glasgow Highlanders, simply being informed the attack was imminent was further complicated by the failure of a number of messages to reach their destination. It was not until the Brigade Major of 100th Brigade person-ally made his way forward to brief them that final preparations could be made.[63] The night passed in terror and discomfort for combatants on both sides. *Leutnant* Heider recalled:

> That evening we were ordered, along with the entire division to shift our front slightly to the left [south], so as to ensure that all units were occupying the Wilhelm Stellung. Reserve Infantry Regiment 230 to our right did not seem to have received this order or to have conformed to it and a gap developed on our flank. Fortunately, this was not spotted by the enemy and I covered it by turning the right flank of the company [to face north]. To our front the scene was one of utter chaos. Dead and wounded lay everywhere – many of them British. We established our strongpoint around two pillboxes. The enemy were about twenty to fifty metres away and enemy machine-guns pointed at us from nearby blockhouses.
>
> During the night a Scotsman blundered into our position. We kept him there to tend to his severely wounded countrymen, who were moaning terribly. One of them had lost both his eyes to a flamethrower. I longed to shoot him and put him out of his misery, but such action was not permitted. I estimate that my company was reduced to thirty to thirty five men. We had to maintain a high standard of alert throughout the night. As I went around the position I saw that many, who had earned the right to sleep, were sleeping their last sleep of all in the miserable muddy shell holes; these, the finest of our faithful people, had been kissed on the forehead by the Angels of Peace.[64]

Opposite *50th Reserve Division*, the organisational miracle whereby 33rd Division relied on battalion commanders, junior officers and NCOs to reorganize and inspire their men to prepare for the forthcoming push ensured the battered division was ready to advance despite the difficult circumstances. Entering the frontline at this time, the

62 Ibid.
63 TNA WO 95/2430/1: 1st Queen's (Royal West Surrey) Regiment War Diary, 26 September 1917.
64 Sheldon, *The German Army at Passchendaele*, pp. 167-68.

battalions of 19th Brigade were bewildered as they made their way to jumping-off positions. The 5/6th Scottish Rifles historian subsequently observed, 'The surrounding ground was a mass of shell holes filled with stinking water and mud and if you fell into one you were lost. It was every man for himself, and no one who passed through that night is ever likely to forget its tragedies.'[65]

Captain Alexander Stewart, commanding C Company of 1st Cameronians, was ordered to send his men forward piecemeal. Having received instructions to do so during the early evening, Stewart immediately sent one officer and 20 men to a neighbouring battalion that had sustained heavy losses.[66] He subsequently recalled relating orders to a young subaltern:

> I could not tell him exactly where he had to go to but told him he must report to the battalion I told him and no other, not to stop till he got there and to hurry. I attempted to impress on him as deeply as I could that he must go to the Battalion he was told to go to and not get drawn into any other fights or seduced into reinforcing any other Battalion that wanted help, as if he did not get to the right place I should get Hell and all the blame. He was a jovial, humorous chap with a thin face, I did not expect to see him again and was sorry to lose him.[67]

The early morning hours of 26 September saw a recurrence of thick mist across the Reutelbeek valley.[68] This, combined with the moon's masking by smoke and mist, disrupted last minute preparations for the early morning assault.[69] Companies of 5/6th Scottish Rifles, previously ordered to join 1/4th Suffolks, failed to arrive at the assembly area by designated rendezvous time. Lieutenant-Colonel H.C. Copeman, the Suffolks CO, requested permission from 98th Brigade to advance at 2:00 a.m., but was refused. With hostile shells still falling into assembly areas, permission was again requested, and finally, at 3:30 a.m., Copeman was permitted to move forward under the condition that he also took immediate responsibility for the complete brigade front where remnants of 1st Middlesex and 2nd A&SHs were still clinging on.[70] Just prior to the Suffolks advance, elements of two Scottish Rifles companies trailed by stragglers arrived from the east. Having missed the rendezvous, they pressed on to the frontline and, in some cases, beyond before turning back.[71]

65   Martin (ed.), *The Fifth Battalion*, p.128.
66   This was the 1st Queen's Regiment.
67   Alexander Stewart, *A Very Unimportant Officer: Life and Death on the Somme and at Passchendaele* (London: Hodder & Stoughton, 2008), pp.251-52.
68   TNA WO 95/2406/3: 33rd Division War Diary, 26 September 1917.
69   Edmonds, *Military Operations 1917*, Vol. 2, p. 286.
70   TNA WO 95/2425/2: 'Report from 1/4th Suffolk Regt, September 1917', 98th Brigade War Diary.
71   Ibid.

Differing accounts of delays experienced in getting troops in position demonstrate confusion and resultant anxiety. The Suffolks reported that the Scottish Rifles failed to move forward when the barrage opened.[72] The latter battalion, as has been previously noted, was dealing with terrain difficulties and a heavy shellfire concentrated on its A and B companies. D Company was completely lost, the company commander calling for a halt to avoid exhausting his men. Having dispatched a volunteer to find battalion headquarters, the company hunkered down to await developments. As the battalion history later observed, 'Daylight made little difference owing to the mist and smoke.'[73] Conditions remaining relatively unchanged, Copeman ordered the half battalion available to remain in place before conforming with pending Suffolk advance.[74]

Battalions finally in place, the assault commenced at 5:50 a.m. Once again, junior leadership excelled despite the confusion. CSM Docherty of the Scottish Rifles recalled the chaos of the first few minutes after Zero:

> Our barrage opened up and at 5.30 a.m. I took two platoons over, just leaving our position in time to avoid a terrific barrage which the enemy put down on it. We took our first objective fairly easily; all the pillboxes had had a good pounding from our heavies and the only Germans left on that position were the dead and wounded. We went through and beyond the pillboxes and lay down; the shell craters in this area had to be seen to be believed. Serjeant Hay and I went along the line to get the men straightened out; dawn had broken by this time and men of the Suffolks and 'B' and 'C' Companies were all mixed up. The shelling was so bad on both sides and the confusion such that some of our men were digging in facing the direction from which our own artillery was firing.

The 1/4th Suffolks pressed forward in platoon rushes, two companies making some progress, whilst one was temporarily stalled after the loss of its commander. As Docherty later asserted, the Suffolks and Scottish Rifles had by this point in time become mixed up, so it would be folly to assert that these battalions were holding distinct lines. Nevertheless, they pressed on to the former frontline from Black Watch Corner to Carlisle Farm, sustaining some casualties opposite the latter, where they linked up with the 4th King's.[75] Remarkably, survivors from the previous day's stand by the Middlesex and A&SH's were discovered to be still holding out in many parts of the line. They had been cut off in some cases for over 24 hours.[76]

72   Ibid.
73   Martin (ed.), *The Fifth Battalion*, p.128.
74   TNA WO 95/2422/3: 5th Battalion Cameronians (Scottish Rifles) War Diary, 26 September 1917.
75   TNA WO 95/2425/2: 'Report from 1/4th Suffolk Regt, September 1917', 98th Brigade War Diary.
76   Dunn, *The War the Infantry Knew*, p.394.

To the immediate north, the Australian 31st Battalion, which had entered the line during the night of the 25/26 September, were making progress inside Polygon Wood. However, they regularly complained of the right flank being exposed by 33rd Division's inability to keep pace. Indeed, 31st Battalion's official report claimed that 'no effort had been made by these troops to advance.' Brigadier-General Elliot, as we shall see, would make similar claims afterwards.[77] Nonetheless, by 11:15 a.m. not much else could have been achieved. Communications breakdowns, as well as battalions becoming hopelessly intermixed, stalled the 33rd Division's assault. In an effort to resume the advance, D Company and half of C of the Scottish Rifles were sent forward, not only to reinforce the line but, as Battalion CO Lieutenant-Colonel H.B. Spens reported, to 'sweep up all parties between battalion headquarters and the line and Black Watch Corner and carry the line on.'[78] To the south, tanks operating on the boundary between 33rd and 39th divisions were encountered by CSM Docherty:

> We had been ordered to stop for 40 minutes on the first objective and then go on, and while we were consolidating this position one of our tanks, which should have attacked with us, came waddling up the Menin Road. The Hun was giving the road 'big licks' and the tank diverged off the road and made in our direction. It stopped just behind us and an officer jumped out and asked me where the Boche was. I pointed out the general direction of the enemy position and asked him to take his 'infernal contraption away to hell out of our vicinity'; I had seen the litter of British dead round derelict tanks in the Hindenburg Line and had decided always to give them a wide berth. The officer was going to put me under arrest and asked for my Company Commander; I told him I was the Company Commander and that the Company was going forward in 15 minutes time. He jumped into the tank, it turned away and as it went I saw the name painted on it was *Auld Reekie*. I remember saying, 'That's the place for me.'[79]

To assist the Australians and further the advance, the 2nd Royal Welch Fusiliers were ordered into Polygon Wood around 10:00 a.m. The battalion arrived in the vicinity of Black Watch Corner by 11:45 a.m. Zero hour was at 12:00 p.m. Fearing 98th Brigade survivors were still holding out in front, smoke shells were employed as cover.[80] Deploying under continuous machine-gun fire, Welch Fusilier CO Major R.A. Poore formed the battalion on a two-company front facing south with one

77 AWM 4 23/48/26, 31st Infantry Battalion War Diary, 26 September 1917.
78 TNA WO 95/2422/3: 5th Battalion Cameronians (Scottish Rifles) War Diary, 26 September 1917.
79 Docherty, '5th Battalion Reminiscences Part II'. Auld Reekie is Scots slang for old smoky – an affectionate sobriquet for Edinburgh.
80 Dunn, *The War the Infantry Knew*, p.395.

company in support and one in reserve.[81]

At noon, the 2nd Royal Welch Fusiliers pushed off to the south. The battalion's mission was to extend the Australian advance and regain momentum on 98th Brigade's front. Almost immediately things began to go awry. The front left company, advancing much too fast, pivoted to face east, and lost touch with the right front company. In response, the support company was immediately ordered forward, and a line extended to Carlisle Farm where the Welch Fusiliers linked up with the Suffolks and Scottish Rifles. Unfortunately, battalion command and control broke down after Major Poore was killed by a direct hit to a shell hole he occupied near Black Watch Corner. His adjutant, Captain J.C. Mann, was shot through the head and killed,

Major R.A. Poore.

and all of the company commanders were down.[82] Following this, as Private Frank Richards subsequently claimed, the battalion medical officer, Captain J.C. Dunn, obtained a rifle and bayonet and, assuming command, 'temporarily resigned from the Royal Army Medical Corps.'[83] By the time the assault's momentum had dissipated, 3:30 p.m., the Welch Fusiliers had made contact with scattered elements of 31st Battalion and 33rd Division. Together, they were in possession of a line extending from Cameron House to Jut Farm.[84] This modest advance was all the more remarkable when the battered state of 33rd Division is taken into consideration. Officers from brigade commanders down had been given independent action permissions by Wood with measurable results. At 3:45 p.m., in a message to 98th Brigade, the GOC 33rd

81   TNA WO 95/2423/1: 2nd Battalion Royal Welch Fusiliers War Diary, 26 September 1917.
82   Richards, *Old Soldiers*, p.248.
83   Ibid., p.249.
84   Dunn, *The War the Infantry Knew*, p.398.

Division reminded them of the importance of keeping touch with the Australians on their left, 'It is of utmost importance that right flank of Australians should be covered by you.'[85] As was commonplace at the time, an enemy counter-attack was anticipated. Meantime, the 100th Brigade had managed to link up with 98th Brigade on the left when, at 4:50 p.m., S.O.S flares rose from positions held by 4th King's and 1st Queen's.[86] Shortly afterwards, the King's reported that the Germans had broken into positions about Jut Farm. More concerning, both 98th Brigade and division head-quarters had received no information from Cameron House and vicinity. On 100th Brigade's front, Worcester and Glasgow Highlanders Lewis Gun and rifle fire drove off the enemy assault with heavy losses.

Throughout the night of the 26/27 September, the situation remained tense and confused. At the divisional level, all that was known was that 100th Brigade had one battalion south and one battalion north of the Reutelbeek. At 10:55 p.m. orders for the Royal Welch Fusiliers to resume the assault with a company of Scottish Rifles next morning were issued by 98th Brigade.[87] Moving forward at 12:30 p.m., the Welch Fusiliers stormed Cameron House only to find it occupied by Australians.[88] However, a pillbox at Jut Farm proved more difficult undertaking until flanked and overrun by the Scottish Rifles, who captured two machine-guns and 14 prisoners.[89] With this minor success 33rd Division, now aligned with 5th Australian Division on the left, had finally achieved its Blue Line objective. As the post-war 5th Scottish Rifles history observed, 'The plan succeeded. "D" Company took the "pillboxes", including prisoners and machine-guns, and further resistance collapsing, the whole position of the Polygon Wood area was occupied by the British.'[90] Lieutenant-General Morland, GOC X Corps, remarked that evening:

> Attack by Second and Fifth Armies at 5:50 a.m. Most objectives gained. 33rd Division heavily shelled at 5 a.m. and do not get on but get on later. Many counter-attacks. 39th Division gain objectives. Visit both divisions in morning … 33rd Division lose some ground in the afternoon and leave Australian flank exposed. Regain some later. Many Germans killed. Heavy day's fighting.[91]

Divisional relief on the night of 27/28 September arrived in the form of 23rd Division. Two battalions of 19th Brigade remained behind until the night of the 28th/29th

---

85 TNA WO 95/2406/3: 33rd Division War Diary, 26 September 1917.
86 Ibid.
87 Ibid.
88 TNA WO 95/2423/1: 2nd Battalion Royal Welch Fusiliers War Diary, 26 September 1917.
89 TNA WO 95/2422/3: 5th Battalion Cameronians (Scottish Rifles) War Diary, 26 September 1917.
90 Martin (ed.), *The Fifth Battalion*, p.129.
91 Thompson (ed.), *General Sir Thomas Morland*, p.230.

when they were withdrawn to re-join the remainder of 33rd Division at Blaringhem and vicinity. There, congratulatory messages from Plumer and Haig, thanking the division for its recent efforts, were disseminated to all ranks.[92] The Polygon Wood fighting had cost it 3,117 men killed, wounded and missing.[93]

Conclusion

Having relieved 23rd Division after its success during the Menin Road push, the 33rd Division has, given the consequences of having a judgmental Dominion ally on its left flank, suffered some reputational damage since late September 1917.[94] Much of the historiography concerning Polygon Wood focuses on the Australian experience and is, therefore, somewhat biased. So it was that the 5th Australian Division history lamented the attention paid to 33rd Division in official GHQ communiques.[95] Moreover, Charles Bean observed that the successful outcome of the fighting 'was largely due to the perfect protection afforded by the artillery, but also largely to the vigour with which the 15th Brigade and the troops reinforcing it snatched complete success from an almost desperate situation on the right.'[96] No doubt 15th Brigade and the entire 5th Australian Division had fought remarkably well. Brigadier-General Elliot, however, was scathing in his criticism of 33rd Division's performance during and after the surprise German riposte. Typical of the tone of his assessment was the perceived failure of Heriot-Maitland's brigade to occupy designated jumping-off positions prior to Zero on the 26th: 'This is on its face a confession of failure of the 98th Brigade troops to get on ...' [97] Nevertheless, subsequent Anzac success would have been impossible had it not been for the defensive/offensive efforts of Elliot's hardpressed but resilient British neighbours.

Field Marshal Haig went on to praise 33rd Division in a message to Plumer on 27 September:

---

92   TNA WO 95/2406/3: 33rd Division War Diary, 26 September 1917.
93   According to collective brigade war diaries, 946 casualties killed, wounded and missing were sustained by 98th Brigade, 654 by 19th Brigade, and 1,517 by 100th Brigade for a total of 3,117 officers and men. Edmonds provides a figure of 2,903 just for 26 September. Hutchison noted in the divisional history that 33rd Division suffered an excess of 5,000 casualties.
94   As per the post-war *Report of the Battles Nomenclature Committee* (1921), the German counter-attack of 25 September was deemed part of the Battle of Menin Road Ridge. See Major A.F. Becke, *Order of Battle Divisions, Part 3B – New Army Divisions (30–41); & 63rd (R.N.) Division* (London: HMSO, 1945), p.38.
95   Ellis, *The Story of the Fifth Australian Division*, p.252.
96   C.E.W. Bean, *The AIF in France 1917*, Vol. IV (Sydney: Angus & Robertson, 1941), p.832.
97   See AWM 111.52, 'REPORT ON OPERATIONS of 15th AUST. INF. BDE. AT POLYGON WOOD ON 24th, 25th, 26th & 27th SEPTEMBER 1917' for Elliot's confidential after-action narrative of events.

Australia at Polygon Wood: A contemporary postcard.

The ground gained by the 2nd Army yesterday under your command, and the heavy losses inflicted on the enemy in the course of the day, constitute a complete defeat of the German forces opposed to you. Please convey to all Corps and Divisions engaged, my heartiest congratulations, and especially to the 33rd Division whose successful attack following a day of hard fighting, is deserving of all praise.[98]

Plumer himself singled out 33rd Division for having 'done fine work under extraordinarily difficult circumstances.' Circumstances of confusion resulting from intense hostile artillery fire; ravaged terrain; poor visibility; communications breakdown and enormous casualties.[99] The means by which the 33rd overcame all of this was due to the overall effectiveness of brigade and battalion commanders, junior officers and NCOs throughout a very trying ordeal during which the divisional line had bent but not broken. Regaining offensive momentum, the division's deadly firepower inflicted crippling losses on the enemy opposite. Indeed, most of *50th Reserve Division* was

---

98   TNA WO 95/2429/1: Special Order of the Day, 29 September 1917, 100th Brigade War Diary.
99   Ibid.

wiped out, *RIR 229* reporting some 2,500 casualties.[100] For all of the ensuing terror, confusion, temporary setbacks and manpower losses, 33rd Division rose to the occasion and demonstrated legendary British tenacity in defence and attack to overcome seemingly insurmountable odds.

100 Lloyd, *Passchendaele,* p.209.

15

'England, and London especially, may well be proud of you'
The 47th Division at Messines Ridge and Bourlon Wood in 1917

Richard Hendry

Introduction

As 1917 dawned, the 47th (formerly 2nd London) Division, a pre-war first-line
Territorial Force [TF] formation composed entirely of London Regiment infantry
battalions, had already been with the BEF on the Western Front for some 21 months.
Having seen action at Festubert, Loos, Vimy Ridge and the Somme, by year's end
it had played notable roles in the assault on Messines Ridge and the closing phase
of the Battle of Cambrai during which it repelled a massive German counter-attack
at Bourlon Wood. This chapter explores what this formation's preparation for and
achievements at Messines and, to some degree, performance at Bourlon, signify about
its post-Somme recovery, development and learning process.

With a sound pre-1917 reputation, it might appear counter-intuitive to select the
47th Division, as opposed to a division of low reputational standing or in need of
re-establishment of an earlier status after 1916, for such consideration. However, in
evaluating the applicability of the 'learning curve' (which remains a useful shorthand
for gradual evolution of BEF tactics), discerning evidence of progress with a battle-
hardened and reputable formation is as instructive as with a 'green' one and arguably,
more so.

The 47th Division faced challenges entering 1917. It had suffered significant
trauma taking High Wood during the Battle of Flers-Courcelette in September
1916. Indeed, this achievement generated enough controversy to prompt an
immediate replacement of its GOC. Moreover, the casualties incurred there and
in follow-up attacks entailed the absorption of sufficient drafts to imperil whatever TF ethos and esprit had survived to mid-1916. Although acknowledging
the High Wood feat, the relevant historiography conveys a hint that the 47th

Division prevailed despite itself and was in need of subsequent rehabilitation.[1] While contentious, this suggestion provides further impetus for this consideration of the division's 1917 experience.

47th Division to Spring 1917

The 47th Division disembarked in France in early March 1915, the second TF formation to do so. At its head was Major-General Charles St Leger Barter, GOC since August 1914.[2] The division enjoyed some advantages. Although two infantry brigades received new GOCs in the autumn of 1914,[3] there was significant continuity in lower commands, with three-quarters of battalion commanding officers [COs] having been in charge for at least six months.[4] The 47th Division had somewhat greater structural stability than other auxiliary formations: its headquarters establishment uniquely permitted the pre-mobilisation appointment of a General Staff Officer Grade 1.[5] Rapid creation of a satisfactorily-manned, administratively-proficient wartime staff function was practicable given the presence of the Post Office (1/8th London) and Civil Service (1/15th) Rifles battalions.[6] The remaining battalions of 140th Brigade were 1/6th (City of London Rifles) and 1/7th (City of London Rifles). In 141st Brigade were 1/17th (Poplar & Stepney Rifles), 1/18th (London Irish Rifles), 1/19th (St Pancras) and 1/20th (Blackheath & Woolwich) battalions. The 142nd Brigade was comprised of 1/21st (First Surrey Rifles), 1/22nd (The Queen's), 1/23rd (County of London) and 1/24th (The Queen's) battalions.[7]

It was during the last days of the Battle of Festubert (15-25 May 1915) that 47th Division broke its 'assault duck', advancing with 'a steadiness and precision worthy of seasoned troops.'[8] It featured prominently when attached to First Army during the Battle of Loos in September. On the extreme right of the British line, right flank exposed, 47th Division was to advance deep into a mile-wide valley bristling with

1   R. Hendry, 'The 47th Division at High Wood, September 1916 – Success against the Odds or an Odd Success?', *Journal of the Society for Army Historical Research*, Vol. 99, No. 396 (Spring 2021), pp.70, 93-94.
2   A. Maude (ed.), *The History of the 47th (London) Division 1914-1919* (London: Amalgamated Press, 1922), pp.3-4, 230 and Appendix D.
3   See Maude, *47th Division* p.232 and Appendix D.
4   K.W. Mitchinson, *The Territorial Force at War 1914-1916* (Basingstoke: Palgrave MacMillan, 2014), p.166.
5   Ibid., p.21
6   Ibid., p.161
7   This order of battle remained until the BEF's reduction of the number of battalions per brigade in early 1918. All numerical references (1/6th Battalion, 1/7th Battalion and so on) in the main text are, unless otherwise stated, to those of the London Regiment.
8   J.E. Edmonds, *Military Operations France & Belgium 1915*, Vol. II (London: MacMillan, 1928), p.75.

fortified coal mining installations prior to forming a flank against counter-attack from the south.[9] The division secured almost all of its objectives within three hours and, notwithstanding heavy casualties, was ready to face counter-attacks soon after, some parties defending positions even after neighbouring units had withdrawn.[10] Then corps commander Lieutenant-General Sir Henry Rawlinson acknowledged that the 47th Division, although having comparatively few casualties (still a note-worthy 1,500-plus), 'did well in establishing the right flank barage [sic] and holding the ground gained with great tenacity.'[11] Lower-profile, but still costly, spells followed at Vimy Ridge and environs in the ensuing 10 months.[12] In late July 1916, infantry manpower strength restored and two brigadiers newly appointed,[13] the division was ordered south to participate in the Somme offensive.

On 15 September, attached to Lieutenant-General William Pulteney's III Corps, the Londoners achieved what had eluded Rawlinson's Fourth Army since mid-July – the capture of High Wood.[14] This highlight of the Flers-Courcelette offensive was attained through a lengthy spell of intensive, sometimes bespoke training, hard fighting, and effective support from flanking units.[15] It owed little to the debutant tanks and not as much as might have been expected to artillery support, misjudge-ments on which contributed to a robust German defence, resultant crowding in the divisional trenches and consequent heavy casualties.[16] The inability of the 47th Division to secure High Wood on schedule or subsequent objectives as per Rawlinson's unre-alistic, Haig influenced battle plan,[17] slowed III Corps and extended Fourth Army's offensive efforts well into November, before seasonal weather halted operations.

9   Ibid., pp.182-86.

10   Edmonds, *Military Operations 1915*, Vol. II, pp.187-91; Maude, *47th Division*, pp.31-32; N. Cherry, *Most Unfavourable Ground: The Battle of Loos 1915* (Solihull: Helion & Co., 2005), p.219.

11   Edmonds, *Military Operations 1915*, Vol. II, p.392; Churchill Archives, Rawlinson, RWLN 1/3: Diary entry, 26 September 1915.

12   J.E. Edmonds, *Military Operations, France & Belgium 1916*, Vol. I (London: MacMillan, 1932), pp.222, 224 Casualties resulting from a German attack at Vimy in May 1916 are given as 1,571; Maude, *47th Division*, p.56 provides a figure in excess of 2,000.

13   The National Archives [TNA] WO 95/2701: 47th Division War Diary, 1 July 1916 – 8,465 across three brigades; Maude, *47th Division*, pp.59-60.

14   For previous attempts, see M. Harrison, *High Wood* (Barnsley: Pen & Sword, 2017); T. Norman, *The Hell They Called High Wood – The Somme* (Barnsley: Pen & Sword, 2007 [1984]).

15   W. Miles, *Military Operations, France & Belgium 1916*, Vol. II (London: MacMillan, 1938), pp.331-36; W. Philpott, *Bloody Victory: The Sacrifice on the Somme and the Making of the Twentieth Century* (London: Little, Brown, 2009), p.366.

16   R. Prior & T. Wilson, *The Somme* (New Haven, Connecticut: Yale University Press, 2006), pp.216-28, 235-36; T. Pidgeon, *The Tanks at Flers: An Account of the First Use of Tanks in War at the Battle of Flers-Courcelette, The Somme, 15th September 1916* (Cobham: Fairmile Books, 1995), p.103.

17   Prior & Wilson, *Somme*, pp.216-19, 226-27; Miles, *1916* Vol. II, p.335.

Barter had little defence when accorded responsibility – justified or contrived – for such 'shortcomings' despite clear commitment to his division's cause.[18] Prior to its assault on Eaucourt l'Abbaye, situated due north of High Wood, in early October, the unfortunate GOC had been sent home to be replaced by Major-General George Gorringe, who, soon after its fraught assault on the notorious Butte de Warlencourt (the first of several Fourth Army failures there), took 47th Division north to the Ypres Salient. Gorringe (a.k.a. 'Blood Orange'), although associated with the recent Kut-al-Amara debacle in Mesopotamia, was deemed a relentless, cool and calm commander. He would remain GOC until the war's end.

Major-General George Gorringe. (Maude, *The 47th (London) Division, 1914-1919*)

Political and Strategic Backdrop

Messines Ridge has been called 'a great victory … with swift completeness … one of the great victories of the war' and 'a textbook operation', a rare set-piece attack which went precisely to plan.[19] Yet, the offensive was, strictly, only ever a preliminary to a larger one which would finally breakout of the Ypres Salient and drive to the Belgian coast.[20] British GHQ's hankering, since 1915, for such a 'Northern Western Front' campaign was delayed whilst the BEF played handmaiden to the French with major efforts at Loos, the Somme and Arras. Notwithstanding their shared desire to initiate major action around the salient, BEF C-in-C Field Marshal Sir Douglas Haig and General Sir Herbert Plumer (GOC Second Army), differed on methodology. That divergence

18 For examples, see Mitchinson, *Territorial Force*, pp.70, 112, 154; Maude, *47th Division*, pp.26-27; Edmonds, *1915,* Vol. II, p.186.

19 J.E. Edmonds, *Military Operations France & Belgium 1917*, Vol. II (London: HMSO, 1948), p.87; R. Neillands, *The Great War Generals on the Western Front 1914-1918* (London: Robinson, 1999), p.376.

20 See Neillands, p.372 for an alternative principal motive; P. Griffith, *Battle Tactics of the Western Front: The British Army's Art of Attack 1916-18* (New Haven, Connecticut: Yale 1996), p.211 for a different emphasis.

between the cavalryman's desire for breakthrough and the infantryman's 'bite and hold' instincts resulted in subterfuge by Haig, who manipulated Plumer out of leading that larger 'centrepiece in the new show', covertly assuring General Sir Hubert Gough early on that his Fifth Army would spearhead it.[21] Further detail of this context is beyond this chapter's purview. Nevertheless, this summary demonstrates that the backdrop to Second Army's final preparations for Messines was not wholly propitious.[22]

Preparation and Planning by GHQ and Second Army

Although benefiting from much thought during 1915-16, the Messines preparations did not, as the Arras and Nivelle offensives stalled, attain full focus until spring 1917. On 7 May Haig finally gave the formal 'go ahead' for a Flanders offensive. Plumer offered a timescale of 'one month' to ready an attack on Messines Ridge. In literal response, 'Z-Day' was set for 7 June, the first Operation Order [O.O.] being issued on 10 May shortly after corps commanders were asked to submit final attack schemes for perusal by Plumer and Haig.[23]

Responsible for the Ypres salient since assuming command of Second Army in May 1915, Plumer knew the Messines Ridge well.[24] Of its dominance by relative height (45 metres maximum), increased with entrenchments, fortification and some 280 miles of wire, the GOC Second Army observed that 'the enemy will not lightly give up the advantage he has held so long …'[25] By early summer 1917, the challenge had grown with German application of 'defence in depth'.[26] Cartographically, the frontline, following the ridge's salient configuration, resembled an archer's bow, while, up to two miles down the rear or eastern edge, the principal deep position – *Sehnen Stellung* or Oosttaverne Line – marked the bow's drawstring. Moreover, surprise would not be the panacea. Despite documented concern about maintaining secrecy and official statements that the imminent assault was a ploy to draw enemy reserves from the Arras front, a combination of Teutonic logic, observation, British over-confidence and lax security advertised Second Army's intentions to the enemy who augmented their artillery assets during April and early May.[27]

---

21   Griffith, *Battle Tactics of the Western Front*, p.211; Edmonds, *Military Operations 1917*, Vol. II, p.20.

22   For a useful summary, see Neillands, *Great War Generals*, pp.364-72.

23   I. Passingham, *Pillars of Fire: The Battle of Messines Ridge, June 1917* (Stroud: Sutton, 1998), p.20; Edmonds, *Military Operations 1917*, Vol. II, pp.32, 416-417 and Appendix VIII; TNA WO 95/275-3(1): 'Second Army O.O. No. 1', 10 May 1917, Second Army War Diary; TNA WO 95/275-3(2): 'G/126', 8 May 1917, Second Army War Diary.

24   Neillands, *Great War Generals*, p.364.

25   Ibid., pp.363, 375.

26   Edmonds, *Military Operations 1917*, Vol. II, pp.43-44.

27   TNA WO 95/275-3(1), p.68, 'G.103', 8 May 1917, Second Army War Diary; TNA WO 95/275-3(1): 'Second Army O.O. No. 1', Second Army War Diary; S. Robbins, *British*

Plumer's assault force, more than 80,000 men,[28] comprised three frontline corps (from north to south, X, IX and II Anzac), each deploying three divisions in line, with XIV Corps in Reserve. The 47th Division was attached to X Corps with 23rd, 41st and, in reserve, 24th divisions.

The operation's initial shape had been discernible since mid-March.[29] On a 10-mile front, from St Yves–Ploegsteert Wood to Mount Sorrel–Observatory Ridge, successive infantry waves would pass through, seizing the crest and summit plateau of Messines Ridge (Blue Line) within eight hours and securing possession of its eastern slope (Black Line) in another similar period. The X Corps had the northernmost stretch, with the 47th Division astride the Ypres–Comines Canal, its boundaries running along the southwest fringe of Verbrandenmolen–Battle Wood (left) and on a south-easterly line from Triangular Wood to Ravine Wood. This scheme, contemplating a general advance of over a mile, was itself only settled after Haig induced Plumer to telescope into one day what the latter had originally envisaged for at least two.[30] Then, with three weeks to Z-Day, Haig changed the final objective to the more distant Oosttaverne Line, entailing waiting time (now five hours) adjustments for all corps to catch up at the Black Line.[31] On 19 May, O.O. No. 2 formally confirmed this extension, at some points to approximately 4,000 yards.[32]

For this task the infantry would be generously supported. On their third major offensive outing of the war, tanks – 76 recently introduced Mark IVs (with enhanced firepower and protection), supported by 12 Mark Is and IIs, each transporting five re-supply 'fills' – were concealed about the rear area in late May.[33] Their offensive task commenced from the Blue Line and, if feasible, extended to the Oosttaverne Line.[34] Underground mines, 24 in number, averaging almost 50,000 lbs of explosive and mostly in readiness by summer 1916, were to be detonated simultaneously at zero hour (3.10 a.m.) from galleries 100 feet below significant points along the German

Generalship on the Western Front: Defeat into Victory (London: Routledge, 2005), pp.73-74; J. Sheldon, *The German Army at Passchendaele* (Barnsley: Pen & Sword, 2007), p.1; Edmonds, *Military Operations 1917,* Vol. II, p.30; Passingham, *Pillars of Fire,* p.45.

28   Passingham, p.35.

29   TNA WO 95/275-1: 'G.288', 18 March 1917, Second Army War Diary.

30   TNA WO 95/275-3(2): 'G.57', 7 May 1917, Second Army War Diary; Edmonds, *Military Operations 1917,* Vol. II, pp.15-19, 32; Neillands, *Great War Generals,* pp.366-67.

31   TNA WO 95/275-3(2): 'G.505', 15 May 1917 and 'G.695', 18 May 1917, Second Army War Diary; G. Powell, *Plumer: The Soldiers' General* (Barnsley: Pen & Sword, 2004), p.184.

32   TNA WO 95/275-3(1): 'Second Army O.O. No. 2', 19 May 1917, Second Army War Diary; Edmonds, *Military Operations 1917,* Vol. II, pp.32, 418 and Appendix IX.

33   Edmonds, *Military Operations 1917,* Vol. II, p.33; TNA WO 95/101-1: 2nd Tank Brigade Diary, 22, 24 and 26 May 1917; A.J. Smithers, *A New Excalibur: The Development of the Tank 1909-1939* (London: Guild, 1986), p.115 (not referenced, but obtained from TNA WO 95/101-3: 'Report', 2nd Tank Brigade War Diary).

34   TNA WO 95/275-3(2): 'G.691' & 'G.695', 18 May, Second Army War Diary; TNA WO 95/275-4: 'SZ.101/6' (2nd Tank Brigade), 2 June 1917, Second Army War Diary; TNA WO 95/852-5: 'Instructions', 1 June 1917, X Corps War Diary.

line.[35] None, however, lay under 47th Division's frontage, the nearest being 500-1,000 yards beyond each flank.

If subterranean mine concentration was to provide the crescendo, accumulated artillery firepower was to set the decisive tempo. Bolstered by batteries transferred from Arras, Second Army's stock totalled 2,266 guns (one for every seven yards).[36] This accumulation was based on a calculative approach, so that the final number of 'heavies', 756, was derived from separate equations for counter-battery work (1:4 for flanking and 1:1 for forward German guns, totalling 341), for infantry-protective fire (one howitzer/45 yards, thus 378 overall) and a 5 percent quotient (38) of 'super heavies' – 6-inch and larger guns plus 12 and 15-inch howitzers.[37] This formidable aggregate represented more than sheer numbers. Particular attention was paid to mathematical and timing calculations; reconnaissance, spotting and ranging work facilitated by the RFC's air superiority; and, to dupe German batteries into revealing themselves for effective counter-battery work, full creeping barrage demonstrations (recommended by *SS 135*) – two by each corps and one on the entire Second Army front – in the first week of June.[38] Centrally, deliberations produced a detailed, two-week fire plan and a barrage timetable, including its extension to the Oosttaverne Line.[39] By the end of May, via effective and expanded railway, tramway and road networks, 144,000 tons of ammunition had been amassed, mostly for a preliminary bombardment originally planned to start five days before Z-Day.[40] The Germans, confident of British intentions, were not surprised when the bombardment started earlier, but were still discomfited by 3.5 million rounds fired in the 10 days before offensive. The last two pre-assault days were largely given over to counter-battery work – under official guidance, an 'unceasing procedure' – against the far from passive enemy emplacements, bringing the full preliminary bombardment's start

35   Edmonds, *Military Operations 1917*, Vol. II, pp.35-38; Passingham, *Pillars of Fire*, pp.56-57, 66; C. Harrington, *Plumer of Messines* (London: John Murray, 1935), p.86. Only 19 mines were detonated on 7 June, three having been side-lined and two subsequently lost.
36   Powell, *Plumer*, p.174.
37   Passingham, *Pillars of Fire*, pp.39-40. It is unclear what account the 1:4 'flanking gun' ratio and resultant total took of the guns of VIII Corps, a non-participant in the infantry attack, but whose guns to the north were well-placed to deal with such enemy pieces. See H. Jones, *The War In The Air: Being the Story of the Part Played in the Great War by the Royal Air Force*, Vol. IV (Oxford: Clarendon, 1934), p.131.
38   *SS 135: Instructions for the Training of Divisions for Offensive Action* (GHQ, December 1916), p.23 (Section III, Para.9(b)); TNA WO 95/275-3(2): 'G.393', 31 May 1917, Second Army War Diary; Edmonds, *Military Operations 1917*, Vol. II, pp.42-43, 47-48; For the RFC, see Jones, *War In The Air*, Vol. IV, pp.109-37.
39   TNA WO 95/275-3(2): 'G.799', 20 May 1917, Second Army War Diary; Edmonds, *Military Operations 1917*, Vol. II, p.35; Griffith, *Battle Tactics of the Western Front*, p.86.
40   TNA WO 95/275-3(2): 'G.125', 8 May, Second Army War Diary; Edmonds, *Military Operations 1917*, Vol. II, pp.39-40, 42.

forward to Z-7.[41] Despite frenetic attempts by *Fourth Army* to reinforce *Gruppe Wytschaete* (responsible for a nine-mile front from St Yves to Mt Sorrel) artillery assets, the 3:1 gun superiority enjoyed by Second Army when the bombardment started was never challenged.[42]

The aggregate of arms for Messines constituted 'an almighty concentration of fighting power.'[43] Major-General Charles 'Tim' Harington, Plumer's Chief of Staff, recalled the final month's preparation as 'wonderful', with Second Army provided with 'everything we wanted.'[44] This might resemble gluttonous self-satisfaction, but, addressing the increased range of and reduced timescale for objectives, Plumer sought to employ and combine weaponry with deliberation. His approach was underpinned by the contents of several early 1917 GHQ publications, that sought to advance tactical appreciation by distilling experience accrued from the BEF's 'decisive reappraisal' prompted by the Somme campaign.[45] Recognising that tactical facility was a product as much of training as battlefield experience, these instructional Stationery Service [SS] pamphlets emphasised the former. Alongside *SS 135*, two others, respectively for battalions and armies,[46] were influential, but February 1917's *SS 143: Instructions for the Training of Platoons for Offensive Action*, was the 'seminal document'.[47] Detailed and prescriptive in parts (although open to differing interpretations),[48] this elevated the platoon to '*the* unit of the attack',[49] self-sufficient and adaptable in battle through its organisation into four sections, delineated by standard issue weapons – rifle and bayonet, Lewis Gun, rifle grenade, and hand grenade.[50]

All *SS* materials were applied to training regimes for corps dissemination, as were lessons from Arras, especially on scheduling artillery barrages, effective

41   *SS 135*, Sec. III, Para. 3 (d); TNA WO 95/275-3(2): 'G.963', 5 May 1917 and 'G.104', 8 May 1917, Second Army War Diary; TNA WO 95/275-4: 'OAD.464', 31 May 1917, Second Army War Diary; TNA WO 95/275-3(2):'G.393', Second Army War Diary.

42   Edmonds, *Military Operations 1917*, Vol. II, pp.44, 48-49, 93; Jones, *War In The Air*, Vol. IV, p.125; P. Strong & S. Marble, *Artillery in the Great War* (Barnsley: Pen & Sword, 2011), p.134.

43   Griffith, *Battle Tactics of the Western Front*, p.86.

44   Harington, *Plumer of Messines*, p.84.

45   Robbins, *British Generalship on the Western Front*, p.95.

46   *SS 144* (February 1917); *SS 152* (June 1917). Although *SS 152* cannot have been directly available for Messines Ridge preparation, most of its content, drawn from earlier learning and published within weeks of the attack, must be taken to have practically influenced preparations. See also Passingham, *Pillars of Fire*, pp.29-30; Robbins, *British Generalship on the Western Front*, p.95; Edmonds, *Military Operations 1917*, Vol. II, p.35.

47   See Introduction by Stephen Bull in (Comp.), *An Officer's Manual of the Western Front 1914-1918* (London: Conway, 2008), p.11.

48   Griffith, *Battle Tactics of the Western Front*, p.95.

49   *SS 143*, Part III – General Remarks (original emphasis) in (Comp.), *Officer's Manual*, p.126; reinforced by *SS 135*, Section 4, Paragraph 5.

50   *SS 143*, Part I, Para.1 in (Comp.), *Officer's Manual*, p.118; Griffith, pp.95-100.

counter-battery work and organising machine-gun barrages.[51] However, Plumer, not the most notable innovator but epitomising 'Trust, Training and Thoroughness',[52] was an excellent administrator. Additionally, notwithstanding further intrusions by Haig in late May,[53] he practised and extended a consultative ethos with frequent liaison and post-exercise de-briefings, ensuring that his staff were trusted and subordinate commanders contributed to assault plans.[54] The celebrated concern of 'Daddy Plumer' or 'Old Plum and Apple' for the 'regimental soldier', encapsulated in his dictum 'waste metal, not flesh', was substantiated by a focus on battleground scale models and training replicas, finessing artillery support and prioritising attention to small details of timing or distance to protect infantrymen.[55]

Notwithstanding tentative discussions about starting several days early (Haig's idea) or late (GOC X Corps Lieutenant-General Sir Thomas Morland seems to have been prominent in that lobby),[56] Z-Day was confirmed as 7 June three days before-hand.[57] Zero-Hour [ZH], 3.10 am, was confirmed on 6 June.[58]

47th Division: Objectives and Preparations

For Messines, on a front of about one mile riven by the canal, the final objective (Black Line) of the 47th Division's two leading brigades, 140th and 142nd – each augmented by one battalion from 141st Brigade – was formed by Oblong and Opal Reserve trenches running behind Ravine Wood and the stables within the grounds of the fortified White Chateau. This would control the plateau on the ridge summit. Enroute, the initial assault units would secure two intermediate objectives, together constituting Phase 1 – first the Red Line (broadly, on the line of Oak Support trench, some 350 yards behind the German front); then the Blue Line, the attainment of which would entail crossing the northern extremity of the raised *Dammstrasse*, seizing the White Chateau itself and occupying a line extending northeast from Oak Reserve Trench. This went beyond *SS 135's* prescription that leading battalion objectives

51   Edmonds, *Military Operations 1917*, Vol. II, p.35.
52   Harington, *Plumer of Messines*, p.79; Simkins, 'Herbert Plumer' in I. Beckett & S. Corvi (eds.), *Haig's Generals* (Barnsley: Pen & Sword, 2006), pp.150-51; Strong & Marble *Artillery*, pp.133-134.
53   Powell, *Plumer*, pp.185-86; Edmonds, *Military Operations 1917*, Vol. II, pp.46-47. See also below.
54   Powell, pp.156, 171; Passingham, *Pillars of Fire*, pp.25, 33; Simkins, 'Herbert Plumer, p.150.
55   Harington, *Plumer of Messines*, pp.82, 87, 89; Passingham, *Pillars of Fire*, pp.24-25, 33; Neillands, *Great War Generals*, p.374; Simkins, 'Herbert Plumer', p.151.
56   TNA WO 95/275-4: 'OAD. 464', 31 May 1917, Second Army War Diary; TNA WO 95/275-4: 'G.452', 1 June 1917, Second Army War Diary.
57   TNA WO 95/275-4: 'G.652', 4 June 1917, Second Army War Diary.
58   TNA WO 95/275-4: 'G.754', 6 June 1917, Second Army War Diary.

be confined to the front-line system.[59] For 142nd Brigade's second wave battalions, progression from second to final objective involved one crossing the canal, as it bent and ran east for about half a mile, to link up with 140th Brigade; the other overcoming the formidable Long Spoil Bank [LSB] fortification on the northern bank.

Harington subsequently opined that Second Army entered battle 'in great heart knowing that their chief had done everything possible for them'.[60] That sentiment seemingly pervaded the 47th. Buoyed by both the visual evidence of Plumer's fastidious preparations and the formidable bombardment that had rained down on the Germans for days, its officers and men were later said to have 'never before … been in better spirits or more confident of success' than on 7 June.[61] This brio also stemmed from the division's own circumstances. Since transferring from the Somme, it had been part of X Corps under Morland (in Haig's eyes, an improved commander since July 1916).[62] In April 1917, after six months engaged in raiding and mine-blowing, the Londoners took up the very positions, astride the Canal,[63] from which they would attack on 7 June; that itself only a minimal lateral shift from their previous sector. Thus, unlike the 47th's introduction to High Wood, when it had moved into Fourth Army's training area near Abbeville only in early August and proceeded to the back areas behind Albert just four weeks before going into action, it was familiar with its ground.

This 'internal' advantage was slightly diminished by some drag factors. First, there was the need to integrate new drafts, trained in basics but still sometimes termed 'backward'.[64] However, this was not unmanageable. Casualties for the post-Somme period (November 1916 to May 1917) were relatively light at a monthly average of 307, under half the figure for the hospitalised (including sick), from whom returners contributed to 'reinforcements'. The latter averaged 1,200 per month. Thus the monthly average for drafts can be estimated at 30-50 per battalion, an extrapolation supported by the relatively few arrivals recorded in diaries. As June opened, the total infantry strength of 47th Division amounted

59   *SS 135*, Section II, Paras. (a) & (d), p.14.
60   Harington, *Plumer*, p.100.
61   Maude, *47th Division*, p.98. See also C. Planck (Comp.), *The History of the 7th (City of London) Battalion, The London Regiment* (London: Old Comrades' Association, 1946), p.113; Anon., *The History of the Prince of Wales' Own Civil Service Rifles* (Uckfield: Naval & Military Press reprint of 1921 edition), p.138; R. Herbert Shaw (ed.), *The 23rd London Regiment 1798-1919* (London: Times Publishing, 1936), p.44.
62   Haig diary, 22 July 1916 and 22 May 1917. G. Sheffield & J. Bourne (eds.), *Douglas Haig: War Diaries and Letters 1914-1918* (London: Phoenix, 2006), pp.208, 295.
63   TNA WO 95/852-2(1): 'X Corps O.O. No. 73', 2 April 1917, X Corps War Diary; TNA WO 95/2702: '47 Div. O.O. No. 133', 4 April 1917 and 'O.O. No. 134', n.d., 47th Division War Diary; TNA WO 95/852-2 (1): 8-9 April 1917, X Corps War Diary.
64   TNA WO 95/2732: 140th Brigade MG Coy War Diary, 4-10 May 1917.

White Chateau stables (top) and Spoil Bank bunker c.1916.

to 12,615.[65] Second, whereas, in August-September 1916 the division's late move towards the line had, at least, allowed full focus on training (including an all-brigade gathering) in back areas,[66] it was never wholly out of the line in the three months preceding 7 June 1917. This resulted from both manning an active sector and limited scope for transfer between armies. The Battle of Arras, involving First and Third armies, ground on until May and Fifth Army was involved in preparations for the Third Ypres offensive. Nonetheless, the high command's longstanding commitment to Messines allowed for efficient use of available time during those three months, the division's training augmenting the esprit generated over earlier successes and firing troop morale and self-confidence, reportedly as far as their 'truly thirsting for blood' by mid-May.[67]

Taped-out ground (replicating trench objectives), which the 47th Division helped to pioneer in 1915,[68] featured heavily in its training programme. In the timing, intensity and sophistication of this technique, now enshrined in *SS 135*,[69] the division's preparations nevertheless differed from High Wood (changes also apparent in the diaries of its flanking divisions – 41st on the left, 23rd on the right).[70] Training with a broad eye for the pending Messines operation was evident from mid-March at least. As early as 4 April, in Second Army's training area beyond St Omer, the 1/22nd Battalion (a first-wave battalion) practised the assault over a course representing trenches 'from the Bluff to Petticoat Lane' (a sector of the enemy line that would attacked for real in two months'). The exercise was repeated the next day as a brigade battle practice with 1/24th Battalion, which was also in the first-wave.[71]

---

65   All figures calculated from data within TNA WO 95/2707: 47th Division Adjutant and Quartermaster General Diary, pp.191-192, 194, 205-207, 209, 217-219, 221, 226-227, 229, 234-236, 238, 248-250, 252, 259-261, 263-264. The total strength (from p.264) was 382 below the 47th Division's 'high water mark' for the period end of February 1917. See TNA WO 95/2707.

66   Hendry, 'The 47th Division at High Wood, September 1916', *JSAHR*, Vol. 99, No. 396 (Spring 2021), p.77

67   TNA WO 95/2729: 1/6th London Regiment War Diary, 6 June 1917; TNA WO 95/2732: 1/21st London Regiment War Diary, 5 June 1917; Anon., *A War Record of the 21st London Regiment (First Surrey Rifles), 1914-1919* (Uckfield: Naval & Military Press reprint of 1927 edition), p.72; Anon., *Civil Service Rifles*, p.137.

68   Maude, *47th Division*, pp.26-27; Edmonds, *Military Operations 1915*, Vol. II, pp.186-87.

69   *SS 135*, Introduction, Para. 7.

70   See the war diaries of 123rd Brigade (TNA WO 95/2636) situated on left of 41st Division, and its first-wave units; 11th Queen's (TNA WO 95/2638); 10th Royal W Kent (TNA WO 95/2639) and 23rd Middlesex (TNA WO 95/2639); 69th Brigade (TNA WO 95/2183) on right of 23rd Division, and component first-wave units: 10th West Riding (TNA WO 95/2184); 8th Yorkshire (TNA WO 95/2184) and 11th W. Yorkshire (TNA WO 95/2184).

71   TNA WO 95/2743: 1/22nd London Regiment War Diary; TNA WO 95/2744: 1/24th London Regiment War Diary. Even at this remove, the document on 1/22nd London's detailed dispositions for 5 April 1917 (TNA WO 95/2743) mentions changes for the 'actual show'.

From 4 April – when 142nd Brigade had already completed eight or nine days more intensive training – until 2 June (the final mention of training in any unit diary), there are, within the division's component units, 44 separately listed practice attacks.[72] And, for battalions whose diaries are lost, vague or obscure, at least 15 additional sessions can be inferred from more forthcoming diaries of units training with them at a relevant time.[73] Some of these inferences arise in the context of brigade exercises, the two forward brigades (140th and 142nd) managing at least two.[74] Of the 44 clear references, only six explicitly mention replicated ground or trenches, but many others imply such, there being no other reason for widespread use of 'marked courses'. The *proportion* of divisional training days over the 12-weeks preceding 7 June, half of that in the six-week preparations for High Wood, was similar to that for 41st Division but markedly lower than 23rd Division.[75] Moreover, the *number* of days devoted to practice attacks, many 'bespoke', was akin to the time accrued by these flanking formations and almost matched that of August-September 1916.[76] This chimes with the most cogent battalion history, which, noting differences between preparations for the two attacks, observed that 1917's training was not as 'strenuous' but 'the Division marched straight to its training ground' and 'the marked out course quickly made its appearance.'[77] The overall increased troop experience that enabled such a direct approach was matched by that of higher command's promotion of maximum efficiency in offensive rehearsals by specifying assault brigades and eliminating non-starters early on.[78] This allowed battalions to

72   Also, variously, 'Tactical Exercise'; 'Open warfare'; 'Brigade Field Day/Exercise'; 'Brigade Attack (Course)' and 'Brigade Tactical Scheme'.
73   The 1/8th London Regiment (TNA WO 95/2731) war diaries are missing for April or May 1917. The 1/15th London Regiment war diary for 16-30 May 1917 (TNA WO 95/2732) records training during 140th Brigade exercises with 1/6th and 1/7th London regiments which performed six practice attacks between 23-29 May. For 1/15th London Regiment, practice attacks are confirmed in general terms by Anon., *Civil Service Rifles*, p.137; 1/18th (war diary, 1-5 and 13-25 April 1917 (TNA WO 95/2737) during 141st Brigade exercises with 1/17th, 1/19th and 1/20th London regiments which did one, three and one practice attack respectively between 18-25 April; 1/21st (war diary, 27-31 March and 1-7 April 1917 (TNA WO 95/2732) records training during 142nd Brigade exercises with 1/22nd, 1/23rd and 1/24th London regiments, at least two of which did practice attacks daily from 4-7 April.
74   140th Brigade on 28 and 29 May 1917, 142nd Brigade on 5 and 7 April 1917. This frequency is consistent with that subsequently advocated by *SS 152*, Section III, Para. 1.
75   See WO 95 war diaries above.
76   The 47th Division eschewed the all-brigade 'Divisional Attack Practice' sessions that had featured in early September 1916 and for which 23rd Division (unusually, relieved in its entirety) had the opportunity during 2-4 May 1917. See TNA WO 95/2168: 23rd Division War Diary.
77   Anon., *Civil Service Rifles*, p.137.
78   Ibid.

be paired as they would be for the coming attack,[79] another contrast with High Wood when archival evidence for such accurate rehearsals is scant.[80]

The form of these rehearsals had not stagnated. As well as site variations and size, special features were integrated in order to obtain realism and address possible contingencies. Fire and movement was given authenticity through firing from the hip during field exercises, a recommendation of *SS 135*.[81] The artillery barrage, with which *SS 135* deemed infantry collaboration essential,[82] was represented by men carrying flags.[83] Communications between the two arms was fostered: officers and telephonists of 235th Brigade RFA joined 140th Brigade at St Omer 'with a view to practising with the Infantry the application of Brigade forward station.'.[84] Work on occupation of an outpost line beyond the enemy trenches was also included.[85] One relevant battalion war diary mentions collaboration with a RFC contact plane for two exercises.[86] To foster initiative in the lower ranks, part of 142nd Brigade repeated practice attacks without platoon or company leaders.[87] Notwithstanding occasional references to exercises being directed or supervised (rather than merely watched) by divisional or corps commanders and staffs,[88] such lower-level confidence was, according to the now-established, platoon-centric doctrine of *SS 143* and *SS 135*, to be encouraged. Thus platoon commanders underwent separate instruction, both in leadership and, feeding into broader practice sessions, in tactical exercises or schemes.[89] And, despite only one diary reference in terms to *SS 143*,[90] it is clear that, amongst the specialist weapons training that the now all-round platoon demanded and the grander-scale practice attacks, much attention was paid to training with platoons and companies.

79   TNA WO 95/2728: 140th Brigade War Diary for 25-26 May 1917. As the designation of attacking brigades was seemingly only made in late April (see TNA WO 95/2702, pp.624-28, '47th (London) Division: General Advance Scheme – General Instructions, G.90/15/2', 29 April 1917, 47th Division War Diary, this being obviously preceded by a 'Warning Order No. 1' on 21 April 1917) it is not clear how 142nd Brigade apparently knew such detail for its appropriately paired work in the first week of April (see above).

80   Hendry, 'The 47th Division at High Wood, September 1916', p.78.

81   *SS 135*, Part V, Para.8, p.27.

82   Ibid., p.15 (Part III, Para.1) and pp.19-20 (Paras.4(d)–5).

83   TNA WO 95/2743: 1/22nd London Regiment War Diary, 5 April 1917.

84   TNA WO 95/2711: 47th Division RHA/RFA War Diary, 13 May 1917.

85   TNA WO 95/2738: 1/20th London Regiment War Diary, 25 April 1917.

86   TNA WO 95/2730: 1/7th London Regiment War Diary, 28-29 May 1917.

87   TNA WO 95/2744: 1/24th Diary London Regiment War Diary, 29-30 May 1917.

88   TNA WO 95/2738: 1/19th London Regiment War Diary, 22 and 25 April 1917. An overarching principle of the later *SS 152*, Chapter II, Part I, Section I, Para.2, which asserted that a division's training should be under 'the personal guidance of its Divisional Commander'.

89   TNA WO 95/2728: 140th Brigade War Diary, 26 April 1917; TNA WO 95/2730: 1/7th London Regiment War Diary, 25 April; TNA WO 95/2744: 1/23rd London Regiment War Diary, 2 and 4 May 1917; TNA WO 95/2744: 1/24th London Regiment War Diary, 10-12 May 1917.

90   TNA WO 95/2729: 1/6th London Regiment War Diary, 21 May 1917.

This mandated approach was 'progressive', both within the unit in question and, as proficiency increased, upwards.[91]

Artillery and Other Positional Firepower

Notwithstanding this efficiency in infantry training, other arms were to be integrated into the assault plans. As previously mentioned, Second Army did not leave to chance the effective combination of infantry and artillery, a major concern of SS 135.[92] And, by June 1917, the dependence of successful infantry assaults on available firepower in a quasi-siege setting was clear to the 47th Division's officers and men, if only because of artillery shortcomings at Loos and High Wood. If official guidance and past battle experience were insufficient, the recent, initially successful Arras offensive and the troops' own experience put the question beyond doubt.[93]

The 47th Division's component field artillery brigades (235th and 236th) were augmented by five from Second Army. This amalgam amassed 120 18-pdrs and 42 4.5-inch howitzers, in six groups (four in 'Double Groups', centred around Swan Chateau and Bedford House respectively). Their positions straddled the canal to a width of about 800 yards on the south side and 1,500 yards to the north. With the exception of 'F Group' (allocated to divisional and brigade commanders for 'special liaison' with the infantry and dispersed on a slightly advanced line between Voormezeele and Maple Copse), they extended back from level with Bedford House to behind Swan Chateau. All of the battery positions selected were capable of laying down a barrage 500 yards beyond the final objective. Some were specified as suitable for wire-cutting and, if required, for 60-pdr batteries to occupy. By 21 May, it was stipulated that, in readiness for operations at short notice (by then a five-day preliminary bombardment was scheduled for early June), all preparations should be completed by month's end. This was readily achieved, the Army artillery brigades completing registration on 31 May.[94] 'Affiliated to' 47th Division for bombardment and destruction purposes, was Second Army's 'Centre Double Siege Group', its 6, 8 and 9.2-inch howitzers ensconced in positions north and west of Dickebusch, some 3-4.5 miles from the German frontline and to the right of the divisional sector. Second Army's 'Northern

---

91   See SS 143, Part II Para 3(ii) in (Comp.), Officer's Manual, p.123, re-incremental training within a platoon and SS 152, Chapter II, Part I, Section I, Para.13 and Appendix XIII with regard to four-week programme, gradually shifting emphasis from section/platoon training to battalion/brigade training.
92   SS 135, Section III.
93   See above.
94   TNA WO 95/2702: 'Instructions No. 9 (Artillery)', 15 May 1917, 47th Division War Diary; TNA WO 95/2711, '47th Div Artillery Instructions No. 1', 21 May 1917, 47th Division RHA/RFA War Diary (positions from Appendix I, p.462); TNA WO 95/2711: 47th Div RHA/RFA War Diary, 31 May 1917.

Counter Battery Double Group' – the majority of its 6-inch and 60-pdr batteries plus 6 to 12-inch howitzers directly behind that sector, but overall ranged from north of Dickebusch to Ypres – made its contribution to the aforementioned negation of 50 percent of German guns on the entire army front even before 7 June had dawned.[95]

For much of May, there were recorded daily stock arrivals by train at the Divisional Ammunition Refilling Point.[96] A lengthy period in situ allowed contemplation of other matters. Early thought was given to liaison, observation posts, Forward Observation Officers (F.O.O.) and wireless stations. By 28 May, locations and individuals assigned specific roles were identified and adjustments to following up the projected advance were under consideration.[97] Moreover, practice/feint barrages would be put down from late April.[98] And, in advance of the full-strength preliminary bombardment, sector familiarity and sufficient artillery presence made it feasible to commence targeted night firing – precluding German aerial spotting – with shelling of enemy communications on 27 May prior to completion of preparations.[99] Bombardment policy was to 'train the enemy' to adopt a limited number of safer overland routes before targeting those locations with concentrated fire.[100] Operational finesse and attention to detail, a Plumer's hallmark, was evident in divisional specification of targets and prescription, with subsequent monitoring, of ammunition expenditure for both specific bombardment activities and the practice barrages that continued through just prior to Z-Day.[101] This, coupled with machine-gun barrages, resulted in a significant interruption of enemy efforts to repair barbed wire defences, an objective stipulated in *SS 135*.[102]

Similar precision characterized the barrage on 7 June, the staging of which owed much to its Vimy Ridge predecessor. Two-thirds of 18-pdrs per Group undertook the creeping barrage close ahead of the advancing infantry with timed lifts of 100 yards every four minutes. The remaining elements of field artillery were tasked with putting down standing barrages 200-700 yards further ahead, the respective firing

95   Positions from TNA WO 95/2711: '47th Div Artillery Instructions No. 1' (Appendix IV), 47th Division RHA/RFA War Diary; Strong & Marble, *Artillery*, p.134.
96   See TNA WO 95/2711: 47th Division RHA/RFA War Diary, 1-31 May 1917.
97   TNA WO 95/2711: '47th Div Artillery Instructions No. 1', 'No. 2', 24 May 1917, 'No. 3', 25 May 1917 and 'No.4', 29 May 1917, 47th Division RHA/RFA War Diary; TNA WO 95/2711: 47th Div RHA/RFA War Diary, 26 May 1917.
98   TNA WO 95/2711: 47th Division RHA/RFA War Diary, 26 April and 1 May 1917.
99   TNA WO 95/2711: '47th Div Artillery Instructions No. 2', 47th Division RHA/RFA War Diary; TNA WO 95/2711: '47th Div Artillery O.O. No. 35', 26 May 1917, 47th Division RHA/RFA War Diary.
100 TNA WO 95/275-3(2): 'G.149', 9 May 1917, Second Army War Diary; TNA WO 95/2711: '47th Div Artillery Instructions No. 2', 47th Division RHA/RFA War Diary.
101 TNA WO 95/2711: '47th Div Artillery O.O. No. 37', 31 May 1917, 'O.O. No. 39' and 'O.O. No. 40', 4 June 1917, 47th Division RHA/RFA War Diary; TNA WO 95/2711: 47th Division RHA/RFA War Diary, 1-6 June 1917.
102 TNA WO 95/2702: '47th (London) Division. Weekly Summary of Operations, May 25th to May 31st 1917', 47th Division War Diary; TNA WO 95/2711: 47th Div RHA/RFA War Diary, 26-29 May 1917; *SS 135*, Section III, Para.3(d).

rates pre-determined (for 18-pdrs, four rounds per minute gradually reducing to one and for 4.5-inch howitzers, half those speeds) for three separate stages of the infantry assault after the Blue Line objective had been secured.[103]

Added to the Royal Artillery's arsenal was that of infantry brigade trench mortar batteries. Situated farther forward – those of 141st Brigade, some providing a substitute barrage where the opposing lines were too close for artillery fire, and 142nd Brigade combined to shell north of the canal about the Bluff and Ravine, whilst, on the opposite side, 140th Brigade's mortars were to bombard Triangular Wood.[104] Divisional machine-guns would also be deployed to provide barrage support. Once all of the infantry objectives had been secured, the creeping barrage would transform into a protective barrage. Four hundred yards beyond this protective barrier, machine-guns would put down a curtain of fire to prevent anticipated enemy counter-attacks.[105]

Other Arms

If infantry's reliance on artillery support and other positional firepower was evident through clear articulation, the same cannot be said of the other arms.

Notwithstanding the pivotal role of air support for artillery effectiveness, especially beyond the ridge and to the German gun line, aircraft occupy little space in the orders and instructions issued by 47th Division prior to the offensive. But this is, perhaps, comprehensible, there being minimal physical co-ordination between the infantry and No. 6 Squadron RFC. Indeed, the two were literally on different planes.[106]

Tanks, which *would* accompany the infantry, provide a stranger case study. Following their harrowing experience at High Wood, the infantry of 47th Division viewed tanks with a mixture of disinterest and suspicion.[107] That perception of tanks as, at best, a

103 TNA WO 95/2702: 'Instructions No. 9 (Artillery)', 15 May 1917, 47th Division War Diary; TNA WO 95/2711: '47th Div Artillery Instructions No. 2', 24 May 1917, 47th Division RHA/RFA War Diary; TNA WO 95/2711: BM 484/61, 4 June 1917, 47th Division RHA/RFA War Diary; Passingham, *Pillars of Fire*, p.44; Edmonds, *Military Operations 1917*, Vol II, p.47. The '47th Div Artillery Instructions No. 2'document also provided for both a deeper heavy artillery barrage, focusing on enemy batteries and strongpoints and discouraging assembly for counter-attacks, and a forward-searching protective barrage for beyond the final objective beyond the ridge.
104 TNA WO 95/2702: 'Instructions No. 6 (Action of Stokes Guns)', 27 April 1917, 47th Division War Diary; TNA WO 95/2711: '47th Div Artillery Instructions No. 1' (Appendix III), 21 May 1917, 47th Division RHA/RFA War Diary; TNA WO 95/2744: 142nd Brigade TM Battery War Diary, 4-5 June 1917; TNA WO 95/2703: 'Report', n.d., 47th War Division War Diary.
105 Edmonds, *Military Operations 1917*, Vol. II, pp.47-48; Passingham, *Pillars of Fire*, p.44.
106 For further details, see Jones, *War In The Air*, Vol. IV, pp.109-37.
107 Griffith, *Battle Tactics of The Western Front*, p.163; Anon., *Civil Service Rifles*, p.138.

peripheral luxury was also prompted by *SS 135, SS 143* and *SS 152*.[108] And, whilst 2nd Tank Brigade, taking part in its first action since formation, would provide X Corps with 12 machines – the fewest of Second Army's corps in light of the shorter distance to the final objective – clearly availed itself of comprehensive preparatory measures, surprisingly little of this made it into divisional operation orders and supplements.[109]

An advanced 2nd Tank Brigade headquarters was established by late-March, after which reconnaissance commenced including work with Second Army counter-intelligence to obtain civilian information on territory under German control.[110] One early result of this was the decision, reversing earlier opinions that tanks could only function on the south side of the canal. This change would deny 142nd Brigade of support whilst, conversely, providing 140th Brigade with increased armour resources.[111] Rail transport, the assigned 47th Division tanks detraining at Ouderdom, was completed without difficulty. Early liaison with the RFC revealed the need to conceal track marks from aerial observation.[112] More substantively, a 'Brigade Liaison Officer' was attached to No. 6 Squadron RFC to expedite the passing of air to ground contact patrol reports to tank battalion headquarters.[113] Ground liaison was sought down to the level of tank commander and infantry battalion headquarters, with telephonic systems ensuring two-way communication for 2nd Tank Brigade (with both X Corps and A Battalion) and for A Battalion (with both its No.3 company, attached to 47th Division, and the division itself).[114]

There were some hindrances[115] but, notwithstanding acknowledgement from the tank officers that the armour was no substitute for the infantry's effort or panacea for its suffering,[116] it is remarkable that little of these thorough preparations were formally shared with infantry commanders. Indeed, few are recorded as having had

---

108 *SS 135*, Section XIV, Paras. 1 and 2; No mention whatsoever in *SS 143* or *SS 152*. Tanks were specifically addressed by *SS 164: Notes on the use of Tanks and on the general principles of their employment as an adjunct to the Infantry attack*' (May 1917), but, published later, it is obviously not mentioned in *SS 135* or *SS 143*.

109 A Battalion, 2nd Tank Brigade (12 tanks) was attached to X Corps. Four vehicles of its No. 3 company were assigned to 47th Division. Passingham, *Pillars of Fire*, p.53.

110 TNA WO 95/101-3: 'Report on operations, June 1917', 2nd Tank Brigade War Diary; J. Beach, 'Scouting for Brigands: British Tank Corps Reconnaissance and Intelligence,1916-1918' in A. Searle (ed.), *Genesis, Employment, Aftermath: First World War Tanks and the New Warfare, 1900-1945* (Solihull: Helion & Co., 2015), p.120.

111 TNA WO 95/101-3: 'Report on operations', 2nd Tank Brigade Diary; TNA WO 95/275-3(2): 'G.172', 9 May, Second Army War Diary. For initial view in March, see TNA WO 95/91-3: 'Project for the Use of Tanks on the Second Army Front', Tank Corps War Diary.

112 TNA WO 95/101-3: 'Report on operations', 2nd Tank Brigade War Diary.

113 Ibid.

114 Ibid.

115 For example, see 2nd Tank Brigade's implicit criticism by omission from the praise for good sand models on other parts of the front. TNA WO 95/101-3: 'Report on operations', 2nd Tank Brigade War Diary.

116 Ibid.

contact with the new MK IV model tank and officers and men were rarely present for armour and infantry tactical exercises.[117] Some documents omitted any reference whatsoever.[118] More typically, others (including documents specifically dealing with tanks) contained quite skeletal, outcome-based descriptions or glancing allusions.[119] Tellingly, orders for 140th Brigade, the only 47th Division unit supported by tanks, were speculative about the feasibility of armour assistance and counselled troops to check the suitability of ground for tank passage beyond the Blue Line once taken.[120] Starting from Arundel House/Farm near the canal, tanks were expected to arrive at White Chateau stables, one pair at ZH+3.45 to support the attack there; the other at ZH+ 4.30 to assist the capture of Opal Trench, Support and Reserve (Black Line).[121]

So, on terra firma, sustained offensive effort would rely on the central partnership of artillery and infantry. The wildcard came in the form of the 19 mines tunnelled beneath the German defences. Scheduled to detonate at 3.10 a.m. on 7 June, none – all of which detonated within a 19-second timespan – were on the 47th Division's front with the closest being at Hill 60-Caterpillar and St. Eloi. Nevertheless, the eruption of 123,500 and 95,600-pound charges provided some advantage to the Londoners' assault.[122]

The defending *Infanterie Regiment Nr. 413 (204th Wurttemberg Division)* which was opposite the extreme left of 142nd Brigade's attack, was severely shaken by the mine detonations.[123] The remainder of 47th Division faced the recently arrived *35th Division*, an experienced Prussian formation diluted by replacements to the point of

---

117 Brig. Gen. Kennedy, GOC 140th Brigade, attended a 'tank demonstration' at Arras. This apparently isolated instance of senior interest occurring at a late stage. See TNA WO 95/2728: 140th Brigade Diary, 30 May 1917; TNA WO 95/91-4: 'Tactical Exercises, Tanks and Infantry: Instructions' (for session on 27 May 1917), Tanks Corps War Diary.

118 TNA WO 95/2702: 'General Instructions', 29 April 1917, 47th Division War Diary; TNA WO 95/2702: 'Instructions No. 15 (Liaison)', 25 May 1917, 47th Division War Diary; TNA WO 95/2729: '1/6th O.O. No. 120', 29 May 1917, 1/6th London Regiment War Diary; TNA WO 95/2730: '1/7th O.O. No. 161', 3 June, 1/7th London Regiment War Diary; TNA WO 95/2731:'1/8th O.O. No. 67', 2 June 1917, 1/8th London Regiment War Diary.

119 TNA WO 95/852-5: 'Instructions', 27 May and 1 June 1917, X Corps War Diary; TNA WO 95/2702: '47th Div O.O. No. 142', 15 May, 47th Division War Diary; TNA WO 95/2702: 'Addendum to O.O. No. 142', 20 May 1917, 47th Division War Diary; TNA WO 95/2702: 'Instructions No. 19 (Tanks)', 30 May 1917, 47th Division War Diary.

120 TNA WO 95/2728: '140th Brigade O.O. No. 167', 22 May 1917, 140th Brigade War Diary; TNA WO 95/2729: 'Addendum No. 2 to 1/6th O.O. No. 120', date unclear but early June, 1/6th London Regiment War Diary.

121 TNA WO 95/91-6: '2nd Brigade Heavy Branch – Tank Operations, Second Army', Tank Corps War Diary; TNA WO 95/852-5: 'Instructions' (Appendix VIII i), 1 June 1917, X Corps War Diary.

122 Edmonds, *Military Operations 1917*, Vol. II, p.60; Passingham, *Pillars of Fire*, p.102; Maude, *47th Division*, p.99; Planck, *History of the 7th*, p.115; Anon., *A History of the Post Office Rifles: 8th Battalion City of London Regiment* (Uckfield: Naval & Military Press reprint of 1919 edition), p.16.

123 Sheldon, *German Army at Passchendaele*, pp.24-29.

mediocrity.[124] Nevertheless, German troop density on X Corps' 6,000 yard frontage was double that of other ridgeline sectors.[125]

7 June 1917: Attack and Assessment

It was all, or mostly, in the preparation. In essence, Second Army's assault on Messines Ridge was executed on schedule and within the day. Typically 500-800 yards apart, the 'intermediate objectives', Red and Blue lines, were overrun by ZH+0.35 and ZH+1.40 respectively. Early momentum and a delayed and weak German counter-barrage denied enemy reserves the opportunity to get forward.[126] Following a planned two-hour pause, by 9:00 a.m. the Black Line was secured and consolidated to the extent necessary for progress beyond.[127] Following another pause until reset ZH (3.10 p.m.) which allowed field artillery batteries to move forward and occupy pre-designated positions, by sunset the final objective, Oosttaverne Line, was in British hands barring a 1,000 yard stretch which was dealt dealt with by the II Anzac Corps in the ensuing 48 hours.[128] Anticipated counter-attacks never materialised, or else were pre-empted by bombardment.[129] Although a victim of its own success – crowding on the ridge during the scheduled pause provided the enemy artillery with ready targets – the rapid advance resulted in some 5,650 prisoners, many averring surprise at its precise date.[130]

Despite this brevity, fewer casualties (11,000) than estimated and consequent accolades about its textbook qualities, it is questionable whether the offensive was 'remarkably easy'.[131] That description is not wholly consonant with 47th Division's experiences, which, in a sector remembered for some of the bitterest fighting, was largely a tale of two heavily defended strongpoints on either side of the canal.[132]

124 Passingham, *Pillars of Fire*, p.110; Intelligence Section of the General Staff American Expeditionary Force, *Histories of Two Hundred and Fifty-One Divisions of the German Army which Participated in the War (1914-1918). Compiled from records of Intelligence section of the General Staff, American Expeditionary Forces, at General Headquarters, Chaumont, France 1919* (Washington, DC: War Department, 1920), pp.414-15.
125 Edmonds, *Military Operations 1917*, Vol. II, p.59.
126 Edmonds, *Military Operations 1917*, Vol. II, pp.61-66; TNA WO 95/852-4: 'Battle Diary', X Corps War Diary.
127 Passingham, *Pillars of Fire*, pp.117-25; Edmonds, *Military Operations 1917*, Vol. II, pp.66-71; TNA WO 95/275-4: 'Operations carried out on June 7th' (appended to 'Summary of Operations Week ending 7th June'), Second Army War Diary.
128 Edmonds, *Military Operations 1917*, Vol. II, pp.76, 81-82, 85-86.
129 Ibid., pp.74-75; TNA WO 95/275-4: Second Army War Diary.
130 Edmonds, *Military Operations 1917*, Vol. II, p.71; TNA WO 95/275-4: Second Army War Diary; TNA WO 95/852-4: 'Battle Diary', X Corps War Diary; TNA WO 95/2703: 'Identification of Enemy Units Established on June 7th', 47th Division War Diary.
131 Sheffield & Bourne, *Haig*, p.298; Strong & Marble, *Artillery*, pp.134-35.
132 Edmonds, *Military Operations 1917*, Vol. II, p.69.

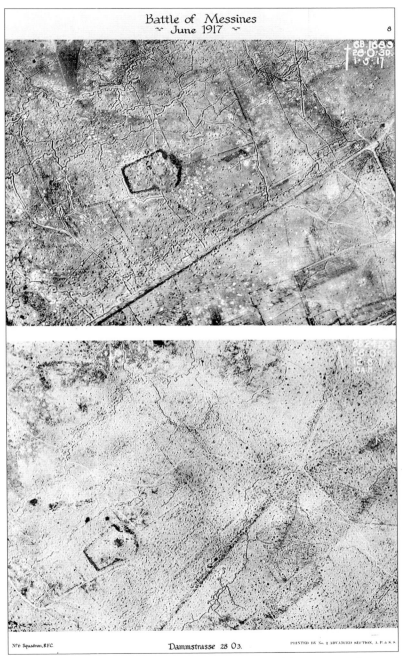

Dammstrasse and vicinity from the air, 1 May and 12 June 1917. The top image depicts the area prior to the Messines bombardment; the bottom afterwards. (Private collection)

To the south, the two most difficult Phase I challenges facing 140th Brigade were a strongpoint protecting the Blue Line (Oak Reserve at the north-eastern extremity of the *Dammstrasse*) and, more importantly, closer to the canal and situated on either side of the Blue Line, the fortified ruins of White Chateau and its stables. The brigade's right flank was led off by the 1/8th Battalion. Knowing its targets well because of the freedom of observation permitted during the preliminary bombardment, the battalion captured the German frontline within five minutes and was only momentarily delayed at the Red Line (Oak Reserve) and then by having to provide assistance to the neighbouring 1/7th Battalion at White Chateau.[133] In occupation of its assigned portion of Blue Line objective by the allotted ZH+47, the 1/8th Battalion proceeded with consolidation until 5.00 a.m.[134] Adhering to the scheduled pause until ZH+3.40, the 1/15th Battalion leap-frogged through the 1/8th enroute to its first Phase II objective, Oak Crescent.[135] Following a brief moment of formation extension, the first wave closed up under the barrage and, as it lifted, overran the objective rendered almost unrecognisable due to shell damage, at 6.50 a.m.[136] The third wave having cleared Oblong Trench, the first and fourth waves rapidly gained control of the final Black Line–Oblong Reserve objective and, as instructed due to the anticipated late arrival of 1/6th Battalion (Phase II left flank unit), turned 90 degrees to form a defensive flank behind Oblong Alley.[137] One party went on to seize Delbske Farm, the small advance allowing patrols to push into Ravine and White Chateau woods, and later to make contact with 1/6th Battalion.[138]

On the left flank, such relatively untroubled progress was not wholly replicated. To the 1/7th Battalion had fallen the 'privilege' of seizing White Chateau before reaching the Blue Line beyond to mark the successful culmination of Phase I. Darkness and smoke caused the battalion's left-hand lead company only belatedly to turn half-right off the canal bank before making its way towards White Chateau. Nevertheless, the company took the Red Line and a section of Oak Reserve beyond on schedule at 3.32 a.m.[139] Events markedly slowed thereafter. The 1/7th Battalion, its later waves

---

133 Anon., *A History of the Post Office Rifles*, p.16; TNA WO 95/2703: 'Report on Attack by 47th (London) Division on June 7th 1917', 47th Division War Diary.
134 TNA WO 95/2728: 'Operations Diary', 140th Brigade War Diary.
135 Anon., *Civil Service Rifles*, p.142.
136 Ibid.; TNA WO 95/2732: 'Record of Operations, 7th June 1917', 1/15th London Regiment War Diary. 6.50 a.m. was ZH+3.40, so capture was almost immediate.
137 TNA WO 95/2728: '140th Brigade O.O. No. 167'; TNA WO 95/2703: 'Detailed Diary of the Operations', 47th Division War Diary: TNA WO 95/2728: 'Operations Diary', 140th Brigade Diary; TNA WO 95/2732: 'Record of Operations', 1/15th London Regiment War Diary; Anon., *Civil Service Rifles*, p.143.
138 TNA WO 95/2703: 'Detailed Diary', 47th Division War Diary; TNA WO 95/2728: 'Operations Diary', 140th Brigade War Diary; TNA WO 95/2732: 'Record of Operations', 1/15th London Regiment War Diary; Anon., *Civil Service Rifles*, p.144.
139 TNA WO 95/2728: 'Operations Diary', 140th Brigade Diary; TNA WO 95/2730: 'Report on Operations of June 7th 1917', 1/7th London Regiment War Diary; Planck,

reinforcing Oak Reserve, was spread out in front and to the sides of the Chateau soon after 4.00 a.m. The left company, having defied enfilade fire from the chateau, took Oak Switch and commenced digging towards the canal.[140] However, the attackers establishing themselves on three sides of the ruins still did not produce an easy resolution. Notwithstanding subsequent reinforcements, two attacks (the second employing Lewis guns and rifle grenades) failed in the face of the defenders' machine-gun fusillades and copious stick bombs.[141] It took a third assault, prefaced by shelling from medium trench mortars, an 18-pdr and, again, employment of Lewis guns, to subdue the objective at 7.50 a.m. This was the only significant, albeit temporary, check to 140th Brigade's assault.[142] Remarking that a lone tank – without specific responsibilities until arrival at the Blue Line objective but still required to assist the infantry whilst in transit – appeared too late to help, the 1/7th Battalion war diarist also recorded that White Chateau was taken without assistance from neighbouring infantry units. This claim overlooked cameo interventions by 1/8th Battalion and, as it proceeded to its Phase II objectives, 1/6th Battalion.[143] Nonetheless, despite enfilade fire emanating from White Chateau, continued resistance there did not greatly impede 1/6th Battalion's progress beyond the Blue Line.[144] One after-action report claimed that the battalion had secured the chateau stables at 7.15 a.m., after which it cleared Opal Trench and, bombing down Opal Support towards the canal, it linked up with 142nd Brigade by 7.30 am.[145] Little more than an hour later, without the expected tank support, 1/6th Battalion approached Opal Reserve (Black Line), which was, by a model application of 'final objective' techniques honed during special training, finally taken by two companies in two waves of two lines each.[146]

History of the 7th, p.115.

140 TNA WO 95/2703: 'Detailed Diary', 47th Division War Diary; TNA WO 95/2728: 'Operations Diary', 140th Brigade Diary; TNA WO 95/2730: 'Report on Operations', 1/7th London Regiment War Diary.

141 TNA WO 95/2730: 'Report on Operations', 1/7th London Regiment War Diary; TNA WO 95/2728: 'Operations Diary', 140th Brigade War Diary.

142 TNA WO 95/2730: 'Report on Operations', 1/7th London Regiment War Diary; TNA WO 95/2703: 'Detailed Diary', 47th Division War Diary; TNA WO 95/2728: 'Operations Diary', 140th Brigade War Diary; TNA WO 95/2703: 'Report on Attack', 47th Division War Diary.

143 TNA WO 95/2730: 'Report on Operations', 1/7th London Regiment War Diary; TNA WO 95/2729: 1/6th London Regiment War Diary; E. Godfrey, *The 'Cast Iron Sixth': A History of the Sixth Battalion London Regiment (The City of London Rifles)* (London: Stapleton for Old Comrades Association, 1938), p.127.

144 TNA WO 95/2703: 'Report on Attack', 47th Division War Diary.

145 TNA WO 95/2703: 'Detailed Diary', 47th Division War Diary; TNA WO 95/2729: 1/6th London Regiment War Diary; TNA WO 95/2729: 'Report of Special Bombing Party in the Assault on 7th June 1917', 1/6th London Regiment War Diary.

146 TNA WO 95/2703:'Report on Attack' and 'Detailed Diary', 47th Division War Diary; TNA WO 95/2728: 'Operations Diary', 140th Brigade War Diary; Godfrey, *'Cast Iron Sixth'*, pp.127-28.

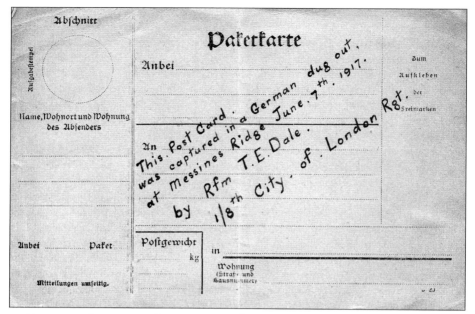

German pro forma personal message postcard captured by a Rifleman of 1/8th Battalion.
(Private collection)

Perhaps explaining orders stating that 'The word "RETIRE" does not exist' and deriding trophy-hunting as 'not playing the game' and risking loss of positions won,[147] 142nd Brigade's task appeared tougher than its devisional partners. And so it proved. Its Black Line front was 1/3 wider than 140th Brigade's and there was no compensatory shorter advance, the assault entailing a push astride 700-yards of canal between the Blue and Black lines. There was, however, a superficial similarity with 140th Brigade in the contrast between its flanks, the right seemingly proceeding without much difficulty if the negligible commentary in secondary sources is the measure. In the vanguard, the 1/24th Battalion advanced on a two-company front in four waves whilst remaining within 40 yards of the meticulously timed barrage to make the Blue Line (Oaf Lane from the canal to just north of the Quarry) in one minute over the allotted ZH+0.47.[148] Whether by accident (smoke and darkness hampering accurate navigation) or design, one party crossed the canal by bridge on the earlier Red Line, linking up with 1/7th Battalion on the south bank.[149] Thus, 1/23rd Battalion, its

---

147 TNA WO 95/2741: '142 Brigade O.O. No. 183', 1 June 1917, 142nd Brigade War Diary.
148 TNA WO 95/2744: 'Narrative of Attack by 1/24th London Regiment, "The Queens", on 7/6/1917', 1/24th London Regiment War Diary.
149 TNA WO 95/2744: 'Narrative of Attack by 1/24th London Regiment, "The Queens", on 7/6/1917', 1/24th London Regiment War Diary; TNA WO 95/2703: 'Report on Attack',

companies remaining within 50 yards of the barrage,[150] was able to depart the Blue Line on time and make for Opal Reserve on the Black Line. Here, a canal crossing *was* part of the plan once the potentially difficult Triangular Spoil Bank was subdued, something achieved shortly after 8.00 a.m.[151] The canal side had been obtained some 30 minutes earlier.[152] Despite a temporary intra-battalion gap caused by one company's premature crossing of the canal, no 'determined opposition' was encountered as 1/23rd Battalion secured Opal Reserve by 9.00 a.m., quickly getting in touch with 1/6th Battalion on its right. Defensive posts with Lewis and Vickers machine-guns were established on its left, a consequence of events affecting the left flank of 142nd Brigade's assault.[153]

The start of this assault was as propitious as that by the canal. Again, moving close (30 yards) behind the barrage, the 1/22nd Battalion's four waves encountered only limited resistance before taking the Blue Line on time. Consolidation in readiness for 1/21st Battalion to pass through towards its Black Line objective followed.[154] However, the first harbinger of difficulty appeared; the left of 1/22nd Battalion's fourth wave encountered heavy machine-gun fire from Battle Wood which was situated in the adjacent 69th Brigade (23rd Division) sector.[155] While the same distraction did not delay 1/21st Battalion's capture of its first objective, Oaf Lane (within 15 minutes),[156] it would contribute to difficulties besetting the battalion as it turned half-right to confront the LSB, guarding access to (and down) the canal. This formidable emplacement, situated on the boundary between *204th* and *35th divisions*, companies of the former's *Infanterie Regiment Nr. 61* augmenting the normal garrison, would be reinforced later that day.[157] Even the LSB's 'morning' strength (reportedly including three machine-gun emplacements), combined with the fire from Battle Wood – by now, over the 1/21st's 'left shoulder' – and from Oaf Keep slightly south, transformed the advance into leapfrog between available shell holes and trenches.[158] In the face of wildly contradictory reports about the neighbouring 69th Brigade's progress and

47th Division War Diary.

150 TNA WO 95/2744: 'Narrative of 2nd Army Offensive Operations of June 7th-9th 1917 as far as they concerned the 1/23 Bn The London Regt', 1/23rd London Regiment War Diary.

151 Ibid.

152 Shaw, *The 23rd London*, p.45.

153 TNA WO 95/2744: 'Narrative of 2nd Army Offensive Operations', 1/23rd London Regiment War Diary; TNA WO 95/2703: 'Report on Attack', 47th Division War Diary.

154 TNA WO 95/2743: 1/22nd London Regiment War Diary; TNA WO 95/2703: 'Detailed Diary', 47th Division War Diary; TNA WO 95/2703: 'Report on Attack', 47th Division War Diary.

155 TNA WO 95/2743: 1/22nd London Regiment War Diary.

156 TNA WO 95/2732:'Report on part taken by Battn in Operations of June 7th-9th', 1/21st London Regiment War Diary; Anon., *War Record of the 21st*, p.73.

157 Edmonds, *Military Operations 1917*, Vol. II, p.69, fn.1; Passingham, *Pillars of Fire*, pp.120-21.

158 TNA WO 95/2732: 'Report on part taken by Battn', 1/21st London Regiment War Diary.

left flank protection,[159] two fragmented attempts at capture failed. Shortly after 8.00 a.m., parts of the second wave companies, later supported by the third and fourth waves, pushed close to LSB's westernmost point and sought to reach the machine-guns at its eastern end. This proved impracticable, a small-scale crossing of the canal to engage the emplacement's underbelly having to withdraw.[160] At 9.30 am, another crossing, seemingly more an essay to by-pass LSB and reach the Black Line but still capable of facilitating its subordination, failed.[161] Capture of LSB before nightfall being considered vital by X Corps, these setbacks prompted a reappraisal, whereby 1/21st Battalion consolidated on the line held (approximately halfway between Oaf Lane and LSB's facing front) and sought to bring its right flank forward to gain better touch with 1/23rd Battalion while another assault was readied.[162] Withdrawal to Oaf Lane itself was subsequently ordered to allow for a five-hour bombardment before an evening attack by three companies of 1/20th Battalion and two platoons of 1/21st Battalion.[163] Timed for 7.00 p.m., it was to drive east, down both canal banks, two companies taking LSB in its entirety and, on the south bank, one company tasked with seizing Oblique Row.[164] Events conspired against this plan when, during assembly, the attackers incurred heavy losses from shellfire.[165] Centre of the three-pronged assault (each company on a two-platoon, two-wave front), A Company made progress along LSB and commenced consolidation. However, its flanking neighbours were constrained by machine-gun fire and a barrage that, it seems, might have been preliminary to a broader German counter-attack which, discouraged by the LSB bombardment, never materialised.[166] Nonetheless, with warnings of imminent counter-attack and A Company exposed on both flanks, the entire force withdrew to the Blue Line around 8.30 p.m.[167] With the 1/21st Battalion still under heavy shelling

159   Ibid.
160   Ibid.; Anon., *War Record of the 21st*, p.74.
161   TNA WO 95/2732: 'Report on part taken by Battn', 1/21st London Regiment War Diary; Anon., *War Record of the 21st*, p.74.
162   TNA WO 95/2703: 'Detailed Diary', 47th Division War Diary; TNA WO 95/2732: 'Report on part taken by Battn', 1/21st London Regiment War Diary; TNA WO 95/2741: 142nd Brigade War Diary.
163   TNA WO 95/2732: 1/21st Diary; TNA WO 95/2741: 'Second Army Offensive – Operations Diary from Zero Hour', 142nd Brigade War Diary.
164   TNA WO 95/2703: '47th Div O.O. No. 150', 7 June 1917, 47th Division War Diary; TNA WO 95/2732: '142nd Brigade O.O. No. 186', 7 June 1917, 1/21st London Regiment War Diary; TNA WO 95/2738: '1/20th O.O. No. 150', 7 June 1917, 1/20th London Regiment War Diary.
165   TNA WO 95/2738: 1/20th London Regiment War Diary.
166   TNA WO 95/2732: '1/20th O.O. No. 150', 7 June 1917, 1/21st London Regiment War Diary; TNA WO 95/2738: 1/20th London Regiment War Diary; TNA WO 95/2732: 1/21st London Regiment War Diary; Anon., *War Record of the 21st*, p.74.
167   TNA WO 95/2732: 'Report on part taken by Battn', 1/21st London Regiment War Diary; TNA WO 95/2738: 1/20th London Regiment War Diary; TNA WO 95/2703: 'Detailed Diary', 47th Division War Diary.

and so badly shaken to be considered unable to resist counter-attacks, its relief was arranged and Gorringe called a halt for the day.[168]

That 'day' was, so far as the main thrust of the Messines offensive was concerned, very much it for 47th Division, which registered 2,046 killed, wounded and missing and 434 prisoners taken.[169] Whilst fighting rumbled on for another week, the division did not participate in the attack on the Oosttaverne Line, having relinquished its right front before day's end to allow 24th Division to deploy for that phase.[170] German shelling was a frequent distraction and some unremarkable counter-attacks were seen off on the following day.[171] Notwithstanding suggestions to the contrary,[172] subsequent sorties on 10 and 13 June never took LSB.[173] Another assault on LSB was planned for 14 June.[174] The 47th Division, however, would be relieved prior to this on 13 June.[175]

The 47th Division's performance, results and demonstrable 1916-17 learning experience might initially be viewed in a qualified light. Against the headline success of Messines Ridge overall, a case, similar in implication to perspectives of its capture of High Wood, could be advanced that it made something of a meal of its particular contribution to victory. As White Chateau was taken in a timescale that did not materially impair progress, front and centre of any such detraction must be the blank drawn at LSB – the subject of later divisional enquiry and censure of 1/20th and 1/21st battalion junior officers for withdrawals resulting from perceived errors of judgment and insufficient determination.[176] Yet, even if one disregards counter-arguments, for example that the remainder of X Corps progressed even without LSB in British hands or that some other formations fell short, the more compelling

168 TNA WO 95/2703: 'Detailed Diary', 47th Division War Diary; TNA WO 95/2741: 'Second Army Offensive – Operations Diary from Midnight June 7/8th to Midnight June 8th/9th', 142nd Brigade War Diary; Passingham, *Pillars of Fire*, p.148.
169 TNA WO 95/2703: 'Report on Attack', 47th Division War Diary. The casualties constitute 30 percent of the X Corps total for 1-12 June 1917. See Edmonds, *Military Operations 1917*, Vol. II, p.87, fn.2.
170 TNA WO 95/2703: '47th Div O.O. No. 151', 47th Division War Diary.
171 TNA WO 95/2732: 1/21st London Regiment War Diary; Anon., *War Record of the 21st*, p.74.
172 TNA WO 95/2744: 'Narrative on 2nd Army Offensive Operations', 1/23rd London Regiment War Diary; Shaw, *The 23rd London*, p.46; Maude, *47th Division*, p.101.
173 Edmonds, *Military Operations 1917*, Vol. II; TNA WO 95/2703: 47th Division War Diary; TNA WO 95/2737: 1/18th London Regiment War Diary.
174 Edmonds, *Military Operations 1917*, Vol. II, pp.85-86; TNA WO 95/852-4: 'X Corps O.O. No. 89', 9 June 1917, 'O.O. No. 91', 10 June 1917, 'O.O. No. 92', 11 June 1917, X Corps War Diary; TNA WO 95/2703: '47th Div O.O. No. 153' & 'O.O. No. 154', 9 June 1917, 47th Division War Diary; TNA WO 95/2703: '47th Div Warning Order No. 1', 11 June 1917, 47th Division War Diary.
175 TNA WO 95/852-4: X Corps War Diary.
176 TNA WO 95/2732: 'GX.3/52', 10 June 1917 and 'M50', 14 June 1917; TNA WO 95/2732: 'GX/3/52', 21 June 1917, 1/21st London Regiment War Diary.

submission is that the 47th Division employed accrued experience alongside learned processes to perform a tough, perhaps the toughest, operational and tactical task creditably.[177]

The infantry, of course, was not operating in a vacuum. Without artillery support – the gunners' largely excellent barrage work was only minimally diminished by occasional short-firing – and the RFC, the task would, almost certainly, have proved impossible.[178] However, that effective collaboration was common throughout Second Army on 7 June. More pertinent here are the variables concerning 47th Division.

Occupied by an unparalleled density of enemy defenders, the 47th Division's sector was the only one divided by a canal, which, though drained and shallow, remained a serious obstacle and, while familiar with their surroundings, officers and men had not previously been required to move down its banks or, in 142nd Brigade's case, cross it in large numbers whilst maintaining rapid forward movement. Moreover, the divisional front did not benefit from the destructive effects of the detonated mines and, if there were ever 'strong points' for neutralisation, the finite speciality of the tank arm, White Chateau and LSB fitted the bill. Yet, with provision of support before the Blue Line almost optional, armour fell behind schedule and arrived too late opposite the former to accomplish anything, thus drawing references that are curt, almost dismissive or damning them with faint praise about their 'moral' effect.[179] Further to this, the terrain north of the canal precluded any use of tanks against the LSB. Here, the prolonged general pause on the Blue Line, criticised by all three divisions in X Corps' post-engagement survey, could have, by allowing reinforcement of the already formidable strongpoint, had a deleterious effect on 142nd Brigade's subsequent efforts.[180] Its attack was greatly undermined anyway by sustained machine-gun fire from Battle Wood, a threat as much from the rear as from the left flank once 1/21st Battalion wheeled half-right. Although 69th Brigade's diarist portrayed this exposure as the result of reluctance to place his brigade's right flank in the air because of 1/21st's travails,[181] contemporaneous information arriving at 47th Division headquarters confirms that 69th Brigade was well behind 1/21st Battalion at the time of the first attempts to secure

177   B. Liddell Hart, *A History of the First World War* (London: Pan, 2014 [1930]), p.391.
178   TNA WO 95/2741: 'Operations Diary from Zero Hour', 142nd Brigade War Diary; TNA WO 95/2703: 'Detailed Diary', 47th Division War Diary.
179   TNA WO 95/2730: 'Report on Operations', 1/7th London Regiment War Diary; TNA WO 95/2729: 'Report by B Coy' and Report 'C Coy', 1/6th London Regiment War Diary; TNA WO 95/852-4: 'Battle Diary', X Corps War Diary.
180   TNA WO 95/852-6: 'Responses by 23, 41 & 47 Divs to Pro forma Questions', X Corps War Diary.
181   TNA WO 95/2183: 'Operations of 69th Infantry Brigade from 5th-13th June, 1917, including the capture of Hill 60 and Battle Wood on 7th June', 69th Brigade War Diary.

the LSB.[182] For its part, the 1/21st Battalion subsequently attributed its difficulties squarely to 69th Brigade's failure to neutralise Battle Wood.[183]

Turning to doctrine, it is arguable that Richard Holmes' observation that the primacy of Messines Ridge offensive's artillery fire plan stifled a certain amount of infantry initiative and flexibility has particular, if unintended, resonance with regard to the unfortunate LSB saga.[184] The ethos of *SS 143* is evident in the frequent company or platoon focus within relevant battalion war diaries and from resultant descriptions of intra- and inter-battalion co-operation between these subunits, the formations adopted and deployment of armed sections. But *SS 143's* credo of the self-sufficient platoon did not translate into 'every man [platoon] for himself' so far as broader support was concerned. Indeed, the importance of artillery cooperation was emphasised *inter alia* in *SS 135*.[185] Yet, although LSB received particular attention from the creeping barrage, timetable rigidity meant that it had passed on by 7.45 a.m., well before 1/21st Battalion's earliest assault.[186] And, as there is no war diary evidence of a barrage callback, it appears that, until commencement of the afternoon bombardment of LSB, the only available support for the infantry came from machine-guns. Thus, notwithstanding undoubtedly brave attempts to seize LSB, tactical flexibility on the ground was restricted. The most enduring instances of initiative by junior leaders were demonstrated by orders to withdraw. Viewed negatively, with plenty of blame to go around, the subsequent search for the guilty found its quarry.[187] Although amply demonstrated by 47th Division's success at Messines, the learning curve was, nevertheless, capable of exhibiting kinks.

Aftermath

The 47th Division remained in the salient for three months, transferring to Fifth Army in mid-August. However, despite its transfer to X Corps reserve during the Battle of Pilckem Ridge (31 July-2 August), it featured in no major operation of the Third Ypres campaign proper according to the official 'Battles and Engagements' list. The division's role during mid-August and early September was limited to raids and

182 TNA WO 95/2703: 'Detailed Diary', 47th Division War Diary; TNA WO 95/2741: 'Operations Diary from Zero Hour', 142nd Brigade War Diary.
183 TNA WO 95/2732: 'M50', 14 June, 1/21st London Regiment War Diary; TNA WO 95/2732: 'Report on part taken by Battn', 1/21st London Regiment War Diary; Anon., *War Record of the 21st*, p.73.
184 R. Holmes, *Army Battlefield Guide: Belgium and Northern France* (London: HMSO, 1995), p.129.
185 *SS 143*, Introduction in (Comp.), *Officer's Manual*, p.117; *SS 135*, Section III, pp.15-23.
186 WO 95/2729: 'Map D2', 1/6th London Regiment War Diary.
187 Although the charges were literally justified by *SS 143*, Part I, Section 9, Para.vi, in (Comp.), *Officer's Manual*, p.122.

line straightening operations, with a positively footnoted contribution to a minor attack near St Julien.[188]

In late September, the 47th Division marched south to join First Army near Arras.[189] Two months later, this relatively agreeable – when compared to Ypres – assignment ended when the division joined Third Army near Cambrai.[190] It was a latecomer to the major offensive (Battle of Cambrai, 20 November-6 December) there. Starting its 10-day cross-country journey to the battlefront as the initial massed tank attack penetrated five kilometres of the Hindenburg Line defensive system, the division was still in transit during unsuccessful and costly efforts (23 to 27 November) to take the high ground about Bourlon village.[191] These resulted in precarious British occupation of much of the adjacent Bourlon Wood where 47th Division entered the line as part of IV Corps (GOC Lieutenant-General Sir C.L. Woollcombe).[192] Despite the contrary impression of *General* Otto von Moser (the opposing *Gruppe Arras* commander),[193] Third Army had, by then, jettisoned offensive operations due to depleted manpower and material resources.[194] Indeed, the 47th, earmarked for transfer to Italy in the aftermath of the Caporetto disaster, was held back to provide much-needed reinforcements.[195] Consolidation of captured territory was the order of the day, although the Bourlon salient, extremely vulnerable to counter-attack, was hardly an ideal setting for the task.

The first substantive words of *SS 135* are 'All training behind the line must be specially directed toward offensive action'.[196] Consequently, the Londoners had had minimal preparation for what confronted them at Bourlon Wood. Relieving 62nd (West Riding) Division on the night of 28/29 November, five battalions (141st Brigade plus 1/15th Battalion) entered the one-mile square expanse under a heavy and prolonged gas shell bombardment. This 'harassing and somewhat costly operation' was aggravated by both the gas lingering in the dense undergrowth and the troop

188 Edmonds, *Military Operations 1917*, Vol. II, pp.88-141; Maude, *47th Division*, pp.105-09; E.A. James, *A Record of the Battles and Engagements of the British Armies in France and Flanders, 1914-1918* (Aldershot: Gale & Polden, 1923), p.22, fn.1; Major A.F. Becke, *Order of Battle of Divisions, Part 2A – The Territorial Force Mounted Divisions and the 1st-Line Territorial Force Divisions* (London: HMSO, 1936), p.75.

189 Maude, *47th Division*, pp.112-17.

190 Ibid., pp.119-121.

191 TNA WO 95/368-1(2): 'G.14/302', 1 December 1917, Third Army War Diary; TNA WO 95/2703: 'IV Corps: Havrincourt–Bourlon Wood Operations, November 20th–December 1st, Part II Narrative of Operations', 47th Division War Diary; W. Miles, *Military Operations France & Belgium 1917*, Vol. III (London: Macmillan, 1947), pp.126-61.

192 Miles, *Military Operations 1917*, Vol. III, p.167.

193 Moser diary, 30 November 1917 quoted in J. Sheldon, *The German Army at Cambrai* (Barnsley: Pen & Sword, 2009), p.256.

194 TNA WO 95/368-2: 'GS 56/234', 27 November, Third Army War Diary; TNA WO 95/2703: 'IV Corps Narrative of Operations', 47th Division War Diary.

195 A.J. Smithers, *Cambrai: The First Great Tank Battle 1917* (London: Leo Cooper, 1992), p.165.

196 *SS 135*, Introduction, Para.1, p.7.

Bourlon Wood and environs, November 1917.

concentration, a decision that three battalions of dismounted cavalry should remain in the wood only being reversed when Gorringe assumed sector command the following morning.[197] With hostile shelling continuing throughout 29 November, disorientation was exacerbated by fatigue resulting from 47th Division's prolonged, stop-start travel from the Ypres front southwards and the limited scope for reconnaissance.[198] The men found existing defences to be either non-existent or in poor condition, necessitating rapid work to extend and improve them. Amongst the units undertaking the work was 1/6th Battalion, on the left (adjacent to 2nd Division) of the divisional line some 300 yards west of the wood.[199] To the particular disadvantage of that battalion, consolidation work was incomplete when, shortly after sunrise on 30 November and intensifying by 8.30 am, a heavy bombardment commenced.[200] This was the precursor to a large-scale German counter-offensive on IV and VI corps that, whilst not unexpected and impossible to conceal anyway (being preceded by attacks against III and VII corps against the other, southern flank of the salient), struck with the force of four *Gruppe Arras* assault divisions.[201]

197 Miles, *Military Operations 1917*, Vol. III, p.167.
198 TNA WO 95/2703: 'IV Corps Narrative of Operations', 47th Division War Diary.
199 TNA WO 95/2738: 1/19th London Regiment War Diary; TNA WO 95/2729: 1/6th London Regiment War Diary; TNA WO 95/2729: 'Narrative of the Operations of November 30th 1917 and of the German Assault on Positions held by the 6th Battn London Regiment, N of Bourlon Wood on that day', 1/6th London Regiment War Diary.
200 TNA WO 95/2729: 1/6th London Regiment War Diary; Godfrey, 'Cast Iron Sixth', p.170.
201 TNA WO 95/2703: 'IV Corps Narrative of Operations', 47th Division War Diary; Miles, *Military Operations 1917*, Vol. III, pp.168, 176-211; Bryn Hammond, *Cambrai 1917: The Myth of the First Great Tank Battle* (London: Phoenix, 2009), p.371. Whether or not attributable to Third Army's view of the likely weight of a German counter-attack, tanks

47th Division's epic fight at Bourlon Wood against *221 Division* on 30 November, mostly occurred outside the actual wood, with the bulk of the fighting taking place on the ridge south southwest of Bourlon village. Here, on 140th Brigade's front, 1/6th Battalion and, to its right, partly amongst the timberland fringe, 1/15th Battalion was, until late morning, efficiently enfilading massed enemy assault waves advancing right to left in a southerly direction towards 2nd Division from their starting point behind Bourlon village and Quarry Wood.[202] Assisted by artillery and machine-guns carefully-positioned north of the main road near the Sugar Factory, they inflicted enormous losses on the attackers before forcing them back over Bourlon Ridge.[203] However, sometime after midday, it became increasingly evident that the enemy had switched his attention to 140th Brigade, massing on its front and then sending out 'feeler' attacks.[204] Throwing back its left flank and reinforcing its right, the 1/6th Battalion violently repulsed these probes. Nevertheless, its predicament grew as small incursions against both flanks allowed the enemy to put down crossfire and move up a small infantry support gun in front of the village.[205] Shortly after 2.00 p.m., in consequence of the battalion's incomplete trenchworks coupled with a breach of the neighbouring 2nd Division's line, the Germans – attacking from a sunken road just beyond the divisional boundary – rolled up 1/6th Battalion's left flank.[206] Severe fighting raged for some time as far back as another sunken road situated in the wood's environs, running due north some 500 yards from and parallel to the wood's edge. Ground was ceded only after 'desperate resistance' when 'almost all' of the defenders had been killed or wounded.[207] With its immediate rear now threatened, 1/15th Battalion, hitherto merely a recipient of shelling and aircraft strafing, was induced to extend a defensive flank down a third sunken road located at the wood's perimeter pending re-establishment of friendly contact.[208] That was not achieved until dusk when 1/8th

had been withdrawn on 28 November 1917. See TNA WO 95/716-7: IV Corps War Diary.

202 TNA WO 95/2728: 'Report on Fighting in Bourlon Wood 30th November 1917', 140th Brigade War Diary; TNA WO 95/2729: Diary entry and 'Narrative of the Operations', 1/6th London Regiment War Diary.

203 TNA WO 95/2703: 'Report on Operations 30th November 1917 (G.90/1/10)', 47th Division War Diary; Maude, *47th Division*, p.125; Miles, *Military Operations 1917*, Vol. III, p.214; Hammond, *Cambrai 1917*, p.374.

204 TNA WO 95/2728: 'Report on Fighting', 140th Brigade War Diary; TNA WO 95/2729: 1/6th London Regiment War Diary.

205 TNA WO 95/2728: 140th Brigade War Diary; TNA WO 95/2729: 1/6th London Regiment War Diary; Godfrey, 'Cast Iron Sixth', p.170.

206 TNA WO 95/2728: 'Report on Fighting', 140th Brigade War Diary; TNA WO 95/2729: 1/6th London Regiment War Diary.

207 TNA WO 95/2729: 1/6th London Regiment War Diary; TNA WO 95/2729: 'Narrative of the Operations', 1/6th London Regiment War Diary; Godfrey, 'Cast Iron Sixth', p.171.

208 TNA WO 95/2732: 'Narrative of Operations covering period from 28th November 1917 to night of 1st/2nd December 1917', 1/15th London Regiment War Diary; Anon., *Civil Service Rifles*, p.166.

Battalion, having assisted remnants of 1/6th to restore much of the ground lost in the preceding hours, deployed three companies northward up the middle sunken road to fill the gap between 1/6th Battalion's right and 1/15th's left.[209] The day's casualties for 1/6th and 1/15th battalions were 382 and 229 respectively.[210]

While all this was occurring on 140th Brigade's front, there was little in the way of infantry action involving 141st Brigade on the right in the wood itself. Uneasy moments from intensive shelling and resultant smoke triggered SOS signals, support movements (including one by 1/22nd Battalion, detached from 142nd Brigade) and preparations for possible withdrawal from Bourlon Wood.[211] The line thus strengthened, nascent enemy assaults notably one emanating from near a railway line 3/4 mile to the northeast, was dispersed. In itself, this was important to the day's outcome, as subsequent intelligence reports suggested that the Germans, wishing to pinch out the Bourlon Salient, had also planned to attack from that direction.[212]

Casualties in 141st Brigade amounted to an estimated 2,000, although only about 100 were fatal.[213] Many were from gas. Situated near the wood's southeast quadrant and southern approaches – areas subjected to the most artillery attention – the 1/19th Battalion was at 50 percent strength even before the hostile advances started.[214] Its ultimate reduction, approximate literal decimation, to 70 men necessitated the formation of a composite battalion with elements of 1/17th and 1/18th battalions.[215] Following a relatively quiet 24 hours involving a postponed transfer to V Corps (GOC Lieutenant-General E.A. Fanshawe), 141st Brigade, plus 1/15th Battalion on its left, was relieved by 142nd Brigade on the night of 1/2 December.[216] Further left

209 TNA WO 95/2728: 'Report on Fighting', 140th Brigade War Diary; TNA WO 95/2729: 1/6th London Regiment War Diary; TNA WO 95/2729: 'Narrative of the Operations', 1/6th London Regiment War Diary; TNA WO 95/2731: 1/8th London Regiment War Diary; TNA WO 95/2728: 'Report on Fighting', 140th Brigade War Diary; TNA WO 95/2731: 1/8th London Regiment War Diary; TNA WO 95/2732: 'Narrative of Operations', 1/15th London Regiment War Diary; Maude, *47th Division*, p.126; Anon., *Civil Service Rifles*, p.166.

210 Maude, *47th Division*, p.127.

211 TNA WO 95/2736: 141st Brigade War Diary; TNA WO 95/2738: 1/20th London Regiment War Diary. The 1/20th, having moved back from the edge of the wood to the Hindenburg Line late on 29 November, was brought forward to Anneux at 1.00 p.m.

212 Maude, *47th Division*, p.126-28; TNA WO 95/2703: 'Report on Operations (G.90/1/10)', 47th Division War Diary; TNA WO 95/2736: 141st Brigade War Diary; TNA WO 95/2737: 1/17th London Regiment War Diary.

213 Maude, *47th Division*, p.127; TNA WO 95/2736: 'Statement of Casualties from 26-11-17 to 31-12-17, practically all sustained during German counter-attack of 30-11-17 to 4-12-17', 141st Brigade War Diary.

214 TNA WO 95/2703: 'Intelligence (G.90/1/11)', 2 December 1917, 47th Division War Diary; TNA WO 95/2738: 1/19th London Regiment War Diary.

215 Maude *47th Division*, pp.126, 133; S. Major, *1/18th Battalion in the First World War* (1973), Chapter 11 <www.londonirishrifles.com>

216 TNA WO 95/748-8: V Corps War Diary; TNA WO 95/748-8: 'Summary of Operations from 1/12/17 – 6/12/17', V Corps War Diary; TNA WO 95/2703: 47th Division War

Eyewitness artist's rendering of the 'great fight in the neighbourhood of Bourlon and Moeuvres', 30 November 1917. (*Illustrated London News*, 2 February 1918)

still, 1/6th Battalion had already been withdrawn and replaced by 1/7th Battalion, the latter now alongside 1/8th Battalion defending the remainder of 140th Brigade's line.[217] On the night of 2/3 December, just prior to 142nd Brigade's own relief, the 1/8th Battalion, situated on the right with 1/23rd Battalion in support, incurred light casualties after both units combined successfully to restore the *status quo ante* in 1/6th Battalion's former sector.[218]

Notwithstanding the remarkable sacrifice to hold and restore the line, Haig was concerned that the Bourlon Salient and its south-easterly extension about Marcoing would remain vulnerable in the long-term. On 2 December, he instructed Third Army GOC General Sir Julian Byng to prepare contingency plans for withdrawal.[219] The next day, Haig ordered a withdrawal to a shorter defensive position, the loss of ground recently won determined to be 'quite secondary' to defensive security and economy of

Diary; TNA WO 95/2728: 'Report on Fighting near Bourlon Wood (1-3 December)', 140th Brigade War Diary; TNA WO 95/2732: 1/15th London Regiment War Diary; TNA WO 95/2742: 142nd Brigade War Diary.

217 TNA WO 95/2742: 142nd Brigade War Diary; TNA WO 95/2730: 1/7th London Regiment War Diary; TNA WO 95/2731: 1/8th London Regiment War Diary.

218 TNA WO 95/2703: 47th Division War Diary; TNA WO 95/2728: 'Report on Fighting', 140th Brigade War Diary; TNA WO 95/2730: 1/7th London Regiment War Diary; TNA WO 95/2731: 1/8th London Regiment War Diary; Maude, *47th Division*, p.128; Planck, *History of the 7th*, p.173; Anon., *A History of the Post Office Rifles*, p.18; TNA WO 95/2742: 142nd Brigade War Diary.

219 Miles, *Military Operations 1917*, Vol. III, p.257.

troops.[220] Following a 4 December conference to determine a precise line (Hindenburg Support–Flesquières Line), Third Army headquarters issued orders to this effect.[221]

Whilst the officers and men of 47th Division were not as sanguine about this directive,[222] their retirement, under cover of darkness on 4-5 December, was almost flawless. The Germans, slow to detect what was happening, allowed 142nd Brigade to commence withdrawal shortly after 11.00pm and to pass through 140th Brigade's covering positions by 3.00 a.m. With rearguards, RE detachments (tasked with destroying abandoned materiel and setting boobytraps) along with the last of the division's component RFA batteries falling back in the remaining 90 minutes, 142nd Brigade completed the evacuation without hindrance by dawn.[223]

Operationally, the withdrawal was the final act of 47th Division's Bourlon Wood ordeal. However, attendant arrangements afforded an opportunity for another feat of 'derring-do'. One of 140th Brigade's covering outposts, just east of Graincourt (approximately 1/2 mile south-west of Anneux), was still manned by C and D companies of 1/15th Battalion early on 5 December. From positions fronting a sunken road running from the village, their combined strength amounted to 120 men. The Germans, on discovering the withdrawal, advanced from Bourlon Wood and its westward slopes in increasing numbers before forming up along the main road whilst parties entered Anneux.[224] Artillery and small arms fire precluded daylight enemy forays farther forward, but by nightfall there was increased enemy infiltration of Graincourt. By the following morning, the Germans had dug in on the village's southern side just behind the outpost's left flank, a continuing menace despite the despatch of a Lewis Gun team to a nearby position on the Flesquières road.[225] The risk of encirclement became critical when the enemy, having earlier moved forward in front of Graincourt, turned half-left to pitch an afternoon advance at 59th (2nd North Midland) Division, to 1/15th Battalion's right.[226] That division's left flank battalion was quickly forced

220 Ibid., p.258; TNA WO 95/368-2: 'GS 56/239', 3 December 1917, Third Army War Diary.

221 TNA WO 95/368-1(1): 'Narrative of Operations on December 4th 1917', Third Army War Diary; TNA WO 95/368-2: 'GS 56/237' and 'GS 56/238', 4 December 1917, Third Army War Diary; TNA WO 95/748-8: 'GS 306/1' and 'GS 306/2', 4 December 1917, V Corps War Diary.

222 Major, *1/18th Battalion in the First World War*, Chapter 11.

223 Miles, *Military Operations 1917* Vol. III, p.264; Maude, *47th Division*, pp.129-130; TNA WO 95/368-1(1): 'Narrative of Operations – December 5th 1917', Third Army War Diary; TNA WO 95/748-8: V Corps War Diary; TNA WO 95/2703: 47th Division War Diary; TNA WO 95/2742: 142nd Brigade War Diary.

224 TNA WO 95/2732: 'Report on Operations December 4th 5th and 6th 1917 around Graincourt', 1/15th London Regiment War Diary; Anon., *Civil Service Rifles*, pp.169-70; TNA WO 95/2728: 'Report on Withdrawal from Bourlon Wood', 140th Brigade War Diary.

225 TNA WO 95/2728: 'Report on Withdrawal from Bourlon Wood', 140th Brigade War Diary; TNA WO 95/2732: 'Report on Operations around Graincourt', 1/15th London Regiment War Diary; Anon., *Civil Service Rifles*, p.170.

226 TNA WO 95/2728: 'Report on Withdrawal from Bourlon Wood', 140th Brigade War Diary; TNA WO 95/2732: 'Report on Operations around Graincourt', 1/15th London

back, the onslaught then developing through Orival Wood, around and behind the right of C and D companies, who, first retiring behind the sunken road, were also fending off incursions down that avenue itself.[227] By the time orders were issued for full withdrawal at 5:30 p.m., the outpost subalterns had already instructed their men to 'cut their way out' and 'make for the sun'.[228] Exposed on all sides when escaping encirclement, the party was reduced by half as it fell back along the 1 1/4 mile route back to a designated strongpoint.[229] Nonetheless, the assailants suffered heavy losses and, as the retreat progressed, 1/15th Battalion 'had the best part of the whole business' including seeing off an enemy party, variously estimated as between 100 and 300 men, before Flesquières.[230] Latterly guided by a cable trench, the survivors were able to reach safety.[231] All covering troops were withdrawn by 8.30 p.m.[232]

As its enormous casualties demonstrate, the division's resourcefulness was sorely challenged at Bourlon Wood.[233] The three phases – defence, attack and withdrawal – constituted 'a complete test of [its] powers and morale.[234] After years of predominantly offensive operations, its performance alongside that of 2nd Division on 30 November, probably facing the most powerful counter-offensive experienced up to that time, has been described as admirable and demonstrating sound discipline and morale.[235] The official historian classified the defence of the Bourlon–Moeuvres sector as 'an outstanding British achievement in the war' and the work of 47th, 2nd and 56th (London) divisions, fighting *Gruppe Arras* 'to a standstill' in 'a soldier's battle ... in the best British infantry tradition.'[236] Haig immediately recognised the defence as 'splendid' and 'magnificent'.[237] Contemporary official approbation was given greater

Regiment War Diary; Anon., *Civil Service Rifles*, p.171.

227 TNA WO 95/2728: 'Report on Withdrawal from Bourlon Wood', 140th Brigade War Diary; TNA WO 95/2732: 'Report on Operations around Graincourt', 1/15th London Regiment War Diary; Anon., *Civil Service Rifles*, p.171.

228 TNA WO 95/2728: 'Report on Withdrawal from Bourlon Wood', 140th Brigade War Diary; TNA WO 95/2732: 'Report on Operations around Graincourt', 1/15th London Regiment War Diary; Maude, *47th Division*, p.131.

229 Anon., *Civil Service Rifles*, pp.171,173.

230 Ibid.

231 Ibid., p.172.

232 TNA WO 95/2728: 'Report on Withdrawal from Bourlon Wood', 140th Brigade War Diary. A and B companies of 1/15th, holding a similar covering position on the other side of Graincourt, had a far less troubled occupation and withdrawal. See TNA WO 95/2732: 'Report on Operations around Graincourt', 1/15th London Regiment War Diary; Anon., *Civil Service Rifles*, p.174.

233 Maude, *47th Division*, p.127 (some 2,600 + for 30 November); TNA WO 95/748-8: 'Summary of Operations from 1/12/17 – 6/12/17', V Corps War Diary (some 1,550 + for 1-6 December).

234 Maude, *47th Division*, p.133.

235 Hammond, *Cambrai 1917*, p.376.

236 Miles, *Military Operations 1917*, Vol. III, p.220, 303.

237 Sheffield & Bourne, *Haig*, p.354; TNA WO 95/748-8: 'G.45', 2 December 1917, V Corps War Diary.

permanence and visibility with the War Office's publication of a didactic account.[238] The accolades appear well-deserved. The 47th Division entered the battle tired and occupied feeble defensive positions but was still capable of facing the highly trained and motivated *221st Division*, whose *Gruppe* commander also registered his admiration.[239] Moreover, with poor communications behind battalion headquarters, such command and control as existed quite necessarily devolved downwards with a corresponding premium placed on the self-sufficiency and confidence of companies, platoons and junior leaders. Clearly, they did not disappoint. Thus, doctrine devised for offensive operations proved its worth in the defence.

Conclusion

As one historian recently observed, 'Learning is a problematic process. In wartime, difficulties snowball.'[240] And, notwithstanding battlefield success in both, 47th Division confronted difficult circumstances during its two major engagements of 1917, one offensive, the other defensive.

Regardless of suggestions that, as a 'single action bite and hold' operation, Messines Ridge only confers credit upon Plumer for not undertaking more than could be achieved, the offensive is simultaneously held up as a straightening of the line in 'exemplary style', all aspects of Second Army's assault being executed highly effectively.[241] Through this lens, the 47th Division's achievements on 7 June can legitimately be perceived as owing much to doctrinal, experiential and anticipatory attention to detail by corps and army command. Furthermore, the pedant, when considering the failure to capture the LSB position, might assert that 47th Division just clipped the high bar cleared by other divisional formations that day. Nonetheless, even though inconvenient and costly, that shortfall, in a zone bereft of mines and tanks and under an unforgiving barrage timetable, became peripheral to Second Army's objectives and timescales. All other operational/tactical aspects of 47th Division's assault astride the canal ensured that the heavily-fortified and densely defended enemy positions were efficiently overcome. In this highly-organised division-level attack, the absorption and practical application of *SS 135, 143* and *144* enabled Gorringe's Londoners, as required, to achieve the Black Line objective.

---

238 Anon. (Captain Christopher Stone), *The Story of a Great Fight (Being an account of the operations of the 47th, 2nd and 56th Divisions in the neighbourhood of Bourlon and Moeuvres, on the 30th November 1917)*, B18/126, Issued by the General Staff 1918. Copy held by Kings College London Military Archives [KCLMA], Montgomery-Massingberd Papers, GB0099, 7/32. Additional copies are also available in TNA WO 95/2703: 47th Division War Diary.

239 Intelligence Section of the General Staff American Expeditionary Force, *Histories of Two Hundred and Fifty-One Divisions of the German Army*, p.698; TNA WO 95/2729: 1/6th London Regiment War Diary; Moser *op. cit.* in Sheldon, *German Army at Cambrai*, p.256.

240 A. Fox, *Learning to Fight: Military Innovation and Change in the British Army, 1914-1918* (Cambridge: Cambridge University Press, 2018), p.76.

241 Griffith, *Battle Tactics of the Western Front*, pp.86, 211.

The 47th Division's resistance at Bourlon Wood certainly cannot be claimed as principally attributable to top-down schemes or foresight from above. Indeed, Third Army staff were inexplicably slow to react to reports of the enemy massing.[242] Whilst benefiting from other divisions' contributions, it was, in essence, a fine example of ex tempore defence and recovery where speed of response, small-group initiative (shaped and driven by *SS 143* and *SS 152*) and esprit came to the fore in lieu of any significant opportunity for preparation or control by senior commanders.

Nineteen-eighteen was a less exemplary year for 47th Division. Without failing unwarrantedly, it took a battering during the spring offensive and did not participate in any 'showpiece' advance and attack moments during the Hundred Days offensives. But there is compelling evidence that, as it exited 1917 with Messines and Bourlon under its belt alongside noteworthy successes in the preceding two years, the division could claim to be a very reliable, conceivably even an elite, formation of the British Army. The former accolade is assured by contemporary contributions from those who had it under their command and the enemy.[243] More recent historians have joined in.[244] Paddy Griffith's elevation of the second, more prestigious categorisation, always one to invite subjectivity, is tantalisingly suggested by the author's previous statistical analysis of 47th Division's actions, offensive and defensive, between October 1916 and the Armistice. This excludes the positives of Loos and High Wood and includes a relatively mediocre 1918 experience.[245] Refining or expanding the assessment techniques of those who had examined the operations of other formations/units, it accords 47th Division an overall success rate of 65 percent against a generally accepted elite benchmark of 70 percent.[246] In any case, regardless of the precise standard attained, during 1917 the 47th (2nd London) Division had exhibited considerable tactical advancement to ride the learning curve and earn Gorringe's late 1917 accolade that 'England, and London especially, may well be proud of you.'[247]

242 C. Falls, *The First World War* (Barnsley: Pen & Sword, 2014 [1960]), p.301.
243 A five-category classification of 74 BEF divisions by the German high command in January 1918 rated 47th Division to second highest – *gute Angriffsdivision* ('good in attack').
244 Mitchinson, *Territorial Force*, pp.152, 196, 210; Griffith, *Battle Tactics of the Western Front*, p.80. The 47th Division 'has a very valid claim [to elite status].'
245 R. Hendry, 'From High Wood to the Armistice – Did the 47th (2nd London) Division become an elite formation of the BEF?', MA Dissertation, University of Wolverhampton, December 2017, pp.50-55 and appendices 25-30.
246 P. Simkins, *From the Somme to Victory: The British Army's Experience on the Western Front 1916-1918* (Barnsley: Pen & Sword, 2014), pp.59-85; P. Simkins, 'Co-stars or Supporting Cast? British Divisions in "The Hundred Days" 1918' in P. Griffith (ed.), *British Fighting Methods in the Great War* (London: Frank Cass, 1996), pp.50-69; G. Inglis, 'Culmination of the Learning Process? Corps and Divisional Performance in the British Third Army in The Hundred Days', MA Dissertation, University of Wolverhampton, December 2016.
247 Maude, *47th Division*, p.133.

16

1917
The 'Dark Days' of the Tank[1]

Tim Gale

On a bleak and unusually cold March day in 1917, a small group of military and civil representatives from France and Great Britain met at the War Office in London to discuss a new weapon – the *char d'assaut* or tank.[2] The importance of this conference can be gauged by the fact that it was presided over by the Deputy Chief of the Imperial General Staff, General Sir Robert Whigham, and the participants included the most senior officers and official representatives of the British and French tank programmes. Within the latter delegation was the originator and commander of the French tank arm (*Artillerie Spéciale* (*AS*), *General de Division* Jean-Baptiste Eugene Estienne, who would play a leading part in the discussions. The conference was quite unusual in that the Anglo-French allies had not hitherto co-operated with regard to their respective tank force arms and had failed to inform the other about current tank projects until they were well underway.[3] Interestingly, all agreed that the concept of a surprise massed tank offensive would be impractical for some time if at all. Nevertheless, the idea would be inaugurated on the battlefield less than eight months later.

Whilst the tank would become central to land warfare for the remainder of the 20th century, this was by no means certain as 1917 opened. The tank had made its battlefield debut at the Battle of Flers–Courcelette (15-22 September 1916) during the closing stages of the Somme offensive. Although far from decisive, there was sufficient promise with the new weapon to continue with its development. By the close of the year Great Britain and France had separate large-scale tank development

---

1   H.J. Elles, Introduction to Clough & A. Williams-Ellis, *The Tank Corps* (London: Country Life, 1919), p. v.
2   TNA WO 32/5154: Report of the Conclusions reached at a Conference on the Tactical Employment of Tanks, held, on the 4th March 1917, at the War Office.
3   It was only with the setting up of the Inter-Allied Tank Commission in May 1918 that a formal process of liaison and co-operation was made possible.

programmes well underway but there were still significant doubts about the potential utility of the tank in the military and political circles of both nations. Moreover, the very conception on how to conduct tank warfare was contested, and it remained unclear as to what was the best method of employing tanks to overcome the Western Front deadlock. By mid-1917, the situation looked bleak, with large-scale deployments of both the British and French tank forces in April having produced mediocre results. However, by the close of the year, two offensives, one British and one French, would cement the tank's role in modern warfare. This chapter is concerned with the evolving fortunes of the tank during 1917, when it faced an uncertain future. Yet the year ended with a successful demonstration of British tank potential during the celebrated Battle of Cambrai (20 November-6 December), and the limited, but equally important, Battle of Malmaison (23-27 October) where French tanks also proved their worth. Although conventionally described as tank battles, in reality both were won by advanced artillery techniques.[4] However, that should not obscure the fact that these offensives were of crucial importance to the development of armoured warfare. Cambrai and Malmaison would ensure that the tank remained at the centre of land warfare for over a century.

Before considering what transpired at the March 1917 War Office conference, it is worth briefly noting the tank's standing in the British and French armies at the start of that year. There are two primary questions facing an army when adopting new military technology: whether the design(s) available can be realised and manufactured in sufficient quantity (and on time) and whether the results of this process can effectively be employed in the context of existing, or possible future, doctrine. There is also the question as to whether it is worth devoting resources to unproven new technology that might be better used elsewhere to enhance existing equipment. Given the technological hurdles to be overcome in tank development, the British and French effort is impressive. Neither nation had much experience in the manufacture of tracked vehicles. Indeed, France had rather an uneven track record in the development of modern weapons prior to 1914, the costliest error being the failure to establish an adequate heavy artillery arm.

Whilst receipt of armoured vehicle proposals were welcomed by French GQG and British GHQ, these ideas encountered resistance in various quarters. There was, for example, a lack of enthusiasm about Estienne's project within the *Direction de Service Automobile* (*DSA*), the organisation responsible for motor transport in the French army. General Mourret, *DSA's* technical service commander, was initially reluctant to provide support because of the heavy demands on the organisation. Indeed, French C-in-C Joseph Joffre informed his government in October 1915 that he required some 1,400 lorries to be delivered by April 1916. Moreover, the *DSA* alone required over

---

4   The best modern study of the Battle of Cambrai is Bryn Hammond, *Cambrai: The Myth of the First Great Tank Battle* (London: Weidenfeld & Nicholson, 2008).

2,000 lorries with 600 replacements needed per month. This was in addition to 500 tractors and 300 lorries that the air service required during this time.[5]

In a similar vein, the British tank programme faced considerable opposition from the Aircraft Production Department, which managed to have the tank programme barred from obtaining aluminium engines, all of which were reserved for aircraft assembly.[6] During a subsequent meeting at the Ministry of Munitions, it was decided that an order for 700 Ricardo engines from five factories made by tank pioneer Albert Stern would be cancelled because there were not enough tanks to install them in.[7] It should also be noted how difficult the engine manufacturing process was in Great Britain and France at this time, with suppliers rarely making deliveries on time.

There was also the issue of personnel. French Schneider tanks had crews of six, whilst the heavier St Chamonds and British tanks had crews of eight. In practice, most French tanks were crewed by NCOs, thus removing valuable junior leaders from other branches of the French army. This was not the case with the British crews, as usually only two of eight crewmen would be officers or senior NCOs. The tank arm, however, still absorbed significant numbers of highly motivated and skilled infantrymen.[8] By 1916, heavy infantry casualties meant that both the French and British armies required large reinforcement drafts and losing them to an untried branch created tension and frustration. Indeed, such were the desired technical skillsets for tank officers and other ranks that the French drafted officers from the *Marine nationale*. Moreover, rather mundane skills were in short supply; the ability to drive was not common at this time, and 200 drivers were brought into the *AS* from the *DSA* and artillery in 1916.[9]

It is also worth noting that tank projects were financially expensive. The French tank project amounted to over 450 million French francs (all indirect costs associated with the project inclusive), slightly over £120 million at exchange rates of the time.[10]

---

5 *Le général commandant en chef à Monsieur le sous-secrétaire d'état de la Guerre (artillerie),* 25 October 1915, Ministère de la Guerre, *Les Armées française dans la grande guerre,* Tome III, Annexes 4, No. 3012. All further references to the French Official History are abbreviated as AFGG, followed by the tome and volume number. Thus, this would be AFGG 3, Annexes 4, No. 3012.

6 Albert Stern, *Tanks 1914-1918: The Log Book of a Pioneer* (London: Hodder & Stoughton, 1919), p.123.

7 Stern, *Notebook,* pp. 124-25. For more on British manufacturing priorities, see Harris, *Men, Ideas and Tanks,* pp. 128-29.

8 For further details, see Chapter 2, Stephen Pope, *The First Tank Crews; The Lives of the Tankmen who fought at the Battle of Flers-Courcelette 15 September 1916* (Solihull: Helion & Co., 2016).

9 GQG, *Le Général commandant en chef à Monsieur le sous-secrétaire d'état de la guerre,* 20 November 1916. Service historique de la défense, French military archives at Vincennes, carton 16N2121. This is referred to as SHD and carton number hereafter.

10 F.J. Deygas, *Les Chars d'assaut – Leur passé, leur avenir* (Paris: Charles-Lavauzelle, 1937), p.300.

Great Britain spent over £5 million on Mark IV tanks alone.[11] However, compared to other military expenditures, British and French tanks were relatively inexpensive, especially when compared to artillery shell expenditure. For example, the Verdun assault on 20 August 1917 cost 700 million francs (£187 million) in artillery ammunition and the Battle of Malmaison cost around 500 million francs (£133 million), the latter being more than France spent on its entire tank programme during the war.[12] Conversely, all resources, human and material, set aside for the tank arm had to be justified by measurable performance on the battlefield.

The noticeably different appearance of British and French tanks is evocative of the fact that all tank designers at this stage were experimenting with new designs without reference to pre-existing templates. With no industrial base for tracked vehicle production in either country, manufacture was, by necessity, awarded to companies that learned about producing tanks as they went along.[13] Unsurprisingly, there were numerous difficulties as Allied tank designers pushed contemporary automobile technology to its limits.

The first British tank was the Mark I. Its familiar rhomboid shape was ideal for crossing trenches but was an inherent limitation in other circumstances. This accounts for the fact that no similarly shaped tank was produced after the war. In contrast, initial French tanks designs were essentially just armoured boxes on a modified American Holt tractor chassis.

The British made some small improvements to their design with the Mark II tank, but it was only with the arrival of the Mark IV in spring 1917 that the 'Heavy Branch Machine Gun Corps'/'Tank Corps'[14] had adopted a relatively reliable tank model.. Weighing 31.4 tons (28.4 tonnes), the Mark IV was 26 feet long with a width just over 13 feet. To increase production speed and to avoid industrial bottlenecks, the Mark IV was armed in two ways; 'Male' tanks with two 6-pounder quick-firing guns and three Lewis machine-guns; 'Female' tanks with five Lewis machine-guns. The Daimler-Foster engine only produced 102 HP so, as with the French tanks, the Mark IV was underpowered and very slow.

In 1917, the French army had two medium tank designs: the Schneider and St. Chamond, with the famous Renault light-tank entering production that year. The first two models were troubled by a series of manufacturing and design faults. The first to go into production was the Schneider (1916), an armoured rectangular box mounted on a Holt tractor chassis. Armed with a short-barrelled 75mm 'Blockhaus'

---

11   John Glanfield, *The Devil's Chariots: The Origins and Secret Battles of Tanks in the First World War* (Stroud: Sutton Publishing, 2001), p.313.
12   Deygas, *Les Chars*, p.300.
13   See Glanfield, *The Devil's Chariots* for a detailed account of the byzantine origins of the British tank and its numerous manufacturers and designers.
14   At this stage of the war the Tank Corps was titled Heavy Branch Machine Gun Corps (HBMGC). The name was officially changed to Tank Corps on 27 July 1917. The latter will be employed throughout this chapter to avoid confusion.

Schneider gun – originally intended for use in fortifications – mounted on the right, it had a very limited arc of fire (just 20°), and a machine-gun on each side. Weighing just over 13 tonnes, its primitive engine struggled to move the vehicle at more than walking pace. In addition to the Schneider, the French Ministry of Armaments independently commissioned the St Chamond. This vehicle was larger (23 tonnes) and armed with a full-size 75mm field gun with an even more limited arc of fire (5°) and four machine-guns. Its tracks were driven by two electric generators that were in turn powered by petrol engine, an ambitious arrangement that French design engineers struggled to make reliable until late in the war.

General de Division Jean-Baptiste Estienne.

French tanks compared poorly with the trench crossing ability of the Mark IV. The Schneider could barely traverse a six-foot wide trench; the St Chamond was only slightly better. The initial tanks were also all under-armed compared to tanks in the next war, with only the St Chamond possessing a full-scale 75mm artillery piece in it. Estienne's view was that a tank's ability to advance under fire was more important than the firepower it carried. He summed up the purpose of the tank's gun as, 'only fire when you can't march'.[15]

Early British and French tank designs needed urgent modifications but wholesale revisions were simply impossible, as by the time most defects became apparent it was too late to alter designs or commission completely new ones. However, these designs, undertaken during wartime with undeveloped technology, were brought from specification to deployment within 13 months – even less in the case of the Renault tank – which was in itself a remarkable achievement.

The novelty of the technology was not the only problem facing the tank arm. Basic supplies were sometimes lacking. Both French and British tank crews encountered difficulties in obtaining good quality fuel for their machines. British petrol was described as 'atrocious' in 1917.[16] An even more serious issue was British and French failure to arrange spare parts manufacture. Nothing was available when Mark I tanks entered action for the first time because manufacturing had been organised on the assumption that no tanks would be in operation until the first 150 models had been

15 Quoted in Tim Gale, *The French Army's Tank Force and Armoured Warfare in the Great War* (Farnham: Ashgate, 2013), p.36. This was a pre-war French infantry slogan.
16 Glanfield, *Devil's Chariots*, p.143.

produced.[17] This meant that spare production had to be hurriedly reorganised prior to the Flers-Courcelette push. French manufacturers had also given little thought to parts supply, a problem that would continue throughout the war.[18]

A further problem was when tanks were prematurely deployed in combat for the first time by the British C-in-C Sir Douglas Haig. His decision to unveil the secret weapon in September 1916 resulted in immediate controversy at home and in France. In Great Britain, Stern and Sir Eustace Tennyson d'Eyncourt of the British Landship Committee opposed the deployment and wrote to the Minister of Munitions, Edwin Montagu, and to CIGS Sir William Robertson, stating their opposition. Stern postulated that the tanks were not ready and the pending deployment was 'courting disaster.'[19] They argued, not unreasonably, that the Mark Is were built as training machines, never intended for fighting, and previous employment as such had significantly worn them from a mechanical point of view.[20] There was also considerable dismay in France. Thus, when General Pierre des Vallières, head of the French Military Mission to GHQ, informed GQG of what the British intended, Joffre warned Armaments Minister Albert Thomas that should the enemy catch wind of the tanks, they could widen their trenches 'in a night'. This meant that current French tank designs would be unable to traverse hostile defences without infantry assistance.[21]

Estienne visited the British tank programme in Lincoln during June 1916 and attempted to persuade the responsible authorities to delay tank deployment until the French models were ready in spring 1917. At this point both armies could then deploy tanks in large numbers.[22] Stern, Director of the Mechanical Supply Department, was asked to intercede with Edwin Montagu who visited Haig to discuss this proposal the following September. The British commander, although sympathetic, was unwilling to change plans at this late stage.[23]

It is difficult to judge who was correct in this case as there were merits in both positions. The French were correct to be concerned that the surprise effect of tanks would be lost. It was also correct to believe that it might provide the Germans with the impetus to develop their own tank arm; indeed it was a noticeable failure of the latter that they did not. However, it was equally prudent of the British to want to test tanks on a small scale, given that no amount of training could replicate combat

---

17   Ibid., p.150.
18   See Gale, *French Army's Tank Force*, pp.68-69.
19   Stern, *Notebook*, pp.89-90.
20   Glanfield, *Devil's Chariots*, p.145.
21   MMF, *Le général des Vallières, chef de la mission, à général en chef (5e bureau)*, 1 August 1916, AFGG IV/2, Annexes 3, 2958 and quote in Elizabeth Greenhalgh, 'Technology Development in Coalition: The Case of the First World War Tank', *The International History Review*, Vol. XXII/4, December 2000, pp.806-1008, p.811.
22   General Estienne, *Compte-rendu d'une mission en Angleterre les 25 et 26 Juin 1916*, 26 June 1916, SHD 16N2121.
23   Stern, *Notebook*, pp.87-90.

lessons. In the event, *OHL* failed to recognise the importance of the introduction of armour in September 1916. They did not accelerate their own programme or develop effective anti-tank weapons, so French fears proved unfounded. However, the arguments against early use remain reasonable. The potential for a decisive surprise was lost in exchange for some insignificant gains on the Somme. However, the French were certainly asking too much if they expected the British to wait until enough of their tanks were available for large-scale operations. This was at least six months away in September 1916. Moreover, the British were well aware of past delays in the French tank programme and had reasons to be concerned that awaiting French readiness could be a long process.[24]

The justification for early deployment was that it would provide invaluable combat experience. There was a great opportunity for the British and French to learn from tank use at the Somme. Unfortunately, it was difficult to discern what aspects of that experience were generally applicable and which were particular to the Flers-Courcelette offensive. For example, the relevant French Military Mission to GHQ's report suggested that direct artillery fire would be no threat to tanks. This was highly misleading.[25] Conversely, GQG abandoned thoughts of mounting a 120mm gun on the St Chamond largely due to British after-action reports.[26] It should be noted that cooperation between Anglo-French tank forces was rendered more difficult because few of the leading personalities spoke each other's language. For example, an important conference at Marly (one of the *AS*'s forward bases), convened to discuss the September 1916 tank attacks had to be conducted largely in German, the only common language between delegates.[27]

For the French, the most disastrous consequence of the premature introduction of tanks on the Somme was exactly what Joffre predicted. Almost immediately, the Germans began to significantly widen their trenches thus ensuring that French tanks could not operate independently of the infantry. With no way to modify existing tank designs, the tanks would now be far more dependent on infantry and could accomplish little by themselves.[28]

This then was the backdrop to the March 1917 War Office conference. Against the advice of British GHQ, it was convened entirely due to pressure on the British War Cabinet from Stern and D'Eyncourt who 'were very much troubled about the future of Mechanical Warfare'. They insisted that a conference be held between those

---

24 For example, see *Le sous-secrétaire d'État de la Guerre (Artillerie) à M. Le général commandant en chef*, AFGG 4/2, Annexes 3, No. 2507.
25 French military mission to GHQ, *Note sur l'emploi des CT le 15 Septembre*, 17 September 1916, AFGG 4/3, Annexes 1, No. 463.
26 GQG, *Le Général commandant en chef à Monsieur le sous-secrétaire d'état de la guerre*, 20 November 1916. SHD 16N2121.
27 Stern, *Notebook*, p.105.
28 Gale, *French Army's Tank Force*, p. 6.

concerned with future tank employment.[29] The military delegates included Major-General Frederick Anley, Administrative Commander of the Heavy Machine Gun Corps (subsequently the Tank Corps), Estienne; *DSA* chief Aimé Doumenc (organiser of the *Voie sacrée* at Verdun the previous year); Jules-Louis Breton, Under Secretary of State for Inventions (then part of the Armaments Ministry); d'Eyncourt and Stern represented the British civilian authorities.

Perusal of both the conference minutes and official report reveals that Estienne dominated the discussion and resultant conclusions.[30] According to the former document, Brigadier-General H.J. Elles, GOC Tank Corps, was silent and Anley's contribution was small, whilst Lieutenant-Colonel J.F.C. Fuller, Tank Corps Chief of Staff, was not in attendance.

Estienne began by stating that the main tactical value of the tanks was to assist the infantry in the advance. He proposed that three types of tank should be employed, heavy (15 to 30 tons); medium (7 to 15 tons), and light (4 to 6 tons). The latter would need to be as light as possible because the French were intending to transport them behind the line with ordinary lorries. Medium tanks were required because heavy tank movement was limited by the availability of adequate bridges that could sustain their weight. Whereas medium tanks would be able to cross temporary bridges and could be easily transported by rail, heavy tanks required special equipment for rail transport. However, heavy tanks were still required because, being long and of great weight, of their inherent ability to traverse obstacles and larger trenches.[31]

Estienne went on to discuss forms of attack available to tanks and asked the delegates to consider two types: surprise without prior artillery bombardment or deliberate attack after thorough artillery preparation as was customary for all offensive operations at this point in the war. He conceded that previous difficulties encountered when concealing assault preparations made it 'improbable' that opportunities would arise for an attack without artillery. However, he also argued that if there was a large mass of tanks available and the terrain favoured concealment, 'great results' might be obtained.[32] In respect to a deliberate attack with normal artillery preparations, tanks were to assist the infantry when the enemy's rear positions were beyond reach of supporting artillery fire.

The idea of a surprise *en masse* tank attack without artillery preparation had been in Estienne's mind since he first approached Joffre and GQG about establishing an

---

29   Stern, *Notebook*, p.121 and TNA WO 32/5154: War Cabinet 44, Extract from the Proceedings of a Meeting of the War Cabinet held at 10, Downing Street, on Thursday, January 25th 1917 at 11.30 am, pp.1-2.
30   See TNA WO 32/5154: Tactical Employment of Tanks and the minutes; Proceedings of a Conference on the Tactical Employment of Tanks, held, on the 4th March 1917, at the War Office.
31   Tactical Employment of Tanks, para. 1.
32   Ibid., para. 2.

armoured vehicle force in 1915.[33] These plans had been ruined by the appearance of British tanks at Flers-Courcelette. However, he still believed that such an attack might be possible. Thus, Estienne advised the assembled delegates about an armoured force concentration followed by an assault with tanks in the vanguard,. Detraining at least 10 kilometres from the enemy line and ensuring that forward assembly positions had sufficient supply and repair facilities, tanks, in the case of an attack without artillery preparation, would precede the infantry. Therefore, they needed to be in position close to the frontline trenches before the assault began. Occupying jumping-off positions at night or under cover of mist or fog, 'great care' was to be taken to conceal their arrival. In attacks where a routine artillery bombardment was to occur, the infantry would advance ahead of the tanks but because zero hour for such operations was more often than not scheduled for daylight hours, it was just as imperative to conceal the tanks prior to jumping-off due to a long approach march.[34]

In line with then current French army doctrine, Estienne believed that the division was the primary combat formation, therefore, tank action had to be coordinated with it. This meant that armoured units should be subordinated to divisional commanders during an assault, although the army commander would always be the ultimate arbiter of tanks. A divisional attack supported by tanks would require two infantry companies to facilitate vehicles' negotiation of obstacles and trenches. Tanks would only deploy when the infantry advance was stalled by enemy strongpoints, after which they would press forward to crush barbed war defences and suppress machine-gun emplacements thus enabling the infantry to carry successive hostile defensive lines.[35]

Estienne proposed that the ideal tank unit organisation would be one heavy and one light tank per three or four medium tanks, the light tanks being reserved for unit and tank battery commanders. He also noted the distinctive roles for the various available tank models. Heavy and medium tanks would be employed where there was little or no surprise and/or manoeuvre. All depended on 'weight of numbers and weight of metal.'[36] During the course of surprise attacks on entrenched positions, medium tanks – taking advantage of their greater manoeuvrability when compared to heavy tanks – would advance ahead of the infantry as a means of overcoming barbed wire defences. Estienne, remarking that 'in open warfare especially the opportunities for light tanks would be very great', conceived light tanks in the role of a rapid reserve with medium tanks tasked to pursue a retreating enemy.[37] These prescient observations were subsequently confirmed during successful operations carried out by Renault and British Whippet light tanks during the second half of 1918.

The French and British General Staff representatives, 'while concurring generally with the principles advocated in the preceding paragraphs by General Estienne', drew

33 Gale, *French Army's Tank Force*, pp.22, 33.
34 *Tactical Employment of Tanks*, para. 3.
35 Ibid., para. 4.
36 Ibid., para. 5.
37 Ibid., para. 6.

attention to some areas of disagreement. They emphasised the 'paramount necessity of careful reconnaissance of the ground' and the necessity for this to be considered when assigning tactical roles to the tanks.[38] They believed that recent British experience indicated it was better to attach tanks to corps command and control rather than division – this was actually a misunderstanding cleared up after the conference. Estienne actually recommended that *in combat* tanks should be subordinate to a divisional commander but in all other circumstances should be under corps control. The General Staff perspective on tank armaments was that it would depend on the type of tank and its projected role on the battlefield. The British declared that the proportion of their gun tanks to machine-gun tanks, being roughly equal, was determined 'to suit manufacture' and that there was not enough evidence for a 'definite opinion' yet.[39]

As the conference was at the instigation of Stern and D'Eyncourt, they, of course, raised the question of tanks as an independent arm and recommended that they should only be employed over ground not subjected to heavy artillery fire. This optimistic view was given a full airing, with Stern suggesting that light tanks might 'perform the role of cavalry in attacking the enemy's gun positions.' D'Eyncourt argued that reliability issues thus far were the result of poorly trained crews and the early heavy tank versions, the new Mark IV model offering significantly higher performance and reliability. With respect to tanks operating independently, he pointed out that armoured vehicles could transport most of their supplies (ammunition, food, etc.) which meant that a surprise attack could be arranged with less preparation and greater depth.[40]

The 'military members of the Commission' rejected Stern and D'Eyncourt's ideas. In their estimation, tanks lacked both the speed and the mechanical reliability (at present) to operate as an independent arm.[41] The military members also agreed that heavily shelled areas were to all intents and purposes impassable to tanks, which is why they should be reserved for deep penetration assaults where the ground would be less damaged than in the proximity of the enemy's forward defences.

The conference concluded with the chairman's summing-up. He postulated four conclusions that were agreed upon by Estienne and the others: '[F]or the present', it was determined that the role of tanks was to support the infantry, particularly during deep penetration advances. Furthermore, all three armoured vehicle classes (heavy, medium and light) should be manufactured. Perhaps, most importantly, it was agreed that surprise attacks without artillery preparation were possible and 'might arise' when large numbers [of tanks] were available and the ground was particularly suitable for concealment.'[42]

The War Office conference is indictive of the dilemmas faced by French and British tank programmes in early 1917. The technology was novel and nothing was certain.

---

38   Ibid., para. 8.
39   Ibid.
40   Ibid., para. 9.
41   Ibid., para. 10.
42   Ibid., para. 11 (3).

The meeting quashed further considerations of armour operating as an independent arm, but it did place on record the idea of a large scale surprise tank attack. Despite this optimism, Anglo-French tank fortunes over the succeeding six months were such that by summer 1917 it appeared unlikely that an armoured force would play a major role in any future offensive, let alone a risky surprise assault without artillery support.

The first French tank attack of the year, part of the Nivelle offensive, was a debacle. Two *AS groupements* (battalions) participated in Fifth Army's offensive at Juvincourt on 16 April 1917. Having been assured that the enemy's artillery would be suppressed, the *groupements* advanced in lengthy single-file columns in broad daylight and in full view of the German artillery observers situated on commanding heights such as the Craonne Plateau. Disaster soon followed. One *groupement* was annihilated by indirect shelling before it had even passed through the first enemy trench system. The other *groupement's* commander was killed when his tank was hit before his subordinate vehicles could deploy. Leaderless, the second *groupement* carried on, with several lone tanks penetrating the enemy defences and some pressing to a depth of more than three kilometres before the attack finally stalled. Unfortunately, this modest success had been costly in men and material: 76 tanks out of the 132 engaged had been put out of action. Fifty-seven were destroyed by German artillery.[43] Stern, accompanied by two British staff officers, attended a meeting of the French Tank Consultative Committee on 23 April 1917. There, Estienne was quite frank about design limitations exposed during the fighting of the preceding two weeks.[44]

Had all three available *groupements* been deployed on 16 April, the subsequent *AS* story might have been different. Fortunately, one *groupement* had not participated in the unfortunate April assaults. Thus, this unit was available for the latter stages of the Nivelle Offensive. This second operation, coming two weeks after the shock of 16 April, was executed in a very different manner from the first. Nineteen Schneiders went into action with only three breaking down, whereas the 12 St Chamonds encountered difficulties when negotiating the local terrain, six breaking down and one being wrecked by artillery.[45] Solely marred by mechanical failures and with just a single vehicle destroyed by enemy action, the assault secured all its objectives with few casualties. It also demonstrated the *AS* organisation's remarkable ability to learn from experience and introduce effective innovations at short notice. The French tank force would not see action again until the Malmaison offensive in October.

The performance of British tanks in the first half of 1917 was little better than those of their French counterparts. For the Battle of Arras (9 April-16 May), the 1st Tank Brigade could only muster 60 vehicles, although the original intention had been to employ two battalions of 96 tanks. Held in reserve for attacks deep into enemy

---

43   Estienne, *Rapport au sujet de la participation aux opérations de la V armée des groupements Bossut et Chaubès de l'artillerie d'assaut, 23 avril 1918, Tableau no. 2*, SHD 16N2120.

44   Ministère de l'Armement, Service Automobile, *Comité consultatif de l'artillerie d'assaut, procès-verbal 8ème réunion, 23 Avril 1917*, SHD 16N2129.

45   Ibid.

Wrecked Schneider CA1 tank, Juvincourt April 1917.

St Chamond tank.

Mark IV Male tank, Messines June 1917.

territory after the infantry had seized the first German line, mechanical difficulties prevented tanks from having a significant impact on operations. This is not surprising when one considers that the models involved were the notoriously unreliable Mark Is and Mark IIs.[46] Some individual British tanks made useful contributions to the fighting at a tactical level, but their overall influence was negligible.

The shambolic British tank assault at Bullecourt on 11 April 1917 was a disheartening setback. As this operation is the subject of a separate chapter in this volume, it will not be addressed here other than to note that it is a prime example of how infantry confidence in tanks could be lost. Once gone, it would prove very hard to regain.

British tanks next participated in the seizure of the Messines–Wytschaete Ridge in West Flanders (7-14 June 1917). A curtain-raiser to the Third Battle of Ypres, this offensive was partially mounted to relieve pressure on the French army which was suffering widespread disorder after the failure of the Nivelle Offensive.[47] Once again, the assault was not organised around tanks, which 'were employed purely as accessories. No reliance was placed on them.'[48] Even in this limited role, it was a difficult operation and the Tank Corps had to concede that only 19 of the 68 tanks

---

46   J.P. Harris, *Men, Ideas and Tanks: British Military Thought and Armoured Forces, 1903-1939* (Manchester: Manchester University Press, 2008), p.96.
47   Ibid., p.98.
48   Quoted in Harris, p.99.

sent forward were of any assistance to the infantry.[49] To be fair, limited tank success at Messines was primarily due to the detonation of 19 underground mines, thorough artillery preparation, and dense creeping barrages that left little for armour to accomplish. When they did come into action, however, tanks added considerable weight to the assault with perhaps the best example being a tank christened *Wytschaete Express* leading the infantry in a successful attack on Wytschaete village. An indication of what the tanks could do if mechanically reliable was demonstrated by the case of one tank pressing on over 3,000 yards to the final Black Line objective in less than two hours.[50]

The Tank Corps would participate in the Third Ypres offensive which opened on 31 July 1917. However, the corps would soon find itself facing deeply unfavourable circumstances for tank action due to torrential rainfall, heavy shelling and inundated ground. All three Tank Corps brigades were to be attached to Fifth Army's subordinate corps (II, XIX and XVIII) with 216 tanks deployed. Whilst the organisation involved in getting the tanks and crews prepared for the operation and bringing them to the battlefield was good, the state of the ground was the final arbiter of how well armour would perform. The area was well-known for being waterlogged and difficult going for transport and this was exacerbated by over four million shells fired by General Sir Hubert Gough's Fifth Army during artillery preparations. Brigadier-General Elles wrote of his 'increasing misgiving' about what the extended preparation was doing to the ground, informing Fifth Army staff that 'our [tanks'] chances fell with every shell fired.'[51] By 31 July, Tank Corps headquarters had forecast that no more than half of the assigned tanks would reach their objectives. In the event, only 19 tanks out of 136 engaged that day were able to assist the infantry attack on the second line.[52] On 19 August a small action known as 'The Cockcroft', the only tank operation worthy of note during the campaign, occurred when 12 MK IVs, advancing in column along a straight road under cover of a smoke barrage, assaulted a series of German blockhouses which had held up 48th (South Midland) Division three days prior. Although five tanks ditched, the remainder were able to suppress the defenders' fire until the strongpoints were isolated and overrun by trailing British infantrymen.[53] This episode provided a welcome advertisement for what armour could do under favourable circumstances. Other tank operations occurred on this front in September and October. Unfortunately, by this time the area had transformed into an impassable swamp and given the appalling conditions, it is remarkable that the Tank Corps was able to send units into action at all.

49   Ibid.
50   J.F.C. Fuller, *Tanks in the Great War 1914-1918* (Nashville, Tennessee: Battery Press 2003 reprint of 1920 edition), pp.110-11.
51   Quoted in J.E. Edmonds, *Military Operations France and Belgium 1917*, Vol. 2 (London: HMSO, 1948), p. 379.
52   Ibid and Harris, *Men, Ideas and Tanks*, p.109.
53   Edmonds, *Military Operations 1917*, Vol. 2, p.202.

Tank Corps headquarters staff, Bermicourt 1917: Brigadier-General H.J Elles (centre); Lieutenant-Colonel J.F.C. Fuller (far left).

By September 1917, the promise of tanks seemed rather tarnished compared to the high hopes expressed at the March War Office conference. French armour had put up a spirited effort and undergone a remarkable recovery, but doubts remained about its usefulness. The Tank Corps had, for the most part, done well given the circumstances but its position as an essential part of the British Army was far from certain.

By late autumn 1917 the British and French armies were in an unenviable position. The vaunted Nivelle Offensive had failed to rupture the front and, by mid-October, it was clear that the Third Battle of Ypres had failed to achieve its strategic goals and was being wound down. The British army was exhausted by its recent Flanders exertions and the French army, having experienced extensive mutinies the previous spring, was in no state to undertake a major offensive. These dire circumstances appeared to have rendered plans for a surprise tank operation null and void. However, a major advance in artillery techniques would make the possibility of an *en masse* assault envisaged at the March War Office conference a reality.

As previously noted, two battles (Malmaison and Cambrai) would be fought before 1917 came to an end. They would determine the tank's future in warfare. The genesis of these offensive operations was rather different. The *AS* had to prove to GQG and the French Army that tanks could be a useful component to operations planned around large quantities of matériel. The British experience was somewhat different. The generally dismal results obtained by the Tank Corps during the Flanders offensive, through no fault of their own, had left this highly-motivated force eager to get into action somewhere more favourable for tank operations. By late autumn, both GQG and GHQ were open to proposals for limited attacks against clearly defined objectives, the criteria of which the Malmaison and Cambrai sectors fulfilled. Thus, tanks would participate in both offensives but only one was to have armour at the very centre of its planning whereas the other would delegate it to a subsidiary role.

There is some debate about who actually devised the Cambrai battle plan. Like much Western Front operational planning at this time, a series of simultaneous ideas were generated and explored in the search for an effective limited attack.[54] The Tank Corps had spent the year searching for a suitable 'tank raid' location. A June 1917 paper produced by corps headquarters identified the area about Cambrai.[55] However, with the Third Ypres offensive soon to begin, it was impossible at this stage to obtain GHQ sanction. Meantime, General Sir Julian Byng's Third Army staff developed a plan, it appears independently, which also involved a limited offensive in the Cambrai sector.[56] In September, Byng proposed a local offensive to GHQ. As the Third Ypres offensive still occupied Haig's attention, Third Army was not granted permission until October. In the interim, the Tank Corps was able to carry out some preliminary preparations.

Operational planning for Malmaison had a different imperative to that of the British prior to Cambrai. The new French C-in-C, General Henri Philippe Pétain, had inherited a seriously demoralized army and his initial efforts were focused on the widespread mutinies that had broken out in the aftermath of the Nivelle offensive. Overall conditions for the frontline troops were significantly improved and the disciplinary response to what amounted to a large-scale military strike was relatively benign. As with Haig, Pétain was enthusiastic about the tank programme and, on initiating a major armaments programme, he significantly increased existing orders for Renault light tanks, as well as ordering a large increase in artillery production. Pétain knew that major operations were out of the question but he also recognised that the army could not remain stationary for rest of the year without seriously undermining its morale and its offensive capability for 1918. He therefore planned a series of limited objective attacks with the intention of carrying out tactical and equipment experimentation. Furthermore, various sectors of the front would be prepared for offensive action during the remainder of 1917 and the following spring and summer. An important aim of these operations was to restore morale, so the proposed assaults had to be successful and relatively light in casualties. One of the prospective operations was to be launched against the German salient on La Malmaison Plateau, an area that had witnessed heavy fighting during the Nivelle Offensive. The French Sixth Army, commanded by General Paul André Maistre, was tasked with carrying out the limited offensive with three reinforced corps and a significant amount of super-heavy artillery.

54   See Harris, *Men, Ideas and Tanks*, pp.108-09.
55   Fuller, *Tanks*, pp. 137-38.
56   Ian Beckett, Timothy Bowman & Mark Connelly, *The British Army and the First World War* (Cambridge: Cambridge University Press, 2017), p.338.

The number of French tanks to be deployed at Malmaison was significantly smaller than the number of tanks set aside for Cambrai. The *Artillerie Spéciale* was anxious to prove its worth after the Aisne disaster of the previous April. Nevertheless, it was too big a gamble to grant tanks the essential role in an operation where mitigating risk was the primary consideration. Instructions to French infantry commanders were quite clear: they were to formulate attack plans as though tanks would be absent; any assistance should be considered a bonus. Thus, at Malmaison, Sixth Army only had 38 Schneider and 30 St Chamond tanks. Their role would be a subsidiary one, for this was to be an artillery battle. Maistre employed some 1,779 guns, including four new and massive 400mm railway guns.[57] There was no attempt at surprise and the French artillery fired 1.5 million shells over five days.[58] The intention was that the lengthy bombardment would destroy the German positions so completely that the infantry could advance with minimal casualties. Nevertheless, some resistance – to be engaged by tanks – was expected after the artillery preparatory phase was over. Maistre was given strict instructions that the offensive was to halt and go no further on reaching the banks of the Aillette River, regardless of success.

Conversely, the British intended to unveil a new form of artillery bombardment that would have surprise at its very core. Most importantly, Brigadier-General H.H. Tudor (BGRA 9th (Scottish) Division) developed the means by which accurate predicted fire was achieved, the result of considerable improvements in mapping, sound-ranging and flash-spotting. This meant that the lengthy artillery destruction bombardments of 1916-17 could be foregone. Whilst the British would be deploying less artillery (approximately 1,000 guns) than the French did at Malmaison, the fact that they would simultaneously commence firing without prior registration would achieve the shock and surprise that the Malmaison preparatory bombardment could not.[59] However, if this bombardment was to commence the moment the British infantry advanced, there was the serious risk that intact enemy barbed wire could present an insurmountable obstacle. Crushing wire defences would be the Tank Corps' primary task. Moreover, British commanders were informed that 'the battle was to be based on tanks and led by them.'[60] This is in stark contrast to French instructions that plans were to be made as though tanks did not exist.[61]

For Malmaison fewer than 70 tanks were distributed amongst seven infantry divisions; for Cambrai five infantry divisions would be supported by 476 tanks of which 378 were the improved Mark IV model. The remainder were described as

---

57 *Le 140e Régiment d'Infanterie pendent la Guerre 1914-1918* (Paris: Berger-Levrault, n.d.), p.41.

58 F. Pellegrin, *La Vie d'une Armée pendant la Grande Guerre* (Paris: Flammarion 1921), pp.172-73.

59 For artillery bombardment particulars, see Wilfred Miles, *Military Operations France and Belgium 1917*, Vol. 3 (London: HMSO, 1948), p.25.

60 Fuller, *Tanks*, p.140.

61 Gale, *French Army's Tank Force*, p.90.

'administrative machines' – support and supply vehicles unsuitable for combat.[62] As the Hindenburg Line trenches were very wide in this sector, tanks were fitted with large fascines to assist crossing. This in itself was a considerable challenge.[63] Fascine installation required 21,000 wood bundles compressed and chained in place by 1,000 Chinese Labour Corps workers.[64] Each tank was limited to one fascine which, when dropped to facilitate crossing, was unretrievable. In order to make this workable, Fuller devised a novel tactical solution. His scheme called for the leading tanks to deposit a fascine in the enemy trench opposite and, on traversing it, they would be overtaken by succeeding tanks which would deposit their fascines in the next trench and so on. A tank section of three vehicles, supported by four infantry sections, was thus the primary tactical unit, the former working in close cooperation, the latter to undertake a complex fire and manoeuvre mission. The entire success of the battle depended on the Tank Corps' ability to break through the four lines of Hindenburg Line defences in a matter of hours, something hitherto unachieved on the Western Front.

The French and British armies recognised the importance of tank cooperation training for both infantry and armour. This, however, was difficult to arrange due to the time available with the added complication that, due to frequent breakdowns, training could be as attritional to tanks as combat. Nonetheless, 14 French infantry battalions undertook the necessary training at Champlieu, the primary *AS* base, between 27 August and 5 October. Each battalion spent up to seven days carrying out tank and infantry exercises.[65] For their part, the British infantry also underwent special training, but only had ten days to arrange it before the offensive opened on 20 November. That this was accomplished is a testament to Fuller's belief that 'the easiest way to coordinate action [between tanks and infantry] was to reduce tactics to a drill … In short, Cambrai was to be a clockwork battle.'[66]

Although Cambrai was not the clockwork battle envisaged, the reverse at Flesquières Ridge being the most egregious setback, for the most part it was a stunning success. The outcome of meticulous planning at all levels, British efforts to keep the offensive secret resulted in complete surprise. Over 4,000 Germans were captured along with 100 guns. Forlorn enemy captives spoke of a feeling of 'helplessness' when confronted by tanks.[67] In some sectors the infantry penetrated the Hindenburg Line defences to a depth of four miles. Thereafter, the promising offensive degenerated into a prolonged, see-saw struggle that lasted until early December. Nevertheless, its opening day was the Tank Corps' first real victory, albeit one that resulted in heavy losses amongst crewmen and vehicles.

---

62   Fuller, *Tanks*, p.144.
63   Ibid., p.140.
64   Harris, *Men, Ideas and Tanks*, p.121.
65   Gale, *French Army's Tank Force*, p.89.
66   Quoted in Hammond, *Cambrai*, p. 69.
67   Miles, *Military Operations France and Belgium*, Vol. 3, p.98.

Mark IV tanks mounted with fascines await the rail journey to the Cambrai front,
November 1917.

When the Malmaison operation concluded (26 October) after three days fighting,
Sixth Army had advanced nearly six kilometres in some places and had captured
over 11,000 prisoners and significant amounts of war material. The victory had been
achieved with the loss of fewer than 12,000 men killed, wounded and missing. This
compared favourably with the 30,000 casualties sustained in the same area during the
previous April and May.[68]

From the *AS* point of view, the Malmaison offensive's most important outcome was
restoration of confidence in tanks throughout the French Army. Unsurprisingly, the
verdict of participant infantry commanders was determined by the effect tanks had in
their sectors. Amongst the myriad after-action narratives, there was only one negative
report.[69] A representative positive example was submitted by one colonel who noted
the considerable effect tanks had on French and German morale, a perspective equally
remarked upon by British tank crews after Cambrai.[70]

68   Robert Doughty, *Pyrrhic Victory: French Strategy and Operations in the Great War* (London:
     Harvard University Press, 2005)., p.389.
69   VI Armée, *Rapport du Lieutenant-colonel De Bailleul du 23 Octobre 1917*, 16N2162.
70   *Rapport de Lieutenant-colonel Lardant sur les Chars d'assaut*, 15 November 1917, 16N2162.

AS losses during the Malmaison offensive amounted to two tanks destroyed and 82 crewmen killed, wounded and missing; light casualties when compared to subsequent fighting.[71] This demonstrated that French armour could suffer comparatively small losses provided that hostile batteries were effectively suppressed. On this occasion, French counter-battery work had been highly effective. Conversely, Tank Corps losses for Cambrai were significant (179 Mark IVs knocked out), for a loss rate of 47 percent. This is understandable when one considers that British tanks were at the centre of operations for most of the first day and used when available for the remainder of the battle. Given the duration and intensity of the fighting, this seemingly high percentage fell well within the range of operational acceptability.

The primary lesson of the Malmaison offensive was that bringing armour into action after a prolonged bombardment was going to be problematic due to the cratered ground; an issue duly recognised at the March conference.[72] However, once the tanks came within close range at Malmaison and Cambrai, it was clear that the Germans had limited options to counter them. Indeed, German captives from both battles expressed dismay that their counter-tank preparations had been to no avail, adding that tanks had caused 'disarray' in their ranks.[73] Thus tanks were of real value to the infantry, especially in relation to reduction of Allied casualties – an issue of pressing concern to Pétain and the French government.

Malmaison and Cambrai also provided the respective Anglo-French participants with a valuable opportunity to reconsider their rather patchy tank doctrine, most of which had been developed without enough experience for it to be anything other than provisional. The French had been working with Estienne's early tanks notes from October 1916 and a revision of this document by Pétain was issued in August 1917. The latter was based on recent Nivelle offensive experience.[74] The British were working from ideas drawn from Lieutenant-Colonel Ernest Swinton's 'Notes on the Employment of Tanks', February 1916 and Fuller's 'Training Note No. 16', February 1917, both by necessity written when the experience of tank warfare was mostly non-existent.[75] The experience of 1917 was considered sufficient enough for GQG to significantly revise tank regulations. A new set, disseminated in late December 1917, formed the basis of French tank tactics and operations for the remainder of the war. The British response was not as straightforward and the cogent arguments emanating

---

71   Gale, *French Army's Tank Force*, p.235.
72   GAN, *Observations sur l'Emploi des Chars d'Assaut le 23 Octobre*, Novembre 1917, 16N2120.
73   Quoted in R. Lafitte, *L'Artillerie d'Assaut de 1916 à 1918* (Paris: Henri-Charles Lavauzelle, 1921), p.38.
74   Gale, *French Army's Tank Force*, pp.35-36.
75   For an excellent discussion of Fuller's note, see Harris, *Men, Ideas and Tanks*, pp 87-91 and E.D. Swinton, 'Notes on the Employment of Tanks, February 1916' in Wilfred Miles, *Military Operations-France and Belgium 1916*, Vol. 2, Appendix XVIII (London: Macmillan, 1938).

from the March conference continued between the War Office and GHQ for some time after Cambrai. This resulted in rather difficult circumstances epitomised by serious disagreements about Stern's ideas on the one hand, and Fuller's on the other.[76]

In retrospect, Malmaison was perhaps the last Allied offensive of the 1916 style and Cambrai arguably the first battle of the 1918 approach. The transition occurred in just a matter of weeks, Cambrai setting the template for Allied offensive operations to the Armistice. However although Malmaison was, as per previous 1916-17 offensives, a primarily an artillery operation, the French army harnessed its experience of old techniques to formulate a new methodology in the conduct of offensive operations. For example, there was a different approach to artillery preparations for Malmaison when compared to that of earlier French offensives. The first three days of the bombardment had undertaken routine destructive fire but, on the fourth day, there was a distinct shift whereby a large proportion of smoke and gas shells was employed along with increased interdiction fire. The primary aim was disruption as opposed to destruction of the enemy's artillery assets and the infantry reserves. After the battle, it was noted that the defending artillery was seriously affected by the neutralisation fire. The success of the second preparatory phase demonstrated that with sufficient air superiority, it was unnecessary to physically destroy the German defences when they could be effectively neutralised instead.[77] Thus, in conjunction with the lessons of Cambrai, the Allies entered 1918 with a firm grasp of the requirements for successful combined-arms operations.

By revealing the nascent tank arm to the enemy in September 1916, GHQ condemned both British and French models to on the battlefield testing under generally unfavourable conditions. With no previous experience of armoured operations to instruct crewmen, it was fortunate that the Allies had competent and innovative senior officers such as Estienne, Elles and Fuller to provide much-needed guidance in the difficult days of 1917.

Malmaison and Cambrai introduced a level of confidence in tank arm utility that was almost non-existent prior to these offensives. Cambrai, in particular, would transform the nature of Allied offensive operations. Moreover, it ensured that General Estienne was finally able to see his 1915 vision of an *en masse* tank assault without artillery preparations realised at the Battle of Soissons (18-22 July 1918) when a large force of light and medium tanks supported a surprise attack by the Franco-American Tenth Army. He might have been able to persuade GQG that this was possible had Cambrai not taken place, but that offensive's early success silenced all remaining doubts.[78] A GQG report on Cambrai of 6 February 1918 is a good indication of this shift in thinking, the document emphatically concluding, 'Surprise is possible in the

76   See Harris, pp.159-68.
77   Lieutenant-Colonel Lucas, *L'Evolution des Idées tactiques en France et en Allemagne pendant la Guerre de 1914-1918*, 3rd Ed. (Paris: Berger-Levrault, 1925), p.193.
78   Gale, *French Army's Tank Force*, p.90.

offensive and counter-offensive'.[79] Likewise, Cambrai justified Tank Corps expansion and consequent tank arm success during the Hundred Days offensives. This included Amiens (8-11 August 1918), possibly its greatest victory of the war. Prior to this, the Allies would have to endure the series of German spring offensives (21 March-18 July 1918), the early success of which was founded on short and disruptive hurricane bombardments. Nevertheless, the 'dark days' of 1917 permanently behind them, tanks would be at the centre Anglo-French offensive operations from spring 1918. Indeed, with regard to the future of land warfare, tanks would be at the centre of Allied offensive operations for the remainder of the 20th century and beyond.

79   GQG, 3 Bureau, 6361, *Note pour les grandes unités au sujet d'une attaque par surprise (bataille de Cambrai)*, 6 February 1918, AFGG VI/1, Annexes 1, 333.

Index

Index of Places

Index of Formations/Units

Wolverhampton Military Studies

www.helion.co.uk/wolverhamptonmilitarystudies

Submissions

The publishers would be pleased to receive submissions for this series. Please contact us via email (info@helion.co.uk), or in writing to Helion & Company Limited, Unit 8 Amherst Business Centre, Budbrooke Road, Warwick, CV34 5WE, England.

Titles